Psychology of Alcohol and Other Drugs

In Memory of Tomy,

Who Withheld His Heart Not From Any Joy

Psychology of Alcohol and Other Drugs

A Research Perspective

John Jung

Sage Publications, Inc.
International Educational and Professional Publisher
Thousand Oaks ▪ London ▪ New Delhi

For information:

Sage Publications, Inc.
2455 Teller Road
Thousand Oaks, California 91320
E-mail: order@sagepub.com

Sage Publications Ltd.
6 Bonhill Street
London EC2A 4PU
United Kingdom

Sage Publications India Pvt. Ltd.
M-32 Market
Greater Kailash I
New Delhi 110 048 India

Printed in the United States of America

Library of Congress Cataloging-in-Publication Data

Jung, John, 1937-
Psychology of alcohol and other drugs: A research perspective / John Jung
p. cm.
Includes bibliographical references and index.
ISBN 0-7619-2100-1 (paper: alk. paper)
1. Alcoholism—Etiology. 2. Drug abuse—Etiology. 3. Drinking of alcoholic beverages. 4. Alcoholism—Psychological aspects. 5. Drug abuse—Psychological aspects. 6. Alcoholism—Treatment. 7. Drug abuse—Treatment. I. Title.
RC565.J858 2000
616.86—dc21 00-008773

This book is printed on acid-free paper.

03 04 05 06 7 6 5 4 3

Acquisition Editors: Jim Brace-Thompson
Editorial Assistant: Anna Howland
Production Editor: Diane S. Foster
Editorial Assistant: Cindy Bear
Typesetter: Rebecca Evans
Cover Designer: Michelle Lee

Contents

Preface

Psychological research has led to considerable progress in understanding the psychology of alcohol and other drug use. Sadly, this important topic receives little attention in the education of psychology students. This oversight is particularly disturbing because major psychological problems such as mood disorders, aggression, stress, poor achievement at work and in school, and problems related to physical health and illness, to name a few, are investigated with little awareness of the significant role played by alcohol and other drug use. Many of the problems studied by clinical, social, industrial, and personality and other psychologists turn out to be causes, effects, or both of abusing alcohol and other drugs.

The psychological study of alcohol and other drug use has always tended to be seen as relevant only to the subfields of abnormal psychology or psychopathology, as if no "normal" use ever occurred. There is no dispute that much research should focus on those who harm themselves and those around them by their substance abuse. Research on methods to bring about recovery for this population is of the highest priority.

Although these aspects are discussed in detail in this book, the content included extends beyond the problematic use of alcohol and other drugs. Attention is first directed toward research on the much larger population of users of these substances who apparently do not develop problems, at least initially. We cannot ignore the fact that most adults do use alcohol in varying degree, with no apparent problems. More than one quarter of adults smoke cigarettes, and although there is evidence they incur harmful health consequences, smokers manage to function ably in their daily activities. The numbers of illicit drug users are more difficult to obtain for obvious reasons, but it is apparent that a sizable minority of the population uses different illicit drugs in ways that do not create problems for themselves or others.

In most societies, attitudes, values, and age restrictions governing licit drug use have unwittingly motivated early and often secretive youthful initiation into the use of alcohol and some drugs. Such activities serve as rites of passage from early adolescence into adulthood. Somehow, most of us will survive this aspect of our socialization without harmful consequences, just as most adolescents manage to learn how to drive a car, but without first frightening the wits of everyone around them. Fortunately, most of us will lose or reduce interest in alcohol and other drugs after the novelty and excitement of experimental use wear off. Other goals, for which a drug lifestyle is incompatible, become more important in our lives. Research on these aspects of substance use receives extensive coverage in this book because understanding how these users avoid substance abuse is potentially useful for the development of strategies for helping those who do not use alcohol and other drugs safely.

Unlike other textbooks on this topic that accord equal space for each major drug, considerably more attention in this book is devoted to alcohol than to other drugs because it is the psychoactive drug of choice for most American adults, consumed by more people, in larger volume, and on more frequent occasions than any other drug. A focus on alcohol also is warranted because it is widely considered to be a "gateway" drug, which supposedly may lead to the subsequent use of illicit drugs. A thorough study of the psychology of licit drugs such as alcohol and nicotine can be useful in determining the extent to which their use or other factors contributes more to the future use of illicit drugs.

One distinctive feature of this book is an emphasis on individual differences. Psychology, in its zeal to establish scientific laws and principles, emphasizes generalizations. Ignored are important subgroup differences along important dimensions such as age, gender, race/ethnicity, and, within each of these physical categories, personality differences. Several chapters on these important factors occur in the middle of the book to draw attention to the critical role they have on alcohol and other drug use and their consequences.

An important goal of the book is to challenge the student to become an "educated" consumer, rather than a docile recipient, of research information. Although most students will never conduct scientific research on alcohol and other drugs themselves, they need and benefit from some knowledge of research methods to help them evaluate claims they will encounter about alcohol and other drugs. For example, much psychological research in this field is correlational in nature and is inconclusive or ambiguous with respect to causality. Still, there is a tendency to interpret negative events related to alcohol and other drugs as consequences of excessive or inappropriate use of these substances. The possibility that the causal relationship, if any exists, might be in the opposite direction is not considered. Thus, when evidence shows that the divorced drink more heavily, the conclusion often jumped to is that alcohol abuse "causes" divorce. Alternative explanations that excessive alcohol use is an "effect" of being divorced or that some personality or situational factors may be leading to both the divorce and the alcohol abuse are considered less often. In this book, methodological issues will be emphasized to help students consider alternative explanations as they examine research findings.

This book can serve as either a primary or supplementary text for upper-division and graduate-level college courses in a variety of disciplines, including basic and applied social sciences such as psychology and sociology, educational psychology, applied human services fields such as social work and criminal justice, and applied health-related fields such as nursing, health science, and physical therapy, and, of course, alcohol and drug counseling. Students in professional fields such as law and medicine, in which critical evaluation about research on the psychological aspects of alcohol and drug use is valuable, will find the book worthwhile as supplementary material.

Acknowledgments

I am indebted for the advice and encouragement of many individuals who have helped improve this book immensely. Valuable suggestions came from Sherry Span and Charles Mason and numerous students in my courses who read portions of early drafts of the manuscript. I am grateful for suggestions provided by the following reviewers: Bethany Neal-Beliroce, Mike Selby, and Sara Dolan. I am especially appreciative of reviews of all or most of the manuscript by Peter Vik of Idaho State University, Perilou Goddard of Northern Kentucky University, and Cynthia Anne Crawford of California State University, San Bernardino. They offered insightful suggestions and generous encouragement that guided improvements to the final version. I owe thanks to my wife, Phyllis, for her aid and expertise in editing and indexing the manuscript.

Finally, I want to acknowledge the outstanding support that Sage Publications offered. Anna Howland provided prompt and thorough editorial advice throughout the production phase. Jim Brace-Thompson was enthusiastic about this project from the beginning. His editorial advice and judgment guided me through some of the difficult choice points every author faces during early stages of a writing project. I appreciate his conviction that my approach offered a needed alternative perspective to the traditional model of textbooks in this area.

- ❖ Focus and Goals of This Book
- ❖ History of Drugs in America
- ❖ Origins of Licit Drugs
- ❖ Origins of Illicit Drugs
- ❖ Some Central Questions
- ❖ Summary
- ❖ Stimulus/Response

1 Psychology of Psychoactive Drugs

Booze, pot, dope, coffin nails, horse, crack, bennies, reds, coke, speed, ice, ecstasy, speedball, junk*—the list of colorful names for psychoactive drugs is a long one that continues to grow. Throughout recorded history in most societies, people have discovered and used substances capable of altering normal experiences and consciousness. Most of these substances have come from natural sources such as plants, seeds, mushrooms, yeast, and grains, but in modern times, synthetic products such as heroin and amphetamines have been added to the list. For a variety of reasons ranging from curiosity to boredom to stress, people are motivated to seek variations in mood, going from high to low as well as from low to high activation. Psychoactive drugs are a potent means of producing these mood states. In addition, many of them, including alcohol, nicotine, hallucinogens, opioids, and marijuana, have been used for medicinal and healing purposes.

Alcohol, tobacco, marijuana, cocaine, heroin, amphetamines, hallucinogens, crack—the list of psychoactive drugs used by humans throughout history is, as already noted, rather extensive. In this book, we will consider all chemical substances as drugs if they are voluntarily consumed for social and recreational purposes to alter mood and conscious states, as opposed to medicinal uses such as treatment of physical and psychological disorders.

Using this definition, alcohol would be classified as a "drug," contrary to a longstanding distinction between alcohol *and* drugs that exists among the public as well as with many professionals working in this area. This separation of alcohol and other drugs into their own domains appears at the highest levels of the federal government, as reflected by the creation in the early 1970s of separate governmental agencies to deal with funding for treatment and prevention research on alcohol (National Institute on Alcohol Abuse and Alcoholism) and drugs (National Institute on Drug Abuse). This separation of alcohol from other drugs has perpetuated the failure of many research, treatment, and prevention activities to acknowledge the reality that many users of psychoactive drugs started with and usually continue the use of alcohol. A more accurate understanding of substance use needs to recognize the central role that use of alcohol plays in the development of using other drugs.

THE APPROACH OF THIS BOOK

This book will emphasize the central role of psychological causes, correlates, and effects of using alcohol and other drugs. A psychology of alcohol and drugs needs no more justification than we require for the study of any other behavior, whether it be watching movies, reading books, attending church, gambling, or working. People use alcohol and other drugs, and it is important to identify and understand the factors that affect such behaviors especially because alcohol and other drug abuse and dependency develop for some users, with destructive and harmful consequences for themselves and others around them. Understanding how these adverse outcomes develop and how to treat them calls for a psychological approach. Furthermore, a psychology of alcohol and drug use is essential for designing effective methods for the intervention and prevention of drug problems.

PSYCHOLOGY PRECEDES PHARMACOLOGY

Multiple factors are involved in alcohol and other drug use. First, the substance must be physically available. A complex process involving cultural, historical, legal, political, and economic factors determines the extent to which a drug is available in a particular society at a given time.

As we grow up, we form many beliefs and attitudes about alcohol and other drugs. We learn that these substances can exert powerful changes on our conscious states, behaviors, and experiences. Such beliefs may increase the desire to use drugs for some people. Without these psychological factors first leading to drug use, the potential pharmacological effects that drugs can produce on the nervous system to affect behavior and experience cannot occur.

And although a drug may be readily available, not everyone will be attracted to use it. Those more concerned about the risks and dangers of drugs than their possible attractions will have less interest in their use. Psychological beliefs and attitudes again are a critical determinant, in this case preventing the use of drugs. Without certain beliefs, motives, and personality characteristics, a drug will not be used even if the opportunity is present.

Understanding why people seek drugs, why they may not seek treatment, or why relapse is so common are important tasks of a psychology of drugs. Thus, psychology may help in developing methods for the prevention of drug use by understanding which reasons motivate users to engage in drug use and which reasons deter nonusers.

A psychology of drugs is also useful for motivating users to want to reduce or stop using drugs. Thus, quitting, or at least the attempt, may work best when it is perceived to be a choice rather than a mandate. But fear of failure may prevent some from even making the attempt to quit. Such efforts may be more likely if positive consequences or alternatives are offered. These psychological considerations may be needed to design effective methods for improving success in quitting. Psychology can help reduce these setbacks by identifying the conditions such as the psychological states and social and physical environments that are associated with relapse.

Focus and Goals of This Book

This book will examine the major psychoactive drugs of current concern to society due to their widespread use or because of the potential harm that may occur from excessive use. Greater attention will be directed to drugs that are used more widely or are associated with greater social problems. Thus, although many prescription and over-the-counter medications such as sedatives, tranquilizers, stimulants, and analgesics can be abused for nonmedical purposes, they will not be included in this book. Considerably more space will be devoted to alcohol because it is the psychoactive drug of choice for most American adults, consumed by more people, in larger volume, and on more frequent occasions than any other drug. Our society approves of and even expects and encourages drinking in a variety of situations.

Alcohol, as with tobacco, is also important as a focus of drug study because it is widely considered to be a "gateway" drug, which may lead to subsequent as well as concurrent use of illicit drugs. An additional justification for centering on alcohol is that it is more thoroughly researched than other drugs, owing in large part to the large population of drinkers. In contrast, relatively less research on illicit drugs is available due to the difficulty of identifying and recruiting large and representative samples of illicit drug users. Most of the research on illicit drug use comes from treatment samples that may not be generalizable to other users. Unlike legal drugs in which controlled studies are available, there are major ethical and legal barriers to conducting experiments with illicit drugs, so findings from these studies are limited to correlational data that do not permit firm causal conclusions.

A secondary goal is to show some of the similarities and differences among these drugs in their origins and their effects. The norms of use patterns will be compared across major demographic factors such as age, sex, and social class or ethnicity. By comparing different major drugs, we hope to identify some common factors underlying the causes and effects of drug use. Issues, methods, and theories of treatment of drug abuse and dependency will be examined.

History of Drugs in America

An overview of the history and background of major psychoactive drugs currently used in the United States is essential for understanding contemporary alcohol and other drug issues and problems. Prior to about 1900, although many states passed drug control legislation, there were no federal laws against any psychoactive drugs in the United States, which were widely available and consumed. How this situation changed and what determined which drugs were regarded as more dangerous than others, warranting penalties for possession and use, is an intriguing tale of politics, prejudice, and propaganda more so than one informed by persuasive scientific evidence.

Alcohol consumption prior to the 20th century was quite extensive, and heavy levels of use were commonplace. The immigrants who settled the American colonies in the late 17th century came from European countries with long histories of alcohol use, and they continued their cultural traditions and practices related to drinking after they settled. In colonial America, drinking was a widespread, generally tolerated, and accepted activity. Alcohol not only was widely available as a beverage but also served as a home remedy for many medicinal purposes. Drunkenness was commonplace then, but it was not considered a social problem for the society of that era (Gusfield, 1963). However, from the early 1700s to the mid-1800s, drunkenness and alcohol problems increased, generating greater societal disruption as the nation changed from an agrarian economy to an urban industrial society.

The widespread social problems such as poverty, crime, and disorderly public conduct created by excessive use of alcohol led to reform movements led by religious groups such as the Quakers and many Protestant denominations. Organized efforts against alcohol were formed such as the American Temperance Society in 1833. As the movement gathered strength, by the late 1800s, calls for temperance yielded to efforts to eliminate alcohol entirely as organizations such as the Women's Christian Temperance Union (WCTU) and the Anti-Saloon League led the fight against the evils of alcohol, tobacco, and other drugs (Gusfield, 1963).

Tobacco was, in contrast, completely unfamiliar to Columbus and his crew in 1492. However, the Indians who met them had begun chewing and smoking tobacco in pipes long ago. By the time the American colonies were settled a little more than a century latter, smoking tobacco was also an established and acceptable drug for the early European immigrants.

Morphine was widely used during the Civil War on the battlefield as an anesthetic for the wounded and dying. Unfortunately, many who survived their battle wounds with the aid of morphine later succumbed to morphine addiction. Interestingly, cocaine injections were initially used to treat morphine withdrawal before it came to be recognized that cocaine itself was an addictive substance. The widely used patent medicines, supposedly good for "whatever ails you," contained alcohol and cocaine and became abused, especially by women.

American cities suffered increasingly from child labor, excessive drug use, crime, and violence, leading social reformers to launch vigorous moral reform campaigns. Many of the poor urban living conditions stemmed from or were exacerbated by alcohol and other drug abuse, but economic oppression, prejudice, and social injustice were also contributory factors. In addition, some substance abuse may have been the effect rather than the cause of poverty and oppression. Nonetheless, political and social pressures encouraged a focus on drugs as the major culprit of society's ills, and the social reformers helped make many of them illegal in the early part of this century.

In contrast to the 19th century, when drugs were unregulated for the most part, state and federal legislation to control drugs increased in the 20th century. Thomas Szasz, a prominent psychiatrist and critic of many social policies restricting choice, contended that drugs served as a convenient scapegoat for the social ills of urban life (Szasz, 1987). He observed that a double standard was used in setting drug policy. Szasz suggested that because alcohol and tobacco are so well ingrained in Christian and English-speaking cultures, we regard them as good, but drugs such as opium and marijuana, which originate from foreign countries, are viewed as bad. Thus, consider the different labels and terms used in connection with legal and illegal drugs: People who sell liquor are retail merchants, not "pushers," and people who buy liquor are citizens, not "dope fiends." The same things go for tobacco, coffee, and tea (Szasz, 1987).

Figure 1.1 identifies some major developments in drug legislation and other aspects of drug control in America over the course of the 20th century. One of the earliest drugs to be controlled in America was opium, banned in San Francisco in 1875. At the federal level, the Pure Food and Drug Act was passed in 1906 due to increasing concern about impurities from opioid drugs in foods and patent medicines. It did not make drugs illegal but required labels to specify the contents.

In 1914, the Harrison Narcotics Act was passed as part of an international effort to reduce the widespread and increasing use of opiate drugs as well as cocaine (Musto, 1987). This law did not make these drugs illegal but required a prescription from a physician before heroin or morphine could be prescribed. During this era, the federal government was prevented from passing national laws by the doctrine that the states held the rights to make these laws for themselves. The federal government adroitly circumvented this problem by placing a tax on opiates by exercising its powers to raise tax revenues.

The restrictions against opium may have been a statement against the Chinese as much as it was toward the drug (Gusfield, 1963). The opium tax was directed toward the Chinese in America, the heaviest users of opium. In the late 1800s, Chinese immigrants were regarded as the "yellow peril" because they provided a large, industrious, and cheap source of labor against which the White population could not compete. Public attitudes were extremely hostile toward this ethnic group, who was easily identifiable due to differences in cultural customs and physical appearance. Similarly, some of the opposition to cocaine was related to prejudices toward Blacks in the South during the reconstruction period after the Civil War (Musto, 1987). Unsubstantiated beliefs that cocaine-using Blacks might become violent toward Whites aroused fear. Restrictions imposed in the 1930s against marijuana were similarly tied to the association of violence and crimes under the influence of marijuana among immigrant Mexican workers in the Southwest, a perception for which there was flimsy evidence (Musto, 1987).

Despite these attempts to control these drugs, after World War I, use of opioids and cocaine expanded rapidly in the United States. Physicians were still able to prescribe narcotics to patients, a practice that soon was halted as law enforcement agencies began to arrest physicians and druggists for using opiates even for medical purposes.

Alcohol was made illegal in 1920 with the Volstead Act, although Prohibition was repealed in 1933 and considered a failure as a means of controlling alcohol use (Musto, 1987). Many who voted in favor of Prohibition were actually unopposed to drinking. Their vote was a means of attacking

Year	National Events and Concerns	Federal Drug Control Legislation
1900s	Temperance movement strong	
1906		Pure Food and Drug Act of 1906 led to decline of patent medicines.
	World War I	Harrison Narcotics Act of 1914 taxed and regulated distribution and sale of narcotics.
1920s	Through the 1920s, attitudes of nationalism, nativism, and fear of anarchy and communism were tied to regulation of alcohol and drugs.	Volstead Act (1920), national alcohol prohibition
1930	Great Depression	Federal Bureau of Narcotics established (1930)
1933	In the 1930s, drug interest dwindled due to concerns with events in Europe; Prohibition repealed in 1933.	
		Marijuana Stamp Tax Act (1937)
1941	World War II (1941-1945)	
1950s	By the end of World War II, there were fewer public drug concerns; Korean War.	Boggs Act (1951), harsher penalties for narcotics and marijuana offenses
	Tolerance of drugs was associated with unpatriotic attitudes in the early 1950s.	Narcotics Control Act (1956), increased penalties for narcotics and marijuana offenses
1960s	Treatment, rehabilitation efforts rose.	Community Mental Health Centers Act of 1963 supports local treatment of addiction classified as mental illness.
	Psychedelics (LSD), marijuana, amphetamines, barbiturates, rise in heroin.	
1964		Surgeon General's Report on Smoking (see U.S. Department of Health, Education, and Welfare, 1964)
	Vietnam War	Bureau of Drug Abuse Control
1970s	War on Drugs	Controlled Substances Act of 1970
	Rise in cocaine use	Drug Abuse Office and Treatment Act of 1972; Drug Enforcement Administration established in 1973
1984	Crack arrives in inner cities	Comprehensive Crime Control Act of 1984
	AIDS epidemic	Anti-Drug Abuse Act (1986) created Office for Substance Abuse Prevention; Anti-Drug Abuse Act (1988) created Office of National Drug Control Policy
1990s	Cigarettes recognized as addictive	
	Tougher control of tobacco, legal cases	

Figure 1.1. Historical Timeline
SOURCE: Adapted from the U.S. Bureau of Justice Statistics (1992).

the powerful saloons and the alcohol industry. Drinking continued illegally, with so many people violating the law that it was unworkable, creating other problems such as crime and corruption associated with the underground manufacture and sale of alcohol. Repeal of Prohibition made it again possible for the alcohol industry to sell and promote its product.

In the 1920s, several federal agencies were established to control narcotics, culminating in the formation of the Federal Bureau of Narcotics in 1930. Its commissioner, Harry Anslinger, was given strong authority for drug interdiction and law enforcement, with the goal of stemming the widespread and increasing narcotics drug problem. The term *narcotic* (sleep inducing) was dropped later because it is inaccurate. Nonetheless, people still refer to "hard drugs," both depressants and stimulants alike, as narcotics. During this period also, there was recognition of a need for treating drug addicts, and hospitals were started in some federal prisons in the mid-1930s.

It might be only coincidental that as alcohol was made less available due to the Prohibition, Americans increased their use of marijuana. Possibly, when a widely used drug declines in availability and/or acceptance, other drugs increase in popularity to fill the void. Thus, when alcohol was being outlawed, immigrant Mexican laborers were introducing marijuana during the 1920s to the southwestern United States (Musto, 1987). They smoked joints made with leaves from one variety of marijuana plant, *cannabis indica.* The drug was depicted as evil and harmful by law enforcement officials and portrayed to the public by newspapers as "the killer drug," linked to violence and crime. Exaggerations of its extremely harmful effects were promoted in propaganda films of the era such as *Reefer Madness.* This hysterical atmosphere led to the Marijuana Stamp Tax Act, passed in 1937, placing controls on its use by imposing a tax for the sale or purchase of marijuana, which incidentally got incorrectly classified as a narcotic.

Drugs designed originally for medical purposes, such as barbiturates and amphetamines, began being widely dispensed by physicians. Before long, these drugs, which could easily be made at home, were being abused for nonmedical purposes and became part of the growing drug problem.

During World War II, drug problems declined, perhaps due to the priorities of the war effort and concerns with national defense. The end of this conflict saw a resumption of illicit drug use, leading the federal government to pass stiffer penalties and mandatory jail sentences for offenders during the 1950s. Heroin use, dormant since the Harrison Act in 1914, started to increase mainly in lower socioeconomic areas. Prices started to rise as well, leading dealers to adulterate the drug by mixing in fillers to meet the demand and increase profits.

During the Vietnam War, a high rate of heroin use by American military personnel occurred due to the almost pure supply of inexpensive heroin in Southeast Asia. As this war wound down, the threat of so many young American military personnel coming back from Vietnam with heroin addiction was a real concern. The danger turned out to be less serious than originally expected because most opiate users in Vietnam were able to quit once they returned to their communities in the United States (Musto, 1987).

One explanation is that the resumption of their former lives reduced the psychological need to use heroin, but it is also possible that the unavailability of pure or high-grade heroin in the United States was a factor. Heroin use became perceived as primarily a problem of the urban poor living in the inner city. The dangers of heroin use increased with the advent of AIDS in the 1980s due to the high risk of HIV infection among heroin users who share needles for their injections.

During the 1960s, social activism in civil rights and other empowerment movements led to major social changes. This activism involved many young people, and it was accompanied by widespread use of many drugs, including marijuana and hallucinogens, which were popularized by the experiences of Timothy Leary, a Harvard professor who was a pioneer in the experimental use of LSD-25. Due to the influence of the hippies and the flower children during this era, alternate lifestyles flourished, including experimentation with drugs.

At the same time, changes in social attitudes, social policy, and drug legislation occurred with a de-emphasis from a law enforcement "lock them up and throw away the key" philosophy toward drug offenders to a focus on treatment and rehabilitation of drug abusers. In 1962, the Supreme Court viewed addiction as a disease, not a criminal activity in itself. The Community Mental Health Centers Act of 1963 facilitated rehabilitation of drug abusers. The Narcotic Addict Rehabilitation Act of 1966 regarded opioid abuse as a disease. The disease conception encouraged a medical treatment rather than an incarceration approach to drugs.

President Nixon launched a "war on drugs" in 1971 and passed significant legislation changing how drug possession, sale, and use were handled in the United States. Law enforcement through the Drug Enforcement Administration (DEA), the successor in 1973 to the Federal Bureau of Narcotics, became the approach for controlling substances rather than the excise tax method of earlier eras. Drug interdiction to cut off the supply of heroin from Turkey became a priority. Greater efforts were made to provide treatment facilities as well.

The Comprehensive Drug Act and Control Action of 1970 was a landmark piece of federal drug legislation that overturned or replaced the existing laws. It authorized the creation of two separate federal agencies for the development of research, prevention, and treatment programs: the National Institute on Alcoholism and Alcohol Abuse (NIAAA) in 1971 to address alcohol issues and a parallel agency, the National Institute on Drug Abuse (NIDA) in 1973 to deal with drug problems.

A new approach for classifying drugs was implemented. Instead of banning classes of drugs and setting penalties for their use based on their chemical structure and pharmacological effect, the Controlled Substances Act of 1970 classified all drugs except nicotine and alcohol by two functional criteria: the drug's medical use and the drug's potential for abuse. Using only those two criteria, all drugs were placed in one of five categories, each with different penalties based on the relative benefits and harm of different drugs.

As shown in Table 1.1, Schedule I drugs, such as heroin, marijuana, and hashish, have little or no medical use but a high potential for abuse. Schedule II drugs, such as certain barbiturates and amphetamines, have some medical use but also a high potential for abuse. Schedule III drugs, such as codeine that is found in prescription cough medicine and is highly addictive, have medical use and a high potential for abuse. Schedule IV drugs, such as sedative-hypnotics and minor tranquilizers, have therapeutic value but less risk of abuse and dependency than Schedule III drugs. Finally, Schedule V drugs, such as many over-the-counter drugs, have high medical use but little potential for abuse and often do not require a prescription.

In the 1960s, as mounting research called into question the seriousness of the harm produced by marijuana, its use began increasing, especially among college students and lower socioeconomic groups. By 1969, due to marijuana's widespread use and growing public sentiment, the government reduced the penalties for marijuana below the level associated with other Schedule I drugs.

A shift in attitudes toward more tolerant positions occurred, as exemplified by the recommendation in 1973 by the National Commission on Marijuana and Drug Abuse that marijuana possession for personal use be "decriminalized." The commission's view was partly based on its conclusions that alcohol and tobacco presented more serious problems. However, President Nixon rejected the commission's report.

Federal drug policies were more relaxed under Nixon's successor, President Ford, who followed a containment approach to drugs aimed to limit damage in contrast to Nixon's all-out war approach. A peak in marijuana use occurred in 1973, and a continuing decline was seen before it began regaining popularity in the 1990s. During this period, there were other unsuccessful attempts to decriminalize marijuana possession of less than an ounce, an effort supported by President Carter.

Before long, new problems began to surface. Cocaine use, which had peaked earlier in the 1920s, began to increase again in the late 1960s, especially among the affluent and upwardly mobile. Initially viewed as a drug

TABLE 1.1 Schedule of drugs according to effects, medical use, and potential for abuse, Drug Enforcement Administration (DEA)

DEA Schedule	*Abuse Potential*	*Examples of Drugs Covered*	*Some of the Effects*	*Medical Use*
I	Highest	Heroin, LSD, hashish, marijuana, methaqualone, designer drugs	Unpredictable effects, severe psychological or physical dependence, or death	No accepted use; some are legal for limited research use only
II	High	Morphine, PCP, codeine, cocaine, methadone, Demerol®, benzedrine, dexedrine	May lead to severe psychological or physical dependence	Accepted use with restrictions
III	Medium	Codeine with aspirin or Tylenol®, some amphetamines, anabolic steroids	May lead to moderate or low physical or high psychological dependence	Accepted use
IV	Low	Darvon®, Talwin®, phenobarbital, Equanil®, Miltown®, Librium®, diazepam	May lead to limited physical or psychological dependence	Accepted use
V	Lowest	Over-the-counter or prescription compounds with codeine, Lomotil®, Robitussin A-C®	May lead to limited physical or psychological dependence	Accepted use

SOURCE: Adapted from the Drug Enforcement Administration (1989).

that had few dangers, its popularity reached a peak in 1982 before it declined (Gfroerer & Brodsky, 1992), according to retrospective data from the National Household Survey on Drug Abuse, between 1962 and 1989. Crack cocaine, a more potent smokable form of the drug that came onto the scene in 1984, caused great concern. A new upsurge in cocaine use occurred, spreading to the streets and to underclass users as well. Heroin made a comeback as new sources of less expensive heroin replaced the supplies from Turkey.

The politics of drug policy shifted back under the administration of President Reagan in the 1980s, who renewed Nixon's strong antidrug campaigns with crusades against illicit drugs such as cocaine, heroin, and marijuana. In Nancy Reagan's terms, the solution was to "just say no." The Anti-Drug Abuse Act of 1986 placed almost $4 billion, primarily for law enforcement, toward a renewed war on drugs.

This brief overview of American drug policies shows how directions can shift back and forth over history depending on the political climate. History seemed to be repeating itself, with the strong fears of cocaine triggering a broad antidrug atmosphere as it had during the early 1900s (Musto, 1987). If one examines the history of drug attitudes and policies from the early years of the nation to the present, a struggle among three types of values—libertarian, medical, and criminal—can be discerned (Institute of Medicine, 1990). During the colonial period, a laissez-faire individual freedom approach seemed adequate. Government involvement with drugs was mainly to impose taxes. As industrialization developed and the nation became more urbanized, the dangers of excessive use of drugs became recognized as a growing social problem, and medical approaches to treating drug problems developed. The third approach, criminalization, more prevalent in the 20th century, emphasized punishment of drug users and legal restriction of availability and consumption of drugs.

Origins of Licit Drugs

DEPRESSANTS

Alcohol

Most civilizations throughout recorded history have used alcoholic beverages such as beer or wine, derived from the fermentation of grains and grapes, respectively. They have been used in rituals and ceremonies as well as for healing purposes since ancient times. The ancient Egyptians honored the god Osiris, who cultivated the vine and created wine and beer. Hippocrates, the Greek father of medicine, is known to have recommended wine for its therapeutic properties. The Greeks paid homage to wine through Dionysus (known to the Romans as Bacchus), the god of wine, with celebrations and festivities. Fermented rice wines were known in the Far East as well as in ancient China and India.

In the 10th century, the Arabians developed the practice of distillation, a process by which the alcohol from fermented beverages is extracted by boiling it until it vaporizes. Then, the alcohol is recaptured after condensation to create more potent beverages with higher concentrations of alcohol.

All alcoholic beverages contain the same active ingredient, ethyl alcohol or ethanol. Ethanol's percentage of the total volume ranges from low levels of around 3% to 4% in beer, around 12% to 14% for wines, and 45% to 50% for distilled spirits such as liquor (Maisto, Galizio, & Conners, 1995).

Alcoholic beverages are consumed for many different reasons, including celebrations, social conviviality, coping with negative emotions, and feelings of intoxication. Sometimes it is consumed to disinhibit or release suppressed feelings, and sometimes it is used to calm or reduce tension and anxiety. The effects can vary with the dose consumed, with low levels generally releasing inhibitions, whereas higher levels often produce drowsiness, lack of concentration, and lack of coordination.

Today, alcohol in its various beverage types has annual sales of billions of dollars in the United States. After the end of Prohibition in 1933, the rise in alcohol consumption grew rapidly, even though there has been a slight decline in the sale of distilled liquor in the past decade. Drinking is widely promoted and advertised. Although societal attitudes against drunkenness have become more negative, drinking is generally accepted in our society.

STIMULANTS

Nicotine

Tobacco is America's homegrown contribution to drugs. Native Americans had been using it for a long time when Columbus arrived in 1492. Nicotine, a potent but highly toxic central nervous system stimulant, comes from the dried tobacco plant, *nicotiana tabacum,* which is native to North America (McKim, 1997).

About 8 mg of nicotine exists in a cigarette, but the amount delivered to the smoker ranges from .1 to .9 mg, depending on specific brands. Cigarettes involve more than nicotine, containing more than 2,500 different compounds, with cigarette smoke involving more than 4,000 compounds. In addition, because there are no legal restrictions on additives to cigarettes, wide variations exist in what manufacturers add to their product, including sugar, preservatives, and taste improvers.

When first introduced to Europe, tobacco was used for various medicinal purposes. It later became a major source of revenue for the American colonies in trade with England, and tobacco use became widespread, so much so that King James I banned smoking. Tobacco use continued in England but in the form of snuff during the early 1700s. Users held a pinch of powdered tobacco near the nose for sniffing, usually until a sneeze was induced, a method that was never popular in the United States, where smokeless or chewing tobacco developed as an alternative to smoking.

By the mid-1800s, temperance movements in America were condemning the moral and health hazards of smoking as its addictive propensities were recognized. As in the case of alcohol, smoking survived these early attempts to restrict its use for pleasure. As a stimulant, nicotine increases alertness and concentration by activating the central nervous system, but it also can paradoxically facilitate relaxation on other occasions (Ray & Ksir, 1993). As with alcohol, its effects are biphasic and reverse direction with higher doses.

The development in 1881 of a machine that could manufacture cigarettes rapidly increased the availability and use of cigarettes. Advertising and promotion, which even had doctors testifying to the relaxing benefits of smoking, aided its growth as a major industry. Increased awareness and scientific evidence about health risks of smoking since the 1960s have led to substantial pressure to regulate smoking.

Caffeine

The methyl xanthines include stimulants such as caffeine, typically consumed in coffee, tea, cocoa, and carbonated soft drinks (McKim, 1997). Beans of the coffee bush in Ethiopia have been used for more than a thousand years. Coffee was thought to have medicinal value. It was highly popular in England as coffeehouses proliferated in London in the 1600s, so much so that in 1674, women published a petition against coffee in which they protested the waste of time and money by men for a "little base, black, thick, nasty bitter stinking, nauseous Puddle water" (Gilbert, 1979).

Although xanthines are widely consumed, they are not commonly viewed as "drugs," and no laws prohibit their use. Large doses may cause insomnia, jitteriness, and tension. Discontinued use may be associated with headaches, fatigue, and lowered alertness.

Use of these beverages does not interfere with holding a job, produce intoxication, or cause automobile accidents. In fact, coffee is commonly regarded as a stimulant, one that may improve alertness, cognitive processes, and work productivity. Coffee drinking is also closely tied to social gatherings, meals, and work breaks. Perhaps no laws or penalties are associated with its use because it does not produce the major social problems associated with alcohol. The health concerns about coffee did not produce legislation restricting its use. The coffee industry responded by successfully promoting decaffeinated alternatives for consumers.

Origins of Illicit Drugs

OPIATES

Opium

Opium comes from the resin of poppy flowers found in the Middle East. As a central nervous system depressant, opium sedates and dulls responsiveness. Pain is deadened, coughing is suppressed, mental alertness is reduced, and drowsiness is induced (McKim, 1997).

From early Egyptian and Greek accounts, opium was widely used for a variety of medical problems, primarily for its analgesic or painkilling capacity. Islamic cultures used opium as well and spread its use to India and China, where it began to be smoked, leading to widespread opium addiction.

Eventually, the Chinese government banned opium, but the British persisted in trading opium to the Chinese to pay for tea from China, which was highly popular in Britain. Finally, the opium wars were waged between the two nations in the mid-1800s, with the victorious British acquiring the rights to Hong Kong in 1842, which they held until 1997.

The British, however, did not avoid their own addiction problems with opium. Leading 19th-century English poets such as Elizabeth Barrett Browning and Samuel Taylor Coleridge fell under its spell and romanticized the drug by attributing it with creative powers. The use of opium in England (Ray & Ksir, 1993) expanded after Thomas De Quincey published a literary account in 1821, *Confessions of an Opium Eater,* in praise of the dreamlike states experienced from his drinking laudanum, a mixture of opium with alcohol.

Morphine

In Germany, the active ingredient in opium was identified in 1803 and named morphine. It is about 10 times as potent as opium itself. That fact, coupled with the development of the hypodermic needle in 1853, which allowed faster delivery of the drug, made it a powerful medical resource. As an analgesic, it found immediate and widespread application during several major wars during the mid-19th century, including the American Civil War, which lasted from 1861 to 1865 (Ray & Ksir, 1993).

Heroin

A synthetic compound, heroin, was developed in 1874 in Germany based on morphine. It has about three times the potency of morphine. Originally thought to be a drug free from addictive propensities, it came to be recognized as a dangerous drug (Ray & Ksir, 1993). Heroin users typically directly inject the drug into their veins with hypodermic needles to produce a stronger effect from the faster delivery of the drug to the brain.

Methadone

Another synthetic drug, methadone, has properties similar to heroin but is less potent, slower acting, and available in tablet form for daily oral use. Due to these features, methadone has less potential for creating addiction or dependency (Ray & Ksir, 1993). Methadone has been used since the 1970s to help heroin abusers deal with their withdrawal reactions when they try to stop using heroin. This method of using one drug to treat another drug is controversial but was widely used in England until abuses in the control of access to the drug became common in the 1960s.

STIMULANTS

Cocaine

Coca shrubs found in the Andes mountains of Peru are the source of cocaine, a potent stimulant extracted from its leaves. Cocaine use leads to short but immediate bursts of energy, strength, and pleasure (McKim, 1997). Its discovery dates back to before the Incas, who chewed its leaves during ceremonies and religious activities until their Spanish conquerors banned its use in the 1500s. It was not until the 1800s that the drug became widely used in Europe for its energizing and stimulating effects on well-being. Extraction of the active ingredient from the leaves provided a more potent form that could be sniffed or injected intravenously. Cocaine became widely used in patent medicines that could be obtained without prescription.

This alkaloid is made into a paste by heating it with hydrochloric acid to produce cocaine hydrochloride. It can be snorted through the nasal passages, intravenously injected, or taken by mouth (Maisto et al., 1995). Cocaine is approximately only 80% to 90% pure because of manufacturing impurities. Drug dealers often "cut" their supply with cheaper substances such as talcum powder, amphetamines, and other fillers until street cocaine is less than 50% pure (Ray & Ksir, 1993).

Cocaine, used in small doses, gradually loses its potency so that the frequency and dosage must be increased to maintain the pleasurable feelings. Higher doses that can be directly inhaled by snorting cocaine powder through nasal passages, injected in veins, or smoked are more stimulating than the low levels that can be obtained from chewing the leaves. However, high doses also may lead to paranoid-like responses, irritability, and hallucinations.

By boiling cocaine in a mixture of strong alkali and explosive solvents, "pure" cocaine is "freed" from many of the impurities. Cocaine without its water-soluble component or "base" is called freebase. Because it is not water soluble, freebase must be vaporized and inhaled to be absorbed by the body.

Crack Cocaine

Another form of cocaine, crack, developed in the mid-1980s, is more concentrated because the water base is boiled out by heating cocaine hydrochloride with a baking soda solution. This procedure does not require dangerous explosive solvents. The product is a crystal or rock, a more concentrated form, that is more dangerous because crack can be smoked, producing a stronger effect than cocaine powder that is used intranasally (Maisto et al., 1995).

Amphetamines

About the same time that use of cocaine declined in the 1920s, another stimulant, amphetamines, with similar effects became popular. This synthetic drug was developed for medicinal purposes such as treatment of asthma, colds, or inducing weight loss through appetite suppression (McKim, 1997). Its chemical structure is similar to ephedrine, the active ingredient in an ancient Chinese herb, *ma huang*, which stimulates the sympathetic nervous system. Between 1930 and the early 1960s, amphetamines were routinely prescribed for treating a variety of clinical problems, including childhood hyperactivity, obesity, and narcolepsy, a sleep disorder.

However, abuse of amphetamines for recreational use soon increased, especially because homemade versions can be made illegally. Amphetamines, as a drug of abuse, were commonly referred to by colorful street names such as speed, uppers, dexies, and bennies. Amphetamines began to be used illegally for the heightened experiences produced by the drug. They were injected intravenously to produce stronger effects than possible in capsule form, but this method increased the likelihood of dependence on the drug (Maisto et al., 1995).

Methamphetamines

Before long, variants of amphetamines that were even more potent were developed. Methamphetamine is the most potent form of amphetamine readily available with or without a prescription, with a duration of effectiveness that is several times that of amphetamines (Ray & Ksir, 1993). Users smoke, swallow, snort, or inject methamphetamines intravenously.

A stronger, smokable form of methamphetamine comes in a crystal rock form and is commonly called *crank, crystal,* or *ice* because of its appearance. The effects of ice resemble those of cocaine but are longer lasting, with highs that last from 2 to 24 hours. Following use, a crash or depression can occur that can last as long as 3 days, during which erratic, violent behavior may occur.

MDMA

A synthetic or "designer drug" receiving much publicity in recent years, MDMA (methylenedioxymethamphetamine), acts simultaneously as a stimulant and a hallucinogen. Ecstasy, as it is glamorously referred to, is derived from both methamphetamine and amphetamine. It is often used during "raves," all-night underground dance parties with techno music accompanied by extensive drug use. Ecstasy stimulates the central nervous system so that users experience hallucinogenic effects and enhanced energy. Using ecstasy at rave parties increases risks of exhaustion and dehydration, and there have been reported cases of fatalities from heat stroke.

DEPRESSANTS

Barbiturates

Barbituarates, a class of synthetic drug used to relieve anxiety and facilitate sleep, were developed in Germany in 1864. Introduced into the United States around the early 1900s for medical purposes, they come in many different types that vary in duration of action. Phenobarbital is a long-acting form, which might calm but not induce sleep, whereas a shorter-acting form such as secobarital would bring about sleep (Maisto et al., 1995). Unfortunately, the faster-acting forms are capable of inducing euphoria and became widely abused street drugs during the 1950s. Clinical use involves the dangers of eventual rebound effects, which impair sleep as well as carry the potential for fatal overdoses (McKim, 1997).

Benzodiazepines

Synthetic antianxiety drugs, called benzodiazepines, became available in the 1960s and were considered much safer than barbiturates, which fell into medical disfavor. The best-known examples, chlordiazepoxide (Librium®), promoted in 1960, and diazepam (Valium®), introduced in 1963, were widely prescribed. Librium®, with a long duration and slow onset, was considered relatively safe, but Valium®, with a more rapid onset, had a greater risk of users developing dependence (Maisto et al., 1995).

One benzodiazepine, flunitrazepam, receiving much attention in the 1990s, is commonly called *roofies.* Marketed as **Rohypnol®**, it is available only by prescription as a short-term treatment of insomnia, as a sedative-hypnotic, and as a preanesthetic medication. It is not manufactured or approved for medical use in the United States but is smuggled because of its low cost and growing popularity among young people. The drug is often taken with alcohol or after cocaine ingestion, possibly to reduce the discomfort experienced after coming down from highs produced by cocaine. The drug has received much notoriety and has been dubbed as the "date rape" drug because of cases in which men have secretly spiked beverages given to their dates to render them incapable of resisting sexual advances. It may lead to reduced blood pressure, memory impairment, drowsiness, visual disturbances, dizziness, confusion, gastrointestinal disturbances, and urinary retention. Some users increase their excitability or aggressive behavior, although the drug is classified as a depressant.

SEDATIVE-HYPNOTICS

Cannabis

Marijuana is extracted from the dried flowers and leaves of hemp, *Cannabis sativa,* a plant found in ancient China about 2800 B.C., where it was used for medicinal and recreational purposes. From China, it spread to many parts of the world, but it was not until the 19th century that marijuana was introduced to Europe (Maisto et al., 1995). The plant also provided hemp, which was important as a source of rope for sailing ships but was no longer a major need in modern ships. The American colonists used the plant for its fiber and also found medicinal applications, but there were no social problems associated with its use during colonial days. During the 1920s, it received a bad reputation because its use by immigrant Mexican laborers in the Southwest was perceived to be associated with violence and crime (Musto, 1987).

Marijuana, colloquially referred to as "grass," "weed," and "pot," usually is smoked in cigarettes ("joints") or in pipes. Users seek the drug for its relaxing and euphoric effects at low levels. Perceptions of time and space can be altered, as with hallucinogens, but high doses can produce hallucinations, panic, and anxiety. The primary active ingredient in marijuana is delta-9-tetrahydrocannabinol (Δ-9 THC), one of 60 cannabinoids found in the plant. Hashish, a related and much stronger drug, is made from the resin of the hemp plant (Maisto et al., 1995).

Hallucinogens

Many drugs are classified as hallucinogens, even though it is not clear what constitutes a hallucination, the altered experience associated with use of these drugs.

The best-known example is lysergic acid diethylamide, more commonly known as LSD-25. This synthetic drug became popular during the drug atmosphere and hippie lifestyle of the 1960s, especially due to the publicity created by its chief proponent, Timothy Leary, a Harvard University professor who championed its use as a means of self-discovery and attainment of personal insight and growth.

LSD-25 comes in different forms that can be swallowed—sugar cubes, capsules, or in blotters. A variety of reactions can occur to psychedelic drugs such as LSD-25, ranging from aesthetic and mystical journeys to frightening and anxiety-producing "bad trips." LSD-25 was made from alkaloids extracted from the ergot molds found on grains. When breads made from infected grains were eaten during famines in medieval France, violent illnesses involving burning sensations, convulsions, and thought disturbances occurred that have been likened to the psychoactive effects of LSD-25.

Mescaline is another hallucinogen that produces effects similar to those of LSD. It is derived from the peyote cactus of the Southwest that the Aztec Indians have used in ceremonies for centuries. Sacramental use of mescaline in rituals is legal in the Native American church. Psilocybin is a less potent hallucinogen than LSD and is obtained from some species of North American mushrooms long regarded as sacred by Aztecs in Mexico and Central America.

A synthetic drug, phencyclidine (commonly called PCP), is of recent origin. It was developed as an anesthetic drug for medical purposes but became a street drug that was popular during the 1970s because of its ability to create trancelike states. It gained notoriety because it was often used to lace marijuana cigarettes given to unsuspecting smokers, which reputedly led them into violent and criminal behaviors.

Some Central Questions

In view of the widespread and significant harmful potential impact of drugs, both licit and illicit, on human behavior, the study of the causes and effects of alcohol and drug consumption is an important undertaking. The following is a preview of some of the broad issues and questions about the psychology of alcohol and drugs that will be raised in this book.

WHO USES ALCOHOL AND OTHER DRUGS?

Before we can answer many questions about alcohol and other drug use, we must reach some agreement on the units of measurement in describing use. Chapter 2 deals with the conceptual and methodological issues involved in defining and measuring substance use. How is use distinguishable from abuse or from dependence? What criteria distinguish abuse from dependence?

Most of Chapter 3 describes survey findings from general household populations that classify respondents into nonusers and users, as shown in Figure 1.2. These surveys determine the relationship of demographic characteristics to the amounts and frequencies of using different types of drugs for specific lengths of time.

Figure 1.2 also shows that among users, a sizable minority has or will eventually develop major difficulties associated with their use, often leading to adverse consequences, including loss of friends, family, jobs, and self-respect. They may become dependent on these substances and possibly move on to more dangerous drugs.

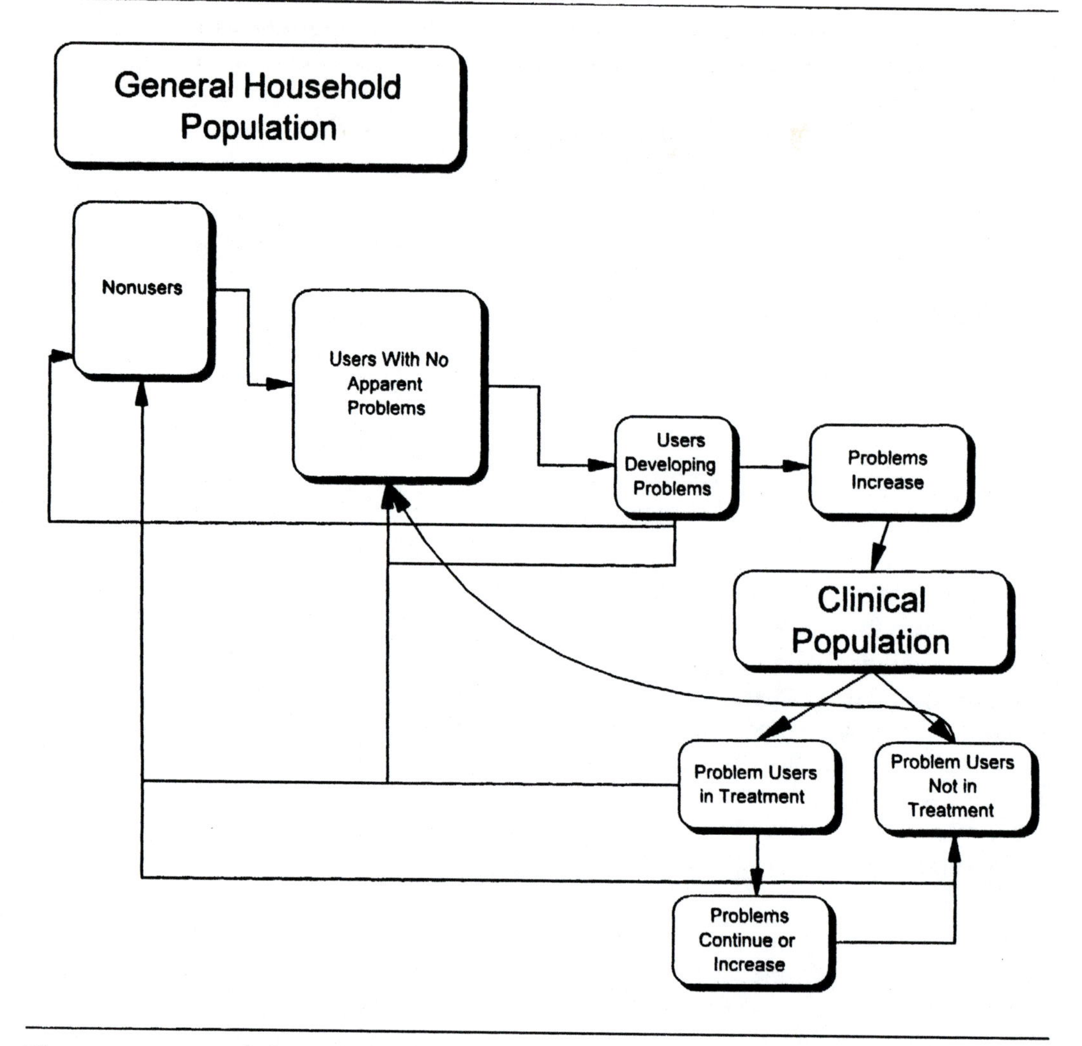

Figure 1.2. Two Different Populations: General Versus Clinical Populations of Alcohol and Other Drug Users

HOW MANY ALCOHOL AND OTHER DRUG USERS DEVELOP PROBLEMS?

Among those with such problems, some will become part of a clinical population (see Figure 1.2). They will seek or be required to accept some type of substance abuse treatment. In later chapters, we will see that this clinical population differs in many characteristics from the general population, and it is important not to assume that generalizations based on one population necessarily apply to the other. In addition, some might benefit from treatment but do not seek or find it. The closing part of Chapter 3 presents evidence on the rates of substance-related abuse and associated problems.

HOW DO ALCOHOL AND OTHER DRUGS AFFECT THE BODY?

A basic understanding of the psychopharmacology and neuropsychology of drugs is presented in Chapter 4. Alcohol and other drugs, to have any effect, must reach the brain centers that control our behavior. Depending on how they enter the body, many factors, including characteristics of the drug and of the user, affect the speed with which they circulate through the body and reach the brain and the rate and means by which they are removed from the body.

Alcohol and drugs affect neurophysiological processes that are the underlying basis of our affective feelings, moods, and emotions as well as cognitive and motivational processes. Information about these processes is essential for the study of how drugs achieve their effects and helps partly explain why drugs are used.

WHAT IS THE RELATIVE ROLE OF HEREDITY AND ENVIRONMENT?

Considerable debate occurs over the roles of heredity and environment on the development of alcohol and drug use. Chapter 5 examines evidence on the relative influence of genetic and environmental factors on drug use. Findings from this research hold implications for developing strategies that may provide the best chances for intervention, treatment, and prevention of alcohol and drug problems.

WHY DO PEOPLE USE ALCOHOL AND OTHER DRUGS?

Theories about the psychology of alcohol and drug use are examined in Chapter 6. Use norms and values differ widely across cultures and fluctuate over time within a given society. These social norms and values associated with the use of different drugs will be examined first because they provide a general context in which individual motives operate.

Different moods and motives precede and accompany the use of psychoactive substances. For example, people who drink alcohol, smoke cigarettes, or take illicit drugs do so when they feel sad, depressed, or lonely. But they also drink or smoke or "do drugs" when they feel happy, elated, and sociable. Psychoactive drugs are used in group settings, but they are also used when people are alone. Social pressure to conform to norms may lead some individuals to engage in drug use to avoid appearing "unsociable." Social factors such as family and parental drug attitudes and behavior influence an individual's drug use. After gaining experience using a drug, some may continue to use, but others may decide to stop using for many different reasons.

Some drugs are illegal in a given society, even though the status of a specific drug may vary over time or place. Most people will avoid the use of these drugs mainly because they are afraid of punishment such as fines and imprisonment or believe that they are addictive. Yet for others, the illegal status may enhance their attraction. Being illegal, they are often expensive and also difficult to obtain readily. Despite these barriers, some may use drugs such as morphine or heroin to relieve pain. Other illicit drugs such as cocaine and amphetamines may be used to produce heightened sensations and stimulation.

HOW DO INDIVIDUAL DIFFERENCES AFFECT ALCOHOL AND OTHER DRUG USE?

Individuals differ in their drug use, as we will detail in the next several chapters. Why do demographic factors have the relationships with alcohol and drug use that have been found as reported in Chapter 3? The role of factors such as age (Chapter 7), gender (Chapter 8), and race or ethnic background (Chapter 9) on alcohol and other drug use with be explored in detail.

Chapter 10 examines how personality differences affect whether an individual takes drugs, if any, as well as the effects of these drugs. Following use of alcohol and other drugs, some people become aggressive and hostile, others show avoidance and uninvolvement, and still others seem more relaxed and friendly. The effects of drugs may vary with personality, but personality also may influence the extent to which alcohol and other drugs are used.

WHAT ARE THE MAJOR PSYCHOLOGICAL EFFECTS OF ALCOHOL AND OTHER DRUGS?

Chapters 11 to 13 look at how alcohol and other drugs affect basic psychological processes such as mood, cognition, emotion, motivation, sensory motor skills, and social interaction. These effects also can be viewed as determinants of subsequent drug use, acting to sustain, increase, or reduce it.

HOW CAN ALCOHOL AND OTHER DRUG ABUSE BE TREATED?

Abuse of many drugs is a major threat to well-being, creating serious physical and mental health problems. Chapters 14 to 16 deal with treatment issues. How effectively can individuals stop drinking, smoking, or using drugs on their own? How successful are mutual help groups such as Alcoholics Anonymous in promoting recovery? How effective are different professional treatment methods for dealing with alcohol and drug dependence? Why do relapses occur in many cases, and how can they be prevented?

HOW CAN ALCOHOL AND OTHER DRUG USE AND RELATED PROBLEMS BE PREVENTED?

Chapter 17 describes psychological approaches to the primary prevention of alcohol and other drug abuse. What types of social policy and control of drug availability and consumption are effective in ameliorating the harmful effects of drugs in our society? How effective are education, taxation, and legislation in influencing drug use?

For each of these broad questions and issues, there have been numerous approaches, theories, and explanations involving physiological, psychological, and sociological factors. In all likelihood, multiple factors act concurrently, sometimes with counteracting influences, to produce the observed differences in drug use behavior, its consequences, and the degree of success in recovery. Theories that focus on single causes probably will not prove as successful as explanations that consider the interplay of multiple determinants ranging from the physiological to the sociological. Similarly, solutions that rely on single factors are also likely to be unsuccessful in treating or preventing alcohol and drug problems.

SUMMARY

Throughout history, humans have used a variety of psychoactive drugs, including depressants, opiates, stimulants, and hallucinogens. In this chapter, a review of the nature and origins of major psychoactive drugs was presented, with emphasis on the history of use in the United States.

Alcohol is the drug most widely used by most American adults. Alcohol may lead eventually to illicit drugs in many cases. We will use research, concepts, and theories developed from the study of alcohol use as a basis for comparison when examining conceptions and evidence about less frequently studied drugs. Use of this strategy is not to deny the seriousness of involvement with the use of other drugs, especially those that are illegal. Many who drink alcohol without any reservations would never think of experimenting with illegal drugs. Use of alcohol is generally tolerated by all but the most moralistic members of society. Understanding the bases for alcohol use may help further our knowledge about the use of illicit drugs.

Major questions about alcohol and other drugs for investigation will include the following: Who uses and in what patterns, what are the effects on the body, what is the relative role of heredity and environment on use, why are they used, how do individual differences affect use, what are the major psychological effects of use, which users develop use-related problems, how can abuse be treated, and how can use and use-related problems be prevented?

STIMULUS/RESPONSE

1. It is instructive to compare the history of social policies that regulate the use of alcohol and various drugs in the United States with those of other societies to get a broader perspective. For example, examine the history of drug policy on heroin in the United Kingdom versus in the United States. Or compare the drug policies on marijuana in the Netherlands with those in the United States. Based on your own views of human behavior, which drug policies in different countries do you think would be most effective or ineffective? Explain your rationale. Do you think adoption of policies from one country would work the same way in another country? Why or why not?

2. Attempts at prohibiting alcohol in the United States as well as in many other countries have failed in general. What do you think are major reasons for this lack of success? What alternative approaches to reducing the problems of alcohol can you suggest that might be better accepted?
3. The annual U.S. social cost of alcohol abuse is nearly $150 billion, according to a report in 1992 from a federal agency. How do you think this determination of the economic costs of alcohol abuse to society is calculated? What categories of outcomes do you think should be considered as a "cost to society"? What problems do you see with the criteria used to define the costs of drugs to society? Do you think alcohol and drugs have any psychological benefits to society? What do you think are some of the economic benefits of alcohol and drug use to society? How would one quantify the benefits of alcohol and drug use?
4. Most alcohol and other drug research examines only the negative effects and consequences. Do you feel this imbalance is due to the reality that negatives exceed the positives, or do you think it reflects a bias of researchers?

- ❖ Defining Use
- ❖ Methods of Measuring Drug Use
- ❖ Use, Abuse, and Dependence
- ❖ Major Conceptions of Alcohol Use Disorders
- ❖ Criteria of Abuse and Dependence
- ❖ Summary
- ❖ Key Terms
- ❖ Stimulus/Response

Defining Use, Abuse, and Dependency 2

One often hears depictions about alcohol and other drug use by others such as, "He's a heavy drinker," "She's a real boozer," "She smokes an awful lot," or "He takes pot sometimes." These descriptions of how much or how often someone uses a drug are vague and do not tell us very much. Compare Cheryl, who drinks a glass of wine every evening at dinner; Brad, who drinks about a six-pack of beer but only on weekends; and Scott, who drinks three or four drinks of scotch and soda about three times a week. Which drinker is the heavier drinker? Which drinker consumes the most alcohol during a typical week? Because the three individuals vary in their temporal pattern of drinking, the type of alcoholic beverage consumed, and the number of drinks per occasion, it is not easy to clearly see which drinker is the "heaviest drinker."

How does one define and measure drug use? "Use" is primarily a descriptive index, typically based on how often a drug is used and in what amounts. The extent of use is related to but not perfectly correlated with the degree of problems for the user or for others. In the first portion of this chapter, we describe the basic methods for defining and obtaining measures of drug use, without consideration of the actual effects of such use levels. As we shall see, the methods needed to determine the use of licit and illicit drugs may differ because of the great difficulty in obtaining information from a representative sample of illicit drug users.

In contrast, other constructs refer to users who have problems for themselves and for others generated by their drug use. Terms such as *addiction, abuse,* and *dependency* are invoked to refer to conditions assumed to underlie these adverse consequences of drug use. The basis for attaching these value-laden terms to drug users is the negative effects of the drugs rather than the actual levels of use. In the second part of this chapter, we will examine the diagnostic criteria used in several major taxonomic classification systems to distinguish use, abuse, and dependency.

Defining Use

The use of any drug is multidimensional, and most measures capture only one or a few of these aspects. Thus far, these indices fall far short in capturing a clear picture of the nature of alcohol and other drug use. To illustrate some of the problems associated with describing the use of any drug, we will describe in detail the measurement of the use of alcohol, the psychoactive drug that has been studied more extensively than any other drug. Due to its wide use and because it is a legal drug that most adult users do not bother to conceal, we are able to obtain more precise information about its use than about the use of illicit substances, which are not as readily reported or observed.

Furthermore, the pharmacological ingredients and potency of alcoholic beverages, like other legal drugs, are regulated and fairly standardized. In contrast, many illicit drugs can vary widely in strength and purity from sample to sample. Because "packaging" of illegal drugs is not standard, users often do not know what dose level they are taking. Even with alcoholic beverages, however, it is not easy to determine the best way to measure the amount of intake, as we shall see.

For any occasion involving alcohol use, there are differences in the type of beverage and number of drinks consumed. Over an extended interval, the frequency of drinking episodes and the amount used differ across drinking occasions for different individuals. The pattern or topography of drinking, which involves the rate of drinking within an episode, also entails different individual consumption patterns for a given beverage. Moreover, different beverage types may be consumed differently (e.g., wine may tend to be sipped delicately, but beer might be gulped down more often).

Alcoholic beverages such as beer, wine, and liquor differ in many respects. Despite these differences, for most research on the causes and effects of alcohol consumption, when researchers refer to a "drink" of alcohol, they usually regard one standard-sized drink of any of these beverages as equivalent in terms of alcohol. In fact, the concentration of alcohol in these different alcohol beverages is not equivalent, with most beer containing about 3% to 4% alcohol by volume, wine 12% to 14%, and liquor 45% to 50%. Because the liquid volume of a typical "drink" of each beverage type also varies, the amount of absolute alcohol is roughly equivalent in a 12-ounce can or bottle of beer, a 5-ounce glass of wine, or a mixed drink or cocktail containing 1½ ounces of liquor.

DEFINING AMOUNT OF DRINKING

The total volume of alcoholic beverages an individual drinks over a given period, such as a day, week, or month, is a widely used convenient summary index of the total amount of alcohol that person consumes. This aggregate index affords convenient comparisons of the drinking of individuals who differ in their patterns of drinking. Thus, the total volume of alcohol consumed can be calculated for individuals with varied drinking habits. Thus, the total alcohol is about the same for Tom, who drinks daily but has only one or two drinks of wine each time; Jeff, who drinks beer occasionally in large quantities coupled with a few occasions involving a small amount of wine; and Brad, who drinks liquor in large quantities but only on weekends.

A volume index of drinking such as a quantity-frequency (QF) score is derived from two more basic dimensions: frequency of consumption and quantity or amount of consumption. For simplicity's sake, assume that people generally drink the same number of times in a period, such as a week or month, and that when they drink they consume about the same number of drinks each time. By simply multiplying the frequency by the quantity consumed per drinking occasion, we obtain a measure that represents the total volume of consumption, known as a quantity-frequency index. Using total volume as the only index of drinking ignores the fact that different combinations of frequency and amount can produce a given total volume, as shown in Table 2.1.

The variables, quantity and frequency, can offset each other in one sense. Thus, a high frequency (30 days in 1 month) of drinking, with a typical low quantity (1 drink) consumed per occasion, yields an aggregate total of 30 drinks per month. Exactly the same total volume of consumption occurs for a drinker with a low frequency (three times a month) of drinking who typically drinks very high quantities (10 drinks) per occasion.

These two extremely different patterns of drinking undoubtedly will have different effects as well as represent individuals with different characteristics and backgrounds. For the same total volume of alcohol, the drinker who engages in heavy drinking, albeit infrequently, is more likely than the one who drinks in smaller amounts, spaced over more occasions, to have problems caused by drinking such as physical harm, cognitive impairment, accidents, and disruption of social relationships.

TABLE 2.1 Very different drinking patterns can produce an identical quantity-frequency (QF) score

Quantity of Drinks	*Frequency of Drinking*	*Quantity Frequency (QF) Score*
1	30	30
2	15	30
3	10	30
5	6	30
6	5	30
10	3	30

NOTE: The same QF score of 30 can be produced by different combinations of quantity of drinks per occasion and frequency of drinking occasions.

The *maximum* or peak consumption levels refer to the highest quantity consumed on an occasion by an individual. This index might be more important than the frequency of consumption when studying factors that are associated with immediate harmful consequences of drinking such as accidents or aggressive behavior. Frequency of drinking might be a reflection of personal values but not necessarily indicate serious physical or psychological harm to drinkers, provided it was at low levels each time. On the other hand, very high-quantity drinking, even if rarely done, would have high risk of harm.

One index of drinking that would likely be associated with harm is a measure of frequency of intoxication, referring to a subjective condition of disorientation and disinhibition more often associated with higher quantities of consumption. A more objective criterion than an index of intoxication associated with impaired behavior is **heavy drinking,** often arbitrarily defined as five or more drinks at a time on several occasions a month.

Individuals show high variability in their use patterns over time. Some drinkers are consistent in using the same amounts and in regular intervals. In contrast, binge drinkers engage in continuous drinking over a period, followed by periods of infrequent drinking or even abstinence. A measure of drinking, such as the QF-V index (Cahalan, 1970), reflects the temporal pattern of drinking by including the degree of variability of drinking over time as a third dimension in addition to quantity and frequency.

Most epidemiological studies focus on the total volume of drinking over a period but need to include measures of patterns of drinking as well (Rehm et al., 1996). The pattern of drinking reflects the social and psychological aspects of the occasion for an individual's drinking such as the social context, drink setting, day of the week, time of the day, and type of drinking companions. Social consequences, both good and bad, may be more strongly tied to drinking patterns than to the volume of consumption.

DEFINING TOBACCO USE

There are also difficulties in obtaining an adequate description of tobacco use. The total number of cigarettes smoked over a given time period is a crude index of smoking that does not consider how cigarettes are smoked. First, the temporal patterns of smoking are ignored when looking only at total consumption. The patterns of cigarette use over the course of a day or week are more like those of caffeine consumption than those of alcohol and many other drugs. Whereas most drinkers restrict their use of alcohol to weekends, mostly in the evening or in conjunction with meals, cigarettes and coffee tend to be consumed many times throughout the day and on most days. Hence, whereas all but the most addicted alcohol user is free of alcohol most of the time, the cigarette smoker is more likely to be under the influence of nicotine almost constantly during waking hours. In part, these differences may reflect the lesser impairment of daily work activities by continuous use of cigarettes than similar involvement with alcohol.

Another reason the number of cigarettes smoked is a poor index of the actual level of smoking is because there is more than one way a cigarette can be smoked. The extent to which each cigarette is smoked and the degree of inhalation of smoke can vary across smokers and even within the same smoker in different situations. For example, low-tar and low-nicotine cigarettes with filters were developed to combat the health threats from nicotine. However, these devices do not work to reduce the hazards of smoking as well as hoped for because smokers of "lights" adjust or titrate nicotine intake levels by smoking more cigarettes; taking more puffs; increasing puff volume, depth, and duration of inhalation; and blocking vents on the filters by covering them with their fingers (Kozlowski, Pillitteri, & Sweeney, 1994). Ironically, these tactics to increase nicotine intake may expose smokers to greater health risks from the tars and carbon monoxide associated with the higher volume of smoke in their lungs. However, studies show no gain in cancer and heart disease risk with low-tar cigarettes.

If one used the approach commonly used for measuring alcohol use, a Q-F smoking index could be computed by determining the typical number of cigarettes smoked each day and the number of days a person smokes during a period. It would have to be adjusted by the amount of nicotine and tar levels contained in different brands and whether the cigarettes were filtered or mentholated.

An aggregate measure of the total number of cigarettes smoked does not adequately reflect variations in the patterns in which individuals smoke their cigarettes. This index would fail to reveal whether that total represented a chain smoker, one who smoked evenly throughout the day, or one who did not smoke every day. Smokers also vary in the number of puffs per cigarette, time between puffs, depth of inhalation, and how much of the entire cigarette is smoked. These factors are important because they affect the amount of nicotine and combustion products such as tars that their lungs receive.

As with **aggregate indices** for any type of drug used, this measure would miss the patterning of use. Cigarettes are typically smoked daily and distributed over the whole day from awakening until bedtime and even in bed for some smokers, unlike alcohol, which may not be used during the week or in the daytime for many drinkers who restrict their use to weekend and evening drinking.

DEFINING ILLEGAL DRUG USE

Attempts to determine the frequency and amount of any illicit drug use may not yield a valid self-report, simply because of the illegal nature of their use. In addition to this problem, the quantity or strength of the dose might prove difficult to measure accurately. Due to the unregulated manufacture of illegal drugs, there is wide variability in the purity or potency of most of these drugs. For example, by the time cocaine reaches the street, it has been adulterated and cut with filler materials to increase the profits for drug dealers. Without standard criteria and regulations, different samples of illicit drugs can vary widely. For example, although morphine constitutes 10% by weight of opium, the samples used by drug abusers can vary from 2.6% to 9.9% (Kalant, 1997). Marijuana obtained from different sources may vary in potency or concentration of its psychoactive substance, *delta 9 THC,* depending on factors such as the subspecies of cannabis plant or the conditions under which it was grown. Cocaine and heroin, cut with fillers by drug dealers to increase their profits, range widely in purity. Without knowledge of the potency and purity of drugs used, it is impossible to accurately determine the dose effect of these drugs on behavior.

Unlike the case for alcohol and tobacco, the route of administration of many illicit drugs varies widely. Injection or smoking the same quantity of heroin or cocaine, for example, allows much more rapid and complete intake of the psychoactive ingredients than oral ingestion. However, this variable must be taken into consideration in addition to the amount consumed because the impact of drugs depends directly on how quickly it gets into the bloodstream to reach the brain.

Methods of Measuring Drug Use

SELF-REPORT MEASURES

Drug research relies heavily on **self-report** of past or current use typically obtained under conditions that protect anonymity. Because admission of using any drug can lead to undesired consequences, an underreporting bias may occur. Even if anonymity is offered, respondents may not trust such promises. For illegal drugs, this problem is obviously much greater.

In addition, retrospective self-reports of drug use are often flawed by inaccuracy of memory. An alternative procedure for legal drugs is to use a prospective self-report in which memory flaws might be minimized or even eliminated if the respondent is motivated to monitor and record future use as it happens. However, such self-monitoring might alter the very behavior being recorded by making individuals realize that they use more than they thought they did or should. Such feedback might change the behavior for some users.

Whether retrospective or prospective, self-reports have been criticized as subjective and apt to be inaccurate or falsified in some contexts. Self-report can sometimes be compared with collateral reports from a family member, spouse, or friend who can provide an independent report about the respondent's drug use, which can be compared with the self-report (Midanik, Klatsky, & Armstrong, 1989). One bias is the tendency to accept the collateral's report as the more objective or accurate measure. For example, if self-reported drinking is lower than what the collateral reports, the drinker is viewed as being in denial. But if the self-reported drinking level is higher than the collateral's report, it is dismissed as inaccurate.

This bias against self-report, in which it is assumed to be the inferior method, may be unwarranted. Many collaterals make estimates based on their expectations about the drug use of the significant other and do not necessarily rely on direct observation, which may be infrequent (Carroll & Carroll, 1995). Indeed, their reports may sometimes be based heavily on the self-reports from the significant other, which can be inflated if the users are bragging to impress others or underestimated when the users are motivated to hide their substance abuse.

Modern technology was used in one study (Searles, Perrine, Mundt, & Helzer, 1995) to measure the validity of self-reports of drinking by providing respondents with pagers to allow a 24-hour surveillance of their real-world drinking for 112 consecutive days. The participants were a heavy-drinking sample, with more than 40% consuming five or more drinks per occasion. Retrospective self-reports of heavy drinkers underreported alcohol use; the beeper data revealed that they engaged in higher use of alcohol than their questionnaire data suggested.

PHYSICAL MEASURES

Many drugs consumed are present in the blood until they are metabolized or excreted. Current alcohol concentrations can be obtained from readings of breath, blood samples, and urine samples. Biochemical measures of **metabolic** products of alcohol such as enzymes, gamma-glutamyltransferase (GGT), as well as physiological indices such as mean corpuscular volume (MCV) are also objective indices of the amount of alcohol that has been consumed.

For nicotine, urine measures of the major metabolite, cotinine, provide some evidence of the extent of cigarette use. Urinanalysis also can detect metabolites of illegal drugs. Cocaine can be detected through the presence of benzoylecgonine, its primary metabolite, in urine for up to about 48 hours after its use. It is not a precise indicator, however, of the amount of use and is apt to overestimate actual use. Marijuana metabolites are more difficult to obtain because most are eliminated in feces rather than in urine.

However, these biological indices have limitations (Carroll & Carroll, 1995). They are limited to measuring very recent usage and must be obtained within a short period following consumption. Moreover, these measures cannot determine the amount of a drug that was consumed over what period of time. For example, a physical index may indicate that drinking occurred, but whether a given reading reflects a small amount recently consumed or a large amount consumed over a longer interval is indeterminate. Moreover, these measures are not tamperproof.

Indirect measures of consumption, such as physical traces, are not perfect and must be assessed along two important dimensions: **sensitivity** and **specificity**. Sensitivity is an index of the extent to which the measure can detect the consumption of a given drug. As Table 2.2 shows, a highly sensitive measure would infrequently miss detecting users. The *specificity* of an index refers to the extent that it does not make false-positive identifications. If other drugs than a specific drug under investigation can produce similar results on the index, specificity of this measure would be low.

TABLE 2.2 Specificity and sensitivity: Two important characteristics of measures for detecting use of alcohol and other drugs

	High-Specificity Measure of Use of a Specific Drug	*Low-Specificity Measure of Use of a Specific Drug*
High-sensitivity measure of using a specific drug	Detects higher percentage of positive cases and makes fewer false-positive errors	Detects higher percentage of positive cases but also makes more false-positive errors
Low-sensitivity measure of using a specific drug	Detects lower percentage of positive cases but does not make many false-positive errors	Detects lower percentage of positive cases and makes more false-positive errors

When other substances also produce high readings on this measure, false-positive cases will occur in which someone who did not use that specific drug will be misclassified as having done so, sometimes with serious legal consequences.

Thus, smoking cigarettes produces cotinine, carbon monoxide, and thiocyanate (SCN), but these products are not specific to smoking because other behaviors also can leave these traces in the body. Dieting, as well as eating broccoli and cauliflower, can increase SCN levels.

SURVEILLANCE INDICATORS

Another indirect source of evidence about legal drug consumption is **surveillance** data or records associated with the sale of alcohol such as tax revenues. Such data merely document levels of possible total consumption but do not reveal patterns of use, heavy or light, or how the total consumption is distributed over different segments of the population. Nor do they deal with how drug use is linked to problems such as health, accidents, or aggression. Obviously, this approach would not be possible for illicit drugs because official sales figures and manufacturing records are not available as they are for alcohol and tobacco products.

Data on adverse consequences related to drug use such as traffic fatalities involving drugs, physical diseases such as cirrhosis of the liver, and admissions to drug treatment facilities provide indirect evidence about the harmful effects of drug use. Such information, however, is correlational and inconclusive about causality. Finally, although sometimes biased or incomplete, historical records and official statistics from government and industry sources can allow insights into the nature of drug use in the historical past.

Use, Abuse, and Dependence

Several distinct but often related aspects of alcohol and other drug use (see Figure 2.1) create social concern: *use* (especially if heavy), *abuse or use-related problems*, and *dependence.*

USE

Light infrequent use of alcohol and many other drugs is not a major concern in terms of adverse physical and psychological consequences. It is heavy or excessive use of drugs that creates social concern. *Heavy* is a rather subjective and relative term, referring to a style of drug use that leads to immediate as well as long-term impaired functioning in the user, conflicts with others, and potential physical health risks to the user. The exact number of drinks that might produce impairment will be affected by other factors such as an individual's past experience with drinking and characteristics such as weight, gender, and genetic background. There is no hard-and-fast objective definition of *heavy* drinking (in many research surveys, it is arbitrarily defined as having five or more drinks on one occasion at least five times in the past month). However, heavy use per se does not necessarily indicate that the alcohol abuser is "addicted" or has no voluntary control over its future use.

Similarly, heavy use of other drugs may or may not constitute addiction to those drugs. Of course, such use might still be cause for alarm due to the risk of harm to self and others. Thus, extensive cigarette smoking has considerable health risks such as coronary and lung disease, even though it does not entail risk for violence or automobile accidents as with heavy alcohol use.

ABUSE OR USE-RELATED PROBLEMS

A second concern about alcohol and other drug use focuses on **abuse** in which use-related problems occur: adverse consequences created during and after alcohol or other drug intake. These **use-related problems** include physical impairment, driving accidents, domestic violence, birth de-

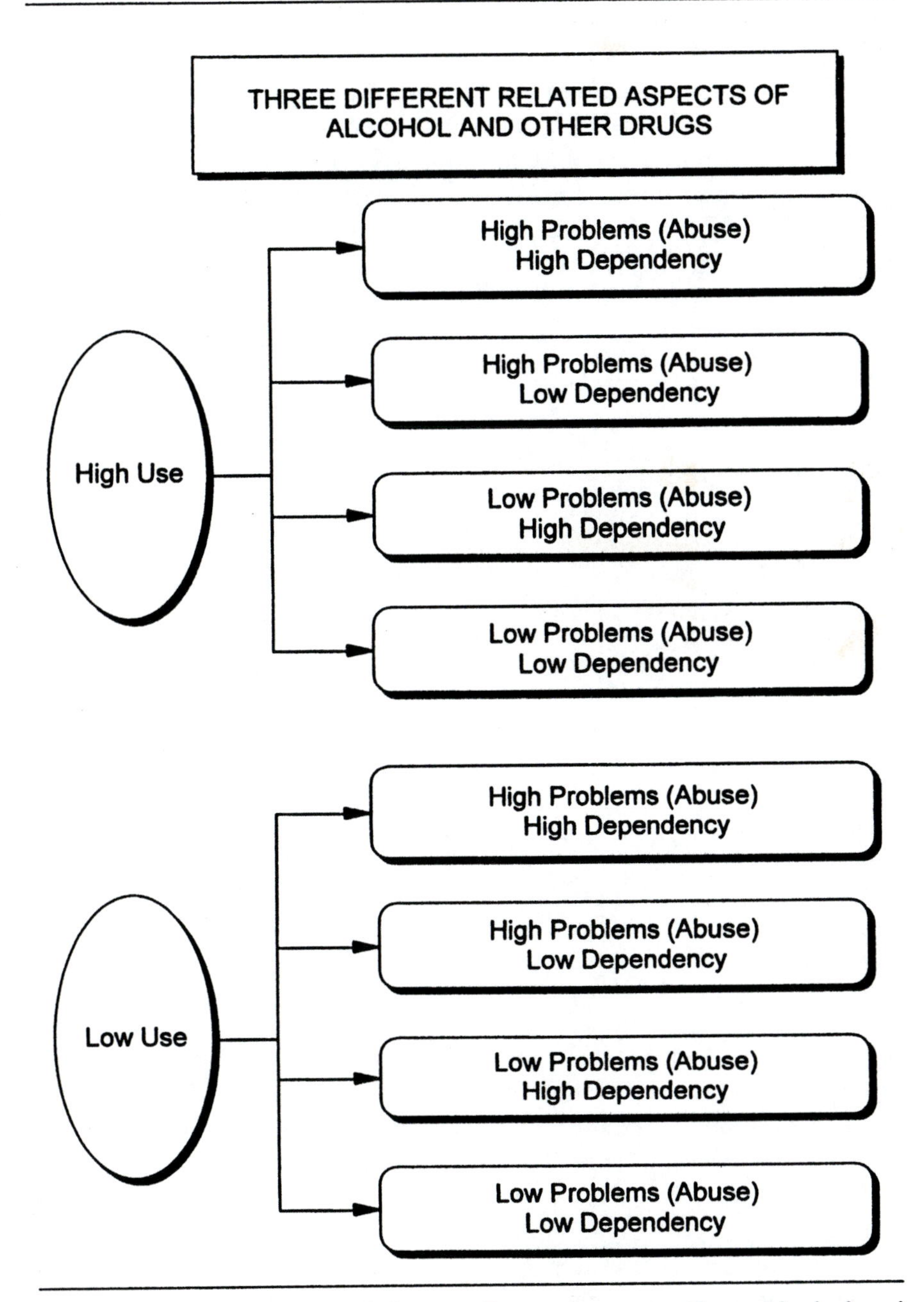

Figure 2.1. Relationship of Three Different Concerns About Alcohol and Other Drugs: Use or Consumption Level, Abuse or Use-Related Problem Level, and Dependence Level

NOTE: Use necessarily must precede abuse and dependence. Although high use is more likely to lead to abuse or dependence, either or both also may exist with low use. Similarly, abuse and dependence can exist together or separately.

fects, work impairment, and legal and financial problems that produce a considerable burden on society as well as on individuals. Although heavier levels of use are more likely to be associated with more adverse psychological and social consequences as well as eventual medical problems, one does not have to ever use alcohol and drugs excessively on a single occasion to encounter these harmful effects, which may occur even for light and occasional users. However, the occurrence of such problems, however serious they might be, is not a basis for establishing the presence of drug dependence.

DEPENDENCE

Dependence is a formulation about substance use developed by psychiatrists and psychologists from extensive clinical observation of drug users in treatment. Dependence is equivalent to the commonly used term *addiction* when referring to the state in which the user no longer seems to be able to control his or her usage. Although some users seem to be able to control their use for many years, it is clear that for others, abuse takes over their lives and disrupts their ability to function normally. This condition, in which either a strong physiological or psychological need to use alcohol or drugs develops, is not a strict function of the amount or frequency of use. It is not limited to heavy and frequent users because even some light or infrequent users may experience dependence.

OVERVIEW

A focus on one of these three dimensions, without recognition of the other aspects, yields an incomplete picture. Each of the three aspects and different combinations of them is unique and should not be considered equivalent to one of the others. Some individuals might have only one or two of these three problems. Thus, one person might engage in heavy use, suffer use-related problems, and yet not show dependence. Another person might be dependent and have use-related problems, despite a low use level. Yet another person might use heavily, be dependent, but not show much evidence of use-related problems. Finally, some users may suffer from all three problems.

How closely are these different aspects of alcohol and drug use related? For example, is use level highly correlated with dependence? Are use-related problems associated strongly with use level? And how closely is dependence related to use-related problems?

Interviews with 22,102 current drinkers in the 1988 National Health Interview Survey (Dawson, 1994) showed that measures based on the frequency of heavy drinking, such as average daily intake, frequency of heavy drinking, and usual quantity and frequency of drinking, were strongly correlated with alcohol dependence during the past year. However, *alcohol consumption measures* were not as sensitive or specific in identifying dependence as were measures based on *alcohol-related problems.*

Drinkers who later develop alcohol dependence may be identifiable from their early consumption patterns. A comparison (York, 1995) of alcoholics and social drinkers assessed drinking patterns over different phases, from the start of regular drinking and continuing up to the present. Drinkers who later became alcoholics began drinking at higher quantities and frequencies as compared to social drinkers. Consumption in alcoholics rose rapidly and peaked near age 40. In contrast, intake of social drinkers remained relatively constant across subsequent drinking phases at about three to four drinks per drinking occasion, with a slight increase in the frequency of drinking over time.

Major Conceptions of Alcohol Use Disorders

DISEASE CONCEPTION OF ALCOHOLISM

An influential formulation was the **disease conception,** a model of alcohol use that is either excessive or generates major problems for users. This formulation, proposed by Jellinek (1960), has had a major influence on the way most people think of alcoholism as well as other drug dependencies to this day. This model, proposed by one of the leading alcohol scholars of his time, was important because it provided a disease model as an alternative to the prevailing moral model that held that alcoholics drank because they lacked willpower. Instead of condemning the alcoholic and denying compassion and treatment, the disease model called for a nonjudgmental response and treatment just as for other physical diseases.

The abuser was seen as unable to control the disease and in need of expert medical attention. A central tenet of Jellinek's (1960) model of alcoholism was that the disease involved a loss of control over drinking, an inability to stop drinking after only one or two drinks. Similarly, a major criterion of an alcoholic, according to Alcoholics Anonymous (AA)—the widely known mutual aid recovery group for alcoholics started in the mid-1930s—is the self-perception that one is "powerless" or has lost control of one's drinking. This is a highly subjective rather than a scientific or medical definition but one that proponents of AA regard as a necessary self-perception before the road to recovery can begin. A fuller discussion of AA and its role in recovery from alcohol problems will be presented in Chapter 14.

Abuse of other substances such as opiates and cocaine also has been conceived of as a disease, leading to behavior that the abuser has no control over once the addiction has been established. Following the lead of AA, similar organizations such as Narcotics Anonymous (NA) and Cocaine Anonymous (CA) have employed a 12-step program for recovery from heroin and cocaine abuse, respectively.

ALCOHOL DEPENDENCE SYNDROME

Currently, even though the term *alcoholism* is still more familiar and used by the public, clinicians and researchers increasingly refer to it as *alcohol dependence*, a formulation that originated with a conception called the **alcohol dependence syndrome** (ADS), proposed by British researchers (Edwards & Gross, 1976). Instead of relying on the drinker's self-perception as the disease concept did, this approach defined dependence in terms of more objective criteria listed below and described briefly in Figure 2.2.

The ADS formulation emphasized a continuum of drinking levels rather than the dichotomy implied by the alcoholic-nonalcoholic distinction. The separation between physical and psychological dependence is blurred under this conception. Impaired control of drinking, rather than a loss of control, was postulated to acknowledge that the phenomenon was not an all-or-none phenomenon.

The ADS is biaxial, involving two separate dimensions: alcohol dependence and alcohol-related problems. Dependence may or may not be associated with alcohol-related problems. Thus, a drinker who is alcohol dependent may be surprisingly free from physical, economic, or social problems from drinking. Also, a drinker who sustained physical damage or adverse social consequences from heavy drinking may not necessarily be alcohol dependent. According to the ADS model, all drinkers who develop alcohol dependence will not go through an invariant progression of stages or "phases" with certain symptoms, in contrast to AA's disease conception of alcoholism.

The **World Health Organization (WHO)** (1978) included the alcohol dependence syndrome (ADS), starting in its ninth revision of the ***International Classification of Diseases*** (*ICD-9*). The concept of alcohol dependence was proposed as an improvement over the disease concept of alcoholism because it does not place as much focus on the physiological basis

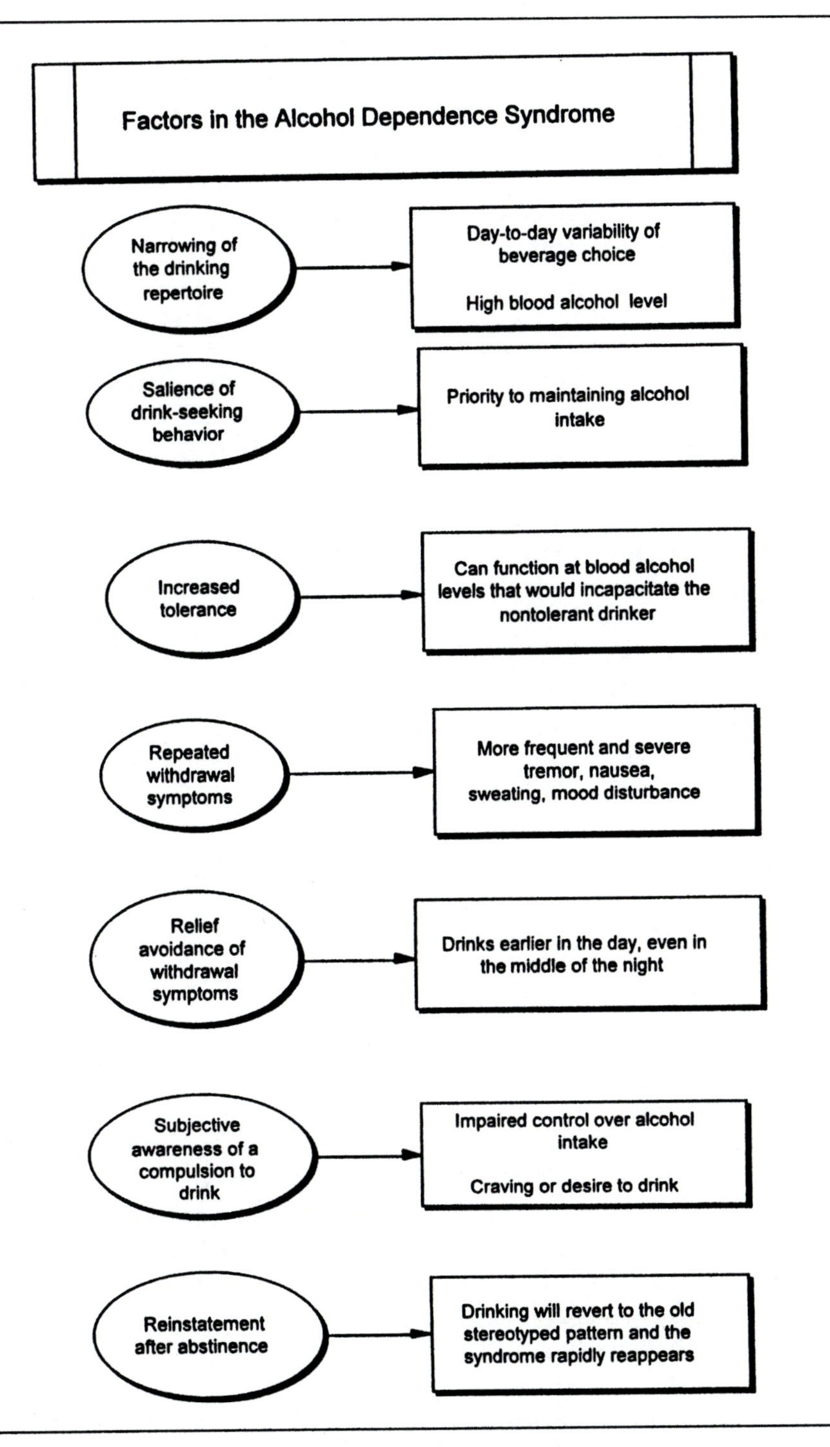

Figure 2.2. Alcohol Dependence Syndrome Characteristics
SOURCE: Adapted from National Institute on Alcohol Abuse and Alcoholism (1990).

of alcohol problems but instead recognizes psychological and sociological factors. Similarly, dependence has been proposed to deal with any drug in which the user is unable to stop using these other drugs.

Criteria of Abuse and Dependence

Controversies and debates in the field have sometimes stemmed from variations in how alcohol and drug dependency were defined and diagnosed. Answers to questions about the causes of alcohol and drug dependency or the best methods for its treatment often depended on which definition was used.

The disease concept of alcoholism advocated by Jellinek and AA involves a high degree of subjectivity because it requires the alcoholic to label himself or herself as an alcoholic. In contrast, three major alternative conceptions relied on more objective criteria for defining alcoholism and drug dependency: two versions of the *Diagnostic and Statistical Manual* criteria (*DSM-III-R* and *DSM-IV;* American Psychiatric Association, 1987, 1994) and the *International Classification of Diseases* (WHO, 1990), now in its 10th version (*ICD-10*). These criteria are periodically revised as more clinical evidence has accumulated, with experts attempting to reach greater consensus on diagnostic criteria.

DIAGNOSTIC AND STATISTICAL MANUAL *CRITERIA (*DSM-III-R*)*

The American Psychiatric Association developed its own set of criteria for defining major psychological disorders, including substance use disorders, known as the ***Diagnostic and Statistical Manual*** **(*DSM*)**. Although the examples of criteria for two different versions of the *DSM* use the term *alcohol,* the *DSM* uses the term *substance* to include other drugs as well. One widely used version, now superceded, is the *DSM-III-R* (1987); it is described here because earlier studies cited in this book used it.

DSM-III-R distinguished between two levels, ***abuse*** and ***dependency.*** A maladaptive pattern of drug use or recurrent use in physically hazardous situations during the past year, lasting at least 1 month or occurring repeatedly over a longer period, was termed *abuse,* as shown in Table 2.3. To be classified as *dependent,* the user had to meet any three of the set of nine criteria shown in Table 2.4, with symptoms in at least two of these criteria occurring two or more times in the past year.

TABLE 2.3 Comparisons of criteria for substance abuse under *DSM-III-R, DSM-IV,* and *ICD-10*

DSM-III-R alcohol abuse

A. A maladaptive pattern of alcohol use indicated by at least one of the following:
   (1) Continued use despite knowledge of having a persistent or recurrent social, occupational, psychological, or physical problem that is caused or exacerbated by the use of alcohol
   (2) Drinking in situations in which use is physically hazardous
B. Some symptoms of the disturbance have persisted for at least 1 month or have occurred repeatedly over a period of time
C. Never met the criteria for alcohol dependence

DSM-IV alcohol abuse

A. A maladaptive pattern of alcohol use leading to clinically significant impairment or distress, as manifested by one (or more) of the following occurring within a 12-month period:
   (1) Recurrent drinking resulting in a failure to fulfill major role obligations at work, school, or home
   (2) Recurrent drinking in situations in which it is physically hazardous
   (3) Recurrent alcohol-related legal problems
   (4) Continued alcohol use despite having persistent or recurrent social or interpersonal problems caused or exacerbated by the effects of alcohol
B. The symptoms have never met the criteria for alcohol dependence

ICD-10 harmful use of alcohol

A. A pattern of alcohol use that is causing damage to health. The damage may be physical or mental. The diagnosis requires that actual damage should have been caused to the mental or physical health of the user.
B. No concurrent diagnosis of the alcohol dependence syndrome

SOURCE: American Psychiatric Association (1987, 1994); World Health Organization (1990). Used with permission.

Using 99 patients differing in degree of the severity of dependence, researchers (Andreatini, Galduroz, Ferri, & Oliveira De Souza Formigioni, 1994) made a test of the validity of the *DSM-III-R* (1987) cutoff point for a positive diagnosis of dependence as the presence of any three out of nine criteria. Only some of the nine symptoms ("excessive drinking," "desire or efforts to control drinking," and "drinking despite major

TABLE 2.4 *DSM-III-R, DSM-IV,* and *ICD-10* diagnostic criteria for alcohol dependence

	DSM-III-R	*DSM-IV*	*ICD-10*
Symptoms	A. At least three of the following:	A. A maladaptive pattern of alcohol use, leading to clinically significant impairment or distress as manifested by three or more of the following occurring at any time in the same 12-month period:	A. Three or more of the following have been experienced or exhibited at some time during the previous year:
Tolerance	(1) Marked tolerance—need for markedly increased amounts of alcohol (i.e., at least 50% increase to achieve intoxication or diminished effect with same amount of alcohol)	(1) Need for markedly increased amounts of alcohol to achieve intoxication or desired effect or markedly diminished effect with continued use of the same amount of alcohol	(1) Evidence of tolerance, such that increased doses are required to achieve effects originally produced by lower doses
Withdrawal	(2) Characteristic withdrawal symptoms for alcohol (3) Alcohol often taken to relieve or avoid alcohol withdrawal syndrome	(2) The characteristic withdrawal syndrome for alcohol, or alcohol (or a closely related substance) is taken to relieve or avoid withdrawal symptoms	(2) A physiological withdrawal state when drinking has ceased or been reduced as evidenced by the characteristic withdrawal symptoms of alcohol (or a closely related substance) to relieve or avoid withdrawal symptoms
Impaired control	(4) Persistent desire or one or more unsuccessful efforts to cut down or control drinking (5) Drinking in larger amounts or over a longer period than the person intended	(3) Persistent desire or one or more unsuccessful efforts to cut down or control drinking (4) Drinking in larger amounts or over a longer period than the person intended	(3) Difficulties in controlling drinking in terms of onset, termination, or levels of use
Neglect of activities	(6) Important social, occupational, or recreational activities given up or reduced because of drinking	(5) Important social, occupational, or recreational activities given up or reduced because of drinking	(4) Progressive neglect of alternative pleasures or interests in favor of drinking
Time spent drinking	(7) A great deal of time spent in activities necessary to obtain alcohol, drink, or recover from its effects	(6) A great deal of time spent in activities necessary to obtain alcohol, drink, or recover from its effects	(5) A great deal of time spent in activities necessary to obtain alcohol, drink, or recover from its effects

	DSM-III-R	*DSM-IV*	*ICD-10*
Inability to fulfill roles	(8) Frequent intoxication or withdrawal symptoms when expected to fulfill major role obligations at work, school, or home	None	None
Hazardous use	When drinking is physically hazardous	None	None
Drinking despite problems	(9) Continued drinking despite knowledge of having a persistent or recurrent social, psychological, or physical problem that is likely to be caused or exacerbated by alcohol use	(7) Continued drinking despite knowledge of having a persistent or recurring physical or psychological problem that is caused or exacerbated by alcohol use	(5) Continued drinking despite clear evidence of overly harmful physical or psychological consequences
Compulsive use	None	None	(6) A strong desire or sense of compulsion to drink
Duration criterion	B. Some symptoms of the disturbance have persisted for at least 1 month or have occurred repeatedly over a longer period of time	B. No duration criterion separately specified. However, three or more dependence criteria must be met within the same year and must occur repeatedly as specified by duration qualifiers associated with criteria (e.g., "often," "persistent," "continued").	B. No duration criterion separately specified. However, three or more dependence criteria must be met during the previous year.
Criterion for subtyping dependence	None	With physiological dependence: Evidence of tolerance or withdrawal (i.e., any of items A (1) or A (2) above are present) Without physiological dependence: No evidence of tolerance or withdrawal (i.e., none of items A (1) or A (2) above are present)	None

SOURCE: American Psychiatric Association (1987, 1994), World Health Organization (1990). Used with permission.

NOTE: The *DSM-III-R, DSM-IV,* and *ICD-10* refer to substance dependence. These criteria have been adapted to focus solely on alcohol.

problems") occurred frequently across the spectrum of dependence severity. In contrast, other symptoms appeared prominently only in the more severe cases ("much time devoted to alcohol," "important activities given up," and "drinking to relieve withdrawal"). Thus, the nine symptoms are not equally important, even though they are treated as if they were when making diagnoses.

DIAGNOSTIC AND STATISTICAL MANUAL *CRITERIA* (DSM-IV)

In the *DSM-IV* (1994), the distinction between abuse and dependence was further refined. *Abuse* requires a maladaptive pattern of drug use, according to the four listed criteria in Table 2.3, assuming that the criteria for dependence for this class of substance have never been met by the individual being diagnosed. To be classified as *dependent,* a drug user must meet three or more of the seven criteria listed in Table 2.4 in the same 12-month period.

In the *DSM-IV* (1994), a diagnosis of dependence no longer required the presence of tolerance or withdrawal as necessary criteria, as was true in the *DSM-III-R* (1987). If *physiological dependence,* defined as either tolerance or withdrawal, is present, the *DSM-IV* indicates that it should be noted but does not require it as a defining characteristic of substance dependence. These changes complicate comparisons between studies using the *DSM-III-R* and *DSM-IV.* Thus, heavy cocaine users who stop do not show clear withdrawal reactions as striking as those seen with a drug such as alcohol, even though they may have other indications of dependency. Under *DSM-III-R* criteria, they would not be diagnosed as dependent as they might be under *DSM-IV* criteria.

Unlike *DSM-III-R* (1987) definitions, in which the duration of symptoms must occur continuously over a month or repeatedly over a longer period of time, the duration requirement in the *DSM-IV* (1994) applies to individual diagnostic criteria and not to the categories of abuse and dependence per se.

A set of psychiatric symptoms that occur in a more or less fixed sequence supports the construct validity of the underlying problem. Is there an orderly onset of the symptoms used in the *DSM-IV* (1994) criteria to define abuse and dependence? In a study of 369 clinical cases (Langenbucher & Chung, 1995), onset of alcoholism appeared to occur in three discrete stages: alcohol abuse, dependence, and accommodation to the illness. This evidence supports the construct validity of alcohol abuse as a discrete first phase from dependence, which is a distinct construct.

A study of alcohol *consumption* provides some support for the lessened emphasis attached to tolerance and withdrawal in the *DSM-IV* (1994) criteria for substance abuse and dependence (Dawson, Grant, & Harford, 1995). The relationship between average daily ethanol intake and the relative frequency of drinking five or more drinks on a drinking occasion in 22,102 current drinking adults was assessed. For selected levels of consumption, drinking outcomes such as impaired control, continued drinking despite problems, and hazardous drinking were about 50% more likely than were tolerance and withdrawal.

INTERNATIONAL CLASSIFICATION OF DISEASES (*ICD-10*)

The 10th revision of the *International Classification of Diseases* (*ICD-10*), containing the WHO (1990) criteria, is also mentioned in Tables 2.3 and 2.4. Because the *ICD* deals with all types of physical health problems, it chose the term *harmful use* instead of *abuse* when referring to problems that are less serious than dependency. As Table 2.3 indicates, harmful use deals only with harm to the user in contrast to the *DSM* category of abuse that extends to cover social harm. *ICD-10* criteria are similar to *DSM* criteria with respect to dependency, as shown in Table 2.4. However, both formulations were vague, using terms such as *often, frequent,* or *progressive neglect.* Moreover, no clear time frame existed for making diagnoses, with the *ICD-10* specifying that the symptoms be present in the past 6 months and the *DSM-III-R* using at least 1 month or repeatedly over a longer period.

RELATIONSHIPS AMONG TAXONOMIES

One study (Schuckit et al., 1994) examined the relationships between *DSM-III-R, DSM-IV,* and *ICD-10* diagnostic criteria for substance use disorders for 1,922 alcohol-dependent probands and their relatives who participated in the Collaborative Study on the Genetics of Alcoholics. Proportions of individuals diagnosed in the three systems were similar, with the highest numbers observed for the *DSM-III-R* and the lowest for the *ICD-10.* Although the same individuals generally received the same diagnosis under the three systems for dependency, diagnosis for *abuse* or harmful use had low agreement across the three systems.

To understand why definitions of dependence differ and also continually undergo change, it is necessary to examine the origins, functions, and goals of these major classification systems (Kendall, 1991). The *ICD-9* is a comprehensive classification covering all "diseases, injuries, and causes of death," and the *ICD-10* (WHO, 1990) deals with all "diseases and related health problems." In contrast, the *DSM* is limited to mental and psychiatric disorders. The *ICD* deals with a broader audience of health professionals than does the *DSM*, and it must be accepted in 140 countries and in at least eight languages. The *DSM* is directed more to mental health professionals and emphasizes problems that are more prominent in Western society than in other cultures (e.g., some types of sexual dysfunction and eating disorders).

It is instructive to trace the history of both taxonomies (Widiger, Frances, Pincus, Davis, & First, 1991). In 1948, the sixth edition of the *ICD* included for the first time a classification of mental disorders, but it did not meet the needs of American psychiatrists, who developed their own nomenclature in 1952 with the first version of the *DSM*. Since then, the two organizations have revised their taxonomies several times in light of new thinking and evidence. Although converging in their definitions, the two approaches still differ. These classification systems are advances over prior systems because they have been empirically tested, with data available on the reliability and validity of diagnostic categories. Both are periodically revised, and the hope is that eventually the definitions will converge.

SUMMARY

Alcohol and drug use involve many different dimensions such as frequency and quantity of use (dose). First, however, before one can measure use of any drug, we must have a unit of measure for that drug. For legal drugs, there are fairly uniform standards, but such is not the case for most illegal drugs. Thus, the amount of alcohol in a bottle of beer or a glass of wine can be readily estimated, but the degree of purity of illegal drugs is not standardized.

Three aspects need to be distinguished. *Use* simply refers to the taking of a drug, irrespective of the level of use. By "use," we are only examining drug taking, without consideration of the effects of drugs. When problems arise from any type or level of use, *abuse* is involved. Finally, *dependency* involves impaired control over use, irrespective of the actual quantity or frequency of use or level of harm.

The second part of this chapter focuses on the evolution of the criteria used by clinicians and researchers to assess and distinguish among drug use, drug abuse, and drug dependency. In the mind of the public, the disease conception is the best known due to its widespread dissemination through AA. Although it originated with alcohol, this formulation has been adapted and extended to many other drugs, as well as to addictions not involving pharmacological substances. The disease conception involves a specific sequence of symptoms that occur over the course of the development of alcoholism or any other dependency. It also entails a theoretical account of the origins of the disease in terms of physical factors, although it also recognizes that a "spiritual" disease also was involved. Ultimately, AA's definition requires that there be a self-recognition of dependency on the part of the individual before recovery can begin.

In contrast, scientifically developed criteria such as the alcohol dependence syndrome and succeeding versions of *DSM* and *ICD* criteria are objective but do not concur among themselves. These formulations will continue to undergo refinement as more research evidence becomes available. It is important to note that these taxonomies are only descriptions of the symptoms. As important as description is, it should not be confused with theoretical or explanatory accounts of the underlying processes, causes, and effects of drug dependency.

KEY TERMS

Abuse
Aggregate indices
Alcohol dependence syndrome
Dependence
Diagnostic and Statistical Manual (DSM)
Disease conception
Heavy drinking
International Classification of Diseases (ICD)
Metabolic (indices of drug use)
Self-report
Sensitivity
Specificity
Surveillance (indicators of use)
Use
Use-related problems
World Health Organization (WHO)

STIMULUS/RESPONSE

1. Most measures in survey research on drugs focus on frequency, quantity, or a combined index of frequency and quantity of use. However, these mea-

sures usually do not identify situational factors such as where, when, or with whom people use drugs. Do you think this additional information would be helpful in understanding why drugs are used and what effects they have?

2. Devise three different ways to measure how much a person drinks or smokes. Assuming your methods do not produce the same estimates, which of your methods might be likely to yield the highest estimates, and which might tend to produce lower estimates of the actual consumption? Explain why estimates might depend on the method of assessment. Which method would be best for the purpose of identifying health risks from drinking?
3. How much use of a drug is "too much"? Base your answer on different criteria such as medical, legal, or social by which such a judgment might be made.

- The Epidemiological Approach
- National Surveys of Alcohol and Other Drug Use
- The Ethnographic Approach
- Stability of Use Patterns
- Abstention
- Rates of Alcohol and Drug Abuse and Dependency
- Summary
- Key Terms
- Stimulus/Response

3 The Extent of Alcohol and Other Drug Use

People use alcohol and other drugs in many different contexts, and the amount they consume may vary on different occasions. Moreover, some individuals have regular use patterns, but others use irregularly, depending on stresses and events in their lives. Alcohol and other drugs often are used together in varying combinations or sequences. Measuring the use patterns for different substances and the correlates of such activity provides important data about the scope of use. Identifying the relationship of patterns of use to different psychological, physical, and behavioral effects offers valuable evidence for evaluating theories about the causes and consequences of alcohol and other drug use.

A thorough description would identify the characteristics of users and specify which substances they prefer. How often and in what amounts are these drugs used? When and where do they use, with whom do they "do drugs," and how do they get the drugs into their bodies? If they use more than one drug, what combination(s) do they use? What causes use, and what are the physiological, psychological, and behavioral effects? In addition to determining these characteristics of current use, it is important to determine the degree and direction of change over time in these aspects of use.

The first half of this chapter parallels the first section of the preceding chapter and presents some major survey findings about the epidemiology of using alcohol and other drugs in the general population in the United States. For the present purpose, use and abuse are not distinguished. Then, using standard diagnostic criteria to define clinical populations described in the second part of the preceding chapter, evidence on prevalence rates of abuse and dependency for alcohol and other drugs will be examined. Due to the difficulty of obtaining detailed illicit drug use data from surveys with large representative samples of the general population, ethnographic observations and interviews with smaller samples, which probably do not reflect the use by the general population, will be included to expand on survey findings on selected illicit drugs such as marijuana, cocaine, and opiates.

The Epidemiological Approach

Epidemiology, a specialty within the field of public health, involves the use of large-scale random samples to obtain information about the number and characteristics of users in the general population. In contrast, instances of drug use that achieve notoriety and public attention such as those associated with overdose deaths, crimes, violence, family dissolution, and other problems represent one extreme sample, typically involving heavy and frequent users or those who use drugs in hazardous environments and circumstances.

Although it is important to acknowledge these extreme cases so they can serve as warnings of the dangers that may occur from alcohol and other drug use, we must ask if these outcomes are typical among all users. Just as we should not assume that the majority of airplanes crash when we hear of one such disaster, we need to determine not only how many substance users suffer adverse consequences but also how many do not experience these negative outcomes.

WHO GETS SURVEYED?

One would not want to generalize about the nature of alcohol and drug use in the general population based on results from surveys conducted with convenience samples such as shoppers at a mall, occupants at a homeless shelter, or clients in a treatment facility. Nor would one want to rely on data from other biased samples such as the regular patrons at the corner bar, residents of a retirement center, or the novitiates at a monastery. Instead, scientific surveys use samples chosen at random to ensure that the respondents represent a cross section of the population to which one wishes to generalize.

National surveys of the general population of the United States usually require thousands of respondents to provide adequate representation from different major subgroups of the whole population. Such surveys entail considerable planning, time, effort, and expense. Useful survey data also can be obtained from more specialized groups, provided some **random selection** of the sample is involved. Thus, one need not conduct a national survey of households if one wanted to draw conclusions about drug use among a special population such as college students, pregnant women, or unemployed men.

It should be pointed out that surveys of alcohol or other drug use or consumption in the general population should not be viewed as a method of determining rates of *dependency*, a construct discussed in Chapter 2. Although some of the respondents in population surveys may indeed be dependent or, more commonly termed, *addicted*, household surveys fail to sample many alcohol- and drug-dependent persons such as homeless persons, inmates of correctional facilities, and residents of other institutions, including inpatient drug treatment facilities.

Epidemiological studies have limitations. On one hand, the total use may be underestimated, especially for illegal drugs, because epidemiological studies tend to not include extreme cases such as inpatients of drug treatment facilities. At the same time, they also may overestimate the total number of users because multiple drug users, those who take several drugs concurrently or sequentially, get counted more than once because they are represented for each drug they use.

Epidemiological studies measure the number of new cases (**incidence**) as well as the number of existing cases (**prevalence**) of various aspects of alcohol and drug use. Surveyors estimate the rates of incidence and prevalence of these variables for specific intervals such as the current month (past 30 days), an extended period such as the past year (past 12 months), or lifetime.

These studies only tell or indicate what use patterns occurred, but they do not provide *explanatory* or theoretical accounts of underlying processes for these use patterns. However, these observations of drug use patterns provide the raw data necessary to develop and test theories or explanations of drug use, assist in the planning of education and intervention programs, and influence public drug policy. These data can be examined to see how important demographic factors such as age, gender, socioeconomic class, and ethnicity are related to drug use and related consequences. This chapter will focus on the basic methods of these surveys, their general findings, and their limitations. More detailed findings about demographic patterns will be presented in subsequent chapters explaining age, gender, and racial/ethnic group alcohol and drug use.

National Surveys of Alcohol and Other Drug Use

Numerous surveys of alcohol and drug use exist, but we will focus on two large-scale annual national surveys, the **Monitoring the Future (MTF)**

Survey conducted with 8th-, 10th-, and 12th-grade high school students administered by the University of Michigan (Johnston, Wadsworth, O'Malley, Bachman, & Schulenberg, 1997) and the **National Household Survey on Drug Abuse (NHSDA)** conducted with persons age 12 and older, sponsored by the Substance Abuse and Mental Health Services Administration (U.S. Department of Health and Human Services, 1997a). Unlike many surveys that are taken only once and use small biased or nonrandom samples, these national surveys employ large and random probability samples and have been administered periodically since the early 1970s.

MONITORING THE FUTURE STUDY

The MTF study reports the percentage of users for several periods—daily, past month, past 12 months, and lifetime (ever used). It should be emphasized that with the exception of the items asking about binge drinking (defined by the MTF as having five or more drinks on one occasion in the past 2 weeks) and heavy drinking (defined here as having five or more drinks on one occasion five or more times in the past month), the amount or level of use is not considered in defining a user. As long as a respondent reports *some* amount of use during the period measured, he or she is counted as a user. Reports of current use for the past month may be more accurate than reports of use over longer intervals such as the past year or lifetime due to greater forgetting and distortion for longer periods.

The category "user" is not as clear-cut as it might appear. This group includes first-time users, continuous or longer-term users, and former users who stopped for a period but have resumed use during the interval in question. Moreover, this definition ignores the fact that users vary widely in use quantities and frequencies.

As noted in Chapter 2, the term *user* includes both those who are not experiencing any physical or psychological problems from their current use as well as those who do have problems such as behavioral impairment, antisocial and violent behavior, undesirable mood changes, or accidents associated with their drug use. Use is not a measure of pathology or dysfunction, although eventually some users may develop psychological and behavioral problems from drug use.

Some indication of the extent to which use is stable over time can be obtained by comparing the percentages of three groups of users in the MTF surveys: those using in the past month, those using during the past year but not in the past month, and those who used sometime during their lifetimes but not in the past year. The differences between rates of current month, past year, and lifetime users should be relatively small for "addictive" drugs if, as commonly believed, users of such drugs find it difficult to stop. If, however, many users are experimental users who try a drug out of curiosity or peer pressure but soon reject its continued use, larger discrepancies should exist between use rates for lifetime, past year, and current month. Similarly, such gaps may be expected if some users are "chippers" rather than addicts, users who drift in and out of drug use, depending on whom they hang around with, the social setting, and their psychological needs.

Drifting in and out of drug use may be a common experience, as attested to by Mark Twain's tongue-in-cheek observation to the effect that he knew it was easy to quit smoking because he had done it many times. His quip implies that he resumed smoking at least as many times as he "quit." If we could have included him in a survey, his current status as a smoker would obviously depend on when he was asked.

Figure 3.1 shows the MTF drug use rates among 12th graders for the past month, the past year but not in the past month, and lifetime or "ever used" but not in the past year (Johnston, Wadsworth, et al., 1997). Although the differences vary with the specific drug, it should be no surprise that the longer the interval, the larger the percentage of users because more time is available. More interestingly, there are large gaps between current, past year, and lifetime use rates of many illegal drugs. For example, among 12th graders, the rate of use of marijuana is about 21.2% for use in the past month, about 34.7% for the past year, and about 41.7% for (ever used) lifetime use in the 1995 MTF survey. Thus, about one in five used marijuana at least once in the past month, but they represented only about half of those who had ever used it and only about two thirds of those who had used it in the past year. Similar large gaps exist for rates of using cocaine, which dropped from 6% (lifetime) to 4% (past year) to 1.8% (past month), and for heroin, which dropped from 1.6% (lifetime) to 1.1% (past year) to 0.6% (past month).

Although the rate of current use for any illicit drug may be seen as the "bad news," the large gap between past year and lifetime use compared to current use could be viewed as the "good news." These differences reflect the possibility that many adolescents do not yet have stable use patterns; some adolescents may experiment with or try a drug and then decide to stop for varying periods. Some may resume or switch to a different drug. Consequently, the higher lifetime use percentage in comparison to the lower number for past year use reflects the fact that many of the users stopped using that drug during the past year.

NATIONAL HOUSEHOLD SURVEY ON DRUG ABUSE STUDY

The National Household Survey on Drug Abuse (NHSDA) is conducted by the Substance Abuse and Mental Health Services Administra-

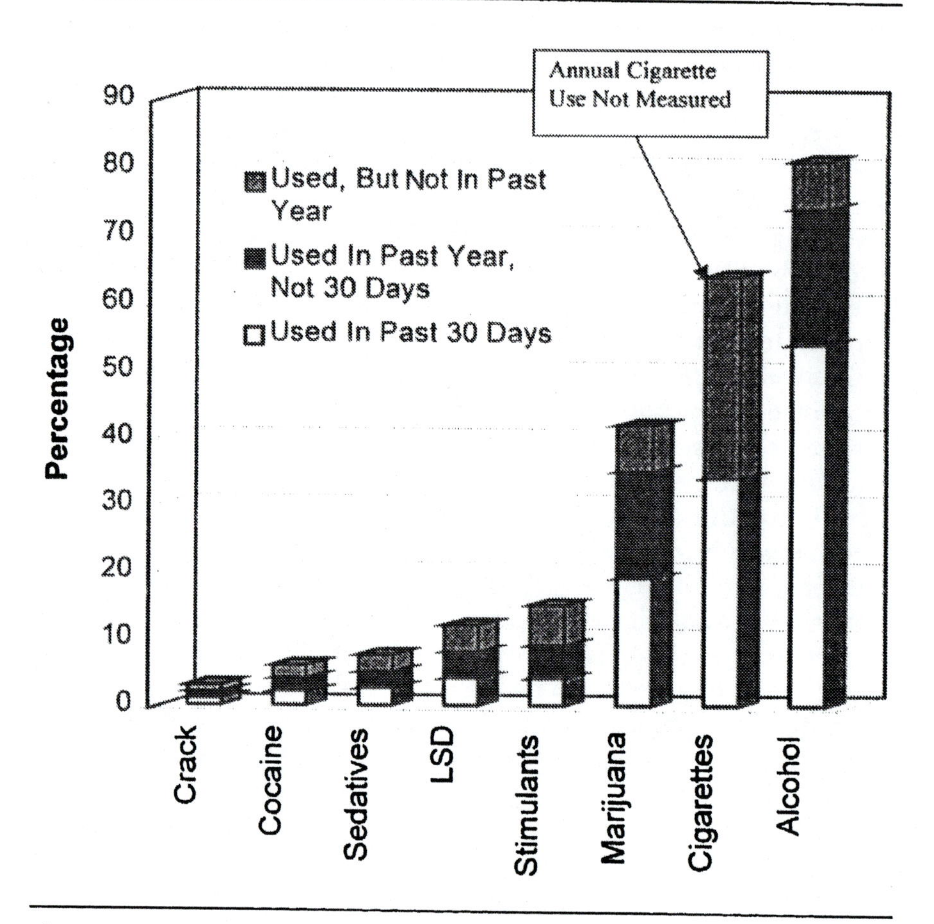

Figure 3.1. Prevalence and Recency of Using Different Drugs in Past 30 Days, Past Year but Not in Past Month, and Lifetime Use but Not in Past Year by 12th Graders
SOURCE: Johnston, O'Malley, and Bachman (1996).

tion, an agency of the U.S. Department of Health and Human Services (1997a). These annual estimates of the prevalence of alcohol, tobacco, and illicit drug use in the United States allow comparisons of demographic differences in drug use and also monitor temporal trends in drug use in society. This survey, started in 1971, was conducted every 3 years until 1988, when it became an annual survey. The NHSDA uses a representative sample of the U.S. population age 12 and older, including persons living in households and in some group quarters such as dormitories and homeless shelters. An underreporting bias might exist due to the face-to-face method of administering portions of the NHSDA survey. Also, the findings may involve underestimates because incarcerated and inpatient treatment samples, which often may involve heavier users, are not included in household surveys.

The NHSDA survey, like the MTF, did not measure frequency of use other than at least once during the interval in question. These surveys focused on the percentage of individuals who used each measured drug but did not identify how often the drug was used. Until 1996, the NHSDA defined a user as anyone who used a drug *at least once* during the past month, past year, or lifetime so that a frequent and an infrequent user would receive the same score as long as their use was within the same time frame. In recognition of this limitation, in 1996, the NHSDA survey began including three categories of frequency of use: more than 51 times a year, more than 12 times a year, and 1 or more times a year.

Prevalence of 30-Day Use

Table 3.1 shows the NHSDA prevalence of drug use rates for the past month from 1979 through 1997 for major drugs for people older than age 12. Due to some changes in the questions used in the 1994 survey, some adjustments were made for findings before 1994 so that comparisons with more recent surveys could be made. In general, there were minor differences between 1996 and 1997, with the exception of increases for ages 12 to 17 (not shown in the table) for use of any illicit drug, particularly marijuana.

In agreement with findings of the MTF study, alcohol was the most widely used substance at 51%, with about 5.9% being heavy drinkers who consumed five or more drinks on at least 5 different days in the past month.

Smokers in the past month represented about 30% of the population older than age 12. Illicit drugs were much lower, with marijuana being the most widely used. Marijuana and hashish users combined were estimated at 5.1%. Among those ages 12 to 17 (not shown in the table), 9.4% used marijuana, reflecting a maintained increased level that started in 1992. Cocaine use occurred for 1.0%. Heroin use is difficult to estimate, and conservative figures showed 0.2% current users in 1997, an increase since 1993. Hallucinogen use was at 0.8% for age 12 and older. Methamphetamine use was reported by 2.3% of the population, but the rate has been stable for the past 3 years. Nonmedical use of psychotherapeutic drugs such as stimulants, sedatives, analgesics, and tranquilizers occurred at the rate of 1.2%.

Use of legal drugs was linked to use of illicit drugs. Thus, alcohol use was a predictor of illicit drug use, as shown in Figure 3.2. Heavy drinkers and binge drinkers were more likely to be users of illicit drugs than were

TABLE 3.1 Percentages reporting past month use of illicit drugs, alcohol, and tobacco in the U.S population age 12 and older: 1979-1997

	1979	*1985*	*1991*	*1992*	*1993*	*1994*	*1995*	*1996*	*1997*
Any illicit drug[a]	14.1[b]	12.1[b]	6.6	5.8	5.9	6.0	6.1	6.1	6.4
Marijuana and hashish	13.2[b]	9.7[b]	5.1	4.7	4.6	4.8	4.7	4.7	5.1
Cocaine	2.6[b]	3.0[b]	1.0	0.7	0.7	0.7	0.7	0.8	0.7
Crack	NA	NA	0.3	0.2	0.3	0.2	0.2	0.3	0.3
Inhalants	NA	0.6	0.4	0.3	0.3	0.4	0.4	0.4	0.4
Hallucinogens	1.9[c]	1.2	0.5	0.4[c]	0.4[b]	0.5[b]	0.7	0.6	0.8
Heroin	0.1	0.1	0.0	0.0	0.0	0.1	0.1	0.1	0.2
Nonmedical use of any psychotherapeutic[d]	NA	3.8[b]	1.9	1.5	1.5	1.2	1.2	1.4	1.2
Stimulants	NA	1.8[b]	0.4	0.3	0.5	0.3	0.4	0.4	0.3
Sedatives	NA	0.5	0.2	0.2	0.2	0.1	0.2	0.1	0.1
Tranquilizers	NA	2.2[b]	1.1[c]	0.8[c]	0.6	0.5	0.4	0.4	0.4
Analgesics	NA	1.4	0.8	0.9	0.8	0.7	0.6	0.9	0.7
Any illicit drug other than marijuana	NA	6.1[b]	3.0	2.4	2.4	2.3	2.6	2.7	2.6
Alcohol	63.2[b]	60.2[b]	52.2	49.0	50.8	53.9	52.2	51.0	51.4
Binge alcohol use[e]	NA	20.2[b]	15.5	14.5	14.6	16.5	15.8	15.5	15.3
Heavy alcohol use[e]	NA	8.3[b]	6.8	6.2	6.7	6.2	5.5	5.4	5.4
Cigarettes	NA	38.7[b]	33.0	31.9	29.6	28.6	28.8	28.9	29.6
Smokeless tobacco	NA	NA	3.7	4.0	3.2	3.3	3.3	3.2	3.2

SOURCE: Substance Abuse and Mental Health Services Administration (1998).

NOTE: NA = Not available. The population distributions for the 1993 through 1997 National Household Survey on Drug Abuse (NHSDA) are poststratified to population projections of totals based on the 1990 decennial census. The 1979 NHSDA used population projections based on the 1970 census; NHSDA, from 1979 through 1982, used projections based on the 1980 census. The change from one census base to another has little effect on estimated percentages reporting drug use but may have a significant effect on estimates of the number of drug users in some subpopulation groups. Estimates here for 1979 through 1993 may differ from estimates for these survey years that were published in other NHSDA reports. The estimates shown here for 1979 through 1993 have been adjusted to improve their comparability with estimates based on the new version of the NHSDA instrument that was fielded in 1994 and subsequent NHSDAs. For 1979, estimates are not shown (as indicated by NA) in which (a) the relevant data were not collected, or (b) the data for those drugs were based on measures that differed appreciably from those used in the other survey years. Consequently, adjustments to the 1979 data were made only for those drugs whose measures were comparable to those in the other survey years. Because of the methodology used to adjust the 1979 through 1993 estimates, some logical inconsistency may exist between estimates for a given drug within the same survey year. For example, some adjusted estimates of past year use may appear to be greater than adjusted lifetime estimates. These inconsistencies tend to be small, rare, and not statistically significant.

a. Any illicit drug indicates use at least once of marijuana/hashish, cocaine (including crack), inhalants, hallucinogens (including PCP and LSD), heroin, or any prescription-type psychotherapeutic used nonmedically. Any illicit drug other than marijuana indicates use at least once of any of these listed drugs, regardless of marijuana/hashish use; marijuana/hashish users who also have used any of the other listed drugs are included.

b. Difference between estimate and 1997 estimate is statistically significant at the .01 level.

c. Difference between estimate and 1997 estimate is statistically significant at the .05 level.

d. Nonmedical use of any prescription-type stimulant, sedative, tranquilizer, or analgesic; does not include over-the-counter drugs.

e. *Binge* alcohol use is defined as drinking five or more drinks on the same occasion on at least 1 day in the past 30 days. By "occasion" is meant at the same time or within a couple of hours of each other. Heavy alcohol use is defined as drinking five or more drinks on the same occasion on each of 5 or more days in the past 30 days; all heavy alcohol users are also "binge" alcohol users.

social drinkers and nondrinkers. Similarly, as Figure 3.3 shows, smoking was a predictor of use of other drugs—specifically, cigarette smokers had higher use of both alcohol and marijuana.

As in the MTF survey, there were disparities between current, past year, and lifetime use rates. Table 3.2 shows these rates for using any illicit drug, marijuana, and cocaine for 1996 for those ages 12 to 17. The gaps in use rates for the three time periods were large. The rate of using any illicit drug in the current month was 9.0; past year, 16.7; and lifetime, 22.1. Similar gaps were found for current, past year, and lifetime use for cocaine and marijuana. These patterns are consistent with the view that many young drug users are experimenters who quit eventually without formal treatment.

Problems of Interpretation and Limitations

In both the MTF and NHDSA surveys, use of a drug is very loosely defined. Quantity of use, as noted earlier, is not usually considered. For example, a person who reported drinking at least one beer, one glass of wine, or one drink of liquor in the past month would be counted the same as a person who reported consuming 20 beers, 20 glasses or wine, or 20 drinks of liquor in the past month. Similarly, for purposes of counting current users, a person who reported smoking 2 ounces of cocaine in the past month would be considered the same as a person who reported injecting 30 lines of cocaine in the past month.

Cross-sectional analyses such as the MTF and NHSDA surveys, which measure use only once, are static portrayals and fail to capture changes in drug use over time within given individuals. As Figure 3.4 suggests, users

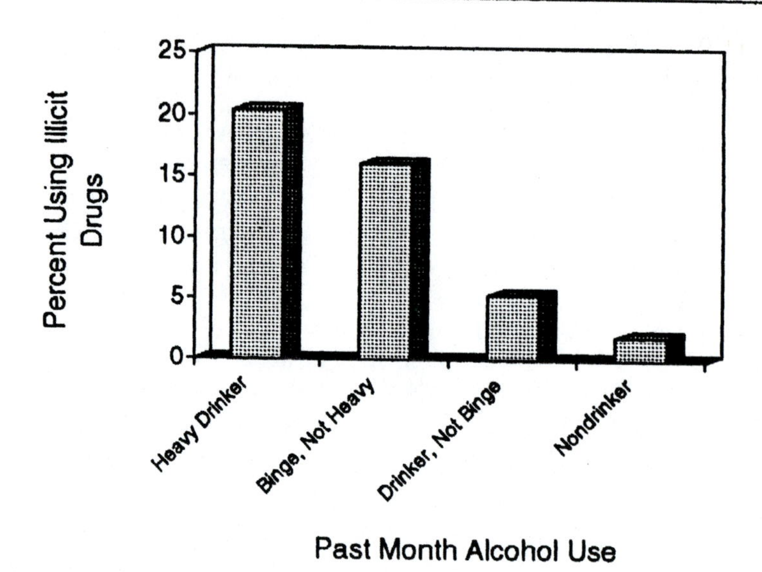

Figure 3.2. Past Month Level of Illicit Drug Use in Relation to Alcohol Use for Ages 12 and Older
SOURCE: U.S. Department of Health and Human Services (1997a).

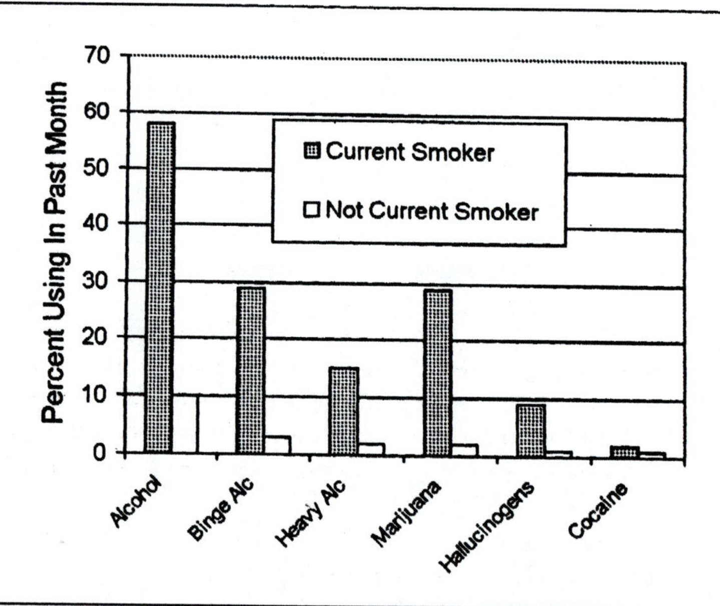

Figure 3.3. Use of Alcohol and Different Illicit Drugs for 12- to 17-Year-Old Smokers Versus Nonsmokers
SOURCE: U.S. Department of Health and Human Services (1997a).

TABLE 3.2 Prevalence rate of drug use for past month, past year, and lifetime, ages 12 to 17: 1996

	Past Month	*Past Year*	*Lifetime*
Any illicit drug	9.0	16.7	22.1
Marijuana	7.1	13.0	16.8
Cocaine	0.6	1.4	1.9
Cigarettes	18.3	24.2	36.3
Alcohol	18.8	NA	NA

SOURCE: U.S. Department of Health and Human Services (1997c).
NOTE: NA = Not available.

may move back and forth between states of use and nonuse, reflecting situational influences on their behavior. Some initiate use, find it unrewarding, and end their use. At a later time, some former users may resume their use. Still other users are chippers, seemingly able to control their use and engage in such activity intermittently, depending on priorities and social circumstances.

Polydrug Abuse. The prevalence of **polydrug abuse** is also overlooked by many surveys, including the MTF and NHSDA. The evidence is presented separately for each drug as if users consumed one drug exclusively, whereas many drugs are frequently used in certain combinations by many drug users. It is obvious that legal drugs are often combined—alcohol with tobacco, tobacco with caffeine, and alcohol followed by caffeine. Less readily observed is the fact that users of illicit drugs report engaging often in polydrug abuse, typically with alcohol (Martin, Clifford, Maisto, Earleywine, & Longabaugh, 1996; Martin, Kaczynski, Maisto, Bukstein, & Moss, 1995). Thus, alcohol is frequently consumed in conjunction with the use of marijuana, cocaine, amphetamines, benzodiazepines, and heroin. Cocaine is often combined with either heroin or amphetamine use. Often, the user is deliberately choosing one type of drug to counter or reduce the effect of another drug, as in using alcohol to take the edge off of a cocaine high.

As a result of interactions among drugs, it is not possible to identify the specific effects of each drug. For example, how mood, motor coordination, sleep, and other behaviors are affected by specific drugs is not determinate. Combinations of drugs from the same category (e.g., sedative-hypnotics) can have additive effects, whereas offsetting effects may occur with drugs from different categories such as depressants and stimulants.

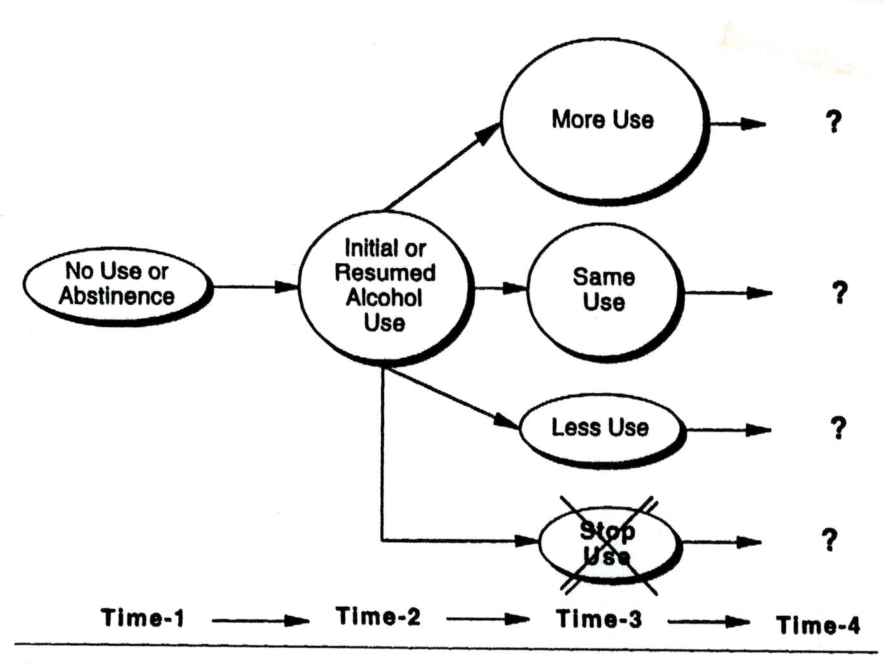

Figure 3.4. Levels of Alcohol and Other Drug Use Can Drift or Change Back and Forth Over Time From Nonuse to Use, Increased Use, or Reduced Use

Some combinations of drugs may involve potentiation in which one drug amplifies the effect of another. Thus, drinking alcohol in combination with a depressant drug can be lethal because the two drugs combine to produce a larger effect than either drug would do alone.

Illicit Drugs

It is not surprising that there are no large-scale surveys of representative users of illegal drugs similar to those done for alcohol. First, it would be difficult, if not impossible, to identify a large and representative sample of users. Second, they would be reluctant to participate for obvious reasons, and if they did, the honesty of their answers would be suspect. Although the MTF and NHSDA national surveys do ask about illicit drug use, they do not provide much detail about patterns and conditions of use.

Figure 3.5 shows 30-day and 12-month prevalence rates for using any illegal drugs from 1987 to 1997 for those ages 19 to 28 from the NHSDA study. The rates are relatively low compared to those for licit drugs and

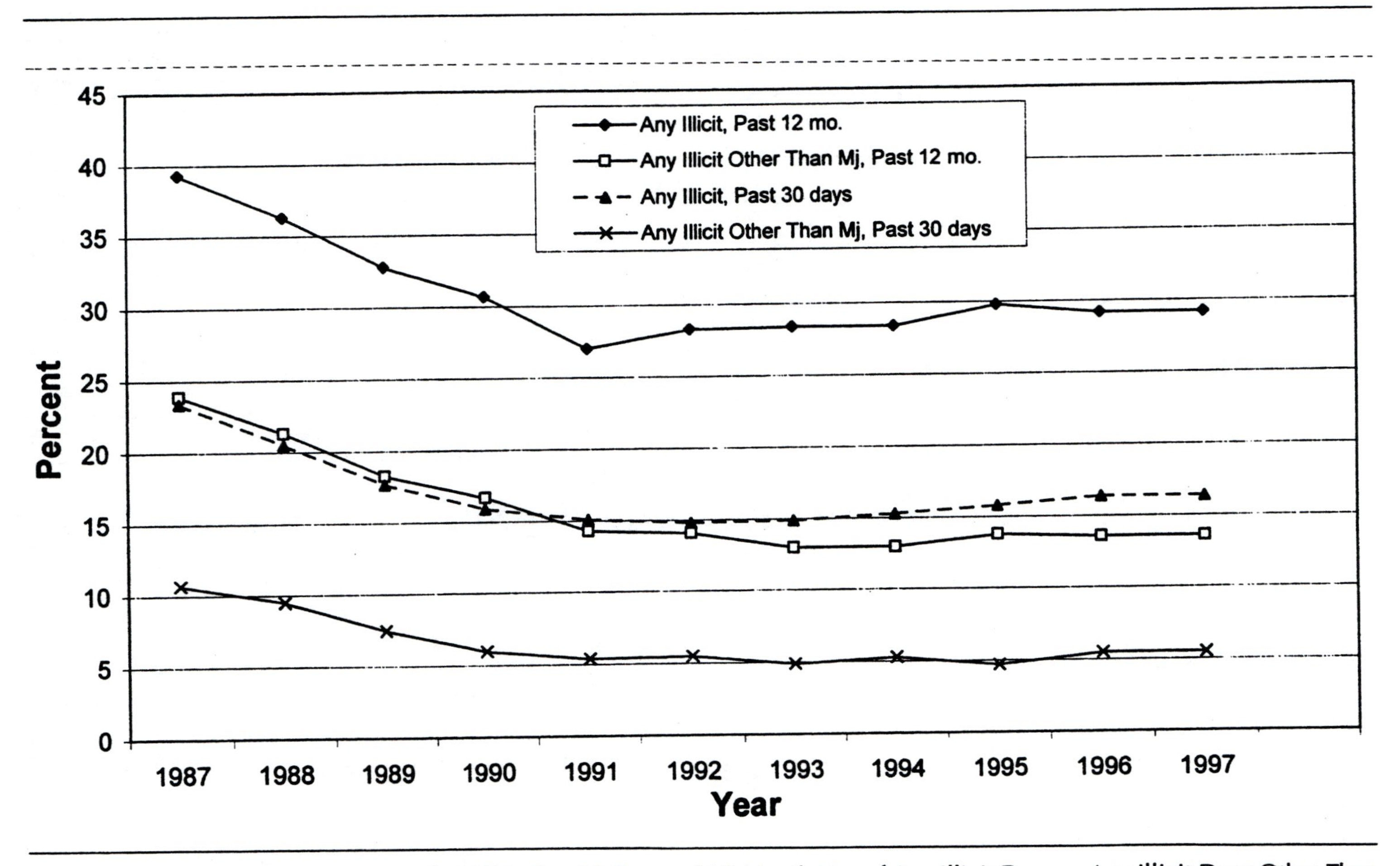

Figure 3.5. Trends Between 1987 and 1997 in Past 30-Day and 12-Month Use of Any Illicit Drug or Any Illicit Drug Other Than Marijuana for 19- to 28-Year-Olds
SOURCE: Johnston et al. (1996).

generally declined over the past decade. However, the frequency and quantity were not assessed in this survey.

Are these rates of illicit drug use applicable to users who are in prisons, treatment facilities, and homeless shelters? And do they apply to upper- and middle-class users, whose use of illicit drugs is easier to hide? Although heavy and frequent use of illicit drugs occurs and produces harmful effects, it may be necessary to use other research methods to study these populations of illicit drug users.

The Ethnographic Approach

The study of illicit drugs relies more on qualitative techniques involving **ethnography** than on epidemiology. These studies are based on highly selective and rather small samples, compared to the large representative samples often used in epidemiological surveys of legal drug use. The researcher may employ a sampling technique based on **snowballing.** First, key informants, typically users, are located, and their trust and confidence are developed so they can identify other users to the researcher. Often, users or indigenous interviewers, rather than the researchers, are recruited and trained intensively to conduct the interviews. It may be easier to establish rapport and trust if other users conduct the confidential and intensive interviews. Users who complete the interview may introduce the researcher to other drug users. Although this procedure has a number of problems—including the highly biased sample, subjective assessment tools, legal risks, and safety concerns for the researcher—it opens a window through which the researcher can begin to observe the nature and characteristics of illicit drug use. Ethnographic methods are by no means beneficial only for the study of illegal drugs but can provide greater understanding of the meaning and function of the use of legal drugs, as illustrated by an ethnographic study of the daily lives of skid row alcoholics (Wiseman, 1970).

Results of some ethnographic studies (Erickson, Aldaf, Murray, & Smart, 1987; Waldorf, Reinarman, & Murphy, 1991; Zinberg, 1984) reveal that illicit drugs such as cocaine, heroin, and marijuana may involve many "controlled users" or chippers who can use without any apparent major problems. Exactly how large this generally unseen part of the "iceberg" of illicit drug users is would be difficult to determine.

A study (Zinberg, 1984) was done based on intensive interviews with more than 200 current and long-term heavy users of marijuana, opiates, and hallucinogens with both controlled and compulsive users of each drug. Opiate users who managed to control their habits had incorporated informal social controls such as the rituals and social sanctions related to their drug use. Other users served as important social factors influencing how the drug would affect the user. Anxiety was common among new users, but using drugs in a social setting with other users who were more experienced had a beneficial effect on the new users. Controlled users were more likely to engage in drug use for social reasons, whereas compulsive users were more inclined to want to experience "highs." The user's expectations, beliefs, values, and setting or social context—and not the pharmacological factor alone—determined the effect of drugs.

A study (Erickson et al., 1987) was done with a middle-class nonclinical sample of 111 Canadians, mostly White middle-class employed males with an average age just younger than 30 who had used cocaine at least once in the past 3 years. Cocaine users in this community sample, as opposed to clinical samples, were recruited by media advertising and posters as well as through personal contacts. This purposive sample, obtained by a snowballing technique, was unlikely to be representative of the Canadian population, although its demographic features were similar to those of other studies using random samples. The researchers wanted to study controlled users to determine their characteristics, their use patterns, and positive as well as negative reactions to drug use. The findings suggested that most users were able to restrict their use to social settings with friends during weekends for relaxation and socializing. Most used other drugs such as cannabis and alcohol. About half had not used in the past month, and about the same percentage could not recall the amount used. Use was controlled in that these occasions were infrequent and involved small drug doses.

In contrast, in-depth interviews (Waldorf et al., 1991) of 267 middle-class, mostly White heavy cocaine users recruited with a snowballing procedure revealed use levels comparable to that of the extreme 5% in norms from national surveys. These users primarily snorted cocaine, which they used infrequently and mostly in social settings with close friends, and generally experienced no problems with their use. Most of them could be considered controlled users, consuming during the past week an average of half a gram. Most of these controlled users took cocaine for recreational rather than for stress management purposes, had structured lives and commitments to families and careers, and invoked rules and routines for controlling when and where they would use it. In addition, almost half of the sample had been able to quit, contrary to the stereotype that heavy users would be unable to do so. Health and financial considerations were paramount factors leading to quitting, which was facilitated by changing social circles and developing new interests. Although quitting is not easy and relapses occurred, most were able to reduce consumption significantly or reach abstinence without concomitant increases in the use of other drugs.

These studies involved small samples of highly selected participants and often relied on uncorroborated self-reports and may not be generalizable to other users of these illicit drugs. On the other hand, if these findings are valid, they show that the effects of these drugs are not based entirely on pharmacological factors, and even if atypical, they do show that some users can engage in controlled use.

Stability of Use Patterns

Most population surveys measure an individual's drug use on only one occasion because of practical and financial cost factors. One important question is whether the pattern of use reported by an individual is a temporary or relatively stable pattern. To answer this question, the same persons must be surveyed on at least two occasions separated by a reasonable interval.

CURRENT FINDINGS

Longitudinal follow-ups (Bachman, Wadswirth, O'Malley, Johnston, & Schulenberg, 1997) were conducted on the high school samples of more than 33,000 students who participated in the annual MTF surveys, with the earliest group studied for 14 years and now in their 30s. Except for cigarette smoking, use of other drugs such as cocaine, marijuana, and alcohol increased for a few years following high school but then declined for most of the sample as they assumed the new responsibilities of careers and family in the years following high school.

Drinking. In a survey that involved two measurements of the same persons over a 6-year period (Harford, 1993) of 10,041 men and women between ages 17 and 24, a large majority of the men but only slightly more than half of the women showed stable drinking patterns over this interval. The demographic correlates of alcohol consumption were similar to those found in most studies, with more consumption by the young, by males, and by Whites.

Onset of current and heavier drinking declined with age over these 6 years. Shifts from drinker to nondrinker status increased with age. Abstinence was unrelated to age for both men and women. Among men, heavier drinking levels did not vary with age.

Self-reported consumption resembled sales trends of alcohol over this period, with a decline in drinking for many indices such as the percentage of the population "currently" drinking, "weekly" drinkers, and heavy drinkers (five or more drinks once a week). This decline in alcohol use in society as a whole does not mean there will necessarily be an immediate or even a delayed drop in alcohol-related problems because other factors besides drinking patterns, such as drinking laws and the degree to which they are enforced, also may affect the extent to which various alcohol-related problems occur.

HISTORICAL TRENDS

Alcohol use levels and alcohol problems have varied over time. Historical events such as Prohibition and its repeal, women's right to vote, global wars, and economic depression are associated with the change of many social attitudes and behaviors that may directly or indirectly affect alcohol use. In addition, changes in the age, sex, and ethnic composition of the population will affect the levels of drinking.

A comparison (Hilton, 1988) of results of the 1964 and 1984 national probability surveys, as well as responses from surveys conducted between 1971 and 1981, provided evidence of temporal differences in drinking. Stability for most indices of drinking such as abstention, frequency, quantity, and frequency of getting drunk or high was found for both men and women.

However, a more detailed analysis (Hilton, 1988) found that there have been increases in heavy drinking (five or more drinks on one or more occasions or eight or more drinks a day), especially among young males between ages 21 and 34—changes that were missed by earlier surveys that used lower consumption criteria in defining heavy drinking.

Comparisons (Hasin, Grant, Harford, Hilton, & Endicott, 1990) across four national surveys conducted between 1967 and 1984 supported the view that there had been a parallel rise in the prevalence of 11 alcohol-related problems among current drinkers between ages 22 and 59. Using an arbitrary criterion score of three or more problems, a large increase occurred for men, from 11.4% to 17.4%. The lower rates for women increased from 2.3% to 5.2%, a doubled rate over this 20-year period in the lifetime prevalence of multiple alcohol-related problems. Current prevalence (during the past 12 months) of multiple problems showed an even larger increase, doubling for men and tripling for women.

Comparisons of drug use for different eras are of dubious validity when the potency of some drugs changes over the years. Heroin, cocaine, and marijuana of the 1990s are more potent than they were in earlier eras. Studies of marijuana users of the 1960s who used milder cannabis have often shown no major impairment of behavior, but they may not be generalizable to the marijuana users of the 1990s who may be smoking a stronger supply.

In addition, even if there are no changes in the drug over time, the effects of a drug for the initial wave of users of a specific drug may differ from that for subsequent users following in their footsteps. Thus, pioneering users of a new drug may have different personality characteristics from those who wait until it seems safe to use the drug. The effects observed may differ because of such preexisting differences among users.

The MTF and NHSDA surveys also provide evidence of drug use trends over the past 25 or more years. From the 1970s, there was a general increase in the percentages of respondents reporting current drug use, which declined for most drugs starting about 1979, especially for alcohol.

It is inconclusive why these changes occur because many uncontrollable events exist. Societal changes and developments, economic factors, political factors, random fluctuations, and specific drug education and prevention campaigns all play some role in producing temporal changes.

Alcohol and drug use rates also are affected by psychological factors. In general, use of a drug is inversely rated to the perceived risk of harm from that drug. Among 12th graders, the perceived risk of harm from marijuana increased from 1979 to 1990, then decreased from 1990 to 1994, but there was no change in perceived risk of harm between 1994 and 1996. This trend in perceived risk was inversely correlated with the trend in the use of marijuana. Thus, higher perceived risk was associated with lower use between 1979 and 1990, when a reversal can be seen with perceived risk dropping and use increasing.

Availability, the extent to which a drug can be easily obtained because of factors such as low cost or convenient access, is also a potential factor. Thus, during Prohibition, although drinking continued, the overall level was reduced based on data such as declines in mortality and morbidity attributable to alcohol.

As shown in Figure 3.6, over the past 20 years, the availability of marijuana was more or less stable. In contrast to the relationship of use with perceived risk, perceived availability proved unrelated to marijuana use levels.

Similar patterns occurred for cocaine. The percentage of 12th graders reporting greater perceived risk of harm in using cocaine in the past year gradually increased from about 30% to around 58% between 1986 and 1997, accompanying a drop in use from about 12% to 9% in the same

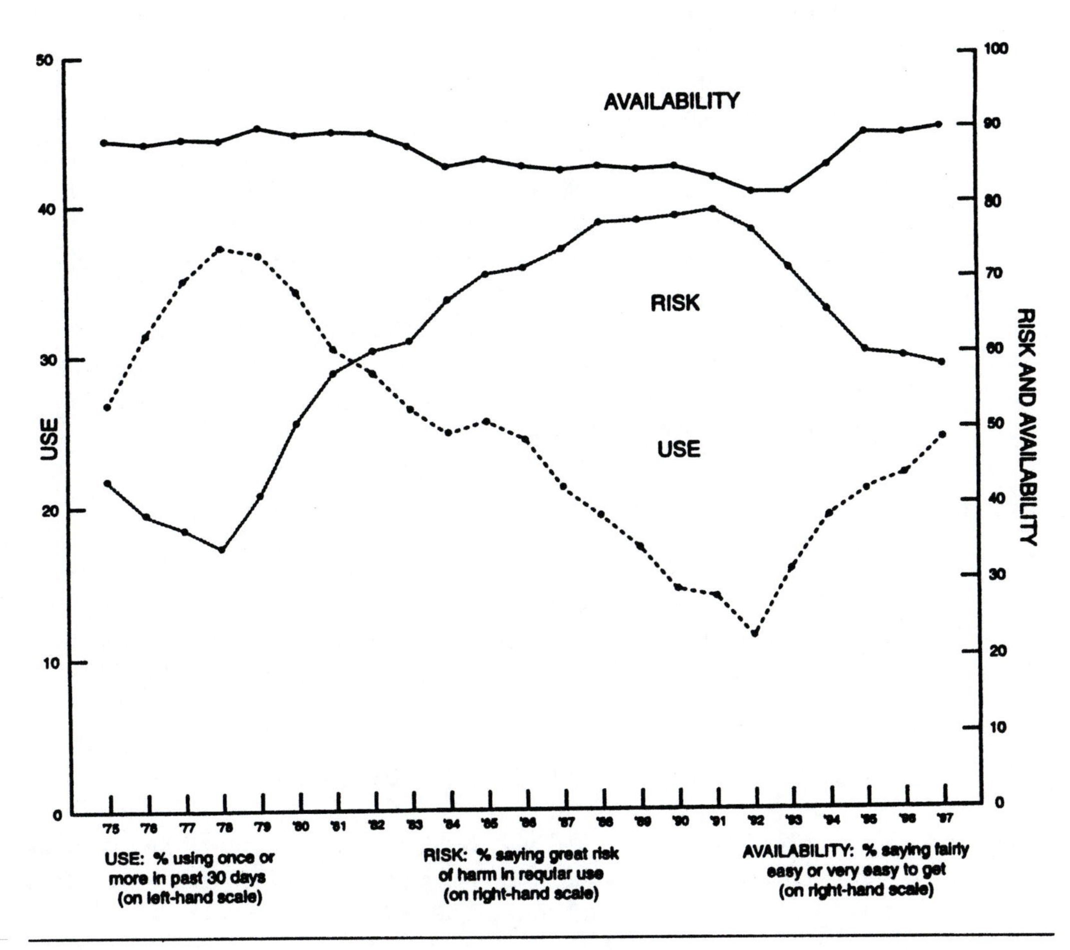

Figure 3.6. Perceived Risk, Availability, and Marijuana Use for 12th Graders
SOURCE: Johnston et al. (1996).

period. Perceived availability, which rose slightly and then declined, was not related to use rates.

Abstention

Abstainers have received less study than drug users have, perhaps because they do not represent problems for society. Different studies of alcohol use have found that 14% to 34% of those surveyed were abstainers, but these studies lump all current abstainers together, failing to recognize the heterogeneity of this category. A 4-year population survey (Goldman & Najman, 1984) of 5,320 Boston adults identified several subtypes of abstainers: lifetime abstainers (58%), current abstainers without a prior drinking problem (34%), and current abstainers with a prior drinking problem (9%). One would expect these subgroups to differ in many ways. Thus, the subgroup of abstainers with a prior drinking problem consisted mostly of males, with higher occupational skills and with moderate to frequent prior consumption habits. Their ideology about abstinence was similar to that of Alcoholics Anonymous (AA).

A comparison (Hilton, 1986) of abstention rates in 1964 and 1979 was based on general population probability surveys. Abstainers (defined in these surveys as those who never drink or drink less than once a year) consistently disapproved of drinking in a variety of contexts. There were four sets of reasons for abstention: moral objection, dislike of drinking consequences, "inconsequential" reasons, and abstinent family background. Militant views against drinking were stronger for lifelong abstainers who had moral reasons for their stance. Abstainers also tended to have more disapproving attitudes about sexual issues such as premarital and extramarital sex than drinkers. Both abstainers and drinkers held negative attitudes on issues related to alcohol-related problems such as belligerence or drinking and driving.

Little or no change in abstention rates occurred over the 15 years between 1964 and 1979 (Hilton, 1986). There was no convergence in abstention rates over time for either sex or age. Regional and religious affiliation differences in abstention did not weaken either. The possibility that the older generation is more abstemious and is being replaced by a wetter younger generation was not supported.

Rates of Alcohol and Drug Abuse and Dependency

As noted in the previous chapter, alcohol and drug use per se is not equivalent to use-related problems or to dependency. It is also important to determine what percentage of users have serious problems such as abuse and dependency and to examine trends over time. Unfortunately, estimates derived from different sets of criteria are not in agreement. One reason why epidemiological studies offer a wide variety of estimates is because the definition is not the same for all researchers, as can be illustrated with the example of alcohol dependency and abuse.

SOURCES OF DATA

Methods for identifying patterns of alcohol and substance dependence and abuse in the general population do not usually involve direct observation but rely on inferences based on several different sources of information.

Official Records

One method uses official records or social indicators such as mortality statistics, hospital admission records, arrest for drunkenness data, sales figures, tax revenues from alcohol sales, and deaths due to liver cirrhosis based on an equation known as the Jellinek formula. Although objective, each of these indices still has its particular limitations. Thus, sales and tax revenues provide one means of determining trends in the total volume of alcohol sold each year, but they do not reveal patterns of actual individual consumption. The purchaser of alcohol is not always the actual consumer, so the term *apparent consumption* is used to reflect that difference. The index is computed by dividing the total amount of alcohol sold by the number of persons age 14 and older.

Another problem in using sales statistics to infer consumption levels is that there is often a temporal lag between purchase and consumption, for example. Although increased sales might imply heavier drinking if the number of drinkers stays the same or decreases during that interval, they call for an opposite interpretation if the number of drinkers increases over that period.

Clinical Population Data

Another index of the extent of alcoholism is more direct, using data from hospital treatment statistics to determine the number of alcoholics. However, there are economic and psychological barriers to using health care facilities so that a biased and smaller sample of those with alcohol problems would be identified with this index. Also, poorer and less educated alcoholics might be less likely to use treatment facilities.

General Population Surveys

Surveys administered to random samples of the general population provide large sets of data obtained with standard instruments that allow estimates of the prevalence of alcoholism for different subgroups.

SPECIFIC ESTIMATES FROM GENERAL POPULATION SURVEYS

National Health Interview Survey

The U.S. prevalence of alcohol dependence and alcohol abuse was estimated (Grant et al., 1991) using the *DSM-III-R* (1987) criteria. Self-reported alcohol use was obtained from 43,809 interviews with respondents age 18 and older in all 50 states and the District of Columbia in 1988 as part of the National Health Interview Survey conducted by the National Center for Health Statistics.

Results showed that 8.63% of the population could be classified as either alcohol dependent (6.25%) or alcohol abusers (2.38%). These estimates translate to a total of 15.2 million Americans age 18 and older.

National Longitudinal Alcohol Epidemiological Survey

The *DSM-IV* (1994) criteria were used in the National Longitudinal Alcohol Epidemiological Survey (NLAES) to determine the prevalence rates of alcohol abuse and alcohol dependence (Grant et al., 1994). A total rate of 7.41%—3.03% for abuse and 4.38% for dependence—was found, which represents 13,760,000 Americans.

Use of *ICD-10* criteria (WHO, 1990) with 1988 survey data on U.S. drinking practices and related problems, as well as estimates of harmful alcohol use and alcohol dependence, were made. A prevalence of 5.2% for the two combined categories was found when the duration criterion of *ICD-10* was met (Grant, 1993).

DSM-IV (1994) criteria for diagnosis of abuse and dependency were applied to findings of the NLAES national survey. Using a standard instrument, the rates of abuse and dependency for alcohol and other major drugs were estimated (Grant, 1996). As shown in Table 3.3, rates of alcohol dependency (13.29) based on *DSM-IV* criteria were considerably higher than those for alcohol abuse (4.88). Cocaine dependency (1.02) was greater than cocaine abuse (.64). Abuse and dependency were about equal for sedatives, tranquilizers, amphetamines, and hallucinogens. Only with cannabis was the rate of abuse (2.86) much higher than for dependence (1.78).

Thus, there are numerous criteria for defining and diagnosing alcohol and other drug dependencies, and each set will generate different estimates. Hence, it is important to consider the particular definition used in each individual study when comparing and interpreting findings across studies. It may be useful to view drug dependency, as Jellinek (1960) did of

TABLE 3.3 Prevalence rates of lifetime *DSM-IV* alcohol and drug use disorders: United States, 1992

Disorder	*Prevalence*
Alcohol abuse, dependence, or both	18.17
Abuse only	4.88
Dependence only	13.29
Any drug abuse, dependence, or both	6.05
Any drug abuse only	3.14
Any drug dependence only	2.91
Prescription drug abuse, dependence, or both	2.01
Prescription drug abuse only	0.98
Prescription drug dependence only	1.03
Sedative abuse, dependence, or both	0.64
Sedative abuse only	0.30
Sedative dependence only	0.34
Tranquilizer abuse, dependence, or both	0.63
Tranquilizer abuse only	0.31
Tranquilizer dependence only	0.32
Amphetamine abuse, dependence, or both	1.48
Amphetamine abuse only	0.76
Amphetamine dependence only	0.72
Cannabis abuse, dependence, or both	4.64
Cannabis abuse only	2.86
Cannabis dependence only	1.78
Cocaine abuse, dependence, or both	1.66
Cocaine abuse only	0.64
Cocaine dependence only	1.02
Hallucinogen abuse, dependence, or both	0.59
Hallucinogen abuse only	0.30
Hallucinogen dependence only	0.29

SOURCE: Grant et al. (1991).

alcoholism, as involving a number of subtypes, all of which have some common features as well as some unique characteristics. The causes and methods for treating each subtype may vary. If clinicians and researchers fail to recognize the existence of subvarieties, controversies and conflicting findings will continue to produce more heat than light.

TABLE 3.4 Lifetime prevalence and odds ratios of selected *DSM-IV* drug use disorders among respondents with and without corresponding *DSM-IV* alcohol use disorder: United States, 1992

	Prevalence of Drug Use Disorders Among Respondents				
	With Corresponding Alcohol Use Disorders		*Without Corresponding Alcohol Use Disorders*		
Drug Use Disorder	*%*	*Standard Error*	*%*	*Standard Error*	*Odds Ratio*
Any drug abuse, dependence, or both	23.1	(0.61)	2.3	(0.09)	9.6
Any drug abuse only	10.6	(0.79)	2.8	(0.10)	2.9
Any drug dependence	14.3	(0.55)	1.7	(0.70)	10.9
Prescription drug abuse, dependence, or both	8.1	(0.38)	0.7	(0.05)	10.6
Prescription drug abuse only	2.7	(0.49)	0.9	(0.06)	2.2
Prescription drug dependence	5.3	(0.34)	0.4	(0.04)	12.6
Sedative abuse, dependence, or both	2.8	(0.22)	0.2	(0.02)	14.6
Sedative abuse only	0.8	(0.25)	0.3	(0.03)	2.1
Sedative dependence	2.0	(0.22)	0.1	(0.01)	22.6
Tranquilizer abuse, dependence, or both	2.8	(0.23)	0.2	(0.02)	16.5
Tranquilizer abuse only	0.7	(0.21)	0.3	(0.03)	1.8
Tranquilizer dependence	1.9	(0.21)	0.1	(0.02)	22.2
Amphetamine abuse, dependence, or both	6.2	(0.33)	0.4	(0.04)	11.4
Amphetamine abuse only	2.1	(0.45)	0.7	(0.05)	2.2
Amphetamine dependence	3.8	(0.30)	0.3	(0.03)	2.3
Cannabis abuse, dependence, or both	18.1	(0.55)	1.6	(0.08)	9.3
Cannabis abuse only	9.7	(0.72)	2.5	(0.10)	2.9
Cannabis dependence	9.3	(0.48)	0.6	(0.05)	11.7
Cocaine abuse, dependence, or both	7.0	(0.33)	0.5	(0.04)	12.0
Cocaine abuse only	2.2	(0.54)	0.8	(0.07)	2.5
Cocaine dependence	5.5	(0.34)	0.3	(0.03)	13.5
Hallucinogen abuse, dependence, or both	2.8	(0.22)	0.1	(0.01)	17.1
Hallucinogen abuse only	0.7	(0.24)	0.3	(0.03)	1.6
Hallucinogen dependence	1.8	(0.22)	0.1	(0.01)	23.2

SOURCE: Grant et al. (1991).

COMORBIDITY OF ALCOHOL AND DRUG USE DISORDERS

Alcohol and other drugs are often used together, sometimes in close succession but often concurrently, rather than separately. Table 3.4 shows the rates of **comorbidity** for alcohol and drug *abuse* using *DSM-IV* (1994) criteria for alcohol and several other major drugs (Grant, 1996). Similarly, *DSM-IV* criteria were used to measure the rates of comorbidity of alcohol and drug *dependency* for these same drugs.

It can be noted that the rates of comorbidity for dependency were always considerably higher than those for abuse. The *odds ratio* indicates how much more likely a person is to have a drug use disorder (abuse or dependency), if the person also has the corresponding alcohol use disorder. Thus, as Table 3.4 indicates, if someone had an alcohol use disorder, 23.1% also had a drug use disorder. In contrast, of those without an alcohol use disorder, only 2.3% had a drug use disorder. Hence, the odds ratio is 9.6, indicating about a tenfold greater risk of a drug abuse disorder if the person had an alcohol use disorder.

Odds ratios for other drugs ranged from 9.3 for cannabis to 17.1 for hallucinogens. The odds ratio for *abuse* disorders was much lower than those for *dependency* disorders, being only about 2.0 for most drugs. Thus, alcohol abusers were about twice as likely to abuse other drugs as those who did not abuse alcohol. These findings generally agree with past studies of the comorbidity of alcohol and drug problems in the general population, such as the Epidemiological Catchment Area Study (Myers et al., 1984) conducted in the early 1980s and the National Comorbidity Study (Kessler et al., 1996) done in the early 1990s, even though those studies used older *DSM-III* (American Psychiatric Association, 1980) and *DSM-III-R* (1987) criteria for dependence.

SUMMARY

Epidemiological studies provide estimates of the prevalence of drug use over specific time periods such as the current month (past 30 days), an extended period such as the past year (past 12 months), or a lifetime. Findings of these studies only indicate what use patterns occurred but do not tell us what causes these use patterns. These results do, however, provide the data necessary to develop and test theories or explanations of drug use, assist in the planning of education and intervention programs, and inform public drug policy.

Two large-scale annual national surveys—the MTF survey, conducted with 8th-, 10th-, and 12th-grade high school students, and the NHSDA, conducted with persons age 12 and older—employ large and random probability samples and have been administered periodically since the early 1970s.

The MTF study reports the percentage of users for daily, past month, past 12 months, and lifetime (ever used). The category "user" includes first-time users, continuous or longer-term users, former users who stopped for a period but are now relapsed, users who vary widely in use quantities and frequencies, and users who may not ever use drugs again in the future. There are large gaps between current, past year, and lifetime use rates of many illegal drugs. The much higher lifetime and annual use compared to current use suggests that some initial use may involve only "experimenting" with a drug and, it is hoped, will soon cease after curiosity is satisfied.

Use of legal drugs is linked to the use of illicit drugs because heavy drinkers and binge drinkers were more likely to be users of an illicit drug than were social drinkers and nondrinkers. Polydrug abuse is overlooked by many surveys. Researchers examine evidence separately for each drug as if users consumed one drug exclusively. In fact, many drugs are frequently used in certain combinations by many drug users. Alcohol abuse or dependency is associated with high rates of comorbidity (i.e., abuse or dependency on some other drug).

Cross-sectional studies, which measure use at one point in time, are static portrayals that fail to capture changes in drug use over time within given individuals. Drug users may move back and forth between states of use and nonuse, reflecting situational influences.

Results from annual surveys suggest that 1979 was a peak year for use of many drugs. However, the interpretation of such trends is ambiguous because many uncontrolled factors at the individual and societal levels are constantly changing and prevent firm conclusions.

The survey method may be less useful for studying illicit drug use. Ethnographic studies, using highly selective and rather small samples, may be preferred to the large representative samples often used for epidemiological surveys of legal drug use. These studies involve small samples of highly selected participants and often depend on uncorroborated self-reports, which may not be generalizable to other users of these illicit drugs.

Estimates of the prevalence of more problematic use involving alcohol and drug abuse and dependency are based on a variety of sources of information, including official records and statistics, data from treatment facilities, and surveys of the general population. The findings derived from such different sets of criteria yield conflicting estimates. For example, surveys conducted in different years have used different definitions of abuse and dependency such as the *DSM-III, DSM-III-R, DSM-IV,* and *ICD-10* criteria.

KEY TERMS

Abstainers
Comorbidity
Epidemiology
Ethnography
Incidence
Monitoring the Future (MTF) Survey
National Household Survey on Drug Abuse (NHSDA)
Polydrug abuse
Prevalence
Random selection
Snowballing

STIMULUS/RESPONSE

1. Suppose you hear a politician report that the rate of annual cocaine use has doubled in the past year. Does it matter whether this increase is from 25% to 50% or from 1% to 2%? Could you also describe the increase as a 25% gain in the first case and a 1% increase in the second case? Which depiction do you think is the fairest representation?
2. Do you think the frequency of drug use is correlated with the quantity consumed? Do people who drink more often also tend to drink larger quantities per occasion? Explain your answer.
3. What types of measures of alcohol use are more likely to be used by a distiller, brewer, or winery in reporting sales? What types of measures of alcohol use are more useful for law enforcement agencies? For moral crusaders?
4. For a given total consumption quantity in a time period, which is worse—high frequency/low quantity or low frequency/high quantity? Why?
5. Which aspect of use—frequency or quantity—do you think is the better predictor of undesirable behavioral consequences? Explain why.

- What Happens After Drugs Are Taken?
- How Drugs Affect the Nervous System
- How Neurons Communicate
- How Alcohol and Other Drugs Affect Neurotransmission
- Physical Effects of Drugs
- Summary
- Key Terms
- Stimulus/Response

Pharmacology and Neurophysiology of Alcohol and Other Drugs

4

People get alcohol and other drugs into their bodies through a variety of means. Whereas they swallow or sip alcoholic beverages, they typically smoke tobacco and marijuana, although some may also chew smokeless tobacco. Heroin is typically injected directly into veins, and cocaine is commonly snorted, sniffed, or smoked. The specific method by which drugs are consumed is an important determinant of how rapidly specific drugs reach the brain. Eventually, drugs are detoxified by metabolic processes or eliminated from the body as waste material. Pharmacology is the study of these processes. Pharmacokinetics refers to how drugs enter, circulate, and exit from our bodies, whereas pharmacodynamics deals with how drugs affect the user's experience and behavior.

Irrespective of how drugs enter the body and find their way through the body to the brain, they affect neurotransmission processes that contribute to their psychological and behavioral impact during the time psychoactive drugs are in the body. The purpose of this chapter is to provide a basic understanding of the pharmacology and neurophysiology of psychoactive drugs.

What Happens After Drugs Are Taken?

ROUTE OF ADMINISTRATION

The speed with which drugs entering the body reach the brain is a major determinant of the potency of their effects. Depending on the specific drug, users prefer different methods of intake. Drugs such as alcohol and caffeine are typically consumed in beverage form. They are first swallowed through the mouth and then go down the esophagus before entering the stomach. Although a small loss occurs for drugs such as alcohol through perspiration or urination, most drugs are absorbed directly and quickly through the linings of the stomach and small intestines into the bloodstream for distribution to the rest of the body. If food has recently been eaten before the drugs are ingested, the absorption rate will be slowed down. This mode of drug use is relatively slow so that the drug user must wait a few minutes or up to an hour before the drug reaches the brain to produce the effects typically sought by the user.

Other drug delivery methods are more direct, such as by **inhalation** as in the case of cocaine snorting, tobacco snuff, or glue sniffing. These methods allow quicker impact because the drugs reach the brain and central nervous system rapidly. Drugs that are typically injected intravenously, such as heroin, also reach the brain quickly.

Smoking cigarettes containing nicotine, cannabis, or the inhalation of crack cocaine are very fast delivery methods and produce potent effects on the brain. For example, about 90% of the nicotine in mainstream cigarette smoke is absorbed from the lungs, and from there it reaches the brain in a few seconds for maximal impact because it does not have to go through the acidic content of the stomach or undergo detoxification by the liver on its first pass through the body. Smoking also produces combustion byproducts such as carbon monoxide (CO), a poison that "captures" the hemoglobin in the blood by binding to it better than it bonds with oxygen. Thus, the ability of hemoglobin to deliver needed oxygen throughout the body is compromised.

DISTRIBUTION

Most psychoactive drugs are weak acids or weak bases. They vary along a chemical dimension of acidity-alkalinity, as measured by values on a **pH scale** that ranges from 1 to 14. Scores of 7 or lower reflect an acid, an environment that converts drugs into an ionized or electrically charged state. Because the acidic condition does not allow easy entry of drugs into cells, the drugs are more readily eliminated. In contrast, in an alkaline or base context with pH levels from 8 to 14, drugs are un-ionized and can easily pass through the body, increasing their retention (McKim, 1997).

Cell membranes are composed of layers of lipid cells that favor the passage of fat-soluble drugs. Alcohol is a drug that is both water and fat soluble. It is rapidly absorbed from the stomach and intestines for distribution throughout the body. A drug that is lipid or fat soluble such as cannabis is much more slowly distributed, enters readily through cellular membranes, and is retained in the body longer.

Because drugs circulate through the body until detoxified or eliminated, it should be possible to measure the concentration of drugs from the blood or urine. However, the feasibility of obtaining measures from blood content varies with different drugs. Thus, cocaine is not readily detectable in blood samples due to its rapid metabolism. In contrast, levels of alcohol consumption can be inferred from the **blood alcohol level** (BAL) or concentration (BAC). Breathalyzers are instruments such as gas chromatographs that appraise ethanol concentrations based on breath samples. They give indirect measures but are more convenient than the use of actual blood or urine samples. However, because ethanol concentrations are not equal throughout all parts of the body, indirect measures are not without flaws. Measures from peripheral areas of the nervous system may not be accurate indices of the BAL in the brain, the organ that has the most impact on behavior. Despite this shortcoming, breath samples are reasonably reliable indices of blood alcohol level.

A specific quantity of a drug consumed by individuals with similar drug use experience will be diluted for larger persons because they have more body liquids. Measures are devised to adjust for variations in body weight across individuals. A commonly used index to measure alcohol effects is the **blood alcohol concentration** (BAC). It is the weight in milligrams of the alcohol present in a volume of 100 milliliters of blood. Larger units also may be used, with the weight expressed in grams (1 gram = 1,000 milligrams) and the volume measured in deciliters (1 deciliter = a tenth of a liter or 100 milliliters). The weight of the alcohol found in a given volume of blood is reported as a percentage such as .10%.

The relationship between BAC and the number of drinks within the past hour for persons of varying weight is depicted separately for men and women in Table 4.1. A "drink" here refers to a mixed drink containing 1¼ ounces of liquor, 5 ounces of wine, or a 12-ounce can of beer, each containing a comparable amount of alcohol. As a rough guide, each of these types of alcoholic drinks consumed within an hour increases the BAC from about .02 to .05%, regardless of whether it is wine, beer, or liquor.

It is commonly believed that different types of alcoholic beverages have different effects. However, whether the beverage is beer, wine, liquor, or any of the myriad variants of these three basic types, if the amount of ethanol consumed is equivalent, the same type of physiological and behavioral effects should occur if pharmacological factors are the sole determinant.

Different beverages may be associated with different effects, even when they are consumed in the same patterns. A study (Klatsky, Armstrong, & Kipp, 1990) of drinking preferences of more than 53,000 White men and women in Northern California showed that beer was preferred by young males, but wine was favored by women, younger drinkers, educated people, and those with low illness. Liquor was preferred by males, heavier

TABLE 4.1 Liquor Control Board, state of Pennsylvania charts for estimated blood alcohol level and impairment as a function of time since drinking for men and women according to body weight

Approximate Blood Alcohol Percentage: Men

	Body Weight in Pounds								
Drinks	*100*	*120*	*140*	*160*	*180*	*200*	*220*	*240*	
0	.00	.00	.00	.00	.00	.00	.00	.00	Only safe driving limit
1	.04	.03	.03	.02	.02	.02	.02	.02	Impairment begins
2	.08	.06	.05	.05	.04	.04	.03	.03	Driving skills significantly affected
3	.11	.09	.08	.07	.06	.06	.05	.05	
4	.15	.12	.11	.09	.08	.08	.07	.06	
5	.19	.16	.13	.12	.11	.09	.09	.08	Possible criminal penalties
6	.23	.19	.16	.14	.13	.11	.10	.09	
7	.26	.22	.19	.16	.15	.13	.12	.11	Legally intoxicated
8	.30	.25	.21	.19	.17	.15	.14	.13	
9	.34	.28	.24	.21	.19	.17	.15	.14	Criminal penalties
10	.38	.31	.27	.23	.21	.19	.17	.16	

Approximate Blood Alcohol Percentage: Women

	Body Weight in Pounds									
Drinks	*90*	*100*	*120*	*140*	*160*	*180*	*200*	*220*	*240*	
0	.00	.00	.00	.00	.00	.00	.00	.00	.00	Only safe driving limit
1	.05	.05	.04	.03	.03	.03	.02	.02	.02	Impairment begins
2	.10	.09	.08	.07	.06	.05	.05	.04	.04	Driving skills significantly affected
3	.15	.14	.11	.10	.09	.08	.07	.06	.06	
4	.20	.18	.15	.13	.11	.10	.09	.08	.08	Possible criminal penalties
5	.25	.23	.19	.16	.14	.13	.11	.10	.09	
6	.30	.27	.23	.19	.17	.15	.14	.12	.11	
7	.35	.32	.27	.23	.20	.18	.16	.14	.13	Legally intoxicated
8	.40	.36	.30	.26	.23	.20	.18	.17	.15	
9	.45	.41	.34	.29	.26	.23	.20	.19	.17	Criminal penalties
10	.51	.45	.38	.32	.28	.25	.23	.21	.19	

SOURCE: Pennsylvania Liquor Control Board (1995). Reprinted with permission.

NOTE: Your body can get rid of one drink per hour. Each 1½ ounces of 80-proof liquor, 12 ounces of beer, or 5 ounces of table wine = 1 drink.

drinkers, less educated people, middle-aged and older people, and those who are at higher risk for major diseases. Consequently, it may appear that different beverages have different effects because the types of individuals who prefer to drink different types of alcoholic beverages are not the same.

The effect of a given dose of alcohol depends on many factors. Consider the case of a driver who has been drinking. The impact of the dose on driving ability also depends on past drinking experience, time since last meal, use of other drugs, and so on. There also will be individual differences depending on the age, size, and health of the drinker.

Nonetheless, in practice, the criterion that receives the critical role in judging driving legality is the BAL. The BAL value used to define unacceptable levels for driving an automobile legally varies in different states, but a reading of .10 is common, although some states have lowered the acceptable limit to .08. A BAC level of .10 indicates that one tenth of 1% of the blood contains alcohol. Using a typical 150-pound male for illustrative purposes, this level might be obtained by drinking three to four drinks within the past hour. A female of equivalent body weight, however, will have a higher concentration due to the higher percentage of body fat in females.

Temporal Aspects

As alcohol or any drug is absorbed into the blood and circulated throughout the body, its concentration rises to a peak. The **ascending limb** of the BAC curve refers to the portion between the end of drinking until a peak level is obtained, as shown in Figure 4.1. As alcohol is metabolized and eliminated from the body, the BAC level declines from the peak level. The **descending limb** of the BAC curve is the section following the peak until the ethanol level is reduced to zero. For any BAC level less than the peak, there are two points where that level occurs, one on the ascending and one on the descending limb.

The *subjective effect* of a specific BAC level differs, depending on whether that given value is on the ascending (see Point A in Figure 4.1) or on the descending limb of the curve (see Point B in Figure 4.1). Due to the process of adaptation by which we tend to notice less and less as time goes by, we tend to feel "less intoxicated" at Point B during the descending limb than at the same BAC level as at Point B during the ascending limb of the curve. Nonetheless, the actual impairment of sensory motor functions may be the same for a given level, regardless of which limb we are dealing with. But because the subjective experience is one of less intoxication on the descending limb, the drinker may be willing to undertake risks such as driving a car even though the BAC level is still dangerously high. Thus, a

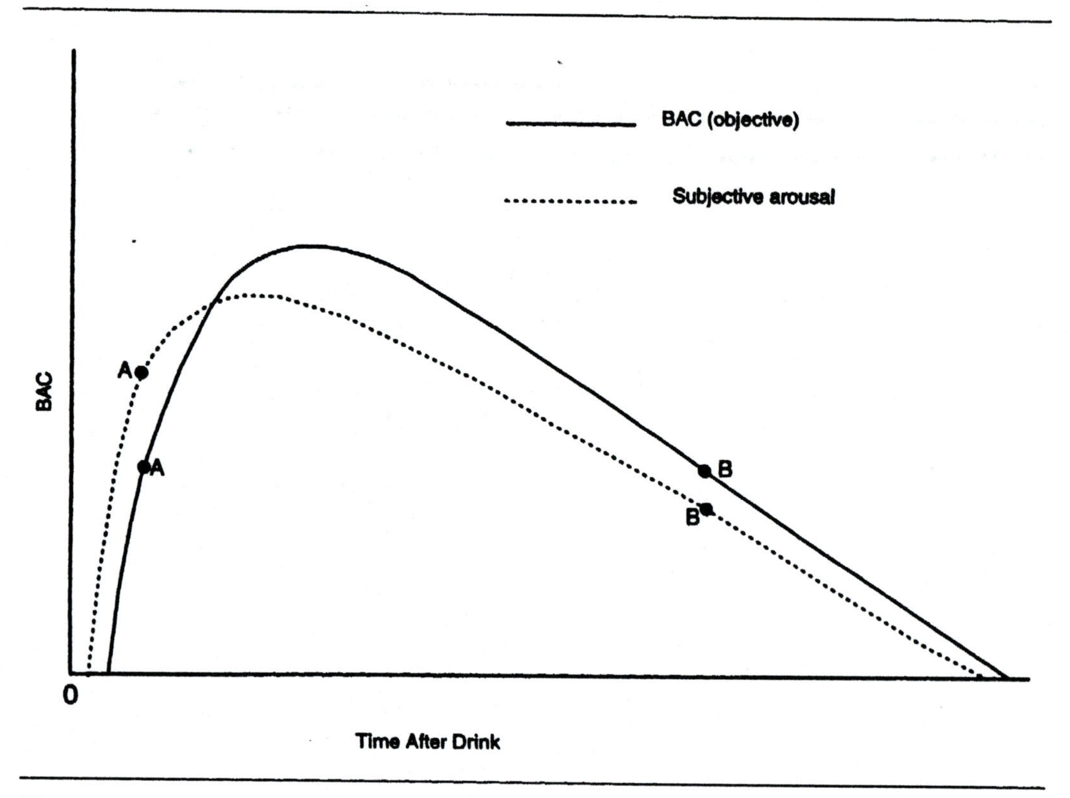

Figure 4.1. Comparison of Subjective and Objective Blood Alcohol Curve and the Different Effects of the Same Objective Levels on Ascending Versus Descending Limbs

drinker may stop drinking well before trying to drive home from a party. The BAC has already peaked and is now on the descending limb, and although it may still be high, the drinker subjectively feels more "sober" than is warranted and therefore feels ready to get behind the wheel and drive.

Thus, a study with college students (Earleywine & Martin, 1993) found that arousing effects were expected on the ascending limb of the blood alcohol curve, but sedative or less intoxicated effects were anticipated on the descending limb. Such effects increased with the size of the dose received, especially with women.

DETOXIFICATION AND ELIMINATION

Most drugs are detoxified or broken down chemically for elimination from the body by the liver. Thus, in the case of alcohol metabolism by the liver, the enzyme alcohol dehydrogenase (ADH) breaks ethanol down into acetaldehyde (ACH). This toxic ingredient is then broken down further by another enzyme called aldehyde dehydrogenase (ALDH) into water and acetate, products that are nontoxic and will be eliminated from the body. If the rate of alcohol ingestion exceeds the capacity of the liver to detoxify ethanol, the result will be an accumulation of alcohol with an attendant "intoxicating effect" on the drinker, as evidenced by slurred speech, staggering, and impaired perceptual motor coordination. On recovery of sobriety, the unpleasant experience of a "hangover" may be encountered as the price for the previous evening's excessive use of alcohol.

For nicotine, the primary product of metabolism by the liver is cotinine and nicotine oxide. During the first pass through the liver, around 90% of nicotine is broken down so that orally ingested tobacco produces little effect in comparison to smoked tobacco, which is delivered from the lungs to the brain in about 7 seconds. Nicotine has a short half-life of about half an hour, with anywhere from 2% to 35% of it excreted unchanged (typically 5%-10%).

Cocaine has a rapid metabolism, with a half-life of about an hour. It is metabolized by the liver, and its metabolite, benzoylecgonoine, has a half-life of about 8 hours. Marijuana is metabolized mainly by the liver. Metabolites are easily eliminated, with about 60% to 70% eliminated in the feces and the remaining 30% through the urine. The total elimination of marijuana is relatively slow, with residual traces found even after several days and up to a month after use because it is lipid soluble.

DOSE RESPONSE CURVES

A major determinant of the effect of a drug is the size of the dose. As the drug dose increases, assuming all else is equal, there is generally an increase in the effect of the drug on physiological or behavior response. The relationship between dose and response is called a **dose response curve.** As shown in Figure 4.2, the effect of increased doses generally is not constant but gradual. At low doses, the effect is small, accelerates with higher doses, and then levels off at even higher doses. For some drugs, higher doses may lead to a reversal, with reduced response at very high levels.

The effect of a given dose will vary across individuals who differ on many factors, including metabolism, age, weight, and gender. For a given individual, the same dose may produce different effects depending on the physical and mental condition. Consequently, it is necessary for pharmacologists to identify *average* responses rather than rely on responses of specific individuals or use occasions.

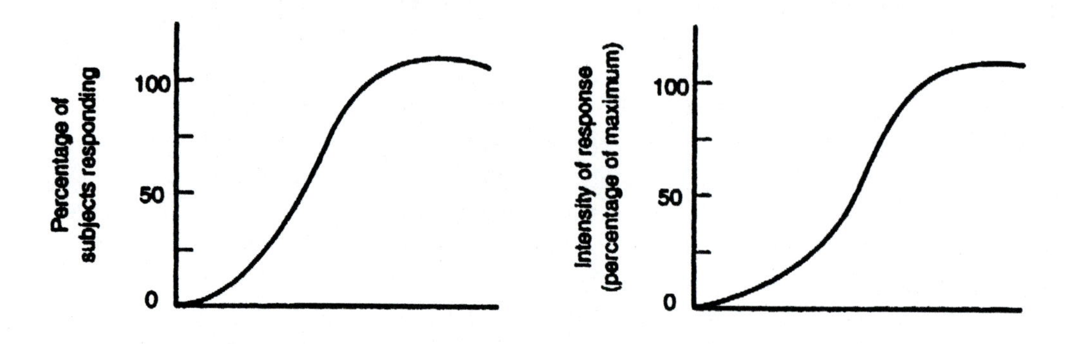

Figure 4.2. Two Types of Dose Response Curves

NOTE: (Left) Curve obtained by plotting the dose of a drug against the percentage of subjects showing a given response at any given dose. (Right) Curve obtained by plotting the dose of a drug against the intensity of response observed in any single individual at a given dose. The intensity of response is plotted as a percentage of the maximum obtainable response.

SOURCE: From *A Primer of Drug Action* by Julien. Copywrited 1998, 1995, 1992, 1988, 1985, 1981, 1978, 1975 by W. H. Freeman and Company. Used with permission.

An alternative type of dose response curve, also shown in Figure 4.2, is to plot the percentage of individuals who experience a given effect at several specific doses. A similar relationship occurs for a given drug, and as the dose increases, a higher percentage of individuals will show an effect of a specific drug dose.

Drug abuse often involves drugs intended for the treatment of medical conditions. Abusers who use these drugs nonmedically are interested in *maximizing* the drug effect, so they seek strong doses even though they often risk adverse side effects. In contrast, physicians may be interested in using lower doses that are sufficient to treat a medical condition, without undue risk of undesired side effects. These drugs have been tested to determine the *effective dose* so that the amount needed to treat a condition effectively but safely is known, especially if the drug is expensive or has serious side effects.

At the other extreme might be dangerous levels—doses that might be lethal and that one would want to avoid. Using laboratory animals, the dose levels of a drug from which half of them died would be termed the *lethal dose* 50. This dose would be adjusted to estimate its equivalence for humans. Dangerous drugs are those with little room for error (i.e., the difference between the effective and the lethal dose is small). Safer drugs have a wide margin for error, with a lethal dose being substantially higher than the effective dose.

How Drugs Affect the Nervous System

What happens in the body at the neurophysiological level after alcohol and other drugs are taken is central to understanding how they affect experience and behavior. Neurochemical and neurophysiological effects occur throughout the body after different drugs are consumed, which affect neuronal processes, resulting in either upward or downward shifts from the prior physiological levels. Often, but not always, these effects are the expected and desired outcomes for the user. On some occasions, however, unexpected and unpleasant consequences may occur when drugs are consumed. Aspects of use such as quantity, quality, or drug combinations can produce variations on behavioral effects.

THE NERVOUS SYSTEM

We will first examine an overview of the nervous system followed by a description of how the neurons communicate. Then an examination of how different drugs influence neurotransmitter substances will provide a basis for understanding how drugs affect behavior and experience. Evidence concerning the short-term or acute effects of drug use on the nervous system will be presented, followed by findings about the long-term effects of chronic drug use on major systems of the body.

Peripheral Nervous System

As Figure 4.3 indicates, the nervous system involves several components. The **peripheral nervous system** (PNS) receives stimuli from outside the body along peripheral nerve receptors to send input to the spinal cord, a set of nerve fibers that runs along the length of the spine, from where they are related to the brain, which sits atop it. The PNS consists of two parts, the *somatic nervous system* (SNS), which controls the striated muscles and receptor organs that we have some voluntary control over, and the **autonomic nervous system** (ANS), which affects smooth muscle and organs over which we have little or no control.

The ANS involves two opposing or reciprocal components, the *sympathetic* and *parasympathetic* nervous systems. In situations that threaten the well-being of the individual, the sympathetic nervous system is activated to enable behaviors to promote survival. Adrenaline or epinephrine is released from the adrenal gland, which activates neural **receptors** to increase

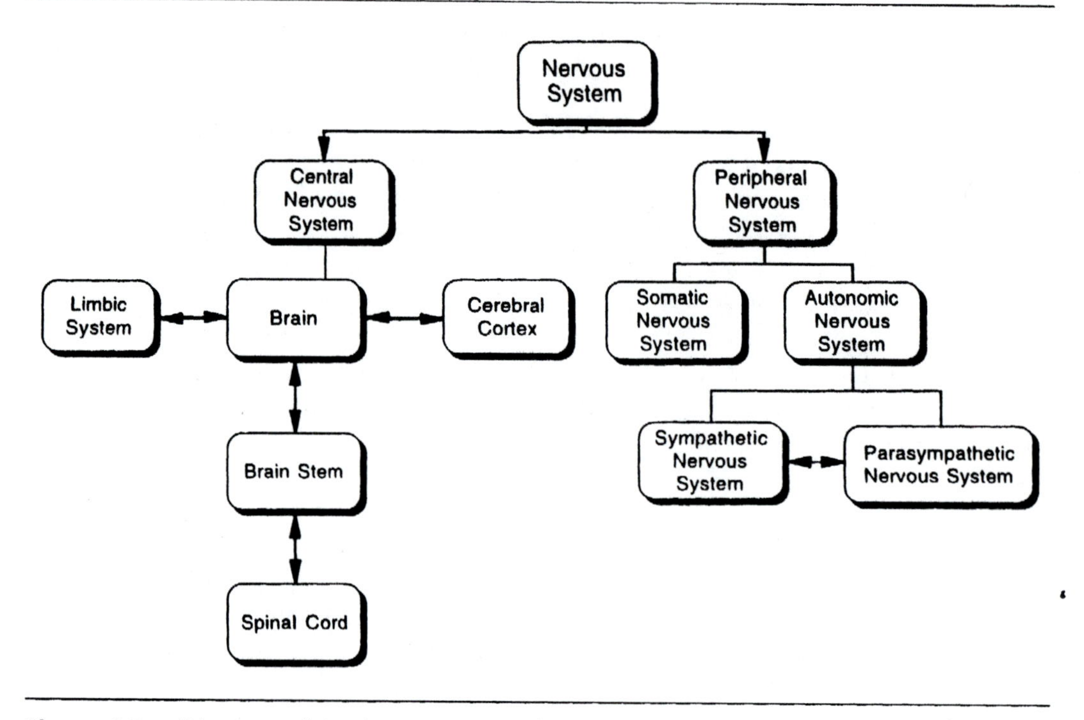

Figure 4.3. Diagram of the Organization of Major Structures of the Nervous System

heart rate and respiration and the release of glucose from the liver to fuel responses to cope with the situation. The parasympathetic nervous system has the opposite function, working through activation of acetylcholine to achieve homeostasis of bodily functions and restore resting levels when the problem is resolved for this system.

Central Nervous System

The **central nervous system (CNS)** comprises the brain and the spinal cord. The CNS processes information from all parts of the body through the PNS to the brain. In turn, messages from the brain are sent back down the spinal cord to direct activity throughout the body.

A highly complex center, the brain is a system of interrelated structures specializing in important functions such as cognition, memory, emotion, movement, sensation, perception, eating, drinking, and sexual function. Figure 4.4 shows the location of important areas of the brain, especially those affected by alcohol and other drugs. The outer covering or cerebral

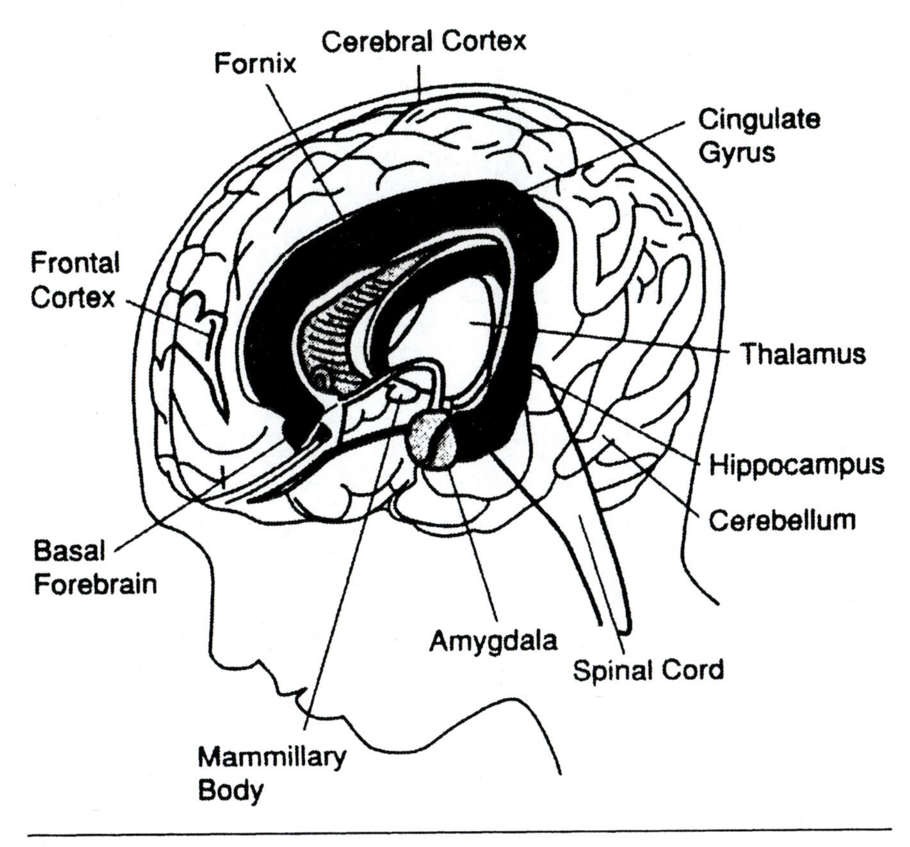

Figure 4.4. Diagram of Primary Brain Areas Related to Alcohol and Other Drugs
SOURCE: U.S. Department of Health and Human Services (1997b).

cortex contains a convoluted surface covering two hemispheres that serves as an association area for sensory and motor functions. At the base or *brain stem* between the brain and the spinal cord is the *medulla,* which governs respiration and vomiting, two functions that drugs may disrupt, leading to fatal or serious harm. Above the medulla is the *cerebellum,* important for motor coordination and balance. The disruption of the ability to walk normally by drugs such as alcohol may involve this center.

A center called the *locus coeruleus* in the lower brain connects with the cortex as well as with mid-brain regions such as the *limbic system,* which contains many of the noradrenergic receptors. This system contains several important structures that regulate many basic emotional functions and behaviors related to physical survival, including hunger, thirst, pain, and sexual activity. A small but very important organ in the limbic system, the *hypothalamus,* is involved with the experience of pleasure and reinforcement. The *amygdala* is implicated as a factor in aggressive behavior. The *ventral tegmental area* of this region connects with the *nucleus accumbens,* which contains many important neurotransmitter sites for dopamine (DA) that are activated by many drugs. A large structure, the *hippocampus,* is involved with spatial location memory. An important midbrain center for pain receptors is the *periaqueductal gray,* which contains many receptors for endogenous opiates that are also activated by opiate drugs such as morphine and heroin.

How Neurons Communicate

An understanding of how drugs affect the body requires an overview of how the nervous system functions, starting at the lowest level. The basic unit of the nervous system is the neuron. Approximately 1 trillion cells send and receive neurochemical information to each other (Charness, 1990). Each neuron has a network of dendrites or fiber endings that extend into the spaces between cells known as synapses to receive information. Then the cells send the information forward to the dendrites of as many as 1,000 adjacent neurons through their single axons, fibers that extend beyond the cell body. Figure 4.5 shows two adjacent neurons, with the sending neuron referred to as the *presynaptic cell* and the receiving neuron termed the *postsynaptic cell.*

NEURONAL PROCESSES

Within a neuron, signal transmission involves changes in electrically charged particles or ions related to chemicals such as sodium (Na^+), potassium (K^+), chloride (Cl^-), and calcium (Ca^+). These ions can pass through the cell membranes through channels that are specific to each type of ion. These ion channels, which are proteins on the neuron membrane, regulate the flow of ions through pores in the cell membrane. Depolarization occurs when the electrical changes produced by these ions involve a decrease in voltage between the outside and inside of a membrane. This process leads to an impulse called the **action potential** that traverses the neuron so that information can move through to the synapse and then on to other neurons.

Ions, in effect, create neural transmission through the cell. The G proteins within the cell, as shown in Figure 4.6, are activated in this process to admit important chemicals known as **neurotransmitters** from one neuron

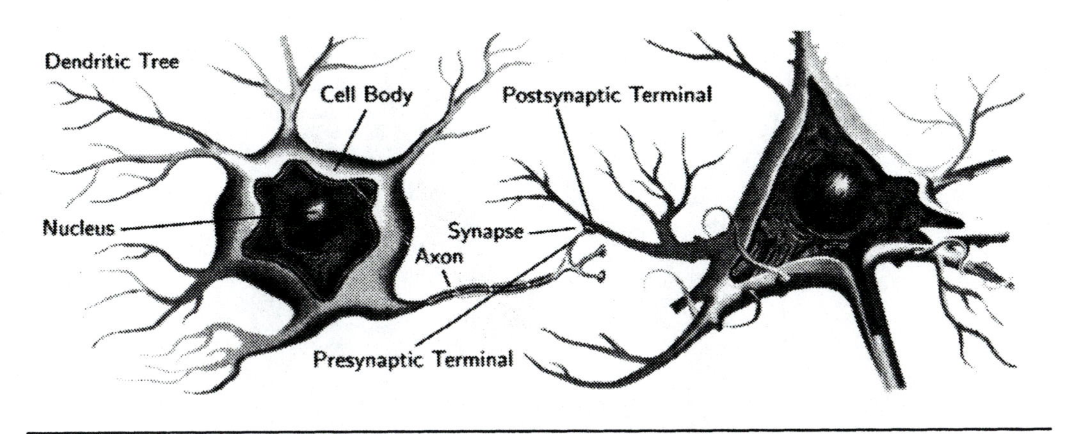

Figure 4.5. Neuronal Structure
SOURCE: Charness (1990).

(presynaptic) across the synapse into adjacent neurons (postsynaptic). If the entering ions have a positive electrical charge, they are termed *excitatory* because they facilitate activation of the cell processes that transmit the signal to the synapse. In contrast, other channels, such as $GABA_A$ receptors, exert inhibitory effects by admitting negatively charged chemicals such as chloride ions (C^-), which reduce the ability of the cell to relay the signal further.

Important regulatory functions and metabolism *within* each neuron involve enzymes called *second messengers,* so named because they pass information from receptors on the membrane to the inner part of the neuron to further excite or inhibit the transmission. This indirect process is slower and may require cascades of stimulation to be activated. One especially important messenger is cyclic guanine monophosphate (cGMP), which is generated by the N-methyl-D-aspartate (NMDA) receptor. Another second messenger, cyclic adenosine monophosphate (cAMP), is valuable for its role in molecular synthesis of RNA.

Alcohol may disrupt adenyl cyclase (AC) function, an important enzyme affecting cAMP, so that transmission of messages from the exterior of neurons to the interior is adversely affected. Disruption of these secondary messenger systems by the actions of ethanol (Tabakoff & Hoffman, 1987) could produce the observed acute effects of alcohol.

NEUROTRANSMITTERS

Neurotransmitters are chemicals created in the neurons and stored in vesicles of cell bodies near the end of the axon, as shown in Figure 4.5.

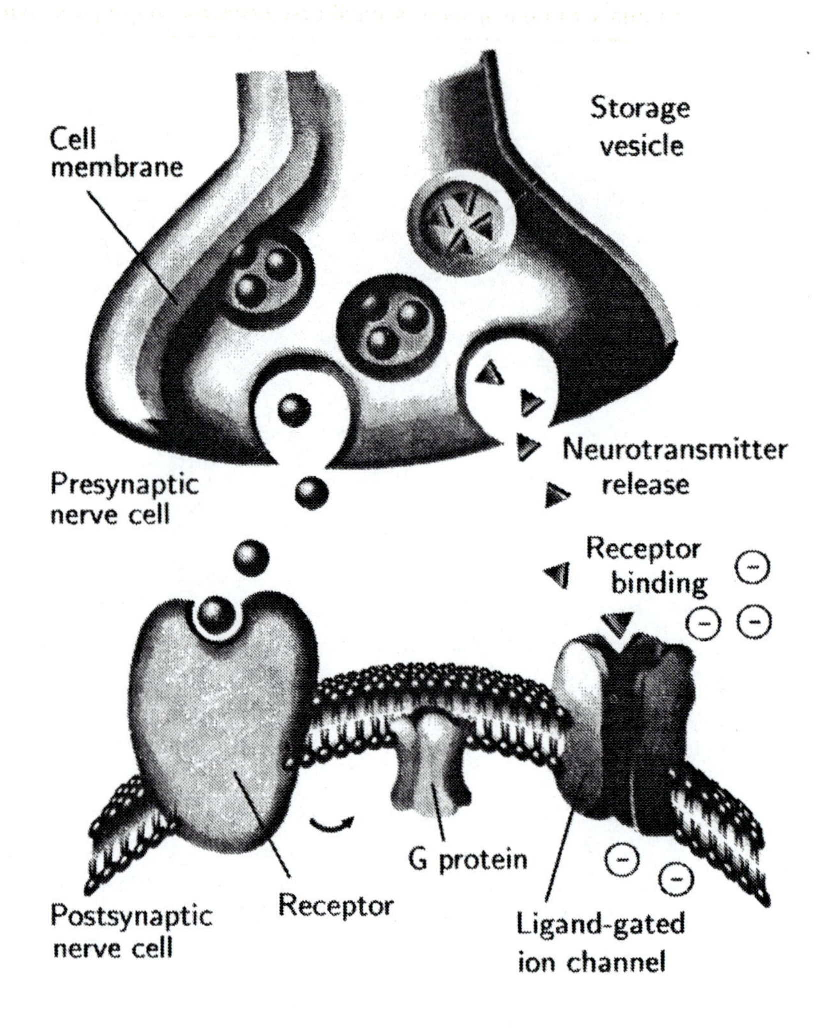

Figure 4.6. Synaptic Transmission
SOURCE: Di Chiara (1997).

When a neuron is activated by impulses from other neurons, these neurotransmitters are released. Thus, neurotransmitters regulate the flow of information among individual neurons throughout the nervous system. Major neurotransmitters include monoamines such as **dopamine (DA)**, *serotonin* (5-HT), and *norepinephrine* (NE). Other important neurotransmitters include excitatory substances, such as *epinephrine* and **glutamate** (NDMA), and inhibitory neurotransmitters that reduce neural activity, such as *acetylcholine* and **gamma aminobutyric acid (GABA).**

TABLE 4.2 Summary of neuropsychological processes for major psychoactive drugs

Drug	*Tolerance for Main Effect*	*Withdrawal*	*Psychological Dependence*	*Major Neuro-transmitter Actions*
Alcohol	Yes	Strong, if high dose	Yes	DA, GABA, glutamate
Nicotine	Fast	Yes	Yes	ACh, DA, NE, beta-endorphin
Caffeine	Yes	Rare	Yes	Block adenosine
Barbiturates	Fast	Strong, if high dose	Yes	GABA
Benzodiazepine	Yes	Slight	Yes	GABA
Opiates, heroin	Fast	Strong, if high dose	Yes	DA, NE, glutamate
Cocaine	Yes	Weak	Yes	Block reuptake of DA, NE
Amphetamines	Slow	Weak	Yes	NE leaks, release and block reuptake of DA, 5-HT
Cannabis	Yes	Mild	Yes	DA, NE, 5-HT, GABA
Hallucinogens	Fast	No	No	Blocks 5-HT

NOTE: DA = dopamine; 5-HT = serotonin; NE = norepinephrine; GABA = gamma animobutyl acid; ACh = acetylcholine.

Each neuron has receptor sites on its membrane that are specific for different neurotransmitters. Each type of receptor appears to recognize or accept a different type of incoming neurotransmitter across the **synaptic junction**, the gap separating each neuron from nearby neurons. When a specific type of neurotransmitter is received at the membrane of the post-synaptic neuron, it "binds" to or fits the receptor site in much the same way a key opens a lock. This process modifies the permeability of the **receptor** so that it increases or decreases the excitability of that cell, depending on the specific neurotransmitter. The levels of these important neurotransmitters appear to be altered in various ways by the consumption of different drugs (Tabakoff, Hoffman, & Petersen, 1990).

Table 4.2 lists the main neurotransmitters involved with different drugs. These synaptic changes in neurotransmitter levels are an important factor in determining the influence that drugs have on behavior and experience. For example, some drugs seem to involve phosphorylation, a process involving the addition of phosphate to the receptor sites, which impairs G protein activity within the cells. These changes, which last for varying duration, impede the process of reuptake by which the neurotransmitters are returned to the originating presynaptic neurons for subsequent use.

Serotonin (5-hydroxytryptamine or 5-HT) is an important regulator of mood and consummatory behavior such as eating. Violent and impulsive behaviors also have been associated with lowered serotonin levels (Lidberg, Tuck, Asberg, Scalia-Tomba, & Bertilsson, 1985). Monamines (MA) such as dopamine, norepinephrine, and serotonin are neurotransmitters that enhance mood. Enzymes such as *monoamine oxidase* (MAO) break down such substances, and the mood enhancement is ended. Drugs that prevent this decomposition of MA, called MAO inhibitors (MAOI), can prolong the benefits of mood enhancers such as dopamine.

A different process for prolonging the mood changes from drug-instigated release of MA involves slowing down the reuptake or removal of the synaptic junction MA back into the cell. One type of antidepressant, the tricyclics such as Elavil® and Tofranil®, works to prevent the reuptake of monoamines such as dopamine and to block cholinergic receptors that receive an inhibitory neurotransmitter, acetylcholine. A newer class of antidepressant drugs such as fluoxetine (Prozac®), which selectively block the reuptake of serotonin from the synaptic area, can also prolong the improved mood states.

The possibility that the body synthesizes its own opiates was raised with the discovery of receptor sites for the opiate morphine in the early 1970s (Pert & Snyder, 1973). It may seem odd that the body would have existing receptors to accept substances that come from outside the body. One plausible hypothesis was that because opiates help the body cope with pain, the receptors for the body's natural or endogenous chemical means of reducing pain would accept exogenous substances such as morphine or other drugs because they also alleviate pain. The eventual discovery that the body has natural or **endogenous opiates** such as *enkephalins* and *beta-endorphins* vindicated this type of reasoning.

How Alcohol and Other Drugs Affect Neurotransmission

As diagrammed in Figure 4.7, there are several ways in which drugs can alter neurotransmission at the synapse. **Agonistic** effects involve facilitation of neurotransmitter function by either increased neurotransmitter production, increased neurotransmitter release, or activation of receptor sites that are normally stimulated by a specific neurotransmitter. In contrast, alcohol and drugs may have **antagonistic** effects on neurotransmitters, either by interfering with their release, usurping the receptor sites that a specific neurotransmitter normally occupies, or causing neurotransmitter leakage from the synaptic vesicles.

Agonistic Effects

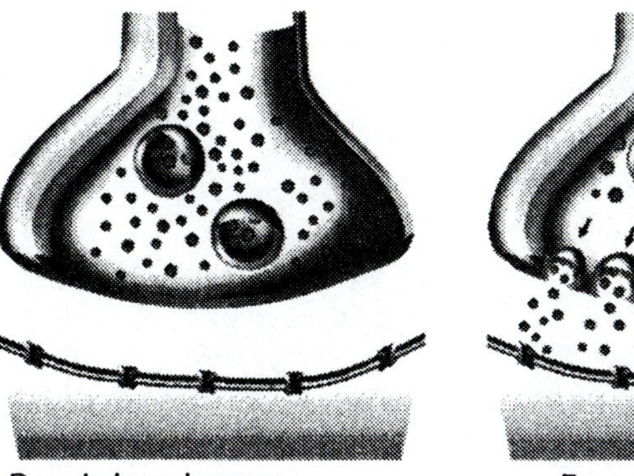

Drug induces increase in synthesis of neurotransmitter

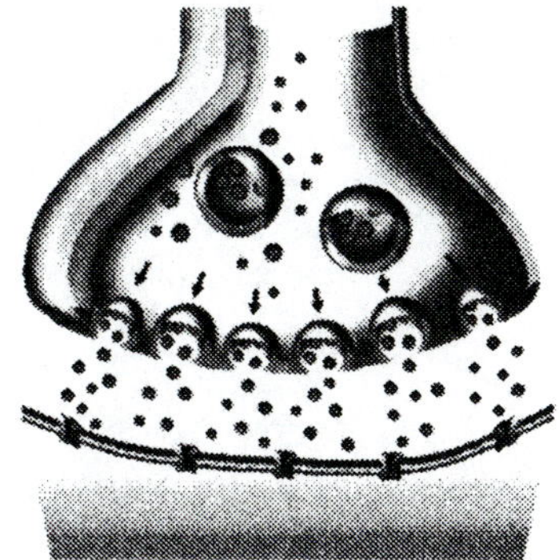

Drug increases release of neurotransmitter

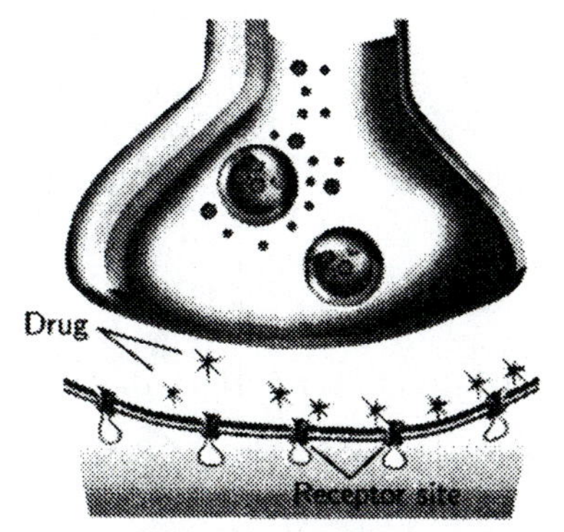

Drug activates receptors that normally respond to neurotransmitter

Antagonistic Effects

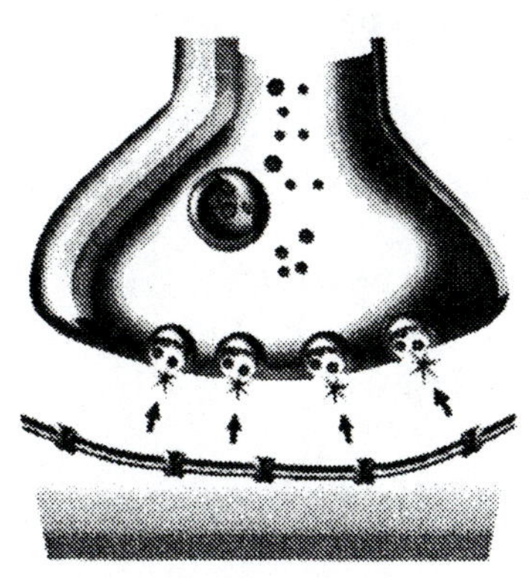

Drug interferes with release of neurotransmitter

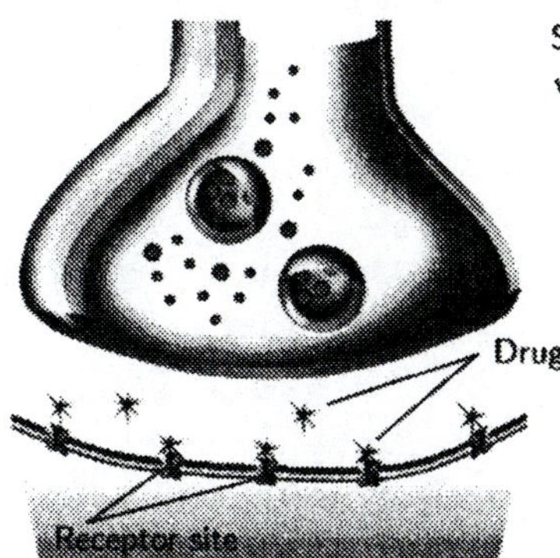

Drug acts as a false transmitter, occupying receptor sites normally sensitive to neurotransmitter

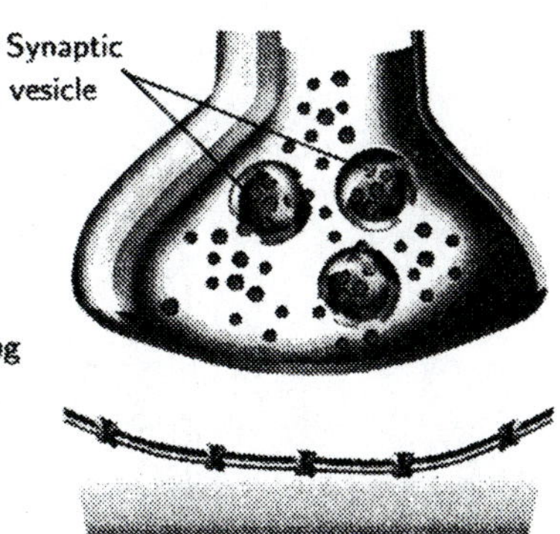

Drug causes leakage of neurotransmitter from synaptic vesicles

Figure 4.7. Six Ways in Which Drugs Affect Reuptake or Depletion of Neurotransmitters at the Synapse

Alcohol

Unlike other drugs, alcohol does not affect specific brain receptors but appears to influence the entire neuronal membrane (Harris & Buck, 1990). Table 4.3 lists some of the main effects. Alcohol disrupts the typical balance of the half-protein and half-lipid composition of the membrane, altering the passage of other chemicals in and out of the neuronal cells. Alcohol increases the chloride ion entry through the actions of GABA, an inhibitory neurotransmitter, so that there is reduced neuronal excitability. Alcohol also inhibits the amino acid *glutamate,* the major excitatory neurotransmitter responsible for allowing higher levels of calcium ions into

TABLE 4.3 Summary of major neuronal processes affected by alcohol

Neuron Membrane: Alter Permeability	*Within Neuron: Disrupt Secondary Messengers*	*At Synapse: Alter Neurotransmitter Levels*
Inhibit glutamate (NMDA)	Cyclic adenosine monophosphate (cAMP)	Dopamine (DA) Serotonin (5-HT) Norepinephrine (NE)
Activate GABA	Cyclic guanine monophosphate (cGMP)	Neuropeptides (endorphins)

cells, primarily through the NMDA receptor, with the net effect of creating a sedative influence.

Dopamine (DA), which may underlie rewarding and pleasurable experiences, appears to first increase with alcohol use but eventually shows a decline with continued drinking. Norepinephrine (NE) is often higher with increasing arousal such as stressful situations. Alcohol seems to be associated with higher levels of NE.

Serotonin is diminished by heavy alcohol use or may be naturally lower for alcoholics. It is possible that alcoholics may be self-medicating their depression with alcohol in a futile attempt to increase their serotonin levels (Tabakoff et al., 1990).

Barbiturates and Benzodiazepines

Other sedative-hypnotic drugs such as barbiturates and benzodiazepines are absorbed readily from the digestive tract. They have specific receptor sites to which these drugs bind, and they release chloride ion channel blockers that inhibit the central nervous system activity of GABA. They can quickly pass through the blood-brain barrier and affect higher functions. Because these drugs are often used in combination with alcohol, their effects can be increased as alcohol slows down their metabolic breakdown.

Nicotine

Nicotine from tobacco is absorbed into the body and activates cholinergic receptors that are affected by the neurotransmitter acetylcholine (ACh), leading to the release of dopamine, norepinephrine, and beta-endorphins.

These *nicotinic receptors* are found in many parts of the central nervous system, particularly in the brain stem. When nicotinic receptors at sites such as the adrenal glands and reticular formation are activated by nicotine, adrenaline (epinephrine) and norepinephrine are released, which also activate the central nervous system, as reflected by increased activation in measures of heart rate, blood pressure, and brain activity measured by the **electroencephalogram (EEG).**

Nicotine-stimulated dopamine release is related to increased activity in the shell of the **nucleus accumbens** (Pontieri, Tanda, Orzi, & Di Chiara, 1996). This region, which connects to the forebrain, includes the amygdala, which deals with emotional and motivational processing. After DA is released and transmits its signals, it is broken down or taken back to the neuron. MAO B is an enzyme that breaks down dopamine in the brain. The finding of lower MAO B in smokers' brains suggests that whatever is inhibiting MAO B could be working with nicotine to enhance dopamine effects by slowing its metabolism. Earlier studies have shown that nicotine did not influence MAO B, so the culprit could be some of the 4,000 or so identified chemicals in cigarette smoke.

Cigarette combustion involves carbon monoxide (CO), which forms carboxyhemoglobin when it binds with blood cells. Nicotine acts to produce electrocortical activation, skeletal muscle relaxation, and cardiovascular and endocrine effects such as the increase of catecholamines, corticosteroids, and pituitary hormones.

Nicotine absorption across membranes depends on it being in its nonionized state or alkaline form. When nicotine is in an acid environment, it enters an ionized state as a cigarette is smoked. The psychoactive effect is weakened because nicotine is not readily absorbed from the acidic environment of the stomach. However, chewing tobacco, snuff, and nicotine gum are effective alternative delivery mechanisms to smoking because absorption of nicotine through the membranes in the mouth directly into the bloodstream maintains its alkaline state.

Caffeine

The caffeine in coffee and carbonated soft drinks is called methylxanthine. It is absorbed from the small intestine and gets distributed to all organs. It acts by blocking adenosine receptors and slowing the reuptake of neurotransmitters such as DA, 5-HT, and NE. Because adenosine acts as an inhibitor of the central nervous system, this action functions to stimulate and activate. Caffeine also acts to release other stimulating neurotransmitters such as epinephrine. **Tolerance** develops for caffeine, and withdrawal reactions occur due to its absence in the form of headaches and lethargy within 12 to 24 hours.

Opiates

Opium is not easily absorbed from the digestive tract. Consequently, oral ingestion does not produce much effect, and opiate users experience more potent effects by injection or smoking it with pipes. Most of it is metabolized during the first pass through the liver. There are five different types of receptors to which opiates bind with different consequences: mu, kappa, sigma, delta, and epsilon. For example, analgesia is mediated mainly by opiates binding to the mu receptor.

Morphine, the active pharmacological ingredient in the opium poppy, is 10 times more potent. Morphine is not easily absorbed because it is not lipid soluble. It is quickly metabolized when smoked or injected.

Heroin, a synthetic opiate developed in the late 1890s, is about three times stronger than morphine, crossing the blood-brain barrier many times faster. It is not lipid soluble. Heroin involves rapid tolerance, with a tenfold increase in dose required within a few months of use. Withdrawal reactions, which include restless agitation, twitching, sweating, drowsiness, goose bumps, vomiting, and cramping, start about 6 to 12 hours after use, peaking in 24 to 72 hours and lasting about a week. Nonetheless, the overall syndrome is relatively mild and can be confused with flu symptoms. The more intense dramatic portrayals are atypical or reflective of either poor-quality drugs with toxic impurities or large doses.

Naloxone and **naltrexone** (ReVia®) are antagonists that block the effects of opiate drugs. They compete with opioids for their receptor sites, and by occupying these locations, they effectively neutralize the opioids by preventing them from producing their effects on the nervous system. Naltrexone is much longer lasting in its effect.

Methadone is a synthetic opiate that is commonly used in treating heroin addiction because its effects are longer lasting with less severe withdrawal that extends over a longer period. Methadone acts as an antagonist to heroin by competing for its receptor sites. One great health advantage is that methadone can be taken orally, avoiding the risk of infections from needle injections.

Cocaine

Cocaine produces its psychoactive effects by blocking the reuptake of dopamine as well as of serotonin. Because these neurotransmitters are retained at the synapse, their mood-enhancing and energizing effects are maintained and produce the high stimulation sought by users. When cocaine is not available to chronic users, the opposite affect of depression occurs, which is commonly referred to as a "crash."

Cocaine has a half-life of only 1 hour, with a longer half-life of 8 hours for its metabolite. A moderate dose (up to 60 mg) elevates mood, enhances performance on physical endurance, and promotes a sense of well-being. However, at higher doses, cocaine can lead to paranoid delusions as well as hallucinations. There is also a risk of overdose as well as interactions with other drugs.

Cocaine mimics the actions of the sympathetic nervous system and its neurotransmitter, epinephrine, which activates the emergency responses such as heightened arousal (increased heart rate, blood pressure, respiration rate, sweating, eye dilation, and increased body temperature). To serve the emergency needs of survival, blood flow goes to the large muscle groups and not to the peripheral organs. Cocaine also has its medical functions as a local anesthetic that can be used to numb the mouth, vagina, rectum, and eyes.

Crack, the potent by-product of cocaine, is the outcome when cocaine and sodium bicarbonate are combined and heated to eliminate the water content.

Amphetamines

The amphetamines are a weak-base substance. These synthetic stimulants originally were used medically to deal with respiratory problems such as asthma, some sleep disorders, and obesity. During World War I, soldiers used them to offset fatigue. Following the war, widespread abuse of amphetamines occurred as they became used as a recreational drug. They stimulate dopamine receptors to increase motor activity and mood changes. Reuptake of dopamine is blocked by amphetamines, and greater release of DA is stimulated. Norepinephrine receptors are stimulated to produce alertness and to counter fatigue.

A more potent form created illegally, methamphetamines, also has been widely abused. A crystal form called ice, which is easily homemade, is a newer form of this category of stimulants that is widely abused.

Marijuana

The active ingredient, delta 9 THC (Δ 9 THC), in cannabis is lipid soluble but does not dissolve in water, so its absorption is slow. Smoking, therefore, is a much faster mode of administration because the drug moves rapidly from the lungs to the rest of the body in a few minutes. Receptors have been found throughout the central nervous system, especially in the *nucleus accumbens.*

Cannabis affects 5-HT and DA levels as well as prostaglandin synthesis. It slows turnover of ACh in animal experiments. Recently, a receptor site for marijuana has been identified (Mechoulam, Hanus, & Martin, 1994) in many areas of the brain, including the cortex, hippocampus, and cerebellum. This finding also has led to the successful discovery of an endogenous neurotransmitter, named *anadamide* (Devane et al., 1992).

Hallucinogens

Psychedelic drugs block acetylcholine sites. For example, LSD-25 blocks the release of serotonin, and atropine and scopalamine block acetylcholine sites. Much of the metabolism is handled by the liver. Although tolerance occurs rapidly, it can disappear in a few days. Because LSD shows no withdrawal reactions, the dangers of physical dependency seem small.

SUMMARY

Answers as to why drug taking is such a strong behavior and why it is so resistant to cessation may depend strongly on the effects that drugs have on neurotransmitters. Even though different drugs involve different sets of neurotransmitters, most involve either direct increases of DA or indirect effects on processes to allow DA to last longer. DA, released in the nucleus accumbens, is widely regarded as a major factor underlying positive reinforcement. Because drug taking is such a powerfully reinforcing behavior, it has been conjectured that drug use acts to increase or maintain levels of DA in the brain. Similarities exist between nicotine, heroin, and cocaine addiction because they all have the ability to selectively increase dopamine transmission and energy metabolism in the shell of the nucleus accumbens (Pontieri et al., 1996). A reward deficiency hypothesis of drug taking assumes that when DA levels are low in the limbic system—either due to situations such as high stress, failure, and depression or to biological differences in the innate tendencies for DA release—drugs can serve as a substitute mechanism for restoring or elevating DA levels (Blum & Payne, 1991).

Stimulant drugs such as cocaine increase the presence of DA by inhibiting its reuptake, so that DA's reinforcing function is prolonged. Nicotine,

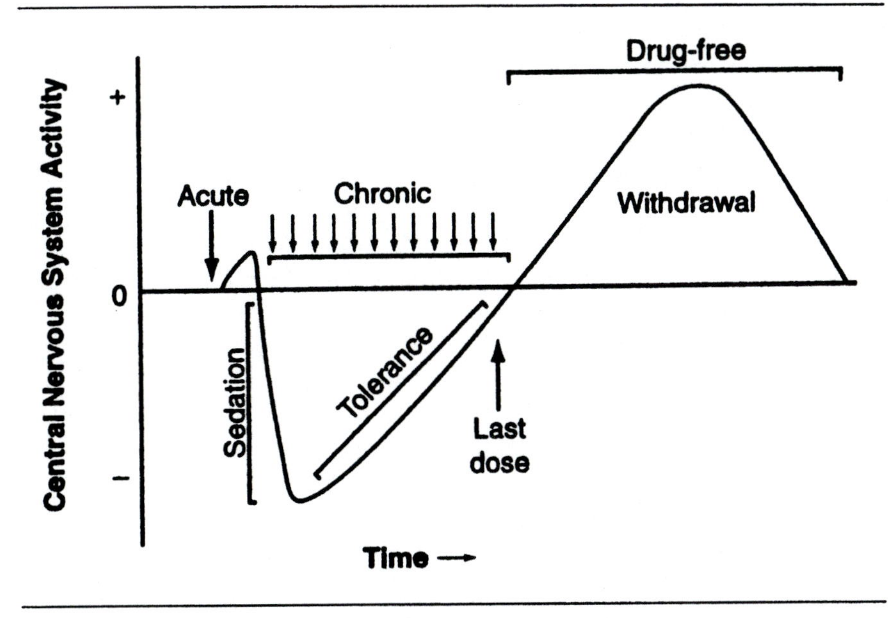

Figure 4.8. Tolerance and Withdrawal From Alcohol Over Time
SOURCE: Mette and Crabbe (1996). Copyrighted by CRC Press. Used with permission.

another stimulant, increases DA as well as ACh. Depressant drugs such as alcohol and the opiates release more DA as well as 5-HT, which may counter depressive affect, at least during early stages of drinking, although there may be a reversal as drinking continues over time.

After prolonged use of many psychoactive drugs, tolerance develops so that the positive reinforcing value declines, but the withdrawal reactions to the cessation of drug use are highly adverse. To avoid or escape these consequences, one must redose with further use of drugs to restore DA levels. Negative reinforcement refers to the process involved when drugs are used to eliminate or reduce withdrawal reactions due to their absence. The development of tolerance over repeated use and its relationship to withdrawal when use ends are diagrammed in Figure 4.8.

TOLERANCE

Continued use of any drug leads to a diminished effect of a given dose. This phenomenon is known as tolerance. In the case of alcohol, use of the same amount that previously produced a given effect is no longer adequate to produce the same effect on later occasions. One danger is that with increased tolerance, the drinker underestimates the true BAC, often leading the drinker to engage in riskier behaviors.

Thus, the gap between anticipated and subjective (actual) reactions to alcohol may differ with the drinker's experience with alcohol. Expected and experienced effects of alcohol in 387 male and female drinkers were compared against observer ratings (Gabrieli, Nagoshi, Rhea, & Wilson, 1991). Based on their drinking history, drinkers were classified into three levels of consumption: high, moderate, and low. They consumed alcohol in the laboratory to produce a BAL that was the equivalent of two drinks an hour over 2 hours before taking a battery of tests measuring sensory motor performance, cognitive and perceptual tasks, and autonomic responses. Assessments of their feelings of intoxication and euphoria were made by drinkers as well as by trained observers.

Anticipated *sensitivity* was measured by drinker ratings to determine the extent to which they expected to experience intoxication, negative emotions, and euphoric emotions after four drinks. Subjective perceptions of mood after drinking were assessed with a mood inventory. In addition, observers rated the drinkers for intoxication, negative emotions, and euphoric emotions. The results showed that heavy drinkers tended to underestimate alcohol effects (objective ratings higher than the subjective ratings), whereas the inexperienced light drinkers tended to overestimate (objective ratings lower than subjective ratings) alcohol effects.

On the basis that observer ratings showed more impairment for the heavy than for the lighter drinkers, it appears that heavy drinkers may underestimate alcohol effects due to tolerance. Observer ratings of the effects of alcohol were generally greater than either the anticipated or the subjective ratings of effects made by the drinkers. Heavy drinkers may be likely to develop further problems because they deny that expected effects and actual effects of alcohol will be as high as they are.

Similarly, use of other drugs involves the development of tolerance, which may be responsible for the increased size of doses of drug consumed on subsequent occasions, although the rate at which it is achieved differs for different effects that each drug produces. For drugs such as amphetamines and heroin, substantial tolerance occurs, with several-fold increases in doses needed after only a few episodes of use. On the other hand, tolerance for cocaine is relatively mild.

Behavioral as opposed to *physiological* tolerance, which occurs at the level of the neuron, involves conditioned or learned responses (McKim, 1997). Thus, expectations and learned associations acquired from using a drug in a specific setting may lead to increased consumption over time in that setting. This form of tolerance may occur even if there is no physiological tolerance at the neurophysiological level.

WITHDRAWAL OR ABSTINENCE SYNDROME

When a long-term user of a drug discontinues its use, a **withdrawal** or **abstinence syndrome** occurs. Acute withdrawal involves highly variable symptoms ranging from sweating, tremors, and anxiety to seizures, hallucinations, and delirium. The irritability and discomfort experienced during the lack of the drug is precisely what triggers the users of some drugs to resume intake of the drug. Drug use acts as a type of self-medication to treat the unpleasant symptoms created by nonuse of some drugs. Hence, a vicious and escalating cycle is generated.

For central nervous system depressants such as alcohol, barbiturates, and benzodiazepines, there is a tendency for a **rebound effect** of hyperexcitability when its effects wear off after a drinking episode ends (McKim, 1997). With higher use levels, this withdrawal reaction is more pronounced.

For stimulants such as cocaine or crack, the withdrawal reaction seems to be relatively mild and involves the opposite affect of depression and lethargy. There is some debate as to whether the cessation of cocaine use produces a withdrawal reaction because of its mild form or whether withdrawal just takes a form that is different from the violent reactions involved in withdrawal from alcohol or heroin (McKim, 1997). Nonetheless, even without a strong withdrawal reaction, there is a strong craving for cocaine or crack. Drugs such as cocaine may be taken mainly for positive reinforcement (i.e., the sense of well-being created by the drug) as opposed to use for reducing unpleasant withdrawal reactions as with alcohol or heroin. Renewed or continued use of cocaine and crack presumably is due to the appetitional features such as the pleasant experiences created by the drug.

Withdrawal symptoms, depending on the drug, generally start from 12 to 24 hours after the drug is no longer used and can last up to several days. The typical medical treatment for alcohol withdrawal involves use of another drug from the same class of depressants, benzodiazepines (e.g., Librium®, Valium®), and vitamins to sedate the hyperexcitability of the nervous system. Barbiturates also have been used but are less often chosen because they involve the risk of cross-tolerance, a condition in which the tolerance to one drug generalizes to other drugs in the same category. If alcoholic patients receive barbiturates to reduce the withdrawal to alcohol, they may adapt too quickly due to cross-tolerance and fail to benefit. The use of newer drugs such as clonidine and beta-adrenergic blockers have been employed successfully (Liskow & Goodwin, 1987). As the withdrawal symptoms abate, the medical treatment is gradually reduced.

Naltrexone, an antagonist for alcohol, has been used to treat alcohol withdrawal (Volpicelli, Watson, King, Sherman, & O'Brien, 1995). Similarly, naloxone has been used to treat heroin withdrawal because it is a heroin antagonist and competes with it for the opiate receptors.

Physical Effects of Drugs

METHODS FOR GETTING EVIDENCE

A variety of methods have been used to determine the long-term effects of alcohol on the nervous system, including anatomical evidence available from autopsies, neurological correlates, and behavioral evidence. The three types of evidence are not always in agreement. For example, anatomical differences observed between alcoholics and nonalcoholics or from before-and-after comparisons of individual alcoholics may reflect causes, effects, or simply correlates of alcoholism. These differences may or may not also be accompanied by detectable neurological and behavioral differences. Similarly, neuropsychological differences may not involve functional consequences for behavior.

The rapid development of more advanced computer techniques has offered impressive new technology for studying the relationship between brain structure, functioning, and alcohol use. A review (Pfefferbaum & Rosenbloom, 1990) described research with tools that examine anatomical structure with three-dimensional images such as scans by computerized tomography (CT) and magnetic resonance imaging (MRI) to improve our visualization of the physical structure of the brain. Research with CT has shown brain tissue shrinkage and more cerebrospinal fluid in the resulting larger ventricles in alcoholics. However, this shrinkage appears to reverse somewhat under abstinence. Use of MRI, which, unlike CT, can distinguish between white and gray matter (two different types of brain tissue), has revealed that alcoholics have greater decreases in both gray and white matter than do age-matched controls.

However, as noted earlier, structural differences do not necessarily imply functional differences. Use of techniques such as positron emission tomography (PET) and cerebral blood flow (CBF) enables measurement of the brain processes, as opposed to structures, by the examination of changes over time in the distribution and accumulation of oxygen and other chemicals in the brain with and without the presence of alcohol. These measures are highly indirect indices of actual physiological processes, obtained through the tracing of radioactive materials introduced into the body, and are still open to interpretation. PET studies (Chao & Foudin, 1986) and research with CBF (Risberg & Berglund, 1987) have suggested that there may be reduced blood flow and cerebral glucose utilization in alcoholics, again with evidence that these processes can be reversed with abstinence.

CHRONIC EFFECTS

Brain

Comparison of alcoholics and nonalcoholics shows that wider sulci (the gaps between the convolutions of the outer layer of the cerebral cortex) and larger cerebral ventricles (cavities) exist among alcoholics that parallel changes typically found with aging. Measures of the electrical activity in areas of the brain with noninvasive techniques such as the electroencephalogram (EEG) and **event-related potentials (ERP)** have shown differences between alcoholics and nonalcoholics (Begleiter, Porjesz, Bihari, & Kissin, 1984). For example, a widely used ERP measure is the **P300 wave**, so called because it occurs 300 milliseconds after a stimulus is presented. It is regarded as a measure of cognitive processing of sensory stimulation and attention to incoming stimuli. Lower amplitudes of the P300 wave have been found in response to sensory tests (Begleiter et al., 1984) among sober alcoholics, suggesting that they may have impaired cognitive or attentional ability.

Such differences also have been found in sons of alcoholics, even prior to the development of alcoholism in the offspring (Patterson, Williams, McLean, Smith, & Schaffer, 1987). Furthermore, this impairment has been found to persist after treatment for alcoholism.

Liver

The liver is the largest organ in the body and serves as the main detoxifier (Lieber, 1984, 1994) for the metabolic breakdown of alcohol through the action of **alcohol dehydrogenase (ADH)**. This enzyme oxidizes alcohol into acetaldehyde, H20, and carbon dioxide, which can be eliminated from the body. In addition, an alternative mechanism for eliminating alcohol has been identified, the **microsomal ethanol oxidizing system (MEOS)**, which seems to allow heavy drinkers to metabolize alcohol more rapidly. As long as the rate of intake does not exceed the elimination rate, the liver should function adequately, but when drinking rates increase, it cannot keep up and may eventually sustain damage. The average adult can oxidize one drink in approximately 1 hour.

Alcohol produces a complication known as portal systemic encephalopathy (PSE), in which the venous blood is shunted away from the liver and fed directly into the circulation. Thus, **detoxification** or elimination of waste products by the liver is prevented, which allows toxins that the liver ordinarily removes such as ammonia to disrupt neurotransmitter functioning.

Chronic heavy alcohol use can also cause a buildup of triglycerides or fatty tissues in the liver, impairing its capability for metabolizing alcohol (Rubin & Lieber, 1968). In addition, hepatitis or inflammation of liver tissue may occur from metabolic by-products of chronic alcohol intake (Maher, 1997). For many but not all cases, hepatitis leads to **cirrhosis** of the liver, which involves scarring tissue so that it can no longer effectively eliminate the ethanol from the body. The extent to which the liver is damaged by alcohol abuse has been found to be greater for women because they have a smaller capacity for metabolizing alcohol during the first "pass" through the liver (Frezza et al., 1990).

Ironically, after heavy chronic drinking damages the liver of alcoholics, a reverse tolerance effect occurs in which less alcohol is needed to produce a given effect. Due to liver disease caused either by alcohol or other factors, there is a reduced capacity for metabolizing the alcohol consumed so that the drinker will become intoxicated at lower levels of consumption.

Normal functions of the liver include the production of bile for digestion of fats; albumin to help regulate fluid balance in cells of the whole body; globulin, which helps fight infections; and prothrombin, which helps clot blood to stop wounds from bleeding. Chronic alcohol abuse can impair all of these vital functions of the liver.

Gastrointestinal Tract

From the mouth, alcohol must traverse the esophagus, stomach, and duodenum to reach the small intestine, where the majority of it is released into the bloodstream. Although low doses of alcohol may stimulate secretion of digestive juices, larger doses act to inhibit them as well as irritate stomach linings and produce adverse effects throughout the gastrointestinal tract. Acute intake of alcohol activates gastric oversecretion, which can lead to gastric hemorrhages, and chronic use of alcohol impairs gastric acid secretion (Cook, 1981). The tendency of alcoholics to use aspirin to reduce their discomfort is another factor affecting bleeding. These processes can produce lesions in the small intestine where nutrients are absorbed into the blood system. The consequence is a reduction in the uptake of important amino acids, glucose, vitamins, and electrolytes.

Other parts of the gastrointestinal tract such as the pancreas are also adversely affected by ducts being blocked by metabolic products of chronic alcohol use (Apte, Wilson, & Korsten, 1997; Silverman et al., 1995). Digestive enzymes ordinarily produced by the pancreas are blocked by alcohol-induced swelling of cells, leading to malnutrition. Eventually, the enzymes break out of the pancreatic linings, creating acute hemorrhagic pancreatitis, which causes severe abdominal pain, nausea, and vomiting. Another function of the pancreas is the production of insulin, which helps convert blood sugars into stored energy. Damage to the pancreas impairs insulin production, resulting in a secondary form of diabetes.

Muscle Systems

Skeletal or striated muscle that is under voluntary control can be damaged by alcohol abuse (Rubin, 1979). Impaired flexor muscle metabolism occurs during aerobic exercise with chronic alcoholics (Yazaki, Haida, Kurita, & Shinohara, 1996). Myopathy, a disorder involving muscle weakness, cramps, and pain, occurs with chronic alcohol consumption.

Cardiovascular System

The cardiovascular system includes the heart and the circulatory system of arteries and veins that extend throughout the body. The heart—which is actually a muscle, although a very vital and special type—pumps blood through this network to carry oxygen and nutrients throughout the body and removes waste materials.

Cardiomyopathy is damage to the heart, which impairs its ability to contract and reduces its effectiveness in pumping blood (Rubin, 1979), leading to shortness of breath, fatigue, palpitations, and eventually, in many cases, congestive heart disorders (Regan, 1990). Although heart disease gradually develops from years of drinking, there is evidence that it can be reversed with abstinence.

There is some controversy, however, about the effects of drinking on the heart. Epidemiological studies (Klatsky, Friedman, & Siegelaub, 1979) of male drinkers found that those who drank a moderate (one to two drinks a day) amount of beer were actually less likely to suffer coronary arterial diseases such as myocardial infarction (heart attacks) than nondrinkers. The conclusion was made that moderate drinking might bestow some protective chemical, possibly high-density lipoprotein cholesterol (Criqui, 1990) associated with more alcohol intake that reduces the risk of heart attack. Alternatively, alcohol may thin out the blood, reducing risks of embolism (blood clots).

However, other interpretations are also possible, dealing with lifestyle factors such as diet, exercise, or coping skills. Perhaps the nondrinkers are too tense and rigid in comparison with moderate drinkers who have a more relaxed attitude. Thus, it might be this general lower reaction to stress rather than consumption of alcohol, per se, that is responsible for the presumed benefits and lower rate of heart attacks for the moderate drinkers. However, it should be noted that among drinkers, those who consumed the most were at the highest risk of heart attacks, possibly due to the acetaldehyde produced by drinking. This toxic metabolic by-product of alcohol may cause enlargement of the mitochondria, impairing their function of providing energy for heart contractions (Lange & Kinnunen, 1987).

One study (Shaper, 1990) questioned conclusions from studies of more than 7,700 middle-aged men in the United Kingdom, showing that one to two drinks a day was associated with lower mortality than for nondrinkers. Many of the nondrinkers may have been heavy ex-drinkers who had to reduce their consumption for health reasons. Therefore, the long-term harm of such earlier abuse, rather than their current lack of drinking, may have contributed to the higher mortality rate found among these now non-drinkers. However, this criticism was challenged by later research (Klatsky, Armstrong, & Friedman, 1986) that found no differences among ex-drinkers, infrequent drinkers, and lifelong abstainers in risk for hospitalization for myocardial infarction. Also, mortality rates did not differ for ex-drinkers and lifelong abstainers (Klatsky, Armstrong, & Friedman, 1990).

Whether or not one or two drinks a day are beneficial in reducing coronary arterial disease, abundant evidence shows that such benefits of drinking are offset by other types of cardiovascular disease attributed to chronic alcohol abuse, such as higher risk for strokes, arrhythmia, and hypertension (MacMahon, 1987).

Some of the protective effects of moderate alcohol consumption related to the risk of cardiovascular disease found in other studies may be due to greater physical activity and other health practices by drinkers as compared to nondrinkers. A survey of 2,072 men and women in a cardiovascular disease prevention project (Barrett, Anda, Croft, Serdula, & Lane, 1995) found that men, especially nonsmokers, who were moderate drinkers had the highest participation in a community physical activity program. Women who were moderate or heavy drinkers were also more likely than nondrinkers to participate and report attempting to lose weight.

Nicotine, in contrast, is incontrovertibly implicated in the genesis of cardiovascular disease. Prior to the 1964 report of the U.S. Surgeon General (U.S. Department of Health, Education, and Welfare, 1964), smoking was not officially recognized as a health risk. Although this report was based on many correlational rather than experimentally controlled studies, the magnitude of the evidence was persuasive in linking the level of smoking with the increasing likelihood of heart disease, respiratory diseases such as emphysema, and lung cancer.

Blood

Alcoholism can be harmful to blood production and function by affecting several vital blood components produced in bone marrow that are necessary for well-being (Ballard, 1997). Deficiencies in the production and function of red blood cells result in anemia, and impairment to white blood cells exposes greater risk of infection. Inadequate platelet quantity or function can prevent clotting to stop loss of blood (including strokes or brain hemorrhages), and abnormal plasma proteins can lead to harmful blood clots as with ischemic strokes. Indirectly, alcoholism affects the blood through malnutrition and loss of vitamins required for blood production.

Endocrine System

The endocrine system, through its hormones, controls and coordinates organs throughout the body. These chemical messengers are released by nerve signals or in response to specific bodily processes. The endocrine system affects diverse outcomes such as physical growth, response to stress, and functioning of cardiovascular, immune, and reproductive systems. Excessive use of alcohol can disrupt these functions (Emanuele & Emanuele, 1997) by disturbing the production of essential hormones, including cortisol, testosterone, estrogen, pituitary growth hormone, and prolactin, to name a few.

Immune System

Alcohol abuse may disrupt the body's abilities to combat certain infectious diseases due to decreased white blood cells such as lymphocytes, macrophages, neutrophils, and cytokines needed to kill bacterial invasions (Lieber, Seitz, Garro, & Worner, 1979; Szabo, 1998). Alcohol alters the immune system functions, eventually leading to viral infections such as the hepatitis B virus, hepatitis C virus, pneumonia, and tuberculosis (Cook, 1998; Seitz, Pöschl, & Simanowski, 1998). In addition, malnutrition, infection, and liver diseases unrelated to alcoholism also may undermine the immune system.

Thus far, there is no evidence of a direct effect of alcohol on the acquired immune deficiency syndrome (AIDS) (Kaslow et al., 1989). Alcohol may indirectly affect AIDS if it serves to increase other behaviors known to contribute to AIDS, such as unsafe sex practices or sharing of needles among drug users. In addition, alcohol might indirectly worsen conditions for those already infected by disrupting their already impaired immune systems.

Reproductive System

Among males, ethanol may lower the male sex hormone, testosterone, at least temporarily (Cicero, 1982). Sexual impotence and impaired performance also may result for male alcoholics (Van Thiel, 1983). Even if they are able to consummate sexual activity, there may be impaired fertility because alcohol reduces the seminal fluids that enable the ejaculated sperm to travel rapidly to fertilize ova.

Alcohol does not spare females from sexual dysfunction either (Hugues et al., 1980; Mello, 1988), as alcohol abuse may be related to impaired menstruation, ovarian atrophy, spontaneous abortion (miscarriage), and infertility. It is unclear whether these outcomes are due to direct toxic effects of alcohol on the hypothalamus, pituitary gland, or ovaries or due to alcohol-induced fluctuations in hormones such as estrogen and progesterone that fluctuate over the menstrual cycle (Lex, 1991). The precise mechanisms for these disruptions are complex and may not entail direct effects of alcohol. For example, other alcohol-related diseases such as liver dysfunction or malnutrition stemming from alcohol abuse could disrupt sex hormones, menstruation, or ovulation.

A review (Mello, Mendelsohn, & Teoh, 1993) found that estradiol levels, a form of estrogen that contributes to increased bone density and reduced risk of coronary artery disease, increased in premenopausal women who consumed slightly more than enough alcohol to reach the legal limit of alcohol.

Fetal Effects

For centuries, there has been a suspicion that alcohol consumption held undesirable effects for pregnant women. Children of alcoholic mothers were observed to be impaired in physical and psychological development. In ancient Carthage, a ritual against drinking alcohol by newlyweds on the wedding night was observed as a precaution against alcohol-induced birth defects (Smith, 1982).

However, it was not until the 1970s that scientific research (Jones, Smith, Ulleland, & Streissguth, 1973; Streissguth, Herman, & Smith, 1978) produced evidence for a **fetal alcohol syndrome (FAS).** A survey (Abel & Sokol, 1987) of 19 studies conducted in various parts of the world found rates as high as 2.9 per 1,000 in retrospective studies, compared to 1.1 per

1,000 in prospective studies. Estimates depend on the methodology. Prospective data based on observations at the time of birth tend to produce lower estimates because some symptoms do not appear until a few years later, whereas retrospective studies that link mental retardation to recall of the mothers' earlier drinking during pregnancy tend to yield much higher rates.

The FAS baby has a low birth weight and a retarded pattern of physical growth. Physical malformations include small head circumference, misshapen eyes, flattened mid-face, sunken nasal bridge, and elongated philtrum (the vertical groove between the nose and mouth). Other malformations may occur in major internal organs as well. The central nervous system shows abnormal functioning, and there is evidence of neurobehavioral impairment (Mattson & Riley, 1998). Behaviorally, the FAS baby may exhibit abnormal neonatal development, sleep problems, childhood hyperactivity, and mental retardation.

The types of impairment vary with the timing of alcohol abuse over the period of gestation. As shown in Figure 4.9, physical damage is sustained during early months of pregnancy, and the impact during later months may be more cognitive and behavioral.

A 10-year follow-up (Streissguth, Clarren, & Jones, 1985) of 8 of the 11 young children (2 had died) in the original study of FAS revealed that their deficits were still pronounced, both in physical and psychological dimensions. They were below average in height and weight and also developed new problems such as hearing and vision problems. Four were severely mentally retarded, and the other 4 were borderline retarded.

Whereas a drink or two might produce a BAC level (e.g., .05%) that might be considered "safe" for an adult woman, it represents a much stronger concentration for the much smaller fetus that shares the same blood content with the mother. The toxic levels may be particularly hazardous during the first trimester of pregnancy when developmental changes are greater, a period when the drinking woman is unfortunately less likely to know she is pregnant.

Only a small percentage of the children of alcoholic mothers suffer FAS, suggesting that a number of factors may combine with the alcohol abuse to exert these damaging irreversible effects. But it seems clear that there is considerable risk to those unborn children of heavy-drinking expectant mothers.

Less extreme but still worrisome problems may occur for pregnant women who drink at much lower levels than alcoholics or problem drinkers. The Seattle Pregnancy and Health Study has examined about 500 children born to White middle-class married women. Subtle neurological and behavioral deficits were found in proportion to the amount of alcohol consumed during pregnancy (Streissguth et al., 1984). The extent to which the

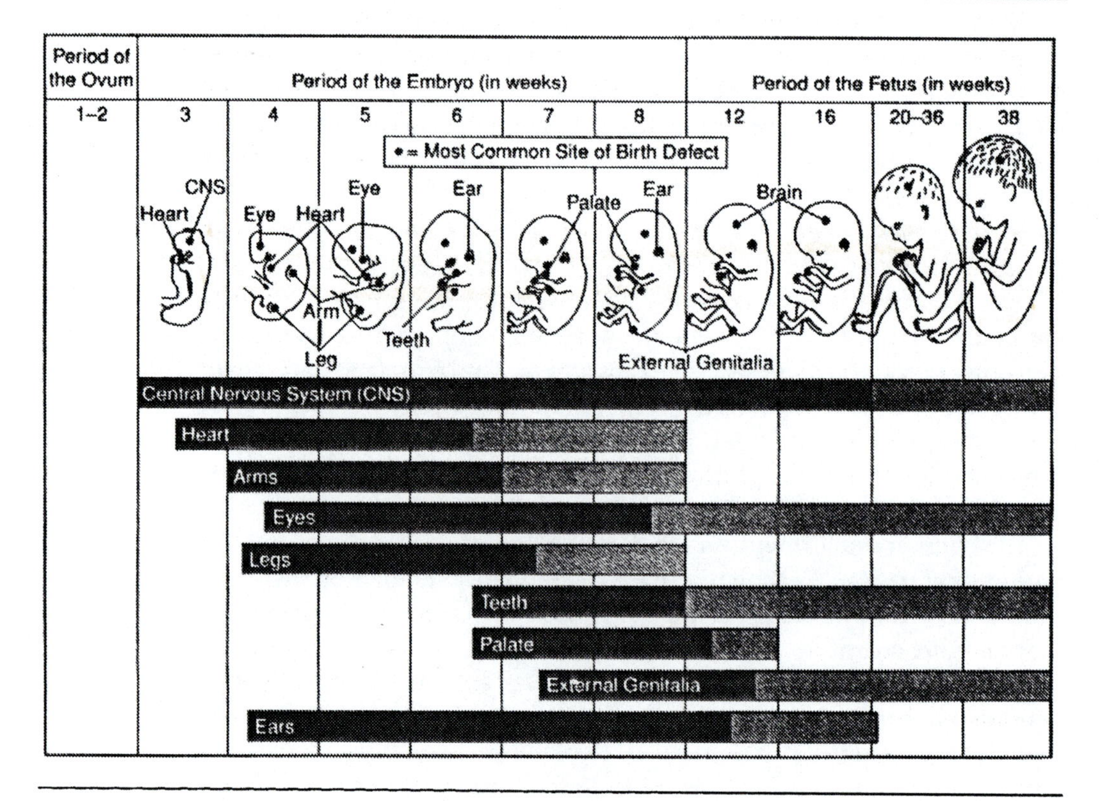

Figure 4.9. Alcohol Affects Different Developmental Processes in the Fetus at Different Stages During Gestation

SOURCE: Moore and Persaud (1993). Copyrighted 1993 by W. B. Saunders. Reprinted by permission.

NOTE: The black portion of the bars represents the most sensitive periods of development, during which teratogenic effects on the sites listed would result in major structural abnormalities in the child. The gray portion of the bars represents periods of development during which physiologic defects and minor structural abnormalities would occur.

mother drank during pregnancy was correlated with the degree to which newborn infants were slower to habituate or fail to attend to a repeated stimulus and slower to begin sucking to an appropriate stimulus.

Deficits on these indices of attention persist throughout childhood. At age 4, children whose mothers drank more during pregnancy scored more poorly on vigilance and reaction time tasks, suggesting that the alcohol may have impaired neonatal neurological development. These less severe effects, referred to as **fetal alcohol effects (FAE)**, as opposed to the more severe fetal alcohol syndrome found with children of alcoholic mothers, occurred even for women with modest levels of drinking.

The study of FAS and FAE focuses on identified severe cases that are referred to clinics and hospitals. A different approach (May, 1995) to the study of **alcohol-related birth defects (ARBD)** involves the study of larger samples in the general population, measures the presence of symptoms associated with drinking, and follows them over the development of the child. The goal is not restricted to the diagnosis of FAS and FAE cases, which are associated with chronic heavy drinking, but to see how a wider range of drinking levels is related to birth defects (Day & Richardson, 1991). One study (Day et al., 1991) compared the offspring of drinking and nondrinking mothers to determine any differences in physical and behavioral symptoms that develop from birth to early childhood. Mothers who consumed one or more drinks daily, on average, throughout pregnancy had babies of lower birth weight, smaller head circumference and length, and slower growth.

Epidemiological studies of the rates of ARBD in the general population will give a more accurate index of the prevalence of these cases than clinic cases and will help guide prevention programs because they assess the social and cultural influences on the rates of ARBD identification (May, 1995).

Abuse of drugs other than alcohol also can adversely affect fetal development in ways that are similar to those attributed to alcohol. Much publicity has been directed toward cocaine-addicted babies over the past decade. Although some physical developmental problems such as low birth weight and small head size existed, they were not always accompanied by behavioral deficits, or the deficits were transitory and no longer apparent in later childhood (Chiriboga, 1998). The evidence on fetal cocaine effects is also difficult to interpret because most cocaine users also drank alcohol, itself a teratogen that is more harmful than cocaine on the fetus (Snodgrass, 1994). When alcohol and cocaine are taken together, a metabolic toxin called cocaethylene, which is stronger than cocaine, is produced.

In addition, many pregnant women who abused different specific drugs have poor appetite and nutrition, both of which can impair neonatal development independently of any harm specific to drugs. Low birth weight and hypoxia are common to newborns from women who used different drugs during pregnancy.

Women cigarette smokers have more pregnancies involving spontaneous abortions and stillbirths. Carbon monoxide from cigarette smoke increases fetal carboxyhemoglobin levels that cross the placenta (Werler, Pober, & Holmes, 1985), possibly creating hypoxia, a condition involving less oxygen that adversely affects the fetus. In this respect, crack cocaine and nicotine smoking have similar cardiovascular effects, but the harm potential may be greater for nicotine because it affects more neurotransmitters over longer duration (Slotkin, 1998).

Newborns of women who abuse opiates during pregnancy show higher irritability and withdrawal-like symptoms as well as poorer motor control, although these characteristics seem to be reduced within a month.

Marijuana use by pregnant women also involves carbon monoxide from smoke that can produce fetal hypoxia. Evidence about the fetal harm of marijuana use during pregnancy is conflicting, with some suggestion of increased irritability, tremors, and sleep disturbances (Scher, Richardson, Coble, Day, & Stoffer, 1988).

Similarly, some women cocaine users have offspring who may have impairments of attention and arousal regulation that are not large enough to produce differences on developmental comparisons with noncocaine mothers, but they might show problems on tasks that are more demanding (Chasnoff, 1991). Some women use multiple drugs during pregnancy, often combining smoking and drinking with one or more illicit drugs (Chasnoff, Griffith, Freier, & Murray, 1992). Some polydrug-abusing women may not remember or admit using certain drugs, so it is difficult to determine the effect of each separate drug used or to measure their complex interactive effects.

Cancers

Cancers of the oral cavity, pharynx, and larynx appear to occur more often in heavy drinkers (Elwood, Pearson, Skippen, & Jackson, 1984). However, because many heavy drinkers also tend to be heavy smokers, any link between drinking and cancer could partially be due to the effect of smoking. More than 80% of squamous carcinomas in these areas are related to alcohol and tobacco use (Thomas, 1995). Other sections of the gastrointestinal tract, such as the colon and rectum, also have shown higher risk for cancer (Glynn et al., 1996; Lieber et al., 1979; Seitz, Gärtner, Egerer, & Simanowski, 1994).

It is not assumed that alcohol itself is a carcinogen, and a number of possible mechanisms by which ethanol might contribute to cancer have been proposed (Lieber, Garro, Leo, & Worner, 1986), including contact-related localized effects, nutritional and vitamin deficiencies, disruptions of DNA metabolism, induction of microsomal enzymes that activate carcinogens, and disruption of the immune system responsiveness. Ethanol may disrupt the enzymes that control carcinogens (Driver & Swann, 1987). In addition, ethanol metabolism involves generation of acetaldehyde, which decreases DNA repair and may lead to chromosomal damage (Seitz et al., 1998).

Among women, one of the leading types of cancer deaths involves breast cancer (Podolsky, 1986). In a study (Williams & Horm, 1977) of the relationship between alcohol use and breast cancer in more than 7,500 cases, the authors concluded that drinkers were from 1.2 to 1.6 times more likely to have breast cancer than nondrinkers. There is some evidence that risk increases with larger amounts consumed (Smith-Warner et al., 1998).

However, other studies (Webster, Wingo, Layde, & Ory, 1983) have not confirmed these findings. Some of the inconclusiveness could be due to methodological problems (Feinstein, 1988; Schatzkin & Longnecker, 1994).

Smoking cigarettes involves combustion, which produces more than 4,000 gases and by-products, most notably carbon monoxide and tars. More than 50 carcinogens have been identified, with the tobacco-specific N-nitrosamines (TSNA) of special significance.

The makeup of cigarettes and the composition of cigarette smoke have changed gradually (Hoffmann & Hoffmann, 1997), a development that makes comparisons over time difficult. In the United States, average tar and nicotine yields have declined. Over the same period, reduction of other smoke constituents was achieved by many factors such as the use of filter tips, selection of tobacco types and varieties, and use of highly porous cigarette paper.

In the United States, nitrate levels in cigarette tobacco rose from 0.3% to 0.5% to 0.6% to 1.35%. This improvement affords more complete combustion, which lowers the levels of one carcinogenic factor, polynuclear aromatic hydrocarbons. However, more combustion increases generation of nitrogen oxides and the formation of carcinogenic N-nitrosamines in the smoke.

Finally, it must be noted that these estimates are based on measures from cigarette smoking "machines" that are programmed to take exactly one 2-second puff with a volume of 35 ml every minute, which does not reflect the more numerous and deeper puffs (averaging two to four per minute with a mean volume of 55 ml) taken by actual smokers using low-nicotine cigarettes.

Alcohol-Related Mortality

A study (Rehm & Sempos, 1995) of the relationship between alcohol consumption and all-cause mortality used data from a 15-year epidemiological study of two age groups (ages 25-59 and 60-75). The study was a follow-up to the National Health and Nutrition Examination Survey (NHANES) and was based on a subsample of 12,036 White men and women. Alcohol consumption and mortality were linearly related under 60 years of age, even after controlling for nutritional variables and smoking.

Different risks exist for different ethnic groups (Sutocky, Shultz, & Kizer, 1993). Blacks and Hispanics had higher rates of mortality from liver cirrhosis than did Whites or Asian Americans, although a higher percentage of Blacks than Whites abstain from using alcohol. Asian and "other" ethnic groups had lower rates of alcohol-related mortality than any other group for most causes of death.

The causes of death vary with racial/ethnic groups. For alcohol dependence and alcoholic hepatitis, Hispanics had similar or lower mortality rates than Whites. However, alcohol-related motor vehicle fatality was highest among Hispanics, followed by Whites and Blacks and lowest for Asian/other.

Among Native Americans, alcohol abuse is involved in the leading causes of death, such as motor vehicle crashes, alcoholism, cirrhosis, suicide, and homicide. Among tribes with high rates of alcoholism, about 75% of all accidents are alcohol related.

Aggregate relationships between suicide and alcohol consumption were analyzed with 1,000 cases from 1969 to 1989 and 532 cases from 1975 to 1989 (Gruenewald, Ponicki, & Mitchell, 1995). Suicide rates increased significantly as a function of increased spirits sales, but beer and wine sales were not associated with suicide rates. The analyses controlled important factors such as age, gender, non-White population, per capita land area, metropolitan size, income, unemployment, religious preferences, and marital status.

SUMMARY

Alcohol and other drugs enter the body in different ways, depending on the drug, but once absorbed into the bloodstream, they affect the functioning of the nervous system. By altering the membranes of neurons, alcohol affects the normal balance of neurotransmitters. These changes produce effects on the central nervous system, either depressing or stimulating activity, depending on the drug. Low or moderate amounts of drugs can be detoxified or eliminated from the body by the liver efficiently so that the toxic by-products of drug metabolism are prevented from accumulating.

Tolerance for drugs develops with continued use so that the same dose produces a diminished effect, which often leads to increased usage at higher doses. However, when the drug is not available, highly unpleasant withdrawal reactions involving physical discomfort, agitation, and irritability occur.

When used excessively over a long period of time, alcohol and other drugs can produce a number of serious physical and medical problems over most major systems of the body. Although some of the effects may be direct, as in the case of fatty liver production from chronic alcohol use, other effects may be indirect, such as malnutrition or bodily injury due to accidents and falls. Chronic effects may occur even for those for whom the acute effects may have been minimal. Long-term excessive alcohol consumption impairs the functioning of all major organs so that eventually, most alcoholics will be confronted with a physical toll of damage stemming from the cumulative effects of alcohol. In particular, damage to the liver disrupts the ability to detoxify alcohol as efficiently as in the past so that reversal in tolerance occurs, with less alcohol producing the same effect that formerly required more alcohol. Due to the long delay usually involved between drinking and these types of adverse effects, it is not surprising that chronic excessive drinking and these types of physical consequences are difficult to detect and prevent.

Alcohol consumption, as well as abuse of many other drugs by pregnant women, may have profoundly damaging irreversible birth effects involving the physical and mental condition of the developing fetus. Higher alcohol use also shows a positive relationship with indices of many causes of mortality as well as increased likelihood of suicides.

KEY TERMS

Action potential
Agonistic
Alcohol dehydrogenase
Alcohol-related birth defects (ARBD)
Antagonistic
Ascending limb
Autonomic nervous system
Blood alcohol concentration (BAC)
Blood alcohol level (BAL)
Central nervous system CNS)
Cirrhosis
Concentration
Descending limb
Detoxification
Dopamine (DA)
Dose response curve
Electroencephalogram (EEG)
Endogenous opiates
Event-related potentials (ERP)
Fetal alcohol effects (FAE)
Fetal alcohol syndrome (FAS)
Gamma aminobutyric acid (GABA)
Glutamate
Inhalation
Ion Channels
Ions
Microsomal ethanol oxidizing system (MEOS)
Naltrexone
Neurotransmitters
Nucleus accumbens
Peripheral nervous system
pH scale
P300 wave
Rebound effect
Receptors
Serotonin
Synaptic junction
Tolerance
Withdrawal or abstinence syndrome

STIMULUS/RESPONSE

1. Have you had the subjective effect of a drug vary depending on the physical and social setting in which it is consumed? Describe the experience and explain how it affected your drug use.
2. Has the effect of some drug on your behavior varied with factors such as time of day or with your physical condition or health? What conditions make drugs more potent in their effects on you?
3. Suppose that psychopharmacologists developed an "antibody" or a substance that could offset a drug's normal neurophysiological effect. Do you think most individuals with problems with that drug would voluntarily take it? If not, would it be ethical for a judge to order that someone with drug problems be treated with such an antibody?
4. Crack babies reportedly have been born to some women who abused cocaine and crack during pregnancy. Is a control group necessary to allow the conclusion that the use of this drug during pregnancy caused the problems for the babies? If so, what do you think would be the appropriate control group?

Heredity and Environment
Alcohol and Other Drug Use 5

Questions about the role of heredity and environment provoke strong and heated debate for many psychological phenomena. The understanding of the determinants of alcohol and drug use, abuse, and dependency is certainly no exception. In this chapter, we will first examine the role of hereditary factors on differences in the use of alcohol and other drugs. Then, we will see how environmental factors, especially early experiences within the family, might affect the likelihood of alcohol and other drug use.

In thinking about heredity as a factor, we do not mean that genes determine the use, abuse, or dependency to a specific drug in the same way that genes might determine physical features such as eye color. The relationship between genetics and behavior is much more complex. Genes may indirectly affect behavior by determining how drugs are metabolized or by creating temperamental characteristics such as impulsivity or anxiety. In turn, these characteristics can influence the likelihood that exposure to drugs may eventually lead to abuse or dependency.

Similarly, environment is a complex factor that includes cultural setting, societal context, interpersonal relations, and physical surroundings. In a broad sense, any factor that is not inherited could be viewed as environmental. These factors can affect the likelihood that individuals use drugs as well as the consequences of such actions.

Hereditary Influences

Differences in biological predispositions that may be genetically determined can lead to wide variations in the reactions of users to the pharmacological ingredients in drugs. Although many users experience unpleasant sensations and reactions to their first use of a drug, some users report positive initial experiences. These initial reactions also may be influenced by expectations learned from others but still suggest that some unlearned or biological differences may be involved.

FAMILY STUDIES

Observations that family members often tend to have similar alcohol and other drug use levels could and have been used to argue that heredity is a major factor underlying drug dependency. But because family members often share a similar environment, particularly during formative years, as well as a common heredity, such evidence also can support environmental explanations. Thus, by observing and modeling one or both drug-dependent parents, children may acquire attitudes and norms that may increase their susceptibility to similar drinking and drug use lifestyles. In addition, growing up with parents who are alcohol or drug dependent, children may develop poor self-esteem, experience abuse or neglect, and later, as adults, turn to drinking and use other drugs to cope with life stressors.

A review of older studies (Cotton, 1979), collectively covering thousands of alcoholics in psychiatric treatment, found that alcoholics were about five times more likely than nonalcoholics to have an alcoholic relative. However, 45% to 80% of the alcoholics did *not* have an alcoholic relative. Therefore, other factors must be involved because a large percentage of children from nonalcoholic families still become alcoholic without the genetic factors that are assumed to contribute to alcoholism for children in alcoholic families.

In research on possible familial links to alcohol and drug problems, the term **proband** is used to refer to those individuals assumed to be at risk for alcohol and other drug dependency due to having at least one biological parent with a similar problem. First-degree male but not female relatives of alcoholic probands were more likely to be alcoholic than for the general population (Reich, Cloninger, Van Eerdewegh, Rice, & Mullaney, 1988; Winokur, Reich, Rimmer, & Pitts, 1970). Figure 5.1 shows that the fathers, brothers, and sons of both male and female alcoholics were more at risk to be alcoholic than were the first-degree female relatives such as mothers, sisters, and daughters (Reich et al., 1988). In addition, the wives of alcoholic men were less likely than the husbands of alcoholic women to also have alcoholism. Although female relatives were at lower risk for alcohol-

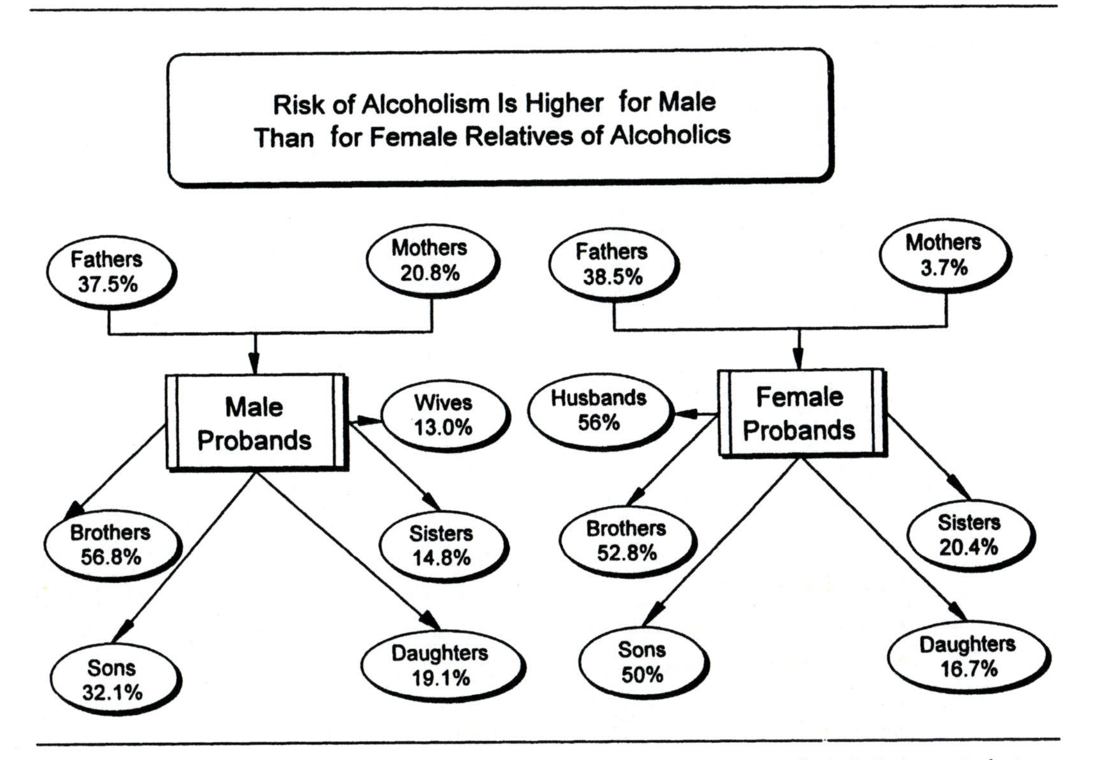

Figure 5.1. Transmissibility of Risk of Alcoholism for Spouses and First-Degree Relatives for Males and Females
SOURCE: Based on data from Reich et al. (1988).

ism (Winokur et al., 1970), they were at greater risk than male relatives for affective or mood disorders such as depression.

Although relatives of alcoholics may share some common genetically transmitted tendencies for different emotional or affective reactions to stressors, societal and cultural conditions may allow different forms of expression for males and females. Because most societies tolerate and even encourage more drinking by males, these tendencies may lead to heavier use of alcohol for them, whereas females who traditionally are restricted from drinking may turn to other drugs such as tranquilizers to deal with stress.

Transmissibility, or the influence of family history of alcoholism, is greater for males (Reich et al., 1988). Furthermore, this effect was greater for more recently born cohorts in terms of a higher lifetime prevalence as well as earlier age of onset of alcoholism. These cohort effects may reflect changes in society that now increase drinking or encourage drinking at an earlier age.

TABLE 5.1 Lifetime dependency rates for different drugs in siblings of drug-dependent probands

	Alcohol-Dependent Siblings		*Non-Alcohol-Dependent Siblings*	
Proband	*Male*	*Female*	*Male*	*Female*
Marijuana dependent				
Yes	56.7	42.8	15.2	7.7
No	31.5	16.2	10.7	4.8
Cocaine dependent				
Yes	43.3	40.5	13.7	8.8
No	18.9	18.2	5.5	2.0
Habitual smoking				
Yes	61.3	60.7	35.7	29.9
No	40.9	37.3	20.3	14.6

SOURCE: Bierut et al. (1998). Copyright 1998 by the American Medical Association. Used with permission.

Two family studies using clinical samples measured the probability for different addictions in relatives of drug and alcohol-dependent persons. One study (Bierut et al., 1998) measured alcohol, marijuana, cocaine, and tobacco use by 1,212 probands (persons classified as alcohol dependent) and their 2,755 siblings. A non-alcohol-dependent comparison sample contained 217 probands and their 254 siblings.

Siblings of alcohol-dependent probands, as compared with siblings of non-alcohol-dependent controls, had higher rates of marijuana dependence, cocaine dependence, and habitual smoking, as shown in Table 5.1.

In addition to providing evidence of common factors underlying dependence for different drugs, the results showed evidence of specific addictive factors. Some differences in drug dependency were independent of whether alcohol dependency was present, suggesting that the development of each type of substance dependence may differ.

In another family study (Merikangas et al., 1998), the vulnerability also varied for different substances. Rates of alcoholism were increased in relatives of alcohol- and cannabis-dependent subjects but not for the relatives of opioid- or cocaine-dependent probands. The study also found higher co-occurrences of the *same* drug disorder, as compared with cross-drug associations, in relatives of the proband (with drug-specific relative risks of 10.2 for opioids, 4.4 for cocaine, and 5.8 for marijuana).

TWIN STUDIES

The study of twins, a longstanding strategy used by researchers trying to marshal evidence for hereditarian views for a variety of characteristics and behaviors, originated with Sir Francis Galton in the late 1800s. Concordance rates, or the extent to which both members of a set of twins show the same outcomes, are compared among identical or **monozygotic (MZ)** twins, fraternal or **dizygotic (DZ)** twins, and siblings. If genetic factors are involved to a great extent, the concordance of outcomes should be highest for MZ twins, followed by DZ twins, and then siblings. If environmental factors are more important, the difference in concordance rates of MZ and DZ twins will be small.

Scandinavian countries, with their extensive and thorough registries of birth and medical treatments and temperance board records of alcohol problems, have provided an excellent source of data for testing theories about the role of heredity on alcoholism as well as other forms of psychopathology. Concordance rates of alcoholism among identical (MZ) twins often have been found to be higher than for fraternal (DZ) twins or siblings (Partanen, Bruun, & Markkanens, 1966).

As Figure 5.2 indicates, three different factors may operate to produce differences between MZ and DZ twins in the liability of an outcome such as alcohol dependency. Outcomes may be due to not only an additive *genetic* factor (A) but also to two types of environment—shared common environment (C) and a specific environment (E) unique to each twin. The higher the *total* influence from all three sources, genetic and environmental, the greater should be the liability of alcohol dependency (Prescott & Kendler, 1995).

A Finnish study (Kaprio et al., 1987) of more than 2,800 pairs of male twins between ages 24 and 49 examined the relationship of genetic and social contact between twins on their drinking and its consequences. Although the obtained higher concordance of alcoholism among identical than among fraternal twins favored a genetic explanation, it also was found that the frequency of social contact between identical twins was greater than for fraternal twins. Thus, the higher concordance of their drinking patterns may also be partly attributable to a greater common environment created by their higher social contact.

These differences were stable, as surveys of 13,404 twins (ages 18-43) in 1975 and 1981 showed that mean consumption levels did not change between 1975 and 1981 (Kaprio, Viken, Koskenvuo, Romanov, & Rose, 1992). Patterns of social drinking were more stable in older (ages 24-43) than younger (ages 18-23) individuals and were more stable among men than women. Heritabilities were higher for twins than for siblings at baseline and at follow-up for both genders and both age groups.

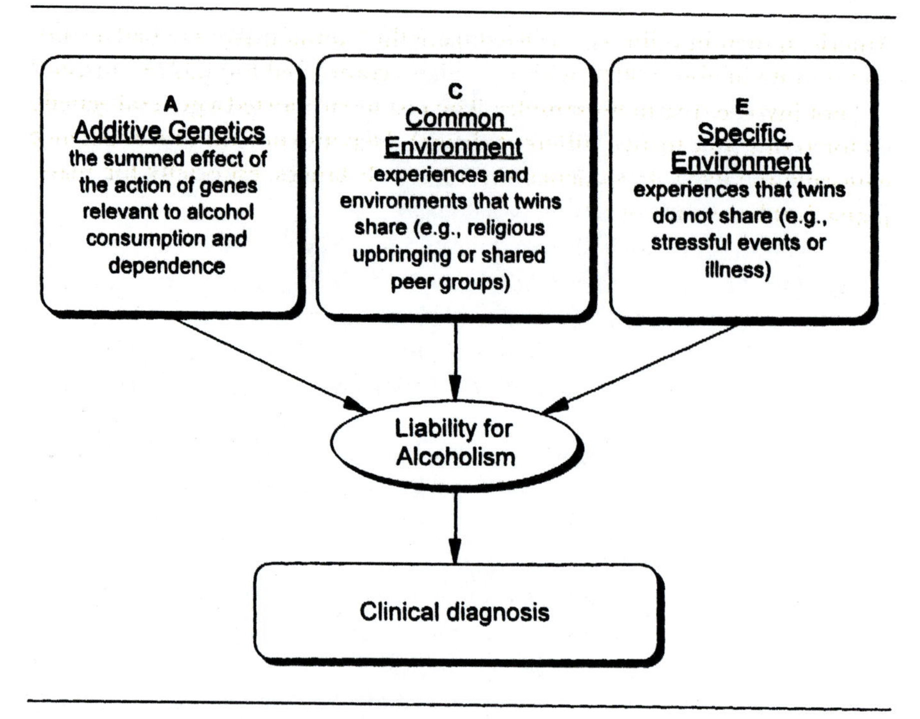

Figure 5.2. Liability Model of Risk for Alcoholism
SOURCE: Prescott and Kendler (1995).

A study (Heath, Jardine, & Martin, 1989) of almost 2,000 female twins in Australia using a birth registry found that concordance of alcoholism was higher among the identical than for the fraternal twins. Frequency of social contact between twins did not seem to affect the alcoholism concordance rates, as had been the case in the Finnish study.

Studies (Pickens et al., 1991) of both male and female same-sexed twins at alcoholism treatment centers revealed a stronger genetic basis for alcoholism for men than for women. The alcoholism rate of monozygotic twins over dizygotic twins was .59 versus .36 for male twins but only .25 versus .05 for female twins. However, twins in alcohol and drug treatment may not be representative of twins who are *not* in treatment. This bias could be serious if twins who are more similar are more likely to be in treatment than are less similar twins. However, this concern may be unwarranted: A study of a nonclinical population (Kendler, Heath, Neale, Kessler, & Eaves, 1992) of female twins identified through the Virginia Twin Registry also discovered higher concordance among monozygotic than for dizygotic twins.

Twin studies also have shown a genetic basis for dependency on drugs other than alcohol. The Vietnam Era Twin Study (Tsuang et al., 1998) of

American men in military service during the Vietnam War era had a completion rate of about 80%, with interviews completed for 3,372 twins, and did not involve treatment samples. The results supported a general genetic factor (common to five different drugs). Dependency on one substance generally involved dependence on other substances, especially for marijuana, but less so for opiates.

Several causal models were proposed and tested in this study. A causal model is similar to a theory in that both hypothesize which factors will lead to certain outcomes. Two of the models supported in this study were a common pathway model and an independent pathway model. A common pathway model holds that the same factors are involved in leading to all forms of substance use, whereas an independent pathway model suggests that the factors affecting use of each type of substance differ. Evaluation of these models involves complex statistical methods to explain the obtained pattern of correlations among variables. The researcher makes a statistical evaluation of the goodness of fit between patterns of relationships in the observed data with predictions derived from alternative models that make different assumptions about the causes. Models with predictions that do not "fit" the observed data are rejected, but any models whose predictions are close matches to the observed data are retained as viable explanations. If more than one model fits, as was the case in this study, the one that is more parsimonious or makes fewer assumptions is adopted. Even though the observed relationships provided some support for both models, this study accepted the common pathway model because it required fewer assumptions.

The extent to which genetic and environmental factors were related to dependency varied widely for specific drugs, being highest for opiates, followed by marijuana, stimulants, and sedatives, and lowest for psychedelics. Overall, these findings point to both general and drug-specific genetic and environmental factors in substance abuse.

ADOPTION STUDIES

When children grow up in the homes of their birth parents, it is not possible to isolate the impact of genetic and environmental factors on their chances of becoming alcohol or drug dependent. In contrast, when children are adopted at an early age, a "natural experiment" exists that offers a somewhat controlled test of the relative role of heredity and environment.

In the case of alcohol dependency, adoption records maintained in Scandinavia have allowed precisely such an opportunity. The reasoning is that if alcoholism has a strong genetic basis, children from alcoholic parents who are adopted to nonalcoholic homes should still be more likely to

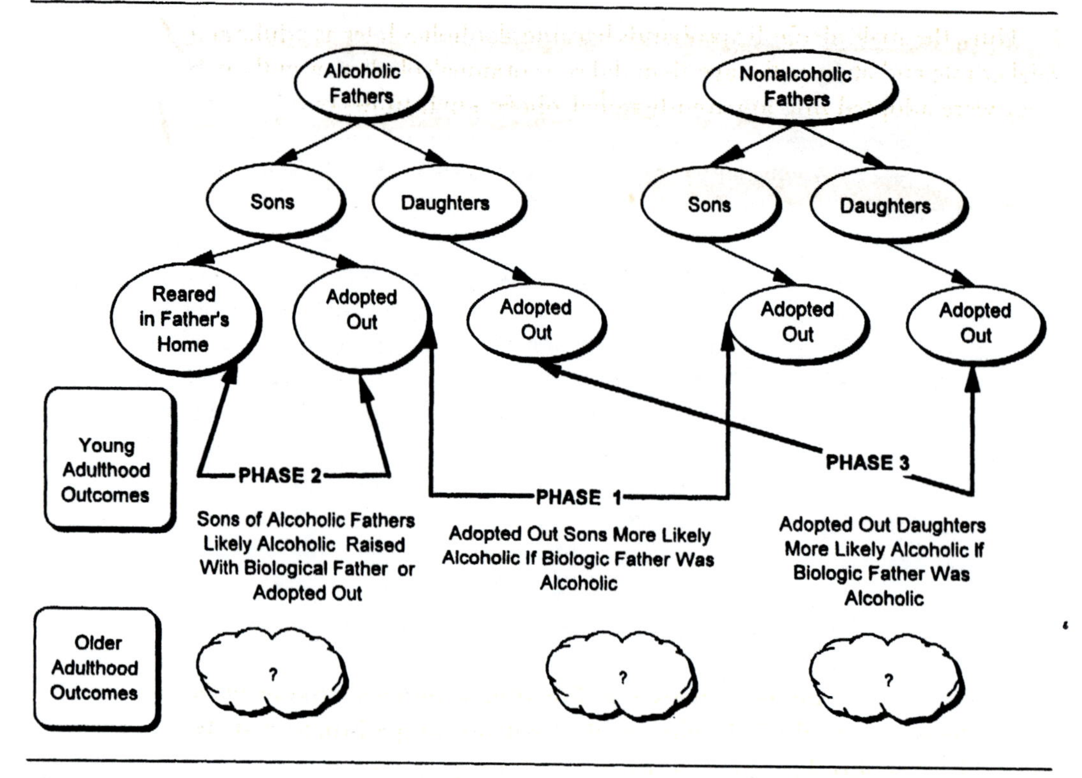

Figure 5.3. Three Phases of a Study of Adopted Children of Alcoholic Fathers in Denmark

become alcoholics as adults than control adoptees who have no alcoholic parent, as illustrated in Figure 5.3. On the other hand, if environment plays a strong role on alcoholism, children should have a lower probability of becoming alcoholics due to their adoption into nonalcoholic homes. This analytical advantage afforded by studies of adoptees has led to several influential investigations.

Danish Studies

Male Adoptees. A pioneering study using adoption records from Denmark (Goodwin, Schulsinger, Hermansen, Guze, & Winokur, 1973) studied male offspring of 55 alcoholic parents, primarily fathers, who were adopted during the first few weeks of life by nonalcoholic families. In Phase 1 of this research, shown in Figure 5.3, comparisons of the adult alcoholism rates of these 55 alcoholic probands with 78 control adoptees from nonalcoholic parents revealed a 4:1 ratio of more alcoholism among those adoptees who had at least one alcoholic parent.

Thus, the male alcoholic probands became alcoholics later as adults at a higher rate and at an earlier age than did sons of nonalcoholics, even though they were adopted into apparently nonalcoholic environments. They also had a much higher rate of divorce than the sons of nonalcoholics, a factor that could have contributed to their alcohol problems as well as any genetic influence. Comparisons on other factors such as psychiatric disorder did not show differences.

As Figure 5.3 shows, Phase 2 of the study (Goodwin et al., 1974) compared adopted sons with 35 other sons who were not adopted but grew up in the homes of their alcoholic biological parent. The nonadopted and adopted siblings did not differ in alcoholism rates, suggesting that being raised in an alcoholic home of the biological parent did not add to the risk of alcoholism among persons known to be at risk biologically. Thus, the biological factor appeared to be the major factor responsible for determining alcoholism rates.

Female Adoptees. A third phase of the same project, diagrammed in Figure 5.3, examined biological factors involved in alcoholism among women (Goodwin, Schulsinger, Moller, Mednick, & Guze, 1977). In contrast to the study of males, no differences were found in alcoholism among 49 female adoptees from alcoholic biological parents in comparison to that observed for 48 control adoptees from nonalcoholic parents.

These adoption studies have proved highly influential, but they are not without a number of problems. The foster parents who adopted the children showed high rates of psychiatric problems as well as a high divorce rate; these problems may add to the influence that any genetic factor of alcoholism would have had. Although alcoholism rates were higher among adopted sons of alcoholics, it should be noted that only about 20% of the probands had become alcoholic at the time they were studied. When the two heaviest drinking categories—alcoholics and problem drinkers—were combined as one group, there was little difference between the adoptees from alcoholic and nonalcoholic parentage.

Most alcoholic parents were the fathers, but no information was obtained about the mothers' status regarding alcoholism (Searles, 1988). It is not unreasonable to expect that some of them were alcoholic as well or at least drinking during pregnancy. If so, this factor of prenatal alcohol abuse complicates the interpretation because any deficits may not reflect only genetic influences.

Swedish Studies

Subsequent studies in Sweden with larger samples corroborated the conclusions from the Danish studies. Alcoholism rates in adoptees and their biological parents among persons born out of wedlock and adopted before age 3 by nonrelatives were examined (Bohman, 1978). Alcohol abuse was defined objectively based on the number of times an individual had been registered for insobriety with the Swedish Temperance Board and whether treatment had been recommended. Three levels of severity of abuse were defined based on this type of information rather than using any clinical or psychiatric criteria. It is likely that use of more conventional diagnostic criteria would have yielded a different classification of cases.

Adopted sons with alcoholic biological fathers were three times as likely to be alcoholic as were adopted sons of nonalcoholic fathers. The ratio was still 2:1 if the alcoholic parent in question was the mother. The proportions of alcoholism for adopted daughters did not seem to be a function of parental alcoholism.

However, a genetic influence for alcoholism in women was suggested in a study using female adoptees (Bohman, Sivardsson, & Cloninger, 1981), which showed an overall prevalence of alcoholism around 4%. The risk of alcoholism was four times greater if the biological mother was alcoholic. The level of alcohol abuse of the foster parents in the adoptive environment did not play as great a role as the alcohol abuse of the birth parent.

A study by Cloninger, Bohman, and Sigvardsson (1981) with 862 male adoptees with alcohol problems had an overall prevalence rate of alcoholism at about 18%. Alcohol abuse of sons and daughters in some families in which both biological parents had mild but untreated alcohol abuse varied in proportion to the amount of environmental demands the children faced.

U.S. Studies

Although the documentation about the biological parents of adoptees is less complete in the United States and the criteria for adoption involve nonrandom assignment of adoptees to homes, adoption studies conducted in Iowa show agreement with the Scandinavian research about the relationship of alcoholism between parents and adopted children. Male and female adoptees separated at birth from parents with psychiatric disturbance were compared to adoptees with parents without mental disturbances (Cadoret & Gath, 1978). The psychiatric background of the parent was not associated with adoptee alcoholism status. Although alcoholism rates were low among the adoptees, there was nonetheless a pattern suggesting that adoptees with alcoholism were more likely to have an alcoholic biological parent than those without alcoholism. However, the criteria for diagnosing parental alcoholism were subjective and based on ratings by social workers rather than by psychiatrists.

Studies of adoptive families examine if there is a stronger link between parental alcohol use and family functioning with alcohol involvement by birth children than for adopted children. One such study (McGue, Sharma, & Benson, 1996) found stronger associations for birth children with their parents but only weak or low relationships between adopted children and their parents.

A test of the effect of shared environment with no biological commonality was possible by studying the siblings. Among the families in this study, 255 sibling pairs were not biologically related, some involving two adopted children and others with a birth child and an adopted child. Results demonstrated the impact of environment as the similarity of alcohol use patterns between siblings was modest, but it was stronger for those siblings who were closer in age and of the same sex.

Adoption studies also have shown evidence that cocaine use and abuse involve hereditary influences. One study of adoptions showed that if biological parents had alcohol problems, there was an increased tendency for illicit drug abuse in their adopted children (Cadoret, Traughon, & O'Gorman, 1987).

However, regardless of how well controlled an adoption study is, the vast majority of children in the general population are not adoptees so that the generalizability of conclusions based on any adopted samples is limited.

GENETIC EVIDENCE

The analysis of genetic material provides some support for an inherited biological basis for alcohol and drug dependency in producing differences in biological vulnerability or susceptibility to using psychoactive drugs. Specifically, individual differences exist in the extent to which dopamine (DA), a neurotransmitter associated with positive states, is activated in the brain by most psychoactive drugs. These variations have been linked to genetic differences in the presence of the **DA transporter gene,** D2, specifically a variant called the A1 allele.

There is also evidence for a genetic basis for other drugs. The acquisition of the smoking habit and its persistence are strongly influenced by hereditary factors. In one twin study (Swan, Carmelli, & Cardon, 1997), a national sample of male twins was surveyed twice, once from 1967 to 1968 and again 16 years later. The long-term pattern of not smoking, smoking, and then quitting smoking were similar across identical twins but not in a control population of nonidentical twins, suggesting a biogenetic component in smoking behavior.

The incidence of the A1 allele was 48% for smokers who had made at least one unsuccessful attempt to stop smoking (Comings et al., 1996). The higher the prevalence of the A1 allele and the earlier the age of onset of smoking, the greater the amount of smoking and the greater the difficulty in attempting to stop smoking. Another study of smokers and nonsmokers found that the prevalence of the A1 allele was highest in current smokers, lower in those who had stopped smoking, and lowest in those who had never smoked (Noble et al., 1994).

About 52% of cocaine addicts have the A1 allele, whereas it was present in only 21% of nonaddicts (Noble et al., 1993). Cocaine users who had a parent who abused drugs, used more potent forms, and had early childhood deviancy were more likely to have the A1 allele.

Gene-Environment Interactions

Genetic influences are complicated because genes may not have the same effect in all environments, as a strict genetic perspective might imply. Thus, individuals with different inherited tendencies for alcohol or drug use are not equally likely to find themselves growing up in the same types of environments. Although many children of alcoholics may grow up in circumstances that add to their chances of developing alcohol problems (e.g., child neglect, abuse, poverty, low self-esteem, etc.), other children of alcoholics do not encounter these environments and may not develop alcohol dependency. Because of such **gene-environment interactions**, a clear distinction between effects attributable to gene versus environment is not always possible.

In summary, individuals who are dependent on a variety of drugs, including alcohol, cocaine, and tobacco, have a greater likelihood than those who are not dependent on these drugs of having the D2 gene, specifically the A1 allele. Perhaps the tendency to use psychoactive drugs that release DA is greater for those who lack sufficient DA from other sources. In other words, the propensity to experience positive reinforcement from using these drugs differs among individuals, and this variation appears to be linked to genetic factors.

Psychiatric Disorders and Genetics

Similar differences in the presence of D2 genes have been found for a variety of psychiatric and behavioral disorders of an impulsive or compulsive nature, including antisocial personality, attention deficit disorders, binge eating, and gambling. Persons with fewer D2 transporter genes may engage in these forms of behavior to release or generate more DA. A dopamine deficit theory (Blum, Sheridan, Wood, Braverman, Chen, & Comings, 1995) holds that people who have too few D2 receptors may engage in activities that compensate for the lowered DA: drug taking, stimulus seeking, and other forms of risk taking such as gambling.

Marker Studies

If, as assumed by a genetic model, children from families with an alcoholic parent are more likely to develop drinking problems, perhaps there are some genetic, physical, biochemical, or neurophysiological differences even prior to the development of drinking problems. Such **marker variables**, factors on which persons from alcoholic (FH+) and nonalcoholic (FH–) family history backgrounds differ, are not necessarily causes. They are factors that help identify individuals who are likely to differ from others in future alcoholism. Some types of markers, such as indicators of ethanol metabolism, may indeed play a causal role because they affect differences in reactions to alcohol. In this type of research, children of FH+ and FH– families are compared to see if they differ on factors that might point toward future differences in drinking behavior.

Genetic Markers. A search for metabolic differences for alcohol between FH+ and FH– groups has not proved fruitful so far (Schuckit, 1981). Schuckit (1987) suggested that sons of alcoholics may differ from sons of nonalcoholics in their sensitivity or reaction to ethanol. Sons of alcoholics had a *lower* arousal from a moderate dose of alcohol than sons of nonalcoholics, a difference that might be part of the basis for why alcoholics need to drink larger amounts of alcohol. Contrary to expectations based on a genetic basis for differences in metabolism, other research (Nagoshi & Wilson, 1987), using both male and female children, found that FH+ subjects tend to show *greater* sensitivity (more disruptive effect) to a dose of alcohol than the FH– subjects.

Biochemical Markers. Monoamine oxidase (MAO) is a genetically controlled enzyme that influences mood states through its regulation of the levels of neurotransmitters such as dopamine and norepinephrine. MAO levels in blood platelets have been found to be lower in alcoholics even after they abstain for long periods. Members of alcoholic families also show lower platelet MAO levels than those from nonalcoholic families. Studies (Pandey, Fawcett, Gibbons, Clark, & Davis, 1988; Von Knorring, Bohman, Von Knorring, & Oreland, 1985) suggest that the MAO-level differences between normals and alcoholics are limited to certain subtypes of alcoholics. It is also not conclusive that this difference in platelet MAO is specific to alcoholism or whether it could be due to general psychopathology.

One hypothesis (Anthenelli & Tabakoff, 1995) suggests that lower MAO levels among alcoholics might contribute to drinking by interfering with the production of serotonin (5-HT). This neurotransmitter has been found to be low in alcoholics. However, the opposite mechanism may be that low serotonin levels could play a causal role in drinking because it has been found to be low in some persons even *prior* to their development of alcoholism (Ballenger, Goodwin, Major, & Brown, 1979). In either case, serotonin levels may serve as a marker variable for alcoholism.

Adenylate cyclase (AC) is another potential marker variable (Anthenelli & Tabakoff, 1995). This important enzyme affects neurotransmission of messages from the exterior of neurons to the interior portions. AC might affect alcoholism by disrupting this process by which the secondary messenger, cAMP, inside cells acts to stimulate or inhibit transmission. One effect is that the reinforcement process involving the production of dopamine is impaired.

Electrophysiological Markers. Differences in brain wave patterns have been observed between FH+ and FH– groups. When visual or auditory stimuli are presented, there is an electrical change known as the P300 wave that peaks about 300 milliseconds later. It is assumed to reflect attention to the presentation of stimuli, and it is smaller for FH+ groups given a dose of alcohol (Volavka, Pollack, Gabrielli, & Mednick, 1985). Similar results were found for young boys from alcoholic fathers in comparison to sons of nonalcoholic controls (Begleiter et al., 1984). These results led to the hypothesis that biological differences between sons of alcoholics and nonalcoholics existed even before these boys began drinking. These findings, although challenged by later research (Tarter, Moss, & Laird, 1990), imply that sons of alcoholics may suffer attentional or perceptual processing deficits.

Although initial studies suggested that females did not have reduced P300, later studies (Hill & Steinhauer, 1993) found that young daughters of alcoholic fathers also had lower P300 than daughters of nonalcoholic controls. However, not all offspring of alcoholics show reduced P300, with only about one third of sons and one fifth of daughters of alcoholics showing this effect.

The Biological Risk Factors Family Study (Hill, 1995) provided substantial evidence for the role of a genetic basis for familial alcoholism among females. An electrical change, N2, which involves a negative peak about 200 milliseconds after a stimulus is presented, is assumed to occur when individuals have a task in which they have to discriminate between stimuli. N2 can be a marker for genetic differences because it is lower among FH+ persons.

Findings of P300 studies at six different research sites comparing alcoholics and their relatives confirm prior findings of reduced P300 in alcoholics (Porjesz & Begleiter, 1997). This result occurred in females and in relatives of probands, even those who are nonalcoholic.

Neuropsychological Markers. Some studies (Nagoshi & Wilson, 1987) have suggested that offspring of alcoholics have impaired cognitive abilities in comparison to controls prior to but not after consuming a moderate dose of alcohol.

After controlling for age, intelligence, and level of drinking, cognitive differences between FH+ and FH– groups were not found (Hesselbrock, Hesselbrock, & Stabenau, 1985). Similarly, no major differences in performance of FH+ and FH– groups on a number of cognitive tests were assumed to reflect different levels of neuropsychological functioning (Workman-Daniels & Hesselbrock, 1987).

Problems With Marker Studies. Overall, the evidence on markers for alcoholism has been inconsistent. One ignored factor throughout this research that may contribute to the conflicting array of findings is the temporal point of measurement following alcohol administration. FH+ and FH– sons may differ in their sensitivity to alcohol in different ways, depending on whether the blood alcohol level is ascending or descending at the time of observation (Newlin & Thomson, 1990), as depicted in Figure 5.4.

Specifically, the **differentiator model** (Newlin & Thomson, 1990) proposed that FH+ sons of alcoholics (SOAs) may experience more positive arousal than FH– sons of nonalcoholics (SONAs) on the ascending limb, which would give them more incentive to drink. In addition, they would also differ on the descending limb in that SOAs would have greater acute tolerance within the test session and return to baseline levels more quickly than the SONAs would, a difference that would lead to less anxiety and also promote more drinking by SOAs. During about the first 30 minutes after a drink, the SOAs would show more intoxication and physiological changes than SONAs, but as time since drinking passed, they would show fewer negative effects of intoxication, as compared with the SONAs.

This model may reconcile some of the confusing results in past research on markers if different studies assessed the effects of alcohol at different times of the day. Alcohol doses in laboratory studies are typically administered at the convenience of the researcher's schedule rather than at times corresponding to when the subjects typically drink. For example, in Schuckit's (1981, 1987) studies, alcohol is given to participants generally at 9 a.m. Light drinkers typically become nauseous when drinking at this atypical time, so some of the differences between FH+ and FH– may be due to nausea rather than to alcohol sensitivity differences, per se. Also, tests are conducted usually in the presence of an experimenter so that so-

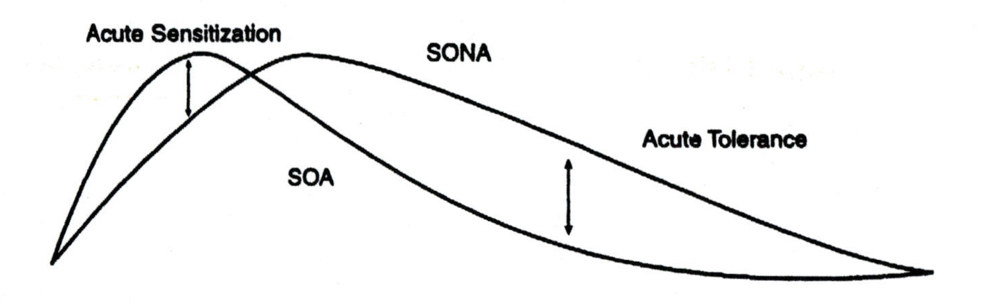

Figure 5.4. Differentiator Model of Alcohol Effects Over Time
SOURCE: Newlin and Thomson (1990). Copyright 1990 by the American Psychological Association. Used with permission.
NOTE: Note the greater acute sensitization during the ascending limb of the blood alcohol curve in sons of alcoholics (SOAs) and the greater acute tolerance in SOAs during the falling limb of the curve. This is indicated by a more rapid and robust onset of the effect of alcohol and a more rapid return to baseline of the falling blood alcohol curve.

cial interaction is required. Thus, differences in reaction could have been affected by social factors as well as by alcohol.

Even when markers seem to have been found, there is no clearly formulated theory to account for the findings. How do markers act as contributors to or as "causes" of alcohol consumption? For example, morphological characteristics such as body size could be viewed as a marker because boys who are physically larger for their age might start drinking sooner because they can more easily be perceived as older (Tarter et al., 1990). We would not conclude that large body size is a direct cause of drinking differences. Instead, it may be that body size has an indirect effect on drinking levels as a factor that is sociologically and psychologically conducive to drinking.

Family Environment Influences

Environmental factors also may be important precursors of subsequent alcohol and drug use in addition to any inherited tendencies. In particular, early experiences in the home such as observation of parental attitudes and behaviors related to alcohol and drugs may influence subsequent alcohol and drug use by children as they grow up.

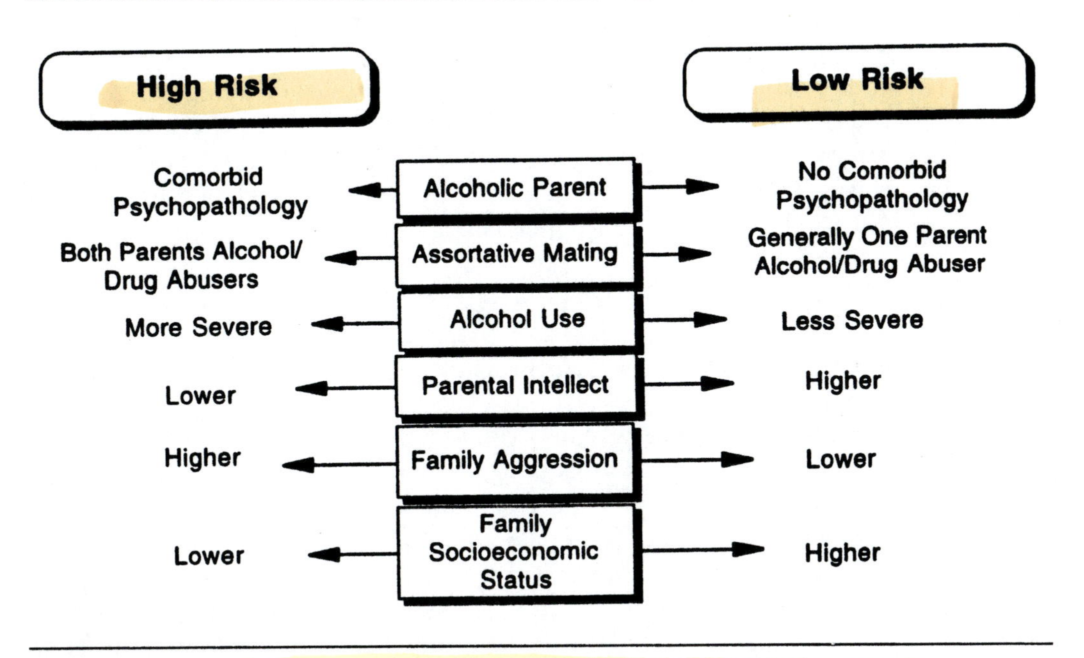

Figure 5.5. High- and Low-Risk Environments for Sons of Alcoholic Fathers
SOURCE: Ellis, Zucker, and Fitzgerald (1997).

GENERAL POPULATION SAMPLES

Alcohol-Specific Influences

Parents may influence their children's drinking through both direct modeling of alcohol use and the transmission of their values about drinking (Bank et al., 1985; Kandel & Andrews, 1987). It is not surprising that similarities in the drinking patterns of parents and their adult children generally have been found in studies with large general population samples (Barnes & Welte, 1990; Dawson, Harford, & Grant, 1992) as well as with smaller clinical samples (Orford & Velleman, 1991; Penick et al., 1987).

Non-Alcohol-Specific Influences

In addition to alcohol-specific family influences, high-risk children in alcoholic homes also face influences that are not alcohol related, as shown in Figure 5.5. There is evidence of more parental psychiatric problems, lower socioeconomic status, family psychopathology, family violence, and parental cognitive impairment. The alcohol-specific and alcohol-nonspecific factors must both be examined to see how they adversely affect the development of children.

Typically, past studies have found that heavier-drinking parents have children who also develop more frequent and heavier patterns of alcohol use. However, other studies with nonclinical samples of college students (Engs, 1990; Wright & Heppner, 1991, 1993) found no relationship between the drinking of parents and their college-age children.

Parent-Child Gender Combination

The effect of each parent's drinking may vary with the gender of the child (Thompson & Wilsnack, 1987). Hence, the degree of similarity of drinking between parent and child may depend on whether one is comparing a parent and child of the same as opposed to opposite sex. Sex role identification theories as diverse as psychoanalytic and social learning (Baldwin, 1967) predict that the same-sex parent should have greater influence than the opposite-sex parent on a child. Consistent with this view, fathers' drinking, as well as mothers' drinking to a lesser degree, was found to be moderately predictive of sons' drinking but was not as predictive of daughters' drinking among adolescents (Wilks, Callan, & Austin, 1989) as well as for college student samples (Jung, 1995).

A large longitudinal investigation known as the Tecumseh Community Health Study (Harburg, Davis, & Caplan, 1982) examined the relationship between the level of fathers' and mothers' drinking with that of their sons and daughters. The heavier the drinking was in the same-sex parent, the heavier the drinking was for the child, up to a point, after which there was a divergence.

Thus, the relative amount of alcohol consumed by sons tended to match that of their fathers but fell behind when fathers were very heavy drinkers. The same trend emerged with respect to the drinking of daughters in relation to the drinking of their mothers. Drinking of daughters also corresponded with their mothers' level of drinking except for the very heavy-drinking mothers, when it dropped off as well.

Weaker correspondences occurred between offspring and their opposite-sex parent. This pattern shows the strong sex role identification influence for both sexes who imitate the same-sex parent more than the opposite-sex parent. Heavy drinking by parents, especially those of the opposite sex, tends to have a reverse effect, lowering the drinking level of offspring.

A follow-up study (Webster, Harburg, Gleiberman, Schork, & DiFranceisco, 1989) examined the relationship between drinking of parents when their children were young and the current levels of drinking by their children as young adults. The study was based on 420 sets of mother, father, and adult offspring. The level of the parents' self-reported drinking in 1960 was compared with the current drinking level reported by their adult offspring in 1977.

Drinking levels of offspring were related to earlier parental use levels. If parents were lifelong abstainers, their children drank less. Parents who drank heavily had high-drinking offspring, especially daughters. Sons' drinking was more similar to fathers' than to mothers' drinking. Overall, offspring drinking levels resembled parents' drinking levels, but still a high percentage of children did not imitate their parents' drinking patterns.

Responses to heavy parental drinking can have varying effects. **Aversion** may occur in which the child adopts a negative attitude toward alcohol use, or **polarization** may occur in which the child may go from one extreme, abstinence, to the other extreme of heavy use (Webster et al., 1989). Because some heavy-drinking parents may often be abusive toward their children, for example, the tendency to model after the drinking of such parents may be reduced. Thus, 56% of the low-volume male drinkers had a heavy-drinking mother whose drinking violated cultural norms. Daughters of heavy-drinking parents were found to be more likely to show the polarization effect.

A follow-up of the Tecumseh study (Harburg, DiFranceisco, Webster, Gleiberman, & Schork, 1990) found that aversion effects were more likely when the opposite-sex parent was a heavy drinker with alcohol-related problems. However, daughters often imitated the drinking levels of heavy-drinking fathers without problems related to their drinking. Daughters showed a polarization effect if their mothers were heavy drinkers, with most of them being abstainers and a sizable minority becoming heavy drinkers themselves. Overall, the highest correspondence of drinking levels between parent and children occurred for abstaining parents, especially if the father was abstinent.

Other research (Orford & Velleman, 1991) found that the relationship of heavy parental drinking to the drinking of offspring varied with the interpersonal relationship between the drinking parent and child. Daughters were more likely to have drinking problems if they had a close relationship to their heavy-drinking fathers. Sons were more likely to have drinking problems if they had heavy-drinking mothers and poor relations with their fathers. These findings, similar in many respects to previous work (Harburg et al., 1990), suggest that the impact of heavy drinking by parents on the drinking of their children is greater for offspring of the opposite sex.

HIGH-RISK SAMPLES

Children growing up in an alcoholic home are assumed to be at high risk for developing psychological problems during childhood and later having alcohol and other drug problems as well. Research on this issue compares high-risk samples, defined as those children who come from families in which there is a positive history of alcoholism (FH+), with children from family histories free of alcoholism (FH–).

Retrospective Studies

Studies based on retrospective recall of alcoholics, diagrammed in Figure 5.6, determine the extent to which parents had alcohol problems while their children were growing up. Self-reports of alcoholics who had an alcoholic parent suggest that alcohol had a stronger effect for them when they first started drinking than for alcoholics who did not have an alcoholic parent. For example, alcoholics with an alcoholic parent or grandparent recalled starting drinking at a younger age and having more problems due to alcohol than either alcoholics without a drinking parent or alcoholics whose drinking relative was someone other than a parent or grandparent (Penick et al., 1987). Thus, the individual's own level of alcohol abuse and a family history of alcoholism appear to produce independent and additive effects. Either factor places one at higher risk, and having both factors increases the likelihood of alcoholism even more.

Inclusion of FH+ subjects who were not alcoholic as a control group in this study allowed an evaluation of the effects of family history of alcoholism on persons not yet afflicted by alcoholism. Because FH+ subjects were found to be more susceptible to problems on most measures than the FH– controls, the study supports the view that a family history of alcoholism places one at higher risk for a variety of psychological and physical health impairments.

Numerous adverse effects are associated with a positive family history for alcoholism. Glenn and Parsons (1989a, 1989b) included 148 middle-aged alcoholics in treatment, about half of whom had an FH+ and half of whom had an FH– background. Control groups of matched nonalcoholics were included, again with about half FH+ and half FH– backgrounds. In one study (Glenn & Parsons, 1989b), health was worse for alcoholics but to a greater extent among those from FH+ backgrounds, where at least one first-degree relative was an alcoholic. Even among nonalcoholic controls, however, health was poorer for those with an FH+ background. Finally, there were few differences in health between males and females that could be attributed to alcoholism, per se, as opposed to biological and sex role differences.

Another analysis (Glenn & Parsons, 1989a) based on the same samples examined psychosocial correlates of family history for alcoholism for the alcoholics and nonalcoholic controls. Family history of alcoholism and the individual's own alcoholism status affected scores on most variables

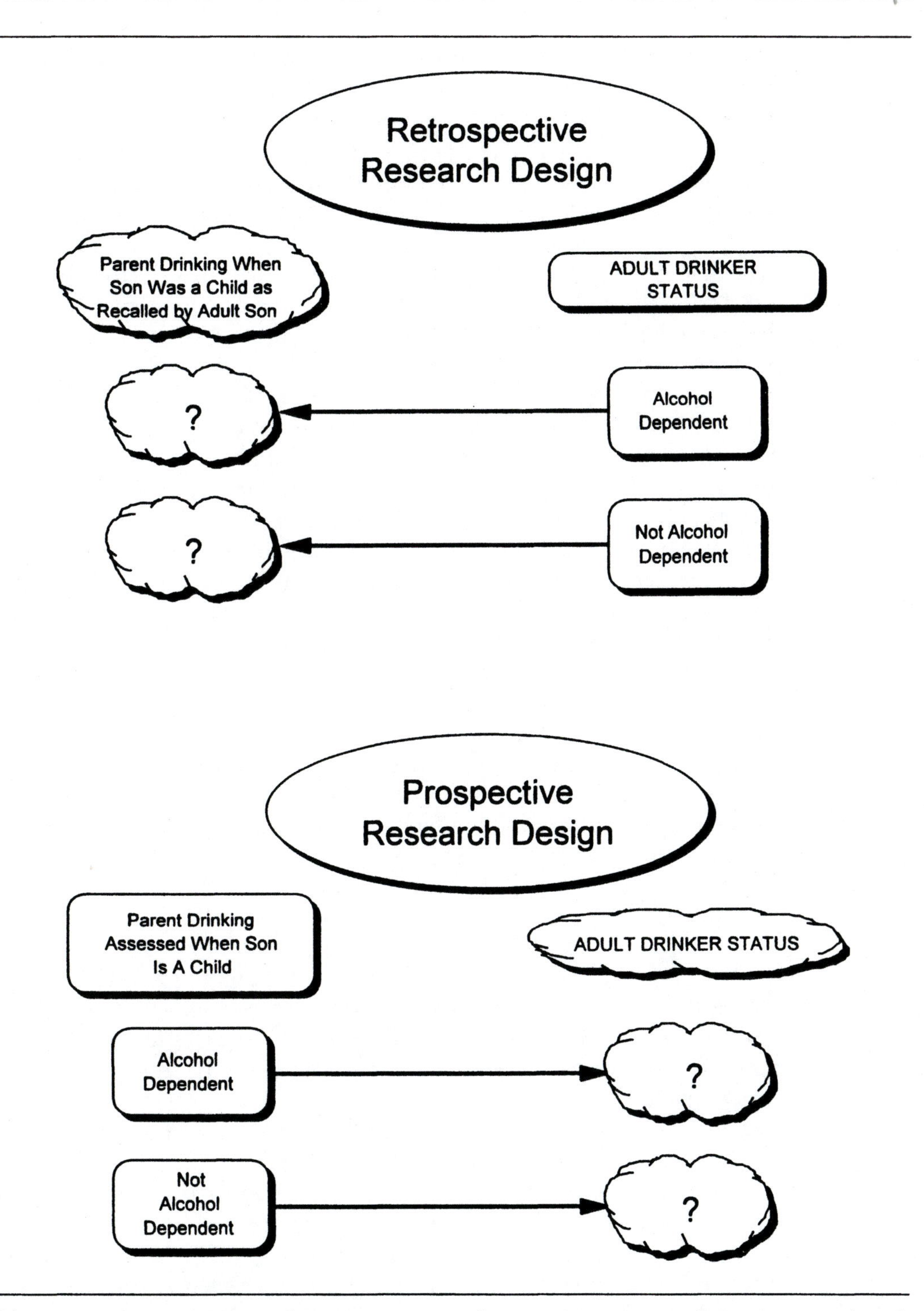

Figure 5.6. Comparison of Retrospective and Prospective Research Designs on the Effects of Family History for Alcoholism

(Glenn & Parsons, 1989a). Those with a positive family history or alcoholism themselves had poorer occupational levels, more turnover, greater family psychopathology, more marriages, and greater anxiety and depression. Similarly, these groups reported more childhood behavior problems such as hyperactivity and conduct problems.

A study (Rodriguez, 1994) of young heroin users found that cognitive tests were within the normal range, but those with a family history of alcoholism started using drugs at earlier ages and performed worse on tasks involving attention, memory, verbal-conceptual abstraction, and nonverbal reasoning. These deficits were attributed to these family antecedents more than with drug consumption per se.

Similar effects of family background occur for smoking (Chassin, Presson, Sherman, & Mulvenon, 1994). Adolescents from an FH+ home typically smoked more cigarettes each day and for more years. They saw themselves as more addicted to cigarettes, had more positive beliefs about the effects of smoking, and reported stronger relaxation and stimulation motives for smoking compared to peers from FH– backgrounds.

Retrospective studies are often based on clinical samples of individuals seeking help for problems not necessarily related to alcohol. These subjects may be likely to search earlier memories for signs of family problems such as parental alcoholism to explain their own problems. This tendency is particularly problematic because most studies rely on self-reports of family history rather than objective or independent assessment. This tendency might produce overestimates of the extent of alcoholism in family backgrounds. It is also likely that clinical samples are an atypical sample reflecting more extreme cases that may not be representative of the general population.

Prospective Studies

Prospective studies assess subjects prior to the onset of alcoholism and follow them afterwards, as shown in Figure 5.6. These before-and-after comparisons of individuals from FH+ and FH– backgrounds offer a stronger basis for inferences about the effects of FH background on the offspring than do retrospective studies.

One prospective study (Pandina & Johnson, 1989) compared an FH+ group of adolescents who had a parent treated for alcoholism, another FH+ group who had at least one parent with heavy drinking, and two groups of FH– background offspring. This was a community rather than a clinical sample, with about 1,400 high school students studied over 3 years. No differences occurred in alcohol problems such as escape drinking, early onset of intoxication, or the frequency of intoxication, but children of alcoholics were more likely to have other problems related to alcohol and drugs sooner.

Positive family history of alcoholism was related to past-year alcohol dependence in a general population sample of 23,152 drinkers (age 18+) in which about 40% reported a positive family history (Dawson et al., 1992). After adjustment for age, race, gender, and poverty, comparisons of FH+ and FH– individuals showed that the odds of alcohol dependence were 45% greater among persons with alcoholism in second- or third-degree relatives only, 86% greater among those with alcoholism in first-degree relatives only, and 167% greater among those with alcoholism in first- and second- or third-degree relatives.

The detrimental effect of alcoholism in a family on offspring includes more alcohol use, greater conduct behavior problems, and symptoms such as depression among FH+ than for FH– groups (Chassin, Rogosch, & Barrera, 1991). Rather than using volunteers or clinical samples, 454 adolescent participants were selected from widely different groups selected from the community. Individuals suspected to be FH– were excluded if there was evidence that their parents had alcohol problems. This study employed a standard objective set of diagnostic criteria for distinguishing alcoholic and nonalcoholic parents rather than the subjective criterion used in many studies based only on the child's feeling that one or both of their parents had "drinking problems."

In a comparison of college students over their 4 years of college (Sher, Walitzer, Wood, & Brent, 1991), drinking history of the parents was not assessed directly but was based on the student's description. Measures also were taken of parental comorbidity and the presence of other psychological disorders often found among alcoholics, so that the specific effect of parental alcoholism could be made independent of these other contributors to alcohol use by their offspring.

The results revealed that a family history of alcoholism is associated with more alcohol and drug problems, stronger expectancies for alcohol use, more behavioral undercontrol, and more psychiatric distress. In addition, FH+ students showed poorer academic performance and lower verbal ability. These differences were present for both men and women for most variables.

It should be noted that some effects attributed to early alcoholic home environment actually might involve processes that precede birth. A 14-year prospective study (Baer, Barr, Bookstein, Sampson, & Streissguth, 1998) of pregnant women showed that the level of prenatal alcohol use measured during pregnancy was a better predictor of adolescent alcohol use than family alcohol environment during childhood.

Problems With High-Risk Sample Studies

Overall, the evidence suggests that children from FH+ backgrounds were more likely to use more alcohol or to develop alcohol problems. One problem with family history studies is the wide variation in the criteria used to define FH levels. Some studies use stringent criteria such as a parent diagnosed and treated for alcoholism, whereas other studies rely on vague and uncorroborated criteria such as the offspring's judgment that a parent had drinking problems sometime in the past. Thus, in some studies, the magnitude of the difference between the FH+ and FH– levels is rather small and unreliable.

As suggested by Figure 5.7, the likelihood of finding differences between FH+ and FH– groups should vary with the criteria used for defining the two groups. Figure 5.7 depicts a continuum of drinking that ranges from nondrinking through moderate to heavy drinking. If groups selected from Points 2 and 3 on the diagram are used to represent FH– and FH+ groups, respectively, there should be less chance of finding differences than if groups are selected from Points 1 and 4. Using a high or stringent criterion to classify drinkers gives fewer but more severe cases of alcoholism that fall further out on the continuum. Using a lenient criterion or broad definition, on the other hand, will lead to the identification of a larger number of cases, but most of them will be less severe or lower on the continuum.

Another problem is that researchers in general have not reported the levels of alcohol use in any absolute or standard values that could be compared across studies. The reported lack of differences could reflect either equally low or high drinking by FH+ and FH– groups. It is conceivable that any effect of FH level among young samples is masked by the tendency for FH– individuals to drink because of adolescent curiosity about alcohol and from peer pressure to drink. If other factors such as these influences combine with family drinking history to determine alcohol use levels, no clear-cut effect of FH level will be found. Finally, the studies thus far may not show strong relationships between parental and offspring drinking simply because they cannot rule out the possibility of alcoholism in children in the future.

The high-risk sample studies cannot separate hereditary and environmental contributions. Instead, they assess the joint influences of heredity and environment on the children from alcoholic and nonalcoholic families. The assumption is that both genetic and home environment factors represent a higher risk for alcoholism for persons from families with a parental drinking problem. However, the genetic and environmental factors could even offset each other in some families. As depicted in Figure 5.8, there may be families in which a genetic factor favoring alcoholism is opposed by a home environment, which lowers the risk for alcoholism, and

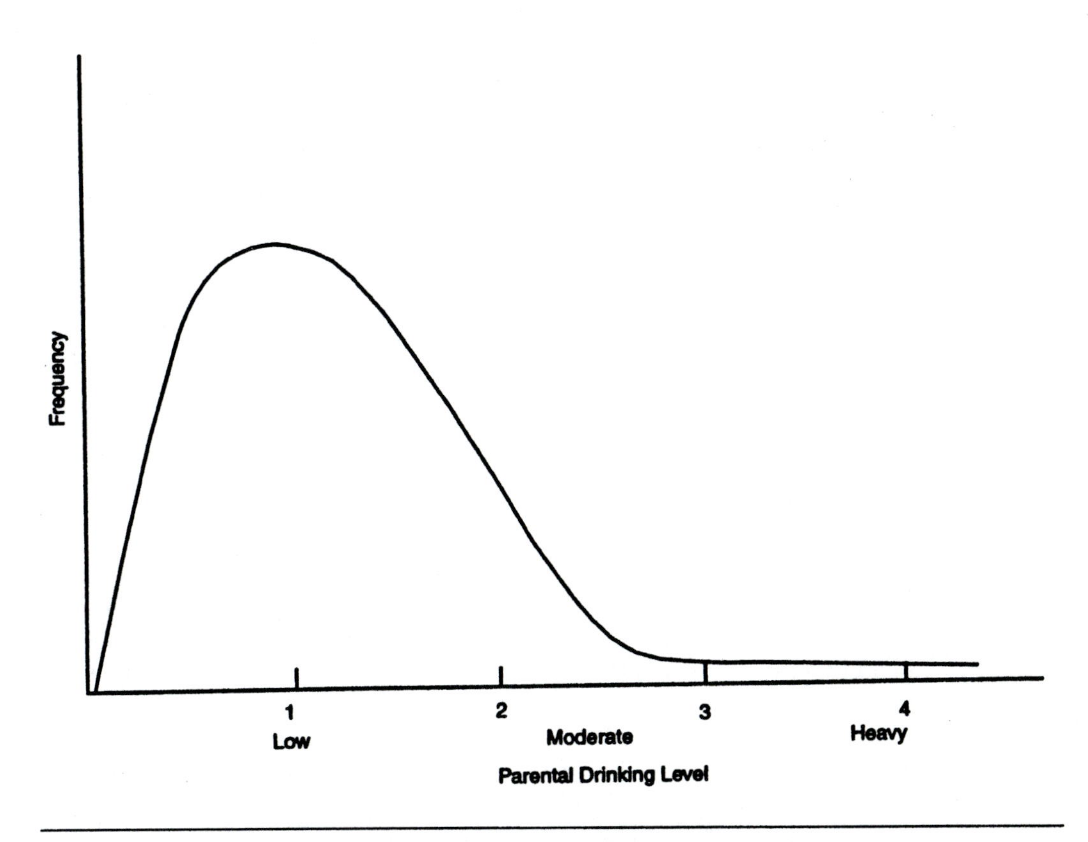

Figure 5.7. Different Cutoffs on the Distribution of the Amount of Alcohol Consumption for Defining FH+ and FH– Can Affect Conclusions From Studies of the Impact of Family History on Alcoholism

NOTE: Studies that use extreme groups (Level 1 to represent FH– and Level 4 to represent FH+) will be more likely to show differences than studies that use intermediate groups (Level 2 to represent FH– and Level 3 to represent FH+).

other families in which a low genetic potential for alcoholism is offset by a home environment that raises the risk for alcoholism.

In other words, the vulnerability or susceptibility of an individual toward alcoholism is based on a combination of both genetic and environmental factors. If either factor is sufficiently strong, alcoholism may occur even if the other factor is weak. For children from FH+ families, both factors are assumed to be high in general. However, it is conceivable that although children of alcoholics may have a high genetic potential for alcoholism, some may have an environment that does not foster alcoholism. Similarly, although children of nonalcoholics may have a low genetic potential for alcoholism, some of them may live in an environment that fosters alcoholism.

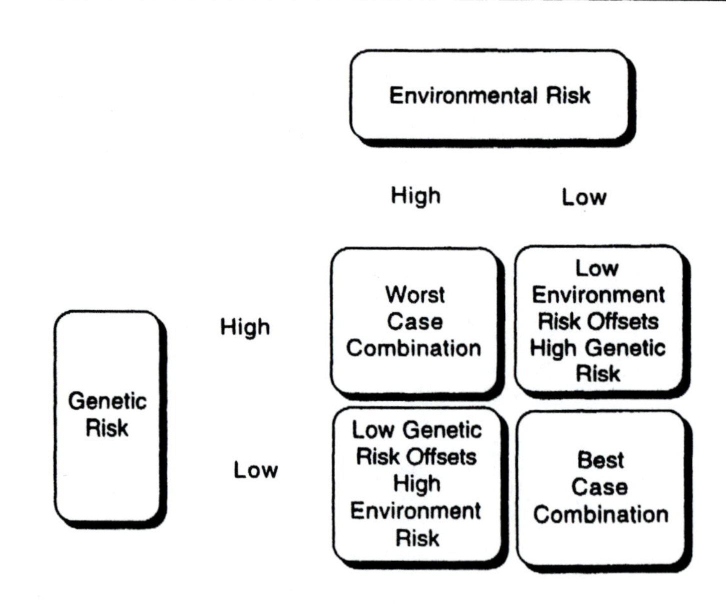

Figure 5.8. Genetic and Environmental Risks for Alcoholism Can Create Either Offsetting or Additive Effects

Integrative Models: Heredity and Environment

Instead of developing explanations that pit heredity and environment against each other, it may be more fruitful to develop models that show the interplay between both sets of factors. One comprehensive model (Pihl, Peterson, & Finn, 1990a; 1990b) examined the interrelationship among inherited tendencies toward alcoholism, localized brain functions, childhood behavior problems, and alcohol abuse. Figure 5.9 assumes that sons of male alcoholics have inherited tendencies that limit cognitive functioning and attention during information-processing tasks. Such cognitive deficits produce consequences that place these children at higher risk for future alcohol abuse. First, these deficits harm learning and academic performance by disrupting attention and preventing the learning of conceptual rules, abstract categories, and rules of social behavior.

A second factor that may predispose these children toward conduct disorders and eventual alcohol abuse is poor socialization about rules of social behavior because these children often come from families with low socioeconomic status, hostility, and alcohol and drug abuse (Hinshaw, 1987). As a consequence, these children may be hyperactive and act out

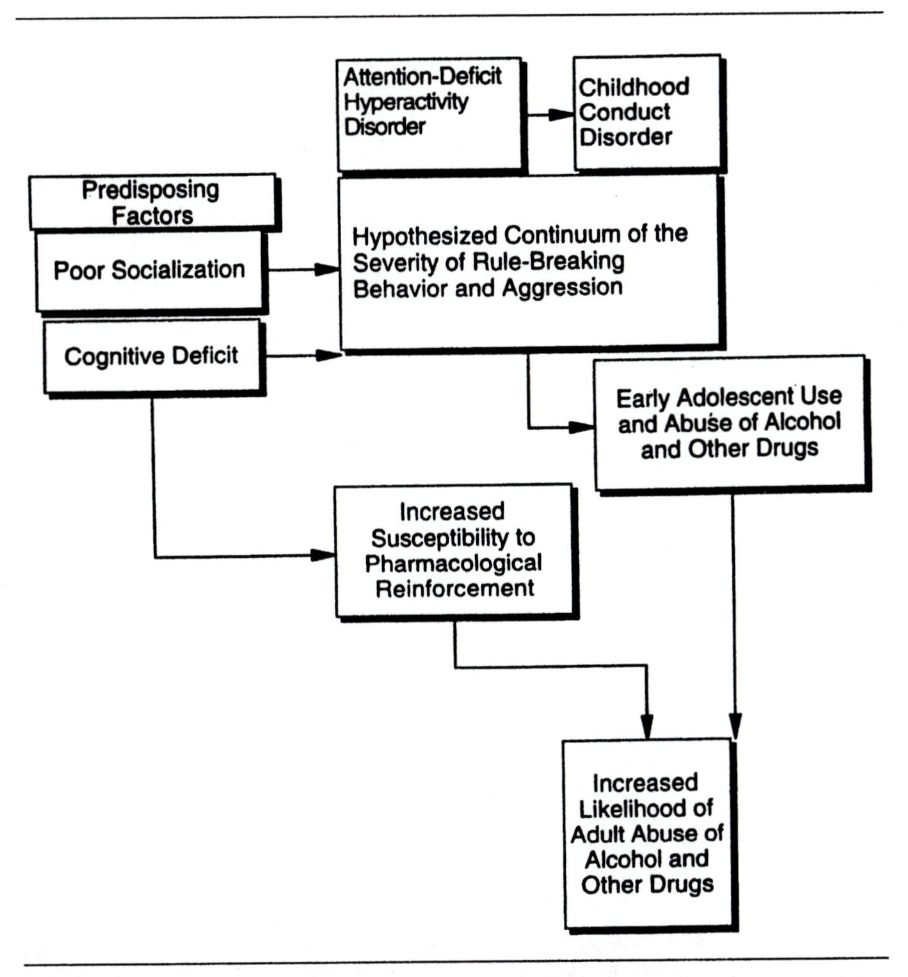

Figure 5.9. Predisposing Childhood Factors Can Lead to Hyperactivity, Conduct Disorders, and Aggression, Increasing the Likelihood of Early Adolescent Alcohol and Other Drug Abuse
SOURCE: Pihl and Peterson (1991).

with conduct disorders at school. Use of alcohol and other drugs may be reinforcing for these children by reducing anxiety in times of stress. However, extended use of alcohol may further disrupt cognitive functions, leading to additional problem behaviors, creating a vicious cycle of more drinking and impairment.

This model is supported by a wide array of evidence from biochemical studies, investigations of the function of specific brain areas involved with organization and categorization, neuropsychological studies of information processing, and childhood behavior problems such as hyperactivity. In their tests of the model, Pihl et al. (1990a, 1990b) focused on young sons of male alcoholics because they have the highest risk of alcohol abuse. In laboratory experiments with tasks involving threats such as a signal followed in a few seconds by electric shock, sons of alcoholics and a control group of sons of nonalcoholics received either a dose of alcohol or a placebo before being compared in their reactions to the task. Psychophysiological measures such as heart rate, evoked potentials, and electroencephalogram (EEG) waves were recorded.

Subjective reports of alcohol effects did not differ appreciably for sons of male alcoholics and nonalcoholics, but the psychophysical indicators suggest that sons of male alcoholics are hyperactive when sober but, after consuming alcohol, achieve a calmer state (Finn & Pihl, 1987, 1988). In contrast, sons of nonalcoholics are less active when sober but more reactive on intoxication. There are also biochemical differences, with sons of male alcoholics showing lower monoamine oxidase and deficits in serotonin.

Overall, the model ties together many differences observed between sons of male alcoholics and controls in behavioral, neurophysiological, and biochemical reactions to alcohol challenge tests. It provides a useful framework for developing and testing hypotheses about the bases for differences in response to alcohol.

That these predispositions are stronger among men may reflect the additional role of the different social norms and attitudes about the role of drinking for men and women. Because women traditionally have not been encouraged to drink at a level comparable to that for men, any biologically based temperamental characteristics that might increase the risk of excessive drinking among women may be countered by these sex role expectations in our society that act as a protective mechanism for women.

In summary, neuropsychological differences are not the only determinants of alcohol and drug use but rather can be viewed as predisposing factors. Biological factors determine initial vulnerability to alcohol and other drug dependence. Biologically based differences in temperament for stimulation and risk taking combine with tendencies acquired from early environmental influences such as expectancies about effects of specific drugs, observed alcohol and drug use by parents, school performance, adequacy of coping skills, and peer influences. Together, all of these factors determine the likelihood of drug use.

SUMMARY

The question of the relative influence of genetic and environmental factors on the development of alcoholism has generated considerable interest and controversy. An explanation emphasizing heredity is more fatalistic because it implies that the "die has already been cast," and the offspring could not alter or control their destiny. Environmental explanations allow more optimism in the sense that interventions can be attempted to counteract or reduce the damage. Children of alcoholics might receive earlier counseling or be placed under foster care, for example. Another possibility would be more education and counseling of parents as to the dangers of parental alcoholism.

At the level of the individual, the answer to this issue would have implications for assigning blame or responsibility between parents and children. If alcoholism were regarded as primarily of genetic origin, the alcoholic would be seemingly absolved of personal responsibility for the problem. At the societal level, the answer to the question carries implications for social attitudes and social policy. If genetic factors were assumed to be the primary determinants of alcoholism, society would be more tolerant than if the alcoholic was seen to be personally responsible.

Naturalistic evidence about the relative role of biology and environment is difficult to evaluate because both variables are always operative and make it impossible to disentangle the effects of each factor from the other. The major evidence that first led to increased awareness about the role of heredity as a risk factor for alcoholism was the adoption studies conducted in the 1950s in Denmark and, subsequently, in Sweden. However, the generalizability of adoptees to the larger population must be evaluated. The circumstances and the types of individuals who place children for adoption and accept adopted children are likely to be significantly different from the more general population. For example, infants placed for adoption are not a random sample of infants but often come from unwed mothers, probably adolescent girls. They may have lower incomes, poor nutrition, and so on. The types of individuals who apply for adoption are not a random sample of the general population either, being screened by social agencies to ensure that they can afford to care for the child and appear to be psychologically stable. Certainly, the answers to these questions may vary in different countries and eras, depending on the social-legal conditions and cultural attitudes related to adoptions.

Other relevant information on the heredity-environment issue involves the study of the far larger number of children who grow up in the homes of their biological parents. Comparing children whose parents vary in their level of alcoholism cannot answer the question of the relative role of heredity and environment as might be possible in twin and adoption studies, but they can be generalized to a much larger segment of the total population. Differences between children from FH+ and FH– families would have to be viewed as due to the joint or combined effects of heredity and environment.

Such studies question the widely held view that children who grow up in an alcoholic family are at risk for not only alcoholism but other types of psychological and behavioral problems. Clinical observations need confirmation from carefully controlled studies. Thus far, there is some support for the conclusion that children from alcoholic environments are different from other children. However, they do not always differ with respect to their drinking practices or its effects on them. Some of the contradictory findings across different studies about the relationship of parental alcoholism and characteristics of their children may be due to the variety of criteria used to define an alcoholic parent in different studies. It is also possible that under some conditions or for some types of individuals, the potentially adverse effects of parental alcohol dependency can be offset, but the nature of these protective factors is not yet fully understood. Because alcohol dependency may require a number of years to become manifest, continued follow-up over another 10 or 20 years may yield other answers.

In much past research, heredity and environment are discussed as if they operated independently. A gene-environment interaction view looks at the joint influence of heredity and environment by looking at how genetic propensities are affected by the environmental opportunities that are available. Thus, even if genetic factors are present that offer high potential for drug use, the environmental factors may either oppose or enhance the expression of these inherited tendencies.

KEY TERMS

Aversion
DA transporter gene
Differentiator model
Dizygotic (DZ) twins
FH+ families
FH– families
Gene-environment interactions
Marker variables
Monozygotic (MZ) twins
Polarization
Proband
Prospective studies
Retrospective studies

STIMULUS/RESPONSE

1. Similar patterns of alcohol or drug use may seemingly occur among family members (e.g., children of alcoholics become alcoholics themselves when they grow up). Psychologists call it a confirmation bias when we notice cases that fit our expectations: You know Joe is an alcoholic, and you then learn his father was also one. "Aha," you say, "just as I suspected. So that's why Joe drinks so much!" But are we as likely to also notice disconfirming instances? For example, do you notice that Bill, also an alcoholic, has a non-alcoholic father? Is Bill just an exception to the rule?
2. Do you know anyone who is a total abstainer from alcohol? Do most members of their immediate family also not drink?
3. What effect do you think current attitudes and social policies about smoking and drinking alcohol in public places will have on the future smoking and drinking by young children?

- Developmental Perspective
- Psychological Perspective
- Theories of Smoking
- Summary
- Key Terms
- Stimulus/Response

Theories of Alcohol and Other Drug Use 6

Why do people use alcohol and other drugs? This is a complex question, and the answer may differ for different individuals, circumstances, and drugs. Factors as diverse as curiosity, rebellion, peer pressure, reinforcement, tension reduction, and others have been proposed as underlying initial use. The promise of rewarding and exciting experiences seems to offset the threat of adverse physical, social, and, in some cases, legal consequences associated with the use of alcohol and other drugs.

Some users initially experience pleasurable consequences for the most part, but others may suffer negative effects and inflict harm on others. Eventually, some will, with varying difficulty, quit using. However, others will become highly dependent or "addicted" and be unable to quit. In view of the considerable physical and social psychological risks involved with the use of many drugs, it is apparent that there must be powerful factors leading to the continued and often increased use of psychoactive drugs.

In this chapter, we will examine major theories about the factors that lead people to use alcohol and other drugs and the nature of the processes, psychological and pharmacological, that occur with the use of these substances. These theories will also explore why it is so difficult to quit using. We will describe the processes proposed in each theory and discuss the research evidence to evaluate its validity. The theories to be presented focus variously on physiological, affective, cognitive, and social psychological factors. These theories should be viewed as complementary rather than as competing rivals. Instead, it may be useful to think of each theory as focusing on different aspects of substance use as well as on different points over time.

Theories that focus on the role of pharmacological properties of alcohol and other drugs overlook the role of psychological variables such as the social and physical setting where they are used, personality and temperament differences, and the prevailing mood and motivation preceding use. Conversely, psychological theories tend to ignore pharmacological changes in neurophysiological processes that underlie some of the psychological and behavioral consequences of drugs. Psychological theories may be more essential in explaining what leads to *initial* drug use. In contrast, theories emphasizing pharmacological and neurophysiological factors may be more relevant in explaining *abuse* and *dependency*, conditions that develop after long-term habitual use, which may no longer involve the conscious or volitional decisions made during early stages of use.

Theories developed primarily to explain drinking are generally applicable to understanding use of most other drugs. Still, it is important to recognize that specific drugs may require additional or different factors from those that pertain to alcohol. For example, the patterns of the frequency and quantity of alcohol use markedly differ from those for nicotine. Whereas alcohol involves oral intake, nicotine is primarily obtained by smoking cigarettes, and many illicit drugs involve intravenous injection. Also, heavy consumption of some drugs such as alcohol or cocaine produces intoxication states that greatly impair cognitive, affective, and motor functions, whereas such risks are negligible for drugs such as nicotine and caffeine.

A similar caution applies to differences between licit and illicit drug use because theories that apply to licit drug use may be incomplete for understanding illicit drug use. Although the pharmacological effects of many illicit drugs may be similar to those of some licit drugs insofar as altering mood states and behavior, the social antecedents and consequences of using each drug are markedly different.

Legal drugs are often consumed publicly by a wide cross section of the adult population. If we use an iceberg to represent the size of the user population, most of the "iceberg" is above the surface and visible for legal drugs. But for illegal drugs, we see only the "tip of the iceberg," and the size of the unseen portion is unknown because illicit drugs generally are used in clandestine settings by a more limited segment of the population. Due to the hidden nature of illicit drug use, less evidence is available about the extent to which such use leads to problems among all users. Aside from any health risks from a specific drug, using an illicit drug carries with it the risk of heavy penalties such as fines or imprisonment, which are absent or minimal for licit drugs. Theories of illicit drug use must explain which individuals assume this additional risk, why they do so, and how this risk might affect the consequences of use.

Use of any drug, licit or illicit, does not just happen. When it occurs, it is in a context of social, cultural, and historical factors that set boundaries and limits for how, where, and when drugs are used. Moreover, alcohol and other drug use does not occur instantaneously but entails a developmental process closely linked to the transition between childhood and adolescence. It is important that developmental factors be included in theories about the use of alcohol and other drugs.

Developmental Perspective

As depicted in Figure 6.1, sociocultural factors such as the societal conditions, cultural values, and drug-specific beliefs, attitudes, and practices provide a stage on which other more immediate or **proximal factors** operate to determine individual alcohol and other drug use. How and when we acquire our beliefs, attitudes, and expectations about alcohol and drugs as we grow up are important for understanding our use of these substances.

As children, long before we use any psychoactive drugs, we have countless opportunities to observe adults, often including our parents and relatives, engage in the use of various drugs, as noted in Figure 6.1. We observe a variety of contexts, motives, and consequences associated with drinking and smoking. In addition to direct observations, we see media portrayals of alcohol and other drug use in movies and on television programs. We are less likely to directly observe the use of illicit drugs but still form preconceptions about the psychological and behavioral effects of such drugs. Thus, prior to our first use of any psychoactive drug, we have expectations and conceptions, right or wrong, about many of these drugs and how they can affect us.

As children, we learn that even licit drugs are for adults only and that children are expected to wait until they reach adulthood before they drink or smoke. In addition to parental, family, and media influences, as we grow up, we observe that some of our peers do use alcohol and other drugs even though they are not of legal age and risk legal punishment. As Figure 6.1 suggests, peers may have stronger influences than parents do on our alcohol and other drug attitudes and use, especially during adolescence. Some of these peers may be perceived by many adolescents as "cool" or sophisticated because they engage in activities designated as adult. Yet at the same time, use of licit drugs is also widely accepted and encouraged as a rite of passage when we come of age.

LICIT DRUGS

Given the social importance attached to licit drug use, it is not unreasonable that initial use of alcohol and other drugs might occur in response

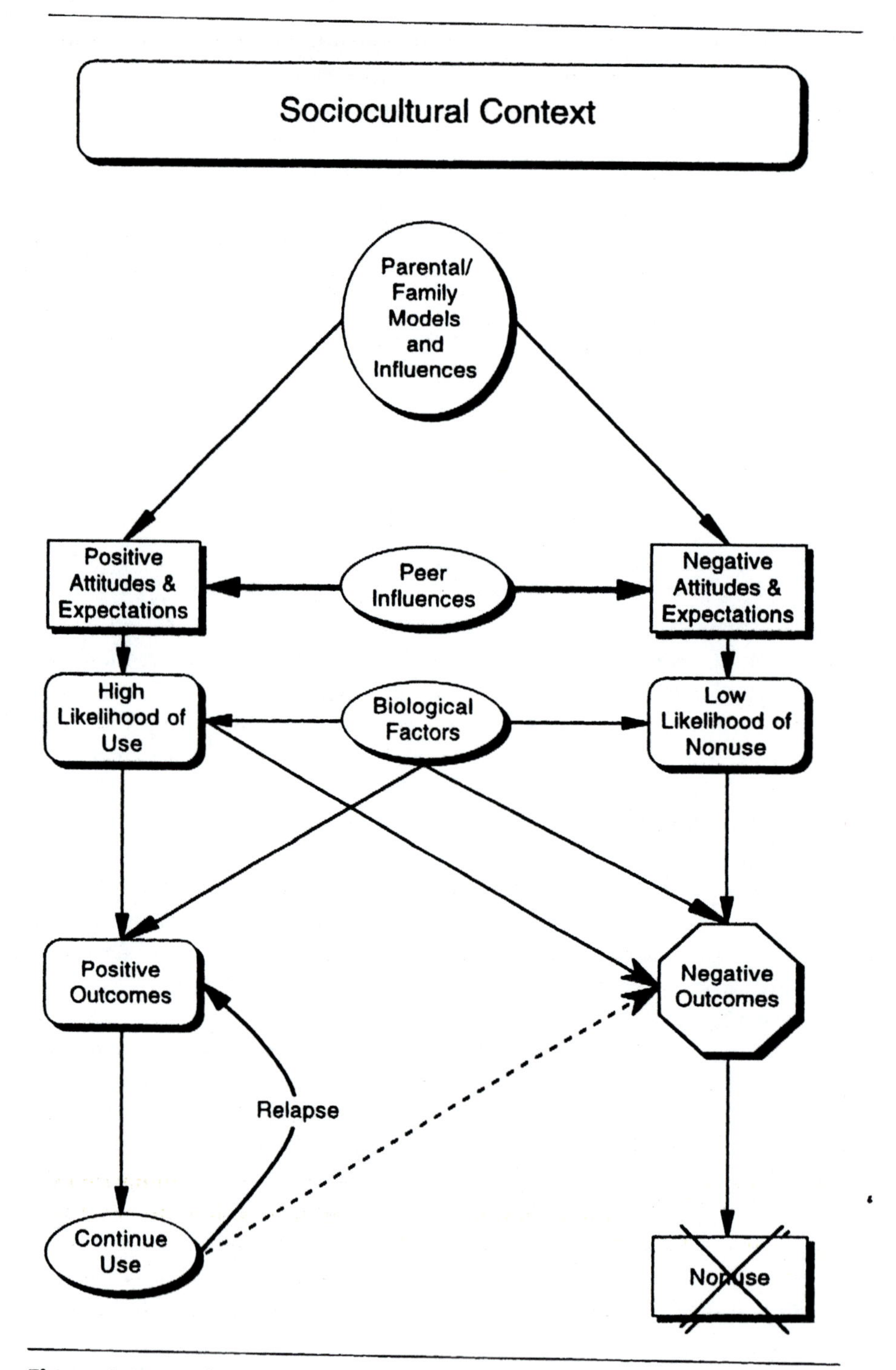

Figure 6.1. Multiple Factors Lead to the Initiation and Subsequent Levels of Alcohol Use, Cessation, and Resumption

to some combination of curiosity, rebellion against authority, and peer influence. For many adolescents, the attractive promise of rewarding and exciting experiences from experimenting with alcohol and drugs will exceed the threat of physical, social, and, in some cases, legal costs. Despite the risks associated with the use of many drugs, powerful psychosocial factors lead to the initial use of alcohol and other drugs.

For some adolescents, the initial foray into drinking, smoking, and doing drugs may be short-lived. Once the curiosity is satisfied, they may not find the rewards of drugs fulfilling. Some may quit, and others may use intermittently without any apparent problems. On the other hand, depending on the specific drug, continued and often increased use will contribute to problems in many areas, including physical, academic, social, and even legal matters. Moreover, use may become "addictive" for some who find they cannot stop or break their dependency on specific drugs.

Biological Factors

If the attitudes and expectations we acquire are positive toward the use of alcohol and other drugs, physiological reactions come into play because those with favorable attitudes will begin to use these substances (see Figure 6.1). Some biological characteristics, probably inherited, may heighten the likelihood of alcohol and other drug problems, at least for males (Tarter, Alterman, & Edwards, 1985). Temperamental factors such as activity level (high), attention span (short), and sociability (high) are associated with a greater likelihood of alcohol problems among males. A neuropsychological model of differences in biological vulnerability (Tarter et al., 1990) has attempted to account for higher risk for alcoholism, at least for early-onset heavy-drinking males with antisocial tendencies. It assumes that alcohol may be inherently more reinforcing for individuals with certain biologically based temperaments that affect their sensitivity to alcohol and other drugs. Figure 6.1 suggests that these positive outcomes should promote continued and possible increased use for these individuals, but negative consequences for others should lead to reduced or discontinued use.

Vulnerability models (Sher, 1991; Sher et al., 1991) also emphasize individual differences in temperament or biological sensitivity to stimulation. In the *enhanced reinforcement model,* innate dispositions of *greater* sensitivity to drugs increase the likelihood that alcohol and other drugs will function as a reinforcer in reducing stress, especially for individuals who have not acquired good psychological coping skills.

In addition, there may be lower sensitivity to intoxication, also attributed to biological differences. Drinking problems could develop because higher alcohol tolerance and lower sensitivity to intoxication allow these individuals to drink to higher levels before they obtain the desired reinforcing effects of alcohol.

The *negative affect model* concentrates on negative feelings that may lead to alcohol and drug use as a form of self-medication. Temperamental factors favoring depression or anxiety, combined with stressful life events and poor coping skills, facilitate the onset of drug abuse.

A generalized vulnerability to drug dependence may exist such that different types of drugs may not represent discrete entities (Tarter, Moss, Arria, Mezzich, & Vanyukov, 1992). Although the neuropharmacological properties of different psychoactive drugs may affect the rate at which dependence develops, the types of individuals who prefer one drug over another are not fundamentally different in any neurophysiological sense. Cultural factors, social norms, and prevailing social policies governing the legal status of different drugs ultimately may determine who uses which drugs.

Consistent with this view is the general finding that most psychoactive drugs affect the release of neurotransmitters (described in Chapter 4) that underlie reward such as dopamine, serotonin, glutamate, and acetylcholine. When deficits in brain neurochemistry associated with reward exist, there may be greater susceptibility for the use and eventual dependence or addiction to many drugs such as alcohol, cocaine, and opiates (Blum et al., 1995). Lack of these reward neurotransmitters activates a cascade of events involving self-sustained craving for drugs that can compensate by activating dopamine release.

In experiments in which amino acid precursors were administered to alcoholics to stimulate release of higher levels of dopamine and serotonin, there was less craving, faster recovery, and lower relapse (Blum, Briggs, & Trachtenberg, 1989).

Social Factors

Most adolescents have learned the same general information about the potential positive and negative effects of alcohol and many other drugs. But wide individual differences in alcohol and drug use nonetheless exist, so it is apparent that other factors must be involved.

Social factors also may influence the variation among adolescents in their drug use. Adolescents differ in the crowds with whom they hang out. For example, with a drug such as alcohol, which is legal (for adults), adolescents who hang around heavier and earlier drinkers differ in many ways from those who associate with lighter drinkers. Academically successful students are less likely to drink as much because it interferes with a valued successful activity. Some adolescents with poor academic achievement or values will drink to cope with this failure; in addition, adolescents who drink excessively probably will harm their academic achievement eventually. Those with weak bonds and low commitment to mainstream societal values will be more likely to be alienated from society and model their behavior after models who engage in frequent and heavy drinking.

Peer Cluster Theory. The peer cluster theory (Oetting & Beauvais, 1987) considers the central role of peers as influences on drug use. Low socioeconomic level, for example, may be associated with environmental conditions that favor choice of peers who engage in drug use; psychological variables such as low self-confidence or poor school performance also may lead to increased association with peers who are involved with deviant behaviors, including drug use.

Are the peers the cause of drug use or vice versa? Explanations for adolescent drug use based on peer influence such as the peer cluster model hold that drug-using peers influence or socialize other adolescents into using drugs. In contrast, another explanation for the same evidence is that peers share similar levels of drug use. A process of **peer selection** (Farrell, 1994) suggests that adolescents who already use drugs seek out or prefer the company of other adolescents who share their involvement with drugs. Those who disdain drugs will tend to choose as friends other non-drug-using adolescents. Thus, drug-using peers do not determine the drug involvement level because there is a tendency for "birds of a feather" to flock together.

Social Development Model. Weak bonds to parents, teachers, family, and conventional role models contribute to drug use in the social development model (Hawkins & Weis, 1985). Poor home and school reinforcements may be linked to lack of academic skills and interpersonal skill. Adolescents with poor family life might find alcohol and other drugs a means of coping with the family and parental conflict they face at home. Thus, nonconforming, rebellious, and alienated youth are more likely to use drugs.

Family Interaction Theory. The family interaction theory (Brook, Brook, Gordon, Whiteman, & Cohen, 1990) proposes that adolescents who have good attachment to parents, affectionate parents, and conventional values experiment less with substance use and have fewer associations with peers who use alcohol and drugs. Adolescents with warm ties to their families might jeopardize these relationships if they use drugs excessively. Maternal control and maternal psychological adjustment minimize the involvement with deviant activities such as drug use.

Social Learning Theory. Parents may influence their children's drinking through both direct modeling of alcohol use (Bandura, 1977) and the transmission of parental values about drinking (Bank et al., 1985; Kandel

& Andrews, 1987). In support of this view, similarities in the drinking patterns of parents and their adult children have been found in studies with general population samples (Barnes & Welte, 1990; Dawson et al., 1992) as well as with smaller clinical samples (Orford & Velleman, 1991; Penick et al., 1987). Parents who drink heavily have children who also develop more frequent and heavier patterns of alcohol use. However, studies with nonclinical samples of college students (Engs, 1990; Wright & Heppner, 1991, 1993) found no relationship between the drinking of parents and their college-age children.

The effect of each parent's drinking may vary with the gender of the child (Thompson & Wilsnack, 1987). Hence, the degree of similarity of drinking between parent and child may depend on whether one is comparing a parent and child of the same as opposed to opposite sex. Views on sex role identification as diverse as psychoanalytic and social learning theory (Baldwin, 1967) predict that the same-sex parent should have greater influence than the opposite-sex parent does on a child. Consistent with this view, fathers' drinking—as well as mothers' drinking, to a lesser degree—was found to be moderately predictive of sons' drinking but was not as predictive of daughters' drinking among adolescents (Wilks et al., 1989) and for college student samples (Jung, 1995). However, in most of these studies of parent-child drinking similarity, the parent-child interpersonal relationships are not examined.

In addition to attitudes and behavior related to specific drugs, general intrapersonal development may influence individual differences in drug use. Self-esteem, social interaction skills, and coping skills play important roles in determining the extent to which drug abuse occurs. Similarly, the family interaction theory (Brook et al., 1990) also recognizes that adolescents with low achievement orientation, depression, low self-esteem, rebelliousness, and poor impulse control, for example, are more apt to engage in experimentation with drugs.

All of the above factors interact to determine the vulnerability of individuals to initiating use and experimenting with alcohol and other licit drugs, but they do not account for why some use only legal drugs and others develop abuse of and dependency on drugs, licit or illicit. The lack of understanding of these differences is partly because most past research has not clearly differentiated between use and abuse (Glantz, 1992). Many studies rely on quantity and frequency measures of consumption to define use and assume these indices also are reflective of abuse or dependency. This assumption is misleading because the correlation of these indices of use with clinical diagnoses of abuse or dependency is not high. Use of clinical diagnoses is needed to identify abuse and dependency.

ILLICIT DRUGS AND DEVIANCE

Social norms encourage most people to at least experiment with or dabble in the use of licit drugs, but this same factor would seemingly minimize the use of illicit drugs. Potential users of illicit drugs might assume that because they are banned, they must be more dangerous and hence to be avoided. In addition, the fear of being caught and either fined or imprisoned is a strong disincentive for using illicit drugs. Nonetheless, a sizable minority does take these risks, and it is important to identify factors that increase vulnerability to illicit drugs.

Biological Factors

Premorbid psychiatric problems have been found to be associated with alcohol and drug problems (Alterman et al., 1998; Tarter et al., 1990). This is the case for both licit and illicit drugs but higher for illicit drugs. Thus, those who abuse and are dependent on illicit drug have high rates of personality disorders such as depression and antisocial personality. They may be using drugs to self-medicate their psychiatric problems. In turn, the psychiatric problem might be exacerbated by the drug abuse.

Individuals who have undercontrol of emotion, high activity, impulsivity, and impaired behavioral self-regulation are at higher risk for drug abuse (Tarter & Edwards, 1988). Other research shows that greater emotional distress and anxiety, coping problems, poor bonding, and low social support are associated with drug abuse (Kandel et al., 1997).

Social Psychological Factors

Biological factors may be important contributors but may be insufficient to explain illicit drug use. Someone with biological vulnerability may still be motivated to obey society's laws and avoid illegal substances. Social and psychological factors may be necessary to motivate the use of these drugs.

Problem Behavior Theory. An undercontrolled behavior style can lead to a set of adolescent problem behaviors involving deviance from social norms, only one of which is excessive use of alcohol and drugs. Problem behavior theory (Jessor & Jessor, 1977) holds that adolescents who experience problems such as deviant sexual activity or criminal behavior also participate in deviant alcohol and drug use.

Several categories of risk factors are postulated in the theory. Background or distal factors associated with increased risk of drug use include the extent to which adolescents are unattached to parents and too attached to peers who use drugs. Higher risk also exists if adolescents are alienated from conventional values and have low self-esteem and external locus of control. More drug use is also likely with adolescents who devalue academic achievement, have low academic expectations, seek independence from parents, and value involvement with drug-using peers. The most immediate or proximal factors associated with more risk of drug use are tolerance of deviant behaviors and beliefs that drug benefits outweigh their costs.

Regular drug users or those committed to an alcohol and drugs lifestyle are found to be higher than nonusers or less frequent users on dimensions such as rebellion, lack of conformity to traditional values, and other socially deviant or illegal behaviors (Jessor & Jessor, 1975). Alienation and distance from family, early sexual activity, and low involvement in school also are associated with the lifestyle of alcohol and drug abusers.

A summary of major factors leading to the use of illicit drugs is provided by a developmental model of vulnerability to drug use (Glantz, 1992). This formulation proposes that risk factors such as parental drug abuse or depressed mood increase the likelihood that a child will develop drug abuse. First, if abuse occurs during pregnancy, impulsivity, attention deficits, and aggressiveness may be more likely. These infants would be more difficult to handle so they may not develop good attachment with their caregivers, jeopardizing the quality of subsequent interactions between parents and the children.

In addition to any biologically based processes that may adversely affect the child, parental drug abuse may lead to child neglect or abuse. Finally, these parents also may serve as models for alcohol and other drug abuse for their young children. These factors may extend later to school adjustment and could interfere with learning. Children who do poorly in school may drop out or develop behavior problems. By adolescence, alienation, self-derogation, hostility, low self-esteem, and depression may have developed. Use and abuse of drugs may be a form of coping with these problems to reduce negative feelings.

On the other hand, protective factors such as high self-esteem or coping skills may reduce the possibility of illicit drug use. The multiple-risk and protective factors are not static components but evolve through interactions with environmental events over time.

Psychological Perspective

Now that we have examined developmental background factors, we turn to a psychological perspective. What functions do alcohol and drugs, licit or illicit, serve for the user?

SOCIAL LEARNING THEORY

Social learning theory (Bandura, 1977) is a cognitive view that emphasizes **expectancies** that we form about the effects of alcohol and other drugs. First, we learn social norms regarding how others use different drugs. We observe what situations permit which amounts of drug use as well as what kinds of effects typically occur with different use patterns. In addition, we learn what effects to expect the drugs to have on our behavior and experiences. Thus, beginning marijuana users have to "learn" how to identify the effects of the drug on them (Becker, 1963). Drugs do not have automatic, universal effects; the user must learn to recognize the physical and psychological effects of drug use.

Original expectations may be revised in line with each individual's actual experience, as determined by factors as varied as sensitivity and tolerance to a specific drug, amounts consumed, and the conditions or context of use. In one study, a user recalled the effects of his first cocaine experience:

> I was looking for bells to ring and stuff. I mean you hear so much about cocaine—cocaine this, cocaine that—so, you know, being ignorant of [what] its effects were, I thought that well, shit, it'd have to be something really spectacular. (Waldorf et al., 1991, p. 18)

First-time users of many drugs, including alcohol, nicotine, and marijuana, report getting nauseous and having to vomit, adding embarrassment to their disappointment. The cocaine user reported, "Later I felt I had to go to the bathroom to urinate."

More often than not, they suffer a letdown as the first experiences with a drug are often negative or at best neutral experiences. As the cocaine user lamented, "And all I felt was something going up my nose that had a slight bite to it and no noticeable change in my functions or anything."

We acquire much "knowledge" about the effects of alcohol and other drugs before we ever actually use a specific drug. Such knowledge is by no means a guarantee that we will use drugs, and for those who do use, it is only one of the many factors contributing to outcomes.

In addition to holding these expectancies about drug use, social learning theory also proposes that we form beliefs about our **self-efficacy**, the extent to which we perceive ourselves to be competent to cope with or control outcomes on tasks. This subjective evaluation can be determined by factors such as the past history of success and failure in specific situations and the reactions of others to our behavior. Affective or mood states can distort this perception, with self-efficacy being enhanced by positive affect and lowered by negative affect.

Social learning theory also recognizes the interaction of cognitive and affective states. If we believe that alcohol or drugs can reduce negative affect, we might try to "drink our troubles away" when we are depressed or anxious. Or at a party where one hopes to experience positive affect, if our expectations are that drinking, smoking, or doing drugs will lower inhibitions and create positive affective states, we will be more likely to engage in these activities.

The relationship of coping skills to drug use also is considered by social learning theory. Individuals who have adequate coping skills and high self-esteem are able to drink at socially acceptable levels and to develop friendships with others who also avoid alcohol abuse. In contrast, those who will probably develop into problem drinkers and alcoholics are those with poor coping skills in general for dealing with life problems. Consequently, they may turn to alcohol and drugs to reduce tension, escape from problems, and feel better. But such excessive drug use will only serve to isolate them from those with drug use levels acceptable in society. Eventually, they will affiliate increasingly with similar drug abusers, and they will mutually reinforce this lifestyle, so that a reciprocal influence exists among members of this group.

Beliefs and Expectancies

Expectancies and beliefs about the effects of alcohol use held by college students fall into six categories on the Alcohol Expectancy Questionnaire (AEQ) (Brown, Goldman, Inn, & Anderson, 1980). These factors are listed in Table 6.1.

The AEQ scale did not assess effects of different dose levels, a factor that should affect expectations. Furthermore, the scale measures only generalized expectancies because the specific situation or context of the drinking is not specified on the instrument.

TABLE 6.1 Summary of expectations for alcohol, marijuana, and cocaine use

Six Alcohol Expectancies	*Six Marijuana Expectancies*	*Five Cocaine Expectancies*
Global positive transforming effect	Cognitive and behavioral impairment	Global positive effects
Social/physical	Relaxation and tension reduction	Global negative effects
Sexual enhancement	Social and sexual facilitation	Generalized arousal
Arousal/power/ aggression	Perceptual and cognitive enhancement	Anxiety
Increased social assertiveness	Global negative effects	Relaxation and tension reduction
Relaxation/tension reduction	Craving and physical effects	

Processes Underlying Expectancy Effects

What is the nature of the underlying mechanisms by which expectancy can actually evoke physical or psychological responses? A strictly pharmacological basis might involve classical conditioning. Thus, we form an association between drug use and certain effects. In the future, the mere belief that one has consumed a specific drug may elicit effects similar to those originally produced by that drug.

After drugs are consumed, original expectancies will be either confirmed or revised, if experiences disconfirm expectancies. Expectancy of social facilitation and actual drinking experience influenced each other in a reciprocal fashion for adolescents over a 2-year period during which many first began to drink (Smith, Goldman, Greenbaum, & Christiansen, 1995). Higher expectancy of social facilitation from alcohol was related to higher subsequent drinking levels. In addition, the higher the drinking levels, the greater the expectancy for subsequent social facilitation. Initial social expectancies of nondrinkers predicted individual differences in the rate of increase of alcohol use over the 2 years.

Expectancies for other drugs are similar to those for alcohol, as illustrated in Table 6.1, which compares the factors identified on the AEQ with those from the Marijuana Effects Expectancy Questionnaire and the

Cocaine Effects Expectancy Questionnaire, developed from self-reports of 704 college students (Schafer & Brown, 1991). Nonusers and users with varying degrees of use of marijuana and cocaine differed in their drug effect expectancies.

Self-reported global positive scores for initial use of marijuana were correlated with shorter latency to next use and with higher lifetime use of the drug by college students, suggesting that abuse potential of marijuana is related to the magnitude of initial positive effect (Davidson & Schenk, 1994). Global negative scores for initial use did not correlate with either measure of future use. A study that examined these responses to cocaine (Davidson, Finch, & Schenk, 1993) showed that subsequent cocaine use also was related to the magnitude of the positive response to first use.

Negative Expectancies

One limitation of the AEQ is that it examines only positive expectancies. *Negative* expectancies about alcohol effects also should be tested as predictors of alcohol use (McMahon & Jones, 1994). Some negative expectations may have weaker effects because they involve distal or delayed consequences—for example, hangovers that may not occur until the morning after drinking. Heavier drinkers expected less impairment but more nastiness and disinhibition from drinking than did lighter drinkers (Leigh, 1987a).

Dose Effects

Dose level is an important determinant of expectancies. For alcohol, moderate doses were associated with expectations of pleasurable disinhibition, whereas higher doses were expected to impair behavior (Southwick, Steele, Marlatt, & Lindell, 1981). Many studies have shown only a modest positive correlation between the magnitude of alcohol expectancies and the extent of drinking, with quantity having a stronger effect than frequency of drinking (Leigh, 1987b).

Heavy Versus Light Drinkers. Drinkers who differ in their typical dose should have different expectancies because they differ in the conditions that prompt them to begin their drinking episodes and in the consequences of their drinking (Southwick & Steele, 1987). The typical light drinker is in a positive mood when drug use starts. The drinking might take place at a party or celebration where a festive mood prevails, and the alcohol is intended to enhance the good time already existing. This mood, coupled with alcohol's ability initially to enhance mood, accentuates the positive affect. After alcohol use ends, negative affect occurs, but it is offset by the positive affect experienced in Phase 1, so there is a gradual decline to a state of neutral or mildly negative feeling. In short, a restoration of balanced emotions occurs.

In contrast, heavy drinkers more often drink when they are in a negative mood already. They may be depressed, lonely, or angry, and they seek drug use to improve their mood. In Phase 1, alcohol may work to counter the negative moods they start out with. A few extra-strong drinks gulped down quickly may give a momentary positive lift. However, in Phase 2, after drinking ends and the effects wear off, negative feelings and fatigue arise. These conditions are apt to prompt drinking episodes in the near future, which repeat the cycle just described with increasing frequency and severity.

Students with higher alcohol consumption levels and more alcohol-related problems have more positive alcohol expectancies, have lower self-efficacy, and cope with avoidant, emotion-focused strategies (Evans & Dunn, 1995). Heavier drinkers, not surprisingly, may believe that adverse drinking effects are less likely than do lighter drinkers. In part, this leniency could be a self-serving rationalization for their behavior, but it might be that heavier drinkers have adapted to heavy use and actually experience less negative impact from their drinking.

In summary, correlations between the use of alcohol and drugs by peers suggest that adolescents imitate drug use of peer models. Consistent with social learning theory, adolescents' own drug use gets reinforced socially by fitting in with the use levels of peers. However, social learning theory is unclear as to why some adolescents choose one type of role model but others choose different ones. Theories emphasizing cognitive factors also do not adequately distinguish between causes and effects of adolescent drug attitudes and behaviors. Drug beliefs might not be *causes* of adolescent drug use, but instead they could be indirect *effects* of their own drug use.

In addition, the situation in which the drug use takes place can modify expectancies. Thus, drug use at a party might be expected to enhance good times, whereas drug use in the classroom might be expected to lead to a number of negative consequences.

Because most expectancy studies are cross sectional in design, they are inconclusive as to questions of causality. Thus, it is possible that the expectancies are the effect, not the cause, of drug use. Longitudinal studies in which the expectancies are measured first and correlated with later drug use help answer this question. Findings in one such study (Bauman,

Fisher, Bryan, & Chenoweth, 1985) support the view that expectancies and alcohol use are related in a complex reciprocal manner, with initial expectancies determining alcohol use, drinking outcomes then modifying those expectancies, and so on.

EXCUSE THEORY

Not uncommonly, when people drink, they attribute some of their behavior to the effects of drinking, especially if they might otherwise be blamed or criticized for any misconduct while drinking. Being under the influence of some drugs such as alcohol is widely accepted by others as a social excuse (MacAndrew & Edgerton, 1969). Similarly, users of other drugs may use such practices to excuse any socially unacceptable behaviors. However, it is possible that illicit drug use may be less acceptable as an excuse.

This excuse mechanism was invoked more frequently for deviant social behaviors such as some forms of aggression or sexual misconduct but less often for nonsocial activities such as mood or memory, for example, when there might be less need for an excuse (Hull & Bond, 1986).

SELF-HANDICAPPING THEORY

Making excuses *prior* to an anticipated shortcoming is a strategy to protect self-esteem, but it can handicap one's performance. Excessive use of alcohol or other drugs may often precede situations when one expects failure or when past success creates anxiety about the likelihood of continued achievement. One test of the self-handicapping theory of drug use (Berglas & Jones, 1978) compared anagram task performance. One group did not know that the anagrams they received had no solutions, but they were told they had "succeeded" on some of the problems. Another group succeeded on anagrams that did have solutions. It was predicted that the group with the unsolvable problems, some of which they apparently "solved," would experience more uncertainty about future performance and have a greater threat to self-esteem when given a second similar task.

Prior to the second anagram task, participants were offered a drug that would supposedly either impair or improve performance (no drug was actually given because the experiment ended after the choice was made). The group with unsolvable problems chose the "harmful" drug more than the group with the solvable problems. By choosing the performance-impairing drug, the group with the inexplicable success on the first task provided themselves with a self-handicap or excuse for the poor performance that they expected would occur on the second task.

SELF-AWARENESS REDUCTION THEORY

A popular conception about alcohol and drug use, often expressed in the lyrics of popular romantic songs, is that it can help one escape or forget troubles. The self-awareness reduction model (Hull, 1987) proposed that alcohol and drug use can impair cognitive processes and hence reduce awareness about one's own situation. It is presumed that drug use interferes with storing new information by disrupting organizational strategies.

In one experiment (Hull, Levenson, Young, & Sher, 1983), participants under a moderate dose of an alcohol or placebo beverage gave speeches about their physical self-perceptions. Self-relevant pronouns such as *I, me, myself, my,* and *mine* were made less frequently in the alcohol condition, suggesting a lowering of self-awareness due to alcohol consumption.

Lowered self-awareness created by alcohol's impairment of cognitive processing may give drinkers an excuse for violating social norms. By reducing self-awareness, alcohol also could reduce compliance with one's typical standards of appropriate behavior.

TENSION REDUCTION HYPOTHESIS

A widely held view of why people use some types of drugs is to relieve stress. According to the tension reduction hypothesis, people use drugs to try to relieve tension and anxiety. When tension is unpleasantly high, people may drink or smoke, expecting that the drug use will lower the tension. If this expectation is upheld, their tendency to resort to these drugs in the future to cope with tension should be increased by this reinforcing experience.

Tension Reduction as an Effect of Drug Use

According to Clark Hull's (1943) learning theory, any response that reduces drive states such as hunger, thirst, or anxiety becomes reinforced. The next time an individual is in a similar situation, he or she will be more likely to perform the same response that was previously successful in lowering the drive state.

However, drinking might increase rather than lower tension in some situations. In the case of alcoholics in treatment who may or may not want to stop alcohol use, the therapists' reminders of the adverse effects of drinking might increase the likelihood that their subsequent alcohol use would increase tension. In contrast, alcohol use might lower tension at a social gathering where most drinkers seek enjoyment.

Finally, alcohol effects are biphasic, leading only initially to tension reduction and positive affective feelings such as relief and pleasure (Southwick et al., 1981). This positive state might continue and rise to a peak as heavier doses are taken as the blood alcohol content from a given dose increases over time. With further passage of time, however, the tension may reverse and start to increase along with negative affective feelings of discomfort and anxiety, reaching a peak and then returning to a state of neutrality (Martin, Earleywine, Musty, Perrine, & Swift, 1993). Thus, drug use can produce both positive and negative affective states, with the dose level and temporal factors being important determinants of the outcome.

Tension as a Cause of Drug Use

Stress and tension actually may cause some forms of drug use. If people believe drug use reduces tension, even if it does not directly do so, stress might motivate drug use.

In laboratory studies, participants may be suspicious of receiving drugs in such a setting and respond differently from the way they normally would. For this reason, a taste-rating task is used in some studies (Marlatt, Kosturn, & Lang, 1975) to hide the true purpose of administering alcohol. Participants are led to believe that they are sampling different wines to assess their taste preferences; in actuality, the goal is to see if participants sample more alcohol when there is higher stress induced by the experimental task. In one study, although none of the participants actually received shock, one group of males was told that they would later encounter painful shock to see how it affected taste reactions, whereas another group of males was told they would receive mild shock for the same purpose. The high-fear condition should lead to more alcohol consumption if it relieved tension. However, no such effect was found with either social drinkers or a group of male alcoholics.

When stress is present, alcohol use may often actually be inhibited, but after the stress is over, drug use may increase (Volpicelli, 1987). For example, male social drinkers worked unsolvable anagrams but received false feedback that their performance was either among the top 15% or the bottom 15% of participants (Pihl & Yankofsky, 1979).

Alcohol use decreased after the feedback for those given stressful negative feedback, suggesting that the presence of tension did not facilitate drinking. For those receiving positive feedback that relieved stress, increased drinking occurred.

A study of the stress-alcohol relationship with a random sample of 1,316 Black and White drinkers showed that coping styles and their expectancy beliefs about drug use were important factors on this relationship for men (Cooper, Russell, Skinner, Frone, & Mudar, 1992). Both higher alcohol use and alcohol problems were related to stress among men who relied on avoidant forms of coping or held strong positive expectancies for alcohol's effects. In contrast, stressors were negatively related to alcohol use among men who were low in both avoidant coping and in positive alcohol expectancies.

Use of alcohol and other drugs, of course, is not the only possible response available in many situations for relieving tension. If other responses such as exercise and recreational social activities are available that can lower the tension, drug use may not be necessary. Furthermore, tension reduction may not be the primary motive for drug use. In fact, when the tired worker comes home and has a drink or two, it probably creates physiological arousal but is paradoxically interpreted as "relaxation" instead of as excitation. Instead, feelings of power and control rather than tension reduction may be important reasons for drug use.

Situations in which no alternatives for coping with tension exist may increase the chance that drugs will be used in hopes of producing a feeling of power. Ironically, excessive drug use may produce adverse consequences that eventually increase rather than lower tension. In contrast, if there are other alternatives for reducing tension, the likelihood of drug use may be lower.

STRESS RESPONSE DAMPENING THEORY

Stress is a determinant of drug use but not a necessary or sufficient one (Sher & Levenson, 1982). The stress response dampening model focuses on the pharmacological effects of drug use. It assumes that there is a complex psychophysiological response to drug use, especially due to factors such as individual differences and social context. In this model, cognitive factors such as expectancies are not as important as psychophysiological factors are.

The stress response dampening theory (Sher, 1987) is a pared-down version of the tension reduction hypothesis discussed earlier. Drug use typically dampens or *reduces* stress, especially cardiovascular reactions, so that drug consumption is reinforcing because it moderates the physical reaction to stress.

Effects on Psychophysiological Indices

Many studies have shown that alcohol use reduces heart rate response levels (Cummings & Marlatt, 1983; Sher & Levenson, 1982), whereas the evidence about its effect on electrodermal indices of stress such as the galvanic skin response is less consistent (Cummings & Marlatt, 1983; Sher & Levenson, 1982). This pattern suggests that alcohol does not have a generalized dampening effect but acts selectively on cardiovascular responses.

Moderators of Stress Dampening Effects

One determinant of whether drugs dampen stress is the amount of drug consumed. To reduce cardiovascular responding levels, high doses of alcohol equivalent to four or five drinks within an hour (e.g., .75 to 1 g/kg) are typically needed.

The type of stressor, physical versus psychological, is also a factor that determines the effect of drugs. Most people do not use drugs to reduce all types of stresses because they realize that they would only add to stress in some situations (e.g., drug use at the office). Instead, they may selectively use drugs for only those stressors that they believe will be alleviated by drug use.

Overview of Theories of Alcohol Use

With so many theoretical approaches, it may be useful to briefly summarize different theories of the use of alcohol. Formulations focus on different aspects of the function served by drinking and the extent to which cognitive and conscious processes seem to be involved. Figure 6.2 suggests that some theories, such as social learning, view drinking as involving a cognitive decision, whereas others, such as stress response dampening, see it as more involuntary and governed by the effects of drinking on affective states and emotions. Theories also differ in whether the drinking primarily serves avoidance or escape from unpleasant states or positive or pleasurable outcomes. Self-awareness reduction and excuse theories emphasize drinking to get away from negative situations. Sometimes, as in self-handicapping theory, this strategy can backfire and make matters worse. As for hedonistic and pleasure-oriented motives for drinking, psy-

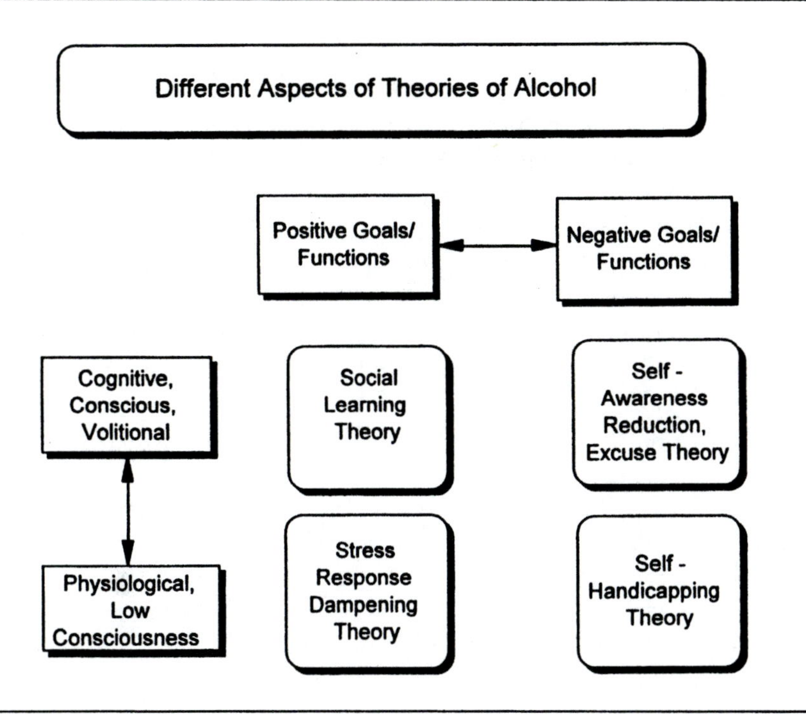

Figure 6.2. Comparison of Theories of Alcohol Use Along the Dimensions of Conscious Control and Positive Versus Negative Functions

chological theories have been remiss and concentrated on negative situations. Although social learning theory does not focus on drinking for pleasure, it can be applied to such motivations.

Theories of Smoking

Although many aspects of theories applying to alcohol and many other drugs pertain to smoking, they do not adequately explain some distinct aspects of smoking. Cigarette smoking occurs periodically throughout the day every day for the dependent smoker, unlike the use of most other drugs. For example, most drinkers, except for highly dependent drinkers, do not drink every day or throughout the course of each day. Furthermore, due to the rapid process by which inhaled smoke carries the nicotine directly to the brain, the impact is much quicker than the effect of alcohol, which must first be absorbed from the gastrointestinal tract into the bloodstream before it can reach the brain.

NICOTINE REGULATION

A pharmacological theory of smoking, the **nicotine regulation** model (Jarvik, 1979), proposes that smokers use cigarettes in a pattern that attempts to maintain a preferred level of **nicotine** in the body. One indication of the importance of nicotine level is that habitual smokers typically need a cigarette to begin the day because their nicotine level from the last cigarette before falling asleep has dropped to an uncomfortably low level during sleep.

A more scientific approach is to conduct an experiment to vary the nicotine level in cigarettes. Smokers, without their knowledge that the cigarettes they received varied in nicotine level, were observed in one study (Schachter et al., 1977). As expected, they inhaled more with low-nicotine cigarettes than they did with regular-strength cigarettes to try to increase the intake of nicotine, even though the cigarettes looked the same.

Another prediction based on this theory is that nicotine replacement therapy with nicotine gum or patch should effectively stop smoking. However, the fact that this approach is not entirely successful points out the need to consider the necessity of additional factors for the maintenance of smoking.

Physical Sensations

The importance of taste as a factor in smoking that is promoted in cigarette ads is probably more a belief than a reality. Smokers show poor taste discrimination among different brands, although taste could be just one of many factors that contributes to the total motivation.

Many smokers enjoy the sensation of blowing smoke out through the mouth and nostrils. Smoke passing through airways might provide airway tract stimulation that reinforces smoking. To test this possibility, one study (Rose, 1988) had participants gargle either lidocaine (a local anesthetic) or saline before smoking. If the tactile sensation of smoke itself is important, then anesthetizing the air passages should make a difference on craving after smoking. Although the amount of nicotine was the same in the two conditions, the lidocaine condition produced more craving. This evidence suggested that smoking is affected, for the short term at least, by the feeling of smoke in the throat. Even though nicotine received in other ways that do not involve smoking (such as chewing) also can be addictive, it may be that the airway sensations from smoking give an extra reward to smokers.

AROUSAL AND SMOKING

Heightened general activation may help explain why smokers try to achieve desired levels of nicotine. Because nicotine is a stimulant, cigarette smoking increases arousal. Although task performance improves with generalized states of arousal up to a point, arousal theory predicts that with very high arousal, competing responses interfere and performance declines, especially on complex tasks.

Instead of viewing arousal as a generalized nonspecific state that affects all processes similarly, it may be more useful to determine how nicotine intake affects specific major neurotransmitters. A two-factor theory (Kassel, 1997) proposes that nicotine acts on *cholinergic* paths to narrow the available cues but also acts on *norepinephrine* in an area of the brain, the *locus coeruleus,* to increase processing capacity and stimulus-processing resources.

MOOD REGULATION AND SMOKING

At the psychological level, mood states play an important role on smoking. Several types of affect may be involved (Tomkins, 1966), with some smokers motivated to smoke for positive affect or pleasure, whereas others are driven to smoke to relieve negative affective states or tension.

Tension reduction or relaxation is a frequent reason smokers give for using cigarettes. This psychological effect seems somewhat paradoxical because it appears to contradict the pharmacological activation created by nicotine. Thus, during breaks from work, employees smoke, presumably to relieve stress. And although nothing might completely relax prisoners who are facing execution, it is a customary act of compassion to offer them a last cigarette before they are executed. Similarly, wounded and dying soldiers on the battlefield are often allowed cigarettes to comfort them.

JOINT ROLE OF PHARMACOLOGICAL AND PSYCHOLOGICAL PROCESSES

A **multiple-regulation model** (Leventhal & McCleary, 1980) acknowledges the role of nicotine regulation as a physical basis for smoking, but it also argues that a parallel psychological process is needed for a more complete theory. This model assumes that the emotional affect activated by nicotine can be conditioned to external cues associated with smoking.

Over time, this psychological factor becomes more critical than the pharmacological factor as the prevailing determinant of smoking.

Under this model, experienced smokers do not consciously smoke to regulate or achieve desired levels of nicotine so much as they strive to modulate emotional states related to past smoking. These affective states originated as conditioned responses to nicotine levels and the bodily feelings generated when smoking occurred in the past. Subsequent smoking, of course, does actually affect nicotine levels, but the mind of the smoker is focused on achieving the emotional, not the pharmacological, states. For example, when smoking occurs, increased arousal from the nicotine occurs, which becomes conditioned to the situation in which smoking occurred. If it is a fearful or anxiety-producing situation, smoking becomes a conditioned response to these negative emotions. Similarly, if the smoking occurs in a joyful and positive situation, the activation from the nicotine becomes conditioned to these positive emotions. Subsequently, when these emotions are aroused, they may trigger the urge to smoke. Smoking itself also may activate these emotions as well. When experienced smokers are unable to smoke, they typically suffer unpleasant withdrawal reactions. This negative affect can become conditioned to those situations in which smoking is not allowed to occur.

Biphasic Effects

It appears that nicotine can produce opposing effects, depending on the circumstances under which smoking occurs. One way to reconcile this apparent contradiction is to view nicotine as a modulator or reducer of existing prior moods, acting to increase arousal for individuals who are depressed or tired while decreasing arousal for those who are tense and anxious. Smokers may cope with different situations by smoking cigarettes to change the prevailing mood toward moderate arousal levels. Other drugs such as cocaine may be sought to promote feelings of highs, whereas other drugs such as heroin are used to generate lows. But perhaps nicotine serves to generate moderation of existing feelings (Krogh, 1991).

Previous research has not paid much attention to mood states prior to smoking. In laboratory studies, the participants are typically in a neutral mood, and the smoking generates the same direction of mood change for everyone.

Absolute or Relative Arousal

Another difficulty with measuring the arousing effect of smoking is that dependent smokers, unlike new or light smokers, will experience negative mood states or withdrawal reactions after they have been abstinent for a short period. Consequently, when they resume smoking, they may experience only relative, rather than absolute, increases in arousal. The nicotine is only allowing them to recover from a depressed state of withdrawal to a "normal" or neutral state but is not producing any absolute gains in arousal. Thus, the addicted smoker still wants to smoke but experiences relief more than pleasure.

SUMMARY

Some theories about why people use psychoactive drugs focus on physiological factors, some on cognitive and affective experiences, and others on social determinants. All of these factors are important, and they can influence each other.

The initiation into alcohol and other drug use needs to be examined separately from the maintenance or escalation of use. Social and psychological factors play a more critical role than pharmacological factors in motivating initial use. After use becomes an established habit, biological vulnerability factors such as temperament may assume more importance in maintaining the behavior.

Expectations about the effects of psychoactive drug use can affect the physiological responses to drugs just as the emotional reactions can alter the cognitive processes occurring while drugs are being used. Social learning theory emphasizes cognitive factors such as the expectancies one has about drug use as determinants of actual drug use. Users learn from watching others and, from past experiences, what effects drug use can produce. They adjust their drug use according to their own needs and values. These expectancies exist for most people before their first actual use of a specific drug. Motivation for initial use can come from social models, peer influence, or sensation-seeking and risk-taking tendencies.

Excuse and self-handicapping theories are useful in explaining how socially learned strategies related to interpersonal interactions affect drug use. For anxiolytic (anxiety-reducing) or depressant drugs such as alcohol, barbiturates, and benzodiazepines, tension reduction and self-awareness reduction theories are relevant. They emphasize use of drugs for coping with stress. These theories also apply to opioids such as heroin and morphine, which often are used to achieve pain reduction.

Tension reduction theory assumes a direct, pharmacological influence of drug use such as relaxation, whereas self-awareness theory assumes an indirect process in which drug use reduces self-awareness of distressful situations.

Although users of some drugs may seek to reduce stress and self-awareness by drug use, sometimes the opposite effect actually may occur due to the impaired functioning and social criticism created by excessive drug use.

The stress response dampening theory focuses on the underlying physiological processes for drug use effects. Cardiovascular responses, in particular, and other physiologic stress reactions are dampened or reduced by drug use. Those for whom these effects occur should be more likely to drink to cope when under stress. This model focuses on how the physiological responses to drug use reduce stress.

Although many of these theories apply to smoking, it may be necessary to develop smoking-specific theories as well. The pattern of cigarette use is markedly different from that of most other drugs; in addition, there is no loss of control or intoxication with excessive use as with alcohol.

Theories that deal with legal drugs are inadequate to fully explain the use of illicit drugs. A theory of illicit drugs needs to explain why users engage in such activities at the additional risk of imprisonment and other strong social disincentives. Although there may be differences in biological vulnerability that increase the reinforcement received from illicit drugs, the potential user must first be sufficiently motivated to transgress societal norms and laws. A social psychological view of illicit drug use is that it is only one of several deviant behaviors engaged in by individuals who have become alienated from society. According to problem behavior theory, a general level of undercontrol by illicit drug users may set in motion a series of consequences that eventually produces many deviant behaviors, of which illicit drug use is only one.

KEY TERMS

Biphasic
Expectancies
Multiple-regulation model
Nicotine
Nicotine regulation
Peer selection
Protective factors
Risk factors
Self-efficacy
Vulnerability

STIMULUS/RESPONSE

1. Do you find that your use of alcohol or other drugs serves to relieve stress in some situations but not in others? Can you identify some of the conditions associated with each type of outcome for the same drug usage?
2. Because most drugs are off-limits to minors, curiosity may play a major role in the initial use of a specific drug. What approaches might be used to satisfy or reduce this curiosity? And if curiosity about a specific drug could be reduced safely, would it lower the risk of future problems with that drug?
3. One motivator for youth to use alcohol and other drugs may be to defy rules and prohibitions against their use. If this hypothesis were valid, if minors were not strictly prohibited from drinking, adult drinking problems would be reduced. Do you agree or disagree?
4. Many people say they drink for positive benefits such as relaxation or to be sociable, but to what extent is this recognized by theories of drinking discussed in this chapter?
5. From your personal experience, describe your expectations before the first time you used alcohol or any other drug. What unexpected experiences, positive or negative, did you encounter from the drug itself?

- Adolescents
- College Students
- Young Adults After College
- Older Populations
- Summary
- Key Terms
- Stimulus/Response

7 Age, Alcohol, and Other Drugs

The nature of alcohol and other drug use, abuse, and dependency changes over the course of life. When children move into adolescence, they want and are expected to become more independent. When adolescents first move out of the home, whether because they get a job and live on their own, drop out of high school, leave to attend college, join the military, or get married, they are no longer directly under the observation or control of their parents. Opportunities become available to engage in new activities, some of which their parents may have disapproved of, including use of many drugs. Not all adolescents will take this route, but for many others, the temptation can be irresistible and the peer pressure overwhelming.

Next, as individuals assume adult roles, they take on the responsibilities of jobs and careers. Most also enter marriage and possibly eventual parenthood. Consequently, many of them lessen the extent of their drug use, which might otherwise interfere with the fulfillment of obligations and commitments of these roles (Grant, Harford, & Grigson, 1988; Johnston, O'Malley, & Bachman, 1997).

At older ages, other role transitions occur. Some will divorce, others will experience widowhood, and some will enter new marriages. Retirement or reduced work may occur. Children grow up and leave the home. These transitions may affect drinking patterns. In addition, most suffer physical decline and increased health problems that may alter the effect of alcohol and drugs so that physical and behavioral impairment occurs with smaller amounts. Accordingly, some older drinkers may reduce their drinking to compensate.

Alcohol and other drug use must be studied across the life span if we are to control its impact on human behavior and experience. These findings can help identify and modify the antecedents and consequences of substance use patterns and problems. This chapter will first examine factors involved in alcohol and other drug use for different age groups. First, findings about alcohol and other drug use and problems among adolescents will be presented, followed by a similar analysis for college students. Finally, evidence on the nature of alcohol and other drug use and problems among older populations will be discussed.

Adolescents

Even before they are old enough to legally use drugs such as tobacco or alcohol, many adolescents will have experimented with these substances, and some may have developed problems from substance abuse and dependency. In addition, some will have sampled illicit drugs such as marijuana and, to a much lesser extent, cocaine and hallucinogens. The factors involved in the initiation into the use of legal drugs during early adolescence are of interest, especially because such behavior is associated with risks of increased future use as well as expansion into the use of other drugs. Moreover, drug use may lead eventually to numerous adverse consequences ranging from accidents to physical health ills to harm of others to fines and imprisonment.

Adolescence is a stage of development with rapid biological, physical, and psychological changes when young people learn the expectations and norms of the adult society into which they will soon be entering. This period involves discovery about oneself and the formation of values and goals. The process of identity development involves trying out different roles and encountering different experiences before deciding what behaviors best fit. This process occurs with respect to a variety of important concerns such as careers, marriage, and parenthood. Thus, adolescents typically date a variety of persons before entering marriage. They work at a variety of jobs to gain knowledge and experience before making commitments about careers.

A similar attitude of experimentation lies behind the initial use of alcohol and other drugs for many youths. Although drinking and smoking are legal activities for individuals age 21 and 18, respectively, in most states, the same behavior is prohibited for minors who are considered "too young" to use these drugs. The added incentives of challenging authority might add to the appeal of drinking and smoking for some younger adolescents. Doing what you are not supposed to do might be a way of impressing peers.

For underage adolescents, unlike for most adults, alcohol and other drugs are more limited in availability or accessibility due to economic and social factors. Thus, not using drugs may not be due to choice but to lack of opportunity. If adolescents cannot buy licit drugs because they are too young or because they do not have enough money, their drug use may be sporadic rather than continuous. Because their alcohol use is of relatively recent onset, dependency involving physical damage may be less likely to occur for adolescents than for older drinkers. Even when alcohol use involves harmful consequences, they often may be immediate and short in duration. In contrast, the physical toll on physical health from prolonged drug use over many years may occur mainly in older people.

Most adolescents, prior to having their first drink, already have acquired firm expectations about how alcohol alters behavior and feelings (Miller, Smith, & Goldman, 1990). They know that when adults are depressed or angry, they often consume more alcohol. Adolescents also recognize that adults also drink at social gatherings and parties to become less inhibited and to have more fun. Adolescents also have learned that drinking too much or too often ruins many lives and creates problems for others, but until they actually have used these drugs, adolescents do not know what the actual effects of drinking will be for them physically and psychologically.

Faced with this background, most young adolescents approach alcohol with curiosity and fascination as well as some fear and anxiety. Alcohol advertising and media images promise that drinking might make life more exciting, alleviate negative moods, and get approval from peers. On the other hand, they realize that there are costs and benefits to drinking. Drinking could be detrimental to academic, social, or athletic success. In addition, many parents and other adults might strongly disapprove of drinking by adolescents.

Although a minority of adolescents will abstain completely, sooner or later, most adolescents will at least "experiment" with alcohol and other drugs. Some will satisfy their curiosity quickly and discontinue use or use infrequently and in small amounts. However, others will increase their frequency of use as well as use higher amounts. A variety of personal and social problems may result from drug use, such as accidents, impaired work and school performance, physical health problems, and interpersonal conflicts and aggression. Adolescents may believe that because they are young and relatively healthy, they can use drugs without losing control over their use.

Similar processes may be involved for the experimental use of illicit drugs but for a much smaller percentage of adolescents (Johnston, O'Malley, & Bachman, 1997). The same blend of curiosity, conformity to

TABLE 7.1 Past month, year, and lifetime prevalence use rates for 8th, 10th, and 12th grades for any illicit drug, any illicit drug excluding marijuana, alcohol, and cigarettes in the 1995 Monitoring the Future survey

	8th Grade			*10th Grade*			*12th Grade*		
	30 Days	*12 Months*	*Lifetime*	*30 Days*	*12 Months*	*Lifetime*	*30 Days*	*12 Months*	*Lifetime*
Any illicit drug	12.4	21.4	28.5	20.2	33.3	40.9	23.8	39	48.4
Any illicit drug except marijuana	9.1	15.8	19.9	17.2	28.7	34.1	21.2	34.7	41.7
Alcohol	24.6	45.3	54.5	38.8	63.5	70.5	51.3	73.7	80.7
Cigarettes	19.1	NA	46.4	27.9	NA	57.6	33.5	NA	64.2

SOURCE: Johnston, O'Malley, and Bachman (1997).
NOTE: NA = not available.

peer pressure, and fear may be present, perhaps coupled with rebellion and defiance among some.

PREVALENCE OF ADOLESCENT ALCOHOL AND OTHER DRUG USE

Although it is illegal to drink alcohol under age 21, many underage adolescents do engage in drinking to some extent and have experimented with a variety of licit and illicit drugs. Table 7.1 shows that the 1995 use rates for licit and illicit drugs over the past month, year, and lifetime all increase with higher grade level. Such early age behaviors may affect subsequent alcohol and drug attitudes and consumption by young people.

Figure 7.1 presents the prevalence rates between 1979 and 1995 for the use of alcohol, cigarettes, any illicit drug, and marijuana during the past month by adolescents, ages 12 to 17. These data come from an annual national survey, Monitoring the Future (MTF), which has documented the extent to which high school students have used different drugs since 1975. After a peak in use rates in 1979, rates dropped over the 1980s but started to increase gradually during the 1990s, especially for marijuana and some other illicit drugs. In general, males are more likely to use all drugs than females are.

By the senior year, more than 80% of high school seniors surveyed in the MTF study of 1996 reported using alcohol at some time in their lives (Johnston, Wadsworth, et al., 1997). Use of alcohol *within the past month*

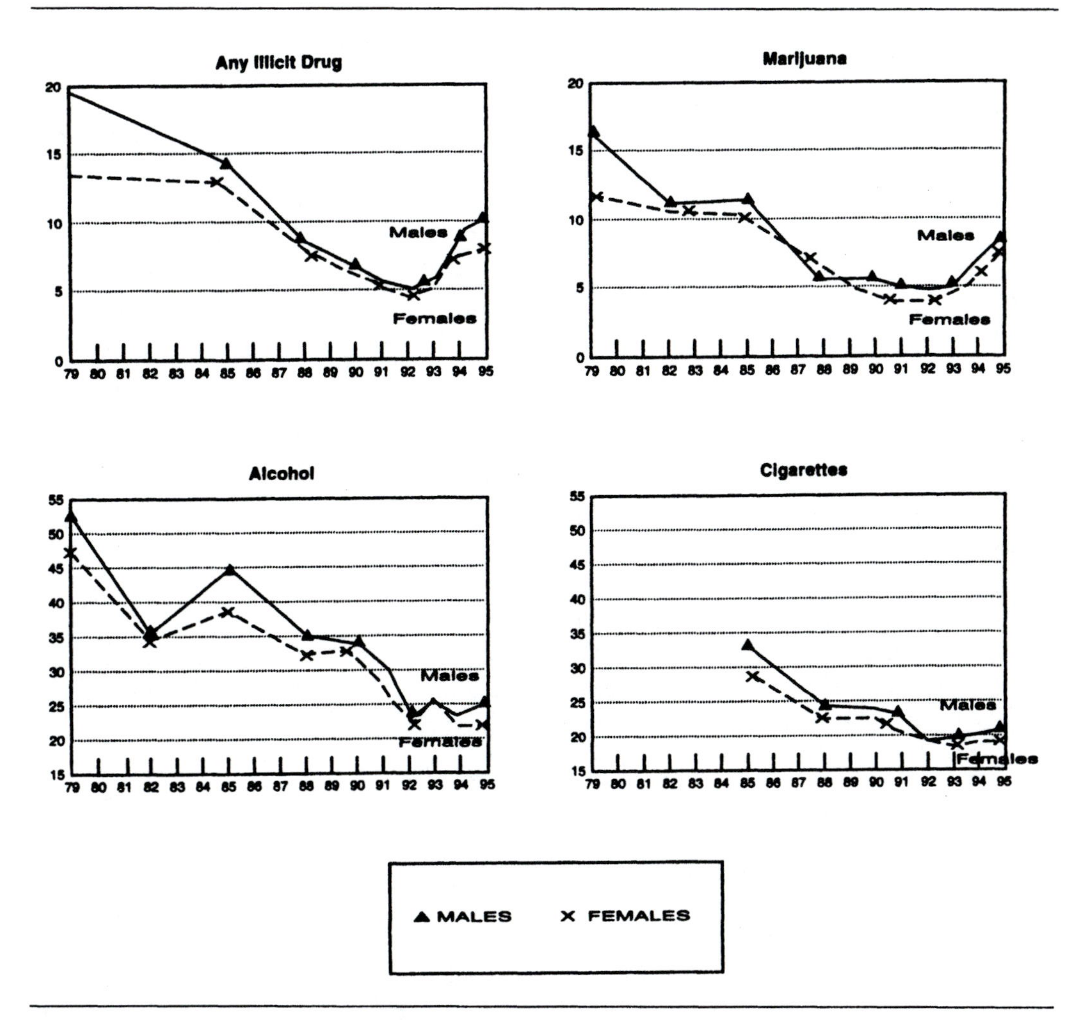

Figure 7.1. Trends From 1979 to 1995 in Prevalence Use Rates of Any Illicit Drug and Marijuana, Alcohol, and Cigarettes for Boys and Girls Ages 12 to 17
SOURCE: U.S. Department of Health and Human Services (1995).

was less prevalent, by about 70% to 75% of males and about 60% to 65% of females. Heavy use or binge drinking (defined as five or more drinks on three or more occasions) was found for 26% of the males and 12% of the females.

Despite the disturbingly high rates of use found, a reduction occurred from 1979 to 1995 in the percentage of high school seniors who consumed alcohol during the month prior to being surveyed. There was also a decline in the percentage who were occasional heavy drinkers (*heavy* is defined in this study as five or more drinks on an occasion in the past 2 weeks), as shown in Figure 7.2.

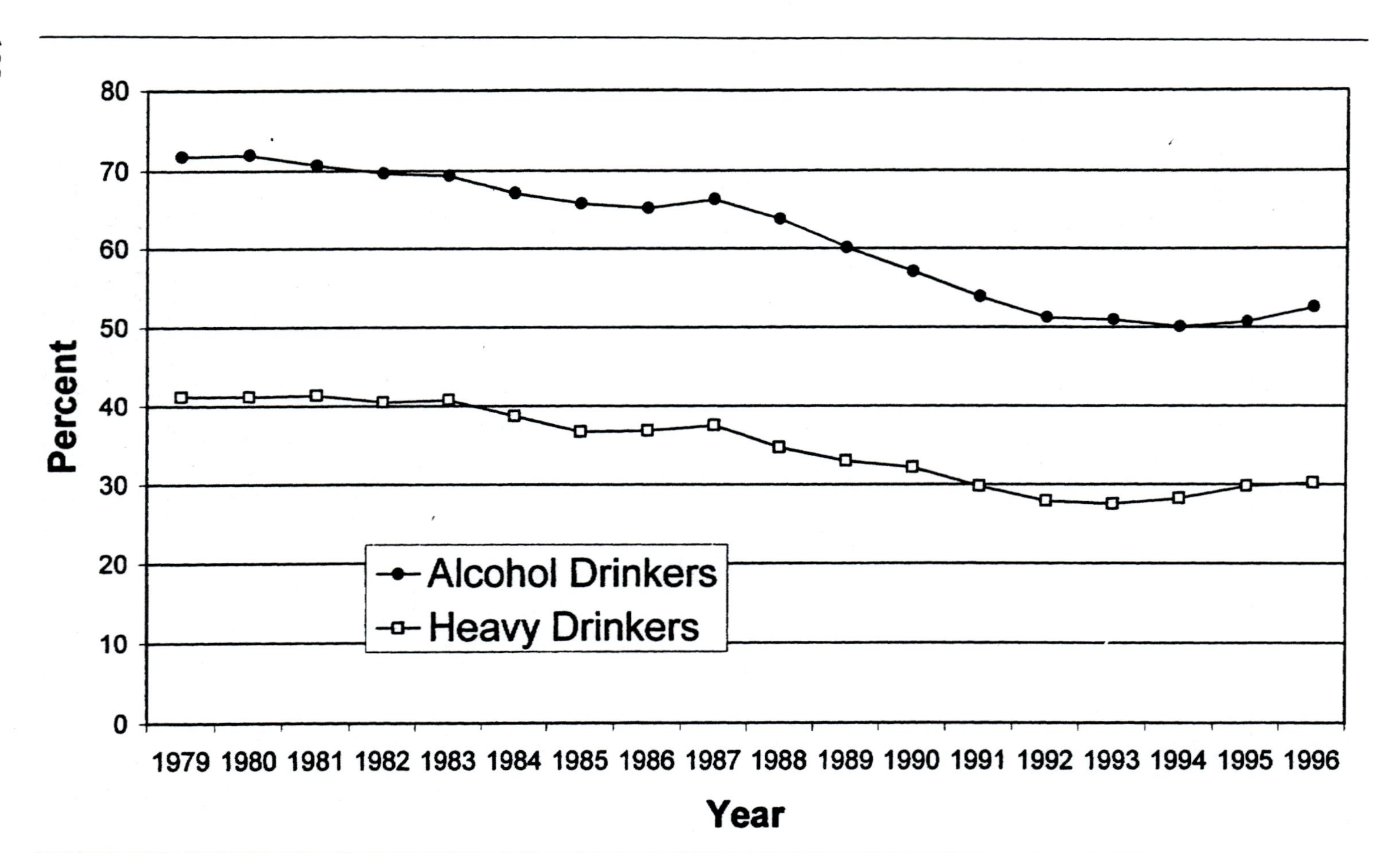

Figure 7.2. Trends From 1979 to 1996 in Any Alcohol Use Versus Heavy Alcohol Use (Five or More Drinks per Occasion) by High School Seniors

SOURCE: Johnston et al. (1996).

The gender gap narrowed in more recent surveys of high school seniors (Johnston, Wadsworth, et al., 1997), as females increased but males decreased their frequency and quantity of drinking. Because most of these seniors had started drinking at a much earlier age, it is likely that many were already drinking at levels that may be dangerous even though they were under the minimum legal drinking age.

Smoking rates were compared for Black and White adolescents (ages 12-17) who participated in the Youth Risk Behavior Survey supplement to the 1992 National Health Interview Survey (Faulkner & Merritt, 1998). Smoking for White adolescents exceeded that of Black adolescents by almost threefold.

Longitudinal Studies

Most major surveys of adolescent drinking have been **cross sectional** in design, comparing individuals in different age groups. However, this method does not allow inferences about underlying developmental processes that occur over time. For an understanding of the processes involved in the initiation and development of drinking, we need **longitudinal studies** that assess the behavior of the same individuals before and after drinking begins.

The stability of alcohol consumption patterns among youth, ages 17 to 24, was studied in the National Longitudinal Survey (NLS) of Labor Market Experience in Youth, conducted by the U.S. Department of Labor in 1982 and 1983 (Grant et al., 1988). Changes in drinking over this 2-year period were measured by charting the drinking of four different groups: new drinkers during the period, drinkers who reverted to nondrinkers during the period, drinkers at both measurement times, and abstainers who did not drink at either measurement time. Most drinkers at the first measurement, 86%, were still drinkers at the second measurement, but the percentage of heavy drinkers declined, especially for women. The prevalence of each consumption category increased between ages 17 to 22 but then declined for ages 23 to 24 for both sexes. This decline in drinking may have occurred at that age because it is a time when many young adults begin to assume more adult responsibilities. These changes reflect a "maturing out" process (Fillmore & Midanik, 1984).

It is encouraging that a high percentage of high school students show reduced use of alcohol only a few years after they hit a peak. Those adolescents who were not involved with other forms of problem behavior were likely to lower their drinking levels later (Donovan, Jessor, & Jessor, 1983), suggesting that their earlier use may have been a form of experimentation rather than a precursor to heavier use. More than half of the adolescent problem drinkers who became nonproblem drinkers by young adulthood had married during the period, in contrast to only 20% of the adolescent problem drinkers who remained so during young adulthood. Similar changes have been found with adolescents during the transition period from late adolescence to adulthood. For alcohol, cocaine, and marijuana, use peaked in the mid-20s for both males and females compared to their use rates as high school seniors. Only cigarette use levels tended to persist (Johnston, O'Malley, & Bachman, 1997).

Trends in adolescent smoking (Nelson et al., 1995) had shown declines in the National Household Survey on Drug Abuse (NHSDA) studies from 1974 to 1980, but from 1985 to 1991, the improvement slowed especially for White adolescents. Only minimal declines in smoking have occurred since 1985.

Gateway Drugs

Alcohol and tobacco have been dubbed **gateway drugs** because use of these drugs preceded the use of illicit drugs in many adolescents (Yamaguchi & Kandel, 1984). The term implies that use of drugs such as alcohol and tobacco opens the way to use of illicit drugs and involvement in other forms of socially deviant behavior. Hence, these drugs are also deemed dangerous because of what they portend by way of future illicit drug use.

Numerous studies have shown that adolescents who drink or smoke are more likely to experiment with illicit drugs. For example, in the 1995 NHSDA study (U.S. Department of Health and Human Services, 1997a), adolescents of high school age who either smoked or drank during the past month were much more likely to use other drugs. Table 7.2 shows that use of any illicit drug, for example, was reported by 35.3% of cigarette smokers but only by 4.7% of nonsmokers. Heavy users of alcohol (54.9%) were more likely to use any illicit drug than nondrinkers were (4.3%).

Although use of alcohol, tobacco, or both does not guarantee use of marijuana and other drugs, it seems to increase the chances substantially because the use of illegal drugs is much lower for those who have not first used alcohol or tobacco. In a temporal sense, it is undoubtedly true that most users of illicit drugs started with alcohol, tobacco, or marijuana. However, there is no evidence for a *pharmacological* gateway in the sense that use of these drugs alters the nervous system in ways that facilitate the use of illicit drugs. Use of licit drugs such as tobacco and alcohol is apt to precede most use of illicit drugs simply because of their easier availability and lower cost. Labeling them as "gateway" drugs only *describes* the sequence in which users move from one drug such as alcohol or tobacco to

TABLE 7.2 Relationship between level of alcohol and cigarette use to use of other licit and illicit drugs in past month for ages 12 to 17 (in percentages)

	Cigarette		*Alcohol*		
	Any Use	*No Use*	*Heavy*	*Use*	*No Use*
Any illicit drug	35.3	4.7	54.9	27.0	4.3
Marijuana/hashish	29.2	2.9	NA	21.1	2.4
Cocaine	3.2	0.2	NA	0.2	0.1
Alcohol	54.6	12.6			
Cigarettes			73.1		11.6

SOURCE: U.S. Department of Health and Human Services (1997c).
NOTE: NA = not available.

other drugs such as cocaine. However, to call them gateway drugs does not *explain* the underlying mechanisms for how they contribute to or influence the use of other drugs. It may mislead us to think that if social policies restricted access to the gateway drugs, there would be less eventual use of the illicit drugs.

An alternative explanation of the relationship of gateway drugs in relation to other drugs is shown in Figure 7.3. Most adults in our society engage in some alcohol use, but only a relatively small percentage ever go on to illicit drugs. Most users of so-called gateway drugs such as alcohol do *not* cross the opened gate to go down the pathway to illicit drugs, as Figure 7.3 indicates. To take an extreme example, about 90% of adults use alcohol, but less than 1% use heroin. Figure 7.3 acknowledges that most illicit drug users started with alcohol, but it also emphasizes that the opposite conclusion that most alcohol users later take illicit drugs is false. Some "third variable," such as a predisposing factor related to different personal backgrounds, may determine why a minority of gateway drug users move on to illicit drugs, but the majority do not.

A longitudinal study (Shedler & Block, 1990) covering children from preschool to age 18 found that those adolescents who engaged in some experimentation with drugs were better adjusted than those who did not. "Experimenters" had lower anxiety and higher social skills. At the other extreme, frequent users were maladjusted and alienated, experiencing more emotional distress. These differences in drug use were related to differences in parenting; closer ties with parents were found for adolescents

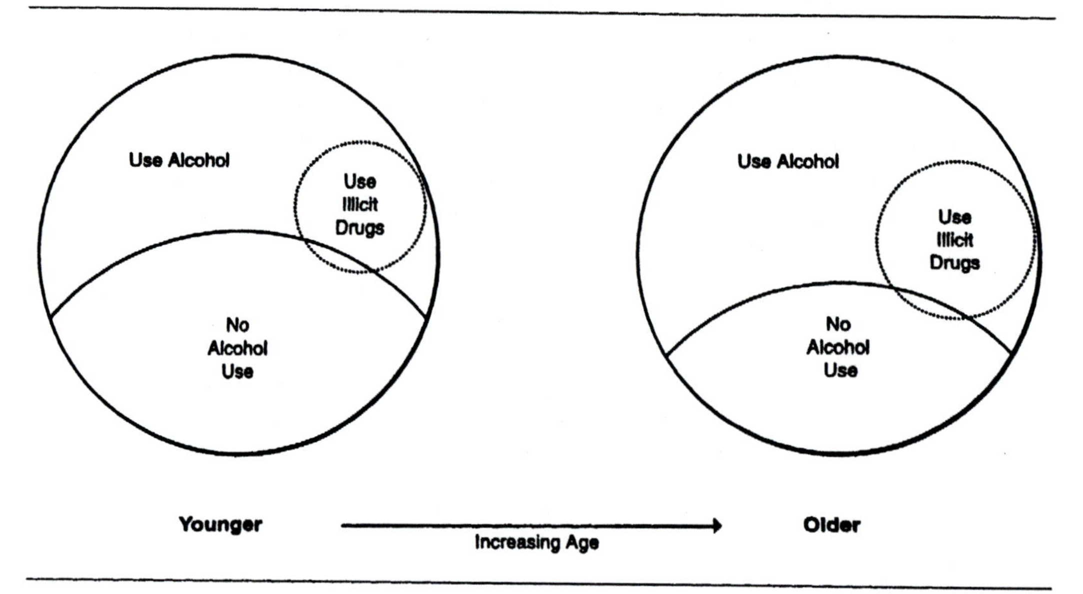

Figure 7.3. Alternative Interpretation of Evidence Used for the Gateway Theory of Drug Use

NOTE: In line with the gateway hypothesis, more adolescents who use alcohol will also use illicit drugs eventually than those who do not use alcohol. However, contrary to the gateway hypothesis, most adolescents will not go on to use illicit drugs, even if they do use alcohol.

who experimented with drugs but did not become heavy users than for either heavy users or nonusers.

Effect of Family Structures

Adolescent alcohol and drug abuse may be related to different family structures. Family structure in America has changed rapidly over the past generation, with a shift from the nuclear family with two parents and their children toward more single-parent, stepparent, and extended family homes.

In the 1995 NHSDA survey (U.S. Department of Health and Human Services, 1997a), 17,747 respondents were surveyed to permit sufficient subsamples to compare different forms of family structure. Using the two biological parent home as the baseline, the results showed that adolescents from one-parent or stepparent families are at higher risk for a number of problems, including poorer school performance, lower college attendance, early sexual initiation and parenthood, own later marital problems, delinquency, and use of alcohol and most other drugs. A general explanation for this pattern is that if families are dissolved due to parental conflict and spousal abuse, the children may experience stress, anxiety, depression, and low self-esteem, which in turn may lead to use of alcohol and drugs.

Complications arise in the causal interpretation of the relationship of family structure with outcomes in studies unless there is control for variables that covary with family structure. Thus, the lower income of single-parent families due to a large percentage of single-mother families may contribute to the adolescent problems more than the nature of the family structure per se.

Still, even with controls for important demographic variables such as age, race/ethnicity, and family income, the finding of lower alcohol use for adolescents from two-parent families persists. Females from mother-only and mother-stepfather families were especially more likely to abuse drugs, even after controlling for demographic factors.

However, the study was limited to examining only family structure but not the *quality* of family interaction, which can vary within each subgroup. Quality of family life may be a more important or at least an additional determinant of adolescent alcohol use.

Moreover, it is not possible to rule out reverse causation in a cross-sectional study. Thus, instead of family structure affecting adolescent drug abuse, it is possible that adolescent alcohol abuse may contribute toward family dissolution by placing stress on the parents. Longitudinal data are needed to see the temporal relationship between important changes in the family structure and adolescent initiation, continuation, or escalation of substances.

DEFINING ADOLESCENT PROBLEM DRINKING

One limitation of past research is the assumption that adolescent problem drinking can be accurately described with the traditional measures and conceptions of alcohol use and abuse developed for adult samples. For example, items on questionnaires designed for adults focus on typical drinking quantities and frequencies. Although these types of questions may be appropriate for many adults, they may be of limited validity for understanding adolescent drinking behavior. A similar problem applies to comparisons of drug use in general among adolescents and adults.

The context and meaning of drinking for adolescents are different from those of their parents and other adults. Drinking patterns of adolescents, in that it is a relatively new behavior for them, fluctuate more over time than for adults for many reasons. Adolescents may be more likely than adults to encounter problems from a single drinking episode, perhaps due to inexperience or lack of knowledge. In contrast, numerous drinking episodes over many years of chronic alcohol use may be more likely associated with the likelihood of problems for alcoholic adults. Physical and medical impairments stemming from such adult drinking histories are less applicable to young people who, as a group, have a briefer history of drinking. In addition, some problems associated with drinking are unique to young people such as troubles with parents or with the law due to underage drinking.

Due to the legal inaccessibility of alcohol for underage adolescents, their problems with alcohol may be more often related to having too much to consume on an *occasion* as compared to adults who may more often have problems of chronic consumption, often with less extreme quantities consumed per occasion. In short, the nature of alcohol problems for nonclinical populations of adults and adolescents may be quite dissimilar.

College Students

After high school, students head off in different directions that have profound impact on their futures. Those with academic talent or at least leanings seek entrance to colleges and universities, others enter careers or trades, and yet others pursue military service. These alternative life paths may in part reflect existing drug use patterns and also may determine future drug use styles. For example, high school students who are heavily into drugs, especially illicit drugs, may be less likely to become college students. College students, if they live away from home, come under the influences of dormitory, fraternity, and sorority norms of alcohol and other drug use, which may differ markedly from the practices acceptable in their parents' home. Thus, college students increase rates of heavy drinking and use of marijuana during their college years, although use of cocaine does not increase. Cigarette use is relatively low among college students and does not change much during college.

PREVALENCE OF COLLEGE STUDENT ALCOHOL AND OTHER DRUG USE

Although most college students are older than age 18, those who are not living at home, which is a large percentage, would not be included as part of national probability surveys. Therefore, surveys of college students may yield different results from surveys of high school students.

In comparing use patterns of high school and college samples, differences in drinking between high school and college students should not be attributed entirely to age differences because the two populations vary in many other respects than age that might affect drinking.

A mail survey of around 7,000 college students at 34 New England colleges and universities (Wechsler & McFadden, 1979) had a return rate ranging from 51% to 87% across different campuses. Compared with the results found in a pioneering study (Straus & Bacon, 1953) done 25 years earlier, drinking among college students has increased substantially, with less than 5% abstainers. Men drank more frequently and in larger quantities than women, with one third of men being classified as frequent heavy drinkers in comparison with one tenth of women. Parental use of alcohol and the extent to which students drank in high school were related to more college drinking. In agreement with other studies, there was an inverse relationship between academic performance and amount of drinking. More than one third of the men and one sixth of the women were drunk at least once a month. Physical fights and difficulties with authorities due to drinking occurred for one fifth of the men.

However, one must be careful in making comparisons of students from different eras because the percentage of the general population that attends college has increased considerably since the early 1950s. Thus, some of the increases in drinking among college students in the 1990s may be due to more recent students coming from a broader section of the general population.

A replication (Meilman, Stone, Gaylor, & Turco, 1990) was conducted at a private rural New England university. Unlike many surveys that use a convenience sample of available participants, a random sampling procedure (everyone in the population of interest has an equal chance of selection) was used to obtain a sample of 350 mainly White respondents between ages 17 and 21, with about 60% males and 40% females. The results suggested a lower rate of daily consumption, especially among males, than found 10 years earlier (Wechsler & McFadden, 1979). In fact, one quarter of the respondents drank less than a drink per week. Nonetheless, alcohol-related problems were still frequent, with more than one quarter of the respondents reporting having a "hangover" and 30% indicating some disruption of normal functioning due to drinking within the past week.

These findings may not be limited to private New England colleges because comparable results occurred at a large public eastern university (O'Hare, 1990). Overall drinking seems to have declined: About one fifth of the respondents indicated they were abstainers, as compared to only

3.7% found a decade earlier (Wechsler & McFadden, 1979). However, rates of heavy drinking were still comparable at about one fifth of the White respondents. Although males drank more than females did, there were comparable levels of alcohol-related problems for both sexes. The combination of smaller body size and differences in alcohol metabolism for women and the possible differences in social attitudes toward drinking by women might contribute to this discrepancy. Finally, a comparison of drinkers older and younger than age 21 showed that the level of consumption and associated problems were equivalent, implying that legal controls were ineffective as factors affecting drinking by college students.

Another large-scale study (Meilman et al., 1990) used a random sample of 45,632 students, with a female-to-male ratio of 3:2, from 89 universities and colleges. The 1992 to 1994 results (Meilman, Cashin, McKillip, & Presley, 1998) are similar to other surveys showing that most students drink at least once a year, but about one fifth do so several times a week. Males reported drinking an average of 6.8 drinks, whereas females reported an average of 2.8 drinks per week. Drinking did vary with some characteristics of the institution; in general, it was higher at the smaller colleges and universities.

The 30-day prevalence rates showed that alcohol, tobacco, and marijuana were the most frequently used drugs, followed by amphetamines, hallucinogens, and cocaine. Use of alcohol, tobacco, and marijuana was higher for males.

The survey also inquired about harmful consequences of drinking, finding that about one quarter of students reported some adverse effects on academic behavior and performance. The heaviest drinkers obtained the lowest grades, especially among males.

About 30% had arguments and fights, and 60% had experienced hangovers. Almost half reported nausea or vomiting, and 12.9% reported being hurt or injured. Although as many as one third expressed regrets over some aspects of their drinking, only 15.6% of the men and 8.0% of the women believed that they had a substance abuse problem. About twice as many men (7.9%) as women (4.2%) tried unsuccessfully to stop using drugs.

Binge Drinking

A survey (Wechsler, Dowdall, Davenport, & Castillo, 1995) in 1993 involving 17,592 students at 140 colleges and universities measured the extent of **binge drinking** (defined as five or more drinks in a row for men and four or more drinks in a row for women in the 2 weeks prior to the survey). A different criterion of binge drinking was used for men and women to reflect the gender differences in metabolism and body mass, as women who typically drink four drinks in a row have about the same likelihood of experiencing drinking-related problems as men who typically drink five drinks in a row (Wechsler, Dowdall, Davenport, & Rimm, 1995). Also referred to as frequent heavy drinking in some studies, binge drinking may be more serious in its adverse consequences for both these drinkers and those around them because it produces more impaired functioning.

About 50% of men and 39% of women binged, although the percentage varied widely across different campuses. About half of these drinkers were considered frequent binge drinkers, defined in this study as engaging in three or more such binges in the past 2 weeks.

Prior bingeing in high school was related to college binge drinking, suggesting that for many students, binge drinking begins before college. Those who binged in high school were three times as likely to do so in college. Being White, members of fraternities and sororities, and involved in athletics were risk factors.

Despite the high percentage of bingers, very few (less than 1%) felt they had a drinking problem. Still, binge drinkers had more alcohol-related problems than nonbinge drinkers following the start of the school year, as summarized in Table 7.3. About 70% of the men and 55% of the women reported having been intoxicated three or more times in the past month, with similar percentages indicating that getting intoxicated was a primary reason for their drinking.

Binge drinkers reported more adverse consequences such as injury and property damage, arguments with friends, and unprotected sex. More frequent bingers had more of these negative consequences than infrequent bingers, who in turn had more than nonbingers.

Heavy drinkers not only suffer harmful psychological consequences of their own behavior but also produce detrimental psychological consequences for others (Wechsler, Moeykens, Davenport, Castillo, & Hanson, 1995). A survey of 28,709 students at 140 campuses across the nation assessed the adverse impact of heavy drinkers on other college students. Returns came from 69% of the students who were predominantly White (81%), with the percentages of ethnic subgroups reflecting their representation in college.

Non-heavy-drinking students living on campuses that were among those with the highest drinking levels (campuses with more than 50% classified as heavy drinkers) were 3.6 times as likely to report having experienced a serious problem such as violence, vandalism, or unwanted sexual advances caused by another student's drinking as were students at a campus with lower drinking levels (campuses with less than 50% classified as heavy drinkers).

TABLE 7.3 Percentage of binge drinkers reporting alcohol-related problems since the beginning of the school year by gender[a]

	Percentage[b]	
Alcohol-Related Problem	*Women*	*Men*
General disorientation		
Have a hangover	81	82
Do something you later regretted	48	50
Forget where you were or what you did	38	41
Sexual activity		
Engage in unplanned sexual activity	26	33
Not use protection when you had sex	15	16
Violence		
Argue with friends	29	32
Damage property	6	24
Disciplinary action		
Get into trouble with the campus or local police	4	10
Personal injury		
Get hurt or injured	14	17
Require medical treatment for an alcohol overdose	<1	1
School performance		
Miss a class	42	45
Get behind in schoolwork	31	34

SOURCE: Wechsler, Dowdall, Davenport, and DeJong (1995).

a. Women binge drinkers report having four or more drinks in a row at least once during the past 2 weeks. Men binge drinkers report having five or more drinks in a row.

b. Percentage of binge drinkers who report that, since the beginning of the school year, their drinking has caused them to experience each problem one or more times.

Drinking Setting

Do aspects of college residential environments contribute to drinking among college students? Alcohol use and related problems in heavy-drinking students between their senior year in high school and the first autumn in college were studied (Baer, Kivlahan, & Marlatt, 1995). Increases in the frequency of drinking over the college years were strongly associated with residence in a fraternity or sorority. Prior conduct problems were also consistently associated with dependence symptoms. However, family history of alcohol problems was not consistently related to changes in use rates or problems.

LONGITUDINAL STUDIES OF COLLEGE STUDENT DRINKING

Follow-ups after 20 and 25 years (Fillmore, 1975; Fillmore & Midanik, 1984) of college student drinkers (Straus & Bacon, 1953) showed that the drinking levels of both males and females during college were closely tied to drinking levels many years later. About 80% of students who were non-problem drinkers during college remained without problems, with about 10% becoming abstainers and about 10% becoming problem drinkers. About one third of current abstainers was found among those who had been abstainers in college, although more than 60% of this group had become nonproblem drinkers over the 25 years. Most interesting, perhaps, was that although the highest percentage (about 20%) of problem drinkers 25 years later came from the group that had been problem drinkers during college, 70% of the men and 81% of the women college problem drinkers had become nonproblem drinkers, and a small percentage even became abstainers.

Many heavy drinkers in college show a reduction or stability in drinking levels only a few years after leaving college. The change in drinking may result also from the departure from the college environment, where the norm is for many students to drink frequently and heavily. In late adolescence, the assumption of adult roles requires greater responsibility and independence. Many abandon their youthful alcohol and drug patterns that they recognized as incompatible with their career and life objectives. Continued overinvolvement with drugs may further interfere with the ability of the adolescent to fit into the norms of adult society. Dropping out of school because of involvement in drugs, for example, limits opportunities to successful careers and jobs.

Surveys of high school seniors who participated in the MTF studies after they became young adults assessed their changes in drinking (Schulenberg, O'Malley, Bachman, Wadsworth, & Johnston, 1996). Many heavy drinkers (five or more drinks on one or more occasions in the past 2 weeks) "matured out" during their 20s, with the frequency of heavy drinking dropping from 55% of 21- to 22-year-old males to about 36% by the time they were ages 31 to 32. Young women showed even greater declines, going from 33% at ages 19 to 20 to about 15% at ages 31 to 32. However, others

(12% of males and 3% of females) maintained their heavy drinking between ages 18 and 24, and some (14% of males and 7% of females) showed increased heavy drinking over this period.

OTHER DRUG USE

Changes in smoking were examined in a 10-year study of 5,115 young adults, ages 18 to 30, who were taking part in a coronary artery risk study (Wagenknecht et al., 1998). Results with this sample, of course, may not be representative of the general population of this age, but they show how different subgroups may change in different patterns. Smoking rates declined in White men and women, remained stable in Black women, but increased in Black men, possibly due to more new smokers among the youngest birth cohort in this group.

Due to the illegal nature of many drugs, there have not been as many surveys of their use as there have been of alcohol use from representative samples of college students. Table 7.4 presents the relationship between self-reported level of use of alcohol, tobacco, and several illicit drugs by 28,709 college students at 140 different colleges and universities (Wechsler, Dowdall, Davenport, & Castillo, 1995). Students, about half of each gender, were predominantly White.

First, it should be noted that only a small percentage of nondrinkers reported use of illegal substances. However, among drinkers, the heavier the drinking, the more likely was the use of illicit drugs as well as cigarettes. Marijuana was the most widely used illicit drug, although the percentage of students who used marijuana varied widely across colleges, ranging from 0% to 52% of the respondents (Bell, Wechsler, & Johnston, 1997). No simple generalization about marijuana use among college students was possible.

Problems of Interpretation

Because college students are a highly selected group for intelligence and academic achievement, as a whole, they should hold higher aspirations and expectations for achievement than their high school classmates who did not go on to college. Accordingly, one might expect that alcohol and other drug use patterns of college students would be lower than for members of their age cohort who are not enrolled in college because such behaviors may interfere with success in college.

College students may *not* drink more than noncollege students of similar age, as commonly assumed. Although college students were more likely

TABLE 7.4 Percentage of students reporting other substance use within the past year by drinking status

Substance	*Student Drinking Status*			
	Nondrinkers	*Nonbinge Drinkers*	*Binge Drinkers*	*Frequent Binge Drinkers*[a]
Marijuana	2	13	31	55
Amphetamines	< 1	2	4	10
LSD	< 1	2	5	11
Other hallucinogens	< 1	2	5	12
Chewing tobacco	< 1	4	12	20
Cigarettes	6	22	42	59

SOURCE: Wechsler, Dowdall, Davenport, and DeJong (1995).

NOTE: Women binge drinkers report having four or more drinks in a row at least once during the past 2 weeks. Men binge drinkers report having five or more drinks in a row. This table reflects the percentage of students who report that they have used each drug within the past year. This list excludes substances that were used by fewer than 10% of the frequent binge drinkers (crack cocaine, other cocaine, barbiturates, tranquilizers, heroin, other opiates, and anabolic steroids).

a. A subset of all binge drinkers, frequent binge drinkers report binge drinking three or more times during the past 2 weeks.

to drink alcohol, they drank a smaller quantity per drinking day than nonstudents of the same age (Crowley, 1991). Sex differences in alcohol use were smaller among college students than among other groups, especially in the proportion of abstainers. Whites were most likely to drink if they were in college, but among Blacks, college students were the least likely to drink.

Most studies of college drinking are cross sectional in design, so trends and changes cannot be determined, even though many cross-sectional findings are interpreted as if they involved longitudinal evidence (Liljestrand, 1993). Many studies give only mean scores for the entire sample presented. This failure to disaggregate the data might hide some real changes for some subgroups that are buried in the overall means. Alternatively, if changes in some subgroups are large enough, aggregated data will make it appear that trends exist for all groups. Therefore, it is difficult to determine if rates of drinking are increasing, unchanging, or decreasing. Studies vary as to whether they report the percentage who drink during some time period, the percentage who drink different quantities, or both (Liljestrand, 1993). These variations make it difficult to compare across studies.

In addition, rarely do studies of college drinking compare students against age-matched noncollege students. Even if such comparisons were made, obvious selective factors determine who goes or does not go to college, making it is difficult to identify all factors associated with attending college that determine drinking among college students.

Young Adults After College

The ages represented in the NHSDA studies go well beyond those of the MTF study, which limited its focus to the initiation and development of alcohol and drug use by adolescents. As shown in Table 7.5, age differences occurred in the percentage of current users of alcohol, cigarettes, and many illicit drugs in the past month, past year, or lifetime. The younger groups, ages 18 to 25 and 26 to 34, were highest, but there was lower use for those age 35 and older.

Figure 7.4 shows the trend in use rates of any illicit drug for the past month from 1979 to 1995. These rates were highest for all groups in the early 1980s and in general declined over the 1990s.

A follow-up study (Bachman et al., 1997) of up to 14 years after high school on a sample of more than 33,000 respondents from a national sample in the MTF survey found evidence of decreases in drug use. With each year after college, increased numbers will marry, and in line with new responsibilities of this new role, there were declines in drug use, particularly when women became pregnant. These patterns were found with alcohol and tobacco as well as with illicit drugs such as marijuana and cocaine. However, the interpretation of these declines is complicated because reduced use of these drugs also occurred throughout society during that period.

Among those who did not go to college, similar changes occurred in the decade following high school graduation as new responsibilities of employment, marriage, and parenthood were assumed after high school. In comparison with high school use, those who entered military service were likely to increase smoking and heavy drinking. However, dramatic declines in rates of using marijuana and cocaine occurred, perhaps in part due to the strong antidrug policies of the military. Women who became full-time homemakers rather than attending college showed lower rates of smoking increase but greater reduction of alcohol consumption, heavy drinking, and illicit drug use. These changes were probably not due to the status of homemaker per se but to the fact that typically homemakers were

TABLE 7.5 Age differences in prevalence of drug use for past month, past year, and lifetime: 1996

	Age			
	12-17	*18-25*	*26-34*	*35+*
Any illicit drug				
Past month	9.0	15.6	8.4	2.9
Past year	16.7	26.8	14.6	5.3
Lifetime	22.1	48.0	53.1	29.0
Marijuana				
Past month	7.1	13.2	6.3	2.0
Past year	13.0	23.8	11.3	3.8
Lifetime	16.8	44.0	50.5	27.0
Cocaine				
Past month	0.6	2.0	1.5	0.4
Past year	1.4	4.7	3.5	0.9
Lifetime	1.9	10.2	20.9	8.9
Cigarettes				
Past month	18.3	38.3	35.0	27.0
Past year	24.2	44.7	39.2	29.1
Lifetime	36.3	68.3	73.3	77.8
Alcohol				
Past month	18.8	60.0	61.6	51.7
Past year	NA	NA	NA	NA
Lifetime	NA	NA	NA	NA

SOURCE: Substance Abuse and Mental Health Services Administration (1997).
NOTE: NA = not available.

often married, sometimes with children or pregnant—all conditions that could account for their changes in alcohol and drug use.

The lower drug use for middle-age respondents also may be partly or entirely a *cohort effect* rather than due to age per se. A cohort refers to a group that represents a unit such as the "baby boomers." Because different age cohorts grow up under different historical circumstances, their drug use may be a reflection of differing attitudes and values toward drugs held in those different eras.

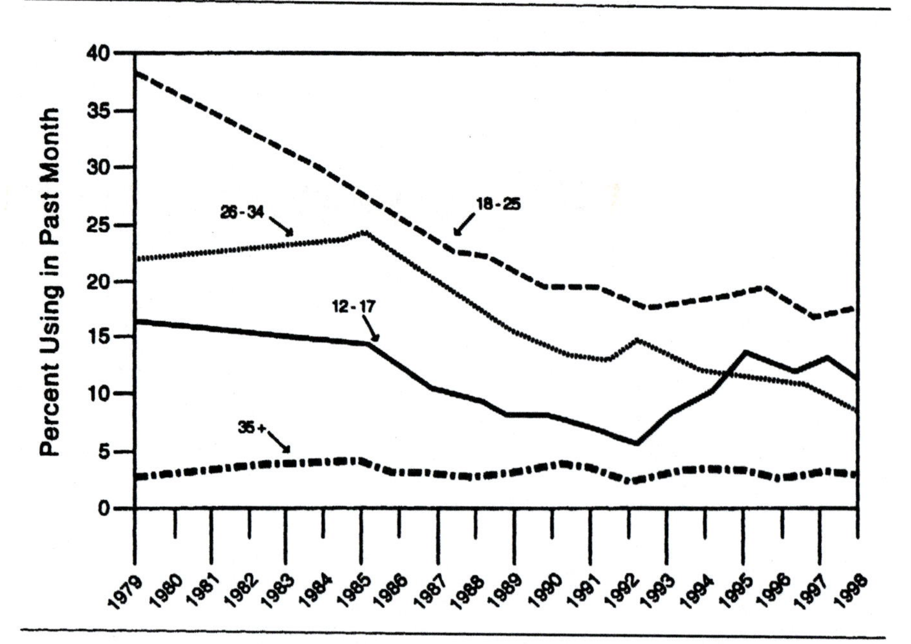

Figure 7.4. Trends in Illicit Drug Use Over the Past Month for Different Age Groups From 1979 to 1998

SOURCE: Substance Abuse and Mental Health Services Administration (1997).

AGE AND COHORT EFFECTS

A major problem of interpretation with cross-sectional data is whether the differences found among groups differing in age reflect a true **age effect** stemming from aging processes or instead represent a generational or **cohort effect.** In Figure 7.5, a hypothetical comparison of 20- and 40-year-old groups can be made for individuals born in different years. For example, we could assess age differences by comparing persons who were age 20 with a different "cohort" of persons who were age 40. Alternatively, we could use a single cohort consisting of the same persons and compare them in different years when they were age 20 versus when they were age 40.

Assume that the first comparison showed a difference. Is it due entirely to age, or could the differences reflect differences due to the cohorts, those who were age 20 in 1980 versus those who were age 20 in 2000?

That is, the groups of different ages in the year 2000 grew up in different social climates with different attitudes and patterns of drinking. The 40-year-old group of the year 2000 grew up in an era (1980) when drug use was peaking relative to the prior decade. Thus, the 40-year-old group of 2000 is not only older than the 20-year-old group of 2000 but also held the drug attitudes and values of the 1980s when they were age 20, which are not the same for those who are age 20 in 2000. These generational or

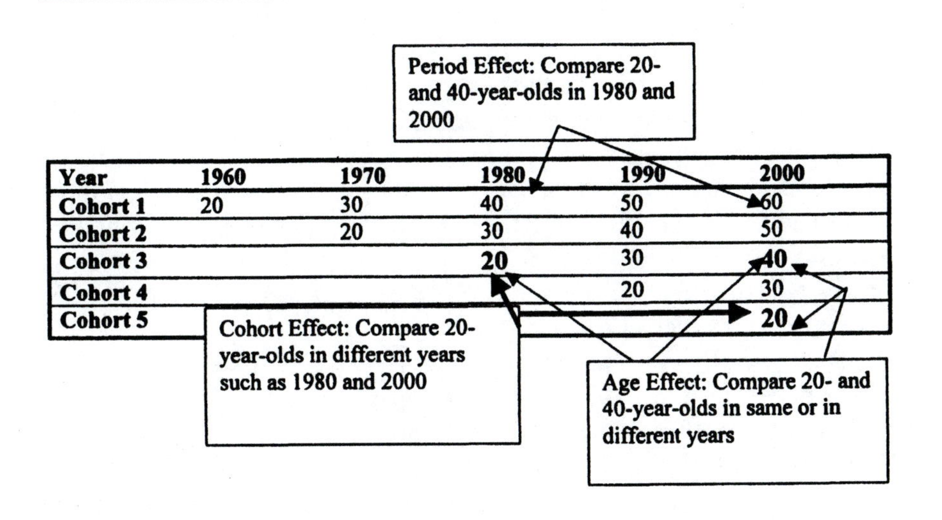

Figure 7.5. Diagram of Hypothetical Age, Cohort, and Period Effects for Samples Assessed From 1960 to 2040 to Compare Ages 20 to 60

cohort differences, rather than age differences per se, could be responsible for some of the drinking differences between the two age groups in a cross-sectional study. Age and cohort are inherently confounded, and it is important to compare age differences across different cohorts to obtain a more conclusive view of age effects.

Alternatively, the differences may reflect changes due to age. As noted earlier, use of drugs may peak in young adulthood due to the demands of changing roles. For some youth, drug use is often an alternative to having nothing to do or lose. However, when the achievement of valued goals may be jeopardized by drug use, a crisis arises. Malcolm X dropped his heroin habit rather abruptly when he discovered his mission of promoting the Black Power movement (Szasz, 1987). One of the most famous cocaine advocates, Sigmund Freud, quit experimenting with cocaine after his initial enthusiasm waned because it failed to be effective in treating morphine withdrawal of a friend. As the use of drugs begins to be perceived as a threat to other goals and there is more to "lose" by continued drug use, it may abate or even end.

Older Populations

As the "graying of America" increases with the baby boomer post–World War II generation now reaching middle and old age, it becomes even more important to understand the nature of alcohol and drug problems among the elderly. In 1990, persons older than age 65 represented 12% of the total U.S. population, but it is estimated to increase to 65 million persons or 22% of the total population by the year 2030 (Spencer, 1989).

Physiological changes due to normal aging can alter the effects of drugs. Older persons have a higher percentage of body fat and less dilution of a given dose of alcohol relative to younger persons. Consequently, a specific dose of alcohol produces a higher blood alcohol level for older persons (Kalant, 1998). However, whether a given dose produces greater impairment for older persons depends on other factors. It is commonly assumed that older persons are more sensitive to alcohol, so a given dose should have more impact on older persons. For example, a dose that would not be problematic for a younger person may be disruptive for an older person. Alcohol-impaired motor coordination among older drinkers occurs possibly because a given dose produces a higher blood alcohol level for older than for younger drinkers (Vogel-Sprott & Barrett, 1984). However, the impairment is not due entirely to the alcohol. Age and correlated factors, such as certain diseases and use of more medications, act like alcohol in that both generally impair performance. However, whether alcohol has a *greater* impairment for older persons is not yet firmly established. Comparisons of younger and older persons receiving the same dose under equivalent conditions are needed to test this assumption.

As older persons face these psychosocial adjustments of normal aging coupled with physical aches and pains, there may be increased use of drugs and medication by older persons in the form of legal prescription and proprietary over-the-counter drugs. There are also reasons to assume that many older individuals drink less due to lower tolerance for alcohol and medical problems that may be seriously affected by alcohol use, as well as due to lower income (Gomberg, 1982). The combination of alcohol with many drugs and medicines taken for old age-related health problems may produce some dangerous outcomes and **cross-tolerances** between the substances.

DIFFICULTIES IN THE STUDY OF AGING AND ALCOHOL AND OTHER DRUG USE

Conceptual and methodological problems exist in research on alcohol problems of the aged (Douglass, 1984). There is a lack of consensus of when an adult becomes "elderly." Usually, a chronological age is imposed, such as age 65 in the United States, rather than one that is meaningful from a psychosocial or biological standpoint. Many of the measures and criteria of alcohol problems that may be appropriate for younger ages may not be valid for older age groups.

Causal interpretation of the relationship of alcohol use to stressful problems such as accidents, health, work performance, relationships with family and friends, and criminal behavior is always difficult to make for any age group. The view that major life stressors may increase drinking among the elderly has an intuitive appeal, but one must recognize that a large percentage of the older population copes with these stressors without becoming problem drinkers (Finney & Moos, 1984).

It is important to include an analysis of sociodemographic and personal factors when analyzing problem drinking among the elderly (Finney & Moos, 1984). The social status and background, as well as the level of self-esteem, coping skills, cognitive appraisal, and availability of social resources, may alter the impact of stressful events and moderate the need for alcohol abuse as a means of coping.

PREVALENCE OF OLDER POPULATION ALCOHOL AND OTHER DRUG USE

Surveys of older persons yield a wide range of estimates about the prevalence of alcohol problems. Community surveys (Bailey, Haberman, & Alksne, 1965) suggested rates from 2% to 10%, whereas hospital counts yield higher figures from 25% and higher due to the high numbers of older psychiatric and medical patients (Gomberg, 1980).

Surveys of household samples indicate that the rate of alcohol problems among older persons is lower than that of other age groups. Several criteria were used in the national survey (Clark & Midanik, 1982) to define alcohol problems: alcohol consumption, alcohol dependence symptoms, and adverse social consequences. Using a definition of *heavy drinking* as an average of 60 or more drinks per month for the past year, 8% of men from ages 61 to 70 (young-old) and 13% of men older than age 70 (old-old) were classified as problem drinkers. Less than 1% of the women in these two age groups were judged as "heavy drinkers." It was also found that older groups drink less, on average, than younger groups.

In terms of an arbitrary cutoff score based on symptoms such as loss of control, blackouts, and so on, 6% of men ages 61 to 70, 2% of men older than age 70, and none of the women were categorized as problem drinkers. Social consequences such as trouble with the law or relationship problems occurred at least once in the past year for 9% of the men in two age groups but for none of the women.

Overall, this evidence suggests that alcohol use and alcohol-related problems are actually lower among older populations than for younger groups. However, this conclusion is qualified by the lack of equivalent criteria to define problem drinking for different age groups. Thus, older drinkers may not have job-related difficulties due to alcohol use simply because many of them have retired.

As noted in the discussion of middle age, a major problem of interpretation with cross-sectional data is whether the differences found between groups differing in age reflect an *age effect* based on biological aging processes or instead represent a *cohort effect* related to the conditions of the era in which each generation grew up. These same concerns apply to the study of older adults.

An alternative to cross-sectional research for assessing age effects is a longitudinal design in which the same individuals are assessed at two or more different time points. As shown in Figure 7.6, a retrospective longitudinal comparison would involve comparing present data with information collected at an earlier date, but often this earlier information was not collected or no longer exists. A prospective longitudinal design would compare present data with information to be collected in the future. The downside to this method is that we would have to wait for many years before the comparison could be completed.

In one study (Fillmore & Kelso, 1987), both longitudinal and cross-sectional designs were used to examine age differences in drinking for men in the general population during the 1960s and 1970s. The longitudinal studies, conducted over periods of 5 and 7 years, showed a modest continuity between drinking levels of adolescence and young adulthood. Incidence of heavy drinking and alcohol problems declined over age among men from ages 21 to 59, with chronicity or persistence of problems highest in middle age, followed by remission.

Cross-sectional age comparisons were made for different cohorts studied 15 years apart in 1964 and 1979, with men who were born during the turn of the century to the 1950s. The era or period in which the men grew up had little effect on drinking, and the age patterns were similar to those found in the longitudinal comparisons.

Other research found no overall age-related drinking changes in a 20-year follow-up of men from two different general population surveys, one beginning in 1964 with men in their 20s and the other in 1967 with men between ages 21 and 59 (Temple & Leino, 1989). Those individuals who did change tended to decrease rather than increase their drinking as they grew older.

Another problem in studying aging, diagrammed in Figure 7.5, is the *period effect*, referring to the influence of the historical era in which a person lived. For example, drinking attitudes and practices during Prohibi-

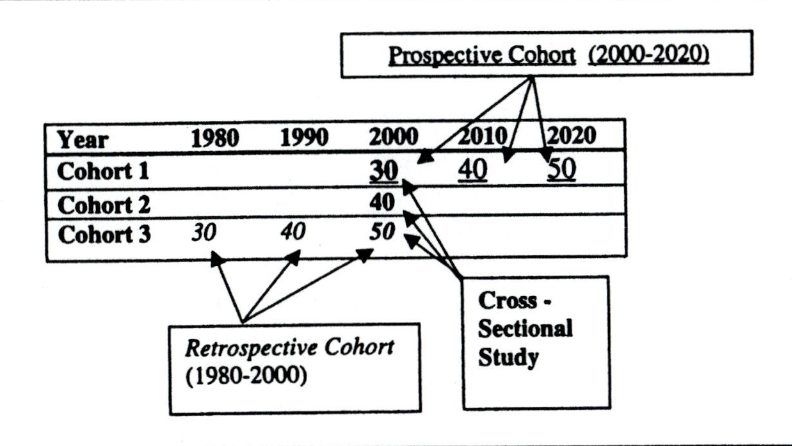

Figure 7.6. Diagram Showing Cross-Sectional, Retrospective Longitudinal Cohort, and Prospective Longitudinal Cohort Designs to Measure Age Differences From Ages 30 to 50

tion were different from those during the drug heydays of the 1960s. As an example, two different longitudinal studies, one done between 1920 and 1940 and one conducted between 1980 and 2000, could each assess age effects while avoiding cohort effects because each study would use the same individuals at all of its time points. However, because the historical periods of the two studies differ, some or all of the differences attributed to age might reflect a period effect.

Data from the Normative Aging Study were used to separate the effects of age, cohort, and period (Levenson, Aldwin, & Spiro, 1998). This longitudinal study followed up 2,280 men who were first studied in the 1960s with mail surveys sent in 1973, 1982, and 1991. A total of 1,267 men, primarily White and from middle and lower socioeconomic levels from the Boston area who were between ages 46 and 72, responded to all three follow-ups. The findings about age effects varied, with only one cohort—those men born between 1919 and 1927—showing a consistent decline in drinking with increasing age.

In contrast, period effects were strong, with all eligible cohorts showing increased drinking from the 1973 to 1982 survey and a decline between the 1982 and 1991 surveys. Cohort effects were weak; only the cohort born between 1928 and 1936 showed consistently higher consumption levels across age and period. In general, problem drinking showed the same patterns as for alcohol consumption, with the exception of the 1928 to 1936 cohort, which had the highest problem drinking at all ages and periods, even though their consumption levels did show a decline in the 1991 survey.

Other factors affecting longitudinal studies such as **differential attrition** produce effects that may get attributed to age. Over the course of a longitudinal study, heavier drinkers may be less likely to continue in the study for many reasons. Problem drinkers may be more transient, less likely to be married, or have unstable employment, so eventually they would be difficult to follow up (Temple & Leino, 1989). Heavy drinking may lead to more accidents, diseases, and other sources of fatality among younger groups, thus leaving the more moderate drinkers as survivors.

Social changes complicate the interpretation of any changes in alcoholism rates observed over long time periods. Also, if alcoholism treatment quality or availability becomes lower over these years, we might expect a rise in the number of alcoholics due to that factor alone. But if we assume that alcoholism treatment has improved or become more available over these years and that increased public awareness and more humane attitudes have led to more alcoholics receiving care, we might find a lower percentage of the older population with drinking problems. Thus, age differences in the prevalence of problems may reflect society's response and the biological effects of aging on the individual.

Age of Onset of Problem Drinking

It is important to distinguish between those older alcoholics who developed their problems with alcohol much earlier in life and those who have a later onset. In addition, there may exist a third group of intermittent or episodic problem drinkers whose levels of drinking have fluctuated widely over their lifetimes. The cumulative effects of alcohol should be greater for those who have been drinking longer, all else being equal. Unfortunately, many age comparison studies do not include the distinction based on age of onset of drinking problems.

Early-onset alcoholics will have had many more years of abusive levels of drinking than other older drinkers. According to a model of accelerated aging (Ryan & Butters, 1984), early-onset alcoholics might have cognitive deficits at later ages. But an alternative model of increased vulnerability holds that the impairment of alcoholics is relatively small at younger ages and widens with increased age. Thus, we would expect early-onset alcoholics who maintain a lifetime of alcohol abuse to show large deficits compared to nonalcoholic elderly cohorts.

Late-onset problem drinkers, or reactive drinkers, are defined as not having problems with alcohol until after about age 40. They may be using alcohol to cope with the medical and physical impairments associated with aging as well as social status changes such as retirement or widowhood. These specific stressors, which are not encountered until older ages, may precipitate the development of drinking problems (Bailey et al.,

1965). Because their history of excessive drinking would be shorter than that of early-onset alcoholics, one might speculate that alcohol might not be disruptive for them. With a definition of late onset set at age 40, however, by age 65, many so-called late-onset alcoholics would have had drinking problems for as long as 25 years (Gomberg, 1990). Perhaps a more meaningful comparison is between early onset and recent onset.

Because late-onset problem drinkers have shown no evidence of a lifelong drinking lifestyle, there is a tendency to assume that the drinking is reactive or a coping response to stress. We may tend to search for some overwhelming negative life event to blame for the drinking. On the other hand, we may fail to detect stressors that instigated drinking for early-onset drinkers because they may not be able to recall specific stressors that may have led to their problem drinking in the distant past. Thus, it may only seem that specific stressors are more often involved in the development of late- as opposed to early-onset problem drinking.

Gender Differences

Research on alcohol in the older population has largely ignored the female drinker, as reflected in the fact that almost all of the preceding research presented here has focused on male drinkers. Inasmuch as gender is an important variable on drinking patterns and consequences (Wilsnack, Wilsnack, & Klassen, 1986), it is important to examine the relationship between age and drinking for women as well as for men.

Several factors make it likely that gender differences may exist. As noted earlier, among younger populations, males generally drink more frequently and in larger amounts. Males also begin their drinking at an earlier age than females do. Consequently, women may develop drinking problems at a later age than men do.

Older women may drink less than men of similar age because they adhere to the traditional sex roles for women that are more clearly defined and, in some respects, less stressful (Wilsnack & Wilsnack, 1992). The motivation for drinking is generally similar for younger and older women: to be sociable, to feel good, to forget worries. However, younger women are much more likely to focus on relaxing effects and forgetting of worries. Younger women are also more likely to report negative consequences of drinking such as physical health consequences, adverse effects on family and social life, and finances.

In contrast to alcohol, evidence exists that women are more likely to use psychoactive drugs (e.g., benzodiazepines such as Librium® and Valium®) and prescription medication than men. Use of psychoactive drugs among older women has been related to widowhood, lower education, higher religiosity, poorer health, higher stress, lower income, and less social support.

Although increased use of medication occurs for both men and women as they age, there is a higher use of tranquilizers, sedatives, and stimulant drugs by women (Mellinger, Balter, & Manheimer, 1971). Elderly women use prescription drugs such as benzodiazepines, barbiturates, and anti-inflammatory drugs because they have a greater increased incidence of major chronic medical disorders than men in old age (Finlayson, 1995). Because alcohol may have dangerous side effects, interactions, and cross-tolerances with many of these prescription drugs, use of alcohol may be particularly disruptive for women.

One study (Gomberg, 1993) compared men and women older than age 55 who were classified as alcohol abusers or as alcohol dependent. In a sample of 124 men and women in treatment (mean age in mid-60s), three times as many women as men were widowed. Education level was comparable, but twice as many men were employed or temporarily laid off; about one third of the women were "homemakers."

An examination of family history revealed that women were more likely than the men to have had fathers, mothers, and siblings who had also had drinking problems. As for their own drinking history, women had later onsets of both initial drinking and their first drinking problem. There were different psychological consequences for older problem-drinking men and women, with men reporting generally positive effects, aside from family conflicts, whereas women experienced negative affects such as depression. Older women in alcohol treatment, especially those who were divorced, separated, or widowed, were also found more likely than older men to have had a significant other (spouse/lover) who was a heavy problem drinker.

In comparison to men, women were more likely to have heavy-drinking current or previous spouses, less frequent public drinking, and greater use of psychoactive drugs such as prescribed medications. Problem drinking occurred for 38% of the women during the last 10 years (late onset) in contrast to only 4% of the men. Finally, women alcoholics were more likely to also be diagnosed with affective disorder, whereas men alcoholics were more frequently diagnosed as also having antisocial personality.

A longitudinal study examined the relationship between depressive symptoms and drinking behavior for 621 late-middle-aged women and 951 late-middle-aged men (Schutte, Moos, & Brennan, 1995). Follow-ups occurred after 1 and 3 years, showing gender differences in the relationships between depression and drinking. Among women, heavier alcohol consumption predicted less depressive symptomatology 1 and 3 years later, as if the drinking was a form of self-medication. In contrast, among men, more depressive symptoms were related to less alcohol consumption on the follow-ups, as if the depressive mood interfered with drinking.

FACTORS AFFECTING OLDER POPULATION ALCOHOL AND OTHER DRUG USE

An overview (Brennan & Moos, 1996) of the major factors influencing late-life drinking and its effects showed the role of personal factors, life context, and treatment factors. Personal factors include demographic variables and past drinking history as well as modes of coping with stress. The life context or environment of the person includes negative life events and chronic stressors as well as the availability of social resources (perceived social support) and the attitudes about and use of alcohol by significant others. Finally, treatment refers to past experiences with alcohol treatment, including treatment seeking and the characteristics of treatment programs. Together, these factors determine drinking behavior and outcomes.

Stress and Coping

Studies (Brennan & Moos, 1990; Brennan, Moos, & Kim, 1993) of 55- to 65-year-old men and women problem drinkers used community rather than clinic samples. Problem drinkers were more likely to be unmarried and male. In terms of personal characteristics, problem drinkers had more stress or negative life events and tended to use avoidance coping responses in dealing with them. Nonproblem drinkers had more social resources and social support and tended to use approach or problem-solving responses in dealing with stressors. Problem-drinking women used psychoactive medicines more and alcohol less, relative to men. Compared with men, they had more recent onset of drinking problems as well as greater depression. The women had more family-related stressors, but they had fewer financial stressors and more social support.

A community study of older persons living in New York State did not show that drinking was higher for persons with more health-related stressors (Welte, 1998). Instead, those who were sick or ill actually drank less, but those who were active and healthy tended to drink more. Although these findings might be interpreted as showing that higher stress, fewer social resources, and avoidance coping "cause" problem drinking, it is also possible that the opposite process may be involved. That is, problem drinking might increase stress, reduce social resources, and lead to avoidance coping.

The study of stress often relies on indices of global or total stress. However, specific types of negative life events may not produce the same effects on drinking, as illustrated by a study of 798 men and 1,242 women (age 65 or older) (Glass, Prigerson, Kasl, & Mendes-de-Leon, 1995). Measures of drinking and negative life event stressors were taken, and a follow-up was conducted 3 years later. In general, alcohol consumption declined over the 3-year period, but how it related to life stressors depended on the type of stressor as well as on gender. Among men, only 4 of the 11 stress events were associated with higher alcohol consumption, whereas 2 others were associated with decreased alcohol consumption. Among women, 2 events were related with higher drinking, and 2 other negative events were associated with decreased drinking at follow-up. Another 4 events had more complex relationships, with higher drinking depending on the level of some other variable.

The type of stressor was also important in a community sample of older persons (Brennan, Moos, & Mertens, 1994). Higher levels of health-specific stressors at the start of the study were related to fewer drinking problems measured 1 to 4 years later. However, non-health-related stressors were associated with increased drinking problems over 1 to 4 years.

How stress has an impact on drinking also appears to be affected by the individual's coping method and level of alcohol use. Increased stress led to more alcohol-related problems for those who relied more on avoidance coping (Brennan & Moos, 1996) or drank at higher levels (Brennan et al., 1994). Heavy drinking can be viewed as a form of avoidance coping that is used if few alternative solutions for dealing with life stressors exist. In contrast, persons with personal and social resources for dealing with their stress were less likely to drink. As indicated in Figure 7.7, those who were lighter drinkers showed reduced drinking a year later if their stress level was higher (Moos, Brennan, & Schutte, 1998). In contrast, those who were heavier drinkers reacted with increased drinking a year later if they had higher stress.

Social Support

Social resources do not always have a beneficial or moderating effect on drinking. One factor is the age of onset of problem drinking (Liberto & Oslin, 1995). Late-onset problem drinkers involve a greater percentage of women. They have greater psychological stability but more likelihood of late-life stress, depression, sadness, or loneliness. Early-onset problem drinkers have more chronic and debilitating conditions; more legal, medical, and financial problems; unstable psychosocial support systems; and family histories of alcoholism.

Among early-onset problem drinkers, the amount of social resources did not predict drinking problems at the follow-up (Brennan & Moos, 1996). For late-onset problem drinkers, those with fewer sources of social support were more likely to cut down their drinking by the follow-up period.

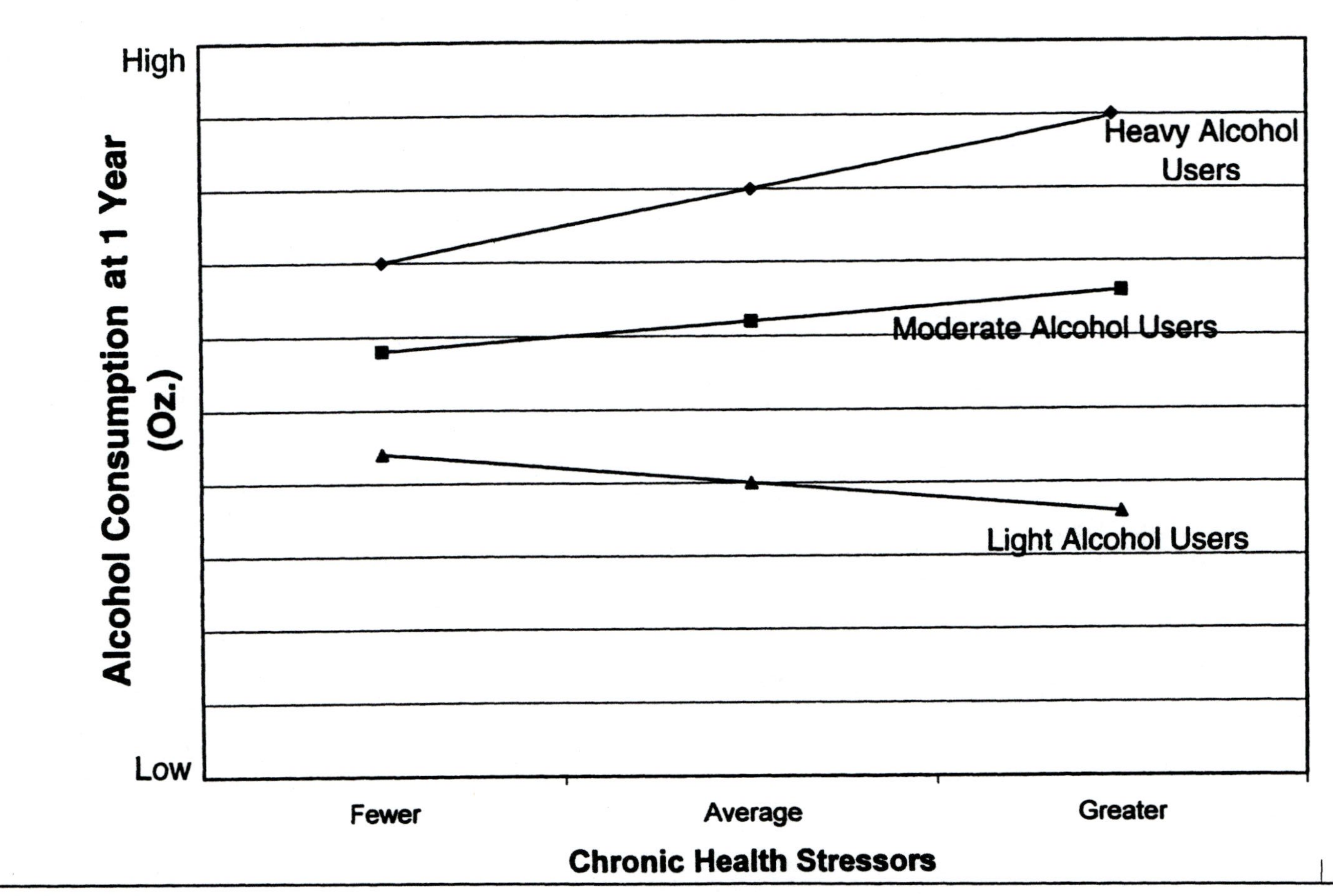

Figure 7.7. Alcohol Consumption 1 Year Later Among the Older Population as a Function of Baseline Alcohol Use and Chronic Health Stressors

SOURCE: Moos et al. (1998).

Somewhat surprisingly, little evidence was found among older persons that problem drinking would have adverse effects on the drinker's relationships with others. In fact, just the opposite seems to happen, with problem-drinking women reporting fewer spouse problems a year later and problem-drinking men reporting fewer conflicts with friends (Brennan et al., 1993). Not only did remission of drinking problems fail to improve relationships with others for men, but it also seemed to lead to increased family stressors for women.

Effects of Retirement on Drinking

The effect of retirement on drinking may vary. On one hand, boredom and increased leisure time may allow more drinking, but retirement may reduce the stresses of work as well as contact with the drinking companions from the workplace. One study (Ekerdt, Labry, Glynn, & Davis, 1989) compared drinking in men over a brief period of 2 years after retirement with a group of men from the same age cohort who remained employed. Retirees showed more variability in drinking levels during this period but overall were not different from the working group. However, retirees were more likely to report problems caused by their drinking toward the end of the 2 years. These results suggest that as retirement continues, problems associated with drinking may become more evident.

Many studies of retirement do not control for sex or age (Finney & Moos, 1984). Because a higher percentage of retirees are women or are older than the employed comparison group, it is not clear if any of the differences in drinking are due specifically to the adjustment to retirement.

Other Drugs

Data from the National Health Interview Survey results from 1965 to 1994 provide prevalence rates of smoking for older persons (Husten et al., 1997). Current smoking among those age 65 and older declined over this period from 17.9% to 12.0%. Among older adults, the prevalence of smoking cessation rose with higher educational attainment and was consistently higher for men than for women and for Whites compared with Blacks. There were no racial differences among women, but older White and Hispanic men were more likely to be former smokers than older Black men.

Less is known about the use of illicit drugs such as cocaine and heroin among older populations (Rosenberg, 1995). Available evidence suggests that very low rates of illicit drug use exist for those older than age 60, except among special groups such as psychiatric and criminal populations (Caracci & Miller, 1991).

Because excessive use of any harmful substance lowers life expectancy, a selective process in which heavy drug users are literally eliminated may occur so that, on average, those with a lower average level of use are more likely to survive. It is also possible that health concerns related to aging may motivate many users to reduce their use of illicit drugs as they age. They may switch to alcohol or prescription drugs, which are less expensive, and have fewer contacts and sources of illicit drugs. In some cases, they may have received effective therapy and counseling so that they are no longer dependent on drugs.

SOCIETAL RESPONSES TO ALCOHOL AND DRUG PROBLEMS OF OLDER USERS

Older persons who are retired may not be regarded by society or by their families as requiring treatment for alcohol and drug problems because their jobs are not jeopardized. Even when family members are embarrassed by older persons' excessive drinking, they may find it more convenient to deny or cover up the problem. Thus, the criterion of what constitutes a substance problem may vary with age. A retired person may drink to the point of intoxication, but unless he or she becomes aggressive or annoying, it may be tolerated, but the same impairment in a younger person would be considered a problem because it could impair job performance.

Older persons are underrepresented in alcohol and drug abuse treatment, suggesting that they may not perceive themselves as having abuse problems. Such perceptions are not entirely independent of societal standards and values. In addition, the elderly may face social and economic barriers to treatment access.

SUMMARY

One's first drink is a rite of passage from adolescence into adulthood. By the time we have our first opportunity to drink, we will have already learned many expectations from adults and media about the effects of alcohol and other drugs.

Early-onset drinkers differ from late-onset drinkers or abstainers even before the first drink. They are often more rebellious, undercontrolled, impulsive, and poorer in academic achievement. Because underage drinking itself is a mild form of social deviance, it is not surprising that many early-onset drinkers also engage in a number of other behaviors that violate social norms such as use of other drugs, sexual activity, delinquency, and even criminal activities.

Attempts by adults to restrict or prohibit underage drinking may backfire by providing the added challenge to some adolescents of defying parental controls. Adolescents who have important activities and goals that are jeopardized by excessive use of alcohol seem better able to avoid alcohol-related problems. However, those adolescents with low self-esteem and little hope of being able to achieve success may be more likely to find excessive use of alcohol and other drugs as a convenient means for coping with their frustrations and failures.

Many college students, living away from home for the first time, may be exposed to more peer pressure and opportunities for drinking than they might have if they lived at home. The academic pressures are more demanding and may be related to alcohol abuse as either a cause or an effect of poor academic performance.

When students leave college, many return to a setting where alcohol use is not expected and drinking levels may decline. Many students who engage in heavy drinking due to participation in fraternities, for example, may revert to lighter drinking after graduation because they are in new environments that are not conducive to excessive drinking.

At the other end of the age distribution, one might expect the transition from full-time work schedules to retirement to affect drinking opportunities. But although the demands of employment might keep drinking in control for most people, the freedom of retirement may be boring and unstructured and allow more drinking to occur without adverse work consequences.

Comparisons of age effects are complicated by the fact that most studies involve cross-sectional comparisons of groups of different ages that also grew up with their own set of historical and cultural experiences. Because our attitudes and behaviors related to alcohol are formed by the norms that prevailed during our formative years, comparisons of the drinking of persons who differ in age are difficult to interpret because differences could be due to either physiological or sociological differences.

Most findings, however, do suggest that alcohol-related problems decline with age. Some of the decrease may reflect the medical complications created by drinking. Thus, if alcohol is recognized as a threat to health, older samples may volunteer or be advised by physicians to cut down consumption. In addition, if alcoholism is a self-limiting disease so that the worse cases die at an earlier age, part of the decline could be due to this attrition process.

KEY TERMS

Age effect
Age of onset
Binge drinking
Cohort effect
Cross sectional
Cross-tolerances
Differential attrition
Gateway drugs
Interactions
Longitudinal studies
Remission

STIMULUS/RESPONSE

1. Based on your own experience and observations of your friends, do you agree with the view that friends tend to have similar drug attitudes and use patterns because "birds of a feather flock together"? Or do you favor the position that one's peer group shapes and molds the behavior of its members? Can you see how both positions could be valid as well?
2. What factors do you think account for the greater amount of alcohol use by members of fraternities and sororities? Do you think that these social organizations tend to attract individuals who have tendencies toward alcohol excess in the first place or that new members change their behavior in ways expected by these organizations to gain acceptance?
3. Many people curtail their alcohol and other drug use as they get older. What evidence would you need to determine the extent to which this reduction is determined by biological, psychological, and sociological factors? Some older people seem to increase their alcohol and other drug use with increased age. How do you think biological, psychological, and sociological factors produce this effect?
4. Have you noticed any change in your parents' drinking patterns as they have gotten older? What factors do you think played important roles in creating these changes?

❖ Gender and Prevalence of Alcohol Use

❖ Gender Correlates of Alcohol and Other Drug Use

❖ Theories of Gender Differences in Alcohol and Drug Use

❖ Women-Specific Issues Related to Alcohol

❖ Smoking and Gender

❖ Summary

❖ Key Terms

❖ Stimulus/Response

8 Gender Differences in Relation to Alcohol and Other Drugs

Alcohol and other drug research has typically focused on the male population in the past and overlooked or ignored the use of alcohol and drugs by women. Perhaps this imbalance reflected the social reality that alcohol and other drug use generally has been more prevalent among men in the past (Lex, 1991). Males drink more frequently, consume larger quantities, and have more alcohol-related symptoms than females (Malin, Croakley, Kaelber, Munch, & Holland, 1982). Moreover, serious social problems with destructive consequences stemming from heavy drinking such as aggressive acts and criminal activities occur at higher levels for men than for women. These conclusions about gender differences are generally applicable as well to many other drugs such as marijuana, cocaine, and opioids (Lex, 1994).

The still influential disease concept of alcoholism (Jellinek, 1952, 1960), which will be described in detail in Chapter 14, ignores women's drinking even though appreciable numbers of women consume alcohol, a trend that has steadily increased since the end of Prohibition (Fillmore, 1986). Of the estimated 15.1 million individuals in the United States with alcohol dependence or abuse, about one third are female (Williams, Grant, Harford, & Noble, 1989).

This chapter describes gender differences in the use of alcohol and other drugs and examines theories that have been proposed for these differences. Factors that may lead to alcohol and drug use, use-related problems, and dependency are examined. In this chapter, alcohol and other drug use are discussed without reference to treatment for abuse and dependency. It is important to first examine the normative use of alcohol and drugs. Discussion of issues and research related to alcohol and drug abuse and dependency and the treatment of such problems will be presented in a later chapter.

Gender and Prevalence of Alcohol Use

As noted in Chapter 3, periodic national surveys such as the Monitoring the Future (MTF) study (Johnston, Wadsworth, et al., 1997) and the National Household Survey of Drug Abuse (NHSDA) find that men generally report higher levels of alcohol and other drug use and problems than women for virtually all psychoactive drugs (Wilsnack et al., 1986). This pattern was confirmed in the 1998 NHSDA, finding that more men (58.7%) than women (45.1%) consumed alcohol to some extent. Men (9.7%) were much more likely than women (2.4%) to be heavy drinkers. Men (23.2%) engaged in binge drinking more than women (8.6%). More men (29.7%) than women (25.7%) used cigarettes as well. These differences have been stable for the past decade.

Use of any illicit drug was also higher in 1998 for men (8.1%) than for women (4.5%). The size of the gender difference was consistent over the 1990s, although the absolute use levels declined for both genders for most drugs. In comparison with 1979, when these surveys began, both men and women have reduced alcohol and other drug use. Table 8.1 illustrates this general pattern with the NHSDA results from 1979 to 1998 for alcohol and any illicit drug use in the past month.

Other factors affect these patterns for both men and women. As Table 8.2 illustrates for 1994 to 1995 NHSDA findings, higher education is associated with lower rates of smoking but with higher rates of alcohol use for both men and women. Use of illicit drugs, especially marijuana, is highest among college students, but for college graduates, the rates are lowest. Employment status also is related to rates of use, with use of licit drugs such as cigarettes and alcohol being generally higher for full- and part-time employees. For illicit drugs, full-time employees are lowest, followed by part-time workers, with highest rates for the unemployed.

Marital status is also a factor on use. Divorced or separated men and women use alcohol and cigarettes at the highest rates, and for illicit drug use, they are second only to those who never married. Lowest rates of using both licit and illicit drugs occurred for the widowed, possibly due in part to the older mean age of this group.

Although these cross-sectional studies can identify differences in drinking among men and women who differ in age at a given point in time, longitudinal designs in which the same individuals are retested are needed to reveal how prevalence, duration, and remission of drinking and problems are related to drinking change in given individuals at different periods of the life span.

A 7-year longitudinal study assessed the drinking patterns of 408 women from 1967 to 1974 (Fillmore, 1987). Drinking patterns of men and

TABLE 8.1 Percentage reporting past month use of alcohol, heavy drinking, and any illicit drug by gender, 1979-1998

	Drug	*1979*	*1985*	*1991*	*1992*	*1993*	*1994*	*1995*	*1996*	*1997*	*1998*
Male	Alcohol	72.4	69.2	59.6	57.2	58.7	60.3	60.1	58.9	58.2	58.7
Female	Alcohol	54.9	52.0	45.4	41.4	43.6	47.9	45.0	43.6	45.1	45.1
Male	Heavy drinking	—	13.0	10.8	10.1	11.9	10.3	9.4	9.3	8.9	9.7
Female	Heavy drinking	—	3.2	3.1	2.7	1.9	2.5	2.0	1.9	2.1	2.4
Male	Any illicit drug	19.2	14.9	7.9	7.6	7.7	7.9	7.8	8.1	8.5	8.1
Female	Any illicit drug	9.4	9.5	5.4	4.2	4.3	4.3	4.5	4.2	4.5	4.5

SOURCE: Substance Abuse and Mental Health Services Administration (1998).

NOTE: Any illicit drug indicates use at least once of marijuana/hashish, cocaine (including crack), inhalants, hallucinogens (including PCP and LSD), heroin, or any prescription-type psychotherapeutic used nonmedically. Any illicit drug other than marijuana indicates use at least once of any of these listed drugs, regardless of marijuana/hashish use; marijuana/hashish users who also have used any of the other listed drugs are included. The population distributions for the 1993 through 1998 NHSDAs are poststratified to population projections of totals based on the 1990 decennial census. The 1979 NHSDA used population projections based on the 1970 census; NHSDAs from 1982 through 1992 used projections based on the 1980 census. The change from one census base to another has little effect on estimated percentages reporting drug use but may have a significant effect on estimates of the number of drug users in some subpopulation groups. Estimates for 1979 through 1993 may differ from estimates for these survey years that were published in other NHSDA reports. The estimates shown here for 1979 through 1993 have been adjusted to improve their comparability with estimates based on the new version of the NHSDA instrument that was fielded in 1994 and subsequent NHSDAs. For 1979, estimates are not shown (as indicated by —) where (a) the relevant data were not collected, or (b) the data for those drugs were based on measures that differed appreciably from those used in the other survey years. Consequently, adjustments to the 1979 data were made only for those drugs whose measures were comparable to those in the other survey years. Because of the methodology used to adjust the 1979 through 1993 estimates, some logical inconsistency may exist between estimates for a given drug within the same survey year. For example, some adjusted estimates of past year use may appear to be greater than adjusted lifetime estimates. These inconsistencies tend to be small, rare, and not statistically significant.

women were compared with the same survey. As Figure 8.1 indicates, the rates for several different aspects of drinking such as frequency, quantity, and consequences were higher for men than for women at all ages, especially in the 20s. Although the percentage of men in their 30s declined on most drinking indices, women had their highest rates on many measures of at-risk drinking during this same decade of life. Convergence of rates for men and women is greatest during their 30s.

Why does drinking peak later for women in comparison to men? Because society tries to protect the vulnerable young female from being vic-

TABLE 8.2 Percentage of males and females age 18 and older reporting substance use in past year by substance type, education, employment, and marital status: 1994-1995

	Cigarettes		*Alcohol*		*Marijuana*		*Any Illicit Drug*	
	Men	*Women*	*Men*	*Women*	*Men*	*Women*	*Men*	*Women*
Education								
Less than high school	44.0	34.8	63.8	45.4	10.1	5.9	12.7	7.5
High school	42.9	32.9	72.8	64.0	10.1	5.6	12.3	8.3
Some college	35.6	32.7	78.7	71.8	13.4	6.5	16.0	8.4
College graduate	20.1	17.7	82.5	77.1	7.9	5.5	9.6	7.2
Employment								
Full-time	36.6	33.7	80.2	75.2	10.7	7.1	13.0	9.3
Part-time	33.2	28.6	78.5	72.5	15.3	7.7	17.9	10.2
Unemployed	54.8	41.9	78.9	68.6	22.6	12.2	26.4	16.7
Other	29.3	25.4	59.1	50.5	4.6	3.1	6.1	4.6
Marital status								
Married	30.6	25.5	72.6	65.1	5.3	2.9	6.7	4.7
Widowed	22.8	21.9	57.8	42.1	1.3	0.5	4.1	0.9
Divorced or separated	54.2	46.8	83.1	70.6	15.1	9.4	18.9	12.4
Never married	42.5	37.4	80.1	73.4	22.8	16.2	26.4	19.0

SOURCE: Adapted from the U.S. Department of Health and Human Services (1995).

timized by drinking, alcohol problems should be delayed among women (Fillmore, 1987). Scores on many drinking measures dropped after age 40 for both men and women. The incidence of self-reports of being "high or tight" dropped sharply for those older than age 40, and many drinkers older than age 60 were abstainers.

Drinking over the duration of the 7 years, an index of the extent of chronic drinking, occurred for a higher percentage of men in their 40s and 50s, but for women, it was highest during their 30s. Men generally were more likely than women to show chronic drinking, but both showed declines with increasing age. These differences suggest that at-risk drinking starts later in life and also occupies a smaller "temporal space" in the lives of women. Finally, women also showed earlier remission than men did across the entire life course. In effect, the duration of alcohol problems is shortened or "telescoped" for women relative to men.

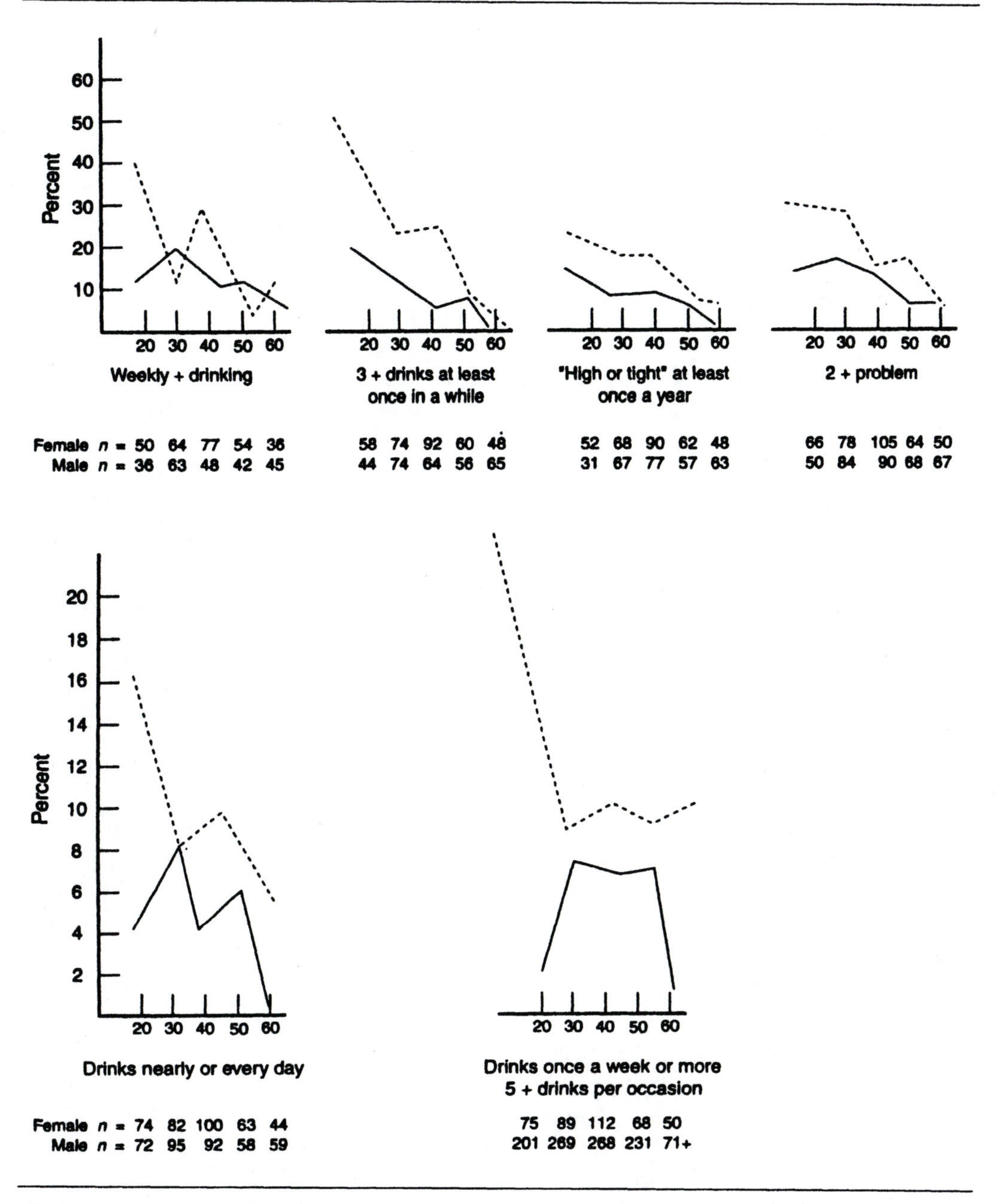

Figure 8.1. Longitudinal Comparison of Alcohol Use for Men and Women

SOURCE: Fillmore (1987). Copyright 1987 by Carfax Publishing, http://www.carfax.co.uk. Used with permission.

NOTE: Dashed lines represent longitudinal measures for men; solid lines represent longitudinal measures for women.

A survey administered first in 1981 and again in 1991 (Wilsnack, 1996) used the same questions to assess quantity and frequency of drinking. Because 696 respondents were surveyed on both occasions, a longitudinal comparison was possible. Only women were surveyed, so no gender comparison was possible.

Some women had considerable shifting of problem drinking over the interval. Thus, 11% of the women who were problem free in 1981 had developed problems associated with drinking by 1986. In the other direction, one third of those who had two or more drinking problems in 1981 were free of those problems by 1986. Such shifts were greatest among younger women, which might reflect the strong effect of situational and contextual factors such as social roles and drinking of partner on their drinking.

The percentage of abstainers increased over the 10 years, but there was no clear relation with age, whereas the percentage of heavy drinkers declined with age. Frequency and quantity of drinking at low (one or more drinks a day) as well as at high (six or more drinks a day) levels declined over this interval, especially for women older than age 40. Problems associated with drinking and symptoms of alcohol dependence declined for all groups, especially for younger ages, when these conditions were higher than for women older than age 40. Younger women tend to drink larger quantities per occasion, often with negative consequences, whereas older women consume lower quantities, even though they drink as frequently as younger women.

Unlike the NHSDA findings described earlier, divorced or separated women showed little difference in drinking rates when compared to married women. The relationships of marital status and drinking might depend on the women's drinking history. For some, drinking could produce marital problems, but for others, domestic problems could be a cause of drinking. Thus, for some women with drinking problems while married, divorce might be an eventual effect of their drinking. For women who do not have drinking problems while married, divorce may sometimes lead to drinking problems. Yet, for other women who leave an unhappy marriage, the drinking may be reduced.

Cohabiting women (living with and having sexual relations with someone to whom they were not married) had the highest levels of drinking and drinking problems. At the time the study was conducted, cohabitation represented an unacceptable lifestyle to society, which added stress or involved women with more rebellious or independent attitudes. As social norms and values have changed, cohabitation has become more acceptable and widespread, so it may no longer be as good a predictor of drinking problems.

Employed women did not have more drinking problems than unemployed women did, even though they did drink more frequently.

However, as with cohabitation, social norms and values about women and work have changed. The relationship of employment status of women to drinking should change from what it was when fewer women had careers or full-time employment.

RACIAL/ETHNIC GROUP GENDER DIFFERENCES

The differences between male and female drinking rates also may vary for different racial/ethnic groups. Analysis of a drinking survey for 1,947 Black and 1,777 White men and women taken from a 1984 national sample of 5,221 men and women showed that a ratio of men to women drinkers was slightly higher among Blacks (1.3:1) than among Whites (1.1:1) (Herd, 1997). A higher percentage of women (49%) than men (26%) abstained among Blacks than among Whites, who had lower rates of abstinence for women (34%) and men (24%). Finally, on a measure based on the quantity and frequency of drinking, the tendency for males to drink more frequently and in larger quantities relative to women was greater among Blacks than among Whites.

The relationship between drinking patterns and problems related to drinking, however, differed across the two racial/ethnic groups. For the same level of drinking, White women were more vulnerable to problems than White men, but among Blacks, the women were less susceptible to problems than men were. Drinking problem rates for women were comparable for Blacks and Whites, but the rates for Black men were much higher than for White men. The ratios of males to females was higher for Blacks than for Whites for binge and symptomatic drinking, job problems, belligerence, financial problems, and problems with relatives.

The lower rates of drinking for Black women are not compatible with the mechanisms posited for White women's drinking. Herd (1997) suggested that there might be higher levels of body weight for Black women, so the same amount of alcohol when consumed by White women produces a lower effect. In addition, excessive drinking among Black women may be more acceptable or less stigmatized.

METHODOLOGICAL AND CONCEPTUAL ISSUES

Comparisons of alcohol and drug use levels between males and females, however, can be misleading. Due to the greater stigma associated with female alcohol and drug abuse, many alcohol- and other drug-dependent women may go undetected. Self-reports of men and women may differ in the extent to which they rationalize their actions. Self-reports of consumption may underestimate drug use and related problems by women. Because alcohol and drug use and abuse are more acceptable for the male sex role, women may be more motivated to try to excuse their deviant drug use by calling attention to extenuating stressful events.

Studies of consumption levels often fail to consider sex differences in body weight and composition, leading to underestimates of alcoholism among women. Because women weigh less and have a higher proportion of body fat to water, the same dose of alcohol should result in greater impairment for women than for men (Lex, 1991).

Measurement biases also may affect studies comparing the drinking of men and women. A review (Schmidt, Klee, & Ames, 1990) of research on women's drinking found that most indicators of alcohol problems such as public intoxication, fights, and arrests while intoxicated may be more applicable to males than to females. The reliance on such male-oriented measures may have underestimated the extent of women's alcohol problems.

Even if there were no methodological problems in obtaining comparable indices, there is the question of sex differences in the meaning or impact of drinking. Does a given level of heavy drinking have the same degree of adverse social and psychological consequences for male and female drinkers?

Drinking styles may differ for men and women. One study (Olenick & Chalmers, 1991) examined the role of mood and marital problems on drinking by alcoholic and nonalcoholic women. Among alcoholics, women were more likely than men to drink to alter mood or deal with marital problems. In contrast, nonalcoholic women drank to alter mood more than nonalcoholic men did, but marital problems did not differ in their effect on the drinking of nonalcoholic men and women.

Women, relative to men, generally drink on less frequent occasions and consume a lower maximum number of drinks per day (Johnson, Gruenewald, Treno, & Taff, 1998). Women tend to develop alcohol-related problems a few years later but have fewer years between the onset of problems and seeking help. Fewer female alcoholics have legal, job, or personal problems related to alcohol. However, the temporal sequence in which these problems arise did not differ much between men and women in a sample of alcohol-dependent respondents in treatment (Schuckit, Anthenelli, Bucholz, Hesselbrock, & Tipp, 1995; Schuckit, Daeppen, Tipp, Hesselbrock, & Bucholz, 1998).

Measures of drinking often combine all beverages, but it is important to examine the type of beverage because the context and effect of different beverages are not the same, especially for men and women. Table 8.3 compares men and women on the frequency and amount of use of three major alcoholic beverages: beer, wine, and liquor. Men were more frequent and heavier drinkers of beer and liquor, but the opposite was true for wine (Dawson, Grant, & Chou, 1995).

TABLE 8.3 Characteristics of past year alcohol consumption by beverage and sex

	Beer		*Wine*		*Liquor*	
Characteristic	*Men*	*Women*	*Men*	*Women*	*Men*	*Women*
Percentage of current drinkers who drank beverage in past year	93.6	71.4	57.0	77.6	70.0	73.4
Percentage distribution by frequency of drinking beverage						
Every/nearly every day	12.11	4.8	4.4	4.4	5.8	4.3
3 to 4 days/week	11.2	5.9	3.3	4.7	4.5	3.0
1 to 2 days/week	31.3	24.2	10.5	15.2	15.3	13.8
2 to 3 days/month	19.7	21.2	13.8	18.5	15.6	16.1
Once a month	13.7	17.7	17.4	19.2	18.2	18.3
Less than once a month	12.1	26.2	50.6	38.0	40.6	44.5
Number of days when drank beverage in past year	94.0	56.0	37.5	44.9	48.7	40.3
Percentage distribution by usual number of drinks of beverage consumed per drinking occasion						
One	25.6	41.8	52.5	49.9	31.2	42.6
Two	28.1	27.6	35.6	37.5	36.3	35.1
Three	15.9	13.9	7.9	7.9	16.3	2.9
Four	9.3	7.4	2.5	3.6	7.1	4.9
Five to eight	16.8	8.1	1.3	1.0	7.4	4.0
Nine or more	4.3	1.2	0.2	0.1	1.7	0.5
Mean number of drinks of beverage usually consumed per drinking occasion	3.2	2.3	1.7	1.7	2.5	2.0
Mean size of usual drink of beverage (ounces)	12.1	1.4	8.1	7.8	1.6	1.3

SOURCE: Dawson, Grant, and Chou (1995).

Because the context or setting in which men and women typically drink also has been found to differ (Clark, 1981), the types of risk that each experiences could differ even for the same level of drinking. Thus, males often drink in public places such as bars and may be more prone to drive after drinking than females are, exposing themselves (and others) to higher risks of accidents. Past research indicates that women list social reasons more frequently than men do for drug use, and the use patterns of their male partners is a major influence on their own level of drinking (Lex, 1994). The same considerations may apply to gender differences in the conditions for using illicit drugs. Furthermore, women who drink or use illicit drugs while pregnant risk damage to the fetus, a biologically based hazard that men are obviously spared.

CONVERGENCE HYPOTHESIS

The view that rapidly changing sex roles in the past generation may have led more women to drink in styles similar to those of men suggests that the gender gap should have decreased over this period. However, a lack of **convergence** of rates for several indices of alcohol consumption or alcohol-related problems for men and women has been corroborated in several studies (Ferrence, 1980; Fillmore, 1984; Temple, 1987; Williams & Morrice, 1992). Comparisons (Hilton, 1988) of several national surveys conducted between 1964 and 1984 found no convergence between men and women in their drinking.

However, other research suggests that signs of convergence may be occurring, at least for younger drinkers (Helzer & Burnam, 1990; Johnston, O'Malley, et al., 1997). Thus, one comparison (Mercer & Khavari, 1990) of drinking among 2,746 college students in 1977 and 1985 suggested convergence, with increased binge drinking and a drop in abstention among women over this interval covered by the two studies.

Age differences also were found (Reich et al., 1988) in the estimated lifetime prevalence of alcohol abuse for men and women that varied with their date of birth. Prevalence rates were 12.3% and 4% for males and females, respectively, for cohorts born before 1940. In contrast, for individuals born after 1955, the estimated rates were higher but more similar, at 22% and 10% for males and females, respectively. Thus, in support of convergence of rates, men were only twice as likely to be alcoholic in the younger cohort, whereas they were three times as likely in the older cohort.

Gender Correlates of Alcohol and Other Drug Use

A number of factors may be related to gender differences in drinking and alcohol-related problems. Biological factors, developmental transitions, and family factors all may have a bearing on gender differences in alcohol use. We will examine each type of factor in this section.

BIOLOGICAL FACTORS

Due to lower total body water in women, gender differences in alcohol metabolism, and effects of alcohol on postmenopausal estrogen levels, the effect of a given dose of alcohol will be greater in women (Lex, 1994). Consequently, women are at risk for some medical problems from lower consumption levels than men are (Bradley, Badrinath, Bush, Boyd-Wickizer, & Anawalt, 1998). In general, chronic higher alcohol consumption by women is associated with hypertension, stroke, breast cancer, and mortality.

Some biological processes related to the reproductive system can be affected by alcohol for both men and women because regulation by the hypothalamic-pituitary-gonadal axis is disrupted by alcohol (Mello, Mendelsohn, & Teoh, 1989) either by direct toxic effects or indirectly by influencing sex hormones such as testosterone, estrogen, and progesterone. Men suffer impotence and lowered sexual interest, and women have menstrual problems as well as childbearing difficulties (Lex, 1994). Alcohol's effect on menstruation, limited to women, may contribute to the later onset of drinking by women, smaller consumption than men, but greater impairment than for men when drinking the same amount (Lex, 1994).

A common belief is that the discomfort during the premenstrual stage might motivate more drinking for women. Poor methodological design and inadequate means of cycle phase identification in this research have produced contradictory results. Drinking was unrelated to menstrual cycle among college women in some studies (Charette, Tate, & Wilson, 1990; Tate & Charette, 1991), and considerable variations in the drinking-menstrual cycle pattern occurred with a small sample of social drinkers (Mello, Mendelsohn, & Lex, 1990). Those who drank more had more hostility and anger during the premenstrual stage, whereas those who drank less experienced more physical discomfort. Another study (Brick, Nathan, Westrick, & Frankenstein, 1986) found that alcohol impairs some functions such as memory and cognition, but the amount of disruption was unrelated to three different points in the menstrual cycle. However, impairment of functions such as reaction time and sensory acuity did vary. Because women eliminate alcohol more rapidly during the mid-luteal phase of the cycle (Gill, 1997), results might disagree if studies were conducted during various points in the cycle. Measures of the expectations and attitudes of women about their menstrual periods also may be needed to account for the relationship between menstrual period and drinking levels (Gomberg & Lisansky, 1984).

Drinking by women may be affected by evidence that heavily drinking women have increased infertility and spontaneous abortion. Similarly, awareness that adverse fetal effects can occur after variable amounts of alcohol consumption during pregnancy may affect drinking (Bradley et al., 1998). For example, women show an early peak in drinking, possibly because many women cut back on drinking during childbearing and child-raising years (Gomberg & Lisansky, 1984).

DEVELOPMENTAL TRANSITIONS

Reaching young adulthood leads to more freedom and independence for both sexes, and increased drinking may be an expression of these changes in social status. There is also increased sexual involvement and activity for both sexes, but the potential of pregnancy and childbearing for women is an important biological difference between the sexes that could differentially affect the impact of excess drinking for men and women. Psychological reactions to gynecological problems, conception or infertility, pregnancy, and possible complications all may help lead to drinking as a coping response among some women. It also must be recognized that excessive use of alcohol also can be the cause of problems related to sexual and reproductive functioning.

In young adulthood, the entrance into the workforce also may be a risk factor for alcohol use for both sexes, but possibly in different ways. Men may drink in response to work pressure, but women often may carry the double burden of holding a full-time job and being a homemaker. As noted earlier, married women who work outside the home have higher rates of alcohol problems than homemakers or unmarried working women (Johnson, 1982). In addition, divorced and separated women younger than age 35 also have high problem-drinking rates, whereas for women older than age 35, problem drinking is higher for married women. Whether the marital discord is a cause of the drinking problem or vice versa is not clear.

Parenting is also a major life transition that is a potential stressor that might lead to problem drinking for either sex. However, because the responsibility of rearing children has traditionally been assigned to women, parenting may involve dual roles for working mothers or the loss of work opportunity for mothers who decide to give up their jobs. Thus, parenting may be a factor affecting the use of alcohol and other drugs to a greater degree for women than men.

On the other hand, as evidence on "maturing out" described in Chapter 7, most young adults seem to reduce their alcohol and other drug use as they assume responsibilities of work, marriage, and parenthood. Thus, for some individuals, these adult roles serve as protective rather than risk factors for substance abuse. These events may be stressors for most people, but some have coping resources and behaviors that do not involve abuse of alcohol and other drugs. Exactly why these life transitions lead to opposite consequences for different people is an important topic for further research.

FAMILY FACTORS

Some risk factors associated with the development of alcohol dependency, such as a positive family history of alcoholism, may be similar for men and women. In addition, other factors may be more likely to differ (Gomberg, 1994). Although alcoholics, as a group, recall experiencing more family disruptions during their early years than nonalcoholics do, women alcoholics do so at a higher rate than men alcoholics do. Possibly, family problems may be more closely related to drug problems for women because interpersonal ties and relationships are more important to women than to men.

Growing up in an alcoholic home can be a stressful and traumatic experience, not only because of the adverse effect of alcohol on the parent but also because of child neglect and abuse, divorced or absent parents, and financial hardships that may contribute to future vulnerability. In some studies, women from alcoholic homes have recalled their family life as involving deprivation and rejection, as well as sexual abuse in some cases, more so than those from nonalcoholic homes. However, these studies did not include males, so it is not possible to determine if these experiences were greater for women than for men.

ADVERSE CONSEQUENCES

A household survey identified gender differences in the nature of problems associated with the use of alcohol and other drugs (Robbins, 1989). The assumption was that men tend to cope with problems by external responses, including antisocial behaviors, whereas women are more likely to internalize problems and suffer emotional distress. Thus, women might hide their use of alcohol and drugs to cope with problems but feel more guilt and anxiety from their use. In contrast, men who abuse alcohol and other drugs were expected to engage in more aggressive and belligerent behavior. The results supported the view that men and women engage in different styles of deviant behavior, with alcohol-abusing women showing more depression and irritability and men having more difficulties with work, school, financial, and legal problems.

Theories of Gender Differences in Alcohol and Drug Use

Most psychological theories about the function of alcohol have developed from observations of males, often those who have been alcoholic. These explanations were assumed to be valid for women as well, an assumption that has been largely untested. Theories that have focused specifically on women have attempted to explain their drinking in terms of their conformance or nonconformance to sex roles. We will look at both clinically based **psychodynamic theories** and behaviorally based **sex role theories** to see how well they can account for gender differences in the use of alcohol.

PSYCHODYNAMIC THEORIES

Early theories about the origins of drinking problems focused on males. Alcohol was seen as a way to deal with dependency conflicts, according to traditional psychoanalytic theories (McCord & McCord, 1960). In addition, drinking also was viewed as a means of fulfilling the need for a feeling of power (McClelland, Davis, Kalin, & Wanner, 1972).

Based heavily on observations of clients in therapy, these views focused on unconscious determinants of behavior, ignoring intentional and conscious processes. The emphasis on biologically determined and early childhood experiences did not recognize the role of current situational and personal factors affecting the individual's use of alcohol and other drugs. Many of the formulations are vague and difficult to test scientifically.

In addition, psychodynamic views seem limited because many factors for drinking are gender specific. Biological differences in the metabolism of alcohol and hormones related to reproductive function may be one source of gender differences in alcohol use. Learning experiences play a vital role in determining sex roles that affect gender differences in attitudes and beliefs about the use of alcohol. In addition, societal values offer different opportunities, encouragement, and approval of drinking for males than for females. It is important to formulate and test other theories that can explain alcohol use by women as well as by men.

SEX ROLE THEORY

Psychosocial explanations for drinking among women emphasize sex roles, a set of learned beliefs and attitudes about the roles for men and women in a culture. In the past, male drinking, even to excess on occasion, generally was acceptable, whereas it was frowned on for females. A man was expected to be able to "hold his liquor," but it was deemed "unladylike" for a woman to get "high" from drinking.

According to one early view, women used alcohol to achieve feelings of "womanliness" or fulfill a feminine sex role (Wilsnack, 1974). This study compared the fantasies of women before and after they consumed a small amount of alcohol. After drinking, women decreased imagery related to achievement but increased thoughts about traditionally feminine activities on the Thematic Apperception Test, a task that requires the respondent to make up a story in response to each series of ambiguous pictures. Women who drink heavily may feel particularly insecure about their femininity, resorting to alcohol to achieve more fantasies about being more womanly (Wilsnack, 1976).

The traditional sex role, centered on hearth and home, might create frustration and depression, leading some women who felt restrained by it to turn to alcohol as an escape. However, due to the strong societal restrictions of drinking by women in the past, it was probably likely that they would have become hidden or closet drinkers.

Sex Role Conflict

The changes in sex roles over the past generation achieved by feminist activism may have altered the picture by allowing more ways for women to achieve. On one hand, one might predict that social changes toward more equality of sex roles would place the traditionally feminine woman under more conflict, either between her traditional domestic role and her actual nontraditional behavior or between her nontraditional behavior and the traditional expectations of society. Either type of conflict might lead to more alcohol use.

Sex role conflict might be the underlying factor for problem drinking among women (Wilsnack, 1973). Conflicts created by having to choose among domestic and work roles could be responsible for excessive drinking. In line with this view, alcoholic women had traditional feminine scores on sex-typed attitudes but masculine tendencies on measures of interpersonal and expressive style (Wilsnack, 1973). Thus, drinking may be a means to relieve conflict related to sex roles. Also consistent with this view, married women working outside the home had higher drinking-problem rates than unmarried working women or married women not working outside the home (Johnson, 1982).

At the other extreme, women who reject values of traditional femininity might experience social ostracism from those expecting them to adhere to feminine values. These women also might experience stress, as a result, and turn to alcohol to cope with this problem (Wilsnack, 1976).

Stress of Multiple Sex Roles

A different aspect of sex roles that might be involved in increasing women's drinking is the stress of the *dual* roles of pursuing a career and being a traditional homemaker. In other words, it may be the multiplicity of roles that creates more stress and is more likely to lead to drinking problems.

Possible support for this view, as well as for the **sex role conflict** view, comes from a study with a sample of 1,367 employed men and women in which greater alcohol use occurred for working women with traditional sex roles and for working men with nontraditional sex roles (Parker & Harford, 1992). These women and men, who had substantial obligations at home and also intense competition at the workplace, consumed more alcohol.

Stress of Sex Role Deprivation

One study (Wilsnack & Cheloha, 1987) found that **sex role deprivation** rather than multiplicity of roles was more likely to be associated with problem drinking among women at all ages. The youngest women were more likely to drink if they lacked stable marital and work roles; middle-aged women drank more if their marriages dissolved or had children growing up and moving out. An additional risk factor for women older than age 50 was working outside the home. Role deprivation may create alienation and feelings of loneliness that allow more time to drink as a coping response for their feelings of despair (Wilsnack & Cheloha, 1987). An alternative explanation, however, is that women who drink excessively may cause the loss of domestic and job relationships.

Thus, a variety of processes related to sex roles have been proposed that create stress and lead to alcohol problems among women. The risk of alcoholism exists not only for women who accept traditional sex roles and for those who do not feel sufficiently feminine (Wilsnack, 1974) but also for women who reject traditional values of femininity (Wilsnack & Wilsnack, 1978).

Findings from retrospective studies with women who are already encountering drinking problems are difficult to interpret because the drinking could be a cause or a consequence of sex role issues or both. Information on this question that would be less ambiguous might come from a prospective study of adolescent girls who have not yet developed strong drinking patterns.

One prospective study (Wilsnack & Wilsnack, 1978) involved a national survey of more than 13,000 students to test the view that girls who drink heavily would reject traditional values of femininity because heavy drinking is not characteristic of traditional females. Measures of the quantity and frequency of drinking, the drinking problems, and symptomatic drinking (e.g., gulping, drinking alone, morning drinking) were taken. Feminine values also were assessed on a scale designed to measure traditional femininity.

The findings were not conclusive. Orientation toward traditional femininity did *not* differentiate between drinking and nondrinking females. Greater drinking and drinking-related problems were related to a rejection of traditional femininity among White, Black, and Hispanic females but not for Native American or Asian American females. By combining the results over all ethnic groups, any relationships of drinking with sex role orientation were obscured.

As sex roles continue to evolve, their relationship to drinking should be expected to change also. In the days when most married women with children were homemakers, it may have been more stressful to also have been employed, but now that most married women with children also work, it could be more stressful to be unemployed and at home. In the future, if and when drinking becomes equally acceptable for both sexes, the need for males to drink to prove their "masculinity" may decrease, and socially acceptable opportunities for females to drink would increase. These simultaneous changes should eventually lower the relationship between sex roles and drinking. Currently, however, drinking is still more important for males than for females in fulfilling their sex roles. Thus, females are less likely than males to drink due to specific sex role demands.

Women-Specific Issues Related to Alcohol

SEXUAL VICTIMIZATION

Although males also can be sexual victims, it is a much greater problem for females. Hence, the discussion will focus on alcohol in relation to sexual victimization of females. A national probability sample of 4,008 women in the National Women's Study (Kilpatrick, Resnick, Saunders, & Best, 1998) indicated that victims of violence were more than twice as likely as nonvictims to have had one major alcohol problem and more than four times as likely to have had two or more major alcohol problems. For 54%, the first intoxication occurred after the first violence experience. About two thirds of sexual abuse victims had their first intoxication after their first sexual abuse.

Different interpretations can apply to these findings. One possibility is that alcohol-abusing women increase the likelihood of being sexually victimized if their lifestyles place them in situations of higher risk for assault. In addition, sexual and physical abuse of women also may lead them to alcohol abuse. It is, of course, possible for a third factor, such as parental alcohol abuse, to increase the likelihood that daughters would face more alcohol abuse and sexual victimization.

Women may be viewed by some as more sexually available or promiscuous when they drink, especially if excessively and in settings such as public bars. Women report feeling more sexually uninhibited when drinking, especially when large quantities are consumed (Wilsnack, Klassen, Schur, & Wilsnack, 1991). Under the influence of alcohol, they may be less likely to avoid or resist victimization due to blackouts or loss of motor control. A review of past research (Miller, 1996) indicated that acquaintance or date rape, rape, and other forms of victimization were more often associated with drinking than with nondrinking women. Because women who drink heavily have or are perceived to have more liberal sexual standards, they may be at greater risk for sexual advances and possible victimization (Klassen & Wilsnack, 1986).

Alcohol may alter cognitive processing by drinking women that would render them more susceptible to sexual situations (Norris & Kerr, 1993). In a study using hypothetical scenarios describing coerced or forced sexual intercourse, intoxicated women viewed the male's behavior as more acceptable and as involving less force than sober women did.

Undoubtedly, both processes may be involved in the relationship between problem drinking and sexual victimization. Thus, a study using a 5-year follow-up (Wilsnack et al., 1991) compared mostly White, middle-aged women who were either problem or nonproblem drinkers. Data collection involved face-to-face interviews with female interviewers. Problem drinkers, reporting sexual dysfunction at the initial interview, were more likely than those without sexual dysfunction to have more drinking problems at the 5-year follow-up.

The opposite causal sequence also was supported in the same study. Women who were nonproblem drinkers at the start of the study but who experienced sexual abuse during the 5-year period were more than twice as likely to develop drinking problems over this interval as those who did not encounter sexual abuse.

A different explanation for this relationship between victimization and alcohol problems is that excessive drinking develops as an escape from guilt, shame, and loss of self-esteem stemming from victimization (Wilsnack, 1984). Posttraumatic stress syndrome (PTSD), a set of adverse reactions to severe trauma, may occur in some victims of violence (Miller & Downs, 1993). Some women may respond to PTSD by excessive use of alcohol and other drugs.

GENERATIONAL DIFFERENCES AND WOMEN'S DRINKING

Due to the large changes in sex roles in America in this century, it is difficult to interpret age-related differences because they are often intertwined with changing cultural values. These generational differences may be greater for women because the relation of drinking to sex role has changed to a greater extent than for men. We will examine generational differences using only an illustration of this problem from a study of age-related differences in alcohol problems (Gomberg, 1984) that examined alcoholic women and age-matched controls in their 20s, 30s, and 40s. It should be pointed out that some of the differences might not be due to age, per se, but to generational changes. In other words, the era in which each group was in their 20s was not the same, and certain social conditions may have affected the drinking behavior of these different groups. Thus, the younger women grew up in an era of greater freedoms for women, with more women working outside the home, more single-parent families, and more couples living together although not married.

A major finding was that the alcoholic women in their 40s did not develop their alcoholism until late in their 30s, whereas the alcoholics who were in their 20s began their alcoholism in their teenage years. Differences in drinking behavior between alcoholic women and the controls were smallest for the women in their 40s. On average, these women were born in 1936, an era of traditional femininity. Alcohol may have been a means of reducing frustration and resentment from lack of fulfillment for some women confined by traditional feminism.

Women in their 20s in this study, born on average in 1956, showed many problems of impulse control and strained relationships with parents. They were more likely to drive after drinking, use other drugs, have potential fetal harm, face workplace problems, and encounter assaults and other violence. The women in their 30s were born, on average, in 1946 and represented the baby boom generation. This group showed more conflict than the other two age groups, perhaps due to the rapid social transition in sex roles during their adolescence.

Middle-aged problem drinkers had fewer problems of impulsivity in their childhood, greater acceptance of traditional sex roles, more use of psychoactive drugs, and more private drinking.

The differences among the women of different ages illustrate how the social context may alter the role of alcohol for different generations. Although all of the alcoholic women drank excessively, it may have stemmed from different types of psychological reasons because of the varying nature of society's demands and expectations for women over this period.

Smoking and Gender

You've come a long way, baby.
—Virginia Slims cigarette slogan

Smoking by women increased to a peak of about one third of the population in the early 1970s. From 1985 to 1995, smoking rates during the past month dropped from 34.5% to 26.8% for women, but smoking by men also dropped, from 43.4% to 31.1% (U.S. Department of Health and Human Services, 1997d). At the same time, the rate of initiation into smoking was greater for women than for men (Pierce, Fiore, Novotny, Hatziandreu, & Davis, 1989). Based on projections made in 1989 from survey data, smoking rates are expected to be higher (23%) for females than for males (20%) as we enter the 2000s (Pierce et al., 1989).

However, comparisons of smoking based only on the number of cigarettes smoked is misleading. Men tend to inhale deeper, so for the same number of cigarettes, they receive more nicotine and other harmful substances from combustion. Men and women prefer different types of cigarettes. Women tend to smoke lower-tar, filtered cigarettes and in smaller amounts than men do. Men are more likely to use smokeless tobacco, pipes, and cigars. Cultural factors also affect gender differences in using specific tobacco products within some cultures but not others. In addition, this gender gap, depending on culture and tobacco product, varies over time (Grunberg, Winders, & Wewers, 1991).

Gender differences in the neurophysiology of nicotine must be considered (Pomerleau, Pomerleau, & Garcia, 1991). Women may differ from men with regard to nicotine intake, effects, or both, especially depending on the menstrual cycle phase, oral contraceptive use, and estrogen replacement therapy. Chronic nicotine use may affect female reproductive endocrinology in ways that affect the extent to which smoking is reinforcing. Finally, pharmacological agents used to treat smoking may have different effects in women than in men.

Daily diaries of smoking maintained by 22 females showed that smoking did not differ as a function of menstrual phase. There was no systematic correlation between symptomatology and smoking within individuals (Pomerleau, Cole, Lumley, Marks, & Pomerleau, 1994): Alcohol and caffeine intake was highly stable across the menstrual cycle in these female smokers.

Some health consequences of smoking such as lung cancer and coronary heart disease are similar for men and women but may occur at different rates. Among women, lung cancer is more likely than breast cancer. Women who smoke have greater risk for cardiovascular disease (U.S. Department of Health and Human Services, 1990). A longitudinal study of more than 199,000 nurses found that the more cigarettes they smoked, the greater the likelihood of coronary heart disease (Willett et al., 1987).

Women uniquely face the risk of reduced fertility, gynecological problems, and earlier menopause, a risk factor for other problems, including osteoporosis, cancer in the reproductive system, and heart disease (U.S. Department of Health and Human Services, 1990). Smoking women who are pregnant have fetuses of lower birth weight, retarded fetal growth, and premature birth, presumably from nicotine and carbon monoxide toxicity, which crosses the placenta and creates carboxyhemoglobin, reducing blood transport of oxygen (U.S. Department of Health and Human Services, 1990).

OTHER DRUG USE AND ABUSE

Drug abuse among women has been recognized only recently for the serious problem it represents historically (Kandall, 1998a, 1998b). Drugs were widely used for medical purposes in the 19th century, especially in treating pain. Virtually all diseases were treated with opiates. Because women were regarded as the "weaker sex" during this period—subject to diagnoses of neurasthenia involving a weak nervous system, leading to chronic mental and physical weakness—cocaine, opiates, and cannabis were routinely dispensed to women for medical purposes. With advances in medical knowledge and recognition of the addictive properties of many drugs, opiate use in the treatment of women declined over the 20th century.

Prevalence Rates

Comparisons of gender differences in the use of different drugs among the general population can be obtained from the NHSDA. However, these surveys underestimate the extent of heaviest drug users because many of them are among incarcerated and hospitalized populations, which are not included in the NHSDA.

We will focus on self-reports of the use of drugs *within the past week* instead of longer time periods typically reported, such as the past year or lifetime use, because this index may reflect more of the committed users. Although not everyone who used in the past week will have used the drug during every week, it is likely that they would be among the more frequent users. On the other hand, a measure of any use during a longer period would not differentiate between individuals who used a drug only once and those who used much more frequently.

Comparisons of gender differences in 1992 for the heaviest using age groups, 18 to 25 and 26 to 34, showed that in the past week, males were about twice as likely (8.8% vs. 3.9%) to have used marijuana, 3.5 times more likely (2.9% vs. 0.8%) to have used cocaine, and twice (0.2% vs. 0.1%) as likely to have used heroin.

Rates of use for the past 30 days were also generally higher for males, with the exception of stimulants, which were about the same or slightly lower than females. The gender gap was smallest for licit drugs such as alcohol and tobacco.

Studies of young methadone patients found that a small percentage of the women were initiated into drug use by a male partner, but males were more likely to be introduced to drugs in a group context (Anglin, Hser, & Booth, 1987; Hser, Anglin, & Booth, 1987). This process probably holds for many other drugs. In addition, women require less time from start of drug use to dependence, as is true for alcohol use (Randall et al., 1999).

Men and women also differ in the progression of drugs that they will use (Kandel, Warner, & Kessler, 1998). Figure 8.2 shows gender differences up to about age 35 in the general sequence of progression. For men, alcohol generally precedes marijuana use, which in turn may lead to illicit drug use. In contrast, for women, cigarette smoking or alcohol use is more often the precursor of marijuana use and subsequent use of other illicit drugs.

The justification and conditions for drug use also may differ for men and women (Lex, 1991). For example, women attribute their use of cocaine to depression, feeling unsociable, family and job pressure, and health problems, whereas men attribute their use to the desire for intoxication. Women may not spend as much for drugs because they are living with a drug-using male partner who provides the drugs. For example, due to the high price of crack, some women may exchange sex to receive the drug.

Psychotropic drugs, including benzodiazepines such as Valium® and Librium®, are widely prescribed for psychological distress, especially for women. They were viewed as safe methods of treating the affective or mood disorders of women but soon became drugs of abuse and dependency. Of all groups, older women receive the most psychoactive prescription drugs (Graham, Carver, & Brett, 1995). Physicians may prescribe different types of drugs for men and women because they present different types of problems or because of preconceptions held by physicians about what drugs work best for each gender (Gomberg, 1996). At older ages, men and women may both use more psychoactive drugs as well as medications such as cardiovascular drugs, analgesics, sedatives, and tranquilizers (Gomberg, 1995). The danger is increased because these drugs can have adverse interactive effects with each other.

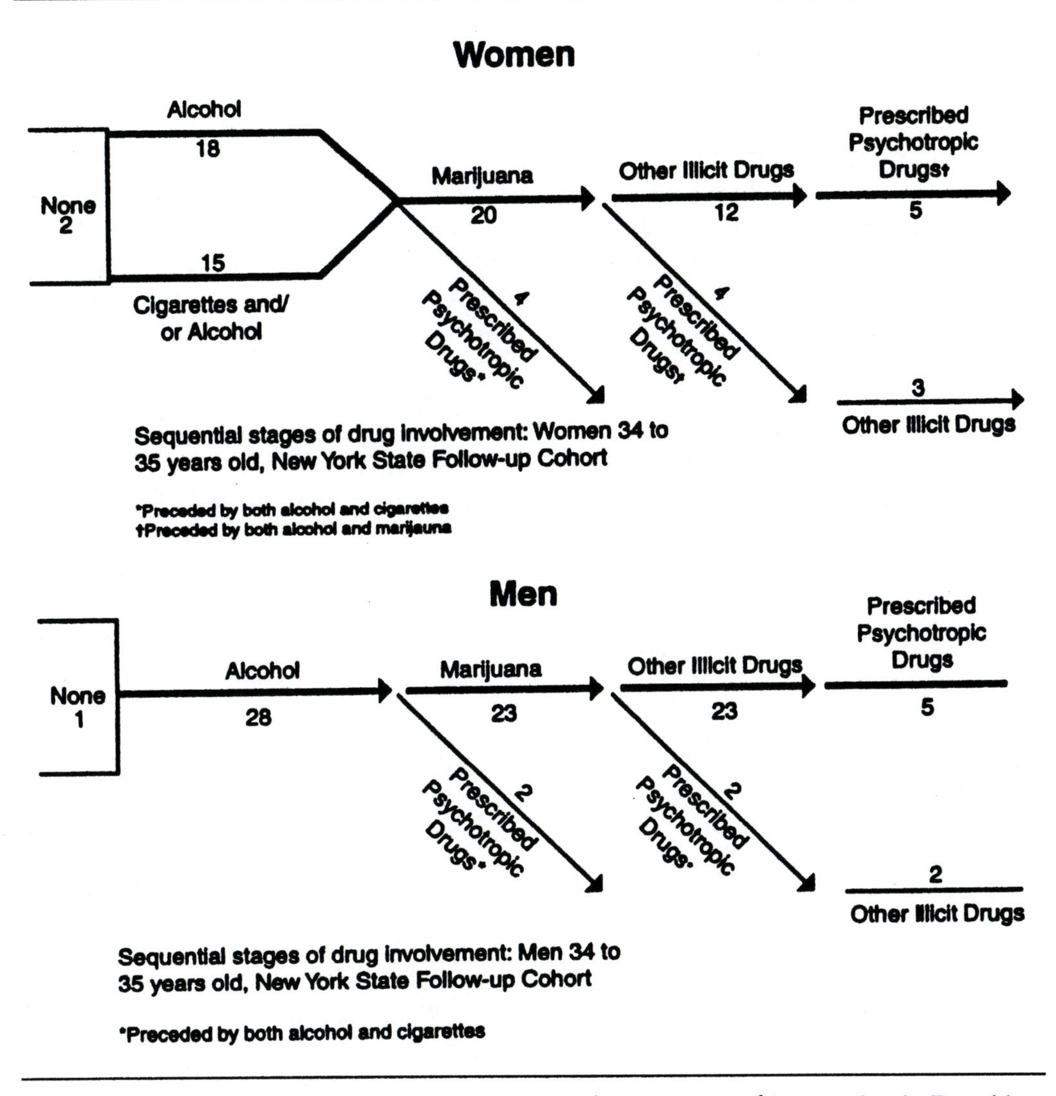

Figure 8.2. Gender Differences (up to Age 35) in the Sequence of Progression in Drug Use
SOURCE: Kandel et al. (1998).

DEPENDENCE ON DIFFERENT DRUGS

The National Comorbidity Survey (Kessler et al., 1994), based on interviews with a national representative sample of more than 8,000 individuals ages 15 to 54, measured the extent of comorbidity of alcohol and drug dependence in the United States. Dependence was measured using the criteria of the *DSM-III-R* (1987), which requires a respondent to meet at least three of nine possible criteria, some of which must exist for at least 1 month or repeatedly over a longer period.

Table 8.4 shows gender differences in dependence during some point in people's lives for different drugs (Anthony, Warner, & Kessler, 1994). Men and women do not differ much in dependence for tobacco, heroin, or cocaine. However, men are twice as likely to experience dependence for alcohol and marijuana during their lifetimes as women are. The reverse holds for psychotropic drugs such as sedatives and tranquilizers: Women are twice as likely to develop dependence as men are.

For both men and women, dependence was most frequent for tobacco. It was followed by alcohol and then illicit drugs for men, but for women the opposite held, with dependence on alcohol at a lower rate than for illicit drugs (Anthony et al., 1994). These data refer only to dependence rates. If one combines dependence with abuse, a less severe state, the rates are about 18% for women but much higher, at 35%, for men.

GENDER DIFFERENCES IN RATES OF PSYCHIATRIC DISORDERS

Substance dependence and abuse together was the highest psychiatric disorder for men (35%), followed by anxiety disorders (19%) and affective disorders (15%). In contrast, for women, substance use disorders were ranked third (18%), following anxiety disorders (31%) and affective disorders (24%) (Kessler et al., 1994).

COMORBIDITY OF ALCOHOL AND DRUG DEPENDENCE WITH OTHER PSYCHIATRIC DISORDERS

About half (51.4%) of the respondents with a substance use disorder in their lifetimes also had at least one other psychiatric disorder in their lifetimes. Occurrence of a substance disorder and some other psychiatric disorder concurrently in a given 12-month period was found in 42.7% of respondents, with the rates being similar for men and women.

Table 8.5 shows the comorbidity of drug dependence with other psychiatric disorders in the National Comorbidity Study for men and women, ages 15 to 54 (Kandel et al., 1998). For women, anxiety, alcohol, and affective disorders had the highest rates of comorbidity with drug dependence. In contrast, the order for men was alcohol, antisocial personal-

TABLE 8.4 Prevalence of lifetime dependence on three classes of drugs among women and men ages 15 to 54, 1990-1992 National Comorbidity Survey

	Women		*Men*		
Drug[a]	%	*Standard Error*	%	*Standard Error*	*z*
Tobacco	30.9	(—)	32.7	(—)	(—)
Alcohol	9.2	(0.8)	21.4	(1.0)	9.5
Illicit drugs	12.6	(1.0)	16.4	(1.2)	2.4
Cannabis	5.5	(0.7)	12.0	(1.1)	5.0
Cocaine	14.9	(2.0)	18.0	(1.9)	1.2
Heroin	25.2	(12.9)	22.3	(6.5)	0.2
Psychotropics	12.3	(2.2)	6.6	(1.0)	2.4

SOURCE: Anthony et al. (1994). Copyright 1994 by American Psychological Association. Reprinted with permission.
a. Base frequencies for users not available.

ity, and conduct disorder, followed by anxiety disorders and then affective disorders.

COMORBIDITY OF ALCOHOL AND OTHER DRUG USE

Studies of alcohol use typically ignore an important contextual aspect of drinking, the extent to which polydrug use occurs. Polydrug abuse occurred in 61% of the 212 problem drinkers in a treatment program (Martin et al., 1996). They were primarily young, male, and unmarried in comparison to those who did not use multiple drugs. The most common combinations were alcohol and cocaine (60%), alcohol and marijuana (51%), and alcohol and sedative (31%).

A higher percentage of women than men in treatment for alcohol problems also abuse other drugs such as antidepressants and tranquilizers, according to the Substance Abuse and Mental Health Services Administration (U.S. Department of Health and Human Services, 1997d).

In the 1997 NHSDA, multiple substances were used by more than one third of the sample, with 18.5% of respondents using two substances in

TABLE 8.5 Comorbidity of drug dependence with other psychiatric disorders among drug-dependent women and men ages 15 to 54, 1990-1992 National Comorbidity Survey

	Women (n = 241)		*Men (n = 369)*		
	%	*Standard Error*	*%*	*Standard Error*	*z*
Anxiety	70.6	(3.5)	43.8	(3.8)	5.2
Affective	55.3	(4.1)	32.7	(3.4)	4.2
Alcohol	68.1	(4.3)	82.2	(2.7)	2.8
Other	34.4	(5.1)	59.2	(4.0)	3.8

SOURCE: Kandel et al. (1998).

their lifetimes and another 16.4% using three or more substances in their lifetimes. No breakdown by gender was provided.

SUMMARY

Although sex roles have undergone substantial changes in U.S. society over the past generation, men are still allowed or encouraged to drink more often, in greater amounts, and in a greater variety of contexts than women are. In addition, the motives and meaning of drinking may vary for men and women.

Epidemiological studies still show more frequent and larger quantities of alcohol consumption by men in the general population. Men are still more likely than women to be seen in alcoholism treatment facilities, although to some degree, the differences may reflect biases of access rather than sex differences in prevalence of alcohol problems.

The role of alcohol and its effects on women may vary markedly at different ages. During adolescence, drinking may be associated with increased sexual activity, and the patterns of drinking developed at this stage may well serve as "scripts" that influence drinking throughout life. Early drinking also may create conflicts with parents. Adolescents face increasingly greater influence from peers and social norms. Boys traditionally have been encouraged to be more independent and are allowed more deviance from social norms, leading to earlier onset, more frequent use, and greater quantity of alcohol consumption than for girls. Although adolescent males still drink more often and more heavily than females do, the gap has been closing.

Changes in sex roles over the past generation may affect the risks of alcohol abuse for women. On one hand, greater career opportunities outside the home offer more freedom for women and reduce the frustration of being limited to domestic roles. For some women, such opportunities might lessen the potential for alcohol and drug use by offering new avenues for personal fulfillment. For other women, the new roles may not be appealing and could create added or at least different types of stress that also might lead to drug abuse for them just as the traditional roles did for women in the past.

As women marry and begin to have children, most women may reduce their drinking and drug use. However, for other women, these role demands may be pressures that increase drinking, which in turn may impair a woman's relationship with her children and spouse, especially if she neglects, rejects, or abuses them.

At middle age, the empty-nest syndrome, along with the decline of physical health and youthfulness, may be stressors that lead to increased alcohol and other drug use. Finally, elderly women who become widowed may experience stigma and loneliness. In addition, the physical aches and pains of aging increase. All of these factors could lead to more alcohol and other drug use as a coping response.

Historically, drugs now considered illicit were legal means of treating women medically. Opiates were acceptable for pain medication until early in the 20th century. Although these substances are now illegal, other psychoactive medications such as tranquilizers and benzodiazepines have been widely prescribed for women since the 1960s to deal with psychological distress. Consequently, a growing concern exists about the higher prevalence of comorbidity, in which dependence on two or more drugs exists at the same time, such as between alcohol and psychotropic drugs such as sedatives. In addition, comorbidity can occur when drug dependence exists with other psychiatric disorders such as depression or anxiety. There are gender differences in the nature of comorbidity, with women more likely to combine alcohol dependency with affective disorders, whereas men are more likely to suffer from alcohol dependency with antisocial personality and conduct disorders.

KEY TERMS

Comorbidity
Convergence
Psychodynamic theories
Sex role conflict
Sex role deprivation
Sex roles
Sex role theories

STIMULUS/RESPONSE

1. In the past, men consumed more alcohol and many other drugs than women. What factors do you think would lead to convergence of alcohol and other drug use levels by men and women?
2. Convergence could involve the use level of men moving lower toward that of women, or it might involve the use level of women moving higher toward that of men. Is one direction more preferable, and why? Which direction seems to be the actual one?
3. Smoking has tended to increase for adolescent females, but it has declined for most other groups as more information about the health risks has become available. What might account for this pattern? What do you think might change this trend for adolescent females?
4. Among couples, the level of alcohol and other drug use by females is more likely to be influenced by their male partners' level of use, but females' use level is less likely to influence males' level of use. What reasons do you think account for this differential influence?

- ❖ Alcohol Use
- ❖ Smoking
- ❖ Illicit Drugs
- ❖ Influence of Acculturation
- ❖ Summary
- ❖ Key Terms
- ❖ Stimulus/Response

9 Racial/Ethnic Minorities and Alcohol and Other Drug Use

Alcohol and other drug use patterns, their consequences, and the treatment of use-related problems and dependency differ considerably across racial/ethnic groups and cannot be understood by relying on data from predominantly European American samples. It is necessary to include analyses of the use of alcohol and drugs by the many other racial/ethnic groups that make up the American population. The racial and ethnic face of the United States has and will continue to change rapidly as we enter the 21st century. Projections for the U.S. population from 1992 to 2050 indicate a continued decline in the non-Hispanic White population. In contrast, there will be a doubling of African Americans, quadrupling of Hispanic Americans, and a 4½-fold increase for Asian and Pacific Islanders (U.S. Bureau of the Census, 1992). It is predicted that more than half of the K-12 student population will come from racial and ethnic minorities by 2020 (U.S. Department of Education, 1994).

In this chapter, we will focus on racial/ethnic groups that have minority group status in the United States and historically have suffered disadvantages of social injustices inflicted by some combination of racism, lack of economic opportunities, and poor living conditions. In the United States, except for Native Americans, these groups descended from immigrants or, in the case of African Americans, slaves. Because of their different cultures, language, and usually darker skin color, these groups were easy to identify, which helped make them targets for prejudice. Ethnic minority groups, in comparison to each other as well as to Whites, have racial or biological as well as ethnic or cultural differences. We will use the awkward term *racial/ethnic group* to acknowledge this complexity.

In the following discussion of drug use and abuse among racial/ethnic minority groups in America, it must be emphasized at the outset that each of the minority groups to be examined—African Americans, Hispanic or

Latino Americans, Native Americans, and Asian Americans—are far from homogeneous groups, as often implied. Considerable heterogeneity exists within ethnic minority groups that is often overlooked (Cheung, 1993). According to one classification, Directive No. 15 of the Office of Management and Budget (U.S. Department of Commerce, 1978), the basic racial categories are as follows. Blacks or African Americans include persons with origins from any of the racial groups of Africa. Latino Americans originate from such diverse regions as Central and South America, Cuba, Puerto Rico, Mexico, or any Spanish culture. Asian and Pacific Islander Americans include persons with origins from the Far East, Southeast Asia, the Indian subcontinent, or the Pacific Islands. American Indians and Alaska Natives have origins in any of the original peoples of North America. Whites or European Americans comprise persons with origins from peoples of Europe, North Africa, or the Middle East. For reasons of convenience and ease, these arbitrary ethnic glosses (Trimble, 1991) are often very misleading. It should be readily apparent that each racial/ethnic group is diverse and that any depiction of the drug use practices and consequences will not accurately represent all of the ethnic groups that have been assigned to each major category.

Alcohol and other drug use will be examined among ethnic minority groups within the United States. Causal interpretations of ethnic group differences must be taken with caution, however, because some of the observed differences can be attributed to other factors that vary across ethnic groups, such as social class and religious differences, rather than to ethnicity per se. Thus, comparisons of race and ethnicity often fail to control for socioeconomic status, two factors that can independently affect drug use. Ethnic differences in drug problems vary with social class (Jones, Webb, Hsiao, & Hannan, 1995). For example, among the less affluent, African American men reported more adverse drinking consequences and total drinking problems than for White men. However, among affluent men, just the reverse was true.

Generalizations about ethnic minority groups are often based on observations of a limited subset of those populations, primarily those who are male, unemployed, or with low incomes (Lex, 1987). We must not ignore the examination of alcohol and drug use among other subgroups among these ethnic minority groups such as women, the employed, and the affluent.

Another important additional factor not to overlook is the impact of minority status in the host culture. Thus, Asians who would be majority group members in China, Korea, or Japan, for example, would be minority group members in the United States, the targets of racial prejudice and discrimination. Lack of education and unfamiliarity with the English language, especially for recent immigrants, would be additional burdens relegating these groups to lower incomes. Thus, minority group members would differ from majority group members not only in culture and heredity but also in social status. These multiple differences make the task of explaining the factors producing differences in drug use among ethnic groups difficult.

Alcohol Use

National surveys using representative samples from the general population (Caetano, 1988; Clark & Midanik, 1982; Herd, 1990) have shown that the patterns and consequences of drinking are widely different across ethnic minority groups in America. Drinking is highest among European Americans and Native Americans, followed by Latino/Hispanic Americans and African Americans, and is lowest for Asian Americans. Moreover, there is a parallel between the drinking levels of these minority groups and the patterns shown in their countries of origin (Bales, 1946; Blane, 1977).

Overall levels of drinking for all groups have declined from 1984 to 1995 (Caetano & Clark, 1998). It is important, however, to examine patterns rather than only the total amounts of use. For example, although Hispanics and Blacks still drank a smaller total amount and less frequently than Whites did, the quantities consumed per occasion were higher for the two minority groups studied, especially for older ages (Johnson et al., 1998).

Heavy frequent drinking, a pattern often found among young males, decreased over the period as they got older, but only for Whites. Abstention increased over this period for all subgroups except among Hispanic women, who showed a stable level of drinking. These racial/ethnic group differences occurred even though education level and socioeconomic status were controlled.

Studies of adult community samples that have focused on minority groups generally agree with the national surveys about aspects of drinking among African Americans (Herd, 1994), Asian Americans (Chi, Lubben, & Kitano, 1989), and Mexican Americans (Gilbert & Cervantes, 1987).

Among secondary students (Welte & Barnes, 1987), the highest percentage of heavy drinkers occurred among Native Americans, followed by European Americans, Hispanic Americans, and then Asian Americans. In California school surveys (Skager, Frifth, & Maddahian, 1989), minority students in the 7th, 9th, and 11th grades typically reported consuming lower amounts and at lower frequencies than European American students.

Gender differences in drinking among most ethnic minorities were similar to those found with general populations for students at college

(Mooney, Fromme, Kivlahan, & Marlatt, 1987) and secondary school levels (Welte & Barnes, 1987), with males typically consuming alcohol at higher levels and more often than females, with this difference being greater for Asian Americans than for European Americans.

PARENT-CHILD INFLUENCE

Racial/ethnic groups differ in how parents try to influence their children's drinking. Thus, parental disapproval of drinking is associated with higher risk of initiating alcohol use by fifth graders for European Americans (Catalano et al., 1992). Parental influence shows an opposite effect for Asian Americans, serving as a protective factor against their alcohol use. Among African American students, a different factor is more important. For this group, parental influence in the choice of friends, rather than parental drinking, acts as a protective factor against alcohol abuse.

Among racial/ethnic minority groups such as Latino Americans and Asian Americans, drinking is much more prevalent for fathers than for mothers in comparison to European American families, in which drinking by mothers is more acceptable. This gender difference leads to the hypothesis that parental influence may be limited to fathers among minorities, especially for sons. However, for majority group students, both parents should be likely to affect their children's drinking, with fathers' drinking affecting that of sons and mothers' drinking affecting that of daughters.

However, the relationship between parental and adolescent alcohol use is rather similar for both African Americans and European Americans (Peterson, Hawkins, Abbott, & Catalano, 1994). Even though African American parents drank less frequently, had stronger norms against alcohol use, and involved their children less frequently in family alcohol use than did European American parents, there were no differences in the relationship between parent and adolescent drinking. In surveys of community samples, no differences were found between European Americans and African Americans in the parental influence on drinking attitudes and norms of children (Herd, 1994). Similarly, a comparison (Li & Rosenblood, 1994) of Chinese Canadians and European Canadians found that even though the Chinese Canadians drank at a lower level, parental alcohol attitudes and drinking patterns predicted the drinking of students for both groups.

Finally, it should be noted that parents can influence their children's drinking by factors other than their own alcohol use. Moreover, these nondrinking factors may differ with ethnicity. Thus, parental disapproval of drinking is associated with higher risk of initiation of alcohol use by fifth graders for European Americans, but it serves as a protective factor against alcohol use for Asian Americans (Catalano et al., 1992). Another factor, parental determination of choice of friends, acts as a protective factor for African Americans.

METHODOLOGICAL ISSUES

Two approaches, which differ widely in methodology, are widely used to provide evidence about the drinking behavior of ethnic minorities (Lex, 1987). The community or population survey uses standard and objective methods to obtain self-reports from a representative sample of the total population, including members from all minority groups. In contrast to community and population studies, ethnography uses the methods of field researchers such as anthropologists. They make field observations and inferences about the meaning or role of drinking in the context of an ethnic group's values and traditions rather than focus narrowly on quantitative descriptions of the quantity and frequency of consuming various types of alcoholic beverages. Moreover, ethnographers typically have used nonrandom samples and relied on **indigenous reports** about drinking. Despite these important differences, each approach is useful, and the data can be meaningfully combined to further understanding of drinking behaviors.

AFRICAN AMERICANS

African Americans, numbering about 29.28 million and representing 11.8% of the population in 1990 (U.S. Bureau of the Census, 1992), are the largest ethnic minority group in the United States. This group has suffered heavily from the adverse effects of alcohol. Economic factors may be related to heavy drinking among Blacks as both contributing factors and consequences. Living in poverty without hope for improvement might lead to more drinking. At the level of individual behavior, Black drinking has been viewed as a reaction to stress or a form of escape to deal with poverty and racism. However, heavy drinking also can reduce one's economic condition by jeopardizing the ability to gain or hold employment.

Alcohol Consumption

In earlier household population surveys (Cahalan, Cisin, & Crossley, 1969), heavy drinking was present in a comparable percentage (21%) for Black and White men but was three times as high for Black women (11%)

TABLE 9.1 Drinking levels of Blacks and Whites as a function of age (in percentages)

	Age									
	18-29		*30-39*		*40-49*		*50-59*		*60+*	
	Blacks	*Whites*	*Blacks*	*Whites*	*Blacks*	*Whites*	*Blacks*	*Whites*	*Blacks*	*Whites*
Abstainers	23	17	15	13	37	21	29	30	60	41
Infrequent	10	8	6	10	8	16	23	7	14	12
Less frequent, low maximum	10	11	8	8	9	14	4	6	6	9
Less frequent, high maximum	13	10	7	9	3	2	3	8	1	0
Frequent low maximum	20	4	15	12	13	10	14	13	7	24
Frequent high maximum	17	20	33	26	17	17	7	19	6	10
Frequent heavier	16	31	17	21	14	19	20	17	5	4

SOURCE: Herd (1990). Copyright 1990 by *Journal of Studies on Alcohol,* Rutgers Center for Alcohol Studies, New Brunswick, New Jersey. Used with permission.

as for White women (4%). Later national surveys (Clark & Midanik, 1982) showed higher drinking for White than for Black males but the reverse among females. Moreover, as shown in Table 9.1, the age distributions differed for Black and White men, with the levels of drinking increasing over age 30 for Blacks but declining after age 3C for Whites (Herd, 1990). Abstention rates were higher for men and women among Blacks than for White men and women.

In a national survey of 1,947 Black and 1,777 White Americans (Herd, 1994), parental influences had a moderate influence on drinking norms and attitudes and were the most powerful predictors of drinking behavior for both Blacks and Whites. However, the exact relationships between social characteristics and norms, parental demographics, parents' drinking attitudes and behavior, and drinking patterns depended on race.

Among Blacks, variations in alcohol use were related to the degree of ethnic identity (Herd & Grube, 1996). Thus, those who were more involved with Black social networks and had greater Black social and political awareness drank at lower levels. These characteristics were assumed to be related to more conservative drinking norms and greater religiosity. However, those with greater exposure to Black mass media, which emphasize drinking, tended to drink at higher levels.

Alcohol Problems

As noted earlier, White and Black males report similar drinking patterns in early surveys (Cahalan et al., 1969), yet Blacks develop higher rates of physical health problems as a result (Herd, 1987). This disparity could be due to factors such as racial prejudice, unemployment, poor health, and poor living conditions. Physical health hazards, which are increased by heavy drinking among Blacks, include higher liver cirrhosis mortality in several urban areas for Black men (Malin et al., 1982). However, lifetime prevalence rates of alcoholism are comparable at around 14% for Black and White males, as defined by *DSM-III* (1980) criteria (Robins et al., 1984).

The use of alcoholism treatment facilities is one index of the extent of drinking problems. However, ethnic comparisons can be misleading because economic and social factors may bias access to treatment. The 1989 report from the National Institute on Drug Abuse/National Institute on Alcoholism and Alcohol Abuse (NIDA/NIAAA, 1990) on alcoholism treatment in the United States showed that 15% of the total clients were Black, a rate exceeding their representation in the population.

Cultural Factors

It is difficult to define a single Black "drinking style" in that both heavy drinking and abstinence orientations can be found (Herd, 1985). The strong influence of fundamentalist Protestant beliefs among many Blacks may contribute to the high level of abstainers, but the need for a coping response to deal with prejudice and poverty might contribute to the high level of problem drinkers.

An ethnohistorical understanding is needed to explain Black alcohol use. In the early days of slavery, alcohol was valued and was a part of an Afro-American tradition that was not accompanied by high rates of disorderly drunkenness. Then came a shift toward temperance in the United States, partly in concert with the move toward abolition of slavery. Blacks assumed a strong attitude of abstinence because alcohol was viewed as a symbol of White oppression. The Black church emerged as a powerful factor for temperance. But when Prohibition came, along with White supremacist and segregationist views, Black attitudes toward alcohol shifted back to viewing it as a form of oppression. Later, mass migration from the rural South to the industrial cities of the North served to loosen Blacks from social forces such as the church, which discouraged excess drinking. Surrounded by the urban environments of nightlife and tavern drinking, alcohol again shifted in its significance toward a symbol of urbanity and freedom. Even today, alcohol represents sophistication, prestige, and affluence for many urban Blacks.

Studies that fail to recognize the historical context tend to focus on deviant drinking by Blacks, particularly by youth who are assumed to engage in alcohol abuse due to alienation with society. In part, this misrepresentation stems from the use of small and usually unrepresentative samples.

Thus, the impact of religion has a stronger relationship with drinking for African American than for White women. A study of about 1,200 Black and White women (Darrow, Russell, Cooper, Midar, & Frone, 1992) found that drinking was unrelated to church attendance among White women but was inversely related among Black women. In agreement with this finding, abstention was more likely among Black women if they attended church more often, were older, or came from a lower socioeconomic background. Overall, heavier drinkers were more likely to be White, be younger, and have a family history for alcoholism.

The social setting for drinking also varies for Black and White women. Black women do more of their drinking at home in comparison to White women, who drink more often in restaurants, in bars, and at parties (Herd & Grube, 1993). However, the relationship between drinking setting and alcohol-related problems may not be an effect of race per se but may be attributable to race differences in attitudes about drinking and socioeconomic status.

The primary measures of alcohol consumption in most studies focus on the quantity and the frequency of use, but for Blacks it is especially important to consider the quality of the beverage and the place of consumption (Gaines, 1985). A concern with quality can be seen in the focus on brand-name liquors as the only suitable beverages. Drinking in public places is disfavored because drinking is regarded as more appropriate for private social gatherings to enhance conviviality. Whether drinking is viewed as a problem is not a simple matter of the amount; rather, it is defined more in terms of type and context of drinking and its impact on family relationships and job performance.

Analysis of data from a 1984 national probability survey by Herd (1989) showed evidence suggesting some major changes in Black drinking behavior. Unlike in the past, in the 1980s, Black men reared in dry areas such as the rural South were drinking more than those growing up in the urban North. No such pattern reversal was found for Whites who drank more heavily if they came from traditionally "wet" areas. Arrests for public drunkenness and driving while intoxicated were more comparable for Blacks and Whites than in the past, when Blacks showed a higher incidence. Heavier drinking for Black males did not cluster along the same social factors found for Whites (e.g., Catholics, high income, residents of urban North).

Contrary to past beliefs that Black drinking was due to psychopathology, the rapid changes in Black drinking behavior suggest that it may be highly responsive to social conditions and changes (Herd, 1987). Analysis of the social meaning of drinking may be needed to understand these patterns and to plan effective interventions. The past emphasis on the familial environment as a determinant of Black drinking may be less important than legal, political, and economic factors.

Treatment for Black alcoholism has not considered the definition of alcoholism as it is viewed in Black communities, and more culturally sensitive approaches are advocated (Brisbane & Wells, 1989). The church and family strongly support a view prevalent among Blacks that the alcoholic person, not the alcohol, is responsible for the problems. Thus, alcoholics could, if they wished, control their behavior. The conception of alcoholism as a disease, promoted by Alcoholics Anonymous, is not consistent with a common view in Black communities of alcoholism as immoral or sinful behavior.

LATINO/HISPANIC AMERICANS

Latino/Hispanic Americans comprise a heterogeneous population of almost 22 million persons primarily with Mexican, Cuban, Puerto Rican, or Central and South American heritage. They represented about 9% of the population in 1990 (U.S. Bureau of the Census, 1992), making it the second largest ethnic minority in the United States. Moreover, this rapidly growing group has a larger proportion of persons at younger ages than does the general population.

Some limitations exist in past surveys. Prior national surveys on drinking focused on the general population and did not adequately measure "Hispanic" drinking (Caetano, 1990). Early anthropological and sociological studies that focused on Hispanics in the Southwest dealt mostly with deviant drinking. Most research with larger samples that are more representative of Hispanics, however, has been on Mexican Americans, who represent only about 60% of Hispanics. Analysis of survey data collected in the 1984 National Alcohol Survey (Caetano, 1988) showed that Mexican Americans have a more serious problem with alcohol than the other Hispanic groups and have a higher incidence of alcohol-related problems such as accidents, homicides, and arrests than the general population. The 1984 National Alcohol Survey showed that Hispanic male drinking was higher among those with higher education and higher income, contrary to expectations based on views that Hispanic drinking might be due to social deprivation (Caetano, 1990).

Alcohol Consumption

In one of the first general population surveys (Cahalan et al., 1969), about 30% of all Hispanics who drank were in the heavy-drinker category, as compared to only about 17% of all Whites who drank. In contrast, later studies (Alcocer, 1982; Caetano, 1984) that compared the drinking of Hispanic groups and the general population with comparable indices of quantity and frequency of drinking showed different results. These analyses, summarized in Figure 9.1, show that Mexican American males, in comparison with national samples, have about the same percentage of drinkers in the two highest categories. Regional factors were also important; Mexican American males from urban areas (Hisp1) were less likely to abstain and more likely to be frequent drinkers than those from inner-city barrios and rural areas (Hisp2). It also was found (not shown) that Mexican American males were much more often intoxicated than Anglo males.

Differences were found between Mexican American and Anglo women in consumption level, with higher percentages of Mexican American women being abstainers or low consumers, whereas a higher percentage of the Anglo women fell in the two heavy-drinker categories. As with the men, regional differences also played a role, with fewer abstainers and infrequent drinkers among urban (Hisp1) Mexican American women than from the barrio and rural areas (Hisp2).

Many studies of Hispanic alcohol and other drug use combine data from such diverse groups as Mexicans, Puerto Ricans, Cubans, and Central and South Americans. This tendency ignores the wide variations that exist among these groups, as shown in Table 9.2, which presents the past month prevalence rates of licit and illicit drug use for men and women, as reported in the 1993 National Household Survey on Drug Abuse (NHSDA) study. Rates for men were typically higher than were those for women, but the degree varies across subgroups and with the specific substance.

Age seems to be another important factor. In national samples (Caetano, 1988), drinking levels appeared to peak before middle age and then decline. However, the peak was at a later age, 30 to 39, for Mexican American males. Unfortunately, these age differences are based only on cross-sectional studies for Hispanics and do not permit firm conclusions that the patterns of younger drinkers will persist as they grow older. This

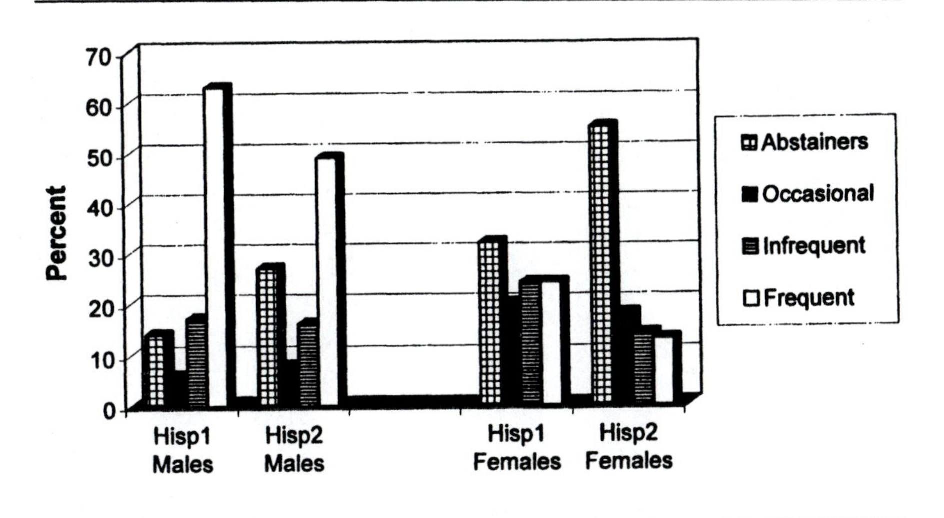

Figure 9.1. Regional Differences in Alcohol Use Among Hispanics, Urban Areas of Northern California (Hisp1) Versus Rural or Barrio Areas of California (Hisp2)
SOURCE: Based on data from Gilbert and Cervantes (1987).

tendency for alcohol use to increase or stay high with older men resembles the pattern in Mexico (Roizen, 1983).

Alcohol Problems

High rates of *DSM-III* (1980) alcohol abuse or dependence occurred for Hispanics in the Los Angeles area (Burnham, 1985). Rates of alcohol abuse or dependence in the past 6 months for those younger than age 40 were higher for Hispanic than for Anglo males (11.2 vs. 7.7), but the opposite held for females (2.0 vs. 4.5). Similar patterns were found for those age 40 and older. Lifetime prevalence rates confirmed the ethnic and gender differences found for the 6-month diagnoses.

According to the National Drug and Alcoholism Treatment Unit Survey (NDATUS) report (NIDA/NIAAA, 1990) on alcoholism treatment in the United States, 10% of alcoholism clients were of Hispanic heritage in 1989. These statistics indicate that Hispanic clients are slightly overrepresented in the proportion of their percentage of the national population, 9%. Such overuse has been consistently reported over the past decade (Gilbert & Cervantes, 1989). The estimated magnitude of Hispanic use of treatment

TABLE 9.2 Prevalence rates of past month drug use among Hispanics in the United States by sex in percentages: 1991-1993

	Male	*Female*	*Total*
Marijuana			
Hispanic	5.6	2.9	4.3
Puerto Rican	6.8	4.0	5.3
Mexican	5.7	2.7	4.3
Cuban	6.3	1.4	3.7
Central American	2.2	0.8	1.4
South American	4.7	1.7	3.2
Other	5.5	5.2	5.3
Cocaine			
Hispanic	1.7	0.9	1.3
Puerto Rican	2.4	0.8	1.5
Mexican	1.9	1.1	1.5
Cuban	1.3	0.3	0.8
Central American	0.9	—[a]	0.4
South American	0.9	0.2	0.5
Other	1.1	0.9	1.0
Alcohol			
Hispanic	58.3	33.9	46.0
Puerto Rican	54.0	34.6	43.5
Mexican	59.0	33.7	47.0
Cuban	59.1	35.8	46.6
Central American	48.8	23.5	34.6
South American	67.5	47.1	57.3
Other	58.9	34.0	45.6
Heavy alcohol			
Hispanic	9.5	1.5	5.5
Puerto Rican	7.3	1.2	4.0
Mexican	11.6	1.7	6.9
Cuban	5.2	0.8	2.8
Central American	4.6	0.3	2.2
South American	5.4	0.7	3.0
Other	6.8	2.2	4.4
Cigarettes			
Hispanic	27.3	17.5	22.4
Puerto Rican	32.7	25.5	28.8
Mexican	27.6	16.6	22.4
Cuban	28.2	16.2	21.8
Central American	19.0	5.8	11.6
South American	28.8	20.5	24.6
Other	21.8	18.1	19.9

SOURCE: U.S. Department of Health and Human Services (1995).

a. Low precision; no estimate reported.

is probably lower than the actual extent. Although the percentage of the Hispanic population younger than age 20 is greater than in the total population, the treatment data do not include many clients younger than that age. Hence, the adult Hispanics receiving treatment represent a much larger percentage of the much smaller adult segments among Hispanic populations.

A comparison (Cervantes, Gilbert, de Snyder, & Padilla, 1990-1991) was made of drinking among U.S.-born Mexican Americans and a mixture of immigrants from Mexico and Central America enrolled in community adult schools in Los Angeles. This sample is unlikely to be representative of most immigrants, and the results may not be highly generalizable. High levels of depression were found, and it was predictive of drinking levels among the men but not for women. Higher positive expectations about the effects of alcohol occurred among men, a factor that may have contributed to greater use of alcohol by men to cope with depression.

Cultural Factors

Machismo makes alcohol consumption play an integral component of the Mexican American male behavior patterns but stigmatizes it for females (Alcocer, 1982). Machismo is a cultural value that emphasizes strength, personal autonomy, and honor but also connotes masculine virility, an aspect that might be seen as promoting heavy drinking. This is a speculation because no studies have clearly defined *machismo* or have measured how it changes over the lifetime in conjunction with alcohol usage.

Cultural explanations for male Hispanic drinking using vaguely defined constructs such as *exaggerated machismo* are simplistic (Caetano, 1990). The item on the 1984 National Alcohol Survey that comes closest to embodying this idea ("a real man can hold his liquor") was endorsed by only 16% of Hispanic males, by 15% of Hispanic females in a national survey, and by even fewer acculturated Hispanics.

NATIVE AMERICANS

The minority group most afflicted with alcohol abuse is Native Americans, estimated to represent 2.02 million, constituting less than 1% of the U.S. population (U.S. Bureau of the Census, 1992). Despite the widely held stereotype of the "drunken Indian," a wide diversity of drinking attitudes and patterns exists among various Native American tribes, as documented by ethnographic or field observations (Weibel-Orlando, 1985). Although there are high rates of heavy drinking among Native Americans, there are also high rates of abstinence. It is also important to consider urban-rural differences because Native Americans in cities have been found to drink at a higher level.

Alcohol Consumption

Native American adolescents consume alcohol at levels that create problems for 42% of the males and 31% of the females in comparison to 34% of White males and 25% of White females. Males between ages 25 and 44 consume the most alcohol, and after age 40, consumption level declines (Lex, 1985).

Alcohol Problems

One index of the severity of alcoholism problems for Native Americans is their disproportionate representation in treatment programs. Although representing less than 1% of the total population, they constitute about 6% of the outpatients treated in federal treatment facilities (National Institute on Alcohol Abuse and Alcoholism, 1981). Another index of the extent of alcoholism among Native Americans is the high liver cirrhosis mortality rate, which is 3½ times the national rate (Indian Health Service, 1982). Other health problems related to alcohol abuse such as pancreatitis, malnutrition, fetal alcohol syndrome, and heart disease were also prevalent (Westermeyer, 1972). Suicide rates (Heath, 1989), as well as homicide rates (Lex, 1985), are about twice the level in the general population.

Cultural Factors

One sociological theory for this situation is that alcohol was new to the American Indians of colonial times, and their culture had no traditions for regulating its use. Another explanation is that the loss of their land and hunting prey as the White settlers expanded the development of the West produced a frustration that was assuaged by excessive use of alcohol. Lack of traditional social roles and loss of autonomy due to these cultural losses might have exposed some Native American tribes such as the Plains tribes to more risk of alcohol problems than others such as the Pueblos (May, 1982).

Although Native Americans are viewed by outsiders as a homogeneous ethnic group and assumed to have common features to their drinking, there are important variations in their attitudes related to alcohol. Anthropologists such as Lévi-Strauss (1966) have distinguished between the "sacred" or spiritual elements and the profane or undesired. Thus, some tribal Native Americans adhere to the myth of the Noble Savage, the unspoiled Native Americans as they supposedly were before the corruptive influence of the European settlers when they arrived on this continent. Alcohol would be the prime example of such a profane influence of the White man that should be scrupulously avoided, especially at any sacred ceremony such as Fifth Sunday Sings, when Native American Christian churches convene.

Profane separation or deviant solidarity is a second stance that might be adopted, one in which there is a collective and public display of flagrant abuse of alcohol. This attitude apparently derives from a rebellion against what may have been once paternalistic Prohibitionist policies restricting Native American access to alcohol, long after it was allowed to every other group. Violating laws and wreaking social havoc, these Native Americans presented a unified reaction to discriminatory policies of the government.

Finally, "maintaining" or controlling one's liquor consumption is a third possible response to alcohol. In the past, powwows, Native American ceremonial events of tribal music and dance, often involved heavy drinking and antisocial behaviors. However, a change toward better monitoring and control of drinking has been observed at powwows through greater physical separation of space allocated for the sacred and the profane activities (Weibel & Weisner, 1980).

There is not, as popularly thought, a single **drinking style** among Native Americans. For example, among the Navajo, there are both recreational and anxiety drinkers (Ferguson, 1968). In the former style, males drink in groups on weekends and special occasions in large quantities for long periods, with the intent to become intoxicated. This style is typified by the solitary and regular use of alcohol by socially marginal individuals, akin to skid row alcoholics, who are rejected by their tribes. Among the Chippewa (Westermeyer, 1972), both unrestrained "Native American" and restrained "White" styles of drinking exist, even in the same individuals, depending on the time and place. Native American drinking styles vary by time and location. One recreational style is accompanied by loud talking, warm interpersonal relationships, and hilarity, which may continue until all financial resources are depleted. This style is generally reserved for drinking among other Native Americans.

These different perspectives hold implications for the types of treatments that might be successful for Native Americans with drinking problems. First, it should be noted that the label *alcoholic* is not used by most Native Americans, although they recognize that some people drink "too much." Typically, Native Americans in an alcoholism treatment facility are there not because they recognize themselves as alcoholics with a treatable disease but because the alternative, usually jail, is worse.

Due to the lack of correspondence between the Native American's view of the drinking and that of the treatment facility, the high failure rate is not surprising. Differences of philosophy exist in various facilities, many of which are culturally sensitive but still short of meeting the typical

Native American client's needs (Weibel-Orlando, 1985). It must be kept in mind that some forms of intoxication have traditionally been an integral part of Native American sacred ceremonies. In contrast, today alcohol is associated with secular or nonreligious activities to a greater extent. Successful treatment programs for Native Americans seem to combine spiritual elements and activities with their treatment procedures.

ASIAN AMERICANS

Asian Americans represent a wide variety of cultures, but the total population is quite small compared to other ethnic minority groups, despite rapid growth in the past decade. Combined, all Asian Americans still make up less than 3% of the U.S. population (U.S. Bureau of the Census, 1992). The category "Asian American" is a designation that is useful as a residual or catch-all grouping rather than as an ethnic or racial group. It is no more culturally valid than one that combined Americans of Swedish, Italian, and German descent into a group called European Americans.

As a whole, Asian Americans come from cultures that have traditionally emphasized Confucian ideals of moderation. Consistent with these views, moderate use of alcohol for males and little or no alcohol consumption for females have been the norm. Public drunkenness is highly frowned on as disgraceful and unacceptable conduct. In view of these cultural roots, one would expect that these groups would have low to moderate use of alcohol and be relatively free from alcohol problems.

Alcohol Consumption

A survey of these groups (Chi et al., 1989) indicates that considerable diversity of drinking levels by these groups exists, as shown in Figure 9.2.

A survey (Kitano & Chi, 1986-1987) of four different Asian cultures in Los Angeles found that Chinese American males drank alcohol in smaller quantities than the general U.S. population, with a higher percentage of abstainers as well. Indirect evidence of low alcoholism rates was found in the low rates of admission for alcoholism treatment for Chinese, although this might reflect a cultural bias against seeking treatment rather than an absence of problems.

Of the four Asian groups, another study (Sue, Kitano, Hatanaka, & Yeung, 1985) showed that Chinese American males had the highest number of abstainers and the lowest number of heavy drinkers. In contrast, higher levels of drinking closer to those of the general population were found in the other Asian American groups. Japanese American drinking practices were surveyed using random households in Los Angeles (Kitano, Hatanaka, Yeung, & Sue, 1985). Higher rates for both the abstainer and

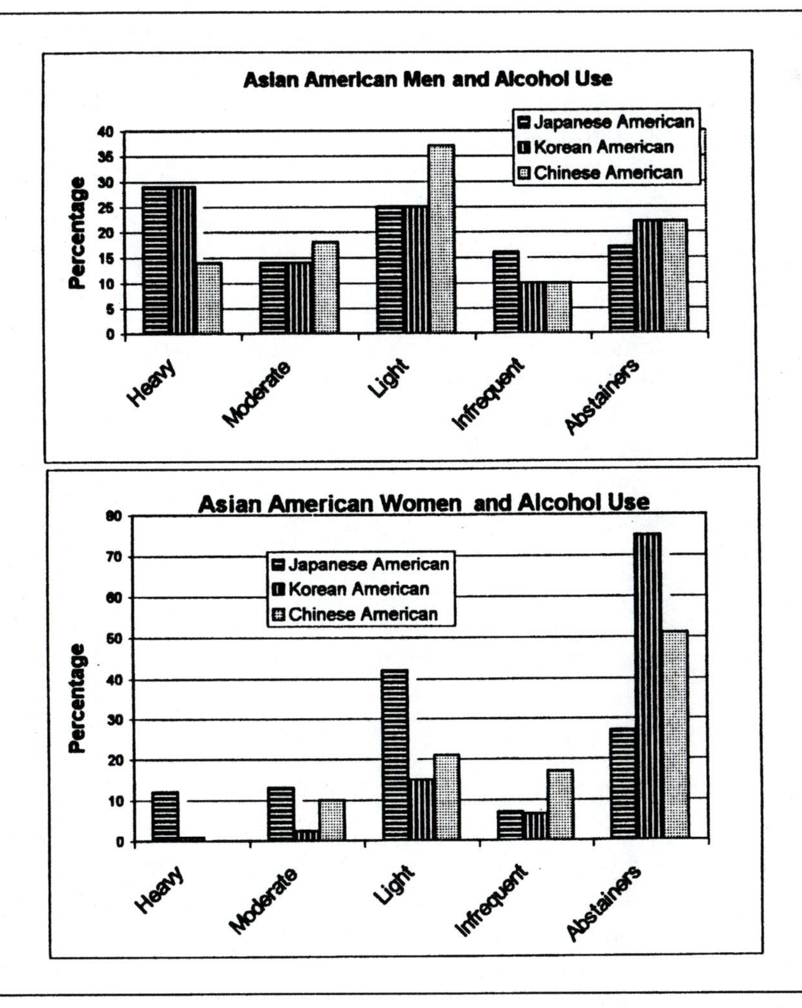

Figure 9.2. Drinking Levels by Chinese, Korean, and Japanese Americans
SOURCE: Based on data from Chi et al. (1989).

heavy drinker categories occurred for Japanese American males more than for other Asian American groups. However, drinking level was not closely related to problem behavior.

A comparison of drinking of Korean American and Chinese American men and women showed that Koreans had higher rates of alcohol use for both sexes (Weatherspoon, Danko, & Johnson, 1994). Men of both groups drank more often and in larger amounts than women. A study (Lubben, Chi, & Kitano, 1988a) of drinking of Filipino Americans, one of the largest Asian American groups, found that a high percentage of Filipino males, more than 29%, were found to be heavy drinkers. Among Korean American males, more than 25% were heavy drinkers, but almost 45% were abstainers (Lubben, Chi, & Kitano, 1988b).

Among Asian American females, alcohol use is low overall (Chi et al., 1989). The highest percentage of heavy drinkers (11.7%) was with Japanese Americans, but this category was virtually nonexistent for the Chinese, Korean, and Filipino groups.

Physiological Factors

The lower use of alcohol by Asian Americans has been attributed to a greater physiological reactivity to alcohol among Asian peoples, as reflected by **facial flushing** that occurs in substantially more Asian than Caucasian adults (Wolff, 1972) and infants (Zeiner & Paredes, 1978). The facial flushing created by vasodilation due to alcohol is one indication that alcohol has a stronger or quicker effect on peoples of Asian descent.

Genetic differences may be involved (Wall, Thomasson, & Ehlers, 1996). After Asian American men (ages 21-25) received a placebo beverage or a 0.75 ml/kg alcohol beverage, the extent of observed flushing was a sensitive and specific predictor of the presence of the allele for the ALDH2 genotype, which is related to how alcohol is metabolized.

Asians seem to metabolize alcohol differently (at a slower rate, so that they have an adverse physiological reaction to a small dose) than other ethnic groups. If this biological factor serves to prevent persons of Asian descent from having serious drinking problems, why do Native Americans, who apparently have similar biological reactions to alcohol, have such serious problems with heavy drinking and alcoholism? One explanation is that Asians place a premium on maintaining "face" so that the threat of losing control of one's behavior due to alcohol reduces the risk of drinking problems. In contrast, it has been argued that Native Americans use alcohol to enhance visionary experiences so that intoxication is congruent with such goals, despite the similar adverse biological reactions.

Cultural Factors

Asian cultures strongly discourage public intoxication, and the alcohol abuser is highly ostracized. The family traditionally plays a strong role in Asian cultures influenced by Confucian ideals, and it discourages public drunkenness in favor of moderation. Integration of drinking with meals also has been suggested (Lin, 1982) as a factor minimizing alcohol problems. Although most Asian cultures have low alcoholism rates, there is still some variability among them. For example, men in Japan seem to drink at higher levels than in the United States, but the opposite is true for women (Kitano, Chi, Rhee, Law, & Lubben, 1992). Differences in cultural values, norms, and institutions regulating alcohol use exist among Asian cultures.

TABLE 9.3 Percentage of adults age 18 and older by current cigarette smoking status and number of cigarettes smoked overall and by sex, race, and Hispanic origin: National Health Interview Surveys, 1987, 1988, 1990, and 1991 (combined)

	Hispanic	*White*	*Black*	*Asian/Pacific Islander*	*American Indian/ Alaska Natives*
Male					
Current	28.6	29.1	35.9	23.9	38.0
Former	21.6	32.1	19.6	19.6	26.0
Female					
Current	17.0	25.7	7.8	7.8	36.2
Former	13.4	20.4	6.9	6.9	17.9
Total					
Current	22.5	27.3	16.0	16.0	37.1
Former	17.2	26.0	13.4	13.4	21.9

SOURCE: Substance Abuse and Mental Health Services Administration (1995).
NOTE: "Current" cigarette smoking status identifies persons who reported smoking at least 100 cigarettes in their lifetimes and who currently smoke cigarettes. "Former" smokers are those who reported smoking at least 100 cigarettes and who are not smoking cigarettes now. "Never" smokers are those who reported that they have not smoked at least 100 cigarettes in their lifetimes.

A comparison (Akutsu, Sue, Zane, & Nakamura, 1989) was made of relative effects on drinking of both physiological differences and cultural differences between Asian Americans and European Americans. Physiological reactivity and attitudes toward drinking were the best predictors of ethnic differences in drinking levels.

Smoking

Tobacco use differs between and within U.S. racial/ethnic minority groups as well as in comparison with non-Hispanic Whites (U.S. Surgeon General, 1998). Among four major racial/ethnic minority groups, Table 9.3 shows that the highest prevalence of adult male smoking occurs for Native Americans and Alaska Natives, followed by African Americans, Hispanics, and, lastly, Asian and Pacific Islanders. In all groups, other than Native Americans and Alaska Natives, men have higher prevalence rates of smoking than women. Decreases in smoking rates between 1978 and 1995 for some groups—such as African Americans, Asian and Pacific Islanders, and Hispanics—were found in the National Health Interview Surveys between 1987 and 1991.

However, among adolescents, there has been a renewed upswing in cigarette smoking among African American and Hispanic youth. This usage has been high since 1978 for young women of childbearing age for most groups, especially Native Americans and Alaska Natives. Education level plays a role, as greater declines in smoking occurred for high school graduates among African American, Hispanic, and White men. Education level was less related to declines for women.

Illicit Drugs

The reasons for illicit drug use among minority groups are complex. Cultural and historical explanations suggest that past traditions and beliefs account for why some groups use illicit drugs. Marijuana was used by Mexican migrant workers in the early 1900s in the American Southwest and later became popular among Black jazz musicians. Opium was used by Chinese immigrants who came to California in the mid-1800s. For many Native American tribes, hallucinogens such as peyote and mescaline have been used for centuries as part of their ceremonies and rituals. A different explanation, based on social status, attributes the use of illicit drugs among some members of minority groups to the lack of opportunity, racial prejudice, unemployment, and poverty.

In the Monitoring the Future (MTF) study (Johnston et al., 1996), racial/ethnic differences in drug use varied somewhat with drug type. As a whole, among 12th graders, Whites had the highest illicit drug use rates, whereas Blacks generally had the lowest rates for illicit drugs. Among 12th graders, Hispanics had the highest rates for many illicit drugs such as cocaine, crack, marijuana, and heroin. Whereas Native Americans generally had the highest overall rates, Asian Americans generally had the lowest rates.

The 1991 to 1993 data for the NHSDA (see Table 9.4) provide prevalence rates of different racial/ethnic groups for licit and illicit drug use during the past 30 days. The use of any illicit drug or, specifically, of marijuana reported in the NHSDA surveys was generally highest for Native Americans and Alaska Natives, followed by Blacks, Whites, and Hispanics. Asian and Pacific Islanders were lowest. Males tended to use at rates dou-

TABLE 9.4 Percentage of past month drug use by race/ethnic group, 1991-1993, combined for men and women

	Any Illicit Drug	*Marijuana*	*Cocaine*	*Alcohol*	*Heavy Alcohol*	*Cigarettes*
White	5.5	4.2	0.5	52.7	23.2	24.7
Black	6.8	5.6	1.3	37.6	17.6	23.4
Hispanic	6.2	4.7	1.1	45.6	17.2	21.2
American Indian/Alaska Native	11.3	8.6	3.1	50.7	6.6	38.7
Asian/Pacific Islander	2.8	1.5	0.3	33.3	1.1	16.9

SOURCE: U.S. Department of Health and Human Services (1995).

TABLE 9.5 Percentage reporting past month use of any illicit drug by race/ethnic group, 1979-1998

	1979	*1985*	*1991*	*1992*	*1993*	*1994*	*1995*	*1996*	*1997*	*1998*
White	14.2	12.3	6.5	6.1	6.1	6.0	6.0	6.1	6.4	6.1
Black	13.3	12.7	8.1	5.6	5.8	7.3	7.9	7.5	7.7	8.2
Hispanic	12.9	8.9	5.3	4.4	5.2	5.4	5.1	5.2	5.9	6.1
Other	15.1	10.7	6.0	3.9	4.3	3.1	4.0	4.8	5.4	3.8

SOURCE: Substance Abuse and Mental Health Services Administration (1997).

ble that of females (not shown in the table), with the exception of Native Americans and Alaska Natives, who had almost equally high rates for males and females.

Trends in illicit drug use over the past month can be compared for different ethnic groups with data from the NHSDA studies from 1979 to 1998. As shown in Table 9.5, during this period, Whites and Blacks had higher rates for any illicit drug in the past month than Hispanics or "Others" (a residual category that included Native Americans and Asian Americans and other small size samples).

However, the "Other" grouping combines highly dissimilar groups only because they are so small in numbers. Yet it is misleading because Asian Americans and Native Americans are at the two extreme ends of the use dimension. The "solution" for this problem in the NHSDA report for 1997 was to delete the "Other" grouping entirely and report data for only Whites, Blacks, and Hispanics.

Influence of Acculturation

Although some stability in drinking patterns occurs over successive generations for several ethnic groups (Greeley, McCready, & Theisen, 1980), the influence of **acculturation** is highly evident for most groups. Drinking patterns move away from those in the country of origin toward those found for the U.S. general population (Blane, 1977). Thus, Irish Americans drink less than the Irish in Ireland, whereas the Jews in America drink more than those in Israel. Similarly, a comparison (Kitano et al., 1992) of alcohol use among Japanese in Japan, Hawaii, and California found that the acculturated Japanese Americans in California drank more in line with American than with Japanese norms.

One study (Caetano & Mora, 1988) investigated the acculturation process through which Mexican immigrants develop changes in drinking after they move to the United States. Responses to a drinking questionnaire by Mexican Americans as part of a national probability sample and by men living in the surroundings of Morelia, Mexico were compared. Although Mexican American men drank more frequently than the Mexicans, they typically drank smaller amounts, suggesting a shift toward U.S. drinking norms. Despite lower amounts of drinking by Mexicans, they reported experiencing more problems related to alcohol than did Mexican Americans. Thus, the impact of drinking is not entirely due to the consumption levels but also depends on cultural values and reactions of the drinker's ethnic group. Mexican American women did tend to drink more often as well as in larger quantities than Mexican women, suggesting that acculturation involves greater change for Mexican women. Hence, a greater increase in drinking occurs among them than for men (Caetano, 1990).

Expectations of Hispanics and non-Hispanic Whites may affect drinking patterns. Low-acculturation Hispanics have greater expectancies of emotional and behavioral impairment and social extroversion from drinking than Whites, but with increased acculturation, these differences in expectations disappear (Marin, Posner, & Kinyon, 1993).

Acculturation and Hispanic drinking do not always have the same relationship; sometimes, they are associated with more abstention, and sometimes they are related to more frequent drinking (Caetano, 1990). The nature of the effect may depend on national origin (Puerto Rico, Mexico, Cuba) and the relocation site. Heavier drinking was found for Hispanics in California than in Texas, reflecting the drinking norms of these locales, as there are more instances of drunkenness and alcohol-related problems in California than in Texas.

A simple acculturation model may not provide a complete explanation of the drinking of minorities. A comparison (Neff, Hoppe, & Perea, 1987) of drinking of Mexican American and Anglo men across a wide age range with controls for social class found that Mexican Americans drank less frequently but in higher quantity than Whites, but they seemed to have comparable levels of problems. Quantity was higher for the *less* acculturated men, suggesting that the stress of marginality led to higher drinking.

The stress of becoming acculturated might produce higher drinking levels (Neff & Hoppe, 1992). Alcohol consumption was examined for Mexican American, White, and Black drinking adults ages 20 to 30. Researchers found higher quantity and frequency of drinking among the *least* acculturated males and moderately acculturated females. There was no support for the acculturation stress model predicting that more acculturated groups would drink at higher levels.

The process underlying acculturation to the ways of a new culture is a complex change involving two concurrent processes (Landrine & Klonoff, 1998). First, extinction of the norms, attitudes, and use patterns of alcohol and tobacco of the country of origin occurs. Concurrently, acquisition of the norms and attitudes of the host culture takes place. Whether an individual group shows increased or decreased use depends on the relative degree of drug use in the host and origin countries. Thus, someone coming from a country where drug use is higher than in the United States will gradually tend to decrease his or her level of use, and vice versa for someone from a country where drug use is lower than in the United States. In accord with this model, smoking and drinking rates of ethnic minority groups coming from countries with lower use than that of the United States *increased* as these groups acculturated to American norms. In contrast, smoking and drinking rates of those coming from countries with higher use *decreased* the longer they lived in the United States.

This model also can account for the often opposite effects of acculturation for men and women. Increased acculturation generally leads to more drinking and smoking for women, but it is associated with declines for men. In most cultures from which U.S. racial/ethnic minorities originate, men drink and smoke at a much higher rate than women do. Hence, when they move to the United States, the men show a drop in use, whereas women show a rise in use.

Finally, immigrants come in different waves or cohorts, and changes due to acculturation can vary with the specific cohort. Thus, the immigrants from Japan to the United States at the turn of the 20th century came from a different background than those coming at the turn of the 21st century.

In addition, the drinking norms in the United States to which they came in the early 1900s have changed drastically and differ for the 21st-century immigrants.

SUMMARY

Although alcohol is consumed almost universally, consumption patterns and problems related to its use vary widely across different cultures. Within U.S. society, racial/ethnic minority subgroups differ among themselves and from the Anglo norms of drinking. In addition to the biological and psychosocial factors that might influence the drinking patterns of any ethnic group, minority groups face the stress of marginality, poverty, and racial prejudice as factors affecting drinking and drinking consequences.

Comparisons of drinking levels and alcohol-related problems between minority groups and Whites can be highly misleading if socioeconomic disparity is not considered. As is true for Whites, social class differences among minority groups also influence drinking styles and consequences.

As among Whites, women drink much less than men among the ethnic minorities examined. Whereas males in some ethnic minorities match or exceed the drinking levels of Whites, the female minorities typically drink less than White females.

Among most racial/ethnic minorities, the distribution of drinking appears to be more bimodal than for Whites, with more abstainers as well as more heavy drinkers. Also, the age at which drinking seems to reach its peak is generally later for racial/ethnic minorities than for Whites. Overall, Latino American and Asian American college students generally consume alcohol less frequently and in lower amounts than European Americans. The highest percentage of heavy drinkers was found among Native Americans, followed by European Americans, Hispanic Americans, and then Asian Americans.

Use of other drugs also varies with racial/ethnic minorities. Cigarette smoking is highest for Native Americans and Alaska Natives and lowest among Asian and Pacific Islanders, with men generally smoking at higher rates than women. Illicit drug use is often thought to be prevalent in racial/ethnic minority groups, but there are wide variations. Among high school students, Whites had the highest rates, but among racial/ethnic minorities, Hispanics and Native Americans had the highest rates, and Blacks and Asian and Pacific Islanders had the lowest rates. These patterns shift slightly with adult populations.

To understand the nature of substance use among minorities, one should consider the historical background of drugs within specific ethnic groups. The factors that lead to alcohol and other drug use and the role it plays are not the same for each minority group. As immigrant groups become acculturated to the United States, their drinking and smoking patterns begin to increase or decrease to resemble more closely those of the host culture than those in the country of origin.

KEY TERMS

Acculturation
Drinking style
Facial flushing
Indigenous reports
Machismo

STIMULUS/RESPONSE

1. Are racial/ethnic group differences in alcohol and other drug use due to socioeconomic factors more than to cultural attitudes? Can you design a study to evaluate the effect of these different factors?
2. Using Asian Americans as an example, consider factors that contribute to different alcohol and other drug use among subgroups such as those of Chinese, Korean, Japanese, and Vietnamese descent.
3. Do you think acculturation to U.S. alcohol and other drug use norms will be faster for men or for women and why? Which racial/ethnic groups will acculturate faster to American alcohol and other drug use norms and why?

- ❖ Methodological Issues
- ❖ Personality Theory and Dependency
- ❖ Different Relationships of Personality to Dependency
- ❖ Psychopathology and Dependency
- ❖ Summary
- ❖ Key Terms
- ❖ Stimulus/Response

10 Personality Differences in Relation to Alcohol and Other Drugs

Is there an **addictive personality**, some pattern of traits typically found more often among those who are dependent on alcohol and other drugs? An addictive personality might be considered to exist if it could be determined that the psychological characteristics of those who were dependent on a particular drug were considerably different from those who were not. However, there would still be the question of whether these characteristics preceded the substance dependency and possibly contributed to its development or whether these traits were primarily the consequences of being drug dependent. Further complicating the issue is the likelihood that some personality correlates might be both causes and effects of dependency rather than one or the other.

However, alcohol and other drug users constitute a heterogeneous group, and the factors leading from use to abuse and dependency may differ widely across individuals as well as across different drugs. Nonetheless, the strong tendency to adopt stereotypes fosters the idea that some set of personality traits exists that differentiates those with drug use disorders from those without them. If such differences could be identified, it might be possible to design more effective methods of intervention, treatment, and prevention. Consequently, researchers have devoted much effort to the search for personality factors associated with dependency on a variety of substances. The concern of this chapter is whether such personality differences exist and how they are related to alcohol and other drug dependencies.

Methodological Issues

A major goal of research on personality is to identify characteristics that distinguish alcoholics from nonalcoholic controls. However, it is also possible that some traits observed among alcoholics may not be specific to this group but also may exist with other forms of psychopathology. Alcoholics may suffer from other psychological disorders such as depression or anxiety, aside from their problems with drinking, and these characteristics may reflect those problems rather than alcohol dependency per se, as will be discussed in more detail later.

NONALCOHOLIC CONTROLS

Unfortunately, many studies of the personality of alcohol and drug-dependent individuals lack control groups of individuals who are not dependent on these substances. Indeed, it is difficult to determine what constitutes an adequate control group. Even studies of institutionalized drug-dependent persons that include a comparison with some other institutionalized groups who are not drug dependent may be inconclusive because their behavior may reflect consequences of institutionalization. Finally, most of these studies are dealing with dependent persons receiving some form of treatment, a population consisting mostly of males from lower socioeconomic levels, persons who may differ from those who are not yet in treatment or with different backgrounds.

Studies with more adequate research designs have used three groups: alcohol or other drug-dependent persons, another psychiatric sample not dependent on alcohol or other drugs, and a noninstitutionalized control group of "normals." Without the inclusion of the psychiatric non-drug-dependent persons, there is the possibility that any impairments found in comparison to the normals may have been due to the effects of being institutionalized rather than to alcohol or other drug dependency per se.

MEASURING ALCOHOL DEPENDENCY

Research on personality uses a variety of measures to identify individuals who are alcohol dependent. Unfortunately, the measures used do not define alcohol dependency with the established criteria used by clinicians such as the *DSM-III-R* (1987).

Many earlier studies relied on the MacAndrew Scale (MacAndrew, 1965), a widely used measure consisting of 49 items from the **Minnesota**

Multiphasic Personality Inventory (MMPI). This scale differentiated male alcoholic outpatients from male nonalcoholic psychiatric outpatients. It should be noted, however, that the average age was around 42 for the alcoholics but only about 35 for the psychiatric controls, so that some differences might be due to this age difference. A serious problem with the scale is that it misclassified about 15% of nonalcoholics as alcoholics and another 15% of alcoholics as nonalcoholics. The scale may allow many false-positive identifications of alcoholics.

The MacAndrew Scale was based on middle-aged White males, so it is less valid for identifying alcoholics among women, adolescents, and minority groups (Gottesman & Prescott, 1989). Furthermore, no evidence was obtained about the alcohol and drug use of the psychiatric controls, nor was there any information about the psychological adjustment of the alcoholics. It is highly unlikely that there would be no overlap between the two groups; that is, we would expect that some psychiatric patients abuse alcohol and that some alcoholics have psychological disturbances. Lack of such information limits the generalizability of the scale to other populations.

The MMPI, as well as other self-report inventories, has shown negative affect and low self-esteem in alcoholics entering treatment. However, as treatment progresses, these characteristics are reduced, implying that they may have been temporary reactions to alcohol problems rather than causes. If they had been "causes" of alcoholism, they should have been less likely to change during treatment for alcoholism.

Although alcoholics had been found to score high on certain MMPI scales such as Scale 4 (psychopathic deviate), there does not seem to be a single MMPI profile that could characterize an "alcoholic personality" (Graham & Strenger, 1988). More attention should be directed toward differences on the MMPI among subgroups.

RETROSPECTIVE STUDIES

Many research studies designed to test theories about the personality of alcoholics have examined alcoholics *after* they have become alcoholic. Inferences often are based mainly on their retrospective recall of earlier aspects of their lives. Interviews with adult alcoholics often may reveal a chaotic childhood, but distortions of memory, selective recall, or deliberate misrepresentation render this type of evidence of uncertain validity. Even if such experiences occurred, it is difficult to know how much they contributed to subsequent drinking problems. Questions of whether an "unhappy" childhood, unresolved dependency needs, parental conflicts, or other factors contributed to alcoholism cannot be tested accurately with this procedure.

The retrospective study of the personality of alcoholics has centered on clients in clinical settings, where there is an overrepresentation of less educated individuals from lower socioeconomic levels of the population. Most of these studies have included no comparisons of males and females. Indeed, most studies have been of males only, and when both sexes have been studied, the results are typically combined across sex, obscuring any differences that might exist.

PROSPECTIVE STUDIES

In contrast to retrospective studies, prospective studies use evidence about the prealcoholic years obtained prior to the appearance of alcoholism. For example, adolescents with no drinking problems took the California Personality Inventory as part of a developmental study (Jones, 1968, 1971). A comparison of those male adolescents with subsequent alcohol problems and a control group without such problems showed that male problem drinkers had been more rebellious and extroverted even before they began to drink. Among females (Jones, 1971), however, there were different antecedents of problem drinking. Middle-aged females were interviewed and classified into five levels of drinking, ranging from abstainer to problem drinker. An examination was made of their personality traits that had been measured during adolescence prior to the onset of using alcohol. Those who were presently heavy drinkers differed from those without problem drinking but in different ways from those observed among males. The heavy-drinking women had been more pessimistic, withdrawn, and less independent as adolescents than their lighter-drinking counterparts.

A problem with any longitudinal study is what happens to the participation rate over the duration of the study. The longer the study, the more attrition and loss of participants for many reasons. If there is no bias in the dropout, such as a random subsample moving out of the area over time, the problem is not as serious if the number is a small percentage. However, it is more likely that heavier alcohol and drug users are probably less likely to be followed up, especially if the study is very lengthy, because they cannot be located or they do not want to be located.

These problems can be reduced with a study of briefer duration. A study involving a short time span may incur fewer dropouts so that generalizability can be maintained. However, this gain comes at some cost. Some effects, especially in the area of drug use, may require many years for measurable differences to be found between those who abuse and are dependent versus those who are not. Failure to find effects may simply reflect the brevity of the time frame of the study.

From a practical point of view, prospective studies are also more expensive to conduct. Finally, the investigator may not be able or want to wait until 20 or more years have elapsed before obtaining data to analyze and report.

Personality Theory and Dependency

PSYCHODYNAMIC THEORY

The psychoanalytic approach emphasizes often unconscious motives for excessive use of alcohol and drug use. These motives may reflect the influence of intensely emotional experiences during infancy or early childhood. In contrast, the biological vulnerability approach (see Chapter 6) focuses on differences in innate physiological reactivity that may produce variations in the effects of alcohol and other drugs.

Early psychological theories of alcoholism had roots in psychoanalytic theory. This emphasis was perhaps due to the fact that many alcoholics sought therapy from psychoanalytically oriented psychiatrists (Cox, 1987). As with psychoanalytic views about many other forms of psychopathology, psychoanalytic explanations of alcoholism focused on unresolved early childhood conflicts of an unconscious nature. Psychosexual development, as proposed by Sigmund Freud (1905/1962), involved a series of stages. Perhaps due to arrested development or fixation at the oral stage of development, a need for alcohol developed as a means of achieving immediate oral gratification and pleasure. Alcoholics were depicted as being immature, dependent, and unable to delay gratification. Use of alcohol was seen as a means to feel good immediately or to achieve a feeling of power.

A classic study (McCord & McCord, 1960) using juvenile delinquents tested the dependency view of alcoholism. A comparison of those who later became alcoholics with those who did not led to the conclusion that *conflict* about dependency rather than dependency per se underlies alcoholism for males. Society demands that males be independent and fulfill the masculine role, which involves aggressiveness. Such a role encourages males to drink alcohol. However, if a potential male alcoholic is fixated or blocked in development at the oral stage, he has unresolved dependency needs that are not in keeping with the male role, and a dilemma exists. Drinking heavily on occasion enables one to fulfill one aspect of the expected masculine role behavior; at the same time, this drinking behavior creates dependence on others without censure because this dependency can be attributed to the influence of alcohol. Consequently, by drinking heavily, males can try to fulfill the need of independence and dependence simultaneously.

A power theory of alcoholism (McClelland et al., 1972) proposed a model of the motivation for drinking in general rather than one limited to the drinking of alcoholics. The independence and aggressiveness often seen in male drinkers were interpreted as a direct manifestation of a drive for power rather than a reaction against dependency. Drinking enables men to engage in fantasies and feelings of power. Thus, lack of power leads to drinking. A series of studies measuring fantasies and imagery in projective test situations before and after the consumption of alcohol was a major line of evidence used to support the theory. As larger amounts of alcohol were consumed, the fantasies revealed greater degrees of personal power.

This approach for explaining the drinking of men was extended to the analysis of drinking among women (Wilsnack, 1974). In contrast to the model proposed for men, this view proposed that drinking served to reduce rather than elicit fantasies of power among women. Women were depicted as having more fantasies about engaging in traditionally feminine activities after drinking. Those women who developed alcoholism were assumed to be more likely to have anxieties about their womanliness. According to this view, alcohol-dependent women might turn to alcohol to help them cope with these feelings of inadequacy (Wilsnack, 1973).

One problem with psychoanalytic theories of the personality processes involved in drinking is that the formulations are difficult to test because they involve assumptions about early experiences about which there is usually no objective evidence. Unconscious processes are controversial because they are not readily amenable to investigation with objective methods. Also, as with the dependency and power formulations, the predictions are sometimes diametrically opposed.

TYPOLOGIES

Although often criticized as simplistic, theories of personality often have involved identifying typologies or classifications of basic groups such as introversion-extraversion, as if everyone could be categorized as one or the other type. Similarly, in the field of alcoholism, several classifications have been proposed.

Type 1 and Type 2 Alcoholism

One typology, based on Swedish studies of adopted children from alcoholic families (Cloninger, 1987), distinguished two forms of alcoholism.

TABLE 10.1 Characteristics of Cloninger's milieu-limited versus male-limited alcoholism compared to Babor's Type A and B typology of alcoholics

	Type 1 (Milieu Limited)	*Type 2 (Male Limited)*
Usual age of onset	After 25	Before 25
Inability to abstain	Less likely	More likely
Fighting and arrests when drinking	Less likely	More likely
Loss of control	Less likely	More likely
Fear and guilt over dependence	Less likely	More likely
	Type A	*Type B*
Usual age of onset	Later	Earlier
Alcohol family history	Less likely	More likely
Alcohol-related problem	Less likely	More likely
Psychopathology	Less likely	More likely

One form, termed *milieu-limited alcoholism* (Type 1), shown in Table 10.1, emerges at a later age, generally after age 25, and in a less severe form. It represented about 13% of the sample. These drinkers did not engage in much aggressive behavior when drinking but did show problems with loss of control or psychological dependence on alcohol along with guilt and fear about this outcome.

A more severe form of alcoholism, typically developing before age 25, was defined as *male-limited alcoholism* (Type 2), as this type seemed absent among women. The biological fathers tended to have severe alcoholism. Variations in the environment of these children did not affect the number of abusers. This type of alcoholism occurred for 4% of the sample. These adoptees had moderate alcohol abuse usually, but such abuse often led to fighting and aggression without much psychological dependence or guilt. Although both types involve heritable factors, the environmental conditions play an additional role with the milieu-limited type but not with the male-limited variety of alcoholism.

Three behavioral dimensions—novelty seeking, harm avoidance, and reward dependence—were proposed as contributors toward the different patterns and consequences of drinking displayed by the two types. As shown in Table 10.1, Type 1 alcoholics would be governed by inhibition. They avoid harm, do not seek novelty, and depend highly on social rewards. They have less severe alcoholism. In contrast, Type 2 individuals seek novelty, do not avoid potential harm, and have low reliance on social rewards; these characteristics may contribute to their likelihood of more severe and earlier problems related to alcohol.

Type A and Type B Alcoholism

A similar typology, based on samples of male and female alcoholics, identified two types: A and B (Babor et al., 1992). The **Type A alcoholic** is similar to Type 1 in taking longer to develop and having less dependence, fewer alcohol-related problems, and less psychopathology. The **Type B alcoholic**, in contrast, is similar to the Type 2 alcoholic, showing earlier onset, more childhood risk factors, family history of alcoholism, and greater psychopathology. The typology was validated with another alcoholic sample (Brown, Babor, Litt, & Kranzler, 1994).

Developmental Types of Alcoholism

An analysis (Zucker, 1987) of drinking from a developmental perspective, with a concern for identifying the origins of drinking, provided a taxonomy that also offers a perspective on the role of personality or individual difference factors. This taxonomy involved four primary alcoholisms: antisocial, developmentally limited, negative affect, and developmentally cumulative. The antisocial form involves early onset, with heavy drinking and alcohol-related problems. It may be transmitted genetically, and a family history for alcoholism usually is involved. The drinking is preceded by childhood antisocial tendencies and behavior conduct problems.

In contrast, a variant called developmentally limited alcoholism involves similar childhood and adolescent drinking excesses and problems. However, as these individuals move into adult roles, they seem to grow out of their drinking problems. Possibly, the risk load they face from environmental demands is less stressful. They also may have stronger parental attachments, higher academic goals and achievements, and other protective factors. Although they risk physical health problems, if they can reach adulthood and assume responsible roles, their drinking excesses seem to abate.

Negative affect alcoholism involves high levels of depression and anxiety and has been more prevalent among women than with men. Drinking serves as a form of self-medication to deal with the negative feelings associated with life stressors.

Finally, developmentally cumulative alcoholism also involves reliance on alcohol as a coping response to environmental stressors. This form of alcoholism reflects a style of drinking that conforms to socially accepted norms. It is cumulative in the sense that drinking experiences over the individual's development from early childhood contribute to the likelihood of future drinking and the conditions in which it occurs. In addition to learned attitudes about the use of alcohol, some biological factors may be involved that predispose these individuals to react more favorably to alcohol than other individuals might.

Different Relationships of Personality to Dependency

We will distinguish between three different ways in which personality can be related to alcohol and other drug dependency: as causes, as moderators, and as effects. Sometimes, researchers interpret findings as evidence of one of these relationships without ruling out the other possibilities.

PERSONALITY VARIABLES AS CAUSES

Factors that are underlying causes of dependency can involve physiological, psychological, or cultural factors. They are variables assumed to mediate or contribute to the likelihood of dependency; the greater the extent to which these variables are present for an individual, the more likely that person should develop dependency. Some of these variables, such as genetic tendencies, may exist well before actual use of alcohol or other drugs begins. But other factors, such as certain life stressors (e.g., divorce or retirement), may not appear until later in life.

Temperament

As an example, Figure 10.1 suggests that some personality variables that exist prior to the development of drinking habits might be a mediator of subsequent drug use and dependency. Some of these factors may be inherited, such as **temperament**. They may predispose some persons to engage in activities that increase their opportunity to drink or to have adverse physical and social consequences when they do drink. They may be impulsive,

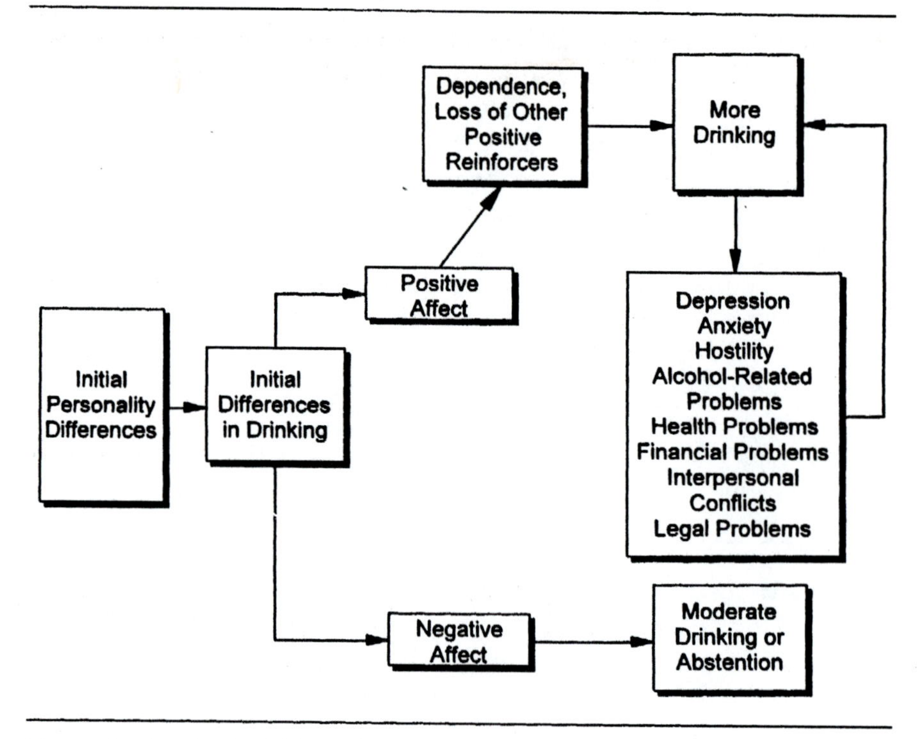

Figure 10.1. A Model Showing How Initial Personality Dispositions Affect Initial Drinking Levels

NOTE: In turn, initial drinking can lead to positive or negative affect, which has different long-term consequences. If drinking leads to positive affect, it may lead to the loss of other sources of positive reinforcement, and drinking becomes more pronounced. As many alcohol-related problems develop, there is further and increased drinking.

aggressive, and hyperactive and in general be undercontrolled in their behavior. A vicious cycle may start in which these tendencies may lead to more punishment, although the punishment may not be highly effective. These individuals may do poorly in school and become hostile and alienated. Eventually, deviant behaviors, including excessive use of alcohol and other drugs, may occur, further removing them from acceptable behavior patterns. The origins of dependency in these cases lie mainly within the individual, who is viewed as the primary "cause" of drinking.

One illustration of how temperament can serve as a mediator of adolescent drug use is a study (Wills, DuHamel, & Vaccaro, 1995) of a sample of 1,826 young urban adolescents (mean age = 12.3 years). Substance (tobacco, alcohol, marijuana) use was related to higher activity level. This temperament was associated with less generalized self-control, maladaptive coping (anger and helplessness), novelty seeking, and affiliation with peer substance users—factors that could lead to higher substance use. In contrast, positive mood was inversely related to use of alcohol, tobacco, and marijuana.

Motivational Factors

A motivational model based on the affective consequences of drinking (Cox & Klinger, 1988) provides a basis for understanding how personality differences might contribute to different amounts of drinking.

For example, male students who are outgoing, extroverted, and antisocial seem to derive more positive affect from their drinking episodes than others do when they begin drinking (Sher & Levenson, 1982). Initially, these young drinkers may drink to achieve positive affect rather than to escape negative affect. Also, as tolerance for alcohol develops, these drinkers must consume greater amounts of alcohol to achieve the level of positive affect previously experienced. In the absence of drinking, they may feel uncomfortable and distressed. At this point, negative affect begins to assume a greater role in motivating continued and increased drinking for these drinkers.

As drinking escalates over time, the factors that control the drinking may change from the original motives. Due to the adverse consequences of frequent and heavy drinking, such as loss of self-esteem, negative reactions from others, and physical and social debilitation, the alcoholic may feel chronic depression and other negative emotions. When alcohol is not consumed, the physical withdrawal symptoms experienced may create added anxiety and tension. Unfortunately, the solution typically adopted by the alcoholic to deal with these overpowering negative effects is to drink even more alcohol, hoping to escape the harsh reality. Thus, the original affective states motivating drinking change as the social drinker is transformed into the alcoholic.

Other Causes

Although personality differences on factors such as temperament and affect might contribute to alcohol and drug problems in the long run, they may not be sufficient or exclusive causes. Numerous other factors such as parental modeling, peer influences, coping skills, and types and amounts of stress encountered can add to the influence of temperament. Thus, a study of Black and White adolescents (Cooper, Peirce, & Tidwell, 1995) found that a chaotic and unsupportive family environment was a better predictor of adolescent substance abuse than the drinking problems of either parent.

Causal Interpretations

The role of personality on alcohol and other drug use is complicated. Characteristics of individuals that exist *prior* to the adoption of a pattern of drug use may be responsible for some of the behavioral correlates of heavy or frequent drug use. Thus, low motivation, aggression, and hostility, which are often seen as outcomes or effects caused by drug abuse, might in some cases actually be precursors or preexisting factors associated with subsequent drug abuse. They may or may not be "causes," but they would not be "effects." The term *risk factors* is often used to describe them because it is neutral with respect to causality or the existence of an addictive personality; it merely indicates that these variables are predictive of drug abuse.

The same interpretative problem arises in comparing users of legal versus illegal drugs. Suppose that prior to the initiation into drug use, those who end up using only legal drugs have different traits from those who use both legal and illegal drugs. Because these correlates existed prior to the use of different classes of drugs, it would be difficult to conclude that these risk factors distinguishing these groups are "effects" of using legal versus illegal drugs. If anything, they might be "causes" of the types of drugs chosen. Thus, higher risk takers and sensation seekers may be more likely to cross the line to use illegal drugs than would law-abiding users who stick with alcohol and tobacco or those who avoid all drugs.

An alternative possibility is that individuals who eventually develop alcohol or drug problems are actually not atypical in their personality or very different in their predrinking years from those who use alcohol and some drugs without serious problems. Consider the case of drinking. Because our society encourages drinking as a normative behavior, most young people, those who later develop use-related problems and those who do not, engage in some social drinking or at least experimental use.

However, some individuals may eventually turn to excessive drinking, drug use, or both as a means of coping by escaping the harsh realities of their lives due to factors beyond their control. Adverse environmental conditions—including poverty, racial prejudice and discrimination, poor education, and low income or personal misfortunes such as child abuse or neglect and chronic poor physical health—all increase the risk of alcohol and other drug dependency.

Causal inferences are difficult also because the connection between personality and drugs is not always direct. The relationship may be indirect in that some personality traits create one set of conditions that in turn promotes substance abuse and dependency. Thus, restlessness and inattentiveness in school may lead to frustration and eventual low achievement. Failing to receive rewards in school may in turn lead to truancy and eventually to dropping out of school. Turning to drugs may help these individuals cope with their alienation. In this scenario, personality factors did not directly lead to drug use, but the personality characteristics contributed to outcomes that increased the likelihood that drugs would become a part of their lifestyles.

PERSONALITY VARIABLES AS MODERATORS

Can some personality traits help protect the individual from conditions that might otherwise lead to alcohol and other drug abuse and dependency? When the effect of some variable is not universal but instead depends on the level of some other variable, such as a personality trait, that trait is referred to as a **moderator variable** (Baron & Kenny, 1986).

Self-Awareness

Self-awareness, the extent to which individuals are conscious of their own behaviors and feelings, was found to lessen the harmful influence of a family history of alcoholism on drinking (Rogosch, Chassin, & Sher, 1990). This may have happened because individuals high in self-awareness reacted to alcohol cautiously because they came from families with a history of alcohol problems. By recognizing their higher risk, they may have taken preventive measures to reduce the chances that they would themselves develop alcohol problems. In contrast, individuals with a similar family history of alcoholism but who were low in self-awareness were less vigilant and thus more likely to develop drinking problems.

In this example, the individual differences in the trait of self-awareness are a moderator variable of the effect of a family history of alcoholism. In other words, although those with the same type of family background who have low self-awareness tend to also develop drinking problems, those with high self-awareness are able to avoid this fate.

Alcohol Expectancies

Expectations about the effectiveness of alcohol to relieve tension appear to moderate the relationship between anxiety and drinking among males (Kushner, Sher, Wood, & Wood, 1994). The higher the anxiety, the more likely men are to drink if they hold beliefs that alcohol would be effective in lowering tension. In contrast, men who do not expect alcohol to relieve tension show an inverse relationship between anxiety and drinking. Thus, expectancies are a cognitive factor that moderates the relationship between anxiety and drinking for males.

PERSONALITY VARIABLES AS EFFECTS

As users become dependent on alcohol and other drugs, they may undergo changes in their outlook on life, as reflected by negative attitudes, hostility, depression, and so on. In other words, certain characteristics may emerge after prolonged excessive use of alcohol and other drugs. Under this view, these individuals are not in control of their environment. Personality here could be viewed as the result or effect, rather than the cause, of higher drug use.

In addition, Figure 10.2 suggests that the reactions of others to the individual's drinking behavior also may shape the eventual characteristics of the personality traits of the drug-dependent individual. For example, as an individual's drug use becomes heavier and more frequent, with its attendant loss of social status and financial, social, and psychological deterioration, he or she may experience adverse social consequences such as embarrassment, ostracism, and social rejection. In turn, increased drinking may occur. Consequently, additional personality differences that distinguish alcoholics from nonalcoholics may begin to emerge. These personality differences could be viewed as *consequences*, rather than *antecedents*, of alcoholism.

One study of personality differences between alcoholics and nonalcoholics concluded that most of these differences were the results, rather than the causes, of their differences in drinking behavior (Vaillant & Milofsky, 1982). Evidence was used from 55-year-old White males who had been part of a classic study (Glueck & Glueck, 1950) of juvenile delinquents. The original control group of 456 inner-city nondelinquent students also was contacted. Blind ratings were made of their alcohol use, personality, and sociopathy. The researchers examined the relationships between adult alcoholism levels and extensive data collected 33 years earlier about infant health problems, childhood emotional well-being, social and academic competence, family drinking levels, and various demographic factors.

Judgments about adult alcohol use and interviews were possible for 367 men. Some had died before age 40 and were not included in the analysis, leaving 260 social drinkers and 71 alcoholics. The results showed no differences between those classifiable as alcoholics and nonalcoholics with regard to most of the boyhood factors such as emotional well-being or family demographics. However, the alcoholics were more likely as adults to have more unemployment, lower education and health, and lower so-

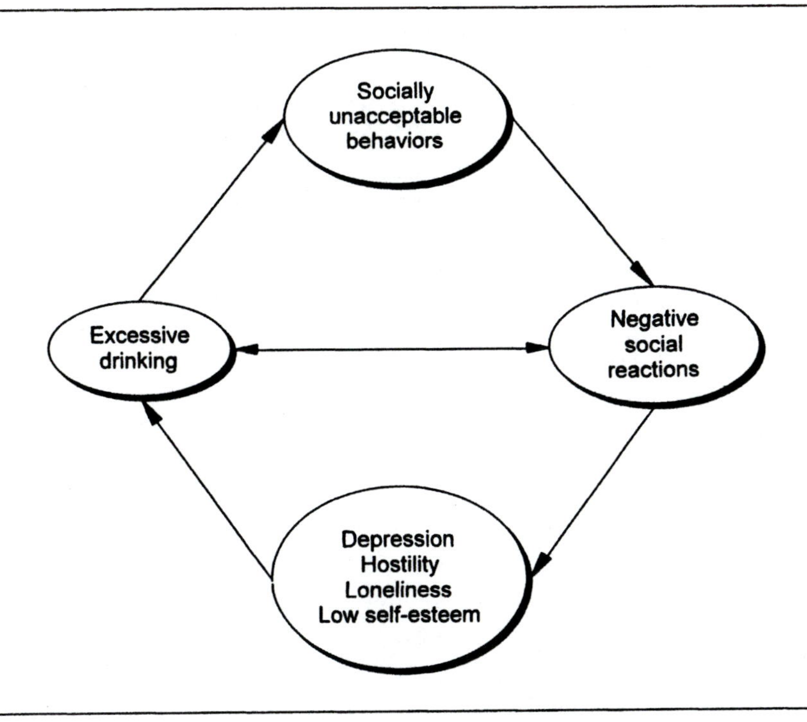

Figure 10.2. Heavy Drinking Leads to Unacceptable Behavior, Which Leads to Negative Social Reactions and Low Self-Esteem

NOTE: In turn, these effects lead to heavier drinking. Heavy drinking also may elicit negative social reactions directly without the need for other unacceptable behaviors occurring.

cial class status. The researchers concluded then that because boyhood competence had been comparable for the two groups, it could not have been the major factor responsible for the differences observed later in life, differences concluded to be the *effects* of alcoholism.

In addition, heredity—as indexed by alcoholism among parents, ancestors, and the individual's cultural background—predicted adult alcoholism better than childhood psychological and sociopathological variables did. When ethnicity and heredity were statistically controlled and equated, the childhood factors did not predict adult alcohol problems, although they did predict adult mental health. Furthermore, factors such as delinquency of parents, childhood environmental weakness, and school problems predicted adult sociopathy but not alcoholism levels. Overall, the pattern supports the role of heredity rather than environment as influencing alcoholism.

However, one challenge (Zucker & Gomberg, 1986) to this interpretation was that the data about early childhood experiences actually had not been collected during those years but later, when the boys were already 14 years old. In other words, this information about early childhood was based on *retrospective* recall and could have been inaccurate or distorted.

Early environment is more critical than heredity as a factor in subsequent alcoholism (Zucker & Gomberg, 1986). For example, family studies in general have shown correlations between adult alcoholism and early environmental factors such as childhood antisocial personality, poor childhood achievement, parental divorce, and parental alcoholism.

Psychopathology and Dependency

Alcohol dependency can occur in conjunction with other forms of **psychopathology** such as antisocial personality, depression, anxiety, and affective disorders. Again, the issue of causality arises. Do the personality disorders represent factors that preceded and hence possibly mediated alcohol dependency, or are they some of the consequences of many years of alcohol abuse and dependency?

COMORBIDITY OF SUBSTANCE USE DISORDERS AND OTHER PSYCHIATRIC DISORDERS

The presence of two or more psychiatric classifications is referred to as comorbidity. Rates of comorbidity of alcoholism with several major psychiatric disorders were analyzed (Helzer, 1987). About half of the 13% of the general population that had experienced alcohol abuse or dependence during their lives also had received an additional psychiatric diagnosis. Women with alcohol problems were more likely than women in the general population to have diagnoses of depression (19% vs. 7%), but there was not much difference in depression between men with alcohol problems and men in the general population (5% vs. 3%). In contrast, alcohol-dependent men were much more likely to have antisocial personality disorder diagnoses than men in the general population (15% vs. 4%). An even larger difference was found for women (10% vs. 0.8%).

As noted in Chapter 8, the National Comorbidity Survey (Kessler et al., 1994) found that about half (51.4%) of the respondents with any type of substance use disorder in their lifetimes also had at least one other psychiatric disorder in their lifetimes. Occurrence of a substance disorder and some other psychiatric disorder concurrently in a given 12-month period was found in 42.7% of the respondents, with the rates being similar for men and women.

For men, substance dependence disorders often were combined with anxiety disorders (19%) and affective disorders (15%). In contrast, substance use disorders occurred with anxiety disorders (31%) and affective disorders (24%).

Among college students (Kushner & Sher, 1993), comorbidity of alcohol disorder and anxiety disorder was higher for males and for students with a positive family history of alcoholism. Another study found that parental alcohol problems were associated with increased risks of *psychiatric* disorders, including substance abuse, conduct, attention deficit, mood, and anxiety disorders in a birth cohort of 1,265 children who were studied to age 15 (Lynskey, Fergusson, & Horwood, 1994). Children of both sexes from alcoholic homes had two to four times higher risks of adolescent psychiatric disorders than children whose parents did not report alcohol problems.

Interpreting Causality

When drug dependency and psychopathology are observed to occur together, several different interpretations can be made. One view is that the drug dependency is one of the "causes" of other forms of psychopathology—that is, alcohol or cocaine dependency is the *primary problem,* and the other problem is a consequence of the drug use. Thus, the excessive drug use may lead to antisocial personality or depression, for example.

A contrasting view is that those with drug dependency are premorbidly pathological or addiction prone. They have personality characteristics that may lead them to eventually develop drug dependency (*secondary*). According to this perspective, some form of psychopathology precedes and perhaps contributes toward alcohol or other drug dependencies. This is a view favored by psychiatry.

For example, the association between alcohol dependency and antisocial personality might involve this process. Past studies have found antisocial personality in approximately 15% to 50% of alcoholics. Antisocial personality is a *DSM-III* (1980) category, formerly referred to as sociopathy, and is found mostly in males. It involves dysphoric moods, sensation seeking, a history of childhood misconduct, and underachievement. Such characteristics increase the risk that the individual will develop drinking problems sooner or later as a secondary outcome of his or her psychiatric problems. Finally, it is possible that the influence is bidirectional, with psychopathology and alcoholism developing concurrently and each problem affecting the other.

In practice, it can be difficult to diagnose specific cases accurately because the criteria for the diagnosis of alcohol dependence and psychopathology categories overlap. Thus, some effects of alcohol dependency such as depression or disorientation can be mistaken for psychiatric symptoms. This overlap of criteria can lead to overestimates of the rates of comorbidity.

Follow-up of cases to observe how changes in one disorder affect the co-occurring problem can be helpful for diagnoses. Thus, if improved personality and mood after detoxification for alcohol dependence occur, it would be more likely that the alcohol problem was primary and the personality disorders were secondary. Similarly, if there is a decline in drinking following psychiatric treatment for mental illness, it would appear that the psychopathology was primary and the alcohol problem was secondary.

Is psychopathology a risk factor for alcohol or other types of drug dependency? There is no simple answer to this question because the *relative* frequency of a characteristic or behavior influences its accuracy as a predictor. To the extent that the predictor in question is common in a given group, it should be less of a risk factor for the pathology. But for more extreme (i.e., less common) behaviors—for example, use of illicit drugs—there will be a stronger link between psychopathology and that predictor. Thus, heavy drinking may not be viewed as a sign of psychopathology in France because drinking is commonplace there. In contrast, such behavior would be a predictor of psychopathology among Jews, for whom heavy drinking is less prevalent.

SUMMARY

Alcoholics have been observed to differ from nonalcoholics in many aspects of their personalities, suggesting the possibility that there is an "alcoholic personality." One important question, assuming such a profile can be identified, is whether these differences existed prior to the onset of alcoholism and hence were part of the causal process, leading to the outcome of alcoholism, or whether the differences primarily reflect the consequences of chronic alcohol abuse and its damaging effects on the physical, psychological, and social well-being of alcoholics.

Longitudinal studies that obtain measures of personality prior and subsequent to the development of alcoholism have suggested that some *general* personality characteristics distinguish the future alcoholic from the nonalcoholic.

These factors may not directly affect drinking but probably operate indirectly over a period of time. Thus, the rebellious and adventuresome youth is more likely to experiment with drinking than the law-abiding and moral youth, who may conform to social norms by not drinking or delaying until a later age. Although many youth who experiment with alcohol may curb or control excesses and never develop dependence on alcohol or engage in other forms of socially disapproved behaviors, others may find that alcohol is a means of coping with life's adversities or providing excitement and stimulation. However, instead of solving problems, their drinking may create additional and larger problems such as academic difficulties, financial woes, interpersonal conflicts, or problems with the law. These unpleasant consequences may further accelerate a dependence on alcohol for dealing with stressors, until eventually alcohol abuse and alcoholism are the consequence. This model appears to account for the origins of differences in behaviors leading to alcohol dependence. In a sense, these personality differences could be considered a "prealcoholic personality." In addition, a complementary model suggests that the alcoholic's stigmatized existence and associated psychological dysfunction may be responsible for creating *additional* personality differences between alcoholics and nonalcoholics. These differences reflect the effects of alcoholism on personality.

Comorbidity refers to the rates of co-occurrence of a substance or drug dependency with a psychiatric disorder, such as antisocial personality or affective disorder. Lifetime prevalence of such comorbidity is high, occurring in about half of those assessed in one study. Some combinations are more likely to occur in males, but others seem more frequent among females. The extent to which biological or sociological factors determine these gender differences is not clear. Another intriguing question is the nature of any causal links between the two disorders within individuals. To what extent does the personality disorder increase the alcohol or drug problem and vice versa?

KEY TERMS

Addictive personality
Minnesota Multiphasic Personality Inventory
Moderator variable
Psychoanalytic approach
Psychopathology
Temperament
Type A (alcoholism)
Type B (alcoholism)
Type 1 (alcoholism)
Type 2 (alcoholism)

STIMULUS/RESPONSE

1. Some personality traits have been found to be associated with heavier alcohol and other drug use. How can you determine the extent to which these characteristics are causes or effects of heavy use? What personality characteristics do you think might be more prevalent among those adolescents who mature out of excessive alcohol and other drug use as they get older?
2. Do you think the personality characteristics associated with risk of drug dependency are the same or different for men and women? If you think they would differ, be specific and explain why you think such differences would exist.
3. If a specific drug were made more widely available than it is currently, would the type of personality associated with use of this drug change? For example, because it is illegal, marijuana is currently used by some but not all types of individuals. If marijuana use were to be decriminalized, would the types of individuals using it be essentially the same or different? Why or why not?

- Methodology
- Mood and Emotion
- Sensory Motor Activity
- Cognition
- Summary
- Key Terms
- Stimulus/Response

Alcohol and Other Drugs *Relationship to Basic Psychological Processes* 11

When I read about the evils of drinking, I gave up reading.

—Henny Youngman

Individuals use alcohol and other drugs for many different reasons. They may expect to achieve pleasurable effects or reduce painful experiences, impress others or yield to social pressure, escape boredom, and forget about problems. Many users seek to achieve these goals by consuming these substances, but unfortunately, there are often unforeseen detrimental effects when large quantities are consumed, especially if repeated often over an extended period.

In this chapter, we will examine research findings about the relationship between alcohol and other drug use and several important psychological processes and outcomes. Pharmacological explanations attribute these effects to chemical factors. However, psychological factors also may be partly or entirely responsible for many "effects" of alcohol and other drugs that are attributed to the pharmacological factors. Due to the social context in which these substances are used and to the expectations of the user, effects attributed to alcohol and other drugs actually may represent the influence of psychological factors. For example, people expect to have a good time when they go to a party. Alcohol and other drugs may be consumed there, and people may later believe these substances were a major factor responsible for the pleasant experiences they had at the party. However, these substances may not have been the primary cause of the happy experiences because most of the people present would have had some degree of positive experience anyway because they came expecting to have fun. Nonetheless, beliefs such as alcohol promotes good times, tobacco relieves social anxiety, and marijuana makes people mellow may have led to the attribution that the alcohol, tobacco, or marijuana produced or at least enhanced the positive experiences. Because these substances may relieve anxiety or tension, they may facilitate the occurrence of pleasurable expe riences by "allowing" the user to forget conscious controls and inhibitions, but they may not be sufficient alone to produce these effects. In other contexts, drugs can lead to quite different effects. For instance, when an angry and frustrated crowd drinks heavily, aggressive and hostile feelings and violent behavior may be unleashed.

Expectancies about the effects of alcohol and other drugs, which were discussed in Chapter 6, are determined by the individual's background, knowledge, and past experiences with the substances used. Whatever the source, these factors are psychological rather than pharmacological in nature. To understand how alcohol and other drugs affect experience and behavior, it is necessary to analyze the contributions of both types of factors. In this chapter, we will focus on important psychological processes such as mood, emotion, sensory-motor activity, and cognition. We begin by first considering the methodology used by researchers to identify alcohol and drug effects on behavior. Understanding the strengths and weaknesses of these methods is essential for analyzing controversies about causal inferences of the effects of alcohol and other drugs.

Methodology

UNCONTROLLED OBSERVATION

Two major research methods have been used to examine how alcohol and other drugs affect behavior and experience. *Naturalistic* or **uncontrolled observation** examines correlations between drug use and behavioral outcomes. Often, several alternative interpretations of an observed relationship are possible, and caution is needed to rule out rival explanations.

As an example, suppose we observed that those who drink several alcoholic beverages during lunch work less efficiently after lunch. One interpretation for this evidence is that alcohol impaired work performance. In jumping to this conclusion, we assumed that these workers were more productive prior to drinking, but we had no direct evidence to support this view. As the top line in Figure 11.1 shows, demonstration of a causal influence of alcohol or any other drug requires that the work quality *before* the drug use was better than it was *after* drug use. In addition, even if work quality was lower after drinking for this group of workers, we also would like to know what the level of work quality was like for comparable peers who did not drink during lunch. This group serves as a baseline for comparison. If these nondrinking peers also showed reduced work quality after lunch, then the drinking workers' deficits could not be due entirely to drinking. Perhaps everyone has a postlunch letdown at work.

On the other hand, if the sober workers had less impairment than the drinking workers after lunch, as shown by the lower line in the hypothetical example in Figure 11.1, we would be safer in attributing the reduced work quality of the drinkers to the effects of the alcohol they drank with their lunch.

Self-Selection

An alternative explanation for our example does not attribute the work impairment to any causal effect of alcohol at all. Instead, a selective process may be operating here, with those workers who drink more alcohol during lunch being different from those who drink less or not at all in some important ways that affect work productivity. For instance, workers who are less motivated, less capable, or under more stress might be more likely to drink more at lunch. Thus, even without the influence of alcohol, their work would likely be inferior to the typical performance of those who drank less. Consequently, we cannot safely attribute the differences in work performance of the two groups to the effects of differences in alcohol consumption.

Whenever some selective process occurs, we may mistakenly conclude that some difference, such as poor work quality by drinkers, is an outcome or effect caused by drug use. Instead, some preexisting difference distinguishing drug users and nonusers is responsible for the observed outcome differences when self-selection occurs. Or both factors may be operative, with some initial differences between drug users and nonusers being enlarged or increased by the influence of the drug.

When we compare individuals who differ in how much they choose to drink on differences in their work, we do not have a before-and-after drinking comparison. Instead, we are measuring whether those who choose to drink more also do poorer work than those who prefer to drink less or not at all.

Figure 11.2 presents a model suggesting that, even when not drinking, those who tend to drink more are also, on average, more likely to suffer impaired behavior than those who drink less or not at all. One basis for this view is that drinkers may be more impulsive and undercontrolled than nondrinkers (Sher & Trull, 1994; Tarter, 1988). For similar reasons, Figure 11.2 also suggests that when drinking does occur, the same amount of alcohol may produce a bigger effect on those who typically drink or drink in large quantities than those who ordinarily do not.

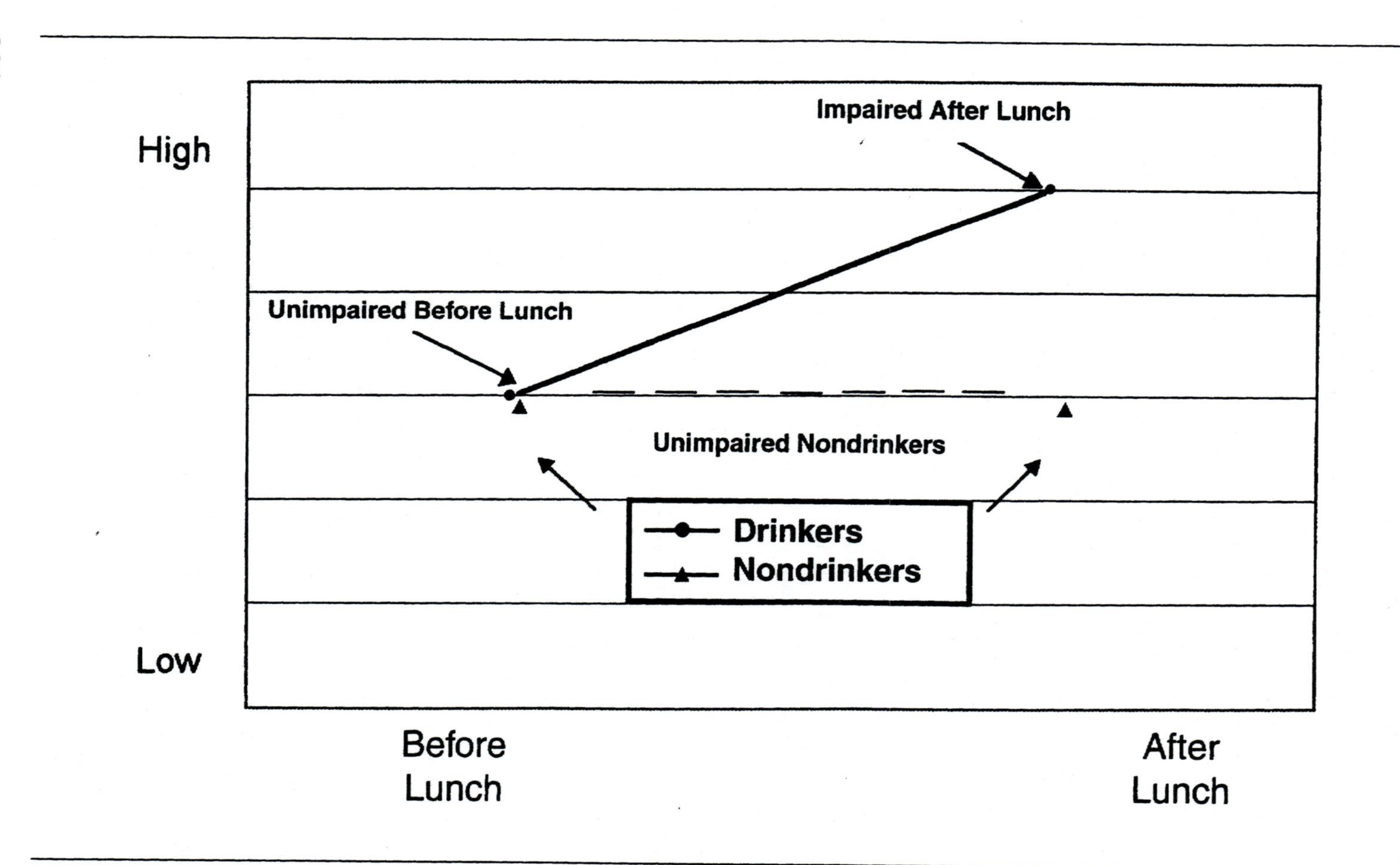

Figure 11.1. Analysis of Evidence Needed to Infer Causal Effects of Alcohol

NOTE: A conclusion that alcohol impairs the behavior of someone known to have consumed alcohol *assumes* that the person would have performed better prior to drinking, as shown in the top line. Also, comparable persons who did *not* drink are *assumed* to perform at better levels than the drinker, as shown in the bottom line. However, causal inferences are often made without evaluating these two assumptions.

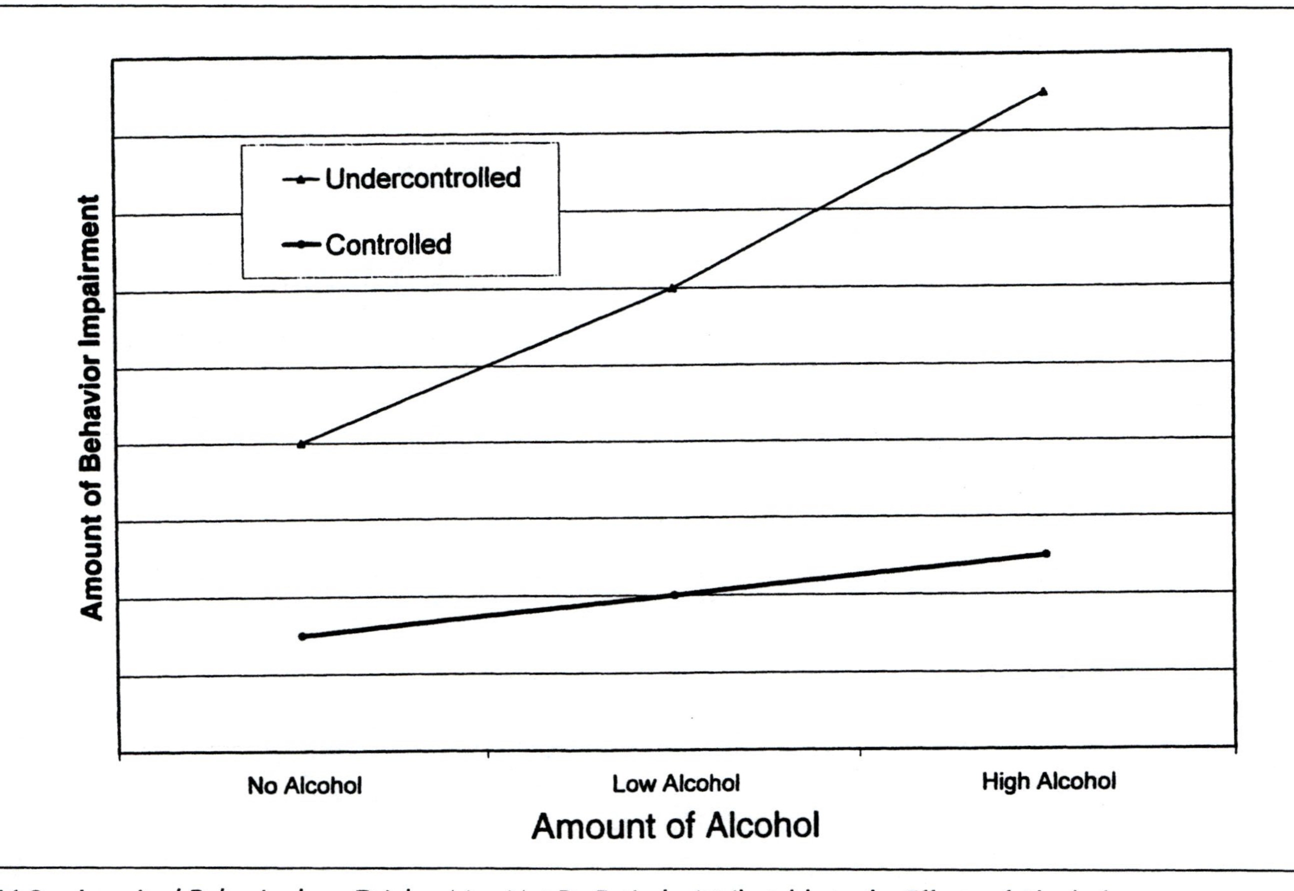

Figure 11.2. Impaired Behavior by a Drinker May Not Be Entirely Attributable to the Effects of Alcohol

NOTE: Self-selection may be involved such that those who drink may be different from nondrinkers in other important ways that affect the observed behavior, such as impulsivity or undercontrol. In addition, the likelihood of impaired behavior is greater for undercontrolled individuals, even when no drinking occurs. After drinking occurs, these differences may widen, with greater impairment for more impulsive and undercontrolled individuals.

CONTROLLED OBSERVATION

The second major method for obtaining evidence about alcohol and other drug effects is the *experiment* or **controlled observation.** An experiment to study the question described earlier might form two groups of workers with a *random assignment method to determine group membership.* One group would arbitrarily be assigned the task of drinking a specified amount of alcohol during lunch. The other group would be instructed to not drink. Under this method, self-selection on the basis of drinking history would be prevented. Any differences in work performance observed after lunch between the two groups could not be attributed to preexisting differences and would be interpreted as stemming from the differences in alcohol consumption.

Because the only systematic difference between the two groups would be the amount of alcohol consumed during lunch, it would be more likely that differences in work performance after lunch could be explained as the effects of alcohol. Although the logic of the experimental method is sound, a practical problem with experimental evidence is that it may not be highly generalizable to behavior under natural conditions. In other words, in the real world, the level of drinking, for example, is not an "assigned" activity but is one that involves free choice or a voluntary behavior.

In the next three chapters, we will discuss research that involves both types of methods to determine any effects that alcohol and other drugs might have on behavior. It is important, when evaluating and interpreting the research findings, to note the strengths and weaknesses of the methodology used. Uncontrolled observations are often useful in generating ideas or hypotheses that can then be evaluated more carefully through controlled observations to rule out alternative explanations. Thus, if smokers are more productive than nonsmokers, is the difference due to smoking per se or to some other factor that also differs between smokers and nonsmokers, such as some personality characteristic? To disentangle the two alternative explanations, one would compare the performance of two groups of workers who were similar in personality traits but one that contained smokers and the other, nonsmokers. This type of controlled observation allows any observed differences to be more safely attributed to smoking rather than to personality. Combining evidence obtained from both methods is often useful to arrive at stronger conclusions.

EXPECTANCY CONTROLS

The mere **expectancy** of receiving drugs can be an influential factor affecting behavior. Laboratory or controlled experiments of the effects of drugs on behavior typically include a *control group* that receives a *placebo* (nondrug) but are told that it contains the drug. In this traditional design, any differences in behavior between these participants and those in the *experimental group,* who expected *and* received the drug, were attributed to the effect of the drug. A variant of this method uses only one group but tests them on more than one occasion by applying the experimental (drug) and control (nondrug) *conditions* in different sequences to subgroups.

But this research paradigm fails to assess any influence that the *expectancy* of receiving the drug per se contributed because both groups expected the drug. Because this type of expectancy existed equally for both groups, investigators could not detect any impact that the mere expectancy of consuming the drug might exert on psychological experiences and behavior. Indeed, if the actual drug had no pharmacological effect, all of the behavior would be due to the expectancy effect.

BALANCED PLACEBO DESIGN

An elaborate research design known as the **balanced placebo** design was developed (Marlatt, Demming, & Reid, 1973) to address the problem of expectancy in alcohol research. As shown in Figure 11.3, this design isolates pharmacological and psychological effects by using four different test conditions. Half the participants receive an alcoholic beverage such as vodka mixed with tonic in a 1:5 proportion, and half receive a nonalcoholic beverage such as tonic water, disguised to resemble a cocktail lounge drink. To increase credibility, a small amount of alcohol may have been rubbed around the top of the glass to provide the odor of alcohol. In addition, half of each of these two groups is told that they have an alcoholic drink, and the other half is told that they have a nonalcoholic beverage.

This complex design allows the evaluation of a *consumption effect* by comparing the combined two groups that receive alcohol (Groups 1 and 3) with those combined two groups that do not (Groups 2 and 4), regardless of whether they expect alcoholic beverages. In addition, it allows assessment of an *expectancy effect* by comparing the combined two groups that expect alcohol (Groups 1 and 2) with those combined two groups that do not expect alcohol (Groups 3 and 4), regardless of what they actually receive. Interaction effects also can be examined with this design to see if the effect of alcohol varies, depending on the type of expectancy. Thus, alcohol consumption might produce a difference in some behavior if the drinkers believe (expect to receive) they are drinking an alcoholic beverage but might not have an effect if they believe they are consuming a nonalcoholic drink.

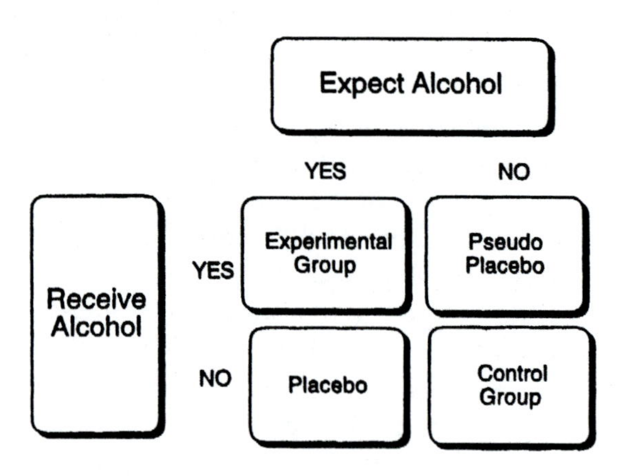

Figure 11.3. The Balanced Placebo Design
NOTE: The balanced placebo design is used in laboratory experiments to measure the expectancy effect of belief that alcohol will be received versus the consumption effects of actually receiving alcohol. Results show that the experimental group that merely expects but does not receive alcohol often shows the same effect as the group that both expects and receives alcohol.

To minimize confusion, it is important to keep in mind that two different types of expectancy will be discussed in this chapter: expectancies about the *effect of alcohol* and expectancies about the *type of beverage* that will be received, alcoholic or nonalcoholic. In natural settings, we receive the type of beverage that we expect to have; hence, we cannot isolate the pharmacological effect of alcohol from the effect of expecting to receive an alcoholic beverage. In contrast, the balanced placebo design used in the laboratory is able to separate these effects. Some drinkers receive the type of beverage that is expected, but others do not receive the type of beverage expected. When the term *expectancy* is used in connection with experiments, most of the time it refers to this expectation about the type of beverage that will be consumed and not to the expected effects of alcohol.

The expectancy of having received even a small dose of alcohol such as one drink has a stronger effect on cognitive processes than whether alcohol was in fact consumed, at least for light to moderate drinkers (Marlatt & Rohsenow, 1980). Thus, expectancy per se may play a major role in affecting behavior, effects that would have been attributed entirely to pharmacological factors in studies that did not use the balanced placebo design.

What is the role of expectations about the amount of alcohol-induced impairment on performance under alcohol and a placebo? Two studies

(Fillmore & Vogel Sprott, 1995) examined the degree of change in performance during an alcohol session on a motor skills task and during a subsequent session for another motor skills task in which alcohol was expected but a placebo was received. A control group completed the second task without expecting alcohol. Expecting greater impairment due to alcohol produced poorer performance under alcohol as well as under a placebo, but expectancies about impairment failed to weaken performance when neither alcohol nor placebo was involved.

One limitation of the balanced placebo design is that not everyone may have identical beliefs or expectancies about alcohol's effects. In the few experiments in which different expectations about alcohol's effects are provided to different groups, they may not be equally credible. All the balanced placebo design can do is control who believes they had alcohol and who does not; it does not determine different expectancies about the effects of alcohol. Another limitation is that it can only be used with low doses of alcohol below a blood alcohol concentration (BAC) of .04 mg % to be effective (Martin, Earleywine, & Finn, 1990). Thus, problems of credibility (as well as ethics) arise if large doses of alcohol are given to participants who are misinformed and told that they are receiving nonalcoholic beverages when in fact they are given alcohol.

On the other hand, some evidence suggests that the balanced placebo method may not be effective even at moderate blood alcohol concentrations (Sayette, Breslin, Wilson, & Rosenblum, 1994). Although misinformed that they were *not* drinking alcohol, 44% of participants who were administered alcohol correctly reported consuming alcohol. Only 6% of those in the placebo control who were misinformed that they had consumed alcohol, when they actually were given tonic water, were not deceived.

Mood and Emotion

Use of alcohol and other drugs is often motivated by the desire to alter the present mood. Many drugs such as alcohol, nicotine, and marijuana can serve both functions, depending on the dose, the situation, the user, and the intended effect on the user. Other drugs such as benzodiazepines are generally used in the belief that they can lower negative affective or mood states such as anxiety and tension. For other drugs such as cocaine or amphetamines, the primary goal is to increase arousal or produce positive or pleasurable moods. Even though the goals for using different drugs are markedly different, it is clear that all drugs are used to influence affective

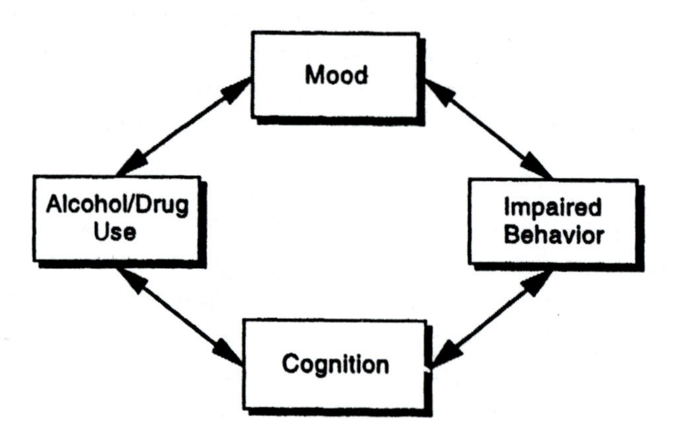

Figure 11.4. Alcohol and Other Drug Use Reciprocally Affect Both Mood and Cognition, Which in Turn Reciprocally Affect Performance

feelings or mood states, changing negative states to less negative or to positive ones, at least for the moment.

Although the present section will focus on how drug use affects mood or affective states, it is important to keep in mind that different psychological processes occur concurrently and affect each other, as illustrated in Figure 11.4. Mood, for example, can alter cognitive processes such as memory, reasoning, and decision making. Mood also can affect motivation and attention, and it may have an indirect impact on behavior through its influence on cognition, sensory processes, and motivation. In turn, these processes also can influence mood in a reciprocal manner. It is not possible to single out one process as more important, but because alcohol and other drugs are typically sought specifically to influence mood, we will first discuss mood states in relation to alcohol and other drug use.

One model of alcohol use (Cooper, Frone, Russell, & Mudar, 1995) assumes that drinkers are motivated to regulate both positive and negative emotions. This model held that enhancement (of positive emotion) and coping (with negative emotions) regulate alcohol use and abuse. Expectancies about the effects of alcohol on affective states can lead to individual differences in drinking. Support was found for the hypothesized model, showing the importance of distinguishing among different psychological motives for alcohol use.

An example of the relationship between life stress, mood, and drug use is a study of about 1,000 middle-aged male employees from the Swedish automobile industry (Rose, Bengtsson, Dimberg, Kumlin, & Eriksson,

1998). Negative life events in the past year were related to depressed mood as well as to more smoking by blue-collar workers but to more drinking by white-collar workers. One possible explanation is that the depressed mood created by the negative life events drove the men to more drug use as a coping response, with the specific drug depending on socioeconomic class.

However, this is a correlational study, and other interpretations cannot be ruled out. For example, some self-selection processes cannot be discounted. The men who drank or smoked at a higher level may have differed from the men who did not engage in these activities in many ways such as health or related attitudes. Some of these differences, as well as the higher use of alcohol and tobacco, could have created more depressed moods. In short, there are many uncontrolled variables in a naturalistic study such as this one.

A second example involves a study of the relationship between marijuana use and academic performance (Andrews & Duncan, 1997). Higher use of marijuana is associated with poorer academic performance, popularly referred to as an "amotivational syndrome," as if a pharmacological effect of marijuana is a direct drain on the motivation of the user. However, the study concluded that for younger adolescents, the relation between marijuana use or cigarette use and academic motivation does not involve such a direct process. Instead, adolescent use of these drugs reflects a deviant pattern of behavior. Students who use drugs heavily are atypical from the general population of students. The drug use is not as likely to be the cause of their poor schoolwork as it is that some third factor, such as a deviant lifestyle, promotes both high drug use and poor academic achievement.

In trying to obtain more definitive evidence about causal roles of drugs, we often turn from naturalistic observations to controlled experiments. We can illustrate this approach with a hypothetical example of how one would use a controlled experiment to investigate the first question raised earlier about the relationship between drug use and mood among autoworkers. We could form equivalent groups of men and then subject them to different levels of life stressors to see if smoking or drinking occurs more for those with higher stress. If so, mood should improve after the drug use. Another hypothetical approach would be to "require" different equivalent groups to smoke or drink in different amounts and then observe if the levels of stress that develop in their lives are higher for those who use drugs more. In this case, mood should worsen with increased drug use.

For ethical and practical reasons, these examples of experiments would probably be unlikely to be conducted. But it is hoped that they would serve to illustrate the differences between naturalistic and experimental evidence. Now, we turn to some examples of actual experiments that examine how alcohol and other drugs affect behavior.

SOME IMPORTANT FACTORS OF ALCOHOL EFFECTS ON MOOD

The determination of the effect of alcohol or, for that matter, any drug in an experiment involves more than comparing the behavior of a treated experimental group receiving the drug and a placebo or control group that does not receive the drug, even though it is told that it has. The factors to be discussed in the following section apply to any type of drug.

Dose Level

An important and obvious aspect of alcohol consumption that affects mood is dose level. Unfortunately, many studies that examine the effect of alcohol on mood with college participants have used only one dose, usually a small amount consisting of one to two drinks, and the results may not be generalizable to larger amounts. It has been recommended that studies compare mood for several dose levels administered to the same participants to provide a more valid test (Tucker, Vuchinich, & Sobell, 1982).

Setting

Drinking in the laboratory experiment setting can be an anxiety-producing experience because the subject is aware of being evaluated. There is no assessment of the subject's existing mood at the start of the experiment, a factor that can influence mood levels during the experiment.

In contrast to the laboratory situation, under real-life circumstances, drinkers ordinarily consume alcohol under a wide variety of moods, both positive and negative. Alcohol may magnify these existing moods when drinking is initiated. The angry or depressed individual may decide to drink to forget problems, but the happy individual may engage in drinking to celebrate a positive event with loved ones. These different types of motives must be considered in determining how alcohol will affect subsequent moods. In addition, an individual may drink for different reasons in different contexts, and these factors must be examined in predicting the effects of alcohol.

Location on the Blood Alcohol Curve

One factor that may lead to conflicting findings across different studies on any behavior is the level on the blood alcohol curve when the experimenter assesses the effects of alcohol. Alcohol effects differ over the course of the curve because it is being metabolized and eliminated over time. In addition, the drinker habituates to the test situation and the subjective influence of the alcohol over time. Because blood alcohol level is a joint function of dose and time since drinking, mood should be assessed at several time points—at baseline before drinking starts and during the ascending and descending limbs of the BAC curve (Tucker et al., 1982).

One study (Sutker, Tabakoff, Goist, & Randall, 1983) assessed the BAC at several points after nonproblem drinkers received a small dose of alcohol. As the BAC was rising, drinkers felt elated and stimulated, but when the BAC had peaked and was descending, they felt depressed and tired. This biphasic effect of alcohol may reflect both physical and psychological factors. At the physical level, the central nervous system is depressed by alcohol, allowing disinhibition of restraints and the experience of pleasurable feelings. Then, after drinking stops and the BAC starts to decline, there is an opposite rebound of negative feeling states. At the psychological level, there may be anticipation of tension relief during the early part of a drinking episode, followed by fatigue and regret after drinking ends and the BAC declines.

Gender Differences

Gender also must be considered as a determinant of how alcohol affects mood (Sutker, Allain, Brantley, & Randall, 1982). The effect of alcohol in reducing negative affect in social drinkers faced with the possibility of receiving electric shock if they made errors on a learning task differed for males and females. Male participants had lowest anxiety if they both expected and received alcohol. In contrast, this condition produced the greatest anxiety among female participants. Among females, the least anxiety occurred when unexpected alcohol was received. This pattern suggests that alcohol relieves anxiety pharmacologically, but that when women know they are receiving alcohol, this awareness counteracts such relief and creates tension.

EFFECT OF ATTENTIONAL DEMANDS

An important additional factor that must be considered is the extent to which the drinker has other tasks to perform. One theory holds that alcohol reduces our capacity to deal with demands on our attention processing. Consequently, when someone is busy with a demanding task that might ordinarily generate tension, consumption of alcohol would serve to reduce tension by interfering with the capacity for attention to it (Steele &

Josephs, 1988). In contrast, if the drinker has few distractors when drinking, alcohol may increase tension because the drinker may focus on worrisome problems.

In one experiment (Josephs & Steele, 1990), intoxicated and sober participants were instructed that they would have to make a speech in 15 minutes about aspects of their body and appearance, which worried them. Half were kept busy with another task while waiting to make their speech, and half were not. As predicted, anxiety was reduced in the group that was both busy and intoxicated, but it increased for the groups that were not busy, not intoxicated, or neither busy nor intoxicated.

The extent to which alcohol might alter stress also may depend on the temporal sequence in which the alcohol and stressor are experienced (Sayette & Wilson, 1991). Most laboratory studies of the effects of alcohol on stress expose the participants to stress after they have consumed the alcohol. Many real-life drinking situations do involve this temporal order, but in other real situations, stress is encountered before drinking has taken place.

The relationship of alcohol to stress may vary, depending on which of these two types of situations are involved. Because alcohol reduces attention, it was predicted (Sayette & Wilson, 1991) that receiving alcohol first would involve less stress because the subject would not attend to the stressor as closely. In contrast, exposure to a stressor prior to receiving alcohol would produce a stronger stress because more attention would be focused on the stressor.

Male moderate-to-heavy social drinkers, given either an alcoholic or a placebo beverage, were required to give a speech for 3 minutes about what they "disliked about their body and appearance." During the waiting period, measures of heart rate were recorded before and after the drink. As predicted, a stress-dampening effect of alcohol on heart rate occurred only if the drink preceded the stressful speech.

Cigarette smoking is also linked to mood alteration. Because nicotine is a stimulant on the central nervous system, it may seem odd that smokers report that sometimes they smoke to relax. A psychological explanation is that the situation or context of smoking (e.g., study or work break, social interactions) may promote the positive mood. In addition, the relief experienced can be pharmacologically based because the smoking occurs following some period of nicotine deprivation, a condition that will produce negative states.

The ability of smoking to relieve anxiety created by a stressful task was measured either with or without a concurrent distraction (Kassel, 1997). A control group of nonsmokers also was given the task to see how distraction would affect their performance. Smoking reduced anxiety only when paired with a distractor, and the distractor did not help the nonsmokers.

Thus, cognitive factors such as a distractor, rather than pharmacological factors, may account for the anxiety relief of smoking. By narrowing the focus of attention, smoking relieves anxiety by distracting the smoker from stressful cognitions.

Smoking cigarettes may enhance attention (Kassel, 1997). According to the stimulus-filter model, nicotine facilitates cognitive performance by screening irrelevant and annoying stimuli from the smoker's awareness. In contrast, consistent with the attention-allocation model (Steele & Josephs, 1988), nicotine enhances attentional processing by inducing attentional narrowing and increasing perceptual processing capacity.

Smoking improved speed and accuracy of college-age males on verbal and spatial learning tasks relative to nonsmoking controls (Algan, Furedy, Demirgoeren, Vincent, & Poeguen, 1997). Smoking improved verbal task performance for females and increased their confidence on the spatial task.

One interpretation of these studies is that by improving mood, cigarette smoking can enhance performance. But is the improvement a net gain in performance or just the restoration of normal function in smokers who perform poorly when deprived of smoking? Smoking may boost performance only to a level comparable to what they would achieve if they had never smoked. Nicotine relieves the unpleasant tension suffered by smokers when they have been abstinent from smoking.

One study compared cigarette smokers who either smoked as they usually would, smokers deprived of smoking overnight, and 20 nonsmokers on a battery of mood questionnaires. Before and after a cigarette/rest period, they performed on cognitive tasks (Parrott & Garnham, 1998). At the initial session, deprived smokers reported significantly greater feelings of stress, irritability, depression, poor concentration, and low pleasure, as compared with both nondeprived smokers and nonsmokers. After the cigarette/ rest break, the mood states of all three groups became generally similar, although the previously deprived smokers still reported elevated depression. A study over a period of a month in which some smokers were allowed to continue smoking but others had to quit showed less negative mood such as depression, anger, and tension among those who smoked (Gilbert et al., 1998). These findings also support the view that mood gains after smoking merely reflect reversal of abstinence distress.

Although some individuals use alcohol and marijuana together, the effects of this drug combination on mood and behavior have not received much study. In one experiment (Chiat & Perry, 1994), four conditions were compared: alcohol alone, marijuana alone, alcohol and marijuana in combination, and no drug treatment. Each drug alone produced moderate levels of subjective intoxication and some degree of behavioral impairment. The combination of both drugs produced the greatest impairment on most tasks and strong overall subjective ratings. Little evidence occurred for subjective or behavioral effects on the day after receiving the drugs.

In another study (Heishman, Arasteh, & Stitzer, 1997), moderate alcohol and marijuana users were administered different doses of alcohol, different doses of marijuana, and placebo in random order. Double-blind tests in which neither the experimenter nor the participant knew which conditions were being administered were given over seven separate sessions. Alcohol and marijuana produced dose-related changes in subjective measures of drug effect. Ratings of perceived impairment were identical for the high doses of alcohol and marijuana. Both drugs produced comparable impairment in digit-symbol substitution and word recall tests but had no effect in time perception and reaction time tests.

OVERVIEW

Naturalistic evidence is abundant that alcohol and other drugs are related to mood states. However, interpretation of the causal role of these substances is difficult, especially due to self-selection affecting who uses drugs. More precision is potentially possible with controlled experiments. However, as Table 11.1 shows, many important differences between alcohol and other drug use in the laboratory and under natural conditions can make it difficult to generalize between results obtained under the two methods.

Under either method, mood and emotional states are not easy to study. Under natural conditions, it is difficult to be on the scene to observe the drug use, so one must often rely on retrospective accounts. In experiments, this problem is avoided, but studying moods is difficult because they can be subtle, subjective, and hard to measure verbally. Moods can change rapidly and can be easily altered by a researcher's attempt to observe or measure them.

In the laboratory, the researcher administers drugs to participants to see their effects. There is no need to ask why the participant is using the drug; use is a requirement of participation. Dose levels are often much higher in the real world than in the laboratory for some users. Anxiety or suspicion may be activated when drugs are given in the laboratory setting because the participant is aware of being evaluated. Often, there is no assessment of the mood prior to or at the start of the experimental session, a factor that could affect how drugs influence subsequent mood states during the session.

In contrast, in the real world, many different moods may exist for different individuals or on different occasions and settings when the choice is made to use drugs. Also, individuals may consume drugs under many moods, positive as well as negative, and these drugs may alter these moods.

TABLE 11.1 Some major differences between studies of drug effects on mood in laboratory and naturalistic conditions

	Mood Prior to Drug Use	*Motivation to Use Drug*	*Dose Level*	*Setting for Observation*	*Duration of Observation*	*Mood After Drug Use*
Natural conditions	Varies widely from positive to negative	User decides; varies widely with individual	Varies widely with individual setting	Varies widely from public to private, alone or group	Varies, can be several hours	Varies widely with drug, dose, setting, individual; can reverse over time
Laboratory experiment	Mildly negative or neutral but not usually measured	Use is a requirement of participation in study	Usually low for ethical concerns	Neutral lab setting, usually alone or with researcher	Short duration, usually an hour or less	Mildly negative or neutral

Thus, an angry or depressed person may decide to drink to forget problems, whereas the happy individual may drink to celebrate a positive occasion with loved ones. These different motives can help determine how the alcohol will affect subsequent moods.

Sensory Motor Activity

Unlike mood, most studies of sensory motor skills, especially reaction time, have been laboratory studies because laboratory equipment to present stimuli and record responses are in general essential for this research. Laboratory situations are highly controlled but also greatly simplified from real-life situations to which we would hope to apply experimental findings. However, laboratory experiments allow firm conclusions about causal influences on alcohol and other drugs on these processes.

ATTENTION AND REACTION TIME

Alcohol has not been found to affect simple reaction time when a person has to detect or react to a single stimulus (Moskowitz & DePry, 1968), but these results may not be highly relevant to tasks outside the laboratory.

Divided attention tasks in which several competing stimuli are present simultaneously, however, are more commonly encountered in naturalistic situations such as driving an automobile or operating equipment in the workplace.

Controlled studies demonstrate disruption of reaction time by alcohol at low doses equivalent to one or two drinks taken within the past hour on tasks requiring divided attention (Moskowitz & Burns, 1971). Participants attended to a primary auditory or visual target and pressed a key when other distractor stimuli occurred at random peripheral background locations. Divided-attention tasks are similar to the demands placed on automobile drivers, such as noticing other vehicles in the periphery, reading street signs while steering through heavy traffic, or talking on a cell phone while merging onto a crowded freeway. Studies of divided attention have implicated alcohol use, even at low to moderate levels below the legal level of .10 mg % in many states, as a factor that may contribute to a high percentage of accidents (Moskowitz, Burns, & Williams, 1985). This effect of alcohol may be indirect, working through its influence on information processing of the central nervous system and brain rather than directly from toxic effects on motor coordination or gross muscle movement.

SENSORY MOTOR COORDINATION

Studies to determine how alcohol and other drugs affect sensory motor coordination have obvious implications for understanding factors contributing to driving accidents. One study (Finnigan, Hammersley, & Millar, 1995) assessed the acute effects of alcohol and expectancy on male social drinkers on a dual tracking and reaction time task analogous to some driving skills and on choice reaction time. A high dose of alcohol had large effects on both tasks, but a low dose had no significant effects. Expecting and receiving a high alcohol dose led to better performance on the primary tracking task than expecting a placebo but receiving the high alcohol dose.

On a driving simulator task involving tracking and braking skills, smokers performed better when they received nicotine than when they had a placebo treatment (Sherwood, 1995). Smoking cigarettes enhanced motor performance, but results seem to involve a relative rather than an absolute improvement. In other words, performance of experienced smokers is impaired when smoking is prevented but restored when smoking is possible (Sherwood, 1993). Nonsmokers and light smokers showed only small benefits of nicotine.

A controlled laboratory experiment used young drivers, ranging from nondrinking drivers to driving while intoxicated (DWI) offenders, to study alcohol's effects on their driving skill (hazard perception latency) and driving style (the perceived level of risk in hazards) (Deery & Love, 1996). Young adults underwent two experimental conditions, no alcohol and moderate alcohol (.05% blood alcohol level [BAL]), in a counterbalanced design. Under alcohol, subjects took longer to detect hazards and responded to them in a more abrupt manner, and these effects were particularly pronounced for DWI offenders. In general, subjects perceived active hazards (as being under their control) as less dangerous than passive hazards (environmental factors).

The effects of marijuana (0, 1.77, or 3.95% delta-9-tetrahydrocannabinol [THC]) on equilibrium and simulated driving were compared (Liguori, Gatto, & Robinson, 1998). Marijuana users smoked one marijuana cigarette at the beginning of each session. Two minutes later, they began a 60-minute test battery that included a computerized test of body sway and brake latency in a driving simulator.

The high but not the low marijuana dose increased body sway. The high dose also marginally increased brake latency by a mean of 55 ms, which is comparable to an increase in stopping distance of nearly 5 feet at 60 mph. The equilibrium and brake latency data with 3.95% THC are similar to results from past studies with participants tested with a moderate dose of alcohol (0.05%).

Self-Selection and Driving Under the Influence (DUI)

Although alcohol and other drugs do contribute to accidents, to what extent is self-selection involved in who engages in drink-drive behavior? Clearly, not everyone who drinks and drives gets arrested or in an accident. Aside from the differences in their involvement in drinking and driving behavior, do DUIs and non-DUIs differ in important other ways such as their driving skills, attitudes, speed, and circumstances? For example, if DUIs tend to drive more recklessly than non-DUIs, even when sober, they might get more tickets and have more accidents than non-DUIs anyway.

Perhaps a subset of drinking drivers may be reckless, impulsive, and irresponsible and hence more likely to be involved in collisions and traffic violations. One approach to this question is to compare drivers with the following: collisions and had been drinking, no collisions but had been drinking, clear driving records, or a previous arrest for DUI. Some research on this issue has involved roadside stops of drivers to measure their drinking frequency and quantity. Although 14% of the drivers in the group with no collision or arrest did show measurable blood alcohol

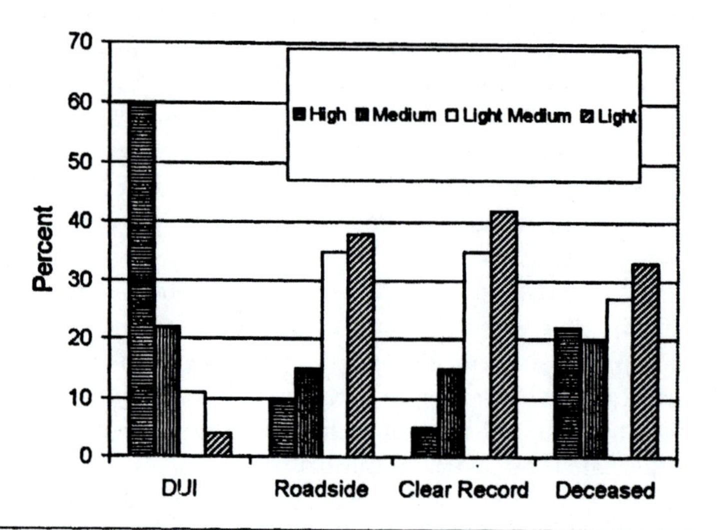

Figure 11.5. Percentage of Four Groups of Drivers Based on Their Drinking Levels
SOURCE: Based on data from Perrine (1990).

levels, only 2% were above .10, the legal limit at that time. This group of drivers "got away" with their drinking and driving up to the time of the study, at least.

As shown in Figure 11.5, DUI offenders had the highest percentage of heavier drinkers, whereas the other categories of drivers primarily consisted of lighter drinkers (Perrine, 1990). (For those who died in car accidents, drinking data were obtained from next of kin.) DUIs may not just be "unlucky" in getting arrested or in accidents. For example, they might drive faster or more aggressively than other drinking drivers, attracting the attention of law enforcement officers and increasing the risk of accidents.

Youth, Alcohol, and Driving

There is a greater representation of young drivers in all types of fatal crashes than from any other age group. To what extent does alcohol have a direct role in producing this effect? In traffic fatalities involving youth in 1987, 31% of those ages 16 to 20 and 45% of those ages 20 to 24 had been drinking alcohol (Fell & Nash, 1989).

However, studies of fatal automobile accidents show a much higher incidence rate among young drivers (ages 16-19) irrespective of alcohol use, suggesting that these fatalities are not entirely due to alcohol. The inexperience of young drivers increases their likelihood of having accidents. Coupled with the use of alcohol, which they also have less experience with, young drivers have a double risk for having accidents, as confirmed by statistics.

Cognition

Alcohol and many other drugs have an effect on cognitive functions such as memory, verbal skills, and visual-spatial-motor coordination. These skills, like sensory motor skills, are more easily studied in controlled laboratory experiments than are mood states. We will examine some examples of controlled studies of the effects of alcohol and other drugs on these functions and the explanations proposed for both the effects of short-term or acute and long-term or chronic use.

ACUTE EFFECTS ON MEMORY

Memory can involve short-term recall of recent information and events or long-term memory of information acquired long ago. Distinctions exist between memory involving knowledge about general versus specific information (**semantic** vs. **episodic memory**) (Tulving, 1983). Different cognitive processes may occur in different aspects of memory such as encoding, storage, and retrieval of information. Acute effects of alcohol are selective, impairing some but not all aspects of memory (Hashtroudi & Parker, 1986).

Effects of alcohol may vary with different depths of cognitive processing (Craik, 1977). In some studies, there were parallels between the types of cognitive deficits associated with aging and those due to intoxication, with both showing greater deficits when the tasks required deeper processing and attention. If the task required reflection or conscious integration of information, intoxication was harmful to performance, but on tasks that activated preexisting semantic structures, there was no noticeable impairment of performance. Thus, sorting words into different categories based on their meaning or comprehending prose passages was unaffected by these levels of intoxication.

Studies with the balanced placebo design generally have shown expectancy but not consumption effects on memory (Marlatt & Rohsenow, 1980). Poorer memory occurred if participants thought they had consumed alcohol. In other words, what they believed they would drink, an alcohol or placebo beverage, was more important than what they actually received.

Consumption but not expectancy effects occurred in another study (Peterson, Rothfleisch, Zelazo, & Pihl, 1990), perhaps because it used a higher alcohol dose. A test battery assessing delayed memory, planning and foresight, word fluency, vocabulary, abstract thinking, reaction time, and pursuit rotor tracking was given to college male social drinkers following one of three dose levels. The highest alcohol dose, which produced BALs of approximately .10 mg %, impaired delayed memory functions, paralleling deficits in clinical patients known to have temporal lobe lesions.

Cognitive functions such as verbal fluency and planning, known to be related to injury to the prefrontal area of the cerebrum, were also disrupted by high doses of alcohol. The pursuit rotor task, which involves more complex motor coordination and also is believed to be controlled by the frontal lobe, was impaired by alcohol. However, speed of motor control as measured by reaction time was not. In contrast, measures of general "intelligence" such as vocabulary and general information were not affected by alcohol.

But plausible explanations for the relationship between alcohol consumption and poorer cognitive function can be offered that are not based on alcohol as a direct causal factor. Less intelligent persons may drink more excessively, or other factors such as anxiety could produce both poorer cognitive performance and higher drinking levels (Grant, 1987), either of which could lead to the observed inverse relationship between drinking levels and cognitive performance. Deficits might be indirectly tied to alcohol through head injuries sustained from accidents while under the influence of alcohol.

Reviews (Grant, 1987; Parsons, 1986) of many studies suggested that the evidence about the effect of alcohol on cognition is inconsistent. One study (Parker & Noble, 1977) found that cognitive skills could be impaired by about four drinks, even with social drinkers. But other studies (Bates & Tracy, 1990) found that the cognitive performance of 21- to 24-year-old men and women was not related to level of drinking.

Some disagreement may be due to the types of tasks and the drinking histories of the participants used in different studies. For example, alcohol produces a subtle impairment not noticed even by the drinker on some but not for all types of memory tasks (Hashtroudi & Parker, 1986). The type of task is important, with those involving nonverbal abstraction, new learning, memory, and perceptual-motor performance being more sensitive to alcohol effects (Parsons, 1986).

Alcohol's effect can vary with the dose and task difficulty. In one study (Lloyd & Rogers, 1997), cognitive tasks, together with mood ratings, were completed before lunch and during the 4 hours following lunch. Participants consumed drinks with no alcohol, low-alcohol dose, or high-alcohol dose with a small lunchtime meal in counterbalanced order on 3 different days. Low alcohol (approximately 0.12 g/kg) significantly increased performance on a difficult vigilance task in comparison to the no-alcohol condition. In contrast, the high-alcohol dose (approximately 0.35 g/kg) tended to impair performance of this task. No effects of alcohol on performance occurred on less demanding tasks. The low dose of alcohol also improved mood by reducing tension. Thus, higher task performance was mediated by the calming effects of the alcohol.

CHRONIC EFFECTS ON MEMORY

A comparison (Williams & Skinner, 1990) of heavy with moderate to infrequent drinkers matched for age, sex, socioeconomic level, and education showed much poorer performance by the heavy drinkers on a battery of cognitive, verbal, and logical reasoning tasks. Deficits were even greater among those with lower education.

One possible physical basis for cognitive deficits stemming from chronic heavy alcohol use is the **Wernicke-Korsakoff syndrome,** a set of disorders attributed to organic brain damage (Berman, 1990). Wernicke's disease, a disorder involving confusion, ataxia (body sway), and ocular disturbances such as diplopia (double vision), is assumed to be due to thiamine deficiency and other vitamin deficits associated with prolonged alcohol use. Korsakoff's psychosis involves a short-term memory impairment (alcoholic amnestic disorder) that occurs despite the ability to engage in other intellectual activities. With this disorder, also known as *anterograde amnesia,* alcoholics have difficulty remembering recent events and learning new information. In addition, alcoholism may result in a dementia, or global deficit of intellectual function, so that abstraction and judgment are impaired.

A different interpretation (Berman, 1990) of these impairments views the memory deficits as part of a syndrome of interrelated disruptions due to alcohol that also involves emotion and motivation. Thus, poorer attention, lower motivation, and diminished affect due to alcohol consumption might all contribute toward poorer performance on memory tasks. Memory is not a function that operates independently of other processes.

State-Dependent Learning

Events experienced while intoxicated may not be recalled when the subject is later tested under sober conditions, a phenomenon commonly referred to as a **blackout.** Blackouts are similar to a laboratory phenomenon known as **state-dependent learning** (Weingartner & Faillace, 1971).

Information learned while under the influence of alcohol is better recalled later if a subsequent test is administered when the individual has been drinking and not, as might be assumed, when sober. This finding suggests that memory is better if the cues associated with the event to be remembered are similar to those that are present when the event is originally experienced.

This consequence of acute heavy drinking is not to be confused with passing out or fainting because the drinker is conscious during blackouts. There is evidence (Goldman, 1983; Ryan & Butters, 1983) that after a period of abstinence, some of these cognitive deficits are partially or completely reversible.

State-dependent learning also occurred when both nicotine and alcohol were consumed (Lowe, 1986). Participants learned a simple route map as they consumed alcohol (0.66 g/kg) and smoked two medium-tar cigarettes (average nicotine content 1.4 mg). On recall 24 hours later, highest recall scores were observed in the group that again received both nicotine and alcohol, the original conditions for the task. It was followed by nicotine only, alcohol only, and finally by the group receiving neither alcohol nor nicotine.

Other Drugs

Performance on cognitive tasks showed no significant differences between smokers, deprived smokers, and nonsmoker groups, either before or after smoking. Deprived and nondeprived smokers attempted more mental arithmetic problems than nonsmokers, both before and after the cigarette/rest break. This pattern suggests that smokers have faster cognitive processing, irrespective of their nicotine status (Parrott & Garnham, 1998).

STRUCTURAL NEUROPSYCHOLOGICAL EXPLANATIONS

Two main approaches (Nixon, Tivis, & Parsons, 1995), structural and process, have been used to develop evidence for neuropsychological explanations of cognitive deficits from alcohol, as summarized in Table 11.2. The structural approach attempts to find a correspondence between behavioral deficits and structural damage to areas of the brain assumed to underlie such behavior. It is assumed that the greater the extent of brain damage, the more impaired the functions governed by that area of the brain should be. One limitation of structural approaches, until relatively recently, was that one could not determine the types of structural prob-

TABLE 11.2 Neuropsychological models of cognitive impairment by alcohol

	Models of Alcohol and Cognition	*Main Impairment*
Structural theories	Generalized/diffuse hypothesis	Functions governed by both hemispheres of the brain
	Frontal lobe hypothesis	Perseverative errors
	Right hemisphere hypothesis	Visual-spatial abilities
Process theories	Premature aging hypothesis	Similar to that found with older persons who are not alcoholics
	Increased vulnerability hypothesis	Occurs in older but not in younger alcoholics

lems unless the person died and autopsies were performed. Now, with more sophisticated neuroimaging tools such as evoked response potentials (ERP), magnetic resonance imaging (MRI), functional magnetic resonance imaging (FMRI), and positron emission tomography (PET), it is possible to observe physical differences in structure in vivo.

There are three different hypotheses for the neuropsychological basis of cognitive deficits among alcoholics: the **diffuse/generalized effects hypothesis**, the **frontal lobe hypothesis**, and the **right hemisphere hypothesis** (Parsons & Leber, 1981).

Generalized/Diffuse Hypothesis

This view holds that alcohol impairs both hemispheres of the brain more or less equally, so that all functions are disrupted by alcohol to the same extent. Parsons (1986) found poorer performance by alcoholics relative to controls on a battery of verbal (left hemisphere) and visual-spatial (right hemisphere) tasks.

Frontal Lobe Hypothesis

Evidence for localized brain damage in the frontal lobes was sought in one study (Parsons & Leber, 1981) that compared the performance of older chronic alcoholics and patients with frontal lobe brain damage due to nondrinking factors such as head trauma on visual-spatial tasks involving a series of problems. Frontal lobe injury generally is associated with poor impulse control, planning, abstraction, and perseverative responding. Alcoholics did as well as controls on initial problems, but with successive problems, they were poorer than controls. Both alcoholics and brain-damaged patients were found to be equally impaired in comparison to control patients. It was concluded that the deficit is not perceptual or verbal per se but involves errors due to perseverative tendencies of responses from earlier problems, creating errors on later problems. Because impairment of attention is associated with the frontal lobe and limbic system, it was inferred that alcoholics might have suffered frontal lobe damage.

Right Hemisphere Hypothesis

Verbal skills were less impaired than the visual-spatial-motor coordination in past research (Ellis & Oscar-Berman, 1989). The lateralization of brain function has been well documented, with evidence showing that the verbal functions are served by the left hemisphere, and the visual-spatial-motor skills are controlled by the right hemisphere. Therefore, the pattern of impairment found with alcoholism led to the hypothesis that the right hemisphere might be an area where damage is likely. Alcoholics, relative to controls, had little impairment on tasks controlled by the left side of the brain (verbal), whereas performance on tasks involving the right side (nonverbal or spatial) of the brain were disrupted. Researchers concluded that chronic alcohol use might have impaired the functioning of the right hemisphere.

Some disagreement exists about the validity of the right hemisphere hypothesis as an explanation for these findings of performance deficits (Ellis & Oscar-Berman, 1989). For one matter, visual and verbal tasks are heterogeneous categories. All tasks of either category may not be controlled by the brain in the same manner. In contrast to studies supporting the right hemisphere hypothesis, other studies (Bolter & Hannon, 1986; Ryan, 1980; Ryan & Butters, 1986) involving tasks with greater attentional demands have shown that alcoholics can show impairment on verbal tasks as well as on nonverbal tasks.

Possibly, when less impairment occurs on verbal than on visual tasks, factors other than differential damage to brain hemispheres may be operating (Ellis & Oscar-Berman, 1989). Thus, the two tasks (verbal and nonverbal) were confounded with task difficulty, with the nonverbal being more difficult. Consequently, the complexity of strategies used by participants would differ for the two types of tasks. Thus, alcoholics may do less well whenever the tasks involve elaboration of strategies, as would be the case for many verbal tasks. But if a verbal task does not require such elaboration, they should not be as impaired.

Studies (e.g., Oscar-Berman, 1988) using perceptual asymmetry tasks such as dichotic listening tasks, in which different stimuli are directed toward each ear, yielded results that also called the right hemisphere hypothesis into question. Alcoholics showed no differences from age-matched controls on these tasks in producing ear advantages of the same type.

PROCESS NEUROPSYCHOLOGICAL EXPLANATIONS

A process approach (see Table 11.2) emphasizes the underlying cognitive functions rather than anatomical areas of the brain that are assumed to be affected by alcohol. Even if alcohol does not produce measurable structural changes, it still might disrupt behavioral and cognitive processing. For example, memory involves several cognitive operations such as storing of information, as indexed by errors on tasks, and retrieval of information, as reflected by speed or latency of response. In addition, a process approach examines efficiency of performance, as reflected by the ability to ignore irrelevant stimuli when performing a task. Alcohol may impair these processes so that memory is poorer even though no structural damages could be detected.

Premature Aging Hypothesis

An example of a process-oriented model is the **premature aging hypothesis,** which holds that chronic alcoholics perform as if they have experienced a premature aging of the central nervous system. Thus, alcoholics have deficits of right hemisphere function similar to impairments found among older nonalcoholics that are generally attributed to aging processes (Jones & Parsons, 1971).

Increased Vulnerability Hypothesis

An alternative account for the similarity of alcoholic and aging effects is the **increased vulnerability hypothesis,** a view that older brains are more vulnerable to alcohol impairment, whereas younger alcoholics are not. This version argues that the results reflect a differential vulnerability in which young alcoholics show no difference from nonalcoholics, but older alcoholics show impairment relative to controls. In general, the impairments due to age differences exceed those found between alcoholics and age-matched controls, implying that the effects of alcoholism on cognition are not the same as those of aging.

RECOVERY OF FUNCTIONS

Some deficits in cognitive functioning found in alcoholics may be recovered following a period of abstinence. Some impairments on cognitive tasks found during the first week of abstinence disappear 2 to 4 weeks later (Goldman, 1983). The abnormal electroencephalogram (EEG) brain wave pattern in alcoholics showed some degree of recovery of function after 3 to 6 weeks of abstinence (Ryan & Butters, 1983). Because recovery of cognitive deficits from aging does not generally occur, this finding challenges the premature aging hypothesis for alcohol's effects.

One study (Reed, Grant, & Rourke, 1992) tested memory defects in non-Korsakoff alcoholics matched for years of drinking but who had different lengths of abstinence varying from 29 days, around 2 years, and 7 years. Recently detoxified alcoholics showed memory impairment relative to controls, but demographically matched long-term abstinent alcoholics with similar drinking histories had performance comparable to the controls.

OVERVIEW

Cognitive impairment from alcohol falls along a continuum. Impaired neurological functioning can slow processing of information, impede new learning, interfere with abstraction, and reduce visual-spatial performance (Evert & Oscar-Berman, 1995). At the extreme end of impairment is the Wernicke-Korsakoff syndrome, which is distinguished by **anterograde amnesia.** Support for a continuum hypothesis would be strengthened if evidence showed a positive correlation between the amount of alcohol consumed and the degree of cognitive impairment. However, such evidence is not available. A clear test is difficult, however, because cognitive impairment is also due to other factors such as age. Gender differences also could be a factor but have not been studied much, and it is difficult to devise a comparable test due to the greater body fat for women (Nixon, 1995). Motivational and emotional factors as well as diet and presence of other diseases also play a role.

A component process model of alcohol effects on memory (Nixon & Parsons, 1993) involved a distinction between an episodic store of specific events and facts, as opposed to a knowledge information store of general concepts and ideas. Alcoholics may be impaired in either store in three different aspects of memory: the *availability* or persistence of information, access or speed of *retrievability* of memory, or the *efficiency* of memory (ability to distinguish between relevant and irrelevant information). Efficiency may be particularly sensitive to impairment among alcoholics.

In one test of this model (Nixon & Parsons, 1991), alcoholics received descriptions of four plants, two that were healthy and two that were unhealthy. Information was provided about the type of care each plant had been receiving such as type of plant food and amount of watering. On the basis of this information, they were told how another plant had been treated. Their task was to predict and explain what the health of another plant would be. Although alcoholics and controls were equal in predicting the physical condition of the plant, the alcoholics were less efficient because they had more difficulty in determining the relevant treatment variable, type of food or amount of watering, that was responsible for the condition of the plant.

In addition, there may be complex interactions between different cognitive functions such as compensatory adjustments. Alcoholics with deficits in one area of cognitive functioning may adapt through the use of other intact capacities (Ham & Parsons, 1997). Verbal skills are generally intact among alcoholics, whereas visual-spatial abilities are impaired. On visual-spatial tasks, alcoholics may try to use verbal skills to compensate for their inability to perform well on them. On the other hand, deficits in cognitive abstraction are closely related to verbal skills, so deficits in problem solving, which involve abstraction, cannot be as readily compensated for by verbal abilities.

Tests of male and female alcoholics (detoxified 3-6 weeks before testing) and nonalcoholic controls found some support for a compensatory model of cognitive functioning (Ham & Parsons, 1997). A similar study (Bates & Tracy, 1990), using heavy-versus light-drinking college students instead of treated alcoholics, failed to support this model. However, the discrepancy between the two studies may not be irreconcilable because the college students were not alcoholics. It is possible that they might show the compensatory behaviors at a later age, especially if they develop alcoholism.

SUMMARY

A variety of methods, naturalistic and experimental, have been used to test hypotheses about the effects of alcohol and other drugs. With experiments, it is possible to "separate" effects of drug use from the influence of beliefs about drug use's effects to determine how much each factor contributes to the observed behavior. An experiment also can help rule out self-selection biases such as when observed differences are not caused by drug use but merely reflect the possibility that those who tend to use drugs more also may differ in other important respects from those who use them less or not at all.

But on the negative side, experiments are usually limited to legal drugs. Experimental situations are artificial, and the behavior may not be reflective of behavior outside the laboratory. Sampling is limited to a small number of participants and unrepresentative samples of the general population; observations are of short duration, and participants know their behavior is being observed. In laboratory settings, participants may be administered drugs, quite unlike the situation in real life, when the person decides when or whether to take a drug.

The balanced placebo design is one method aimed at examining the combined and separate influences of the expectancy of consuming alcohol and the pharmacological factor. Studies using this paradigm have shown that for light to moderate drinkers, many behaviors are altered by the belief or expectancy that they have consumed alcohol. However, the method is limited to the study of acute effects of small doses of alcohol due to ethical problems and issues of credibility. Outside the laboratory and its controlled experiments, expectancy and pharmacological effects are inseparable and may even reinforce each other.

In laboratory experiments, opportunity for alcohol consumption is determined on a random basis by the researcher. But under naturalistic circumstances, individual psychological and physiological factors determine who may be more disposed to use and abuse alcohol. Consequently, the reactions to alcohol consumption may differ for light and heavy drinkers, even before drinking problems develop. Thus, the psychological effects of alcohol cannot be fully understood without including consideration of other differences among individuals who differ in their voluntary levels of alcohol consumption.

The psychological effects of a given amount of alcohol for chronic abusers and alcoholics differ from those of light to moderate drinkers. Depending on the extent of alcohol abuse, chronic use may have produced tolerance, organic damage, and nutritional deficits. Also, the psychosocial deterioration associated with alcoholism may alter the expectancies and motives for drinking. Such differences should lead to different behavioral and experiential consequences of alcohol consumption for those who are versus those who are not alcohol dependent.

We hope to ultimately understand the real-life drug use, but too many uncontrollable variables impede our comprehension. Laboratory studies afford a more precise form of observation but at the cost of reduced generalizability. Using evidence from both methods may enable us to gradually refine our models and derive more valid conclusions from our observations.

KEY TERMS

Anterograde amnesia
Balanced placebo
Blackout
Controlled observation
Diffuse/generalized effects hypothesis
Episodic memory
Expectancy
Frontal lobe hypothesis
Increased vulnerability hypothesis
Premature aging hypothesis
Right hemisphere hypothesis
Semantic memory
State-dependent learning
Uncontrolled observation
Wernicke-Korsakoff syndrome

STIMULUS/RESPONSE

1. Use your own experience to describe how mood states have been both an antecedent and consequence of alcohol and other drug use.
2. Students who drink excessively have been found to get lower grades. Does this prove that alcohol impairs learning? Suggest alternative explanations for this correlation. What study would you suggest to provide more conclusive evidence?
3. Stimulants such as cocaine, crack, and methamphetamines are thought to cause hyperactivity. Marijuana is thought to cause "a motivational syndrome" and mood changes. Could self-selection be involved in these examples? How can you test this possible alternative explanation for these correlations?
4. Mothers Against Drunk Driving (MADD) conducted a survey in 1998 and found that Americans support tougher anti-drunk-driving laws. Most Americans (70.1%) support lowering the legal drunk-driving limit to .08 blood alcohol level. More than 80% (81.8%) support impounding repeat offenders' vehicles, and 64.7% support permanent vehicle confiscation. Alcohol treatment was backed by 91.5% and jail sentences by 85.2%. How effective do you think each of the proposed changes would be in deterring drinking and driving? Can you think of other measures that might be as effective? Are there some measures that would be especially relevant for younger drivers?

- ❖ Aggression
- ❖ Sexual Activity
- ❖ Summary
- ❖ Key Terms
- ❖ Stimulus/Response

12 Alcohol and Other Drugs
Relationship to Interpersonal Processes

Alcohol and other drugs are often consumed, publicly or privately, in a social context. In some situations, such as at a party, almost everyone also may be using alcohol or other drugs, but in other circumstances, there may be few or no other users. In either circumstance, use of these substances can produce immediate and delayed consequences on the nature of social interactions between the users and other individuals.

In this chapter, we will examine the relationship between the use of alcohol and other drugs and two important forms of interpersonal behavior, aggression and sexual behaviors. Although they are highly dissimilar, they share one common feature: Societal restrictions and prohibitions against their expression are often in place for both behaviors. Aggression, which will be discussed first, refers mainly to behavior that involves harm to others or, at least, intent to harm. In extreme cases, some aggression involves criminal behavior such as violence toward others. Then, we will examine the relationship of alcohol and other drugs to sexual behavior, both consensual sexual relationships and unwanted sexual advances.

Aggression

What is the relationship between the use of alcohol and other drugs and the occurrence of aggression? Because alcohol is commonly believed to be a disinhibitor, aggressive tendencies may increase with drinking either because of pharmacological effects operating at the neurophysiological level or the influence of expectations or learned beliefs about the effect of alcohol.

CORRELATIONAL EVIDENCE

Ample naturalistic evidence suggests that alcohol use often precedes or accompanies violent behavior. Almost daily, one hears about homicides, assaults, attempted murders, burglaries, and robberies in which alcohol was used by either the perpetrator, the victims, or both. In Pasadena, California, for example, a study of crime during two 2-week periods in the early 1990s found that about half of all arrests, 60% of rape cases, more than half of domestic assaults, and 100% of homicides involved alcohol. Similar statistics probably can be found in many other communities.

In more than half to two thirds of homicides and assaults, the offender, the victim, or both had been drinking (Welte & Abel, 1989). In cases in which victims appeared to have been instigators of the fatal incidents, they were more likely to be intoxicated than when defendants were the provokers. In a large-scale study (Pernanen, 1991) in Thunder Bay, Ontario, about half of the sample (n = 900) reported being victims of violence, although in about 40% of cases, the incident had occurred as long as 8 years earlier. In about half of these violence incidents, alcohol was involved for at least one party, with the offender being the drinker in 51% of these cases, whereas the victim was the solitary drinker in 30% of the cases.

A high incidence of alcohol use has been reported in date or acquaintance rape (Abbey, 1991) and in rape cases overall (Amir, 1967), with estimates of at least 50% of rape cases (Koss, Gidycz, & Wisniewski, 1987). About 60% of 913 women interviewed in one national survey sample (Klassen & Wilsnack, 1986) reported experiencing some form of sexual aggression from men who had been drinking. Victims of violent drinkers tend to be similar to the aggressors, being young, never married, and frequenters of bars (Fillmore, 1985). The victims typically are acquaintances of the aggressors.

Despite the many accounts of incidents of violence reported in the news and portrayed in dramatic presentations, violence occurs relatively infrequently (Roizen, 1997). Most people, fortunately, do not commit violent actions or do them very rarely. Low violence is desirable in a good society, but for research purposes, it is easier to study if a larger sample of cases occurs in a relatively brief time span.

Prison Populations

An alternative source of evidence that can provide large samples are prison inmates. High rates of aggression exist for this population, where many have been arrested for violent crimes. Almost half of prison inmates in the United States claim to have been affected by alcohol, other drugs, or both alcohol and other drugs at the time they committed the offenses for which they were arrested (Mumola, 1999).

A review (Collins, 1986) of studies of incarcerated violent offenders showed a greater prevalence of alcohol problems for these inmates as compared to the general population. An examination of data for more than 1,300 male felons that controlled for background variables such as age, race, educational level, marital status, and number of prior arrests revealed that violent offenders were more likely to have reported drinking prior to their arrest than were nonviolent inmates (Collins & Schlenger, 1988).

However, a similar comparison (Pernanen, 1981) showed that whether the inmate met the criteria for alcohol dependence was unrelated to the type of offense. This suggests that it is more likely that the acute effect of alcohol, rather than some personality factor related to chronic use, is the factor contributing to the violence. Intoxication may impair cognitive processes and judgments, leading to the misinterpretation of cues and in turn leading to violent interactions.

Illicit Drugs and Aggression

Due to the illegal status of many drugs, there is less objective evidence and research about their relationship to aggression or, for that matter, many other behaviors. Much of the "evidence" is anecdotal, involving case examples, and is not based on large samples representative of the general population.

The most widely used illicit drug, marijuana, is stereotypically viewed as a drug that may lead to reduced aggression and "mellow" feelings among its users. Heroin is commonly seen as producing lethargy and, except for some violent crimes to obtain drug money, is thought unlikely to provoke aggression as a direct pharmacological effect.

In contrast, stimulants such as amphetamines, cocaine, and crack generally are believed to produce heightened arousal as well as feelings of paranoia that can lead to higher levels of violent aggression. In particular, the agitation and confusion accompanying withdrawal from the lack of access to stimulant drugs may activate aggression in chronic users and not reflect a pharmacological effect of the drug's actions.

Clinical observations and some controlled observations in laboratory experiments using competitive tasks (Taylor & Hulsizer, 1998) generally have supported these beliefs. Although these experiments have their limitations because they use small doses over short periods with individuals who are not dependent on drugs, they do have the advantage of objective evidence obtained while the drugs are being consumed.

However, commonly held beliefs about drug effects on aggression are not upheld for all drugs. Specifically, users of benzodiazepines (minor tranquilizers) should display less aggression because these drugs are sedative and reduce anxiety. Paradoxically, there is clinical evidence that some users of this class of drugs often display anger and hostility.

Another important source of violence derives from the circumstances surrounding drug dealing. Battles over turf or territory, fraudulent selling of inferior grades of an illicit drug, or disputes over money from drug transactions lead to "systemic violence." In other words, although these violent behaviors are nonetheless serious problems associated with illicit drug use, they must be recognized as socially and psychologically rather than pharmacologically determined.

However, many of these "effects" may not even be due to pharmacological aspects of the drugs. Psychiatric problems may be greater among users of illicit drugs, and these characteristics, possibly in combination with these drugs, may activate aggression in certain circumstances. Illicit drugs may not be causes of aggressive behavior so much as aggressive individuals are more prone to seek illicit drugs and, under their influence, may become more violent.

Alcohol Versus Illicit Drugs

The U.S. Bureau of Justice Statistics report compared the relationship of using alcohol versus illicit drugs to crime for 1997. The report (Mumola, 1999) concluded that there was a relationship between past *use* of illicit drugs, but not of alcohol, with crime.

However, the report used *different* criteria in defining alcohol use and illicit drug use, leaving the conclusion in question. Whereas juvenile *illicit drug use* was defined in terms of rates of lifetime use and monthly use, *alcohol use* was more stringently defined in terms of more problematic use levels, such as binge drinking and alcohol dependence. These different criteria bias the results in favor of alcohol because a heavier level of alcohol than illicit drug use was required before it was linked to crimes.

When comparable criteria were used, such as the extent of use occurring *at the time the offense* was committed for which an individual was incarcerated, as Table 12.1 shows, there were no differences between the relationship of crime with alcohol and with illicit drugs. They have roughly equal roles in crime: 37% of state inmates reported using alcohol, and 33% of state inmates said they were using drugs at the time of their crimes. About 34% of federal inmates reported being under the influence of alcohol at the time of their offenses, and 22% of federal offenders said

TABLE 12.1 Relationship between crime and drug use among prison inmates

	% of Prisoners	
Self-Reports	*1997*	*1991*
Drug use in month before offense		
State	57	50
Federal	45	32
Drug use at time of offense		
State	33	31
Federal	22	17
Alcohol use at time of offense		
State	37	32
Federal	20	11
Alcohol drug use at time of offense		
State	52	49
Federal	34	24

SOURCE: Mumola (1999).

they were under the influence of illicit drugs when they committed their crimes.

In the 1997 survey of the inmates of federal prisons, 51% reported the use of alcohol or drugs while committing their offenses. Although only one fifth of inmates in state prisons were drug offenders, 83% reported past drug use, and 57% were using drugs in the month before their offense, compared to 79% and 50%, respectively, in 1991. Also, 37% of state prisoners in 1997 reported drinking at the time of their offense, up from 32% in 1991.

Although the proportion of federal prisoners held for drug offenses rose from 58% in 1991 to 63% in 1997, the percentage of all federal inmates who reported using drugs in the month before the offense rose from 32% to 45%. One fifth of federal prisoners reported drinking at the time of their offense in 1997, up from one tenth in 1991.

Alcohol may be more dangerous than illicit drugs in some situations such as those involving violent crime such as assault, murder, and sexual assault. In fact, 42% of state prisoners and 25% of federal prisoners convicted of violent offenses reported using alcohol at the time they committed their crimes, compared to 29% of violent state offenders and 25% of violent federal offenders who said they were high on drugs when they committed their crimes. Not surprisingly, many drug offenders were in prisons primarily or only because of drug law violations. In addition, one in six drug offenders reported that they committed their crimes to get money to buy illicit drugs.

Critical Evaluation

The overall evidence would appear to establish alcohol and drugs as dangerous substances that contribute to many undesirable social consequences. One limitation to this evidence, however, is that it is largely based on self-reports, which may be inaccurate due to faulty memory.

In addition to forgetting, overestimates of drinking may occur if drunkenness is invoked as an "excuse" (MacAndrew & Edgerton, 1969). Thus, if offenders think they may receive lighter punishment when their misdeeds are perceived as due to the influence of alcohol, they may claim they were drinking more than they actually were.

Measurement. Assessing the level of alcohol use is difficult. With retrospective recall, there is often no accurate information about how close in time the drinking occurred in relation to the offense. The accuracy of measuring drinking may not be equivalent for all offenses, being higher for offenses in which the offender is apprehended on the scene or shortly thereafter than those in which weeks or months have passed since the incident. Often, only dichotomous yes-no assessments, rather than measures of degree of drinking, are used to determine if drinking occurred in association with a violent incident. Thus, the evidence usually cannot accurately answer the question of whether alcohol and other drugs directly "caused" criminal activities.

Sampling. Another problem with evidence from prison inmates is that it involves atypical samples that may not be easily generalizable to the general population. The relationship of alcohol with violent crimes may be inflated among inmates because intoxicated offenders may be more likely to be apprehended than lighter drinkers or nondrinkers (Murdoch, Pihl, & Ross, 1990). In addition, some cases could involve mistaken or false charges.

Controls. Regardless of whether a general or a prison population is studied, a sample of sober individuals is needed as a baseline comparison to determine how much aggression occurs in the absence of drinking (Lipsey, Wilson, Cohen, & Derzon, 1997). Often, this control group is ab-

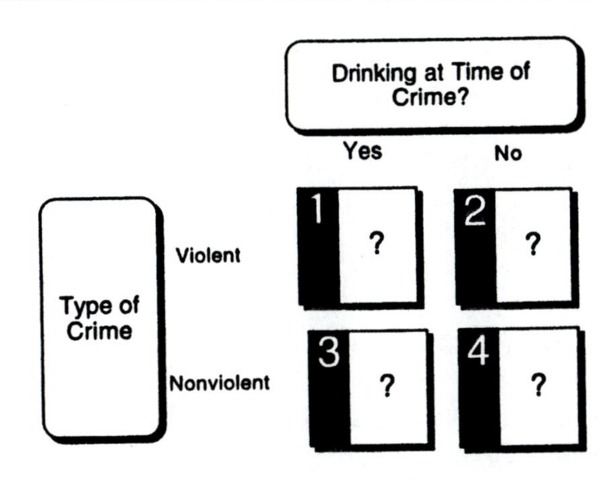

Figure 12.1. Hypothetical Comparisons Needed to Determine the Role of Alcohol on Violent Crime

NOTE: Even if alcohol is consumed by arrestees for violent crimes, we cannot conclude that alcohol was a major cause of the violence unless we compare the violence of drinking arrestees (Cell 1) with the baseline level of violence in sober arrestees (Cell 2). In addition, we also need a before-and-after drinking comparison (Cells 3 vs. 4) of rates of nonviolent crimes among drinking arrestees.

sent when statistics are cited about the extent of alcohol use among offenders (Roizen, 1997). To argue that a link exists between violence and drinking, one must realize that it is not sufficient to demonstrate that a certain percentage of violent offenders had been drinking at the time of arrest. In Figure 12.1, the percentage of violent offenders among drinking arrestees (Cell 1) should be compared with the percentage of violent offenders who were sober when arrested (Cell 2) and found to be higher. Even so, alcohol may still not be the primary cause of the violence and drinking combination; third-variable explanations also might account for why some people both drink more and are more violent. For example, some psychiatric conditions might lead some individuals to engage in more drinking and more violent behavior. Finally, assuming that alcohol use is related to violent crimes, is the relationship any stronger than that between drinking and nonviolent crimes (comparison of Cells 3 and 4 in Figure 12.1)? Hypotheses about the type of processes that enable alcohol to increase crime would depend on whether drinking increases violent and nonviolent crimes to the same extent.

Solitary Versus Dyadic Drinking. An analysis of the alcohol-aggression correlation also must distinguish between situations in which only the offender was drinking, only the victim was drinking, and both were drinking.

The first situation implicates alcohol as a possible cause of violence by the drinker, the second situation is somewhat at odds with a causal interpretation, and the third situation is ambiguous about causality (Murdoch et al., 1990). Thus, if both parties involved in an assault had been drinking, it is difficult to determine whether alcohol instigated violence on the part of the offender, victim, or both. Also, in some cases, it may not be certain which party was the offender and which party was the victim. Finally, in addition to alcohol possibly leading to aggression, an opposite consequence also may occur for heavy drinkers. They themselves become targets for violent victimization because their intoxication may render them more vulnerable.

A similar problem arises in explaining cases of acquaintance rape in which both parties had been drinking. Alcohol does not automatically activate sexual aggression but may facilitate it through many processes that could have been affected by drinking (Abbey, 1991), as suggested by Figure 12.2. In this model, culturally learned aspects of gender roles serve as background factors. The male's expectation that alcohol increases sexual feelings may encourage his advances. The female's drinking may act as a stereotypical signal of sexual readiness that the male misinterprets. Once the alcohol is consumed by the male, he may be less likely to interpret resistance as refusal and regard it as playing hard to get. As for the female, her drinking also might lower her ability to continue her resistance.

Pharmacological Versus Psychological Factors. Alcohol and other drugs may influence behavior through either *pharmacological* or *psychological* processes or both factors. Drugs such as alcohol, barbiturates, and benzodiazepines act as central nervous system depressants, whereas other drugs such as amphetamines and cocaine increase arousal and stimulation. All psychoactive drugs alter mood and conscious experience in some manner, and these effects may influence social behaviors such as aggression and sexually intimate behaviors.

In addition, or alternatively, alcohol and other drugs may influence social behavior through their influence on cognitive and affective factors that determine the appraisal and meaning of social situations. These *psychological* factors, such as beliefs and expectations about drug effects, may affect social interactions.

For example, a comment made in jest that would ordinarily be taken in stride by someone who is sober may be misinterpreted as hostile by someone who has been drinking. In contrast, someone who is lighthearted from drinking who is criticized might ignore or not interpret the comments as threatening.

In the realm of sexual behavior, cues and behaviors in interpersonal interactions also may be interpreted differently when the person is sober as

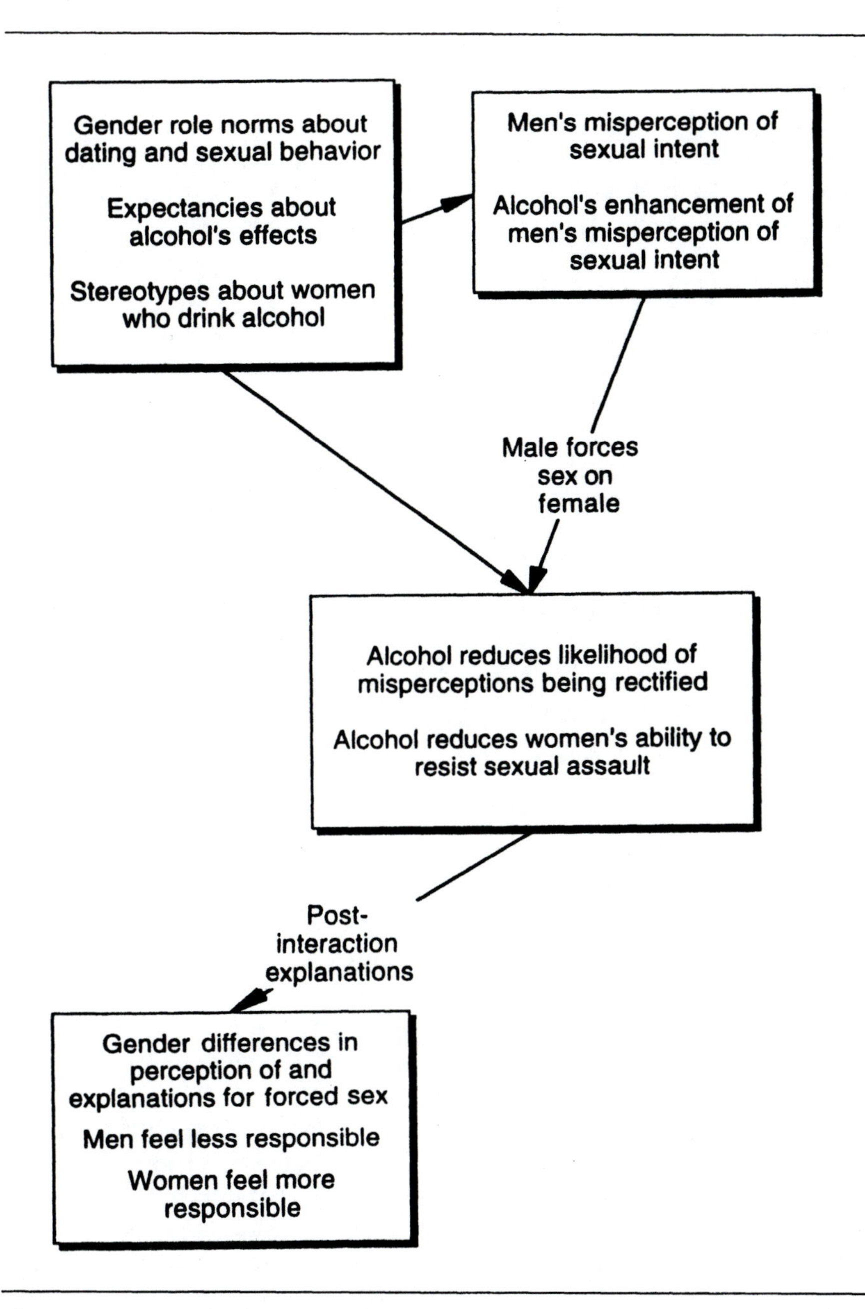

Figure 12.2. Multiple Factors Determine How Alcohol Can Be Involved in Acquaintance Rape

SOURCE: Abbey, Ross, and McDuffie (1994). Copyrighted 1994 by Humana Press. Reprinted with permission.

NOTE: Psychological beliefs and expectations about drinking in mixed-sex situations differ for men and women; these factors determine how any physiological effect of alcohol will influence sexual aggression.

compared to when he or she is under the influence of alcohol. These differences have implications for how an individual reacts to sexual overtures involving potential sexual partners.

It is difficult, if not impossible, to separate the pharmacological and psychological effects in natural circumstances, so researchers use controlled experiments to determine their relative contributions.

EXPERIMENTAL EVIDENCE

Studies using an experimental group that receives alcohol and a control group that receives a nonalcoholic placebo beverage generally show that the alcohol condition leads to more aggression than the control condition (Bushman & Cooper, 1990; Taylor & Leonard, 1983). However, a review (Hull & Bond, 1986) of balanced placebo design studies, which control for expectancy as well as for alcohol per se, found that the effects of both consumption and expectancy of alcohol on aggression were inconsistent across different studies. The heterogeneous results about expectancy effects on aggression could be due to individual differences in the need for expressing aggression. For example, among individuals expecting alcohol, only those who experienced recent frustration might display aggression.

Laboratory Paradigms

The experimental method allows objective and standard measurement of the intensity and duration of the stimuli. In experiments, for ethical reasons, the goal is not to provoke realistic and possibly uncontrollable aggression but to make the participant in the study think that someone has aggressed against them. Then, an opportunity to retaliate against the aggressor is provided to the victim.

To achieve these goals in the laboratory, a face-to-face confrontation between the aggressor and the victim is undesirable and unnecessary. In these experiments, college student participants are typically paired with strangers who are potential targets for aggression either because they provoke the participant or because they are convenient targets for the displacement of aggression. Actually, an accomplice of the experimenter pretends to be another research participant. Using a so-called "aggression machine" (Buss, 1961), the real participant is supposed to teach a concept to the bogus participant over a series of trials by providing "feedback" in the form of varying intensities of shock whenever a mistake is made. The accomplice, who performs the task in an adjoining room, does not actually receive shocks. This paradigm allows the researcher to measure the effects of different factors on these aggressive tendencies of the participants.

Another procedure (Taylor, 1967) involves having the accomplice (in an adjoining cubicle) pretend to compete with the participant on several trials on a reaction time task. The real participant is led to believe that the winner of each trial can select some level of electric shock to "punish" the loser. In actuality, the shock levels are selected in a predetermined sequence of increasing intensity that is independent of actual performance. The participant receives shock on trials when he "loses." When the real participant "wins" a trial, he gets a chance to see what level his opponent had intended for him. Accordingly, if he is provoked by the threat posed by the opponent's intent to deliver strong shock to him, the participant may retaliate by administering high shock intensities on subsequent trials to the fake participant.

These studies are intended as analogues of aggressive behavior, but their generalizability to real-life situations is limited because the two opponents do not have face-to-face interactions. Laboratory studies of aggression are mostly limited to the use of electric shock for instigating aggression. Although the deceptions are realistic, some participants may not fully believe they are harming the other participant because they may assume that the researchers would not have them perform a task that inflicts real harm to others.

Expectancy Controls

A comparison (Chermack & Taylor, 1995) of the influences of pharmacological and expectancy effects on the alcohol-aggression relationship involved interviews of males about their alcohol expectancies. They were randomly divided into two groups: placebo or high-alcohol dose. They had the opportunity to behave in an aggressive manner (administer shocks to opponent) toward an unseen "opponent" on a competitive reaction time task.

High doses of alcohol resulted in higher levels of aggression compared to the placebo condition, regardless of which beverage they expected to receive. Thus, pharmacological factors are needed to fully account for the relationship between alcohol ingestion and aggression.

Factors Moderating Effects of Alcohol

Alcohol does not automatically release aggression, as often assumed. If alcohol only acted by releasing inhibitions for aggression, we should find more aggression across all situations for all individuals when aggressive feelings are activated. However, many situational and personal factors have been found that moderate the effect of alcohol.

A model (Chermack & Giancola, 1997) that summarizes some of the complex set of factors involved in determining whether alcohol might affect aggression is presented in Figure 12.3. As shown in the left-hand box of the model, past learning during childhood development about aggression and personal experiences with violence serve as a distant background factor against which the present situation an individual is in determines the likelihood that alcohol use would lead to aggression. The middle section of Figure 12.3 shows numerous factors that affect the outcome, such as the setting, the relationship to the other person or persons, and the amount of threat involved. The individual's own personality and present mood combine with these situational factors to determine the use of alcohol and drugs as well as how such use may lead to the expression of violence, represented in the box on the far right of the diagram. There are many reciprocal, rather than unidirectional, effects among the components. Thus, alcohol consumption can affect mood, which in turn affects violent behavior, but the reverse also occurs. Violent behavior can alter mood, which in turn can determine alcohol and other drug consumption. Some of these moderators of alcohol's effect on aggression will now be examined in more detail.

Provocation. Many studies using a competitive reaction time task, with the winner in each trial getting to shock the loser, have found an alcohol-aggression link under certain conditions such as provocation, threat, and dose. Provocation was necessary before alcohol would increase aggressive responding on the Taylor competitive reaction time task. When there was no provocation, the alcohol and sober conditions were both low on aggression (Gustafson, 1993; Taylor & Chermack, 1993).

The relationships between provocation, acute alcohol intoxication, and aggressive behavior were studied in 48 men who had impaired cognitive performance on tasks associated with frontal lobe function (Lau, Pihl, & Peterson, 1995) to see if reduced cognitive functioning may reduce inhibition of aggression.

Half completed an aggression task while intoxicated, and the other half performed the task while sober. Aggression, defined in terms of shock level delivered to a fictitious unseen opponent, increased with provocation, alcohol consumption, and poorer cognitive performance. Furthermore, men with the lower cognitive performance and presumably more frontal lobe damage, showed the greatest aggression when provoked.

Situational Conflict. The effects of alcohol consumption on aggression also may vary depending on the extent to which ambivalence about expressing aggression may exist in the situation. Thus, alcohol consumption effects are present only when the aggressive behavior in the situation involves high conflict (Steele & Southwick, 1985). Even when people are an-

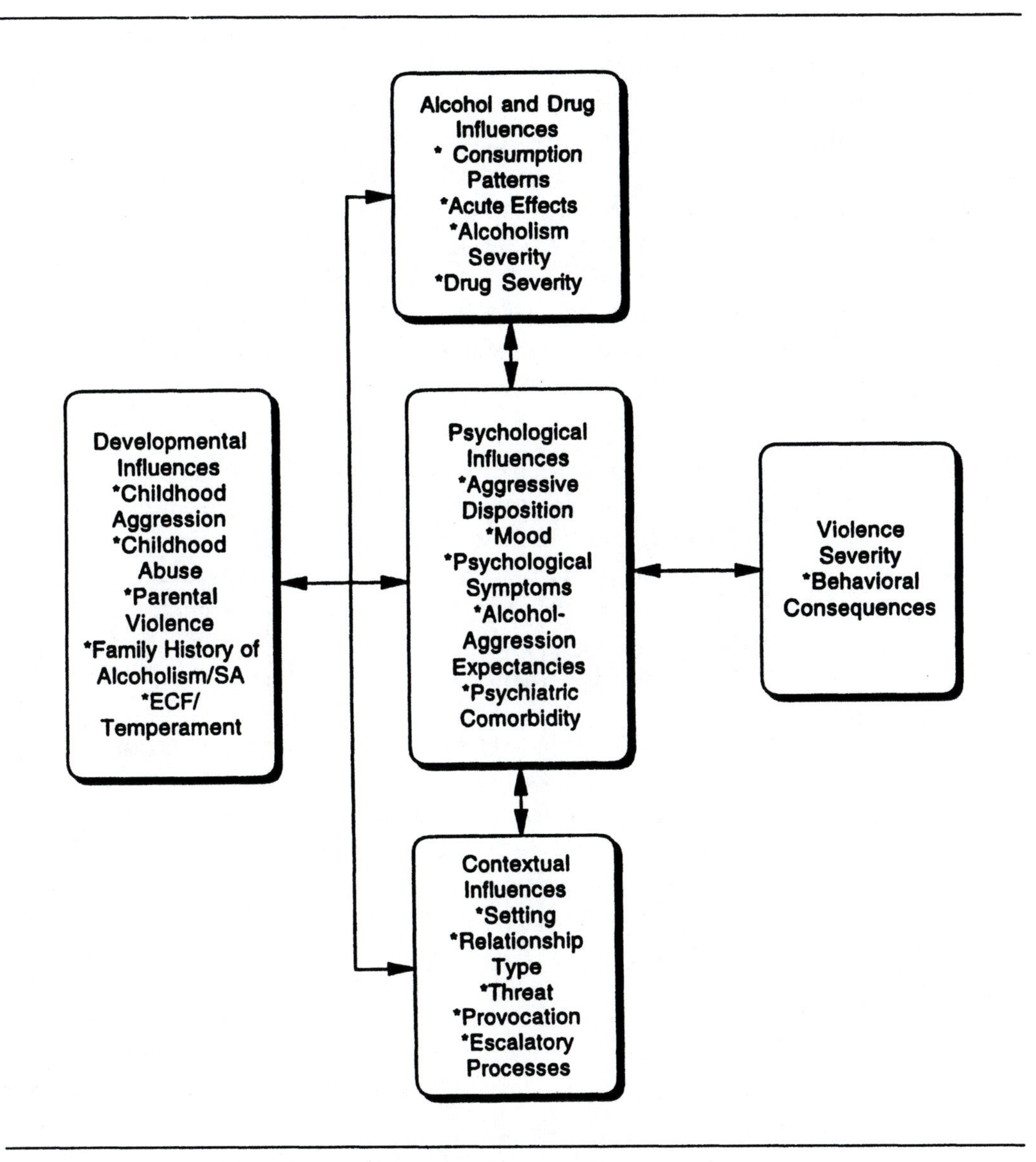

Figure 12.3. Model of Moderators of Aggression

SOURCE: Chermack and Giancola (1997). Copyright 1997 by Elsevier Science. Used with permission.

NOTE: The immediate setting and psychological factors are proximal determinants of the effects of alcohol on aggression. In addition, distal background factors from childhood and family experiences also play a role.

gry with other people, they often have some conflict or reluctance to engage in aggression because of potential adverse social consequences, especially when sober. However, when people have consumed large amounts of alcohol, they are more prone to act on these aggressive urges.

This tendency of alcohol to release our inhibitions of aggression is termed **alcohol myopia** (Josephs & Steele, 1990), a situation in which our short-sighted impulses are dominant over our long-range interests. This effect is due to the disruptive effects of even a few drinks on our attention. When we are sober, we can weigh the pros and cons of engaging in a specific behavior, but when we are intoxicated, attention allocation is diminished so that such considerations are obstructed.

In addition, external cues in a situation that might ordinarily inhibit aggression (e.g., police are present) might not be noticed, so aggression could occur. By reducing *inhibition conflict* about aggressive feelings, alcohol can facilitate the expression of aggression.

Situational Anxiety. When cues suggest that retaliation or social disapproval will occur for aggression, anxiety may be aroused that may inhibit aggression (anxiety inhibition model).

Alcohol consumed before receiving these cues may weaken the anxiety and hence increase the level of aggression. When sober, increased anxiety cues act to inhibit aggression, whereas when intoxicated, these cues should make less difference because they may be less noticed and fail to inhibit aggression.

A different view holds that alcohol consumption may lead to more aggression because it restricts attention (myopia) (Josephs & Steele, 1990). Both theories predict that alcohol use increases aggression, but the anxiety disinhibition model deals only with cues of anxiety, whereas the inhibition conflict model views the relative strength of two opposed factors—one inhibiting and one instigating aggression—as the determinant of outcomes.

A **meta-analysis** (Ito, Miller, & Pollock, 1996) was performed on studies examining the relationship between anxiety and aggression. In this procedure of comparing different studies, the results of available studies on a topic of interest are statistically combined and treated as if they represented one very large study. This method allows an evaluation of the effect of different factors with a much larger sample than possible within a single study. The analysis concluded that there is support for both models.

Personality. In one study (Giancola & Zeichner, 1995), 60 young, White, intoxicated social drinkers competed against a fictitious opponent. They both received and delivered electric shocks to their fictitious opponents under either provoking or nonprovoking conditions. In the high-provocation condition, aggressive personality traits, subjective intoxication, and blood alcohol level were effective predictors of physical aggression. In the low-provocation condition, only aggressive personality traits and blood alcohol level predicted aggression. None of the variables was related to aggression for intoxicated females.

Dose Size. The effect of a larger dose size could be due to alcohol reducing self-focus or awareness of one's inner states (Hull & Young, 1983). Most participants in an aggression experiment might be reluctant to inflict harm on another because it conflicts with their values. If higher doses produced less self-focus, external cues such as instructions from the experimenter to administer shock to another participant in the study might elicit the aggressive response more readily.

Temporal Factors. Any effect of alcohol on aggression that might occur due to stress may depend on the temporal relationship between drinking and the stressor. For example, how alcohol affects aggression may depend on whether the drinking precedes or follows a stressor. In one study (Sayette & Wilson, 1991), more anxiety reduction occurred if alcohol was consumed *before,* rather than *after,* facing the stressor. Although aggression was not examined in this study, one might infer that the greater anxiety reduction due to drinking prior to the stressor would be associated with less aggression.

Ascending Versus Descending Blood Alcohol Level. A controlled experiment (Giancola & Zeichner, 1997) tested male college students, sober versus .08 mg % alcohol, competing on a modified aggression machine against a fictitious opponent. Half of each group was tested on the ascending and half on the descending limb of blood alcohol level.

More aggression occurred when tests occurred on the ascending limb, when alcohol has an activating effect, but it had a sedating influence on the descending limb, reducing energy. These results disagree with expectancy theory, which would not predict a difference in effect over time.

CAUSAL EXPLANATIONS

Correlational evidence linking alcohol and aggression is ambiguous as to causality. Drinking may reduce inhibitions, releasing aggressive behaviors. Conversely, aggressive behaviors could activate guilt or fear that may increase drinking. Finally, a process involving a third factor, such as personality, could increase both drinking and aggression independently.

A prospective longitudinal study can help provide some answers. Behaviors that precede other behaviors are eligible to be considered causes of the later behaviors. In contrast, later behaviors cannot logically be viewed as causes of earlier behaviors. One such study (White, Brick, & Hansell, 1993), conducted over 3 years using a random telephone survey, examined the transition in alcohol use, aggression, and their relation to each other over early adolescence. Three different cohorts were tested—mainly White working-class and middle-class samples who were ages 12, 15, and 18.

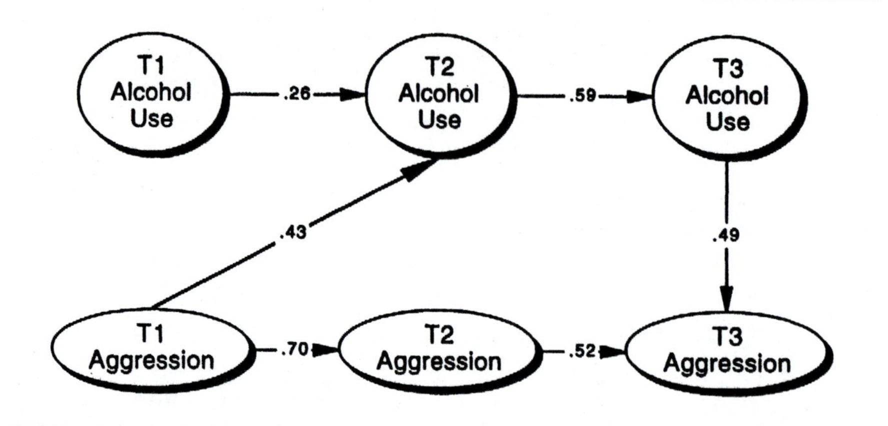

Figure 12.4. Longitudinal Relationship of Aggression and Alcohol Use by Adolescents

SOURCE: White et al. (1993). Copyright 1993 by *Journal of Studies on Alcohol,* Rutgers Center for Alcohol Studies, New Brunswick, New Jersey. Used with permission.

They were studied to assess the temporal sequence of aggression and alcohol consumption, the stability of the relationship, and how changes in one affect the other.

Results did not support a reciprocal model whereby alcohol and aggression each affect the other. Instead, at least for males, early aggression tendencies at age 12 appear to lead to early alcohol use by age 15, but this early use of alcohol did not increase later aggression, as shown in Figure 12.4. Moreover, early aggression was a better predictor of later alcohol problems than was early alcohol use.

The results favor the model in which early aggressive tendencies lead to increased later drinking. This naturalistic study shows that over an extended period of several years, the more aggressive individuals tend to drink heavily and behave aggressively when intoxicated. These findings might seem in conflict with laboratory experiments in which the opposite sequence occurs, with higher alcohol use preceding the aggression. It must be kept in mind that laboratory experiments deal with behavior within a specific short-term period, whereas naturalistic studies typically cover several years.

Finally, a model in which the alcohol-aggression correlation is viewed as "spurious" may be tenable. Thus, a third factor, such as genetic temperamental differences on dimensions such as impulsiveness or hyperactivity or shared environment (family pathology or childhood victimization), could act as a common antecedent of both higher alcohol use and increased aggression.

Consistent with the view that a personality factor may act as a moderator of the alcohol-aggression relationship is evidence of the much higher

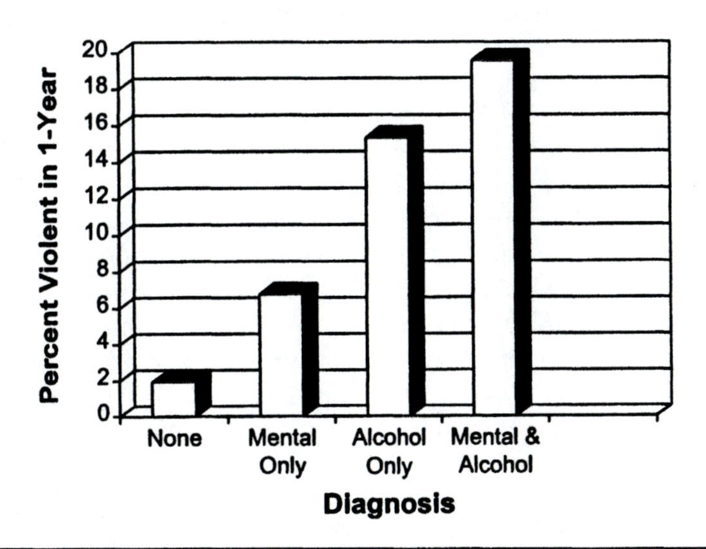

Figure 12.5. Comorbidity of Alcohol Abuse and Mental Disorder Affects Aggression

SOURCE: Swanson (1993).

NOTE: Alcohol use disorders are more likely to be related to violent behavior than are mental disorders; having both disorders slightly increases the level of violence over having only alcohol use disorder.

risk of aggression among men who abuse alcohol and have been diagnosed with mental disorders. Analysis (Swanson, 1993) of data from the Epidemiological Catchment Area Study (Regier et al., 1984), a national study of mental disorders, found that comorbidity of alcohol and major mental disorders was associated with much higher rates of violent behavior, as shown in Figure 12.5.

Males with dual diagnoses of major mental disorders and alcohol abuse or dependence had the highest rates of aggression, followed by those with only alcohol disorders and those with only major mental disorders, with the lowest violence among men with neither problem.

Sexual Activity

> Candy is dandy
> But liquor is quicker
>
> —Ogden Nash

Intimate sexual encounters may involve the use of alcohol and other drugs because they are widely believed to enhance sexual arousal and lower inhibitions, intensifying the advances and passion of the initiating partner. Alcohol and other drugs are also widely thought to act as aphrodisiacs so that suitors ply their potential partners with these substances to weaken any resistance. Drinking may precede, accompany, and follow sexual activity. The questions of interest are whether drinking or using other drugs directly or indirectly increases sexual activity, and, if so, what are the underlying psychological or physiological processes?

A major concern is the increased risk for AIDS and other sexually transmitted diseases if alcohol use increases "unsafe" sex practices such as intercourse without the use of condoms, especially with multiple partners. The issue of whether the likelihood of unsafe sex practices might be greater because alcohol may impair judgment is particularly relevant.

Alternatively, some third factor may independently promote both drinking and sexual activity. For example, among young adolescents, both activities can be viewed as normatively deviant behaviors. Hence, they might occur in rebellion to parental and societal norms and expectations leading to the development of alcohol use and sexual activity as separate forms of delinquency.

SURVEY EVIDENCE

As adolescents mature, they become involved in activities that were previously forbidden to them and are generally restricted to adults, such as alcohol consumption and sexual intimacy. Because alcohol is popularly viewed as a disinhibitor, it would hardly be surprising that alcohol is associated with sexual activities.

Overall Activity

About half of the adolescents in one study (Robertson & Plant, 1988) reported drinking alcohol at the time of their first sexual intercourse. Sexually active adolescents were found to be more likely to use alcohol than those who had not engaged in sexual intercourse (Coles & Stokes, 1985).

The Youth Risk Behavior Survey provides annual self-reports about a broad range of health risk behaviors from a representative sample of high school students in the United States. An analysis of the 1990 report, based on more than 11,000 students (Lowry et al., 1994), found that students who reported no substance use were least likely to report having had sexual intercourse, having had four or more sex partners, and not having used a condom at last sexual intercourse. After controlling for differences in age, sex, and race/ethnicity, these sexual risk behaviors were highest for those who had used marijuana, cocaine, or other illicit drugs. Students who had used only alcohol or cigarettes had smaller increases in the likelihood of having had sexual intercourse and having had four or more sex partners.

A random survey of 439 college students (Meilman, 1993) found that 35% reported some form of sexual activity after starting college that was influenced by drinking. While under the influence of alcohol, 18% had engaged in sexual intercourse, and 15% had not used safe-sex techniques. Three categories—any form of sexual activity, sexual intercourse, and abandonment of safe-sex techniques—showed a positive relationship with heavier alcohol use and binge drinking.

The use of alcohol and other drugs was related to sexual risk taking in a representative sample of 12,069 younger men and women after controlling for age, education, and family income (Parker, Harford, & Rosenstock, 1994). A survey of 398 undergraduates (Desiderato & Crawford, 1995) found that within a 3-month period, two thirds of the students had engaged in sexual intercourse, and one third of these reported having more than one sexual partner. Almost half of the sexually active students did not use a condom during their last sexual encounter, and only one fourth reported using condoms consistently. Alcohol use was related to inconsistent condom use among students with multiple sexual partners.

Alcohol use was more strongly related to unprotected sex among adolescents than that for adults (Leigh, 1990). These differences may reflect the fact that drinking and sexual activities are new experiences during adolescence, both of which usually involve breaking strong inhibitions (Leigh & Morrison, 1991). Alcohol may therefore serve as a more powerful disinhibitor for adolescents than for adults for whom these activities are generally more established.

Specific Incidents

Many studies on this issue are based on retrospective global recall of sexual activity in general. Results from a study requiring recall of specific discrete sexual incidents could suggest different conclusions. Surveys dealing with behaviors during *specific* sexual incidents can provide stronger evidence about the role of alcohol use in sexual behavior because the *temporal relationship* between them can be determined.

Studies based on event-specific data reveal a different aspect of the link between drinking and sex. In one survey, 968 adults were asked about the circumstances of two sexual encounters: their most recent sexual experience and their most recent encounter involving a new sexual partner (Temple & Leigh, 1992). Encounters with new partners were more likely to involve alcohol, but the use of alcohol was not significantly associated with risky sexual activity. Sexual attitudes proved to be a stronger predictor of unsafe sex.

A clearer picture of any causal relationship between drinking and sexual practices may be obtained if data were obtained on a daily basis rather than retrospectively. A study (Leigh, 1993) based on daily diaries of drinking and sexual events of 99 men and women over a 10-week period showed that alcohol consumption was associated with a general *reduction* of sexual activity, with *no* effects on risky sexual behaviors related to AIDS transmission. Apparently, lapses in judgment about sexual practices as a consequence of alcohol consumption may not be as strong as retrospective recall studies suggest.

Other Drugs

Associations between the development of adolescent alcohol, cigarette, and marijuana use and risky sexual behavior were examined over an 18-month period (Duncan, Strycker, & Duncan, 1999). Participants were 257 adolescent boys and girls assessed at three time points. Use of all three substances was significantly related with risky sexual behavior. Similar patterns in these relationships occurred for boys and girls.

Substance use and risky sexual behavior were examined for 125 substance-abusing female adolescents and 78 controls between ages 14 and 18 (Mezzich et al., 1997) in relation to psychological variables. Uncontrolled behavior, negative affectivity, and childhood victimization were related to both substance use and risky sexual behavior. Antisocial behavior mediated the associations between uncontrolled behavior, negative affectivity, and childhood victimization with substance use and risky sexual behavior. Affiliation with an adult boyfriend was directly associated with substance use involvement and accounted for the relationship between chronological age and risky sexual behavior.

The Massachusetts Youth Risk Behavior Survey was administered to a sample of 3,054 students from randomly selected high schools and classrooms (Shrier, Emans, Woods, & DuRant, 1997). More than one third of the sample had experienced sexual intercourse. Increased frequency and severity of drugs such as marijuana, cocaine, crack, and alcohol, as well as more years of sexual intercourse, were associated with an increased number of sexual partners and recent condom nonuse.

Substance use and sexual activity were studied with a nationally representative, probability-based sample of young adults ages 18 to 30 in 1990 (Graves & Leigh, 1995). Respondents who drank more frequently, were heavy drinkers, smoked cigarettes, and used marijuana in the past year

TABLE 12.2 Percentage of respondents reporting alcohol problems: General population versus homosexual sample, by age group and gender

	General Population		*Homosexual Sample*	
Age Group	*Men*	*Women*	*Men*	*Women*
18-25	29	16	26	24
26-30	25	7	25	21
31-40	16	8	24	25
41-60	7	4.5	19	15
(Overall)	(16)	(8)	(23)	(23)

SOURCE: General population data from Clark and Midanik (1982); McKirnan and Peterson (1989).

were more likely to be sexually active. Those who had five or more drinks at a sitting and who used marijuana were more likely to have had more than one sexual partner. Heavy drinkers were also less likely to use condoms; however, no association occurred between alcohol use and engaging in unsafe sexual practices.

Gay and Lesbian Populations

Generalizations about the relation between alcohol use and sexual practices based on heterosexual populations may not prove valid for gay and lesbian populations. A review (Donovan & McEwan, 1995) of studies of alcohol and sexual risk-taking behaviors held that the concept of sexual risk taking must recognize the context of the behavior rather than basing the definition only in terms of sexual acts.

In one study (McKirnan & Peterson, 1989), 3,400 readers of a gay newspaper reported alcohol problems to a greater extent than shown in earlier studies with less representative samples. Table 12.2 presents the rates of problem drinking for male and female homosexual adults in three age groups in comparison to rates for corresponding samples of heterosexuals obtained from a national survey (Clark & Midanik, 1982).

Only 14% of gay men and lesbians in this Chicago sample abstained from alcohol use, as compared to 29% in national general population surveys. In addition, alcohol problems were higher in the gay sample (23% vs. 12%);

however, the rate of heavy drinking of 15% was comparable to the 14% found in the general population. Lower rates but similar patterns of drinking and drinking problems were found among lesbians in comparison to heterosexual women. If drinking problems of homosexuals are in part a response to the historical stigmatization of homosexuality, one would predict a decline in such problems as societal attitudes toward homosexuals become more accepting, as they have over the past generation. Similar comparisons were made for cocaine and marijuana use, based on data from other researchers (Clayton, Voss, Robbins, & Skinner, 1986).

Earlier studies with clinical samples found rates of alcohol problems to be around 30% for homosexual men (Lohrenz, Connelly, Coyne, & Spare, 1978), much higher than the 10% to 15% estimates usually found for men in general population surveys. Estimates based on clinical samples may not reflect an accurate picture for the whole population of homosexuals. The other convenient source of evidence has been gay bars because they have been a major social gathering place for homosexuals. However, drinking might still be expected to be higher among bar patrons than for the homosexual population as a whole. Previous estimates may be artificially high, although alcohol problem rates are higher for homosexuals than for the general population (Paul, Stall, & Bloomfield, 1991).

With respect to the level of drinking among homosexual populations, one review (Bux, 1996) of recent research about problem drinking among gay men and lesbians found that they are not at a significantly higher risk for drinking heavily or for developing drinking problems than heterosexual men. However, both gay males and lesbians appear to be less likely to abstain from alcohol than their heterosexual counterparts.

However, those who have alcohol problems may have greater risks of unsafe sexual practices. Self-reported sexual risk taking for 383 sexually active gay and bisexual men (ages 18-60) entering substance abuse treatment revealed that risky sexual practices such as engaging in anal intercourse without a condom in a 90-day period were reported by 55% (Paul, Stall, Crosby, Barrett, & Midanik, 1994). In general, sexual risk behaviors were greater for those who used more drugs.

Overall, the evidence suggests that alcohol and other drug use may contribute to early sexual activity, more frequent sexual involvement, and riskier sexual practices such as unprotected intercourse among sexually active adolescents. However, these correlational studies are cross-sectional and do not prove that alcohol per se "causes" adolescents to take greater risks such as engaging in unprotected sexual intimacy. Some third factor such as personality characteristics might contribute toward both higher alcohol and other drug consumption as well as toward earlier sexual intimacy and risky sexual behaviors.

CLINICAL EVIDENCE

Clinical studies deal with a more restricted population of individuals who are seeking treatment for alcohol abuse. They may also have other problems, such as **sexual dysfunction**, that may stem from their alcohol abuse. In research that directly measured sexual dysfunction with couples in a laboratory setting, the reverse situation existed. The pioneering team of Masters and Johnson (1966) studied a sample that consisted of individuals who were seeking treatment for sexual dysfunction, not for alcoholism. However, alcohol was found to be a possible contributing factor in many instances. Impaired sexual performance among this population may have been due to the acute effects of alcohol in some cases but may have been due to the chronic effects of alcohol abuse in other instances. As the gatekeeper observed in Shakespeare's *Macbeth,* Act II, Scene 3, "Much drink may be said to be an equivocator of lechery."

As Figure 12.6 indicates, heavy alcohol abuse eventually may lead to risky sexual behaviors and to sexual dysfunction. In turn, sexual impairment could activate a cycle of further alcohol abuse as a form of self-medication to cope that actually further impairs sexual performance. Thus, among chronic alcoholics, impaired sexual performance may be a possible consequence of alcoholism (Lemere & Smith, 1973). Impotence occurred in only 8% of males, due primarily to the inability to have erections rather than to loss of desire.

A comparison (Beckman, 1979) of women alcoholics was made with a control group of "normals" as well as a control group of psychiatric patients. Alcoholic women, as contrasted with the control groups, reported the strongest desire for sexual intercourse when drinking, engaged in it most often when drinking, and enjoyed it most often when drinking. However, their reported levels of sexual satisfaction were lower than for women in the control groups.

A survey of women in the general population (Wilsnack, Wilsnack, & Klassen, 1984) found similarly that those who drank at high levels had greater sexual dysfunction (lack of sexual interest, low frequency or lack of orgasm) than light drinkers. Moderate levels of drinking were associated with the lowest frequency of sexual dysfunction.

In identifying the causes of sexual dysfunction, most views have placed the blame on some aspect of the impaired individual. However, because dysfunction also may be a function of the partner, this may be an oversimplification. Thus, alcoholic wives are often married to alcoholic husbands. If the wives are sexually unsatisfied, to what extent are these conditions created or influenced by the alcoholism of their husbands? If the husbands themselves are physiologically impaired by alcohol or are less attractive

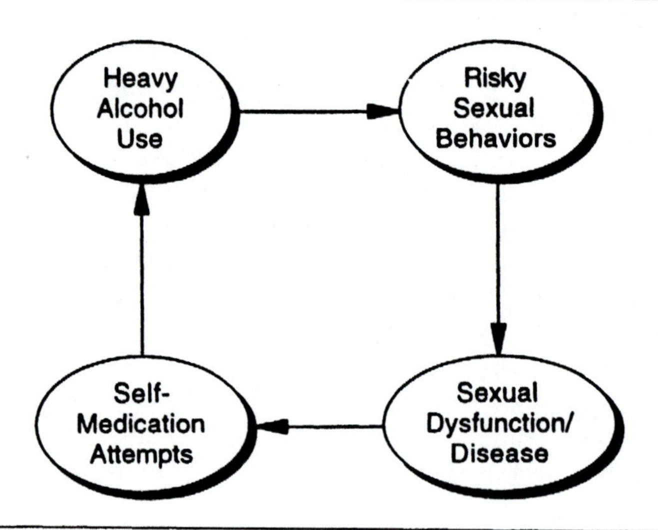

Figure 12.6. Heavy Alcohol Use Can Increase Risky Sexual Behaviors, Which May Lead to Sexual Dysfunction and Increased Alcohol Use

psychologically due to their intoxicated condition, they may contribute to the wives' lack of sexual responsiveness.

Conversely, sexually inhibited wives may turn to alcohol or be encouraged by their husbands to drink to overcome inhibitions. Reliance on alcohol to engage in sex for many years may eventually lead the wife to become alcoholic and, in turn, become less attractive to her husband. This creates a vicious circle, with further impairment of sexual interest and performance.

Marital Conflict

Although marital conflict probably exists in most marriages involving alcohol dependency, most studies have not explicitly examined the role of marital conflict on male alcoholics' sexual satisfaction. One study (O'Farrell, Choquette, Cutter, & Birchler, 1997) on this issue included married couples with an alcoholic husband ($n = 26$), maritally conflicted couples ($n = 26$), and nonconflicted couples ($n = 26$) without alcohol-related problems on both sexual dysfunction and sexual satisfaction.

In comparison to the nonconflicted couples, male alcoholics and their wives experienced less sexual satisfaction across a range of variables and more sexual dysfunction, including husbands' diminished sexual interest, impotence, and premature ejaculation and wives' painful intercourse.

However, when contrasted with maritally conflicted couples, impotence was the only area where alcoholics reported more difficulties. Also, there was a greater decline in the frequency of intercourse with older age among the alcoholic than among the conflicted couples. Thus, marital conflict is a major contributing factor to most of these problems. For alcoholic couples, both marital conflict and the physical effects of chronic alcohol abuse combine to create sexual dysfunction.

Sex Offenders

Some studies of alcohol's influence on sexual activity involve retrospective analysis of special populations. One example is a study of sex offenders such as rapists and pedophiles (Gebhard, Gagnon, Pomeroy, & Christianson, 1965). The researchers attempted to determine whether drinking had been involved in these offenses. Interviews showed that about two thirds of offenders reported being intoxicated at the time of the offense, but this type of evidence is suspect due to its self-serving nature. It does not explain how the alcohol contributed to the offense. Many drinkers do not commit such crimes, even though they have the "opportunity." A more complete picture of the role of alcohol in these crimes also requires data about the effects of alcohol use on sex offenses by a "control" group of sex offenders who did not get caught.

EXPERIMENTAL EVIDENCE

Experiments, unlike surveys, can be used to directly study the effect of alcohol on actual physical aspects of human sexual response. However, this method raises issues of ethics and generalizability due to the artificial nature of the laboratory setting. In one early study (Farkas & Rosen, 1976), male college students received drinks that produced blood alcohol concentrations (BACs) of 0, .025, .050, or .075 mg % while they watched an erotic film. A plethysmograph was attached around the penis to measure the degree of penile tumescence or erection continuously during the film viewing. Low doses of alcohol slightly enhanced sexual arousal, but higher doses actually weakened sexual response for males.

A similar study (Wilson & Lawson, 1976a) was conducted with college women who viewed an erotic film after four different doses of alcohol received on separate occasions while wearing a vaginal plethysmograph consisting of a photocell inside a Plexiglas tube to assess changes in vaginal blood pressure as an index of sexual arousal. The immediate BACs measured after drinking were 0, 0.026, 0.049, and 0.079 mg % for the four different doses. Thus, the highest level is near the amount considered to be illegal for driving an automobile in many states. Increased alcohol dose reduced sexual arousal at the physiological level, as measured by vaginal pressure-pulse scores, although the women reported enhanced subjective arousal.

Use of the balanced placebo design allows a separation of pharmacological and psychological influences on sexual arousal (Wilson & Lawson, 1976b). This design varied the expectancies about the type of beverage male college subjects would receive, alcoholic or nonalcoholic, as well as the type of beverage consumed, alcoholic or nonalcoholic. College students viewed erotic films depicting both heterosexual and homosexual content. An expectancy effect occurred, with more physical and subjective arousal in the group expecting to receive alcohol than in the group that did not expect to receive alcohol. There was no alcohol consumption effect, but the results are limited because only one small dose level (.04 mg %) was used.

A replication of this study (Wilson & Lawson, 1978) used women participants. Expectancy did not increase physiological arousal, even though it did lead to increased subjective arousal. Alcohol consumption, however, impaired physical arousal.

It should be recognized, however, that studies in laboratory settings are highly artificial and involve relatively low doses for ethical reasons. Low doses are especially dictated to maintain credibility when the balanced placebo is used. These studies rely on samples of college students who are hardly representative of the general population. Even among college students, they can be viewed as a biased sample because those who volunteer for sex research have had greater sexual experience and more liberal sexual attitudes as well as more sexual problems (Wolchik, Braver, & Jensen, 1985).

The general implication of these findings is that contrary to popular belief, alcohol's effect on sexual arousal is not mediated through a physiological basis but through a psychological process in which one's expectancies are more critical, at least at low dose levels. The correspondence between physiological and psychological sexual arousal is much weaker for women than it is for men. Social and anatomical factors could account for this difference (Wilson & Lawson, 1978). Men may form stronger associations between genital sensations and cognitive information, such as the type of beverage consumed, because penile arousal may be easier for males to label or identify than it is for females to detect vaginal arousal.

It is possible that the pattern of results from laboratory studies of alcohol effects on sexual arousal was compatible with the excuse function of alcohol use (Crowe & George, 1989). Sexual arousal may be increased by alcohol expectancy when excuses are needed (i.e., when inhibition may exist). Thus, in one study (George & Marlatt, 1986), participants viewed slides showing erotic, violent, and violent-erotic content, materials that presumably create inhibition in the participants in a research study. Both the amount of viewing time and self-reported sexual arousal were higher for the group that expected alcohol than the group that did not, especially for a set of slides depicting highly deviant behaviors. Viewing of such stimuli, especially in an experiment conducted at a university, is a type of "deviant" activity that is likely to generate inhibition. Therefore, the expectancy of alcohol should disinhibit or enhance sexual arousal.

The societal context should be considered when interpreting the pattern of findings (Crowe & George, 1989). Society imposes a double standard, with greater tolerance of sexual arousal and deviance among men than with women; it should not be surprising that alcohol expectancy generally produces less sexual arousal among women than for men.

The fact that alcohol at higher doses can often increase sexual responsiveness, even when it is socially unacceptable, may be due to the impairment of cognitive processing. A model of alcohol-related disinhibitory effects proposes that higher doses disrupt awareness of inhibitory cues that ordinarily restrain antisocial behaviors such as sexually inappropriate behaviors (Steele & Southwick, 1985). Evidence for the model came from previous studies of the effects of alcohol that were classified in terms of whether the observed behavior or situation involved high or low conflict. A method, known as meta-analysis, was used to combine results from different studies to evaluate the effects of alcohol consumption and expectancy for low- and high-conflict contexts. Consistent with the model, expectancy effects exceeded consumption effects in low-conflict situations, but the opposite was found for high-conflict situations.

Overall, experiments on alcohol and sexual response seem to find paradoxical effects, with both enhanced and suppressed sexual responses (George & Norris, 1991). Although *psychological* arousal may increase with more alcohol, there is an inverse relationship between the amount of alcohol consumed and the level of *physical* sexual arousal. With higher blood alcohol levels, sexual arousal diminishes.

OVERVIEW

Although behaviors involving aggressive violence and risky sexual practices are markedly different, there are some similarities in how alcohol and other drugs may affect these behaviors. Figure 12.7 illustrates a model involving how either aggression or risky sexual behaviors might be increased by heavy alcohol use.

Initially, impulsive or undercontrolled individuals drink heavily, and this behavior eventually increases the instigation of violence or the initia-

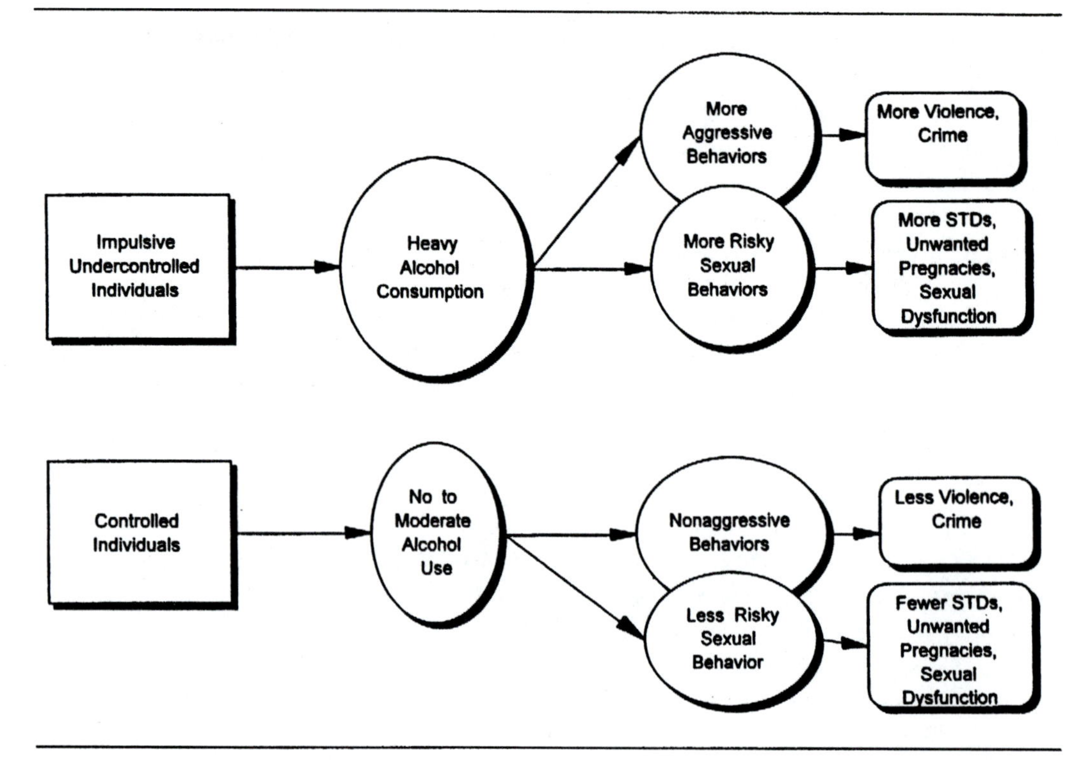

Figure 12.7. Hypothetical Model of the Relationship Between Impulsivity and Either Aggression or Sexual Activity

NOTE: Each behavior can have adverse consequences and lead to subsequent continued or increased alcohol consumption.

tion of sexual risk taking. Heavy involvement with alcohol at an early age may increase other delinquent activities. Risks of violence increase, with attendant risk of criminal offenses. Early entry into drinking increases having sexual intimacy, which can lead to complications such as sexually transmitted diseases, unwanted early pregnancies, and, in some cases, sexual dysfunction. Young females also may become sexual victims, exploited by older men. For females who become pregnant, there are the additional physical and psychological risks of abortion.

To deal with guilt and anxiety, harmful consequences, and stresses associated with aggression and sexual intimacy that were facilitated by early and heavy alcohol use, individuals may increase subsequent alcohol use (not diagrammed in Figure 12.7) as a form of self-medication to help escape or forget their miserable lives. Such drinking responses may be more likely for aggression among males, but for females, it may occur in relation to sexual activities.

SUMMARY

Alcohol is popularly viewed as a disinhibitor, so it is not surprising that its use is associated with behaviors that are ordinarily inhibited or restrained in most circumstances, such as violence or sexual intimacy.

Incidents of natural aggression are difficult to interpret due to many uncontrolled variables. Much of the evidence is retrospective recall and not easily validated. The incidents that are available for researchers to study are relatively infrequent and may not involve random samples. Evidence from studies of prison inmates convicted of violent crimes, which suggest that use of alcohol and other drugs may have played a role in these crimes, may not be generalizable to the general population.

Laboratory studies allow controlled observation to help rule out alternative explanations for the correlation between alcohol use and aggression. Alcohol generally releases aggression in laboratory studies, although the situation is also an important factor. The more conflict involved in the situation, the more likely alcohol will produce higher aggression.

Depending on the dose, different effects may occur. At levels that produce intoxication, some drinkers may perceive certain situations as more threatening and therefore may react in ways that may either evoke or provoke aggression. Cues such as anxiety, which ordinarily would inhibit an individual from aggressive behavior, might not be noticed when intoxication occurs, so these inhibitors no longer function to keep violence under control. Or if a person is more likely to become angered when drinking, the likelihood that he or she may initiate aggression may increase in certain circumstances.

Control of aggressive tendencies may be less effective after drinking occurs because alcohol may restrict attention and reduce the salience of inhibiting cues. Higher cognitive controls in the forms of self- and social criticism that ordinarily restrain behaviors also may be weakened under the influence of alcohol.

Sexually intimate behavior also is affected by alcohol and other drugs. Anxiety, fear, and guilt, which might be inhibitors of sexual behavior, might be reduced by alcohol consumption. Alcohol use also can serve as an "excuse" later if sexual activities are condemned. Research clearly has shown correlations between alcohol use and involvement in sexual intimacy. In addition, risky sexual practices associated with potential HIV infection are higher for those with more alcohol involvement.

Among alcoholics, alcohol use has been found to be associated with sexual dysfunction. Due to the correlational nature of the evidence, however, it is unclear whether the alcohol abuse produced the sexual impairment or vice versa.

Laboratory studies of the effects of alcohol on sexual arousal are limited to relatively small doses given on single occasions to a select group of college students who are willing to volunteer for studies that most students might not. Although the generalizability to real-life sexual behavior is questionable, these studies demonstrate the influence of alcohol expectancies on sexual arousal, apart from any pharmacological effect.

Aggression and sexual intimacy are similar in that they are both often highly restricted behaviors. When alcohol is consumed at levels and in circumstances that narrow the attention of the drinker, these inhibitors are less effective in restraining either of these behaviors. Pharmacological and psychological factors may both affect how people behave when they consume alcohol and other drugs.

Alcohol or other drugs per se may not be the primary factor responsible when their use is associated with incidents having negative outcomes. Instead, some combination of the personality of the transgressor and the use of alcohol may be responsible. To blame alcohol or other drugs, without considering the characteristics of the user who commits the crime, is to scapegoat the substance.

KEY TERMS

Alcohol myopia
Expectancy controls
Meta-analysis
Sexual dysfunction

STIMULUS/RESPONSE

1. Think of different methods that you could use to determine the effect of alcohol or some other drug on a specific crime.
2. How accurately do you think you could determine the effect of alcohol for these hypothetical cases?
   a. A man murders his wife but is not apprehended for 3 weeks.
   b. A bank robber is arrested as he flees the bank.
   c. A clerk, known to be an alcoholic, confesses to embezzlement.

3. On the basis of your "practice" on these criminal cases above, how accurate do you find the following statement: As much as 80% to 90% of all crime in the United States is committed by people under the influence of alcohol or drugs (National Institute of Justice, 1995).
4. Research shows a correlation between heavy use of some drugs and violent crime. Do the drugs cause these forms of aggression, or do aggressive persons both use more drugs and also commit more aggressive acts?
5. The popular media often present sensationalistic depictions of drug use. Headlines such as "Drug-Crazed Man Commits a Crime" are often used to describe events. How can we know that a drug "caused" a specific man to commit a crime? Maybe he would have done it even if he were drug free. And could it be that a person could actually be less likely to commit the crime under the influence of a drug?
6. Do you think that alcohol releases sexual inhibitions due to a pharmacological effect on sexual arousal or because of expectations and beliefs? How could you determine the relative influence of each factor?
7. Sexual assault and rape are often associated with drinking by the offender. Discuss possible alternative processes that might be responsible for this relationship.

- ❖ Alcohol and Marital Status
- ❖ Effects of Parental Alcohol Abuse on Children
- ❖ Alcoholic Family Interactions
- ❖ Children of Alcoholics
- ❖ Codependency
- ❖ Summary
- ❖ Key Terms
- ❖ Stimulus/Response

Alcohol and Other Drugs *Relationship to Family Processes* 13

Mid pleasures and palaces, though we may roam,
Be it ever so humble, there's no place like home.

The well-known last phrase of this expression about the security and comfort of home actually comes from a lament about the domestic ravages of alcoholism, titled "Ruined by Drink," by Nobil Adkisson, composed around 1860. It goes on to describe the domestic tragedy: "but the father lies drunk on the floor, The table is empty, the wolf's at the door, and mother sobs loud in her broken-back'd chair, Her garments in tatters, her soul in despair." This depiction dramatically shows the devastation that parental alcoholism may wreak on the well-being of the family. It is not surprising, then, that considerable efforts are devoted to understanding the impact of the father's alcoholism on the mother as well as on the children.

Due to the rapid and major changes in the structure of the "family" that have occurred over the past quarter century, previous perspectives may need revision. The model of the nuclear family—two parents and two children, possibly one of each sex—has become a rarity. Research in this area needs to recognize the wide variety of family constellations and arrangements (McCubbin, McCubbin, Thompson, & Han, 1999). According to the 1994 U.S. census, married-couple families in 1994 represented only 55% of households, down from 71% in 1970. Single-parent households, of which mothers were 86%, represented about 31% of families in 1994, and they are increasing. At the same time, the average size of families has declined from 3.14 persons per household in 1970 to 2.62 in 1994. These statistics are averaged over the entire population and are not accurate for different racial/ethnic groups.

The definition of the family has changed as first marriage rates have declined and cohabitation has increased. In addition, remarriages are commonplace; 67% of Blacks and 55% of Whites live in stepparent families.

Marriage occurs at high rates for cohabiting stepfamilies, with 25% marrying within 1 year. These and many other changes in the definition of *family* may yield different rates of alcohol and other drug use from those found in traditionally defined families.

Finally, as increasing numbers of women have been recognized as alcohol dependent over the past generation, the risks to children are no longer limited to excessive-drinking fathers. Evidence indicates that mothers with alcohol and other drug problems display high levels of punitiveness toward their children.

Alcohol and Marital Status

SELECTION INTO MARRIAGE

Mate selection in our society is obviously not a random process but may often involve a process called *assortative mating*. People do not select mates on a random basis; rather, they prefer to choose their marriage partners, and usually they select mates who are similar in important ways to themselves.

Drinking might be one of the many dimensions of similarity that is related, even if indirectly, to attraction. Thus, impulsive and aggressive males who also drink heavily may be more sexually attractive to young females, especially if they also engage in drinking actively. Although drinking problems may not exist or be apparent during courtship or early years of marriage, eventually drinking problems may arise for these couples. Past clinical research suggests that if one member of a marriage has a drinking problem, there is a greater chance that the partner also has a drinking problem. However, these studies involve treatment samples that may overestimate the extent to which spouses in the entire population are similar in drinking.

In a study of 5,310 young adult women in a national longitudinal survey (Windle, 1997), problem-drinking women were twice as likely to be married to problem-drinking husbands as were nondrinking women. The overall problem-drinking prevalence rate was only about 10%, much lower than reported in other studies. However, because this sample used women younger than age 30, the rates should increase somewhat over time. In addition, women who had heavier lifetime use of marijuana and cocaine were twice as likely to have husbands who were problem drinkers. There were also some racial/ethnic differences, with this tendency being lowest among African American women. Similar ethnic group patterns existed for other drugs such as marijuana or cocaine.

MARRIAGE EFFECT AND ALCOHOL

The **marriage effect** (Leonard & Rothbard, 1999) refers to the lower drinking rates found among married than with single individuals. Many cross-sectional studies have demonstrated this relationship. However, because single and married groups differ in their average age and young persons tend to drink more heavily, one might suspect that the drinking differences attributed to marital status could be due more to age differences. However, the marriage effect remains even after controlling for age, gender, and socioeconomic status.

Cross-sectional studies may not detect actual declines in drinking as individuals move from single to married status. It is possible that self-selection occurs in which lighter drinkers are more likely to marry sooner than are heavier drinkers. The evidence on this issue is mixed (Bachman et al., 1997; Kandel, Davies, Karus, & Yamaguchi, 1986). Longitudinal studies that examine the drinking levels of the same individuals before and after marriage are needed to determine if the differences between single and married individuals actually reflect temporal changes within individuals.

Longitudinal studies demonstrate that within a year or two after marriage, many individuals have indeed decreased their drinking (Bachman et al., 1997). Studies conducted within a year or two after marriage (Bachman et al., 1997; Miller-Tutzauer, Leonard, & Windle, 1991) find reductions for men and women during the first year after marriage but not for single individuals for the same time period.

A study of 500 newlyweds in their first year of marriage (Leonard & Rothbard, 1999) found that both husbands and wives drink at similar levels. This similarity could reflect their common interests, values, and lifestyles. It might also stem from their similar reactions to shared experiences, both positive and negative.

Husbands seem to influence wives more, as men's heavy drinking may lead women to drink up to their level. On the other hand, the wife's typically lower level of drinking does not seem to have any protective effect in reducing the alcohol consumption of a heavier-drinking husband. This asymmetrical influence could be due to many reasons. Husbands may drink with men at work and be more influenced by them than by the drinking of their wives. Wives, on the other hand, may not have other drinking partners, so their drinking may be primarily influenced by their husbands' drinking.

Reduction of using other drugs also may occur for married as opposed to single individuals (Burton, Johnson, Ritter, & Clayton, 1996). However, studies that have measured drinking over 5 years after marriage (Horwitz, White, & Howell-White, 1996; Power & Estaugh, 1990) have not shown a consistent marriage effect.

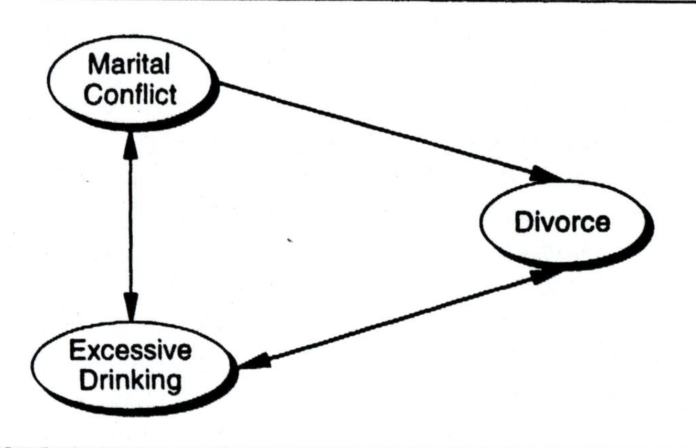

Figure 13.1. Hypothetical Relationship Between Heavy Drinking, Marital Conflict, and Divorce

EFFECT OF DRINKING ON MARRIAGE

In marriages in which heavy drinking exists over long periods, marital quality eventually deteriorates. Among those who marry at a young age, for example, this risk may be very high; most of these marriages dissolved by age 23 in a British study (Burton et al., 1996). Continued drinking problems by one or both spouses may lead to conflict and eventually, for some couples, the end of the marriage. Heavy drinkers may be abusive or depressed, which may lead to divorce at a higher rate for couples with a heavy drinker. Differential selection out of marriage may occur, as shown in Figure 13.1, in which heavy drinking may lead to marriage dissolution directly, or indirectly due to the conflict in the marriage associated with the drinking. However, the influence could be in the opposite direction as well in some marriages, with the divorce leading to the excessive drinking.

Domestic Violence

Close to half of the wives of men at an alcoholism clinic reported violence and physical harm from their husbands (Orford et al., 1975). However, without data on rates of domestic violence for a comparison group of nonalcoholics, it is not possible to know how much of the violence can be attributed to the influence of alcohol. One comparison that did include such a control group (O'Farrell & Murphy, 1995) found that married men undergoing alcoholism treatment were four times more likely to have physically abused their wives than demographically matched nonalcoholic males.

The manner in which alcohol is related to domestic violence may not be the same in all marriages. Structured interviews (Frieze & Schafer, 1984) showed that for some couples, both drank excessively, and drinking was often causally related to the violence. However, for other couples, drinking was not excessive, nor were the couples especially violent unless drinking occurred. Yet a third group had high levels of violence but few problems with excessive drinking, so that their drinking may not have contributed to their domestic violence.

One study (Van Hesselt, Morrison, & Bellack, 1985) compared wife-abusive, maritally discordant but nonabusive, or happily married couples. The level of drinking by wives was not a predictor of the spousal abuse received, whereas the level of the husbands' drinking was directly related to greater spouse abuse. In contrast, one study found that wives who were alcoholics were more likely than nonalcoholic wives to be victims of spousal violence (Miller, Downs, & Gondoli, 1989), possibly because they were perceived as not deserving better treatment because of their alcoholism.

Evaluation. Domestic violence is usually attributed to the amount of alcohol consumed by the abuser (Leonard & Senchak, 1996). However, distal factors such as social class, personality, and upbringing also must be considered as determinants. These factors should be controlled for because any of them might lead to both the violent tendencies and the drinking levels. After these distal factors have been controlled, the amount of alcohol consumed still is found to contribute to the probability of violence.

Various explanations have been offered to account for these correlations between alcohol abuse and domestic violence. In a specific episode, domestic violence related to alcohol abuse may be due to lack of attention to cues that ordinarily inhibit aggression while directing more attention to cues that instigate aggression. However, pharmacological effects of alcohol and psychological factors, such as the drinker's expectancies about the influence of drinking, cannot completely explain marital aggression because there are individual differences among alcoholic husbands.

One hypothesis is that violent and nonviolent alcoholics may have different drinking patterns. Thus, binge drinkers are more likely to be violent than steady drinkers (Murphy & O'Farrell, 1994). Binge drinking could create a higher level of intoxication than steady drinking. Finally, the effect of intoxication on spousal communication differs for violent and nonviolent alcoholics, with greater defensiveness and hostility among those who resort to violence (Murphy & O'Farrell, 1996, 1997).

Another possibility is self-selection. For example, alcoholics who are prone to domestic violence might differ from nonviolent alcoholics in some important factor, such as their beliefs and expectancies about the relationship between drinking and violence or in their temperamental dispositions toward aggression or hostility. Thus, as suggested in Chapter 12, those men with antisocial personalities not only may be more prone to aggression but also may show increases in aggression with alcohol, whereas other men may not.

However, explanations based on self-selection in which some types of persons who are prone to violence also tend to drink excessively cannot explain easily why violence often declines after alcoholics stop using alcohol following treatment (O'Farrell & Murphy, 1995). Additional mechanisms must be involved. Reduced information processing under the influence of alcohol can only account for short-term effects of drinking because the intoxicating effects of drinking eventually wear off. An explanation of the effect of long-term drinking on marital quality also is needed.

A third model suggests that marital difficulties might mediate the relationship between alcoholism and marital violence. Couples may have conflict and stress over financial, work, or legal problems that have an adverse impact on the quality of the marriage. If these circumstances lower the threshold for violence after drinking, then it would follow that counseling or improvements that benefit marital satisfaction should reduce domestic violence. Thus far, the evidence on this issue is mixed.

SELECTION OUT OF MARRIAGE

It seems reasonable to think that higher drinking could contribute toward divorce because it could be a source of conflict in a marriage. National cross-sectional surveys show that married persons drink less than those who are single, separated, or divorced.

Marital quality was related to husband's drinking quantity and to problem drinking of either spouse in one study (Leonard & Roberts, 1998). Marital stability ratings were predicted only by husbands' drinking quantity. These results support the view that heavier drinking could lead to differential selection out of marriage.

EFFECT OF DIVORCE ON DRINKING

However, evidence from a cross-sectional study does not prove that drinking caused the divorce, especially because it is also likely that many individuals increase their drinking *after* the divorce. A longitudinal study would be necessary to see if increased drinking occurred from before to after the divorce within individuals. One national longitudinal study of young women (Hanna, Faden, & Harford, 1993) found that those who were separated or divorced increased their alcohol use subsequently.

Not only do divorced individuals drink more later, but they also have more alcohol-related problems. However, different mechanisms are possible. One hypothesis sees alcohol abuse as a means of coping with depression and low self-esteem following divorce. A different explanation focuses on changes in roles and lifestyles (e.g., being single again often places one in situations that facilitate and promote drinking).

It is likely that there is a bidirectional influence between divorce and alcohol dependency. Thus, as alcohol abuse increases, divorce is more likely; after the divorce, alcohol abuse may be a response for dealing with the emotional problems related to the failed marriage. The findings, based on samples of couples, are supported by evidence using aggregated measures over the entire nation between total alcohol sales and consumption, divorce rates, and expenditures on alcohol (Caces, Harford, Williams, & Hanna, 1999). As per capita consumption increases by an average of 1 liter, divorce rates increase 20%. Increased divorce rates of 1/1,000 have been associated with a 10% rise in alcohol expenditures.

SAMPLING PROBLEMS

It must be kept in mind that the families available for these studies of family processes in alcoholic homes are not a random sample (Leonard, 1990). Families in which one or both parents have reduced previous problem drinking to acceptable levels would not be included. Also excluded would be families with extreme or prolonged alcohol problems because they would probably have divorced. The remaining families most likely would be those managing to put up with or tolerate the alcoholic's drinking thus far.

It is also likely that the families that get studied seek treatment or counseling, but those that do not seek help would not be studied. In some of these families, the problems may not be sufficiently serious for the family to seek counseling or treatment, but in other families, other factors such as attitudes may be preventing treatment, even though the problems warrant help.

Effects of Parental Alcohol Abuse on Children

As noted in Chapter 5, genetic influences might affect the subsequent alcohol and drug use and abuse by children with an alcohol-dependent parent. In addition, the family environment of alcoholic homes may affect the eventual level of alcohol and drug use by the children as well as aspects of their personality. Thus, for children who grow up in the homes of their alcoholic biological parents, it is likely that experiences related to drinking by alcoholic parents may adversely affect them.

Relatively little study of the effects of alcoholism on the family has been done, especially on identifying the underlying process for such effects. Many early studies used clinical observations based on small samples that were unrepresentative of both the alcoholic and general population. Poor measurement instruments, usually based on retrospective self-reports, yielded observations that were of unknown reliability and validity. As we shall see soon, direct observations of family members in alcoholic families interacting with each other have been useful in furthering the understanding of how alcohol affects family processes.

DIRECT EFFECTS ON CHILDREN'S LATER DRINKING

Parents may influence their children's drinking by direct modeling of alcohol use and by the transmission of their values about drinking (Bank et al., 1985; Kandel & Andrews, 1987). Hence, it is not surprising that similarities in the drinking patterns of parents and their adult children exist with large general population samples (Barnes & Welte, 1990; Dawson et al., 1992) as well as for smaller clinical samples (Orford & Velleman, 1991; Penick et al., 1987).

Typically, these studies agree that heavier-drinking parents have children who also develop more frequent and heavier patterns of alcohol use. It also should be noted that other studies with nonclinical samples of college students (Engs, 1990; Wright & Heppner, 1991, 1993) have found no relationship between the drinking of parents and their college-age children.

There is evidence that the effect of each parent's drinking may also vary with the gender of the child (Thompson & Wilsnack, 1987). Hence, the degree of similarity of drinking between parent and child may depend on whether one is comparing a parent and child of the same as opposed to the opposite sex. Sex role identification theories (Baldwin, 1967) as diverse as psychoanalytic and social learning predict that the same-sex parent should have greater influence than the opposite-sex parent does on a child. Consistent with this view, fathers' drinking—as well as mothers' drinking, to a lesser degree—was found to be moderately predictive of sons' drinking but was not as predictive of daughters' drinking among adolescents (Wilks et al., 1989) and college student samples (Jung, 1995).

INDIRECT EFFECTS ON CHILDREN'S LATER DRINKING

In addition to being potential models for alcohol abuse, how alcoholic parents treat and interact with their children could have adverse effects on them. These negative experiences may be psychologically disruptive and, in some cases, may increase the likelihood that the children will develop their own alcohol problems as adults.

The emotional strife and turmoil found in many homes where parents abuse alcohol and other drugs may have a destructive effect on the psychological development of children and possibly increase their own future likelihood of using alcohol and drugs to cope. A comparison of the home environments of children of alcoholics and nonalcoholics found more marital conflict, parent-child conflict, psychiatric problems among the children, and poor adaptive functioning by parents in the alcoholic homes.

These conflictual and stressful family environments may impair the children's self-esteem. However, conflict and stress are by no means specific or limited to alcoholic homes but occur in families with nonalcoholic psychiatric problems as well. Thus, any impairments observed in children of alcoholics may reflect the effects of growing up in a dysfunctional family rather than of alcoholism per se. Still, when children of alcoholics are compared with control groups of children of nonalcoholic parents who are in therapy for problems unrelated to alcohol, differences have not been as strong as might be assumed (West & Prinz, 1987).

A different avenue by which alcoholic parents may indirectly contribute to adverse outcomes for their children could involve poor parenting skills. For example, alcoholic parents may fail to monitor or screen children's behavior or their choice of friends so that they may develop delinquent behaviors and fall under the influence of persons who may lead them astray (Chassin, Curran, Hussong, & Colder, 1996).

EFFECTS OF PARENT ALCOHOL ABUSE ON CHILD ABUSE

Under the influence of alcohol, some parents may act abusively toward their children in many ways (Langeland & Hartgers, 1998; Widom, Ireland, & Glynn, 1995). One category of abuse is nonsexual and involves behaviors such as hitting or slapping, verbal abuse such as insults or threats, and physical harm with a weapon. Such treatment could have serious harmful consequences that continue into adulthood.

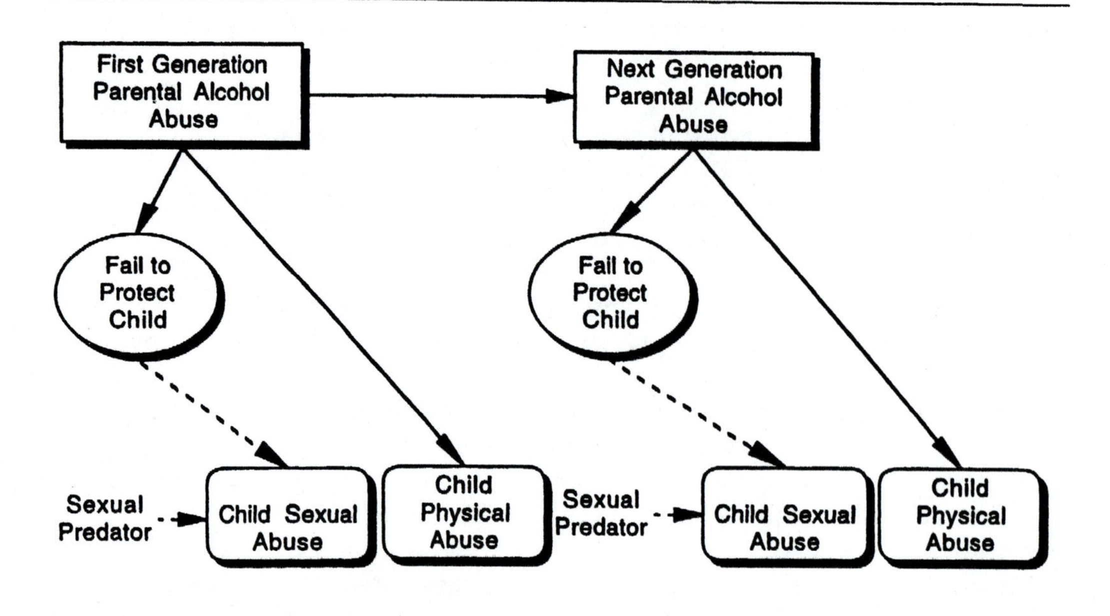

Figure 13.2. Model of Parental Alcohol Abuse and Child Abuse Across Successive Generations

A second form of violence involves sexual abuse, when unwanted sexual behaviors, from exposure to touching to penetration, are inflicted on the child. Unlike cases of physical abuse, most sexual abuse incidents involve perpetrators other than the parents. Within the family, the most likely sexual abuse involves fathers or stepfathers and their daughters. One reason why children of alcoholic parents have a higher risk for sexual abuse is that the parents are less able to protect them from sexual predators. For example, if the father is the perpetrator, mothers may be unable or unwilling to call authorities, leave home with the children, remove the children to a safe place, or make the husband leave. In some cases, the mother herself may have been sexually abused as a child, have substance abuse problems herself, and have an abusive partner so that she is unable to protect her children.

In addition to the immediate but long-lasting harmful consequences such as physical and psychological trauma for the children who are abused, there may be delayed consequences. In effect, a perpetuating cycle may develop, as shown in Figure 13.2, in which parental alcohol abuse may increase the likelihood of physical and/or sexual abuse of their children. When these children later grow up, they will have a higher likelihood of abusing alcohol, which in turn may lead them to abuse their own children.

EFFECTS OF CHILD ABUSE ON CHILDREN'S LATER ALCOHOL ABUSE

Victims of **child abuse** may subsequently develop alcohol and other drug dependency to cope with the shame, fear, and pain of these experiences (Miller, Maguin, & Downs, 1997). Most research on this topic uses clinical samples of individuals with alcohol abuse problems. These cases may represent the extreme cases, assuming recall is valid, which may not be generalizable to the general population. Other studies that are also retrospective include samples seeking help for mental health problems that do not involve alcohol or samples from the general population.

Clinical Samples

Self-reported childhood abuse by women who were in alcohol treatment, drinking and driving programs, and mental health facilities were compared to a control group of women from a household sample (Miller & Downs, 1993; Miller, Downs, & Testa, 1993). Substantially higher percentages of the women in the alcohol programs reported experiences of some form of nonsexual violence as well as sexual abuse toward them as children.

Table 13.1 shows these percentages for different forms of nonsexual and sexual abuse experienced by one group of women, those in alcoholic treatment programs, in comparison to a control group of household women. Women in alcohol treatment programs were also more likely to have been sexually abused than were women in mental health clinics for problems that were not alcohol related. However, women in mental health treatment programs who also had alcohol problems were more likely to have been victimized as children than those without alcohol problems (Miller & Downs, 1995).

A questionnaire to 89 men and 37 women in three London alcohol treatment centers showed that 54% of women and 24% of men identified themselves as victims of childhood sexual abuse or assault (Moncrieff, Drummond, Candy, Checinski, & Farmer, 1996). Abuse generally started before age 16 and involved nonrelatives. Sexual abuse victims tended to be younger, started drinking earlier, and had more alcohol-related

TABLE 13.1 Rates of sexual abuse and physical abuse for women in alcohol treatment, mental health treatment, or random households (in percentages)

	Treatment for Alcohol Problems (n = 178)	*Treatment Not for Alcohol Problems (n = 92)*	*Random Household (n = 82)*
Any sexual abuse	70	52	35
Exposure	58	43	26
Touch	60	41	21
Penetration	44	27	9
Father			
Verbal aggression	67	49	31
Moderate violence	57	46	35
Severe violence	40	27	13
Mother			
Verbal aggression	73	68	50
Moderate violence	71	63	51
Severe violence	49	41	28
Parental			
Severe violence and sexual abuse			
Both	47	37	14
Neither	12	28	41

SOURCE: Miller, Downs, and Testa (1993). Copyright 1993 by the *Journal of Studies on Alcohol*, Rutgers Center for Alcohol Studies, New Brunswick, New Jersey. Used with permission.

problems than nonabused respondents. Many of them came from families with a history of alcohol misuse.

Community Samples

Clinical and community samples may yield different findings. Those who have not yet sought or received treatment may have less serious problems, but it is also possible that some could have serious problems that they are denying.

The relationship of childhood sexual abuse to alcohol problems of women was explored through interviews of 917 adult women from the general population as part of the National Study of Health and Life Experiences of Women (Wilsnack et al., 1984). Retrospective reports of childhood sex abuse among problem drinkers were more than double the reports for nonproblem drinkers.

An analysis of several studies found that a higher prevalence of alcohol problems occurred in the general population among females if they had been sexually or physically abused as children (Langeland & Hartgers, 1998). For men, the evidence about relationships between child sexual or physical abuse and alcoholism was inconclusive.

A study of childhood sexual abuse and alcohol and drug abuse was conducted with 4,790 students in Washington state public schools in Grades 8, 10, and 12 (Bensley, Spieker, Van Eenwyk, & Schoder, 1999). The strongest association was between combined sexual abuse and molestation and heavy drinking by the youngest group, the 8th graders.

For drug use, the associations with reported abuse history were slightly stronger, at higher levels of severity and for combined abuse and molestation compared to nonsexual abuse. For early initiation into drug use, the associations with sexual and nonsexual abuse combined were stronger for marijuana use and regular drinking than for alcohol and cigarette experimentation.

The relationship between physical and sexual abuse, physical symptoms, psychological symptoms, alcohol abuse, and street drug use was examined with 1,931 women from a wide range of backgrounds (McCauley et al., 1997). About 22% reported childhood or adolescent physical or sexual abuse.

Compared with women who reported never having experienced abuse ($n = 1{,}257$), women who reported abuse as children but not as adults ($n = 204$) had more physical symptoms, depression, anxiety, somatization, and low self-esteem. They were more likely to be abusing drugs or alcohol and more likely to have attempted suicide and to have had a psychiatric admission. Patients who reported both childhood and adult abuse had more psychological problems and physical symptoms than those with only childhood or adult abuse.

Gender Differences Among Victims

Most child sexual abuse studies have focused on female victims, who constitute the large majority of cases, but it must be recognized that males also can be targets of sexual abuse. A study of a psychiatric sample (Windle, Windle, Scheidt, & Miller, 1995) found that 49% of the women and 12% of the men reported sexual abuse, 33% of the women and 24% of the men reported physical abuse, and 23% of the women and 5% of the men reported dual abuse.

Although both women and men had higher rates of antisocial personality disorder and suicide attempts (Windle et al., 1995), other reactions to such abuse by male and female victims may not be the same. Females may develop generalized anxiety and cope with alcohol and other drugs, but males may be more likely to display violent and aggressive responses as well as depression. One reason for the gender differential is that the norm for male drinking is already so high that it may not show a higher rate for victims of child abuse. In contrast, females generally drink at a lower rate so that higher drinking by child sexual abuse victims may be more noticed.

Gender Differences Among Perpetrators

Although most child sexual abusers are probably males, such may not be the case for physical abuse. Most research on the relationship of alcohol abuse and child abuse does not identify which parent is the primary perpetrator of the physical abuse. Fathers with alcohol problems are often assumed to be the perpetrators, perhaps because more males than females seem to be treated for alcohol-related problems (Blume, 1994).

However, women with alcohol and other drug problems are also more likely to physically abuse their children (Miller, Smyth, & Mudar, 1999). Many of these mothers themselves report being victims of abuse when they were children or being abused by their spouses (Hotaling & Sugarman, 1986), suggestive of intergenerational cycles of family violence repeating themselves (Velleman, 1992a, 1992b). Interestingly, although mothers were harsher in their punitiveness toward their children if they had been victims of childhood *physical* abuse or spousal abuse, they were actually less punitive if they had been victims of childhood *sexual* abuse.

Methodological Problems

There are variations in the definition of *sexual abuse,* as well as variations in the degree and timing of abuse, that make comparisons difficult across studies. Similar problems exist in lack of agreement on the definition of alcohol misuse or dependence. Other problems involve the methods of data collection, sample selection, the presence or absence of control groups, possible recall bias, and difficulties with conducting prospective studies.

Retrospective studies are more common because they are easier to conduct, but they generally involve treatment samples. However, the relationship between child abuse and adult alcohol abuse can be obscured if the treatment interventions are highly effective. Nonetheless, a literature review found a relationship with child abuse in retrospective studies of *alcoholic* women.

Prospective studies with samples from the general population avoid this problem but are expensive and require long periods of time to complete. A review of prospective studies did not find a strong association between child sexual or physical abuse and alcohol problems.

One prospective study (Widom et al., 1995) compared documented court cases (611) of child abuse, neglect, or both with 457 nonabused and nonneglected children. Most of the cases were from lower socioeconomic status levels, and the childhood sexual abuse rate was about three times that found in a national survey. Examination of these cases about 20 years later showed a relationship between childhood victimization and subsequent alcohol abuse for women but not for men, even when controlling for parental alcohol or drug problems, childhood poverty, race, and age. Interestingly, child neglect, not abuse, was a better predictor of later alcohol problems for women.

Another study used data from a national survey of women's drinking in which 1,099 women were asked about their sexual experiences prior to age 18. Those who reported abusive sexual experiences were compared to women who did not (Wilsnack, Vogeltanz, Klassen, & Harris, 1997). Controlling for age, ethnicity, and parental education, women with histories of childhood sexual abuse were more likely than women without such histories to report recent alcohol use, intoxication, drinking-related problems, alcohol dependence symptoms, and lifetime use of prescribed psychoactive drugs and illicit drugs. These national sample findings were consistent with those from clinical samples.

In addition to alcohol abuse, women who suffered childhood sexual abuse also had more problems in other areas. They had higher depression and anxiety, pain that prevented intercourse, sexual intercourse before age 15, less sexual satisfaction, and more sexual dysfunction. One might conjecture that some of these problems either stemmed from or contributed to the alcohol abuse.

Problems of Causal Interpretation

Although the evidence generally agrees that childhood sexual abuse and, to some extent, physical abuse are related to later alcohol abuse, the underlying process for this relationship is not clear. Causal interpretation of research on the relationship between childhood sexual and physical abuse to subsequent alcohol abuse has numerous problems. Some studies do not include a control group of nonabused children. Such control groups need to be matched with the abused group on important demographic variables that are related to child abuse. Thus, it is useful to match for age, socioeconomic level, and parental education because more sexual abuse has been found for younger individuals and for those from families with lower socioeconomic status and lower parental education. Those studies that do include a control group may not be able to rule out other factors that are associated with child abuse, such as family problems unrelated to alcohol abuse, child neglect, or other forms of victimization.

Most analyses of childhood abuse have focused on the factors that increase the likelihood of dysfunctional consequences while ignoring the possibility that other factors may be associated with *lower* future alcohol abuse. For example, one study (Fleming, Mullen, Sibthorpe, & Bammer, 1999) of 710 Australian women who reported childhood sexual abuse illustrates the role of an additional factor, family background. Specifically, childhood sexual abuse was associated with adult alcohol problems only for those women who also had a mother perceived to be cold, who had an alcoholic partner, or who believed that alcohol was a sexual disinhibitor.

In sum, the alcoholic parent may adversely affect the child in several different ways. However, not all children seem to be harmed by living with an alcoholic parent. Some children deal with the stress of living with an alcoholic parent well, just as children who must deal with problems of a parent unrelated to substance abuse can cope well. Identifying the sources of this resiliency of some children is an important task for researchers.

Alcoholic Family Interactions

Observing the interactions of members of alcoholic families may provide important insights about the process of family disruption from the alcoholic's drinking. Correlations of parent and child behaviors do not assess the actual dynamics of family interactions.

Due to the fallibility and unreliability of self-reports about these interactions, some researchers bring families into the clinic or the laboratory and observe their interactions directly. This type of research is expensive and time-consuming but offers the advantage that the observations are made directly by the researchers. One shortcoming is that the clinic may involve biased samples of families. Moreover, family interactions in the laboratory or the clinic may yield artificial or atypical behavior.

However, direct observation of families in their own homes is obviously difficult to achieve due to the amount of time required and the intrusiveness of the observers, which may distort the typical behaviors. It is also possible that expectations and biases of the observers might distort their observations. Moreover, families that might allow such observation may be quite different from those that would not participate in such research. Nonetheless, such research involving direct observation of families (Steinglass, Bennett, Wolin, & Reiss, 1987; Wolin, Bennett, Noonan, & Teitelbaum, 1980) offers the advantage of studying family interaction patterns as they actually occur.

WET VERSUS DRY INTERACTIONS

One strategy has been to compare interactions when the alcoholic has been and has not been drinking (Jacob & Seilhamer, 1989). Comparisons of discussions by alcoholic and control families found more negative affect by both the alcoholic and nonalcoholic spouse when the alcoholic had been drinking (Jacob, Ritchey, Cvitkovic, & Blane, 1981). Husbands in nonalcoholic families were more influential in problem-solving communications, but the opposite was found for alcoholic couples.

A series of studies that involved direct observations of family interactions led to the idea that the use of alcohol may act as a stabilizer for the alcoholic family that has developed a homeostasis centered on the drinking of the alcoholic (Steinglass, 1981). In one study, an alcoholic who was being treated in a residential facility volunteered to be a research participant. However, he was reluctant to give up alcohol and had stated his intention to resume drinking following discharge. He agreed to be observed in an interview session while sober, along with his wife and two teenage children and a psychiatrist. The session was marked by confrontations between him and the other family members who attacked his behavior.

A week later, another interview occurred with one important difference. Prior to the interview, the alcoholic was allowed to drink 6 ounces of alcohol and told he could drink during the interview. Family members were informed about this procedure and agreed to participate as part of a research project. The alcoholic was less depressed than in the first interview and was assertive with his family. Similarly, the family members were more animated, whereas in the first interview, they had sat rigidly in their seats, avoiding eye contact with each other. Verbal interactions increased dramatically. Surprisingly, there was also considerable laughter among all members, even when references were made to some of the alcoholic's past alcoholic behaviors.

In part, some of the differences may have occurred if the families felt more at ease in the second or alcohol interview. However, most of the difference may reflect a cycle between behaviors associated with sobriety and those related to intoxication (Steinglass, 1981). The family acts as if it believes that certain behaviors are caused by the alcohol, behaviors that do not occur when the alcoholic is sober. These intoxicated state behaviors are highly predictable over drinking occasions for any given family, although they may not be the same for all alcoholic families.

More important than their regularity is that these behaviors serve the function of short-term problem-solving strategies for dealing with family problems (e.g., feelings, role conflicts, sexual difficulties, or problems external to the family such as neighbors, work issues, etc.). Thus, alcohol might act to make one person assertive in dealing with a problem when assertion is desirable, or it might lead another person to withdraw from conflict when such retreat helps promote interpersonal harmony. Such habits or strategies inspired by alcohol become stronger over time. The family is not typically aware of this function served by the alcohol. In fact, the family usually views the alcoholism as the problem rather than as the strategy for coping with everyday problems. Although alcohol may work for short-term solutions, it does not work in the long run and also creates the additional problems of alcohol dependency and its disintegrative effects on the family.

An observational study (Steinglass, 1981) of 31 families from a wide background involved nine separate 4-hour home visits spread over 6 months. Two observers made systematic records about minute-by-minute verbal and nonverbal interaction patterns. These findings may not be specific to alcoholic families because no observations of families with other psychopathologies were made.

Different patterns of family interaction occurred when the alcoholic had been drinking compared to when he or she had not. Moreover, although observed families showed dramatically different behavior patterns when the alcoholic member was wet versus dry, the nature of the difference between the "wet" and the "dry" state interactions was not universal but varied across families.

Observations (Jacob, Krahn, & Leonard, 1991) were made of adolescent children of alcoholic, depressed, and nondistressed fathers during problem-solving discussions with their fathers, mothers, and both parents together. Comparisons were made of sessions when parents were and were not drinking alcohol. Nondistressed father-child dyads differed from both clinical samples in showing higher rates of congeniality and problem solving, whereas the impact of alcohol consumption on father-child, mother-child, or triadic interactions was not related to the diagnostic status of the father.

In one study (Jacob & Leonard, 1992), researchers videotaped interactions between the members of alcoholic couples to study the sequences of responses between them. Alcoholic husbands reacted with negative behavior to problem-solving attempts of their wives; when the husbands' behavior was positive, it had no effect on their wives. In comparison, with depressed couples, alcoholic husbands were less positive in their responses to the problem-solving efforts of their wives. Even during sober interactions, there were differences between alcoholic and other couples, with more complaints and hostility in marriage for the alcoholics. Alcoholic husbands were less unhappy than their wives were, and they were also less aware of wives' complaints.

EPISODIC VERSUS STEADY DRINKERS

A distinction between **episodic** (binge) and **steady** (regular pattern) drinkers may improve our understanding of the effects of alcoholism on family interactions (Jacob & Leonard, 1988). Drinking comes to serve as a strategy for facilitating problem solving among steady drinkers. In contrast, it functions as a means of avoidance that allows episodic drinkers to express hostility when they are faced with conflictful situations. Observations of sober interactions showed no differences between these two types of alcoholics. However, after drinking had occurred, more problem solving and greater negativity were found for couples with a steady drinker, except for spouses of episodic drinkers. Overall, these studies suggest that alcoholic family interactions when the alcoholic is drinking differ from those observed under sobriety, but the exact pattern may differ for alcoholics with different drinking styles. The assumption that all alcoholic couples are similar should be questioned (McCrady & Epstein, 1995) because the drinking style is an important factor on the couples' interactions.

FAMILY RITUALS

A ritual is a valued routine that a family engages in around some important activity such as dinner times, holidays, and vacations. Rituals are stable behavior patterns repeated regularly, with each family member having a consistent role to play. Alcoholism may either disrupt (subsume) or not interfere with these rituals. Research (Bennett & Wolin, 1990; Wolin, Bennett, & Jacobs, 1988) on the role of alcoholism on **family rituals** has examined the extent to which alcohol abuse subsumed the family rituals and took over as the central theme of the family life. Members of two generations of 25 families, in which at least one parent was an alcoholic, were interviewed in depth with structured interviews. It was hypothesized that transmission of alcoholism from one generation to the next is more likely to the extent that the alcoholism disrupts such family rituals. If the adult offspring of alcoholics are "deliberate" in rejecting alcohol as a central theme of their own families when they marry by forming new nonalcoholic rituals or by marrying nonalcoholics, they may avoid some of the adverse effects of growing up in an alcoholic home.

Children of Alcoholics

Various forms of psychopathology, not limited to alcohol and other drug abuse, have been noted (Cermak, 1986) among **children of alcoholics** (COAs). Clinical observations have suggested that they develop problems stemming from growing up in an alcoholic home that range from insecurity and low self-esteem to an extreme tendency to please others and to rescue the family (Beattie, 1987). They judge themselves without mercy, feel different from other people, and have difficulty having fun. These consequences could lead these children to alcohol and other drug abuse as they grow up. Understanding how children of alcoholics are affected by growing up in alcoholic families may be useful in seeing how alcohol-related problems continue from one generation to the next.

Alcoholism of parents leads to a dysfunctional family (Black, 1981). However, the children react in various ways to their parental drinking (Wegsheider, 1981). Many experience anger and resentment or even suppression of feelings. Some children cope by withdrawal, and others may try to placate and mediate. Many children may come to blame themselves for the problem. These different reactions are adaptations to a dysfunctional family situation that will eventually entail serious psychological cost to the well-being of the child (Wegsheider, 1981).

COMPARISONS OF CHILDREN OF ALCOHOLICS AND NONALCOHOLICS

A review (West & Prinz, 1987) examined the extent to which parental alcoholism affects children. Weak support was found in six of seven reviewed studies for the idea that children of alcoholics are more hyperactive. Interpretation of these findings is unclear. Because hyperactivity involves attention deficit and is related to aggression, hyperactivity rather than alcoholism could be the basis for the relationship between parental alcoholism and problems in the children. Moreover, a number of questions are raised. For example, how much of any observed differences could be due to prenatal factors? Is the impairment the same for children living with an alcoholic mother, with an alcoholic father, or with two alcoholic parents? When one parent is alcoholic, does it matter whether the nonalcoholic parent also lives in the home?

Children from alcoholic families have more mental health problems (Moos & Billings, 1982) and engage in substance abuse more often (Beardslee, Son, & Vaillant, 1986), but other variables such as socioeconomic status cannot be ruled out as alternative causes of these problems. Although a poorer family home environment exists among children of alcoholics than among controls, many of them function as well or better than children from the nonalcoholic control families (Clair & Genest, 1987).

Adolescent children of alcoholics have lower self-esteem, more depression, and heavier drinking in comparison to controls from nonalcoholic families, but the evidence is based mostly on self-report and ignores other causes such as physical abuse and other family psychopathologies (Roosa, Sandler, Beals, & Short, 1988). Sampling also may have been biased because only those children of alcoholics seeking counseling were included, and they may have had other problems not directly derived from the parents' alcoholism.

A middle-aged, middle-class community sample of female COAs had higher levels of depression and lower levels of self-esteem than controls (Domenico & Windle, 1993). COAs also reported lower levels of perceived social support, family cohesion, control over their children, and marital satisfaction and higher levels of marital conflict. No significant differences in alcohol use were found. However, drinking by COAs was more likely for coping purposes.

When COAs were compared with children from families with a different problem (divorce), no differences were found on current outcomes of functioning, nor did they differ from a control group (Senchak, Leonard, Greene, & Carroll, 1995). This similarity occurred despite the fact that COAs recalled that their fathers were cold to a greater extent than did children from divorced or control families, and the two groups receiving counseling (children from families with divorce or alcoholism) recalled more parental conflict than did the controls.

The degree of risk for children may differ, depending on the type of alcohol-dependent parent. One study (Zucker, Ellis, Bingham, & Fitzgerald, 1996) compared parenting by fathers who were antisocial alcoholics (AAL) with those who were nonantisocial alcoholics (NAAL). The AAL fathers came from families with a greater density of alcoholism, lower intellectual functioning, and higher levels of nonalcoholic psychopathology in comparison to NAAL fathers (Ellis, Zucker, & Fitzgerald, 1997; Zucker et al., 1996). Moreover, the wives of AAL fathers had higher levels of antisocial behaviors than those of NAAL fathers. AAL families showed more aggressive behavior and conflict and had lower socioeconomic status than NAAL families.

Paternal depression and alcohol problems were higher in AAL than in NAAL families, and the control families were lowest. The differences were not as wide among mothers but were apparent for antisocial behavior and

TABLE 13.2 Differences in risk factor levels for children of alcoholics (COAs) and nonalcoholics (NCOAs)

Childhood Risk Indicators	*Degree to Which Indicator Is Present in Children*
Preschool years (ages 3-5)	
Child externalizing behavior problems[a]	AAL > NAAL > Control
Child internalizing behavior problems[b]	AAL > NAAL > Control
Child hyperactivity[c]	AAL > NAAL > Control
Child risky temperament	AAL > NAAL > Control
Early school years (ages 6-8)	
Child externalizing behavior problems	AAL > NAAL > Control
Child internalizing behavior problems	AAL > NAAL = Control

SOURCE: Ellis et al. (1997).

NOTE: AAL = antisocial alcoholics; NAAL = nonantisocial alcoholics; Control = matched nonalcohlics from the same communities.

a. Aggressivity and delinquency.

b. Depressed or uncommunicative behavior.

c. Restlessness and short attention span.

current depression levels. Finally, spousal aggression was highest for AAL, followed by NAAL and then by control families.

These differences could provide a basis for greater risk of problems for the children of AAL families. The different family backgrounds and experiences of AAL and NAAL affect how parents treat their children and possibly affect the degree of risk their children face for subsequent alcohol dependency. Table 13.2 shows that for preschool children, as well as for early elementary school children, aggression (externalizing behavior) as well as depression (internalizing behavior), hyperactivity, and risky temperament (a composite index of activity and emotional reactivity level) were higher for children of alcoholics, especially those from AAL families, than for control nonalcoholic families.

WHY DO SOME BUT NOT OTHER COAs BECOME ALCOHOLICS?

For those COAs who do become alcoholics, what is the underlying mechanism? The lower self-esteem of some COAs derives from the greater amount of life stresses experienced in the home, which in turn leads to depression and other symptoms (Roosa et al., 1988). Eventually, this process might increase the risk of alcohol abuse as a means of coping with the low self-esteem. However, for those children in alcoholic homes who do not experience as many threats to their self-esteem, there may be a weaker impact of parental alcoholism.

The family environment may sometimes affect the likelihood of COAs becoming alcoholics as adults in complex ways. A follow-up of a longitudinal study of adolescent boys started in the 1940s examined factors that affected the drinking of sons of alcoholics (McCord, 1988). If the mother had held the alcoholic father in high esteem, the sons were more likely to show alcoholic tendencies. In nonalcoholic families in which sons became alcoholics, a better predictor than the mother's attitude toward the father was the extent to which the sons were undercontrolled during adolescence. Thus, different pathways to alcoholism may exist in different families.

INVULNERABLES

More variability exists among children of alcoholics than the formulations of self-help organizations such as Adult Children of Alcoholics (ACOA) would suggest (Werner, 1986). A large percentage of these children seem to function ably and have been termed **invulnerables.** It would be worthwhile to examine the factors that enable them to do so well while others do not.

All alcoholic parents do not have the same severity of alcoholism, or the alcoholism does not lead to divorce or a splitting of the family in all cases. The age of the child when the parent develops alcoholism, the child's relationship in general with parents, the size of the family, and other forms of parental psychopathology are added factors that might prove important in determining how detrimental the alcoholism of a parent is on the mental health of the children.

Protective Factors

In addition to the risk factors presented by alcoholism in the family, shown in Figure 13.3, there may also be counterforces that protect against the development of alcohol and other drug use. For example, children might be "protected" by nonalcoholic mothers, who might offset the negative influences of alcoholic fathers (Curran & Chassin, 1996).

Children of alcoholics could be protected by parents in several ways. For example, parental monitoring of the adolescents' involvement with peers who abuse drugs seems to help prevent their adoption of such

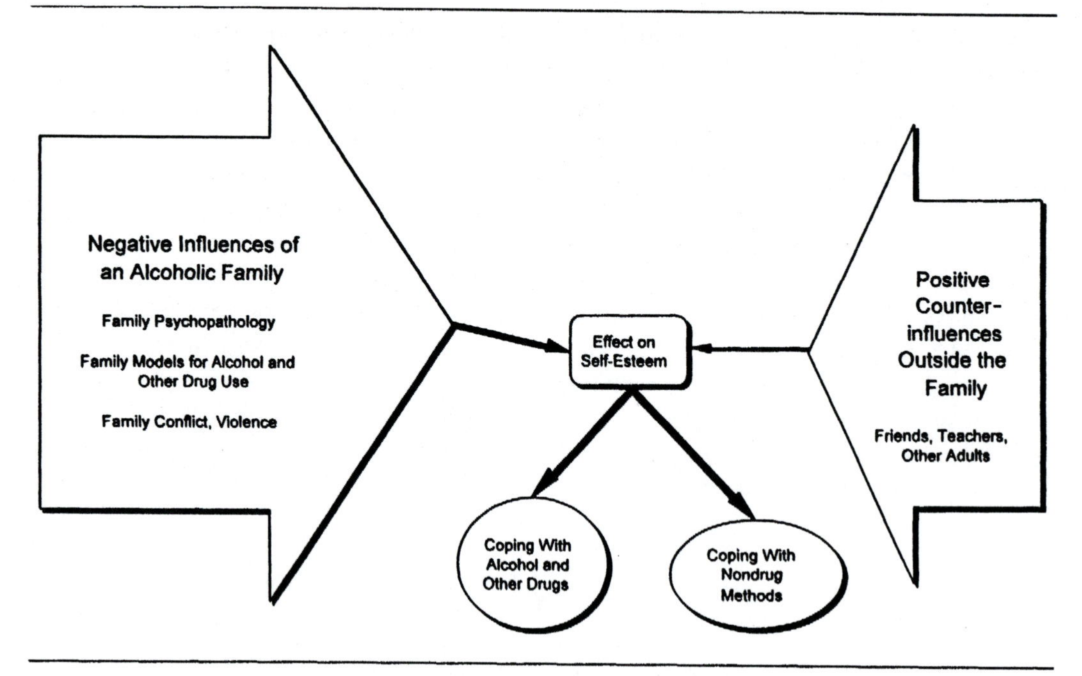

Figure 13.3. Model Showing How Positive Factors Outside the Alcoholic Family May Counter the Adverse Effect of Family Alcohol Abuse on the Child's Self-Esteem
NOTE: The total set of factors determines the likelihood of using drugs to cope.

practices (Chassin et al., 1996). However, alcohol-abusing parents are probably less likely to practice this vigilance.

The nonalcoholic parent, other relatives, older siblings, and friends could nurture COAs to help offset the negative impact of the alcoholic parent on the children's self-esteem. COAs also may develop a sense of self-worth through associations with nonalcoholic friends. In addition, the children may be fortunate enough to encounter some sources of rewarding experiences from adults at school or in the community that may offset any adverse effects of an alcoholic home.

Parenting by COAs

How do COAs relate to their own children when they later become parents? After the experience of having been reared by one or more alcoholic parents, do they differ from children of nonalcoholics in how they bring up their children?

One study (Bensley, Spieker, & McMahon, 1994) found that COA mothers and their children showed dyadic behaviors that were less problematic than those of other mothers on mother-child teaching interactions at 1 year of age, mother-child interactions during structured play at preschool age, and child attachment behavior at preschool age.

Although COAs reported more historical life stress, more family disruption, and more drug use, these problems did not appear to be related to their own performance as parents. They recalled feeling relatively more rejection than love from their alcoholic parent, but this was not related to their own parenting behaviors. Perhaps some COAs, as parents, make more efforts to avoid the shortcomings of the parenting they received themselves.

A CRITIQUE OF COA STUDIES

There is a risk of overgeneralizations from studies of COAs who receive counseling (Heller, Sher, & Benson, 1982). Those COAs who do not have adjustment problems are overlooked. There is a lack of controlled research to evaluate the validity of COA typologies, and few comparisons are made between alcoholic and nonalcoholic families (Blane, 1988). The definition of the alcoholic parent is often vague and varies widely across different studies (Searles & Windle, 1990). When controls are included, only small differences in psychological functioning and well-being have been found between children of alcoholics and nonalcoholics.

For example, a comparison (Tweed & Ryff, 1991) of 114 adults who were children of alcoholics with 125 adult children of nonalcoholics found that although the children of alcoholics showed higher anxiety and depression scores than the children of nonalcoholics (possibly due to their awareness of the risks of growing up in an alcoholic home), no differences were found in the overall functioning of the two groups. One reason why these results do not agree with many earlier studies is that they involved community rather than clinical samples. Thus, it is possible that the home environment may be more harmful for children coming from families in which the alcoholic parent needs treatment than for those coming from homes in which the alcoholic parent does not go into treatment.

Moreover, research evaluating various types of interventions is sorely needed. It is important to determine whether different types of programs are needed, depending on the age of the child. Psychological interventions might even have harmful effects for some children of alcoholics, especially if the labeling of such individuals promotes self-fulfilling prophecies (Burk & Sher, 1988). Studies (Burk & Sher, 1990) have demonstrated that adolescents hold more negative stereotypes of "children of alcoholics" than they hold of "typical teenagers." In a second study, mental health professionals watched a brief videotape of an adolescent with a soundtrack describing the home background. They gave lower evaluations when the adolescent was labeled as a child of an alcoholic than of a nonalcoholic, regardless of whether the description of the adolescent was positive or negative.

Most naturalistic and clinical studies of adolescent and adult children of alcoholics are retrospective, relying on inferences and self-reports about earlier events (Sher et al., 1991). The implication is that the present differences in characteristics differentiating children of alcoholic versus nonalcoholic parental environments can be attributed to this factor alone. However, objective and thorough comparisons of early life events experienced by children of alcoholics and those of nonalcoholics are rarely available. Nevertheless, strong beliefs are widely held that COAs are uniquely dysfunctional. This situation could be an example of a "Barum effect" in which vague descriptions of characteristics caused by growing up in an alcoholic home are accepted readily as true by anyone with low self-esteem (Sher, 1997).

Many research studies of COAs first identify alcoholic parents, usually in treatment, and then compare their children with those of nonalcoholic parents. One problem with the use of a sample of alcoholic parents in treatment is that they may not be comparable with nontreated alcoholics who could be either more or less impaired as a group in their alcoholism. Similarly, the children of treated alcoholics may not be equivalent to those of nontreated alcoholics. Other studies focus first on the identification of problem children and then examine drinking levels of the parents in comparison with those of parents of nonproblem children.

These two methods may not produce the same results because it is unlikely that as many of the parents with drinking problems identified with the second method would be receiving treatment for alcohol problems as with the first method, in which all of them are in treatment. If one assumes that treatment benefits the alcoholic and the family, the children identified with the first method may show fewer problems than those selected under the second approach.

Another major problem with these methods, which both involve cross-sectional designs comparing different groups at one point in time, is the difficulty of establishing causal inferences. If there is a correlation between the drinking levels of the parents and children, it could be that the parents' alcoholism is producing the problems in their children or vice versa, or both processes could be involved. The use of longitudinal designs in which measures are taken of the same individuals at different points in time would permit such inferences, but these methods are expensive and obviously require a longer time frame.

It also might be important to differentiate among alcoholic families in which one versus both parents are alcoholic. If both parents are alcoholic, this might appear to be worse than if only one parent is alcoholic. On the other hand, if one parent is alcoholic and the other is not, there might be more conflicts between the two parents. When only one parent is alcoholic, comparisons of the effect of the sex of the alcoholic might prove important. Furthermore, the effect of the alcoholic parent could very well differ for sons and daughters. Whether the alcoholic parent is the same or the opposite sex of the child may have different implications for that child. Unfortunately, little research has examined these aspects of the alcoholic parent-child relationship.

Codependency

The discussion thus far has focused on the family environment of an alcoholic home as it might affect the children and nonalcoholic members of the family. It is assumed that the family wants the drinking to stop or be reduced and that the family will try to influence the alcoholic in this direction. However, it is also important to examine the possibility that the reactions of the nonalcoholics may paradoxically contribute to or enable the continued or increased drinking of the alcoholic.

A systems theory view of the family focuses on the influence of each member's behavior on other members (Bowen, 1974). These models hold that, in general, the family achieves a balance or homeostasis from which it resists change. In alcoholic families, alcoholism becomes the focal point to which adjustments are made, and family interactions can become highly dysfunctional in maintaining this equilibrium. The concept of **codependency** (Wegsheider, 1981) refers to this reciprocal relationship between the alcoholic and one or more nonalcoholics who may unwittingly aid and abet the alcoholic's excessive drinking and irresponsible nondrinking behaviors created by the drinking.

Change occurs within the family as it adjusts to the drinking problem (Jackson, 1954). There is an understandable tendency for nonalcoholic family members to deny that there is a problem for a long time. The alcoholic becomes the focus of the family, and adjustments are made to the alcoholic. Thus, the codependents sacrifice their own independence and autonomy by reacting to the alcoholic's behavior in a futile attempt to regain control. By covering up and excusing the alcoholic's shortcomings, the codependent could be faulted as an accomplice.

Due to the stigma of alcoholism, it is not surprising that many nonalcoholic family members would be inclined to hide the fact of alcoholism from the outside world by making up excuses for the alcoholic when necessary. In addition, they may blame themselves or be blamed by others for their role in facilitating and maintaining the drinking of the alcoholic member. Codependent behavior, however, generally has not been seen in a negative light until recently. Indeed, in the past, a heroic vision of the martyred family members of the alcoholic has been a more prevalent portrayal. However, the view that the nonalcoholic members of a family could contribute toward maintaining the alcoholic's drinking has gained acceptance. Codependency is regarded as a problem in its own right (Cermak, 1986; Woititz, 1983). By continually adjusting and reacting to the alcoholic's drinking, but without success, the codependent suffers a loss of self-esteem and experiences a mixture of depression, helplessness, and self-blame. As the alcoholic becomes less able to perform his or her family roles, the codependent may try to "rescue" the family and assume the responsibility by trying to perform those tasks in addition to his or her own. Using concepts from 12-step programs such as Alcoholics Anonymous, Adult Children of Alcoholics (ACOA) has actively called attention to the dysfunctional aspects of codependency among codependents and encouraged them to toss aside the need to control the lives of others.

This line of thinking is not limited to alcoholism but has been applied to an array of addictions, including dependency on other people as well as to substances. Pop psychology and self-help books call for codependents to recognize and overcome their codependent relationships. Critics (Gordon & Barrett, 1993) of the construct see it as a popular social movement that tends to stigmatize and blame the victim for being dysfunctional.

There have been clinical observations and anecdotal evidence about the nature of codependency but relatively few rigorous scientific investigations conducted to validate these impressions, identify correlates, and determine consequences.

One study compared couples in which one member was a recovering alcoholic with a group of matched couples without an alcoholic member. Higher codependency levels occurred for the clinical sample (Prest, Benson, & Protinsky, 1998). Moreover, within the clinical group, alcoholics and their spouses had similar dysfunction in their families of origin, current families, and codependency levels.

WIVES OF ALCOHOLICS

Alcoholism often has been referred to as a family disease in the sense that all members are adversely afflicted. It was not until the 1950s that the family dynamics of alcoholism began to receive attention. The early focus came from clinical studies of alcoholic men and their nonalcoholic wives (Ablon, 1984). At that time, it was suspected that the wife often might have been a factor causing the alcoholic to drink because she was frequently observed to have psychological problems. Thus, the alcoholism of the husband was blamed on the wife as if her psychological disturbances somehow "drove him to drink" or that she had some characteristics that facilitated her husband's drinking.

Comparisons (deBlois & Stewart, 1983) of wives of alcoholics and nonalcoholics found that those whose first husbands had been alcoholics had married at an earlier age after knowing their husbands for briefer periods and had more marital problems, lower education, and lower socioeconomic status. However, the study was limited in that the sample had women who were mothers of boys attending a child psychiatry clinic, which suggests that they may have not been a representative sample of mothers. A different type of explanation (assortative mating) for the correlation between the husband's drinking and the wife's psychological problems assumes that certain types of people are attracted to each other. Thus, antisocial and rebellious men who drink excessively may tend to be matched with women who have psychological problems (Stewart & duBlois, 1981).

However, yet another explanation is that the psychological problems of the wife of an alcoholic might be viewed as some of the consequences of living with an alcoholic husband (Jackson, 1962). A seven-stage model has described how the wives of alcoholics might cope, starting with denial and ending with recovery as the final stage, although it was not assumed that all families would successfully reach recovery. This formulation was based on observations at Al-Anon meetings. Al-Anon membership comprises the family members of alcoholics who feel the need to find support from persons facing the same problems. Members believe they must recognize that they are powerless over the alcoholic and that they need to accept a higher power. The goal is not to cure the alcoholic, whom they are told to "release with love," but for members to find a means of dealing with their own feelings and to stop trying to save the alcoholic who has usually led the wives and other family members to engage in irrational and dysfunctional modes of behavior as they cope with the alcoholic family member.

SUMMARY

Marriage partners tend to use alcohol at similar levels, as people may tend to select mates who share similar characteristics and behavior patterns. Initially, alcohol consumption declines during marriage. Over time, alcohol use will increase for some individuals. Those marriages in which one or both partners develop alcohol abuse or dependency may generate conflict and even end in divorce. Following divorce, alcohol abuse may begin or continue to increase.

Children living in alcoholic family environments may be affected in several ways by the alcoholism of one or both parents. Direct effects on early childhood development may occur because the parents' drinking behavior serves as a model for the children to imitate later. However, it appears that for some children, there is a drop-off in the tendency to imitate the cross-sex parent's drinking if it is heavy. Parental alcoholism may produce adverse effects in the form of neglect or abuse of children, consequences that may eventually lead to excessive drinking in the children when they become older.

Indirect paths of influence are also possible when alcoholism leads to domestic strife or divorce, which could create a home environment that might impair the children's psychological development of self-esteem, regardless of whether they eventually develop drinking problems.

In addition to affecting the levels of alcohol abuse in their children, some alcoholic parents may harm their children with physical and sexual abuse. Some evidence shows that childhood sexual abuse and, to some extent, childhood physical abuse are related to adult alcohol abuse, especially for women.

Direct observations of interactions of families in clinical treatment reveal that the family members behave differently when the alcoholic is dry versus sober, but the nature of the differences may vary with the family or whether the alcoholic is a binge or steady drinker. Alcohol may function as a short-term coping response for problems that eventually fails. Alcoholic drinking may disrupt established family rituals or established patterns of interaction. These studies are based on small samples that agree to be observed; thus, the findings may not be generalizable to other families, but they offer important opportunities to develop hypotheses about the impact of alcoholism on family interactions.

Nonalcoholic family members may inadvertently contribute to or "enable" the alcoholic's drinking. By adjusting their behavior to accommodate that of the alcoholic, they may hope to avoid conflict and arguments.

Children of alcoholics are hypothesized to have higher risks of being alcoholics themselves as adults than are children of nonalcoholics. Although some research supports this view, many children of alcoholics do not appear to be harmed by having alcoholic parents. It is important to also study which factors are protective in preventing these at-risk children from following in the footsteps of their alcoholic parents.

Codependency may develop when nonalcoholic family members try to please or not annoy the alcoholic. Thus, the blame is shifted, partially at least, from the alcoholic to the nonalcoholic family members. Al-Anon encourages nonalcoholic spouses to seek help to learn how to break their codependent addictive relationships with alcoholics.

KEY TERMS

Child abuse
Children of alcoholics
Codependency
Domestic violence
Episodic (drinking)
Family rituals
Invulnerables
Marriage effect
Steady (drinking)

STIMULUS/RESPONSE

1. Marriage partners generally seem to be similar in their levels of drinking. Do you think this outcome involves conscious awareness of similarity of their alcohol use by the couples during courtship, or do you think a more subtle process is involved?
2. Some research indicates that following divorce, alcohol consumption may increase due to the feeling of loss following the breakup. Can you make any arguments for predicting *reduced* drinking by some individuals following divorce?
3. How does drinking alter the pattern and nature of interactions between drinkers and nondrinkers in a family? Can you identify both positive and negative interactions?
4. Do you think that parents who drink heavily treat their children differently when they are sober than when they have been drinking? If so, describe the nature of the different responses and speculate on why such differences exist.

- ❖ Motivating Change
- ❖ Alcoholics Anonymous and Related Mutual Help Groups
- ❖ Self-Help Treatment for the Families of Alcoholics
- ❖ Summary
- ❖ Key Terms
- ❖ Stimulus/Response

14 Recovering From Alcohol and Other Drug Dependency

You can lead a horse to water,
but can you make him drink?

The problem facing the treatment of abuse and dependency of alcohol and other drugs is just the opposite from that involved with the proverbial horse and water. How do you lead the alcoholic away from alcohol, and how can you stop the drinking?

Many users of alcohol and other drugs will experience serious impairment sooner or later. There is no single pattern of development for the transition from recreational and casual use of alcohol and other drugs to abuse and dependency. Unfortunately, the user is often the last to recognize the problem, which deteriorates from bad to worse. Alcohol-dependent and other drug-dependent persons often inflict harmful consequences on themselves as well as on others. Even friends and family may ignore or fail to recognize the problem, or when they do recognize it, they may be reluctant or unable to confront their loved ones about their alcohol or other drug problem.

Irrational thought processes allow alcoholics to defend their drinking (Denzin, 1987). Alcoholics could be said to hold a "lay theory" of drinking that centers on **denial**. Alcoholics believe that alcohol conveys power and control; any challenge to their drinking evokes powerful rationalizations and defenses of their drinking. They often shift the blame from themselves to others such as nondrinking spouses, who allegedly "made" them drink. Instead of viewing alcohol use as the problem, alcoholics reverse things and regard alcohol as the solution. Even alcoholics in treatment may nostalgically recall earlier days when their drinking was associated with positive outcomes, a tendency that may sustain the denial. Alcoholics may think that they can still regain the power to indulge in "successful drinking," despite the present setbacks associated with drinking.

Eventually, many individuals who drink alcohol excessively will develop problems that necessitate intervention and treatment. They may experience physical symptoms such as craving and withdrawal or suffer alcohol-related health problems. In addition, some may manifest antisocial or violent behavior, poor work performance, depression, and hostility. Eventually, they will be referred or mandated by legal authorities to attend some form of alcoholism treatment and counseling.

Motivating Change

Until an alcoholic is diagnosed, the process of treatment and rehabilitation cannot be effective. Even then, there is often much resistance. How do alcohol-dependent and other drug-dependent individuals break their addictions? The answer to this problem involves a series of questions. First, what motivates or prevents alcohol-dependent and other drug-dependent individuals from even considering quitting? Next, what moves them to actually try to quit? What procedures do they use in trying to quit? Why is quitting so difficult to maintain, with many attempts ending in relapse? Finally, how do they achieve success in quitting over the long term?

In extreme cases in which alcohol and other drug abuse leads to legal difficulties, the motivation may involve coercion in the form of court-mandated treatment. In other cases, individuals may come to recognize that the dependency is costing them too much in the form of work and school performance, mental and physical well-being, and interpersonal relationships. Irrespective of the original impetus for change, individuals will seek a variety of treatment methods ranging from self-help groups such as **Alcoholics Anonymous** to more formal treatment from professional treatment providers in clinics and hospitals.

On the other hand, there are obstacles to wanting to stop. Fear of not being able to quit also may deter some from trying. Embarrassment in admitting addiction and the inability to control one's drug use are other factors. For example, one impediment to successful long-term smoking cessation is weight gain, especially among women (Murray & Lawrence, 1984).

STAGES OF CHANGE

Quitting is often discussed as if it were an all-or-none process, leading to a user or nonuser outcome. An alternative conceptualization (DiClemente et al., 1991) views quitting as a process involving different **stages of change,** as diagrammed in Figure 14.1. Originally proposed to deal with self-change in smoking, this model also can be applied to other drug dependencies. The progress through stages is not without occasional reversals, when setbacks to an earlier stage occur. Hence, the model involves a spiral, rather than a linear, pattern over time. First, there is a *precontemplation stage* when drug abusers do not see any problem and feel that everything is under control. In this period, they may seriously consider but do not actually try to quit. They are ambivalent, but the seeds of change may be beginning to grow.

However, if problems associated with alcohol and other drug use start to develop, a process of self-change may start. Hints and negative feedback from others, interpersonal conflict, poor school and work performance, and so on may serve to raise consciousness to the possibility that they may have a substance abuse problem. During this *contemplation stage,* they may consider cutting back on their drug use to see if the situation improves. It is a period of identifying and weighing the costs and benefits of change.

Some move on to the *preparation* or *determination stage* in which they not only think seriously about change but also start making efforts to cut down. Over the next 6 months, an *action* period occurs in which serious efforts to stop using are made. Efforts may or may not involve or require professional treatment, depending on individual circumstances, and sometimes self-change or support groups may be effective. The next stage, *maintenance,* begins about 6 months after action is initiated and continues until successful quitting is achieved. However, because drug habits are difficult to eliminate, considerable vigilance must be employed during this stage to prevent a breakdown or relapse. Social support is important in helping those who want to quit using alcohol and other drugs adhere to their goals.

MOTIVATIONAL INTERVIEWING

There are some similarities between the approaches used by friends, counselors, clergy, and other laypersons who are not professionally trained to treat alcohol and other drug abusers. By helping friends with alcohol and drug problems appraise the consequences of their current alcohol or drug lifestyle, they can sometimes get individuals with drug problems to take that first step.

Motivational interviewing (Miller, 1996) is one technique—developed for use by professional therapists to help alcohol and other drug abusers—that is very similar to methods also used by laypersons. Whether used by a counselor or a friend, the strategy involves guiding the individual into completing a decision balance sheet by identifying the perceived pros and cons of continuing to use or stopping the use of drugs. This process can help the individual move from the precontemplation to the contemplation stage for taking action against alcohol abuse and dependency.

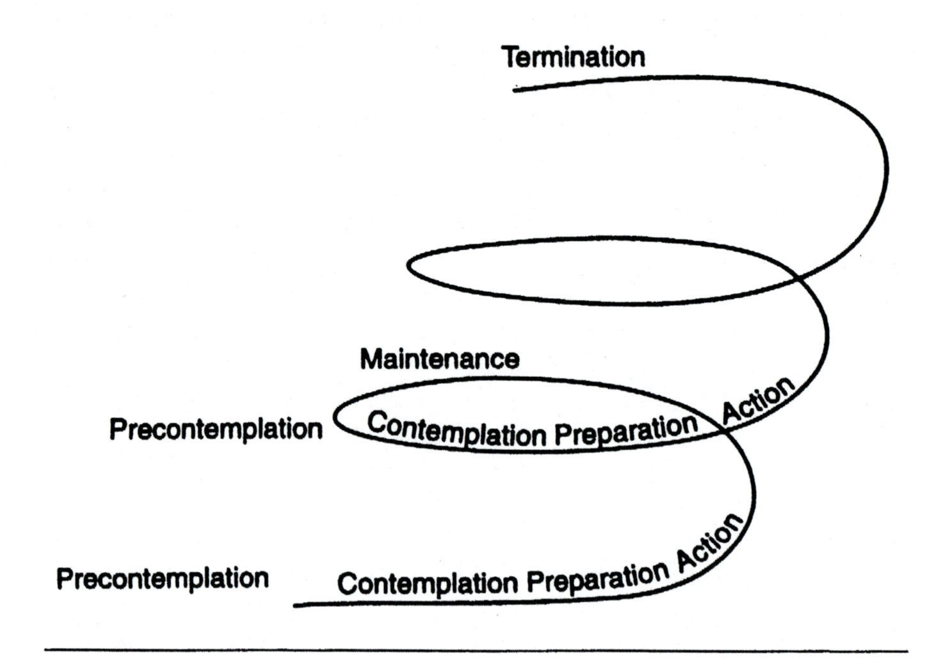

Figure 14.1. Spiral Model of the Stages of Change in Recovery From Drug Addictions

SOURCE: Prochaska, DiClemente, and Norcross (1992). Copyright 1992 by the American Psychological Association. Used with permission.

Motivational interviewing uses structured interviews that avoid confrontation or argument; instead, the approach is to plant seeds or ideas in the minds of individuals that their drug dependency is creating problems. When individuals analyze the costs and benefits of their alcohol and other drug use, it increases their awareness of the extent to which this behavior affects their current lives. The hope is to create sufficient discomfort to motivate them to want to change. In contrast to widely used informal methods of help for alcohol abuse and dependency such as Alcoholics Anonymous, the approach does not require admission of powerlessness or acceptance of the label of alcoholic. It encourages personal choices and responsibility about the role of future drug use in their lives.

METHODS OF RECOVERY

A variety of approaches exist for the treatment of alcoholism and alcohol abuse, but they can be grouped under two major categories: informal self-help groups, such as Alcoholics Anonymous and related 12-step programs, and formal or professional treatment, including individual or group psychotherapy, cognitive-behavioral methods, and pharmacologically based treatments. Typically, some combination of approaches will be used.

In this chapter, the focus will be on informal treatment through mutual help groups such as Alcoholics Anonymous. Many of the issues discussed below apply more or less to the development and treatment of problems associated with the use of other drugs. It is hardly surprising, then, that similar mutual help groups (McCrady & Delaney, 1995) based on 12-step concepts such as Cocaine Anonymous and Narcotics Anonymous have been developed for people with problems with other drugs such as cocaine and narcotics, respectively. In addition, we will describe newer recovery programs that have challenged and provided alternatives to the approach of Alcoholics Anonymous, such as Rational Recovery®, SMART Recovery, and Women for Sobriety. Then, in the following chapter, we will examine more formal treatment approaches involving professionally trained therapists using psychotherapy, behavioral methods, and pharmacotherapy.

Alcoholics Anonymous and Related Mutual Help Groups

HISTORY OF AA

During the temperance and Prohibition eras, the prevalent view of alcoholism involved the moral judgment that excessive drinking was sinful behavior and reflected a lack of willpower. Blame was placed primarily on the alcoholic, who was held to be responsible for his or her own predicament. Little sympathy was given to the drunkard, who was ridiculed as a "skid row bum," ignoring the reality that many otherwise respectable citizens who were gainfully employed might also be drinking excessively.

It was in this social climate in the mid- to late 1930s that two strange bedfellows fostered the movement that led to a major shift in the societal stance toward alcoholism away from the moral model. One party consisted of perhaps the most influential grassroots mental health development in U.S. history, **Alcoholics Anonymous (AA)**. In addition to its impact on alcoholism, it also has served as a model for innumerable other self-help groups formed to deal with a variety of other psychological and societal problems throughout the world.

The inauspicious founding in 1935 of this organization in Akron, Ohio, involved informal meetings that developed from a chance encounter of two alcoholics, a stockbroker named Bill Wilson and a physician, Dr. Bob Smith. They discovered they were able to help each other achieve something that had eluded each of them individually—sobriety. By first acknowledging their powerlessness over alcohol, they were able to start on the road to recovery. Many of the ideas and the philosophy underlying AA had been developed by earlier temperance groups, including the Washingtonians in the 1840s and by an evangelical religious movement known as the Oxford Group in the early part of the twentieth century. However, it was not until AA emerged that the underlying philosophy of these approaches achieved its highest success. Bill W. and Dr. Bob, as they called themselves to protect their anonymity for fear of being stigmatized as alcoholics, discovered that recovery occurred from meeting with other alcoholics to share personal accounts of their drinking problems and to read and discuss inspirational materials. Through this program for recovery, alcoholics achieved a spiritual reawakening and regained control of their lives with the support of one another.

From this humble beginning was born the self-help program of AA. Bill Wilson began to disseminate this ideology and these techniques to any alcoholic who sincerely wanted to stop drinking. The original publication of *Alcoholics Anonymous* in 1935 (Alcoholics Anonymous World Services, 1935), now in its third revision, was a major factor in spreading the AA program. This book, affectionately termed the *Big Book* by AA members, contains the story of Bill Wilson's battle with alcoholism as well as personal stories of the recovery of other alcoholic men and women that provide inspiration for many alcoholics toward recovery. AA meetings are now held throughout the world, not only for alcoholism but for other forms of addiction as well. At the same time, challenges have come from alternative approaches such as Rational Recovery® and SMART Recovery, which regard AA as a cult that emphasizes fatalistic views.

SCIENTIFIC MODELS

Another party opposing the moral model of alcoholism, scientific researchers, had fewer personal motives for their interest in alcoholism. As objective observers, they wanted to apply the empirical methods of rigorous science to study alcoholism and alcohol abuse just as scientists do when studying any type of phenomenon. The approach, espoused by scientific investigators, emphasized reliance on objective data, quantifiable variables, controlled experiments, and theories that generated testable hypotheses. This approach encompassed several different models.

Medical Model

In the influential formulation of a noted scientist, E. M. Jellinek (1960), alcoholism is regarded as a disease, one that can be and should be amenable to treatment and cure in much the same manner as many physical diseases. The idea that alcoholism is a disease was not original with Jellinek but dates back as early as 1785, with the views of Benjamin Rush, an eminent American physician. However, during the 1800s, the moral view prevailed, and drunkenness was regarded as sinfulness. If alcoholism had been recognized as a disease rather than a character defect, a number of significant implications would have followed. The medical profession, due to its commitment to the treatment of diseases, could no longer justify ignoring the plight of alcoholics. Society would not be able to continue to blame alcoholics for their problem because diseases are medical problems and uncontrollable by those afflicted. This view of alcoholism as a disease fit AA's views on the physical nature of the origins of alcoholism and was wholeheartedly promoted in their philosophy.

The original formulation (Jellinek, 1952) distinguished between addictive and nonaddictive forms of alcoholism, maintaining that the disease model applied only to the addictive variety in which there is the susceptibility of eventual loss of control over drinking after years of excessive drinking. As to the causes of the differences between addictive and nonaddictive forms, Jellinek speculated that a so-called "Factor X" existed, possibly a predisposing metabolic or physiological difference, although he did not rule out differences in lifestyle as a determinant either. But he later modified his definition of alcoholism by broadening its scope to cover "any use of alcoholic beverage that cause[s] any damage to the individual or to society" (Jellinek, 1960, p. 35), hoping to direct more awareness to alcohol problems.

Stages of Alcoholism. From a small sample of 98 AA members who completed a questionnaire about the course of development of their drinking problems, Jellinek (1946) proposed a model of alcoholism by identifying a syndrome of symptoms to describe its temporal course, as shown in Figure 14.2. Later, a larger sample of about 2,000 AA members was used to refine the model (Jellinek, 1952).

In the early stage, referred to as the prealcoholic phase, social factors often lead to drinking for relief from tension. Eventually, tolerance to alcohol develops so that a larger dose is needed to produce the same level of relief previously generated by a smaller amount. The disease enters the prodromal phase with the occurrence of blackouts, a type of amnesia for events experienced during drinking episodes, especially when the drinker is physically fatigued. Later, when sober, the drinker may not recall experiences encountered during previous drinking bouts. Surreptitious drink-

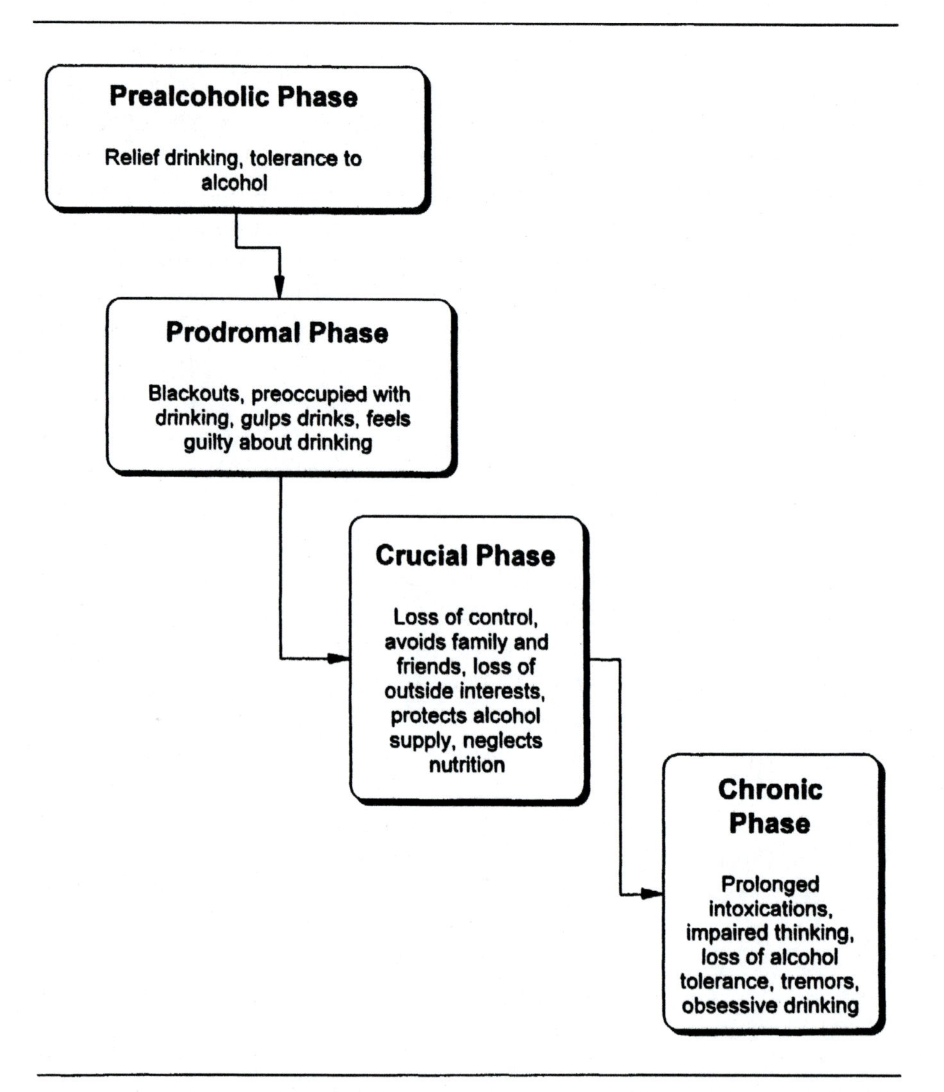

Figure 14.2. Major Aspects of the Different Phases of Alcoholism in Jellinek's Model

ing begins in which the alcoholic sneaks drinks to prevent others from knowing. Preoccupation with drinking develops so that the alcohol takes on a greater importance than previously.

In the third phase, the crucial phase, loss of control occurs in which drinking is difficult to stop once it begins. There may still be control over whether to start drinking on a specific occasion. As drinking takes over, the alcoholic begins to rationalize his or her drinking more frequently, often with defensiveness and hostility. Other major changes occur in the life of the alcoholic: family frictions, loss of friends, work impairment, poor nutrition, and medical problems, which might also increase drinking.

Finally, in the fourth phase, the chronic phase, prolonged intoxication or "benders" occur, along with a reversal in tolerance for alcohol so that less alcohol is needed to produce impairment than previously. When alcohol is not available, withdrawal reactions occur involving pronounced physical discomfort, anxiety, shakes, tremors, and irritability. Although the length of the phases may vary with the individual and other factors, Jellinek (1952) proposed that the sequence of the phases is universal.

This model, proposed by one of the leading alcohol researchers of the time, was important because it provided a disease model as an alternative to the prevailing moral model, which held that alcoholics drank because they lacked willpower. Instead of condemning the alcoholic and denying compassion and treatment, the disease model called for a nonjudgmental response and treatment just as for other physical diseases.

The views of AA and Jellinek were not developed independently of each other because, as noted earlier, Jellinek relied heavily on the personal experiences of alcoholism from AA members. It should hardly be surprising, then, if the self-reports of self-labeled alcoholics fit the primary model proposed by Jellinek and AA very closely. Interestingly, it also may be noted that none of the interview responses of females was included because they often differed with those provided by males (Fingarette, 1988).

Subtypes of Alcoholics. If other types of alcoholics than those studied by Jellinek exist who, for whatever reason, do not participate in AA, the disease model may have less validity for them. In his formulation (Jellinek, 1960), derived from interviews with AA members, Jellinek did describe several types of alcoholics, using Greek letter designations to identify them. The gamma alcoholic, characterized by psychological and physical dependence as well as loss of control, is the type most commonly seen by AA and is assumed to be the prototypical American male alcoholic. Chronic and progressive in nature, this type of alcoholism involves psychological and physical dependence on alcohol. The alcoholic loses control over drinking and is unable to voluntarily stop.

Jellinek also proposed the existence of several other types: the alpha alcoholic, who is a purely psychologically dependent case and presumably does not exhibit loss of control or show evidence of physical addiction to alcohol. In contrast, the beta alcoholic, an infrequent variety, shows only organic damage and nutritional deficiencies, probably due to heavy drinking, but no psychological or physical dependence. A delta alcoholic was proposed, who is similar to the gamma alcoholic but without loss of control. This drinker seems to drink continuously throughout the day but not in quantities that typically produce intoxication. This type is more commonly observed in wine-consuming nations such as France. Finally, there is the epsilon or periodic alcoholic, who would be described as an infrequent binge drinker but one who shows no chronic physical dependence. This type of alcoholic can go for long periods without drinking, but when drinking occurs, it is excessive. Although the types seem to be mutually exclusive, Jellinek did allow that individuals drink in different patterns at different times and hence might be classified as a different type on various occasions.

Instead of acknowledging some type of variation among alcoholics, many conceptions about alcoholism assume that all alcoholics are alike and that an individual can readily be identified as either an alcoholic or a nonalcoholic. Jellinek's typology was generally ignored, and alcoholism was viewed as a homogeneous disease. Recognizing the value of examining subtypes of alcoholics is warranted because it may provide a better understanding of both the origins of and treatments for the different types of alcoholisms than possible under a unitary model of the disease.

The **medical model** or disease conception of alcoholism has proved influential in altering negative societal attitudes toward alcoholics, leading to a more humane concern with their plight. Treatment and rehabilitation, not condemnation and ostracism, have been accepted as the more appropriate response to alcoholism.

In addition, during this era when the medical model was being developed, other important strides toward greater scientific investigation of the biomedical and psychological aspects of alcoholism were made. Jellinek and other researchers developed a Center for Alcohol Studies at Yale University, since relocated to Rutgers University, which was at the forefront in encouraging and promoting research on alcohol problems as a legitimate goal of scientific investigation. The establishment of a major scientific periodical (now named the *Journal of Studies on Alcohol*) provided a prestigious and influential outlet for researchers to disseminate their findings.

Behavioral Model

In the 1960s, the study of alcohol use was based on a different emphasis in the work of behaviorally oriented researchers who focused more on the *drinking behavior* of alcoholics than on any internal disease associated with drinking. They conceptualized alcoholism as a learned response that, like any other form of acquired behavior, could be reinforced or controlled by its consequences. They avoided speculation about intrapsychic states such as denial, craving, and loss of control that were major aspects of lay beliefs about alcoholism as well as of influential organizations such as Alcoholics Anonymous.

Behaviorists questioned the validity of the disease conception of alcoholism. Although they would not deny that alcoholics might develop physical diseases from drinking, they rejected the view that alcoholism itself is a physical disease. They held that medical diseases have an identifiable set of symptoms that develop in a certain sequence, whereas alcoholism does not. Defenders of the disease conception countered that the behaviorists held too narrow a definition of disease and that many physical diseases involve substantial variations in symptomatology.

These researchers studied alcoholics in clinical and experimental settings and used laboratory animals under better-controlled but artificial conditions. They emphasized objective observation of quantifiable aspects of behavior under the influence of alcohol, in comparison to behavior under a sober state. The goal was to find methods of modifying drinking behavior to bring it to acceptable levels.

The controversy between AA and behaviorists over the question of whether alcoholism is a disease, a continuing issue of debate, is complicated by the common use of *disease* as a metaphor. *Disease* is often used to symbolize any pathological condition. Thus, *dishonesty* is a term used to refer to someone who engages in behaviors such as lying and cheating. Metaphorically speaking, we condemn dishonesty as a "cancer" or disease because as it spreads, it destroys the quality of our social relationships.

The metaphorical use of the term *disease* should be distinguished from the view that alcoholism is a medical "disease." Thus, one would not call on a surgeon to "treat" dishonest persons for this "disease" with a scalpel. Instead, one might try to modify these behaviors through a variety of psychological techniques, including counseling, punishment, guilt, and social modeling. The dishonest person would be expected to assume responsibility for changing these behaviors. In the same respect, staunch critics (Peele, 1989) of the disease concept of alcoholism viewed excessive drinking behavior, or dependence on alcohol, as an unacceptable and harmful form of behavior, not as a disease in the medical sense.

THE ALCOHOLICS ANONYMOUS PROGRAM

Alcoholics Anonymous, undoubtedly the most publicized and familiar recovery program, is unique because of its self-help orientation and philosophy that alcoholics are the ones who can best help other alcoholics to recover. Since its beginnings in the mid-1930s, it has offered hope to countless alcoholics all over the world. The concepts underlying Alcoholics Anonymous are not entirely original, having been used by earlier social reformers (Trice & Staudemeier, 1989). The 19th-century temperance movement in the United States produced one of the forerunners of AA in the mid-1800s: the Washingtonians, a group of alcoholics who took a pledge of abstinence and relied on mutual support and hope as a means for recovery. A later movement of a quasi-religious nature, called the Oxford Group, emphasized the importance for alcoholics of recognizing or admitting their powerlessness over alcohol. As with the Washingtonians who preceded them and with AA, which followed them, the Oxford Group strongly believed in the value of mutual support and help.

AA is a program based on **12 steps** (Alcoholics Anonymous, 1985) (see Table 14.1), a set of practices designed to help the alcoholic achieve a lasting recovery. Although not based on any formal religion, concepts and processes resemble features of many religious ceremonies and rituals. First is the recognition that the alcoholic is powerless over alcohol because the belief of control over drinking ensures defeat by it. The alcoholic must move from arrogance and pride to humility. Unless this first step is achieved, the prognosis for improvement is poor because individuals will feel that others are imposing the treatment on them for a nonexistent problem. In contrast, once they can change their self-perception and admit frailty, progress can begin. Critics of the view that alcoholics are powerless sometimes have interpreted this as implying that alcoholics are not responsible.

Alcoholics are then encouraged to believe that a **higher power** (Step 2) can restore them to sanity and next, in Step 3, to decide to turn their lives over to the care of the higher power or God "as we understood Him." These two steps often represent major hurdles for those who do not believe in the concept of God, even though AA expands the definition of God to allow even nonreligious conceptions. A spiritual awakening and an attitude of surrender to a higher power infuse this step in which the drinker seeks and accepts help.

Some of the 12 steps involve highly specific behavioral objectives, starting with the making of a "fearless moral inventory" (Step 4) to increase awareness of one's strengths and weaknesses. This is a difficult hurdle because it entails admission of failures. Although people may admit to excessive drinking, they think that sobriety alone will restore their lives. The drinking, in their eyes, is the cause of any character defects they might have; therefore, they try to avoid a moral inventory.

Step 5 involves confession not only to oneself and a higher power but also to another person of the wrongs committed against others. As with religious confessions, humility is achieved by such admissions. In confessing to another person, one may be embarrassed but still benefit from the relief experienced.

Knowledge of one's faults is not enough. Step 6 calls for the readiness for change with the help of the higher power. This requires submission be-

TABLE 14.1 The 12 steps of AA

1. We admitted we were powerless over alcohol in that our lives had become unmanageable.
2. Came to believe that a Power greater than ourselves could restore us to sanity.
3. Made a decision to turn our will and our lives over to the care of God as we understood Him.
4. Made a searching and fearless moral inventory of ourselves.
5. Admitted to God, to ourselves and to another human being the exact nature of our wrongs.
6. Were entirely ready to have God remove all these defects of character.
7. Humbly asked Him to remove our shortcomings.
8. Made a list of all persons we had harmed and became willing to make amends to them all.
9. Made direct amends to such people wherever possible except when to do so would injure them or others.
10. Continued to take moral inventory and when we were wrong promptly admitted it.
11. Sought through prayer and meditation to improve our conscious contact with God as we understood Him, praying only for knowledge of His will for us and the power to carry that out.
12. Having had a spiritual awakening as the result of these steps, we tried to carry this message to alcoholics, and to practice these principles in all our affairs.

SOURCE: Alcoholics Anonymous (1952). The 12 steps are reprinted with permission of Alcoholics Anonymous World Services, Inc. Permission to reprint the 12 steps does not mean that AA has reviewed or approved the contents of this publication or that AA agrees with the views expressed herein. AA is a program of recovery from alcoholism only; use of the 12 steps in connection with programs and activities that are patterned after AA but that address other problems, or in any other non-AA context, does not imply otherwise.

cause the alcoholic must admit the need of the assistance of the higher power.

Step 7 directs the alcoholic to humbly ask for the removal of shortcomings. Without the attitude of humility, AA feels that the alcoholic cannot maintain sobriety. Humility comes about only through repeated humiliations that stem from overreliance on self-sufficiency.

Step 8 calls for a commitment to make amends whenever possible to the persons they have harmed. Some find this difficult and become defensive, or they focus instead on the harm that these persons may have done to them.

Step 9 requires actual fulfillment of these good intentions. At first, the experience might prove even exhilarating because of the sense of relief, but AA warns against resting on one's laurels and procrastinating in making amends for more serious offenses. Hence, Step 10 reminds the alcoholic to continue taking personal inventory and admitting errors.

Step 11 invokes a religious tone, reminding the alcoholic of the importance of prayer and meditation to maintain contact with the higher power. This step is spiritual and urges the alcoholic not to pray for what he or she wants but for insight into what the higher power wants. By working the 12 steps of the program, the alcoholic achieves humility and atonement and eventually carries forth the message to help other alcoholics, as specified in the 12th step.

Aspects of the AA program could easily be related to other approaches. A behaviorist would notice that AA uses procedures that are the same as self-monitoring, social learning, and covert sensitization. Although the theoretical foundations, view of the change process, and treatment practices of AA are often seen as at odds with those of behavior therapy, many similarities may allow integration of the two models (McCrady, 1994). Similarly, the focus of psychotherapy on the development of insight or the reliance on realistic goal setting is compatible with the AA attitude of taking "one day at a time."

As shown in Figure 14.3, the stages of change model (DiClemente, 1993) parallels different processes advocated by AA. Whereas AA speaks of "hitting rock bottom" before change can begin, the change model refers to precontemplation. Some of the first few steps of AA, such as recognizing that their lives had "become unmanageable," correspond to the contemplation stage of change. When AA calls for reliance on a higher power, the change model calls for preparation for change. AA participation in meetings and "making amends" to those harmed by their drinking are comparable to the action stage of change. Continuing to work the AA program is essentially the maintenance stage in the change model.

Members attend free AA group meetings as often as they wish. These meetings are held in most communities throughout the week in public facilities such as churches, community centers, and hospitals. Some meetings are open to any interested person with or without a personal drinking problem, but other meetings are closed to nonmembers. During the typical speaker's meeting, one or more recovering alcoholics will make a personal statement about their own lives and how they were adversely affected by drinking before they came to AA. They then relate how their lives were changed through "working the program" of AA to achieve sobriety. There is a formal structure, beginning with an inspirational reading from an AA publication and ending with a prayer.

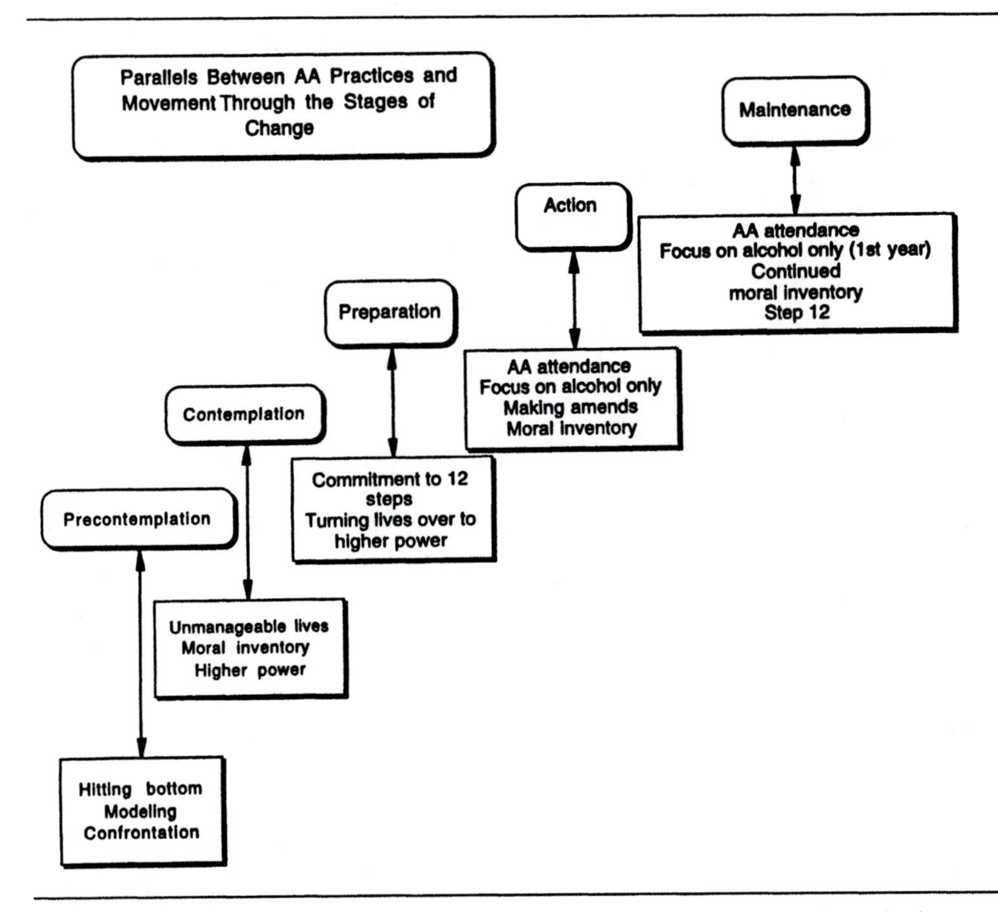

Figure 14.3. Comparison Between AA Practices and Movement Through the Stages of Change Model
SOURCE: DiClemente (1993). Copyright 1993 by Rutgers Center of Alcohol Studies, New Brunswick, New Jersey. Used with permission.

"God grant me the serenity to accept the things I cannot change, the courage to change the things I can, and the wisdom to know the difference." This prayer makes the important distinction between those things that are not changeable and those that are. It then urges appropriate responding by asking one to learn to accept the things that cannot be changed. Failure to accept things that cannot be changed leads to anger, frustration, and resentment—conditions often associated with excessive drinking. However, it is also important to act to modify those things that can be changed. Passive acceptance of a bad marriage, a boring or unfulfilling job, and modifiable health status can all lead to escape through excessive drinking. Finally, the prayer recognizes the difficulty in sometimes accurately knowing which situations are unchangeable and which are changeable by asking for wisdom in being able to distinguish the two.

Some of the benefits of AA participation can be interpreted in terms of attributions (Beckman, 1980). AA involvement helps alcoholics modify their attributions of responsibility for their drinking. Alcoholics' realization that many drinkers do not suffer the harmful effects of alcohol that are experienced by alcoholics leads them to blame themselves for their plight. The feeling that "I'm a no-good drunk" adds to their burden and maintains the drinking. By affiliating with AA, alcoholics reinforce each other's belief that the disease of alcoholism, not their own doing, is responsible for their condition. Acceptance of AA ideology allows a shift of attributions about their drinking from internal to external factors, a change that may be helpful in reducing their self-blame and facilitating recovery.

Critics and skeptics often have rejected the religious connotation of many tenets of AA, especially the requirement of surrendering to God, even though AA allows considerable latitude in defining God or a power greater than ourselves. The AA group itself could represent the power that is greater than the self. The concept of a higher power should not be an obstacle for alcoholics because, in a sense, alcohol is their higher power: "The trick is for the addict to switch from a destructive higher power to a constructive and beneficial one" (Wallace, 1996, p. 27). Nevertheless, the view that AA is a type of religious cult with rigid rules and ideas dies hard and is often an obstacle to newcomers. Skeptics also ridicule AA participants for their excessive smoking and coffee drinking, arguing that even if they give up alcohol, they are still addicts to other substances or to AA meetings themselves.

Who Goes to AA?

It should not be assumed that everyone referred to AA attends regularly or at all. Only around 20% of those referred to AA actually attend (Brandsma, Maultry, & Welsh, 1980). Earlier studies described the typical AA member as male, older than age 40, White, upper middle class, and with an authoritarian personality, strong affiliative needs, susceptibility to guilt, external locus of control, field dependence, cognitive simplicity, formalistic thinking, low conceptual level, religious orientation, existential anxiety, and a tendency to conform (Ogborne & Glaser, 1981).

However, later studies (Emrick, 1987) refuted this negative profile by showing there was no relationship between AA involvement and socioeconomic status, social competence, social stability, or religion. AA members have been found to be more internal, hold more positive treatment expectations, and have less existential anxiety (Gianetti, 1981). Treated alcoholics who were AA members were psychologically healthier than those whose treatment did not include AA (Hurlburt, Gade, & Fuqua, 1984).

These conflicting views could all be tenable if the nature of AA membership has changed over the years. Although the membership surveys conducted by AA do not assess psychological dimensions of participants, they do indicate a shift in demographic features. Surveys by AA indicate more female members, increasing from 30% to 34% from 1984 to 1987, and more members younger than age 30 than in the past. Thus, the male over-40 group represented only about 45% of participants in 1987, whereas in previous years, members were overwhelmingly male. These shifts in the composition of AA membership may be due in part to changing drinking norms and demographic changes. In addition, the reputation of AA as a successful program has led to many treatment facilities and social agencies referring alcohol-dependent individuals to AA who in the past would not have chosen to attend.

Evaluation of AA

Due to the anonymous nature of AA participation—a feature intended to facilitate the seeking of help by protecting individuals with this highly stigmatized problem—it is not possible to obtain scientifically rigorous evidence about the benefits of AA (McCrady & Miller, 1993; Ogborne, 1989). Little is known about who attends AA and drops out or continues but does not benefit. Of course, an abundance of testimonials and anecdotal evidence attest to the many positive changes achieved through AA, so it is likely that benefits are real and substantial for large numbers of participants. Nonetheless, without more thorough information, it is difficult to understand the underlying basis for improvement.

AA conducts its own anonymous survey of participants. These surveys, conducted every 3 years, are not based on random samples and may involve some biased samples of those who choose to complete them. The 1987 report (Alcoholics Anonymous, 1987) showed a 10% increase, with 36% of members reporting that professional treatment helped lead them to AA. This cooperation between professionals and AA is not surprising, given that about 60% of therapists are also members of AA. The AA surveys reported an increased number of members with 3 or more months of attendance, but this includes many who already have achieved sobriety but may be coming to meetings for "booster shots."

One strategy for evaluating the effectiveness of AA involves comparing alcoholics in a treatment program who have and have not participated in AA. A serious problem, however, is that these two groups may differ in many other aspects, such as severity of their alcoholism or motivation for improvement, so interpretations must be cautious.

The fact that many participants do benefit and achieve abstinence might reflect a selective process in which those who are more motivated or ready to accept the goal of abstinence are more likely to attend AA meetings than those who are not. However, none of the demographic variables distinguished between those who did or did not benefit from AA participation (Emrick, 1989). This analysis of AA survey responses showed that the degree of AA involvement before, during, or after a treatment program was unrelated to drinking levels.

Controlled studies (Brandsma et al., 1980) of the effectiveness of AA assigned alcoholics randomly to AA and several other types of formal treatment and found no differential improvement. However, these studies may have underestimated the effects of treatment because they used poorly motivated court-referred clients to AA, as suggested by high dropout rates. Moreover, the extent to which participants actually engaged in the different steps advocated by AA was not measured in these evaluations (Ogborne, 1993).

The difficulty in evaluating AA is not just due to anonymity of participants or to methodological problems but also to vague definitions and concepts (Bradley, 1988). These problems add to the lack of progress in understanding how AA works.

The scientific approach to evaluating AA attempts to measure processes of disease and recovery with objective methods. However, the approach of AA is holistic and phenomenological, not scientific. Thus, the "outcome" is not achieved at a specific, measurable point in time. Dropouts should not be viewed as "failures" because the definition of *dropout* can be relative, as "someone not ready" at that point for AA, rather than absolute.

Racial/Ethnic Minorities and AA. It is somewhat surprising, given the history of AA and the middle-class Protestant and Anglo-Saxon roots of the movement, that racial/ethnic minority group members would find AA participation effective (Caetano, 1993). Although no official statistics are available about the ethnic background of participants, there is sufficient observational evidence that racial/ethnic minorities do attend AA in sizable numbers. For example, AA meetings that consist of predominantly Hispanic participants (Gilbert & Cervantes, 1987) may be more acceptable to this minority group. However, without further study, we do not know what aspects of AA are embraced by minority participants (Glaser & Ogborne, 1982). These groups may participate in AA in different ways than White middle-class attendees do, adapting the program to meet their values. Not all participants, for example, may accept the higher power concept of AA, even though they might recognize the usefulness of humility or the value of social support (Morgenstern & McCrady, 1993).

Alternatives to Alcoholics Anonymous

AA is a group-oriented approach that some may find oppressive. Others object to its formal structure and authoritarian tone. Although AA's philosophy calls for voluntary involvement, participation is increasingly mandated by outsiders such as courts, prisons, and substance abuse treatment programs. Because Alcoholics Anonymous has acquired such a dominant place in recovery programs, alternative approaches have developed that make different assumptions about the nature of addiction and the appropriate methods for recovery.

Rational Recovery®. An organization, **Rational Recovery® (RR)**, created in the late 1980s, vehemently opposes the AA and 12-step program philosophy (Trimpey, 1992). RR is a for-profit organization that believes individuals can quit on their own and are not powerless under alcohol as AA dogmatically proclaims. Based on concepts from rational emotive therapy (Ellis, McInerney, DiGuiseppe, & Yeager, 1988), RR teaches individuals how to recognize and ignore what they term the *addictive voice* of AA ideology. Alcoholism is not a disease, according to RR. Learning skills to cope with problems can lead to plans for achieving abstinence.

RR attacks the vast addiction treatment industry that has developed as an indication that society is hooked on the concept of addiction, as much as it is on drugs. Unlike AA, no group meetings are involved. RR refers to its primary reading resource (Trimpey, 1992) as the *Small Book,* to emphasize its differences from AA, which refers to its primary source of literature as the *Big Book.*

SMART (Self-Management and Recovery Training). In the early 1990s, a split developed among the leaders of RR, and one group separated to form SMART, which is maintained as a nonprofit organization. Like RR, **SMART Recovery** relies on rational emotive therapy (Ellis et al., 1988) and urges independent self-reliance in recovery using techniques related to cognitive-behavioral modification. It opposes the 12-step philosophy that emphasizes powerlessness.

Women for Sobriety. AA started as and still is a male-oriented organization. Middle-class, middle-aged White, educated women may find the requirements of AA that alcohol-dependent women must make atonements and strive for humility objectionable because women generally have lower power in many aspects of their lives (Beckman, 1993). In 1975, Jean Kirkpatrick started **Women for Sobriety,** a self-help organization for women with alcohol problems that emphasized taking responsibility for one's actions and adopting positive thinking (Kaskutas, 1996). The philosophy emphasizes self-reliance, feelings of competent, emotional and spiritual growth, and abstinence. The meeting format is less hierarchical than that of AA in the sense that all women at a meeting take turns sharing their recent experiences, especially positive events, rather than dwelling on presenting historical accounts of their personal drinking. Although not highly publicized, this small and relatively new mutual aid organization provides an alternative to AA for women with alcohol dependency problems.

Self-Help Treatment for the Families of Alcoholics

It has been noted in the preceding chapter that family members are seriously damaged by the drinking of the alcoholic member of the family and are often in need of counseling and psychological treatment. Al-Anon, a program that borrows heavily from AA concepts, was developed for the treatment of the family members separately from the treatment of the alcoholic.

THE AL-ANON PROGRAM

Al-Anon is a recovery program related to AA in approach that was developed for the significant others of alcoholics. Started in 1935 by Lois Wilson, the wife of the cofounder of AA, its philosophy closely mirrors that of AA and its 12 steps. Al-Anon (1984, 1986) encourages its members to admit their powerlessness over their alcoholics and the unmanageability of their lives as the first step toward recovery. Without this first step of detachment, members might continue to find ways to stop the alcoholics from drinking or feel guilty that they had failed.

Al-Anon holds that nonalcoholic family members need to be concerned about their own recovery from strong tendencies to be overcontrolling and assuming too much responsibility for the lives of others. Before the term *codependency* was coined, Al-Anon was dealing with the underlying phenomenon in which the nonalcoholic unintentionally enables or contributes to the maintenance of the alcoholic's drinking. Many nonalcoholic spouses try to prevent their alcoholics from drinking, using a variety of means such as hiding the bottles or emptying the alcohol down the sink. These attempts to control the drinking of the alcoholics are rarely effective in changing the drinking; eventually, the codependents feel despair, resentment, and a sense of hopelessness. At the same time, they deny that alcoholism exists. They are embarrassed by the stigma associated with alcoholism. They also "cover up" and clean up after the alcoholics, despite the physical and psychological damage created by the drinking. Because the alcoholics are spared some of the adverse effects of the drinking, they are unlikely to assume responsibility for the drinking.

Al-Anon recognized that nonalcoholic spouses had problems separate from those of the alcoholics, and to meet those problems, it was first necessary for them to recognize that they were not personally responsible or to blame for their alcoholics' drinking or for getting the alcoholics to stop drinking. As in AA, alcoholics' drinking is viewed as a disease, not a willful act. The task of stopping the drinking, according to Al-Anon, can only be solved by the alcoholics, and the tasks of the nonalcoholics or codependents are to learn to "release with love" their alcoholics and to stop overcontrolling them. After the first step of detachment, the codependent is urged to turn the matter over to a higher power. As with AA, members of Al-Anon gain support from each other to facilitate recovery through a 12-step program of self-improvement and personal growth based on similar concepts developed by AA.

Evaluation of Al-Anon

A 1984 survey conducted across the United States by Al-Anon showed that most participants were White (96%) and predominantly female (88%) (Cermak, 1989). They were mostly middle-aged, with about half of them having had some college education. There may be some bias in the types of persons who completed the survey, so this demographic portrait of membership may only be a rough approximation.

As is true of AA, little objective evaluation of the effectiveness of Al-Anon participation has been done. Self-reports of wives who participated in Al-Anon claimed a reduction of enabling behaviors—making excuses, covering up, checking up on spouses' drinking—as well as fewer emotional outbursts and nagging about the spouses' drinking (Gorman & Rooney, 1979). However, even assuming these self-reports are valid, it is unknown if such changes by wives reduced the husbands' drinking behavior.

NATURAL RECOVERY

Natural recovery or remission may occur for some alcoholic and drug-dependent persons who did not receive formal treatment but still managed to end their substance abuse (Tuchfield, 1981). Interviews (Ludwig, 1986) of alcoholics who experienced spontaneous recovery suggested that certain life events motivated change, but there is a wide variety of such events, ranging from social pressure to major life changes, on one hand, to "strangely trivial" events (Knupfer, 1972), on the other.

The pioneering 18th-century American physician, Benjamin Rush, described several cases of natural recovery in his discourse on the effects of alcohol (Jellinek, 1943). In one instance, a farmer who was habitually drunk happened to rush home from the local tavern one day due to an impending storm before he had a chance to become intoxicated. Surprised by his unusual sobriety, his 6-year-old son announced his father's arrival to his mother, emphasizing that he was not drunk. Shamed by his realization of how he was regarded by his son, the farmer suddenly reformed his drinking habits.

Another tale of a natural recovery involved a drunkard who was followed one day to the tavern by his goat, whom he proceeded to drench with liquor so that they both had to stagger home. The next day, the loyal goat again followed the master to the tavern but balked at the entrance despite the master's entreaties to enter. The apparently greater intelligence of the goat so shamed the master that from that point, he ceased to drink liquor.

These anecdotes suggest that sudden changes in drinking attitudes and behaviors can occur. Overall, however, not much attention has been given to such natural recoveries. Some problem drinkers may not need formal treatment to recover. Natural recoveries may be much more frequent than suspected. One study (Sobell, Sobell, & Toneatto, 1991) recruited 120 ex-drinkers through newspaper ads, asking, "Have you successfully overcome a drinking problem without formal treatment?" After screening, there were 71 who were abstinent and 49 who were nonabstinent. In addition, a group of 28 alcoholics was discovered who had had some formal treatment but did not consider it as a factor in their recovery.

Unlike in previous studies of natural recoveries, a control group of problem drinkers was included by recruiting 62 drinkers with newspaper ads asking, "Do you have a drinking problem now?" The ad indicated that this was a research study to obtain information to help those with problems and seeking treatment, but participants in this study would not be given a treatment program. Only those who had never sought formal treatment were studied.

More than 96% of the 182 participants in the study met the *DSM-III-R* 1987) criteria for alcohol dependence, although only 21% were considered highly dependent. The demographic profile of the participants was similar to that found for alcoholics in seven major outcome studies (Foy, Nunn, & Rychtarik, 1984).

The first phase of the study identified the variables related to stopping and maintaining the cessation of drinking, distinguishing between those who achieved abstinent and nonabstinent (controlled drinking) recovery. The reasons for choosing abstinent or controlled drinking were related to the respondents' self-confidence that they could control their drinking, with those choosing abstinence being less optimistic.

Not seeking formal treatment was related to embarrassment, no perception of a problem, unwillingness to share the problem with others, and stigma. Almost all claimed that they felt they could handle the problem themselves. Paradoxically, they also admitted having a drinking problem. Failure to identify with the stereotype of an "alcoholic" was often a barrier to seeking treatment. Perhaps there should be more attempts to offer programs for those who recognize that they have drinking problems but do not want formal treatment.

Self-Quitting Among Smokers

Is it possible to quit smoking without formal treatment? Self-reported and observer-rated nicotine withdrawal in self-quitters after 30 days showed that anxiety, difficulty concentrating, hunger, irritability, restlessness, and weight increased, and heart rate decreased after cessation for up to 180 days (Hughes, 1992).

Except for hunger and weight gain, these symptoms returned to original levels by 30 days after quitting. Craving, depression, and alcohol or caffeine intake did not reliably increase. Relapse was predicted by postquitting depression rather than by withdrawal symptoms, craving, or weight gain.

A comparison of 10 large-scale studies at different research sites studying self-quitting found widely varying success rates at typically low levels (Cohen & Shiffman, 1989). Part of the variation in success rates may depend on the severity of the smoking. Heavier smokers are less likely to succeed in quitting on their own. Failing to quit on their own may lead them to eventually turn to clinical treatment, but their success rates may be low compared to self-quitters showing high success rates simply because these smokers may be relatively light or infrequent smokers.

In addition, success rates depend on the definition of quitting. For example, the *duration* of quitting must be considered. The longer the follow-up interval, the more likely there will be more relapse to resumption of smoking. Thus, it is impossible to evaluate a study of psychology faculty that reported high rates of successful self-quitting (Schachter, 1982) because the duration of quitting was not examined.

Even when the same time interval is used, rates of quitting can depend on how continuous each success is. Someone who quit and did not smoke continuously over a 6-month period would be counted as only one success, whereas someone who "quit" on four different occasions over the same period, having relapsed on three of the attempts, would get counted as four successes. When longer duration of cessation is used as the criterion, the rates of successful self-quitting are lower.

Natural recovery also has been reported with heroin addicts (Biernacki, 1986). These middle-class users who led otherwise normal lives were able to stop using heroin without formal treatment. After facing many crises from their drug use, they managed to modify their social settings by dissociating themselves from other users and developing new social networks that supported their recovery, often participating in self-help groups with other recovering users.

A study of natural recovery (Granfield & Cloud, 1996) of middle-class male and female alcoholics and drug addicts found that despite little or no exposure to either formal treatment or self-help groups, they reported being abstinent for more than 5 years, on average. They reported an average period of more than 9 years of prior drug dependency. It must be recognized, however, that this nonrandom sample was small and that self-report was the only evidence of prior dependency and present abstinence.

SUMMARY

Alcoholics Anonymous is the best-known and most widely publicized approach to the treatment of alcoholism and alcohol abuse. Although it describes itself as a program of spiritual recovery more than as a "treatment" for alcoholism, AA's philosophy and methods have exerted a strong influence on formal treatment programs. Through self-evaluation and mutual support, AA members engage in a spiritual program to abstain from alcohol as they rebuild their lives. Countless numbers of individuals have attended AA group meetings all over the world. The 12 steps, beginning with an admission of powerlessness over alcohol, provide a structured series of tasks of self-examination and improvement that will help overcome alcoholism.

Due to its informal and subjective nature, the program of AA is difficult to evaluate objectively. Nonetheless, professional or formal treatments often involve AA participation as an adjunct to a treatment package consisting of education and counseling as well as more specialized components that differ across programs. The failure to include control groups makes it impossible to determine the relative effectiveness of different parts of a treatment package. AA's reputation as an effective means for recovery from alcoholism, although difficult to rigorously evaluate, has led to the development of similar organizations for other types of psychological problems.

Al-Anon is a self-help organization for family and friends of alcoholics. It is modeled after AA in concept and offers a similar 12-step program for codependents to help them realize that they are powerless over the drinking of their alcoholic family members. It is believed that this first step of detachment is needed before codependents can begin to recover from their own addiction of trying to control their alcoholic family members' drinking. Alcoholism is viewed as a family disease, not limited to the alcoholic member, because the nonalcoholic family members are also dysfunctional. The codependents must be led to focus primarily on their own recovery, not that of the alcoholics.

Natural recovery from drug dependency apparently happens, but most of the evidence is anecdotal. The existence of such successes does not mean that everyone is capable of natural recovery, but it also does suggest that formal treatment is not always necessary. It is possible that some types of personalities or environmental circumstances are more likely to be associated with such successes. Such cases warrant more investigation to identify the techniques and factors that are involved.

KEY TERMS

Al-Anon
Alcoholics Anonymous (AA)
Denial
Higher power
Medical model
Motivational interviewing
Natural recovery
Rational Recovery®
SMART Recovery
Stages of change
12 steps
Women for Sobriety

STIMULUS/RESPONSE

1. Motivating change: Have you ever tried to get someone to reduce their frequency or quantity of drinking? Which tactics have you found to work best, and which tactics have you found to be ineffective? Has anyone tried to get you to reduce the use of any drug? If so, which tactics worked and which did not?
2. AA believes that alcoholics must admit that they are helpless over their drinking and need to seek a higher power. Do you think this approach is compatible with or in opposition to a view that everyone has to take responsibility and control over their own lives?
3. Because there are many parallels between the ideology and rituals of AA and those of organized religion, do you think AA would be more effective with individuals who also hold firm religious commitments?
4. Do you know someone or have you ever overcome a strong bad habit without any formal intervention or treatment? Describe which processes were helpful in this natural recovery.

- ❖ Psychotherapeutic Approaches
- ❖ Behavioral Approaches
- ❖ Family Therapy
- ❖ Pharmacological Approaches
- ❖ Evaluation of Treatment Programs
- ❖ Other Treatment Issues
- ❖ Treatment of Abuse and Dependency on Other Drugs
- ❖ Summary
- ❖ Key Terms
- ❖ Stimulus/Response

Treatment of Alcohol and Other Drug Dependency 15

In marked contrast to the approach to "therapy" for alcohol and other drug abuse and dependency used by grassroots or lay organizations such as Alcoholics Anonymous, Cocaine Anonymous, and Narcotics Anonymous, formal treatment requires specialized professional knowledge of fields such as psychology, pharmacology, and neurophysiology. As we shall see in this chapter, most formal treatment programs involve some combination of a wide range of techniques and approaches, including psychotherapy, cognitive-behavioral skill training, aversive conditioning, pharmacotherapy, hypnosis, physical exercise, and social skill training rather than a single technique (Institute of Medicine, 1990). Three general categories—pharmacological, psychotherapeutic, and behavioral—encompass most approaches. Our focus in this chapter will be on psychotherapeutic and behavioral approaches, although this distinction is often blurred because they overlap or are often used together.

SIZE OF THE TREATMENT POPULATION

Before examining treatment approaches, it is useful to determine the scope of the problem in terms of the number of individuals who receive alcohol and drug abuse treatment. It is worth noting that an estimated 27% of the general population has suffered some type of drug abuse or dependence during their lifetimes, but only 8% has received formal treatment (Kessler et al., 1994).

Although the number who receive treatment is only the tip of the iceberg of those in need, it is still useful to identify those who seek and receive treatment. An estimate of the number of drug abusers under treatment in the United States can be obtained from the National Drug and

TABLE 15.1 Number of alcohol and other drug clients in treatment

	Unit Orientation			
Unit Function	*Alcohol Only*	*Drug Only*	*Combined Alcohol and Drug*	*Total*
Treatment units	1,472	1,266	5,021	7,759
Clients in treatment				
Drug clients	0	178,651	172,779	351,430
Alcoholism clients	131,555	0	251,970	383,525
Total clients	131,555	178,651	424,749	734,955
Prevention education units	960	674	4,162	5,796
Other units	609	472	2,552	3,633
Total number of units	1,782	1,449	6,377	9,608

SOURCE: National Institute on Drug Abuse/National Institute on Alcoholism and Alcohol Abuse (1990).

Alcoholism Treatment Unit Survey (NDATUS). Started in 1974 by the National Institute on Drug Abuse (NIDA), it has been jointly conducted since 1979 with the National Institute on Alcoholism and Alcohol Abuse (NIAAA) to survey all private and public alcohol and drug treatment facilities in the United States periodically to determine the number and type of treatment facilities and the extent to which they are used.

The 1989 report (National Institute on Drug Abuse/National Institute on Alcoholism and Alcohol Abuse [NIDA/NIAAA], 1990) showed that only about 80% of the available treatment capacity was used. Table 15.1 shows that the 1,472 alcoholics-only and 5,021 combined alcohol and drug abuse facilities were used by 383,525 alcoholic clients. The vast majority of patients, 86%, were seen on an outpatient basis in these facilities, of which 64% were privately supported. During the 12 months prior to the survey, an estimated total of 1,450,000 patients (inflated because those who entered different facilities on different occasions would have been counted more than once) were in treatment.

Table 15.1 also indicates that facilities treated a comparable number of drug abuse clients (351,430) in the 1,266 drug abuse only and 5,021 combined drug abuse and alcohol units. The overall use rate was also close to the 80% found for alcohol units. Most (4,350) units were outpatient facilities, serving 290,712 of the drug abuse clients. About one third of the clientele were young (ages 25-34), and about one third were female. Blacks represented about one quarter and Hispanics about one sixth of the total client population for whom ethnicity was known.

Psychotherapeutic Approaches

Psychotherapy comes in many forms, but the emphasis is on verbal communication between patient and therapist, either in individual or group settings. The communication focuses on the patient's background, current life situation, and motives for drinking in an attempt to give the patient an understanding of the causes of the drinking. After achieving insight about the psychological origins of the drinking, presumably the alcoholic can gain control over the drinking problem.

PSYCHODYNAMIC APPROACHES

Psychodynamic schools of thought interpret alcohol and other drug abuse as a reflection of conflicts (often unconscious) or characterological defects in earlier stages of development. For example, psychoanalytic views hold drug use to be a sign of a negative fixation at the oral stage of development due to negative experiences associated with feeding during infancy. They regard the drug abuser as adept at the use of defense mechanisms and unconscious processes such as denial, rationalization, and projection to cope with the threat represented by the excessive drug use.

Interpretation of the past by the therapist is assumed to break down client defenses, provide insight, and facilitate recovery. However, it may be unwise to strip away the "preferred defense structure" (Wallace, 1985) developed by alcoholics too early in the therapeutic process. These defenses, although maladaptive in the long run, are the only immediate means of coping that the alcoholic has. Other methods must be developed before they will give them up.

Psychodynamic approaches view alcoholism as a symptom of underlying conflict (Leeds & Morgenstern, 1996). Personality precursors are assumed to cause the excessive drinking. Research to evaluate the validity of therapy for alcoholism often has involved poor methodology, with reliance on single cases and no controls. The degree of severity and heterogeneity of alcoholics has been ignored in drawing conclusions.

One proposal for improvement calls for an integration of psychoanalytic concepts with aspects of cognitive behavior modification therapy (E. L. Keller, 1996). This approach is a mixture of Marlatt's relapse prevention model (Marlatt & Gordon, 1985) that uses a behavioral approach to treat the drinking in combination with a psychodynamic model to better identify the underlying factors leading to alcohol and other drug abuse.

Therapy involves a "working alliance" (Greenson, 1967) in which the clients come to identify with the therapist, as they work together on agreed goals. Patient resistance, which refers to patient defenses that impede the operation of the working alliance, is a psychoanalytically based concept. The task of the psychodynamic therapist is then to explore defenses and unconscious conflicts to help establish a working alliance so that the behaviorally based relapse prevention skills can be developed (D. S. Keller, 1996, p. 94).

Critics of psychodynamic approaches question the usefulness of concepts such as denial, which is assumed to be characteristic of alcoholics. This assumption may be unwarranted because a survey (Grant, 1997) of a sample of respondents with a lifetime *DSM-IV* (1994) alcohol use disorder revealed that only 12.7% had at some time recognized a need for alcohol treatment but had not undertaken it.

It was also enlightening to learn what the respondents reported as the reasons for failure to seek treatment. Instead of "denial" or a failure to realize they had a drinking problem, many indicated ambivalence, fear, or embarrassment about public disclosure of a stigmatized problem such as alcoholism. Other reasons reflected feelings that they should be strong enough to handle the problem or that the problem would get better by itself. Because the study relied on self-reports, some of the reasons may have been excuses or rationalizations, but overall they do not support widespread denial among those who did not seek treatment. The use of denial as an explanation for failure to seek treatment is somewhat circular because the only index is the fact that others think you should be in treatment but you are not.

RATIONAL EMOTIVE THERAPY

Rational emotive therapy (RET) places more focus on increasing the client's awareness of present and future motivators of drug use rather than on past or unconscious factors. Based on the views of Albert Ellis (Ellis et al., 1988) that many psychological problems stem from irrational beliefs, the therapist attempts to dispel and correct misconceptions about alcoholism held by the client. By continually questioning and confronting the alcoholic with evidence, the goal is to help the clients realize the illogical and erroneous views they have. Denial is often the reaction of alcoholics to such confrontation who seem to think, "I can't be alcoholic because I don't drink in the morning" or "I only drink wine and beer."

Later, after facts are presented that convince the alcoholic that he or she has a drinking problem, the goal is to help the client realize why he or she is drinking and how to find alternative ways of achieving such goals. RET also helps the client understand the need for abstinence and learn how to overcome irrational beliefs such as, "I need alcohol to relax" or "I am too weak to handle the situation without a drink." Abstinence is difficult to maintain because of other irrational beliefs such as, "No one will like me if I don't drink" or "I'll never have any more fun without alcohol." The therapist tries to modify these cognitions by helping the client obtain disconfirming evidence.

Behavioral Approaches

Behavioral orientations regard alcohol and other drug abuse as similar to any other learned behavior that may be reinforced by outcomes. Thus, initiation into the use of alcohol and other drugs may provide peer acceptance, generate excitement, or release tension and anxiety. Continued use may develop into abuse and dependency so that the user loses control over the voluntary use of the drug. Drug abuse, however, also has negative consequences ranging from physical discomfort to social ostracism. These consequences may deter some from continued use, but others may actually increase drug use to cope with these discomforts.

The behavioral approach to treating alcohol and other drug dependency is based on principles of learning and conditioning theory, many of which were discovered with laboratory studies of humans and other animals. This approach assumes that behaviors such as use of drugs are sustained or reinforced by outcomes such as the physiological and psychological states they produce. Stimuli such as the physical and social context associated with these outcomes from drug use acquire the power to activate future drug use. The same processes should allow us to "unlearn" prior associations and habits or to develop new ones. Hence, one general strategy for treatment might be to attempt to remove these sources of reinforcement, drugs, and the associated stimuli that trigger the motivation to use them. This strategy could be supplemented by the reinforcement of alternative behaviors that interfere with drug taking.

CLASSICAL CONDITIONING

Classical conditioning, a major tradition of learning theory pioneered by Pavlov (1927), involves a relatively passive role for the individual. According to classical conditioning, a subject develops associations between neutral stimuli and consequences so that eventually those stimuli acquire the ability to elicit these responses.

Applying this paradigm, one method of alcoholism treatment—aversive conditioning—pairs unpleasant stimuli with alcohol or alcohol-related stimuli so that eventually the latter elicit negative reactions on their own. Benjamin Rush (1745-1813) observed that mixing a tartar emetic with rum produced an aversion to alcohol in a man who loved to drink (Jellinek, 1943). It is assumed that repeated pairing of drugs or stimuli associated with their use, such as taste and visual cues, with a negative or painful stimulus will make drug users want to avoid the drug in the future. External cues associated with drug use such as hypodermic needles, in the case of injected drugs, could similarly be paired with aversive consequences to create negative associations to drug use.

Aversive conditioning (Rachman & Teasdale, 1969) builds on classical conditioning by repeatedly pairing strong negative stimuli such as electric shock or nausea-producing drugs called emetics with the drinking of alcoholic beverages to reduce the attractiveness of such drinking. Following a series of trials in which alcohol drinking is immediately paired with one of these noxious stimuli, the drinker will experience negative feelings at the very thought of drinking and eventually will avoid alcohol because of the expected noxious outcomes. This paradigm has been the basis for the commercial use of aversive conditioning in alcoholism treatment. A review (Wilson, 1987) of research on aversive conditioning concluded that the benefits of chemical aversion conditioning are low in comparison to the physical risks involved. Another study (Elkins, 1991) concluded that emetic conditioning has a success rate of around 60% in private hospitals.

Irrespective of the effectiveness of aversive conditioning, not all alcoholics are willing to accept this type of treatment, and success may be limited to those who are motivated to participate. Aside from queasiness about the discomfort involved, there is also the real danger of physical harm if the noxious stimuli are too strong.

OPERANT CONDITIONING

Another major tradition in learning theory, **operant conditioning,** holds a view of the learner as an active participant in behavior change. Trial-and-error behavior (Thorndike, 1911) may be involved in which the learner comes to identify which responses lead to which outcomes. The outcomes serve as reinforcers (Skinner, 1938) that are contingent on the responses being made by the individual. Drug use is similar to any other behavior in the sense that it can be reinforced by consequences of that behavior. The user initially finds that the drug leads to positive or pleasurable outcomes and begins to use the drug more often or more heavily.

In theory, drug use should be reduced if it leads to negative consequences. Yet drug abusers often experience severe negative physical and social consequences from their drinking but do not easily reduce their drug use drinking. One reason for this failure of negative consequences lowering the drug behavior drinking is the long temporal gap between the beginning of a specific drinking occasion and the unpleasant consequences.

Some treatment programs have employed *contingency contracting* to reinforce drug abusers when they abstain and when they participate in treatment program activities. For example, requirement of sizable monetary deposits from patients, which they would forfeit if they did not complete the program, was effective in improving attendance (Pomerleau, Pertschuk, Adkins, & Brady, 1978). Use of employment opportunities as a consequence of sobriety was found (Nathan, 1984) to be another effective form of contingency management for alcohol self-regulation.

MOTIVATIONAL ENHANCEMENT

Motivational enhancement training (MET) (Miller, 1995; Miller, Zweben, DiClemente, & Rychtarik, 1995; Monti, Rohsenow, Colby, & Abrams, 1995) emphasizes the use of nonconfrontational techniques to help alcohol abusers develop their own motivation for reducing their drinking. Behavior change is regarded as an active process involving cognitive appraisal by the client rather than a passive process in which therapists control outcomes. The goal is to have the client assume responsibility for wanting to make changes rather than to require change or to directly teach techniques for change.

An initial assessment battery determines the client's drinking patterns, performance on some neuropsychological tasks, results of blood tests, and negative consequences of their drinking. Feedback and explanations are provided to the client and often a significant other during the first of four sessions. In these few counseling sessions, the therapist tries to help clients recognize discrepancies between their current life situations and how they would like their lives to be. The therapist is empathic and supportive. When the client shows resistance by arguing or sidetracking from the issue, the therapist does not challenge the client but instead rolls with the situation. By offering suggestions of ways to change and encouraging clients to actively decide which route to take, MET helps clients develop self-efficacy, the belief that they can influence outcomes.

SOCIAL LEARNING

Social learning theory (Bandura, 1977, 1999) emphasizes processes that allow alcoholics to learn through observation of consequences to others that reductions in drinking behavior lead to desirable consequences or reinforcers such as social approval or better work performance. By imitating other people who have successfully reduced their drinking, alcoholics acquire self-efficacy, the feeling that they can control their drinking. This approach views excessive drinking as a maladaptive and avoidance form of coping with problems, and the goal is to teach active forms of coping that do not involve alcohol when the individual is in situations that entail high risk for drinking. Accordingly, the cognitive-behavioral treatment approach applies learning principles to teach drinkers to change their drinking behavior by changing the outcomes or contingencies of alcohol consumption. In addition, the alcoholic is taught alternative coping behaviors for reducing stress through techniques such as relaxation training and stress management. By mastering these skills, self-control develops. Instead of there being a unidirectional influence in which the environment controls the individual, now there is a bidirectional relationship of reciprocal determinism as the individual's behavior can influence the environment.

An example of one approach emphasizing coping skills (Monti, Gulliver, & Myers, 1994) teaches alcoholics to cope more effectively with interpersonal relationships and intrapersonal feelings and moods such as anger and stress that could lead to the resumption of problematic drinking. The overall perception of stress in a high-risk situation may be lowered if the individual learns coping responses for managing the situation, reducing the need for drinking. Social skills training with models and behavioral rehearsal to improve assertiveness and communication skills can enable the clients to elicit more social support for sobriety. In addition, exposure to alcoholic drinks and related cues is used to help clients learn urge coping skills, including use of alternative coping, distraction, and thinking about the benefits of sobriety and the negative consequences of drinking when tempted by alcohol.

Family Therapy

Family therapy, an approach that shifts the focus of treatment from the individual to the family, has grown rapidly since the 1950s. Originally developed for a variety of psychological problems, it also has been increasingly used for the treatment of the alcoholic family. There is no single type of family therapy because diverse orientations such as psychodynamic and behavioral approaches exist. They differ from the view of Al-Anon, the self-help group described in the preceding chapter, which regards alcoholism as a family disease. Al-Anon urges the nondrinking members to detach from the alcoholic rather than remain as enabling codependents who might contribute toward continued drinking by the alcoholic.

In contrast, family systems theories emphasize the dynamic interactions among family members, requiring a treatment program involving all of them. Family therapists believe it is insufficient to treat only the substance abuser. If other family members know about the drug abuse, as in most cases involving alcohol, they are part of a system of interrelated members who interact with the alcoholic. Just as the alcoholic's drinking and behavior affects them, family members can in turn have a strong effect on the alcoholic.

Comparisons of interactions when alcoholics have been drinking with those that occur when alcoholics have not been drinking are a central goal. Families come to see how their alcoholic family members' drinking disrupts their interactions in harmful ways. Therapy focuses on changing family communication and interaction patterns that occur when alcoholics have been drinking to more constructive and positive behavior.

PSYCHODYNAMIC APPROACHES

Ackerman (1958) was a pioneer in family therapy. Coming from a Freudian psychoanalytic orientation, which emphasizes unconscious intrapsychic conflicts and defense mechanisms as underlying alcoholism, he recognized the need to work with the entire family as an interrelated system in treating any type of psychological problem. Each member of a family system has a role, and boundaries or rules more or less define each member's function. When conflicts arise among family members, communication may break down. Family members may become defensive, anxious, and unable to deal with each other. The therapist must help the family overcome resistance and achieve a new balance of roles among members after its homeostasis has been disrupted by disturbances such as alcoholism.

STRUCTURAL FAMILY THERAPY

Bowen (1978) also viewed many psychological problems as rooted in family relationships. Tensions between any two family members may spread to include a third member, a process called **triangulation.** When two persons have a breakdown of communication, one party may draw a third party into the conflict, someone who may take sides. This process may be repeated so that more interlocking triangles are created, until eventually all family members become enmeshed in the problem.

The therapist also can be regarded as part of a triangle. To be effective, the therapist must not take sides but must maintain emotional contact with both parties in a conflict. Placing more emphasis on cognitive than on emotional reactions, the therapist must help individuals differentiate between their intellectual and emotional feelings. If they fail to do so, they will be less adaptable when faced with stress and be overwhelmed by their emotions. In addition to this intrapsychic goal, individuals need to differentiate "self" from the other family members of "undifferentiated family ego mass." If they succeed, they can freely express their own feelings and not be dominated by the feelings of other family members.

In the case of alcoholism, family members who have the greatest dependence on the alcoholic member are assumed to be the most overly anxious about the problem. This anxiety may lead to criticism of the drinker and emotional isolation from the drinker, factors that might increase the drinking, creating an escalating cycle of events. The family therapist's task is to interrupt and reverse this process by helping family members lower their anxiety and restore emotional contact with the alcoholic member.

Despite clinical evidence of the usefulness of family therapy, the comparative effectiveness of different approaches to family therapy has not been determined (Kaufman, 1985), and controlled evaluations are rare (Thomas, 1989). One problem in comparing studies of family therapy is that there are so many variables in family composition, such as marital status, number of children, living arrangements, and number of drinkers in the family. Also, there is the generalizability issue of whether families willing to enter family therapy are more similar on other important factors than those who do not enter family therapy (Institute of Medicine, 1990).

BEHAVIORAL APPROACHES

Marital family treatment programs involve highly structured sessions with both the alcoholic and nonalcoholic spouse present to work together on improving their relationship (O'Farrell, 1995). The first goal is to reduce abusive drinking. Couples discuss their feelings about the drinking of the alcoholic and may form written contracts about goals for the behavior of each. In later sessions, the focus is on repairing the marital relationship and increasing positive behavioral exchanges between the spouses. The long-term goal is to help prevent relapse and deal with other marital issues.

Behavioral treatment methods for family therapy (McCrady, 1989) emphasize the reciprocal reinforcement system between spouses. The development of improved positive communications involves the nondrinking spouse providing reinforcement to the alcoholic for achieving sobriety.

Spouses are taught how to reinforce nondrinking and to cope with the spouse when drinking does occur.

Studies comparing recovering alcoholics with nonalcoholic controls from the community suggested that marital therapy could be effective in improving the psychological functioning of the spouses and children. One study (Moos, Finney, & Chan, 1981) compared the family environments of alcoholics 2 years after marital therapy with those of nonalcoholic community controls. Two subgroups of alcoholics were identified: the remitted group that had maintained sobriety and the relapsed group that had not. Cohesive, expressive environments relatively free of conflict were found in the homes of both the remitted alcoholics and controls. In contrast, the home environments of relapsed alcoholics were not cohesive, expressive, organized, or free of conflict. Remitted patients were similar to controls in some respects such as depression and physical symptoms, but they still were poorer in other respects such as more use of medical treatment and greater anxiety. The relapsed patients were poorest on all dimensions.

Follow-up studies (Finney & Moos, 1991, 1992) of the 83 members of the original sample of 113 alcoholics who were alive 10 years later upheld the findings observed after the first 2 years at the 10-year follow-up. For more than two thirds of the patients, drinking status and remission or relapse at the 10-year follow-up were the same as they had been at 2 years after treatment.

Alcoholics with more cohesive families, experiencing lower life stress and using active cognitive coping at the 2-year follow-up, were more likely to have better 10-year outcomes. At 10 years, those who showed remission functioned at a level comparable to the matched community control group, and both were superior to the relapsed group.

Unfortunately, evaluative studies such as these, especially those involving random assignment, have high attrition rates and inadequate follow-ups. As more systematic research is conducted, a better understanding of the factors affecting the usefulness of family therapy will be achieved.

TYPICAL 28-DAY TREATMENT PROGRAM

Although variations exist among treatment programs, some common features exist among most 28- to 30-day inpatient alcoholism and drug treatment programs that follow the **Minnesota model of treatment** (Miller, 1998). First, if the patient enters the hospital in a crisis due to excessive drug use, detoxification for several days is needed before counseling and psychotherapy can begin. Severe withdrawal reactions may occur because of the sudden unavailability of drugs such as alcohol and heroin. Medical supervision, drug treatment with benzodiazepines, and nutritional treatment are required to safely manage the detoxification phase.

Then, a mixture of individual and group therapy is used along with didactic educational films and lectures about the physical effects of the drug in question. There is some question as to whether much of the cognitive information is comprehended because even after detoxification, cognitive processes are impaired for a period (McCrady, 1987).

These standard components of the treatment program are often supplemented by recreational and occupational therapy. Self-help in the form of Alcoholics Anonymous, Cocaine Anonymous, or Narcotics Anonymous meetings, depending on which drug is involved, are recommended as supplements, especially after the patient is discharged from the inpatient program.

Pharmacological Approaches

The use of drugs for the treatment of alcoholism has typically been in an adjunct role to ensure the physical safety of intoxicated patients undergoing the adverse effects of withdrawal reactions during detoxification. Benzodiazepines such as Librium® or Valium® are used as an adjunct to relieve anxiety and depression in patients to facilitate their psychological treatment.

A different application is the use of drugs such as disulfiram (Antabuse®) to block the elimination of acetaldehyde, a toxic by-product of alcohol metabolism by the liver. This procedure is a deterrent to drinking by patients in treatment because alcohol consumption while taking this medication produces strong unpleasant physical reactions (Brewer, 1993).

One interesting new use of drugs is the use of naltrexone, an opioid antagonist that is believed to block the effects of alcohol (Volpicelli, Clay, Watson, & Volpicelli, 1995). Some studies have found naltrexone effective in reducing craving and relapse among alcoholics. Finally, increasing the use of antidepressants (Kranzler, 1995) such as desipamine to counter depression and anti-anxiety agents such as imipramine (McGrath, Nunes, & Stewart, 1996) have been employed as adjuncts for treating alcohol dependency.

Evaluation of Treatment Programs

The primary goals of clinical practitioners who conduct psychotherapy with alcohol and other drug abusers are not the same as those of research-oriented evaluators of treatment outcomes. Therapists, depending on their years of training and actual practice in dealing with drug abusers, may be convinced that an effective program does not need scientific evaluation. Psychotherapeutic treatment of individuals does not include controlled evaluation of the effectiveness of procedures or identification of the underlying processes that may be involved in any improvement in the patients. Instead, psychotherapists rely on clinical experience and expertise and attribute any improvement to be due to treatment. Although effective treatment indeed may occur in the absence of objective and rigorous evaluation, such evaluation is vital to scientific researchers in their efforts to identify ineffective or even harmful treatments.

CONTROLS

In practice, sound evaluation of therapy is difficult for a number of reasons. A researcher might want to use an experimental design in which a group of treated drug abusers receives treatment (experimental group), and an otherwise comparable group of drug abusers selected on a random basis (control group) does not receive treatment. However, most treatment facilities do not permit clients to be assigned to untreated control groups, partly because they assume that their program is valid and partly because they cannot ethically justify withholding it from persons in need. Ethical concerns would make therapists reluctant to use untreated control groups, whereas *researchers* would require their inclusion to achieve scientific rigor.

However, alcohol and other drug users who do not receive treatment but do *not* represent a random sample can provide an approximate "control" group for comparison. For example, as Figure 15.1 indicates, some alcohol or other drug users may not seek or accept treatment. Still others may want treatment but may be unable to afford or obtain it. However, when treated groups are compared with these types of untreated groups, it is not clear that any differences can be attributed to the treatment.

Because patients (as well as the therapists) are *not* randomly assigned to the different treated and untreated conditions, they are quite likely to be unequal in respects other than the treatment. Instead, some selective bias may be involved in determining who gets which treatment or who even gets treated at all. For example, the treated patients may be more motivated than the untreated ones. Or they may differ in social class, education level, or some other factor that affects drug use. This selective process is not "wrong" or undesirable, from a practical perspective. If those people who, for whatever reason, receive treatment show improvement, that is a worthwhile outcome. On the other hand, this bias in the methodology compromises the evaluation of the factors responsible for the treatment outcomes and limits the generalizability of outcomes.

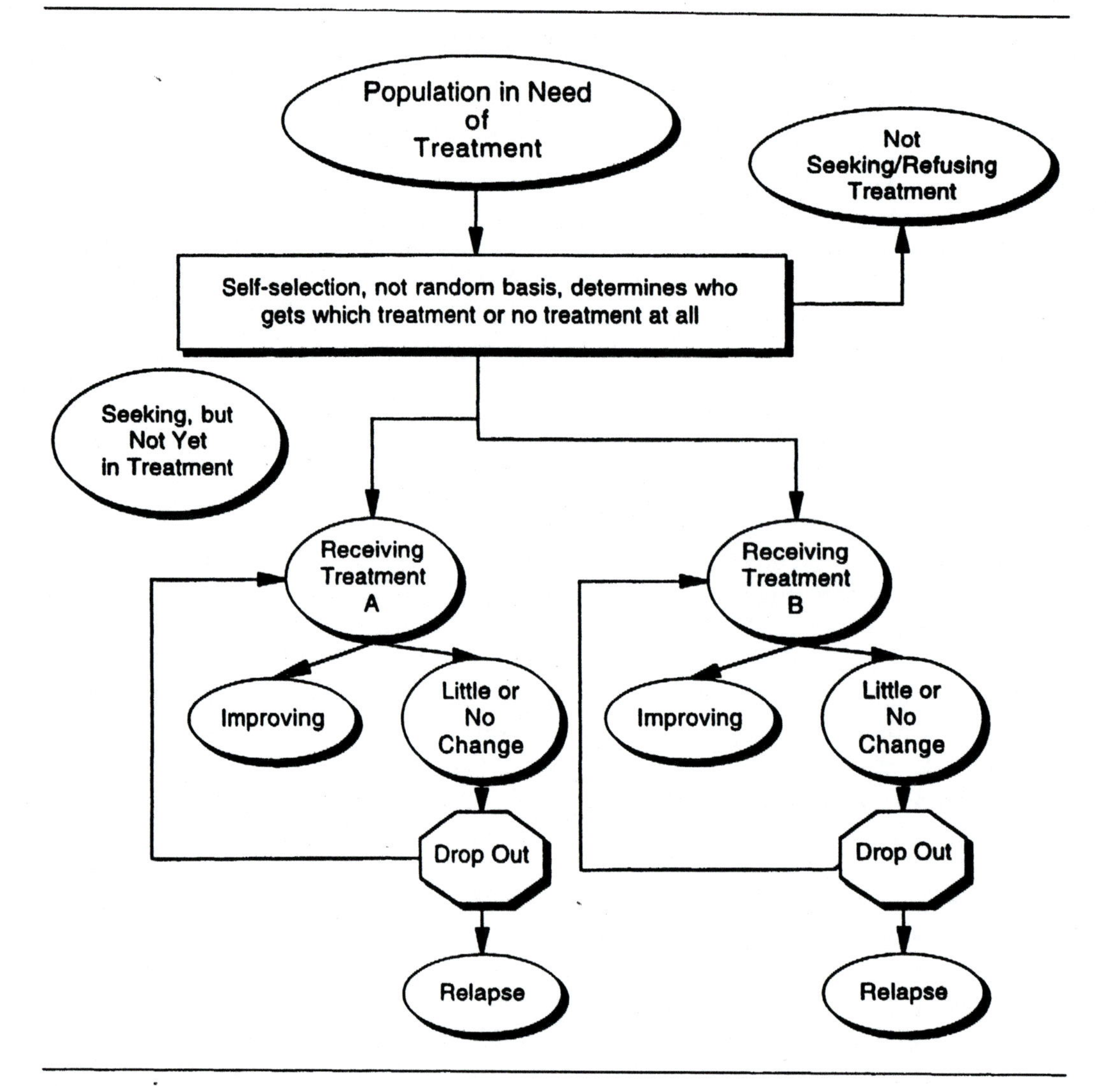

Figure 15.1. Who Gets Which Treatment, If Any, and What Happens to Them?
NOTE: Nonrandom samples make causal interpretation of outcomes difficult, especially if the attrition from different treatments is not comparable.

Figure 15.2 presents a model illustrating how treatment outcomes are affected jointly by various aspects of the treatment, such as its length, setting, or technique, as well as by client characteristics, such as drinking or drug use patterns, physical and psychological attributes, and social background. A focus on either treatment or client variables to the exclusion of the other can present an incomplete picture of the determinants of success or failure from treatment.

Another problem in evaluating treatment is identifying the most effective procedures within a program. Treatments usually involve a "package"

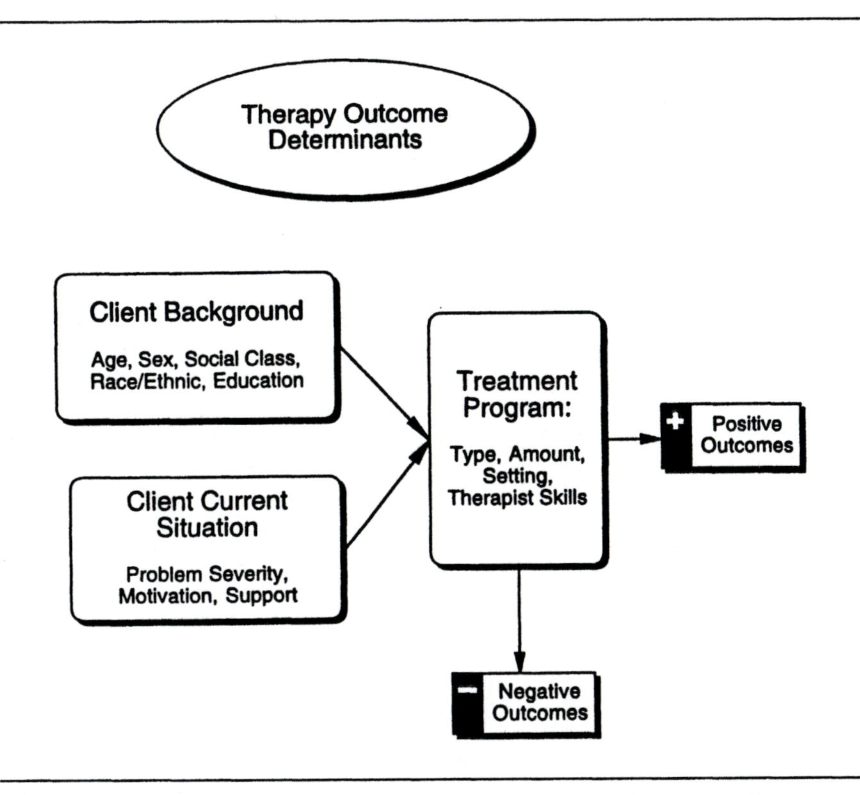

Figure 15.2. Model of Client and Therapist Variables That May Affect Treatment Outcomes

or set of components, as illustrated by Figure 15.3. A typical program may include individual and group psychotherapy, family therapy, exercise, nutrition, and educational films and lectures. If changes occur following treatment, can we determine how much each component contributed to the changes? It is conceivable that some of the components even could have had adverse effects that were masked by the beneficial effects of other components. It is rare to include any types of control groups that do not receive treatment to establish baselines for change over time. Without appropriate control groups, it is not possible to determine the type of effect each treatment component has on client status outcomes, so only the total effect can be established.

ATTRITION

Clients may drop out before the end of a program, as shown earlier in Figure 15.1, creating some difficulties of interpretation. Thus, if the more severe cases drop out, leaving cases that are more amenable to improve-

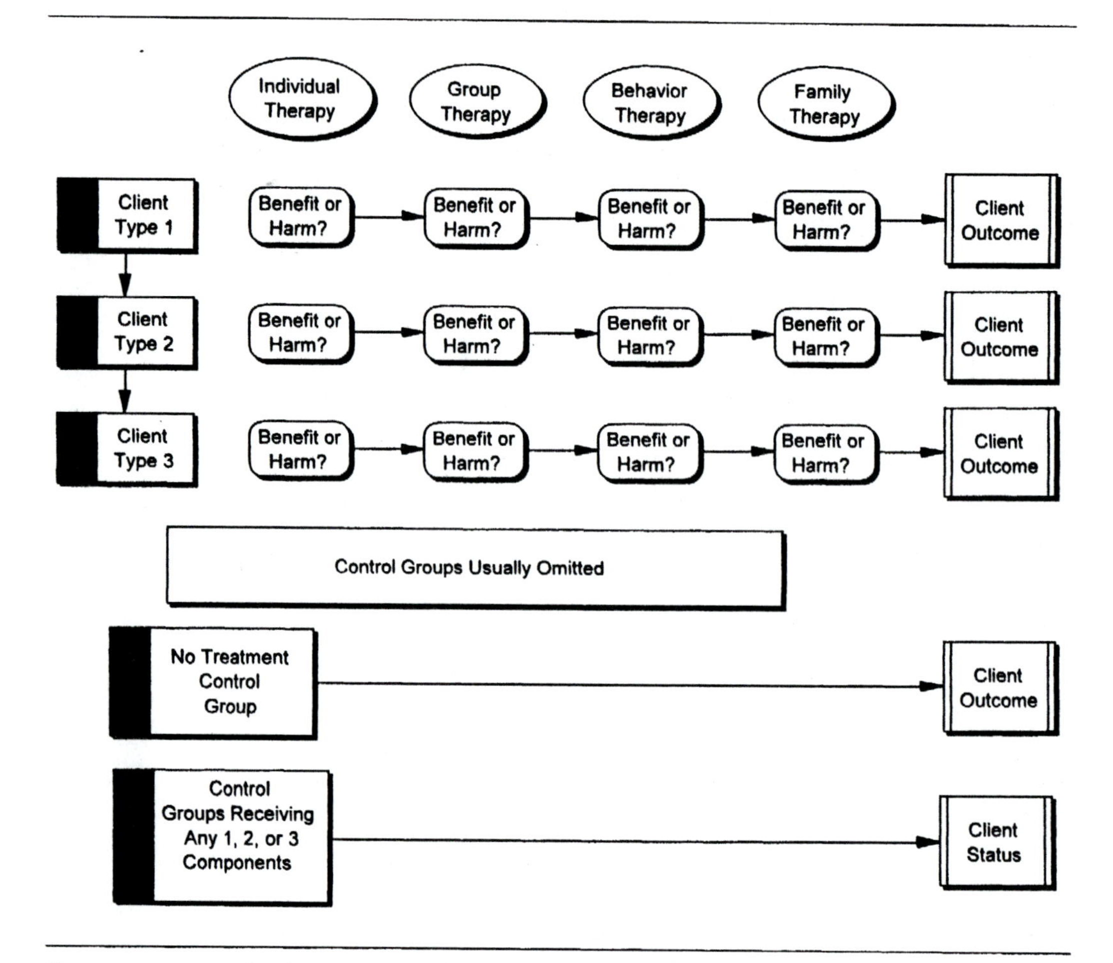

Figure 15.3. Lack of Appropriate Control Groups Make It Difficult to Identify the Effect of Different Components of Treatment Packages on Outcomes

ment, one may conclude erroneously that the treatment was the sole factor responsible for the success. If, for the two programs in Figure 15.1, Treatment A has a greater reduction in drinking than Treatment B, the conclusion that it was more effective would be incorrect if the heavier drinkers dropped out of Treatment A.

Long-term follow-ups, essential for evaluation, are difficult to conduct for alcohol and other drug treatment populations. Once released from treatment, those patients who have no families to return to or steady employment opportunities may become transients with little chance of being relocated later. If contacted, they may have little interest in participating in research, especially if they have suffered relapse from their treatment gains.

SUCCESS RATE

Widely divergent claims of treatment success exist for alcoholism treatment. Individual hospital treatment programs claim success rates as high as 90% (Emrick & Hansen, 1983). A much less optimistic estimate of 7% was made in a study at the nonprofit Rand Corporation (Polich, Armor, & Braiker, 1981). Closer examination of the two reports showed that self-selection bias occurred in the treatment program with the 90% success rate, but the evaluation was based on only the 10% of patients who participated in aftercare programs. The high success rate also may have been due to about one third of the patients being treated twice before they achieved success.

In the Rand study, with only a 7% success rate, more thorough assessment with objective procedures was used. Random sampling of 474 patients at eight different NIAAA-funded alcohol treatment programs were studied over 4.5 years. Less **attrition** occurred, with about 85% of the original patients located for another interview, or they were found to be deceased. In addition, independent measures of drinking levels were obtained and checked against blood alcohol content readings.

TYPE OF TREATMENT

A review (Maisto & Carey, 1987) of 26 published evaluation studies of alcoholism treatment avoided the problem of selective bias affecting the assignment of subjects to treatment conditions. The review looked only at studies involving either random assignment of clients to two or more treatment groups or studies in which clients in different treatment groups were matched on variables related to the outcome measures. A wide variety of treatment approaches were represented in this set of studies. The treatments usually were added as supplements to other prior forms of treatment. Furthermore, pretreatment measures were obtained before administering the treatments. The evaluation was made from 1 to 19 or more months later, depending on the study, with the modal period being 12 months.

The review revealed that the type of treatment was not a factor in effectiveness. Observed improvements across the 26 studies were stable over the observed period of 1 to 2 years. One conclusion might be that improvement was due to a few common aspects embedded throughout the variety of methods used and that some of the differences in treatment were not having any effect. However, the lack of differences in improvement may reflect a "ceiling effect" (Maisto & Carey, 1987), in that the level of improvement was already approaching the maximum when these supplemental treatments were imposed. Another explanation involves the failure to try to match patients to the type of therapy. Treating all alcoholics with the same treatment method may have masked some genuine effects (Finney & Moos, 1986). Thus, if some alcoholics benefit more from one technique but others improve more with a different procedure, the overall results obtained with a single method applied to both populations would show a less impressive average effect.

A comparison (Miller, Brown, et al., 1995) of therapy evaluation studies published since the late 1970s attempted to determine the effectiveness of different treatment programs by combining the results across studies. Each of the 211 studies that were acceptable for the analysis had to have at least two groups—an experimental or treatment group and a control or untreated group or two experimental groups—each receiving a different treatment. In addition, a study must have used random assignment of patients to the different treatments to be included in the analysis. This requirement allows one to rule out other explanations for any differences between the treatment groups.

Results from all studies evaluating a specific type of treatment were combined to provide a measure of overall effectiveness that was based mainly on two factors. One factor, based on several indices, reflected the quality of the evaluation methodology as measured by criteria such as use of objective methods, use of follow-up, proof of no differential attrition or dropout, use of collateral corroboration, adequacy of statistical analyses, and replication.

The second factor was based on the type of research design. If a no-treatment control was used, a score of +2 was given if the treatment was better than the control. If a no-treatment control was omitted, a score of +1 was given if the one treatment was better than the other treatment. The basis for a greater weight when a no-treatment control group was included was that this design can determine if the superior treatment was better (or worse) than no treatment. In contrast, the design without a no-treatment control group can only inform regarding relative benefits (or harm) of the two treatments but cannot indicate if either of the two treatments differed from no treatment.

Conversely, if the treatment being evaluated provided poorer outcomes, it was assigned a score of –2 when there was a no-treatment control and –1 when there was no control group. If no differences were obtained, the study was given a 0 score.

The scores on the two factors for each study were multiplied and totaled across all studies using a specific treatment. The criteria and definitions used in this analysis to measure the effectiveness and methodological rigor of studies may not be acceptable to everyone. Also, conclusions based on cumulative results rather than on specific studies may be misleading.

Using this procedure, the most widely used procedures were among the lowest in demonstrated effectiveness. Thus, educational films, general alcoholism counseling, and psychotherapy—the major components found in the widely used general alcoholism treatment programs following the Minnesota model—were among those with the lowest scores. It must be kept in mind that this index does not prove they were ineffective; it means the studies did not prove they were effective.

In contrast, studies evaluating brief intervention, social skills training, and motivational enhancement and community reinforcement were able to demonstrate that they had high effectiveness. Because Alcoholics Anonymous (AA) had no controlled evaluation studies, it was not possible to evaluate AA with this procedure.

TREATMENT GOALS: ABSTINENCE VERSUS MODERATION

An emotionally charged issue is the question of whether alcoholics in treatment should be abstinent or only reduce drinking to moderate or controlled levels. The ideology of AA and other self-help groups clearly insists on abstinence as the goal. The dictum for an alcoholic to heed is "one drink is too many and a thousand is not enough." Behavioral psychologists, on the other hand, have argued that more alcoholics and other drug abusers might undergo treatment if they were allowed to use their drug moderately rather than to stop completely.

Some clinical studies (Davies, 1962; Lovibond & Caddy, 1970) have provided evidence suggesting it is possible for alcoholics to achieve **controlled drinking**, contrary to the views held by AA. The alcoholics studied seemed to be able to function normally on jobs without relapse, even though they had, on average, up to 5 ounces of absolute alcohol daily; this seemed to refute the assertion that abstinence was a necessary goal for recovery.

Advocates of abstinence hold that it is dangerous for recovering alcoholics to drink at all because they might lose control. Whether recovering alcoholics *should* drink, even at a moderate level, and whether they *can* drink moderately are separate questions. Behaviorists have insisted that the latter issue be resolved empirically by comparison of alcoholics treated under the two different criteria of abstinence and controlled drinking.

CONTROLLED DRINKING CONTROVERSY

In the 1960s, psychologists with a behavioral orientation challenged the disease conception of alcoholism that held that alcoholics had to achieve abstinence before treatment could be successful. Jellinek (1960) argued that once an alcoholic drinks, the alcohol activates loss of control physiologically.

However, operant conditioning techniques that were successful in reinforcing contingencies between specific behaviors and rewarding consequences in many other areas have been applied to drinking behavior. Thus, contrary to Jellinek's view, some evidence suggests that alcoholics could be trained to drink at levels that do not lead to problems. A controlled experiment in Australia (Lovibond & Caddy, 1970) found that alcoholics could maintain moderate drinking levels even after periods up to 2 years after treatment.

Evidence of controlled drinking (Sobell & Sobell, 1973) was found in male alcoholics under treatment for 4 weeks in an inpatient hospital setting. A randomized control group design involved two experimental groups that received a package of treatments, with one group given a criterion of abstinence and the other a goal of controlled drinking. This treatment included procedures such as blood alcohol content discrimination training, aversive conditioning, assertion training, and counseling. Two control groups received the conventional programs used in the past at the hospital, again with one having a controlled drinking goal and one given an abstinence criterion.

At both the 6-month and 1-year follow-ups, the treated experimental groups showed better improvement than the control groups. Importantly, the abstinent groups were no better than the groups that had been allowed to drink moderately, leading to the conclusion that controlled drinking was possible for alcoholics.

AA advocates and others criticized the findings because they felt it would tempt many recovering alcoholics to abandon their abstinence and to experiment with controlled drinking, a practice with the potential to undermine their continued sobriety. In addition, questions about the authenticity of the data led critics (Pendery, Maltzman, & West, 1982) to conduct their own investigation with a follow-up of the controlled drinking patients who had been in Sobell and Sobell's (1973) study 10 years earlier. It revealed a high number of relapses in the first year among this group. Also, the follow-up revealed that several of the treated alcoholics in this group had relapsed into alcoholic drinking, and four had died of alcohol-related complications. Unfortunately, they made no follow-up of the abstinence group, so it is not possible to interpret these results meaningfully.

Eventually, allegations of fraud were raised against the Sobells (Boffey, 1982). After a thorough evaluation, no proof of fraud could be established by a special committee of independent investigators (Dickens, Doob, Warwick, & Winegard, 1982) formed by the Addiction Research Foundation of Canada to study the evidence.

Analysis of data from a study of a random sample of more than 1,300 male alcoholics treated at 8 of the 44 federally funded alcoholism treatment centers located across the nation is relevant to this issue (Armor, Polich, & Stambul, 1978). Some of these alcoholics had resumed "controlled" drinking, defined at a somewhat high level of 3 to 5 ounces on a typical day, but were not reporting any problems. In comparison to an untreated control group of alcoholics that had a remission of drinking problems for only 50%, the treated alcoholics, overall, showed a 70% remission rate a year later. However, a controversial finding was that the relapse rates at 18 months after treatment were no different among those who had been engaged in controlled drinking and those who were totally abstinent when assessed at 6 months after treatment assessment. The implication was that it did not make any difference whether alcoholics were abstinent or drinking in moderation 6 months after treatment because relapse was at the same rate for both groups 18 months after treatment.

AA advocates and others attacked the study on a number of procedural grounds. The charge also was made that even if the results were valid, it was irresponsible to publish them because it might undermine the recovery of many alcoholics who would be tempted to try to drink in moderation but not be able to succeed. It was also held that the alcoholics tested were probably not really alcoholics, only heavy drinkers. In other words, critics of controlled drinking defined alcoholics as drinkers who cannot drink in moderation. By this definition, any evidence that some alcoholics can drink moderately can simply be dismissed on the grounds that this sample could not have consisted of true alcoholics. Thus, circular definitions prevent the issue from being tested. An objective definition of *alcoholic* is needed, but there is no consensus of what it should be.

A 4-year follow-up (Polich et al., 1981) further studied 922 of the male alcoholics of the first study (Armor et al., 1978). Relapse was found in 41% of the alcoholics who had been drinking in moderation 18 months after treatment as compared with only 30% of alcoholics who were abstinent 18 months after treatment. In other words, when a longer time period than the 18-month interval of the original study was used, abstinence appeared to have been more successful in preventing relapse. If alcoholism is not viewed as a condition that involves a steady progression, as is popularly thought, but rather as one of unstable fluctuation, use of too short a period for defining abstinence may lead to inaccurate and unreliable measurement (Polich et al., 1981). Longer periods of evaluation following treatment are needed to measure accurately the effects of treatment.

A review of 22 independent studies (Miller, 1983) found only one in which controlled drinking was unsuccessful for large percentages of varying types of patients throughout the country. Less than 5% of alcoholics examined were able to exercise controlled drinking (Helzer, Robins, & Taylor, 1986). However, techniques for monitoring drinking were not taught to these patients as part of their treatment, so these findings are not strong evidence that controlled drinking cannot work.

In one study (Foy et al., 1984) that directly compared controlled drinking and abstinence goals, controlled drinking was associated with more alcohol abuse at a 6-month follow-up, but there was no difference at 1 year after treatment. A follow-up of clients after 5 to 6 years (Rychtarik, Foy, Scott, Lokey, & Prue, 1987) also found no difference between the two treatment criteria, but interestingly, controlled drinking occurred for about one fifth of the patients. In contrast, controlled drinking was associated with fewer relapses for a follow-up about 20 years later of 60 Swedish male alcoholics (Nordstrom & Berglund, 1987). Some of the conflicting evidence may be because the severity of alcoholism may determine which goal works, with controlled drinking succeeding only for those with lower dependence and abstinence being more effective for those with severe dependence (Miller, Leckman, Delaney, & Tinkcom, 1992).

The interest in controlled drinking as a treatment option has declined since the 1970s. Abstinence now appears to be the primary treatment goal. Nathan (1992), an early advocate of controlled drinking, became a proponent for abstinence and maintained that the evidence had not upheld the original promise that controlled drinking showed in the 1970s. On the other side, Peele (1992) charged that the politically charged atmosphere intimidated the controlled drinking proponents from further evaluation of its potential.

INPATIENT VERSUS OUTPATIENT TREATMENT

Alcoholism treatment often involves inpatient (residential) treatment, at least for acute withdrawal. One advantage of inpatient care is the continual supervision of the patient by a staff of professionals, but the cost for the typical 28-day hospital stay for alcoholism often exceeds $15,000, whereas outpatient treatment typically costs about 10% of that amount. In the 1970s, patients with health insurance received inpatient treatment, but with the changing trend toward containment of health care costs in the 1990s, there is more reliance on outpatient care. In contrast, with illegal drugs such as cocaine or heroin, therapy has been based primarily on outpatient programs and residential treatment facilities known as therapeutic communities (TC) such as Synanon and Phoenix House. These publicly funded programs offer a supportive and highly structured living environment that deals not only with drug problems but provides counseling, education, and discipline.

Do inpatient programs provide more effective treatment than outpatient care? A review (Miller & Hester, 1986a) of 26 controlled studies of alcohol treatment concluded that the more costly residential programs did not show more effective treatment. Inpatient programs varying in duration of stay did not show any differences in success either. Some studies have indicated otherwise, finding that longer stays led to less remission, but such studies are typically confounded by factors such as higher motivation or socioeconomic status of patients undergoing lengthier and more costly treatment.

DURATION OF TREATMENT

Treatment programs vary in duration, with most ranging from a few weeks to 1 or 2 months for alcohol dependency. Does the duration or amount of treatment affect treatment outcomes? Comparisons of treatment effectiveness often are measured by abstinence rates at follow-up after intervals from a few months to 1 or 2 years after treatment. Examination of success across programs of varying duration has shown more abstinence with longer treatment programs (Welte, Hynes, Sokolov, & Lyons, 1981a, 1981b). However, it is not clear that length of treatment is responsible for these outcomes because those who can afford lengthier treatment may improve for other reasons.

Similarly, conclusions from comparisons of treatment duration within a given treatment program also must be qualified. Those who receive shorter treatment may have dropped out because they were less motivated or not showing improvement, whereas those who remain for the full treatment may have been less severe cases (Chapman & Huygens, 1988; Welte et al., 1981a). A review of research on this issue (Smart, 1978) found that those who received longer treatment showed better outcomes, but because the duration of treatment was not randomly assigned to clients, causal interpretations of the length of treatment are not warranted.

Studies that employed random assignment of alcoholics to different durations of treatment have failed to show that longer treatment is any better than briefer treatment. One study (Walker, Donovan, Kivlahan, & O'Leary, 1983) that randomly assigned alcoholics to 2 or 7 weeks of hospital treatment found no differences in the amount of improvement. Those who did continue with weekly aftercare meetings for 9 months, however, were more likely to remain abstinent. Another study (Powell, Penick, Read, & Ludwig, 1985) used random assignment of male alcoholics to one of three outpatient treatments that varied in intensity. All groups improved, but none was superior.

NONDRINKING OUTCOMES

In evaluating treatment effectiveness, one must specify one or more outcomes that are expected to occur. What should be the criteria of success of a program? Although it would seem obvious that reduction or cessation of alcohol use is necessary, it is important to include other criteria such as psychological well-being, work productivity, interpersonal relationships, and family behavior. If drinking stops but other problems persist, it would be difficult to conclude that success has occurred.

Other Treatment Issues

Other issues relating to treatment of alcohol and drug dependency include the question of the effectiveness of brief therapy, the importance of early detection, the importance of matching patients to treatment, the role of motivation in treatment, and the possibility of natural recovery.

BRIEF THERAPY

In addition to the major approaches to therapy already discussed, some forms of "brief therapy" may be effective, at least for some individuals. For example, a provocative study of 99 married male alcoholics (Orford & Edwards, 1977) suggested that conventional treatment involving abstinence for a randomly selected subgroup was no more effective than a single session of advice and counseling regarding the need to reduce drinking. Each couple in the advice group met with a psychiatrist who told them that the husband had alcoholism and should abstain from drinking and that it was up to them to handle the problem. In the treatment group, the couple were offered a yearlong program, including AA and access to prescription drugs to reduce withdrawal symptoms. By the end of the treatment, only 11 of the total sample were abstainers, and there was no difference between the advice and treatment groups. On the surface, this study would appear to suggest that at least some types of alcoholics could achieve effective change with the briefest of treatments. However, it would be dangerous to generalize this conclusion to all types of alcoholics. This effect may be limited to alcoholics who have milder levels of alcohol dependence. Furthermore, the duration of the effectiveness of this brief therapy also needs to be determined.

Other forms of brief therapy include *bibliotherapy*, a term referring to the use of a handbook or manual instructing the alcoholic how to manage his or her own drinking levels. Self-therapy guides have been developed (Miller & Taylor, 1980; Sobell & Sobell, 1993) to help problem drinkers achieve controlled drinking through a variety of self-monitoring activities and stress reduction exercises. One study (Sanchez-Craig, Leigh, Spivak, & Lei, 1989) compared men and women problem drinkers who were randomly assigned to three forms of brief therapy based on cognitive and behavioral change. Two therapy programs involved self-help manuals, and the other employed a therapist teaching the same concepts. Females were found to benefit more, especially with the self-help versions of the therapy.

EARLY DETECTION

For any type of psychological disorder, earlier detection allows earlier participation in treatment. A major goal of alcohol and drug treatment, therefore, has been to find ways of early detection in hopes that more severe problems can be prevented from occurring.

Screening

For instance, if individuals simply complete a short written questionnaire and self-diagnose the extent to which they may be having problems, it might help identify alcohol and drug problems at an earlier stage. Such an instrument would be inexpensive and readily available so that large numbers of people could, if they wished, be tested. Early **screening**, if accurate, could facilitate early intervention.

The Michigan Alcoholism Screening Test (MAST) (Selzer, 1971) was one of the first such surveys. It consists of 25 items dealing with questions of drinking, opinions of friends and relatives about their drinking, alcohol-related problems, and symptoms related to alcohol dependence. A shorter 10-item form, the Brief MAST, is shown in Figure 15.4.

Use of this screening test with alcoholics has been effective in accurately identifying a high percentage of them as alcoholic. However, the test requires that honest answers be given, and it is easy to fake because it is obvious which answers indicate alcohol problems. Treated alcoholics already

Questions *Circle Correct Answers*		
1. Do you feel you are a normal drinker?	Yes (0)	No (2)
2. Do friends or relatives think you are a normal drinker?	Yes (0)	No (2)
3. Have you ever attended a meeting of Alcoholics Anonymous (AA)?	Yes (5)	No (0)
4. Have you ever lost friends or girlfriends/boyfriends because of drinking?	Yes (2)	No (0)
5. Have you ever gotten into trouble at work because of drinking?	Yes (2)	No (0)
6. Have you ever neglected your obligations, your family, or your work for 2 or more days in a row because you were drinking?	Yes (2)	No (0)
7. Have you ever had delirium tremens (DTs), severe shaking, heard voices, or seen things that weren't there after heavy drinking?	Yes (2)	No (0)
8. Have you ever gone to anyone for help about your drinking?	Yes (5)	No (0)
9. Have you ever been in a hospital because of drinking?	Yes (5)	No (0)
10. Have you ever been arrested for drunk driving or driving after drinking?	Yes (2)	No (0)

Figure 15.4. Brief Alcoholism Screening Test (MAST)
SOURCE: Allen and Columbus (1995).

have come to admit or accept their diagnosis of alcoholism; however, whether the scale would be as successful in identifying alcoholics who are not yet in treatment is a different issue. Another question is the level of false positives, individuals who are erroneously classified as alcoholics.

A review (Storgaard, Nielsen, & Gluud, 1994) of validity studies of the MAST found wide variations in validity for studies conducted over 20 years because they varied considerably in the prevalence of alcohol problems, diagnostic criteria, and the examined patient categories. Factors with the largest effect on predictive values were the prevalence of alcohol problems, the diagnostic method against which the MAST was validated, and the populations on which the MAST was applied.

MATCHING PATIENTS AND TREATMENTS

All alcohol- and drug-dependent individuals do not have the same patterns, causes, or consequences of their drinking. Moreover, individual differences in the types of treatments are acceptable to different drug-dependent persons. Consequently, a given treatment method might be effective for some patients but prove useless for others. Accordingly, the strategy of treatment matching developed, which attempted to provide different types of alcoholics with different treatment methods.

Matching is a form of screening to identify which alcoholics are more likely to be successful with a particular treatment (Miller & Hester,

1986b). There is nothing to be gained trying to treat patients with a specific program if they probably would not benefit from it. If treatment resources are scarce, as is usually the case, matching might allow someone who could benefit from a specific treatment to have a better chance of receiving it.

In one study, researchers (Babor, Kranzler, & Lauerman, 1989) used a battery of tests—including a physical exam, lab tests, diagnostic interviews, personality tests, and two self-report inventories administered to alcoholic and nonalcoholic males and females—in an attempt to determine if any one screening test worked best. Scores on these tests correlated reasonably well with established screening tests such as the MAST and MacAndrew alcoholism scales. Self-report items dealing specifically with alcohol content were best at differentiating among males but were less effective at identifying high-risk females. There may be no one best method for screening because the purpose of the screening and the characteristics of the sample also must be considered.

One study (Kadden, Getter, Cooney, & Litt, 1989) illustrated the usefulness of matching alcoholics for either a coping skills treatment or an interactional group therapy treatment. The coping skills treatment attempted to teach behavioral skills for coping with situations that lead to drinking, and the interactional group therapy treatment promoted cohesive groups involved in emotional closeness and self-disclosure. Male and female alcoholics were randomly assigned to one of the approaches. Coping skills training was more successful for alcoholics considered high in sociopathy and psychopathology, whereas interactional group therapy was more effective for those low in sociopathy.

In another study (Cooney, Kadden, Litt, & Getter, 1991), patients who were found to be mismatched with type of therapy were found to be less successful than matched patients in outcomes 2 years later. Inpatient clients were randomly assigned to aftercare group treatment with either coping skills training or interactional therapy. It was hypothesized that individuals scoring high on measures of sociopathy or global psychopathology have better outcomes in coping skills treatment, whereas patients low on these dimensions have better outcomes in interactional treatment. Contrary to the original hypothesis, patients with cognitive impairment had better outcomes in interactional treatment, and patients without cognitive impairment did better in coping skills treatment.

One study compared three different treatments over 18 months: brief broad spectrum (BBS), extended relationship enhancement (ERE), or extended cognitive-behavioral (ECB) with 188 patients randomly assigned to one of the three treatments (Longabaugh, Wirtz, Beattie, Noel, & Stout, 1995). The ERE treatment was significantly more effective in increasing abstinence of patients entering treatment with a network unsupportive of

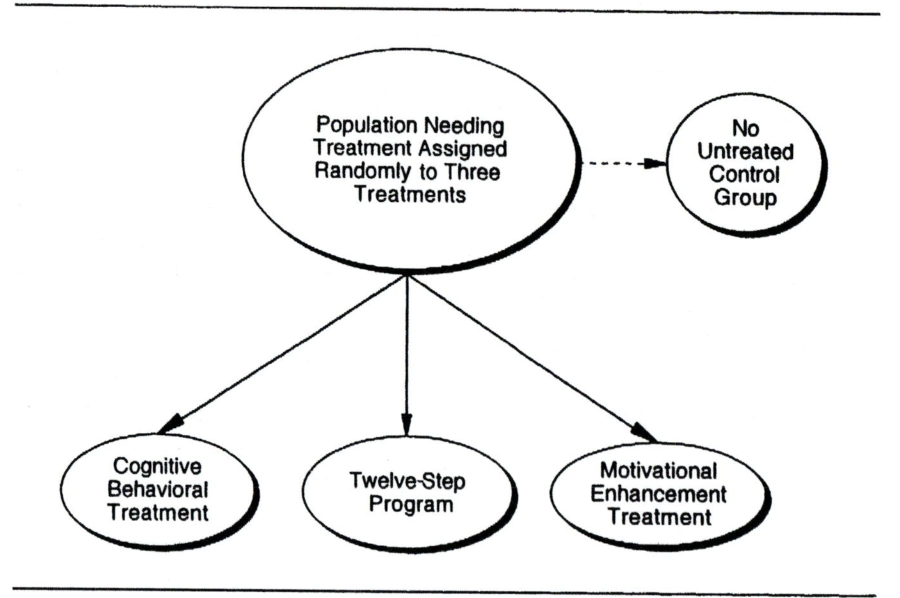

Figure 15.5. Project MATCH Design Showing How Clients Are Randomly Assigned to Three Different Treatments
NOTE: A no-treatment control condition was not included.

abstinence or with a low level of investment in their network, whereas BBS treatment was more effective for patients with either (a) both a social network unsupportive of abstinence and a low level of network investment or (b) high investment in a network supportive of abstinence.

Outcomes for the ECB condition were neither as good as for those who were matched nor as bad as for those who were mismatched to the different exposures of relationship enhancement. This suggests that dose of relationship enhancement should be determined after assessing patient relationships.

A major evaluation (National Institute on Alcohol Abuse and Alcoholism, Alcoholism Treatments to Client Heterogeneity) was sponsored by the NIAAA at a cost of $27 million and requiring more than 8 years to conduct. Using *DSM-IV* (1994) criteria to define alcohol dependency, 774 inpatients and 952 outpatients, mostly male, were randomly assigned to one of three individually administered treatments, cognitive-behavioral coping skills, 12-step facilitation treatment (which involves aspects of AA), and motivational enhancement treatment (MET), as diagrammed in Figure 15.5.

The cognitive-behavioral therapy program was based on social learning use of alcohol to cope with problems. The goal of this approach was to teach alternative coping and problem-solving techniques for dealing with situations that represent high risk for drinking. Twelve weekly sessions were used to teach coping skills for dealing with intra- and interpersonal problems, including anger, depression, and anxiety. Active participation accompanied by modeling and practice with positive corrective feedback were essential aspects of the program.

The 12-step facilitation program was a structured program based on the 12 steps of the well-known AA program. Indeed, patients were encouraged to also attend AA meetings. The emphasis of this program of 12 weekly sessions was on a view of alcoholism as a spiritual as well as a medical disease.

Finally, motivational enhancement therapy involved four sessions distributed over 12 weeks that used techniques for initiating immediate internally motivated changes. Two sessions were directed toward identification of present and future plans and toward instigating motivation for change. Two final sessions offered reinforcement from the therapist for progress and assessment with feedback to the client.

Demonstration of matching would refute extreme views about treatment that "everything works about equally well" or "there is one superior treatment," both of which are probably myths (Miller, 1990). It was hypothesized that one type of treatment would work well for some alcoholics, but another type of treatment would be better for others. In other words, there would be an interaction between type of method and characteristics of alcoholics.

Ten client characteristics that previous research had suggested might be useful as matching variables were measured. For example, both cognitive-behavioral and 12-step therapies were expected to work for patients with higher alcohol involvement because they needed the more extensive treatments. Motivational enhancement was hypothesized to be best for clients with high conceptual ability and low readiness to change.

Clients were evaluated at intake and every 3 months from the 3rd to the 15th month. Assessments were taken of drinking, psychological functioning, and consequences of drinking. Compliance of patients was extraordinarily high, and they all received substantial amounts of treatment. Although a high percentage of clients showed improvement in achieving abstinence (National Institute on Alcohol Abuse and Alcoholism, 1997), the overall success rates did not significantly differ across methods. Unfortunately, for the matching hypothesis, the predicted interactions between treatment method and type of alcoholic were not found. However, unexpectedly, psychiatric severity did interact with treatment. Thus, for low-psychiatric severity outpatients, 12-step facilitation treatment led to more abstinent days than did cognitive-behavioral therapy, but there were no differences between methods for outpatients with high psychiatric severity.

On the positive side, all groups showed improvements for most of the first year, suggesting that lack of differences between treatment might have reflected a ceiling effect in which there was little room for improvement. However, by the end of the year, a high percentage of patients relapsed according to the definition of using alcohol again. But when measured by the number of abstinent days, large increases occurred between the beginning and the end of the treatment.

Critique

A no-treatment control group was not included in the research design, but the researchers held that the improvement from baseline to follow-up points was so pronounced as to leave little doubt that the treatments all worked, but equally well. Still, having a no-treatment control would have been worthwhile because some improvement may occur without formal treatment. All of the gains in the treated groups may not be attributable to specific treatments because some remission may occur over the duration of the treatment.

A key methodological procedure was the random assignment of patients to the type of treatment, a design feature that can be viewed as either a strength or weakness of the study. Under typical procedures, different types of persons may be selectively attracted to different types of programs. However, under such conditions, rates of success of different programs cannot be clearly attributed to the nature of the program because the types of clients attending each type of program also would differ. The program with the highest success might just happen to have fewer severely impaired drinkers, and these drinkers might have done just as well even if they had received one of the other types of treatment.

Random assignment of patients to treatment method avoids this problem of interpretation of findings because it prevents self-selection into different treatment by patients. On the other hand, patients who might have strong preferences for one type of program but who are assigned to a different type may not do as well as they might if they had been allowed to receive their preferred type of treatment. Although randomized assignment is scientifically necessary and justifiable, in the real world, patients are not randomly assigned to treatment. They often select methods in which they have faith and expect to have success. When treatments are randomly assigned, many alcoholics may not have confidence in the efficacy of the method to which they were assigned and consequently not do as well.

Despite the thoroughness and magnitude of the study, it compared only three treatment methods. It is conceivable that there might have been support for the matching hypothesis if other methods had been included or if other delivery systems had been used (e.g., group vs. individual or inpatient vs. outpatient). The outcomes were assessed after 1 year only; a longer-term evaluation might yet disclose differences that would support the matching hypothesis. Over time, relapse rates, for example, might differ for different treatment methods and different types of alcoholics.

Although the sample was diverse, it cannot be claimed that it included all types of alcoholics. It is conceivable that patients with different attributes may have reacted differently to the treatments used. Thus, most of the patients were male, and different results may have occurred with female patients.

A review of studies on matching (Mattson & Allen, 1991) concluded that the best variables to use for matching are not yet known. Moreover, the improvements in treatment outcomes have been modest, typically around 10%. In view of the added costs and effort, it remains to be seen whether many treatment providers will undertake the changes involved in offering more individualized treatment programs for different types of clients.

THE ROLE OF MOTIVATION IN TREATMENT

When treatment fails, it is often attributed to the client's lack of motivation, not to the lack of therapist skill or to the inappropriateness of the treatment. In keeping with the general view of the alcoholic as someone with inadequate coping skills or low self-esteem, this accusation of low motivation is not surprising. There is the danger of self-fulfilling prophecies whereby the therapists' expectations that the alcoholics will not be motivated increase the likelihood that treatment will fail (Miller, 1985). Of course, those patients who do successfully complete treatment are credited with high motivation. The definition of motivation, then, is circular and irrefutable and hardly useful as an explanation.

Internalized motivations (IMs) and external motivations (EMs) of patients for treatment, as well as confidence in the treatment and orientation toward interpersonal help seeking, may all be involved. IM was associated with greater patient involvement and retention in treatment (Ryan, Plant, & O'Malley, 1995). Patients high in both IM and EM demonstrated the best attendance and treatment retention, and those low in IM showed the poorest treatment response, regardless of the level of EM.

A two-session motivational checkup was given in one study (Miller, Benefield, & Tonigan, 1993) to male and female problem drinkers who were randomly assigned to three groups: (a) immediate checkup with directive-confrontational counseling, (b) immediate checkup with client-centered counseling, or (c) delayed checkup (waiting list control). Overall, there was a 57% reduction in drinking within 6 weeks, which was maintained at 1 year. Immediate checkup clients had a significant reduction in drinking relative to controls. The two counseling styles were discriminable on therapist behaviors. The directive-confrontational style yielded significantly more resistance from clients, which in turn predicted poorer outcomes at 1 year. Therapist styles did not differ in overall impact on drinking, but the more the therapist confronted the client, the more the client drank at the 1-year follow-up.

Treatment of Abuse and Dependency on Other Drugs

Many of the same issues related to the evaluation of alcoholism treatment apply to treatment of dependency with other drugs. Since the 1970s, three major large-scale national evaluations of drug treatment effectiveness have included thousands of drug users receiving treatment in many hospitals and clinics across the United States. The first study, prompted by the recognition of the rapidly growing drug problem, was conducted in the early 1970s. Started as a patient-reporting database, the **Drug Abuse Reporting Program (DARP)** was based on 44,000 clients in 52 federally funded treatment programs. Results showed that community-based drug abuse treatment reduced drug use and criminal behavior (Simpson, Chatham, & Brown, 1995).

In the late 1970s, the **Treatment Outcome Prospective Study (TOPS)** provided longitudinal evidence up to 5 years on the effectiveness of federally funded treatment facilities (Ginsburg, 1978). This study involved 11,000 patients in 41 treatment programs in 10 cities. It expanded on the DARP by examining the relationship of patient characteristics, program environments, and available treatment services to outcomes. Results showed that treatment reduced use of heroin and other illicit drugs during as well as following treatment. The reduction in social costs related to predatory crime showed that the treatment was cost-beneficial (Hubbard et al., 1989).

By the early 1980s, the "war on drugs" seemed to be winning, and drug abuse dimmed in public and governmental priority. Economic inflation and federal budgetary problems also lessened the fiscal support of drug treatment. Funding dropped about 25% in the 1981 Omnibus Budget Reconciliation Act, and funds were allocated to the states via block grants that eliminated the federal control of how the monies were used. About the same time, several major developments created upward shifts in the levels and types of drug use and related problems. Cocaine became cheaper, more widely available, and available in its more potent smokable form, crack. Heroin use increased, and the use of needles increased the risk of infection from the rapidly rising HIV and AIDS epidemic (Fletcher, Tims, & Brown, 1997).

DATOS

The rapidly changing drug scene made it likely that the evidence on drug abuse from the earlier evaluations might no longer be valid. Consequently, the National Institute on Drug Abuse initiated a major study, the **Drug Abuse Treatment Outcome Study (DATOS)**, which tracked 10,010 drug abusers in nearly 100 treatment programs in 11 cities from 1991 to 1993. Only about 75% of the original sample could be located after 1 year, of which about 70% were successfully interviewed.

The patients in different types of programs differed in their characteristics and drug use pattern. Most programs fell into one of four major types of drug abuse treatment: outpatient methadone treatment (OMT), outpatient drug-free (ODF) behavioral treatment, long-term residential treatment (LTR), and short-term inpatient (STI) treatment, as indicated in Figure 15.6, which identifies the major methods for each type of facility. All four treatment modalities typically included supportive group therapy, urine monitoring during treatment, relapse prevention, and posttreatment involvement in self-help groups (Flynn, Craddock, Hubbard, Anderson, & Etheridge, 1997).

Overall, most patients were male (66%); 47% were African American, and 13% were Hispanic. Most of these patients were young but had been long-term drug users with the average age at first treatment being 29.5 years and patients reporting having been addicted for 10 to 15 years on average before first entering treatment. The average age of a patient entering treatment was 32.6 years.

Figure 15.7 presents some of the characteristics of patients for each of the four treatment types. Although the treatments were similar in the percentage of male clients, they differed considerably on some other factors. OMT clients tended to be older and had longer treatment duration; LTR clients were least likely to be married or have health insurance. ODF clients were most likely to be referred by courts and to be African American or Hispanic. STI patients were most likely to be married, have health insurance, and have the least likelihood of treatment more than 3 months.

Although patients were often described in terms of their primary drug problem, most of them were polydrug abusers; 97% had used alcohol, 95% used cocaine, and 46% reported having used heroin before entering treatment. A random sample was selected for follow-up, and nearly 3,000 patients were interviewed a year later to assess drug use and behavioral

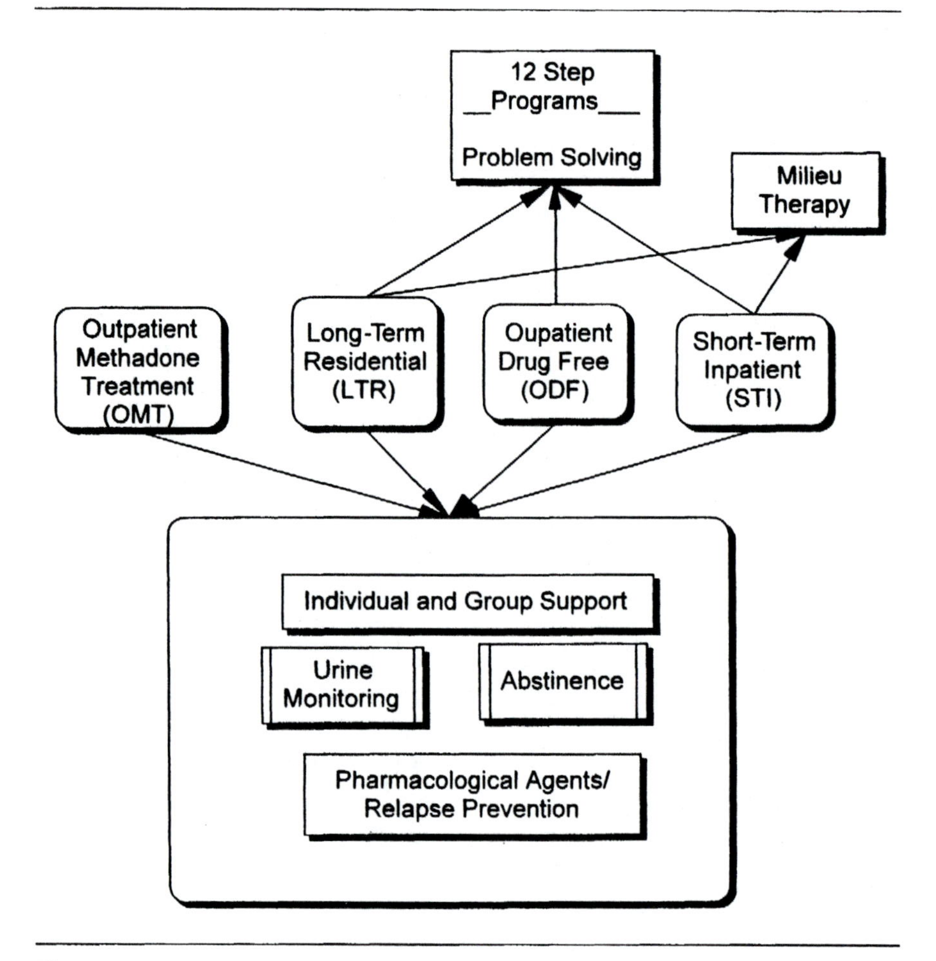

Figure 15.6. Major Components in Four Drug Treatment Programs in the Drug Abuse Treatment Outcome Study (DATOS)

functioning. Self-report was used widely, although urine testing also was employed, so that gross distortions in reports of drug use could be detected.

All treatment programs were successful to some degree at a 1-year follow-up (Hubbard, Craddock, Flynn, Anderson, & Etheridge, 1997). Length of treatment was important because reductions in drug use were significantly greater for patients with moderate to severe problems if they were in treatment for 3 months or more (Simpson, Joe, Fletcher, Hubbard, & Anglin, 1999).

Figure 15.8 indicates that between admission and the 1-year follow-up, there was less overall drug use. Methadone treatment reduced heroin use by 60%. In the follow-up year, only 27.8% of OMT patients reported weekly or more frequent heroin use, compared to 89.4% reporting heroin

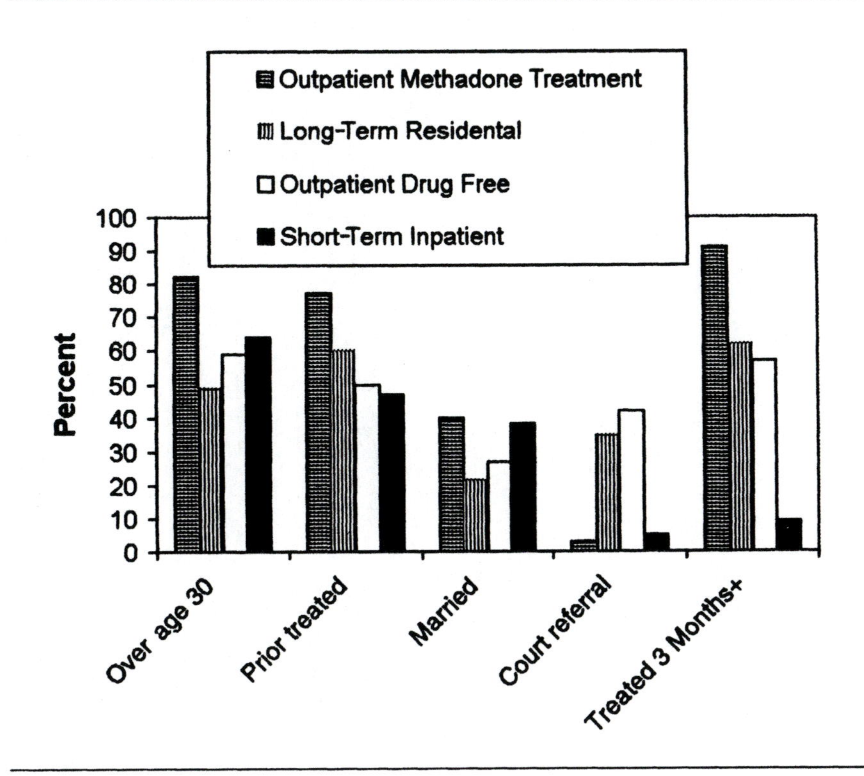

Figure 15.7. Client Characteristics in Four Drug Treatment Programs in the Drug Abuse Treatment Outcome Study (DATOS)
SOURCE: Based on data from Flynn et al. (1997).

use prior to admission. Both LTR and ODF treatments resulted in more than 50% reductions in weekly or more frequent cocaine use at the 1-year follow-up of 1,648 cocaine-dependent patients.

In addition, Figure 15.8 shows that behaviors other than drug use also improved, with reduced suicide attempts, predatory illegal activities, risky sexual behaviors, and other health-limiting behaviors. For most treatment modalities, increases in full-time work also occurred (not shown).

The DATOS findings also showed that many drug abuse treatment patients received a decreasing number of health and social services in the past decade (Etheridge, Hubbard, Anderson, Craddock, & Flynn, 1997). More than half of patients in all four types of treatment reported that they received no aftercare services specifically for medical, psychological, vocational, family, social, or legal problems. Thus, even as the need for these services increased, available services declined due to reduced funding, managed care, and the use of block grant allocations to individual states that are not under federal control.

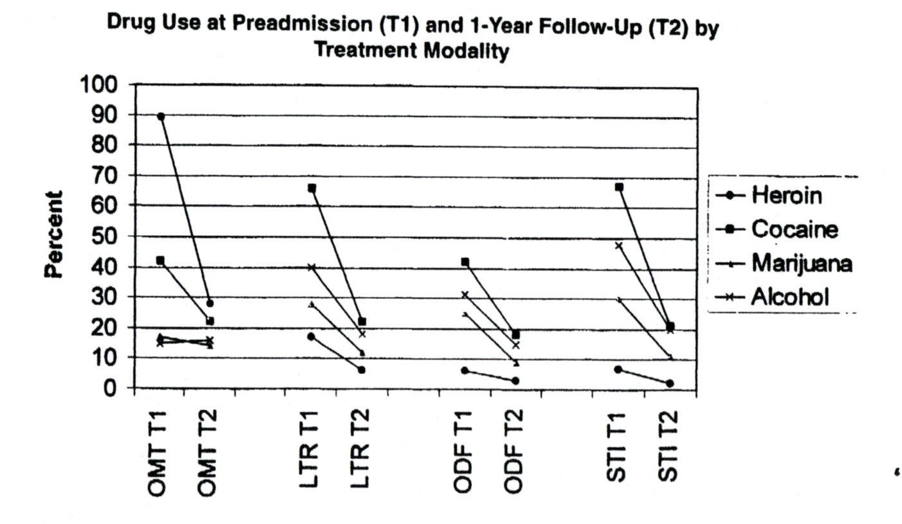

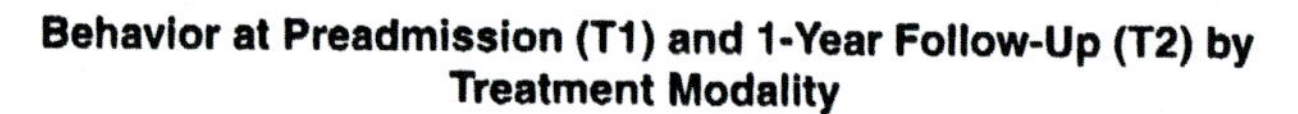

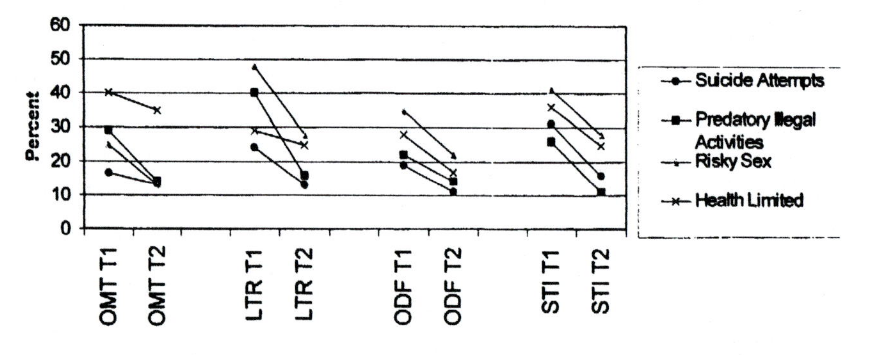

Figure 15.8. Baseline (T1) and 1-Year Follow-Up (T2) in Four Drug Treatment Programs in the Drug Abuse Treatment Outcome Study (DATOS)
SOURCE: Based on data from Hubbard et al. (1997).

It is important to recognize that DATOS was an evaluation of treatment under naturalistic conditions rather than a controlled experiment. There was no nontreatment control condition, and the patients were not assigned randomly to treatment modality. There were ethical and practical considerations that precluded any use of randomized trials, so there was no alternative procedure that would have been acceptable. Consequently, the results must be cautiously interpreted. It is possible for self-selection to have occurred, with the types of clients in the different treatments varying in some important way such as severity of dependency that could affect treatment outcome. Because there were no nontreated controls, it is not possible to identify how much of the improvements were specific to the treatment components.

Drug Replacement Approaches

For some drugs, a major strategy is to employ replacing a drug under treatment with a weaker drug. Programs to treat dependency to opiate drugs such as heroin include many components of programs used for alcohol dependency. In addition, the use of methadone is a distinct component of many, but not all, heroin treatments. In this type of therapy, patients receive a standard dose of methadone, a less psychoactive drug as a replacement for heroin, on an outpatient basis. Patients also must undergo counseling, take routine urine tests, and refrain from any illegal drugs. Such use of methadone has been praised as well as condemned. Properly administered, methadone has been effective in reducing use of heroin (Anglin & Hser, 1992), cutting down criminal activities related to heroin use (Hubbard et al., 1997), and improving health (Ginsburg, 1978). However, methadone maintenance has raised criticism because under this program, patients are still taking a psychoactive drug.

Other pharmacological approaches to countering the effects of heroin include the use of opioid antagonists, such as naltrexone (ReVia®) and LAAM (levo-alpha-acetylmethodol), which work like methadone but require lower doses.

SMOKING TREATMENTS

> Quitting smoking is easy. I've done it many times.
>
> —Mark Twain

Anyone can quit smoking for a short time. However, quitting for an extended period is much more difficult, and relapse into smoking is a common problem.

Measurement Issues

Comparing rates of quitting and evaluating smoking treatment success rates are difficult because of the many measurement problems (Velicer,

Prochaska, Rossi, & Snow, 1992). Estimates of rates of smoking cessation will depend in part on the temporal duration of the quitting. Shorter intervals should yield higher rates of success, but as the interval is increased, the success rate should diminish. The *point prevalence* rate refers to the level of quitting at a particular observation point that usually covers a brief interval. "Quitters," using this criterion, would be a heterogeneous group because it would include smokers who have quit for a long period as well as those who have only quit recently. Not surprisingly, then, point prevalence is not highly related to health outcomes for the group as a whole. *Continuous abstinence* involves the percentage of smokers who quit since an intervention was initiated and involves a longer interval with more stable levels of change. *Prolonged abstinence* refers to the percentage of smokers who are continuously abstinent for a prolonged period preceding the assessment but not necessarily starting at the time of intervention. Because most studies of quitting do not make these distinctions, comparisons across many studies are often meaningless because different studies used different criteria of quitting.

Quitting Methods

Many techniques for smoking cessation are based on behavior modification principles such as fading or extinction. Other established behavioral methods involve conditioning procedures such as counterconditioning and aversive conditioning (Hajek, 1994). The treatments for smokers include diverse approaches such as acupuncture and hypnosis to reduce rapid smoking gradually and cue exposure.

Pharmacologic treatments (Haxby, 1995) such as nicotine chewing gum lozenges, skin patches, and nasal sprays are effective, especially the nicotine skin patch and chewing gum. Nicotine still enters the body, but the smoke is eliminated because cigarette smoking is not involved. Whatever harmful effects nicotine produces should still occur. About 20% to 25% of smokers receiving these adjuncts stop smoking at least for 6 months. However, given that about 10% of smokers are able to stop smoking without these aids, the net improvement is actually only 10% to 15%.

Nicotine gum has an unpleasant taste that may deter its use. In addition, gum chewing is not always socially acceptable. Use of gum requires more effort and control by the smoker, whereas nicotine patches automatically release nicotine. Aside from remembering to apply the patches, the smoker needs to make less effort to receive the nicotine with patches than with gum.

Evidence suggests that these approaches can be effective, and this method has not received objections on the grounds that smokers are still receiving nicotine. Another drug, bupropion hydrochloride (Wellbutrin®), which is an antidepressant, was approved by the Food and Drug Administration in 1997 for use in conjunction with nicotine gum and patches. Because tobacco is a legal drug that is widely used and freely marketed, nicotine replacement is acceptable in our society, whereas methadone as a replacement for an illegal drug such as heroin is not without controversy.

Behavioral techniques based on operant conditioning theory involve sensitization and desensitization as well as contingency contracting. There is little evidence that any single form of behavior therapy is more effective than other forms (Hajek, 1996). In addition, nicotine replacement treatment can add substantially to the success of behavioral treatments; however, the addition of behavioral methods to nicotine replacement therapy is of little value.

Cognitive interventions help smokers identify reasons to quit and cues that trigger smoking, devise alternative coping skills, and provide social support for quitting. Minimal-contact approaches that emphasize self-help also have been developed (e.g., manuals or guides); they are inexpensive but of unknown effectiveness.

In addition to individual-level treatments, either in clinics or self-help programs, there are community-oriented approaches. Unlike clinical approaches that deal with changing the smoking of individuals, community programs focus on reducing smoking by changing environments, media messages, and information campaigns.

Different types of programs appeal to different individuals; what works for one person may not work for another, so care is needed in generalizing from overall success rates of different techniques. A match between the motivation level of the smoker for quitting and the type of intervention may be an important factor on success rates. Smokers who are willing to expend much time, effort, and money to quit may do better simply because they are more motivated to quit (Strecher, 1983).

SUMMARY

A variety of treatment approaches have been developed for alcoholism. Treatment outcomes depend not only on the treatment method and its setting but also vary with client variables such as drinking history, other forms of psychopathology, and demographic factors. Evaluation of treatment effectiveness in an objective and scientifically rigorous manner is difficult because random assignment to treatments and the use of no-treatment control groups are usually not feasible.

The issue of whether the treatment criterion should be abstinence or controlled drinking pits one of AA's central tenets about alcoholism against the scientific skepticism of the empirically oriented behavioral researchers who believe alcoholics could, in principle, learn to drink in moderation. This question, as it was posed, did not allow a scientific answer, and the political fallout from the controversy has distracted researchers and practitioners from more immediate concerns that can be evaluated empirically.

Although these rival approaches have been bitter opponents in their perspectives on the nature of alcoholism and how to promote recovery, some areas of overlap and agreement between them may be overlooked because of differences in terminology. For example, the social learning focus on the acquisition of coping skills to reduce stress is not incompatible with AA, which urges alcoholics to make attitudinal and behavioral changes through its 12 steps, all of which can relieve stress.

The alcoholic member's drinking disrupts family functioning and is harmful to the well-being of family members, but it is also possible that the family may often contribute to the alcoholic member's drinking. Recognition of the reciprocal influence between the alcoholic and other members of the family system provides a fuller understanding of the complex interpersonal factors that must be addressed when treating alcoholism. Use of family therapy when the nonalcoholic family members undergo therapy with the alcoholic member is growing and offers a promising approach.

Most treatment methods seem to be effective for some alcoholics. Alcoholics vary in their psychological and sociological backgrounds, factors that may determine which treatment method, type of therapist, or amount of treatment will be most effective. It is important that we eventually identify the type of alcoholic that each technique can help in the hope that we can match each alcoholic to the appropriate treatment.

Treatment for abuse and dependency of other drugs such as heroin and cocaine can use similar principles and methods to those employed for alcoholism. The types of clientele at different drug treatment modalities vary along dimensions such as age, social background, type of drug, and severity of problem, so comparisons of relative effectiveness can be misleading. In general, longer treatment duration is associated with better outcomes at a 1-year follow-up for all treatment modalities.

KEY TERMS

Attrition
Aversive conditioning
Classical conditioning
Controlled drinking
Drug Abuse Reporting Program (DARP)
Drug Abuse Treatment Outcome Study (DATOS)
Family systems
Marital family treatment
Matching
Minnesota model of treatment
Motivational enhancement training (MET)
National Drug and Alcoholism Treatment Unit Survey (NDATUS)
Operant conditioning
Project MATCH
Psychodynamic approaches
Rational emotive therapy (RET)
Screening
Treatment Outcome Prospective Study (TOPS)
Triangulation

STIMULUS/RESPONSE

1. Behavioral approaches to alcoholism treatment seek to reinforce alternatives to the use of alcohol. What do you think would be some attractive alternatives, and how would you reinforce these other behaviors?
2. One method of cognitive behavior modification for treating drug problems is to change some of the cognitions that prompt drug use. What are some of these cognitions, and how do you think they might be changed?
3. Family therapy assumes that both the alcoholic and other family members are willing to work on the problem. What difficulties can you foresee in getting such participation, and how would you overcome them?

4a. Coerced drug treatment is rare for civilian populations, but for incarcerated populations, it can be mandated. In fact, some research on the California prison system's drug treatment program claims some success. At one prison in San Diego, only 16% of its inmates who also completed an aftercare program came back into the system within 2 years of their release. In contrast, statewide, the recidivism rate is about 70%. Does this result mean that most of the treated inmates actually reduced their drinking or that they do not commit crimes (or do not get caught) at the levels of untreated inmates in other prisons? What follow-up study would you do to answer this question?

4b. Many prisoners resented involuntary requirements. Prison officials, however, felt that this was a case of inmates not knowing what was best for them. About 80% of the prisoners who were asked to attend drug treatment programs said they wanted nothing to do with them. But because the treatment program was involuntary, inmates who did not attend would lose good-time credits and privileges. Do you feel the prisoners were justified, or do they not have the same rights as nonprisoners?

4c. In a follow-up study of treatment programs for incarcerated felony offenders, 79% of participants were employed on release. Only 35% were rearrested, compared with a national rearrest rate of 63%. Do you think that this evidence justifies the use of coerced treatment?

- Lapse Versus Relapse
- Models of Relapse
- Overview of Relapse Process
- Relapse Prevention
- Summary
- Key Terms
- Stimulus/Response

Relapse After Alcohol and Other Drug Treatment 16

One of the most frustrating and frequent obstacles to successful treatment and recovery is the high likelihood of relapse among individuals suffering from dependency on any drug. For example, following treatment leading to abstinence or even reduced use, "cravings" for the drug arise. These insidious experiences involving strong temptations to return to drug use can be overpowering. The rationalization, often made by alcoholics as well as by those who cannot enjoy their own drinking if others are abstaining, is that "just one little drink can't hurt." The inability to cope with these temptations that frequently confront treated patients who have achieved abstinence jeopardizes maintenance of their recovery. Estimated relapse rates of 50% to 90% occur within 6 months following treatment for many drugs, including alcohol, smoking, and heroin (Hunt & Matarazzo, 1973).

Much evidence concerning relapse is based on clinical case histories and concentrates on failures to maintain abstinence. Evidence about the factors that precipitate or predict relapse is lacking (Brownell, Marlatt, Lichenstein, & Wilson, 1986). We also lack evidence on how one can prevent relapse. A "natural history" of relapse, which would include the identification of processes underlying successful resistance as well as the analysis of factors involved in relapses or the failure to overcome temptation, would be instructive and provide a basis for improving understanding.

Lapse Versus Relapse

It may be useful to distinguish between a **lapse**, a single episode of a slip from sobriety, and a **relapse**, which refers to a process entailing a series of lapses (Brownell et al., 1986). Important questions about the relationship of lapses to relapse and recovery exist. The line between lapse and relapse is vague. Each lapse could be viewed as a step further along the path to the end of a cliff culminating inevitably with a fall that could be regarded as the relapse. Expectations of failure might occur after a lapse so that an attitude of futility develops. This linear view is the prevalent conception of relapse, but an alternative view is that lapses are a possibly beneficial factor, if the patient could learn or be taught what caused the slip and how it could be prevented.

If relapse occurs, how does the individual interpret it? If it is seen as a failure, the individual may give up efforts to stop using. However, if an incident involving renewed use can be seen as only a temporary setback, the individual can renew a commitment to overcome the undesired behavior so that eventual control may be achieved. Thus, relapse is viewed as a "circular" rather than a linear process, a perspective that would also allow the possibility that lapses could be informative and instructive. If the individual can identify the factors and situations that lead to lapses, successful change can be achieved in the long run. Learning from one's mistakes helps prevent recurrence of the same mistakes.

RETROSPECTIVE EVIDENCE

Negative emotional states have been found to precede relapse in many instances, according to retrospective self-reports from alcoholics (Marlatt, 1985a). Interviews with alcoholics (Ludwig, 1986) reveal their phenomenological experiences about the nature of the Pavlovian "bells" that triggered their relapses. Only 11 of the 150 alcoholics could not identify any "bell," with 71% reporting one or two cues. Social situations and internal tensions were prominent. Also mentioned were external stressors, mealtimes, depression, music, alcohol advertisements, and idiosyncratic cues such as reading in the bathtub or plowing the garden in the spring. It would appear, then, that a wide variety of internal and external cues are believed by alcoholics to trigger their drinking. However, caution is necessary because some of the answers might be excuses offered as attempts to justify their relapse (e.g., the stress "made me do it").

Self-reported causes of relapse were identified in more than 300 individuals with a variety of addictions, including nonpharmacological prob-

TABLE 16.1 Comparison of relapse factors for different addictive behaviors (in percentages)

Relapse Situation	*Alcoholics*	*Smokers*	*Heroin Addicts*	*Gamblers*	*Over-eaters*	*Total*
Intrapersonal determinants						
Negative emotional states	38	37	19	47	33	35
Negative physical states	3	2	9			3
Positive emotional states		6	10		3	4
Testing personal control	9		2	16		5
Urges and temptations	11	5	5	16	10	9
Total	61	50	45	79	46	56
Interpersonal determinants						
Interpersonal conflict	18	15	14	16	14	16
Social pressure	18	32	36	5	10	20
Positive emotional states	3	3	5		28	8
Total	39	50	55	21	52	44

SOURCE: Marlatt and Gordon (1985). Copyright 1985 by Guilford. Used with permission.

lems (Cummings, Gordon, & Marlatt, 1980). Negative emotional states such as depression or anger were found in about 35% of cases (Marlatt & Gordon, 1985), as shown in Table 16.1. This factor accounts for more than one third of the relapses not only among alcoholics but also for smokers, gamblers, and overeaters, as well as, but somewhat lower for, heroin addicts.

Other major causes were interpersonal conflict (16%) and social pressure (20%). An intriguing cause for some relapses was the tendency of a small percentage to deliberately place themselves in risky situations to test their personal control or "willpower."

Limitations of Self-Report

A problem with self-report evidence is that it can be biased by attempts to avoid looking bad. That is, someone who has experienced a slip might find that reporting stress and negative emotions as causes of lapses are acceptable extenuating excuses. However, the claim that the lapse was caused by the discomfort of tremors from not drinking might be seen as a sign of weakness and hence avoided. Furthermore, these states may overlap and be confused with each other by the alcoholic.

PROSPECTIVE EVIDENCE

Overall, relapse research is limited by its heavy dependence on retrospective self-reports, which are difficult to validate even when there is no intent to distort. Studies with a prospective orientation take measures of clients at varying points from the end of a treatment program up to the time of relapse. When relapse occurs, determination of factors that are correlated with relapse is possible. Newer studies (Shiffman et al., 1994) using "near real-time" methodology employ electronic beepers and palmtop computers so that clients having a lapse can record information about the setting, urges, mood, and coping close to the moment of crisis.

In one prospective study of 100 alcoholics and 100 heroin addicts examined over a 12-year span, relapse was less likely if the user had a substitute dependence, compulsory supervision, new relationships, or inspirational group membership (Vaillant, 1988, 1992). In addition, the level of social competence or stability prior to development of a drug problem was a better predictor of treatment success than was the severity of the drug dependency. Lower social competence was related to less successful treatment.

Thus, both exteroceptive cues such as the physical setting associated with substance abuse and interoceptive cues such as emotional and physiological signals are potential triggers of relapse. Cues associated with the external physical setting, as well as internal cues such as olfactory and gustatory cues related to the substances, could activate relapse. In addition, social influences such as pressure and modeling also have been found to be associated with the urge to drink (Marlatt & Rohsenow, 1980).

Conclusions based on studies using prospective designs and near real-time measures generally find results similar to those from retrospective methods about the factors involved with relapse (McKay, 1999). Nonetheless, reliance on self-reports can lead to overestimations of the extent that relapse involves conscious awareness. It is likely that many relapses may be of "an absent-minded quality" (Tiffany, 1990), but when interviewed, people who relapse will construct accounts, but they may not be reflective of actual processes.

CAUSES OF RELAPSE

The causes of relapse can be divided into individual or intrapsychic versus interpersonal and social-environmental cues. The first type could include physical sensations as well as psychological states such as cognitions and emotions. The second type could include cues such as other individuals using drugs, the smell of drugs, or the sight of drugs as well as the physical surroundings associated with drug use.

Role of Craving

Cues are commonly assumed to activate internal feelings referred to as cravings, which then trigger resumed use of drugs after a period of abstinence. However, it is unclear whether these cues are necessary or, in many cases, a type of retrospective rationalization for relapse. There is little agreement on what **craving** for alcohol means or how to best measure it. Moreover, there is some question as to how closely it is tied to drug use (Singleton & Gorelick, 1998).

One review of past studies found that reports of craving showed only an overall modest correlation with consumption measures of different drugs (Tiffany, 1990). The general assumption that subjective cravings are invariably associated with increased drug use was not upheld and implies that cravings are not necessary or sufficient for drug use.

The role of conscious desire or craving for drugs during abstinence and withdrawal was studied with data from more than 1,600 patients with a variety of addictions, including alcohol, cocaine, and alcohol with some drug other than cocaine in a primary rehabilitation center (Miller & Gold, 1994). Craving was not a major self-reported cause of relapse for any type of patients. Relapse was not related to conscious craving, and it was rarely the first reason given for relapse. Drug use is such a highly ritualized and automatic behavior that conscious thoughts or distinct craving states may not be needed for relapse to occur (Miller & Gold, 1994).

Individual differences may exist in the extent to which different cues lead to craving, based on past drinking experience, biological factors, and coping skills. In other words, reactivity to cues that affect craving may not be the same across individuals, with it possibly being stronger for more addicted drinkers.

Cognitive Factors

Positive and negative alcohol expectancies of 50 male alcoholics measured at admission to a nonresidential alcohol dependence treatment were examined as possible precursors to relapse to a first drink following treatment (Jones & McMahon, 1994). Negative alcohol expectancies, especially for longer-term outcomes, were predictive of more relapse.

Affective States

Affective reactions may play a role, although theories disagree as to whether negative emotions (Wikler, 1965) or positive appetitional motives (Stewart, deWit, & Eikelboom, 1984) are primarily responsible. Positive affective states may activate cravings in alcoholics, but physiological factors such as the discomfort and pain experienced during withdrawal are also potent conditions leading to relapse (Marlatt, 1985b).

Negative mood may have a role in precipitating relapses and crises among alcoholics. A relationship between negative bias and the extent of negative mood when tested was found when retrospective reports of relapses were studied (Hodgins, el-Guebaly, & Armstrong, 1995). The most frequent precipitant of relapses and crises was negative emotional states, although minor relapses were more likely to be precipitated by social pressure. Females were more likely to report interpersonal and less likely to report intrapersonal determinants than males.

Stress

In addition to negative mood on a specific occasion, longer-term situations such as stressful life events also have been linked to relapse. A study (Cooper et al., 1992) of Black and White males found that avoidant coping and positive expectation about alcohol were likely to lead to relapse during high stress. In contrast, higher stress had less relapse for men who were low on both variables and was not a factor among women, regardless of their coping style or alcohol expectancies. In another study, males who had higher stress following treatment had more relapse than those for whom treatment lowered their life stress (Brown, Vik, Patterson, Grant, & Schuckit, 1995).

LABORATORY STUDIES

Due to the potential self-justification bias and fallibility of memory with retrospective report, researchers must obtain direct evidence about the cues that lead to relapse among alcoholics. Some have used controlled experiments to seek more objective evidence.

The balanced placebo design (Marlatt et al., 1973), discussed in Chapter 11, has been used to isolate the role of expectancy of drinking alcohol as a factor on the craving to drink. More drinking occurs among alcoholics who are led to believe they have consumed alcohol, regardless of whether they actually did, demonstrating that alcohol consumption per se is not needed to create craving (Laberg, 1986; Stockwell, Hodgson, Rankin, & Taylor, 1982). Thus, psychological factors such as expectancies about beverage content are important factors in relapse.

Responsiveness to alcohol-related cues that trigger drinking may be stronger for alcoholics. In a study (Monti et al., 1987) in which alcoholics were exposed to alcohol but not allowed to drink, cue reactivity or physiological responsiveness was greater among alcoholics exposed to these alcohol cues. Using salivation as an index of cue reactivity, they presented alcoholics and nonalcoholics with the sight and smell of both their favorite brands of an alcoholic beverage and a control beverage. The results showed that alcoholics salivated more to the alcoholic drink, whereas there was no difference for the nonalcoholics. Both groups had stronger urges to drink the alcoholic beverage.

Another study (Cooney, Gillespie, Baker, & Kaplan, 1987) found that alcoholics experienced more physical symptoms, lower confidence about being able to resist temptation, and more guilt than nonalcoholics after being allowed to hold and sniff but not drink their favorite alcoholic beverage. Both groups had an increased desire to drink and expected pleasurable consequences.

In conclusion, it appears that cue reactivity is greater for alcoholics than for controls and may play an important role on relapse following treatment. In the next section, several models are presented that suggest how these cues might trigger relapse.

Models of Relapse

CONDITIONING MODELS

According to the classical conditioning paradigm used by Pavlov (1927), stimuli that are originally neutral as cues for specific responses may come to acquire the power to elicit these responses. Thus, the well-known experiments of Pavlov with laboratory dogs showed that the presentation of stimuli such as a light or tone repeatedly in association with food powder came to elicit salivation. Such a light or tone was initially incapable of causing salivation, which is an unconditioned response (UCR)

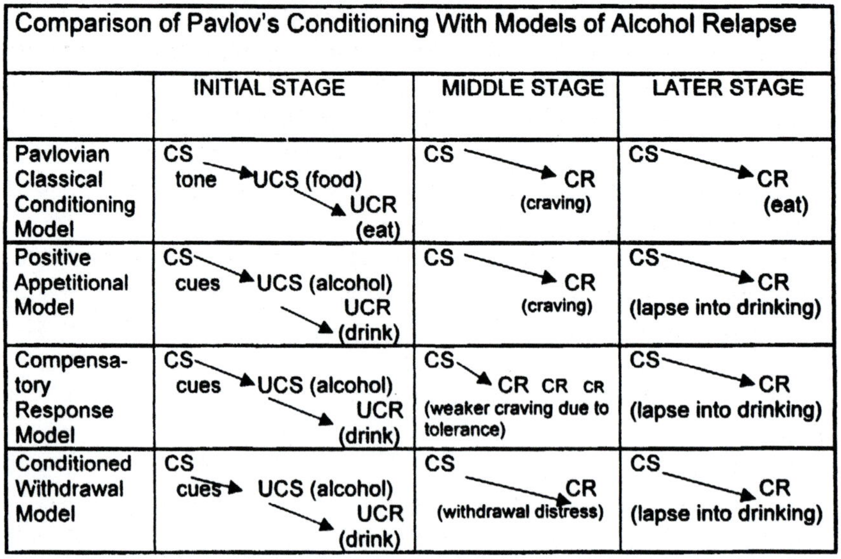

Comparison of Pavlov's Conditioning With Models of Alcohol Relapse

	INITIAL STAGE	MIDDLE STAGE	LATER STAGE
Pavlovian Classical Conditioning Model	CS tone → UCS (food) → UCR (eat)	CS → CR (craving)	CS → CR (eat)
Positive Appetitional Model	CS cues → UCS (alcohol) → UCR (drink)	CS → CR (craving)	CS → CR (lapse into drinking)
Compensatory Response Model	CS cues → UCS (alcohol) → UCR (drink)	CS → CR CR CR (weaker craving due to tolerance)	CS → CR (lapse into drinking)
Conditioned Withdrawal Model	CS cues → UCS (alcohol) → UCR (drink)	CS → CR (withdrawal distress)	CS → CR (lapse into drinking)

Figure 16.1. Relationship of the Classical Conditioning Paradigm to Different Models of Alcohol Relapse

to the unconditioned stimulus (UCS) of food. But by pairing these stimuli that are unrelated to food frequently with the presentation of food, these stimuli became conditioned stimuli (CS) capable of eliciting salivation even in the absence of food, as shown in the top row of Figure 16.1. Because the salivation is in response to the CS rather than to the actual food, it is called the CR, whereas it is termed an *unconditioned response* when it occurs in the presence of food.

In the case of alcohol, as the bottom three rows of Figure 16.1 shows, certain physiological and psychological reactions or unconditioned responses (UCR) occur when alcohol (UCS) is consumed. If stimuli (CS) such as the taste, smell, or visual cues associated with the drinking of alcohol occur alone later, there should be some partial activation of the responses (CR) that alcohol itself elicits. Thus, these cues act as conditioned stimuli that produce conditioned responses such as craving, physiological arousal, and drug-seeking responses. The strength of the CR is in proportion to factors such as the length of prior drinking, recency of past drinking, and the similarity between past drinking settings and the present one. Three models of relapse based on the classical conditioning paradigm will be described in the following section.

Positive Appetitional Model

One model based on classical conditioning (Stewart et al., 1984) emphasizes the positive incentive value of alcohol as a determinant of relapse. The **positive appetitional model** focuses on events that occur prior to when alcohol is consumed. The drinking of alcohol produces a positive affective state, one that is conditioned to other stimuli such as the sight and smell associated with drinking that later have the capacity to trigger subjective desire or craving for alcohol and evoke the motivation to use the substance again. As Figure 16.1 indicates, this model may apply more to early stages of drinking.

Compensatory Response Model

Although derived from the same Pavlovian paradigm, the **compensatory response model** (Siegel, 1983) holds that conditioning involves responses that are opposite in direction from the original unconditioned responses, presumably to restore homeostasis. Alcohol, for example, intensifies physiological arousal, so this reaction is followed by the attempt of the nervous system to suppress arousal. This process may be one explanation for the phenomenon of tolerance discussed in Chapter 4, whereby increasingly larger doses eventually are needed to produce an earlier level of arousal generated by a smaller amount. Because these conditioned cues act to reduce the effect of a drug, they could activate resumed use in an attempt to generate the arousal state associated with their drug. Figure 16.1 suggests that this model may be more applicable to experienced users who are not yet alcohol dependent.

Opponent Process Theory

The **opponent process theory** (Solomon, 1980) is a general model of addictive behaviors and not limited to drugs. It is based on the role of affective reactions to the receipt and termination of strong stimuli. Because the model distinguishes between early and later stages of affective experiences, it is suited for explaining the transition from normal to addictive drug use.

Drug use, itself, is a strong stimulus that produces an affective state, A, as shown in Figure 16.2. Thus, having a few drinks or smoking cocaine will produce a strong arousal. When the effect dissipates, an affective aftereffect, B, occurs that is opposite in emotional tone to that produced by the

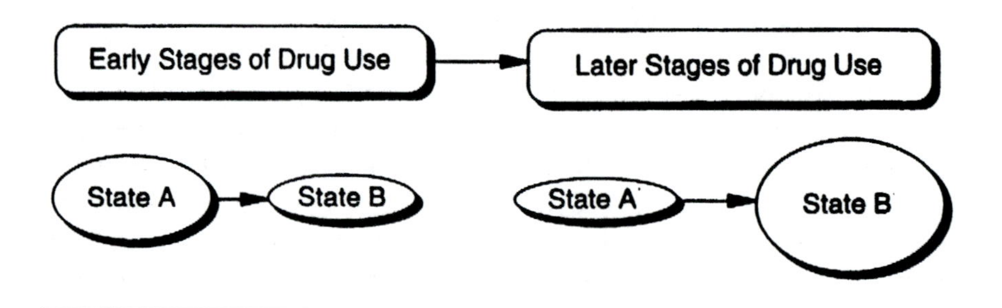

Figure 16.2. Opponent Process Theory Showing Relative Magnitude of the A and B Opponents in the Early and Later Stages of Drug Use

consumption of a drug. It works like a compensatory response to restore the body to a neutral state. If the drug use produced positive affect, its removal or termination leaves a feeling of negative tone, akin to disappointment. In contrast, a drug that produced a negative affect would leave a positive feeling after the original affect ended, similar to relief. Taken together, the two states, A and B, represent opponent processes.

Early Versus Later Stages. The opponent process theory explains why the relationship between these two opposing affective states shifts over time as the drinker becomes more experienced with a drug. For beginning or light drinkers, a small amount of drug is capable of producing a strong positive affect (State A), and the negative aftereffect (State B) is relatively weak. However, as drug use continues and becomes heavier over time, tolerance develops. The small dose that originally was capable of producing a given amount of positive affect now generates a weaker positive A state, which is followed by a larger negative B state.

Thus, when the heavy user does not have access to drugs, the negative opponent process or B state is now much stronger than it was when drug use was lighter. The typical "solution" adopted by the heavy user is to try to forestall both the shrinking positive affect and the mushrooming negative aftereffect that occur with repeated use by increasing the quantity and frequency of drug use. In essence, addiction involves the increased use of the drug to treat the unpleasant symptoms associated with withdrawal from the drug. Unfortunately, this strategy is doomed and entraps the drug user into a spiral of deepening addiction.

Due to conditioning processes, these affective states become associated with environmental stimuli. Consequently, even if a user becomes abstinent, these conditioned stimuli can activate feelings previously related to the drugs and hence increase the likelihood of relapse into drug use.

Conditioned Withdrawal

One model of **conditioned withdrawal** (Wikler, 1973) focuses on negative interoceptive cues such as physiological reactions associated with the withdrawal reaction to the absence of alcohol. As with the preceding model, these internal cues are conditioned to external cues such as the room or physical setting where excessive drinking previously ended. Later, these cues can act as conditioned stimuli to activate conditioned withdrawal reactions and experiences of craving. To reduce or eliminate these aversive withdrawal responses, one might relapse into drinking. This model deals with processes more likely to occur in drug-dependent individuals, as indicated in Figure 16.1.

INCENTIVE SENSITIZATION MODEL

A different conception of the processes involved in the development of addiction focuses on neurophysiological changes produced by drugs. It contrasts two different psychological aspects of drug use: "wanting" and "liking" drugs. Among beginning users, wanting a drug and liking its effects are linked, with both tending to increase together. However, for the addicted or long-term user, the two states become dissociated. For those dependent on drugs, wanting the drug stays high with continued use, but liking the drug (receiving pleasure from its use) actually decreases with repeated use.

According to the incentive sensitization model, these effects may be based on changes in the neurophysiological processes created by drugs as the course of drug use continues. The model (Berridge & Robinson, 1995; Robinson & Berridge, 1993) postulates that the divergence between wanting and liking a drug with repeated use is due to the development of a third factor, **incentive sensitization.** Prolonged drug use can produce neuroadaptations that lead to a hypersensitivity to drugs, as reflected by a strong wanting to use the drug. The basis for this change may lie with changes in brain processes (Koob & Le Moal, 1996) due to prolonged drug use, specifically in the *nucleus accumbens.* A reduction in dopamine, a major neurotransmitter presumably underlying pleasure, may be responsible for wanting a drug capable of increasing dopamine levels. In contrast, the neural system underlying the "liking" dimension is not affected by long-term drug use and is unlikely to generate hypersensitivity. Hence, the drug user experiences more wanting, but less liking or pleasure occurs when the drug is consumed.

This model suggests that the persistent nature of drug addiction may not be mainly pharmacological but is dependent on the heightened attention of the drug user to environmental and psychological stimuli previously associated with drug use. Hypersensitivity to drugs is more likely to occur in the same context in which a drug was usually taken in the past. For the long-term user, these cues still can arouse renewed "wanting," even though "liking" experiences following use are diminished. This craving in response to cues associated with drug use in the past increases the likelihood of relapse. Hence, limiting exposure to environmental cues that trigger wanting may be essential if the sensitization to stimuli is to be prevented.

SOCIAL LEARNING THEORY

In contrast to the preceding models in which relapse is attributed to factors that may operate with low awareness or volition on the part of the drinker, social learning models (Bandura, 1977; Marlatt & Gordon, 1985) emphasize factors such as the modeling of others and the individual's cognitive appraisal of the factors. Instead of viewing alcoholism as a disease over which the victim has no control, social learning theory views alcoholism and other addictions as a set of strong habits with undesirable consequences that can be offset by the conscious decision to acquire a new set of habits.

Social learning theory holds an opposing view to that of AA about abstinence. It believes that AA's view of alcoholics as weak and powerless victims ironically can increase the likelihood of relapse because alcoholics will come to believe that after a single slip, they will suffer a full-blown relapse (Marlatt & Gordon, 1985). Thus, the goal of abstinence offers no margin for error and is equivalent to being "out after only one strike." Such expectations may then become self-fulfilling prophecies for any unfortunate alcoholics who have a slip that will escalate into further drinking.

A drinker who yields to temptation and returns to the use of alcohol creates an **abstinence violation effect** (AVE) whereby the realization of the lapse creates cognitive dissonance with his or her goals of abstinence (Marlatt, 1978). It may increase negative affect such as guilt, lower feelings of self-efficacy, and lower attributions of internal control. The magnitude of the AVE is assumed to be a function of factors such as degree of prior commitment to abstinence, the duration of the abstinence period, the immediate subjective effect of the drug used, and the attributions for the lapse.

The social learning model also focuses on the expectations held about self-efficacy, one's perceived ability to deal effectively with problems in general as well as specifically related to drug use. As shown in Figure 16.3, the likelihood of a relapse can be related to whether a coping response en-

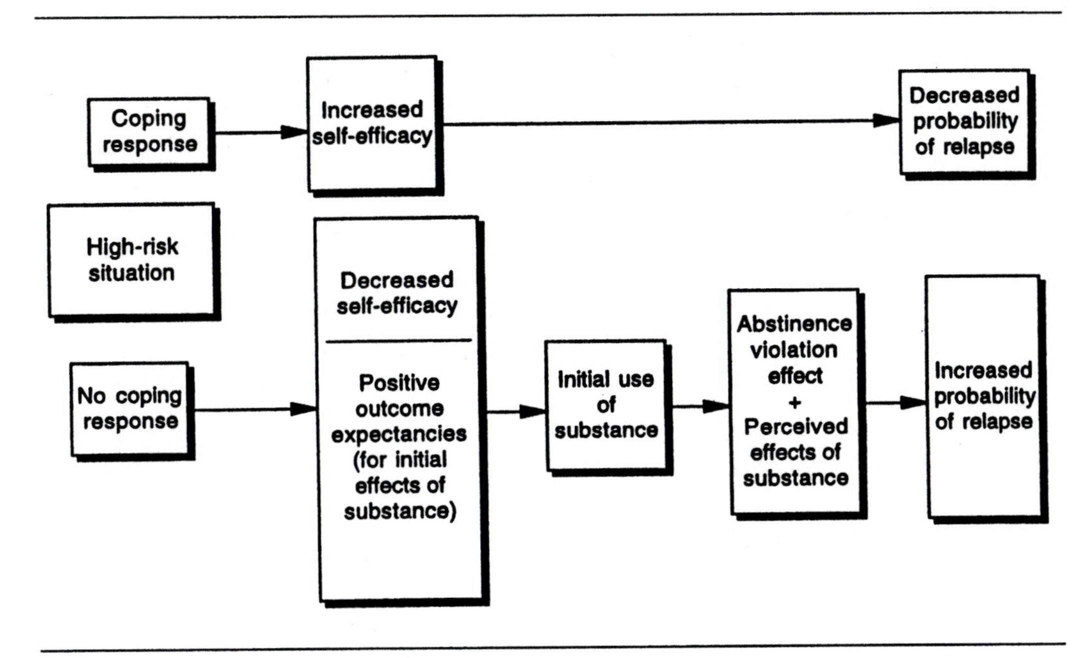

Figure 16.3. A Cognitive-Behavioral Model of Relapse
SOURCE: From Marlatt and Gordon (1985). Copyright 1985 by Guilford. Used with permission.

hanced or reduced one's feelings of self-efficacy in a situation with high risk for relapse.

Social learning theory predicts that relapse can be minimized by methods that help the alcoholic develop coping skills, both cognitive and behavioral, to aid in resisting temptation. Furthermore, the social support and encouragement of significant others for recovery can help prevent relapse.

Strong negative affect might lower personal feelings of self-efficacy for dealing with a problem and lead to the appraisal that alcohol would lower the negative affect. Positive expectations of disinhibition also might stimulate drinking. In theory, a person with adequate coping skills could handle such situations without alcohol, even if he or she had previously used it for coping.

Attributions are the causal explanations that people generate to account for outcomes (Weiner, 1985). These attributions can vary along several dimensions such as internal-external (e.g., self vs. other), stable-unstable (e.g., constant vs. variable), and global-specific (e.g., universal vs. unique). Following an event such as a lapse in which an offered drink is accepted, an alcoholic might try to explain "what happened." An example might be the following: My drinking is due to my own weakness in self-control in refusing the offer (internal), I am always weak when offered a drink (stable), and I am weak in all situations when alcohol is offered (global). Different types of attributions hold different consequences. Internal, stable, and global attributions for an AVE, as in this example, will lead to more negative affect, including conflict and guilt. The larger the AVE, the greater the chances of relapse if the individual regards alcohol to be an effective method of alleviating these feelings.

Self-efficacy is a key to recovery and avoidance of relapse. Individuals must acquire a sense of control and believe that they can overcome their dependence through their efforts (Bandura, 1999). For example, learning how to cope with stress without drinking or learning social skills to know how to refuse a drink could help increase this self-efficacy.

Overview of Relapse Process

A model (Niaura et al., 1988) of what happens after a lapse occurs, as well as the likelihood of a relapse that incorporates many of the factors proposed by conditioning as well as social learning models, is diagrammed in Figure 16.4. The figure shows how a complex interplay of cognitive/affective, physiological, and behavioral factors might influence the eventual consequences of a return to drinking by an alcoholic.

First, a combination of contextual or environmental cues in conjunction with affective states, both positive and negative, determine the arousal of urges to drink, physiological activation, and expectations about the effect of a drink. These effects can loop back and alter the initial affective states. Thus, at a party where most people are drinking, the craving to drink while thinking about having a good time from drinking and experiencing physiological arousal might promote positive affective feelings. In contrast, craving a drink while being alone at home, thinking about feeling sick after drinking, and expecting guilt over drinking might activate more negative affective states.

At the next stage of the process illustrated in Figure 16.4, feelings of self-efficacy will be activated. Do the individuals feel that they can control the situation, or do they feel that it is hopeless? Individuals will have different levels or types of cognitive and behavioral coping responses for dealing with such situations. They also may make attributions about the causes of their behavior and urges. These different factors influence each other, as suggested by the bidirectional arrows in the diagram between these components. Thus, urges to drink can lower one's feelings of self-control; conversely, feeling self-control may be associated with a reduction

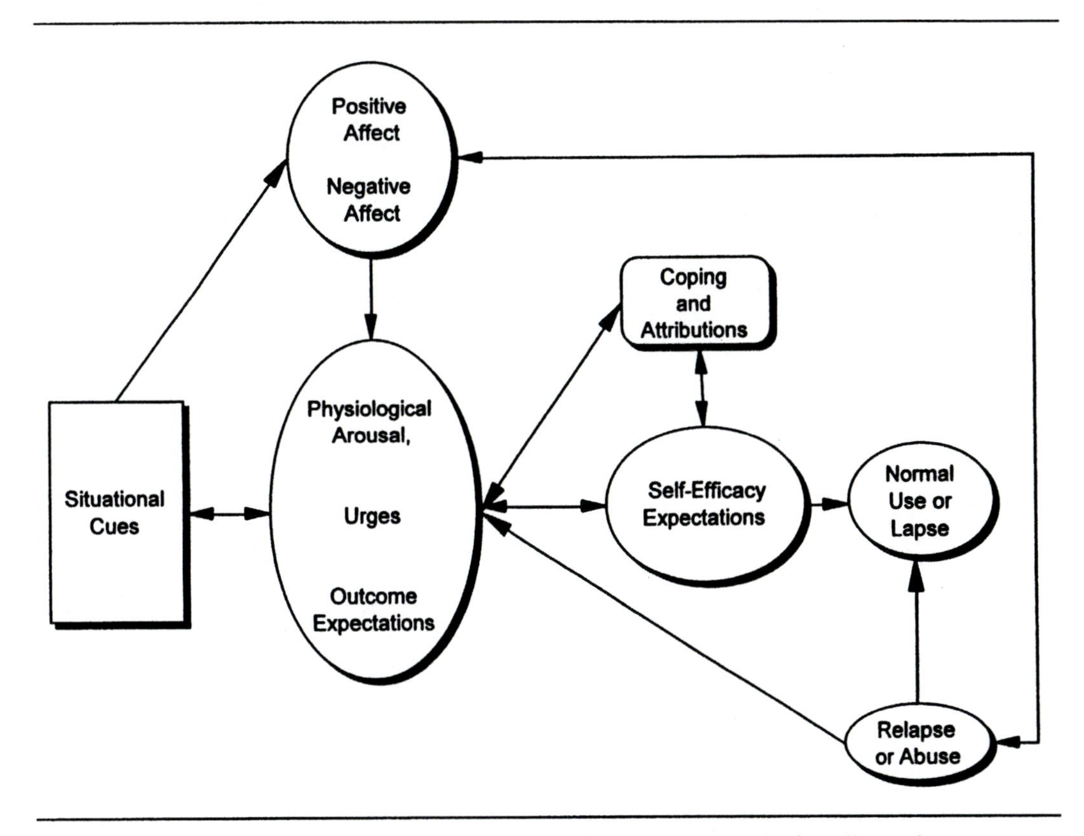

Figure 16.4. A Regulatory Feedback System Linking Constructs Related to Relapse
SOURCE: Adapted from Niaura et al. (1988).

of urges. Similarly, the availability of good coping skills for dealing with a situation in which drinking urges are high can reduce those urges and physiological arousal, but the presence of compelling urges might weaken availability or use of these coping skills.

Depending on whether the urges to drink or the inhibitory coping and attributional responses prevail, the outcome will be a lapse, normal use, or nonuse of alcohol. Depending on the types of attributions made about the lapse and the effects of the alcohol itself on the affective consequences, lapses may eventuate in further lapses and total relapse. If the drinker concludes that the causes of the lapse are internal, stable, and global, or the alcohol diminishes negative affect, the chances of further deterioration are strong. Conversely, if the lapse is attributed to external, unstable, and specific factors, or the drink has little influence on the affective state, the lapse may be an isolated event.

Relapse Prevention

Different approaches for preventing relapse reflect different assumptions about the factors responsible for relapse. Conditioning models assume that relapse is an automatic or involuntary outcome and employ relatively passive methods for prevention such as cue extinction and pharmacological methods. In contrast, active methods involving decision making, coping skills, and problem solving are more compatible for those holding social learning views of relapse.

PASSIVE METHODS

Cue Extinction

Cue extinction, whereby the environmental stimuli that trigger cravings for alcohol are weakened, may be beneficial. Extinction deals with the process by which prior conditioned responses are weakened or eliminated. According to this concept from classical conditioning, exposure to alcohol cues in the absence of actual consumption of alcohol eventually will weaken drinking urges as the associations lose their strength. This process is known as covert sensitization.

Prolonged exposure to alcohol under conditions that prevent actual consumption may reduce craving (Laberg & Ellertson, 1987). Sixteen detoxified alcoholics received either a small priming dose of alcohol or a soft drink. The prime was expected to act like a conditioned stimulus. Then they were presented with bottles of either alcohol or a soft drink. Six sessions were used.

Measures of arousal such as skin conductance and heart rate as well as self-rated arousal were obtained before and after priming. The results showed increased arousal and craving only if subjects had been primed with alcohol before exposure to additional alcohol. Merely being exposed to the sight of alcoholic beverages did not increase arousal. Moreover, these reactions to exposure to alcohol cues decreased over the six successive sessions of cue exposure, indicating that extinction was occurring.

The clinical effectiveness of cue exposure treatment in alcohol dependence was tested (Drummond & Glautier, 1994) using a controlled trial with 35 severely alcohol-dependent men who received either cue exposure or relaxation control following detoxification. Cue exposure involved 400 minutes of exposure to the sight and smell of preferred drinks provided over 10 days in a laboratory setting. The relaxation therapy control group spent identical time in the laboratory but received only 20 minutes of exposure to alcohol cues. Results supported the extinction view. At a 6-month follow-up, the cue exposure group showed a more favorable outcome with a delayed relapse of heavy drinking and less total alcohol consumption.

On the other hand, given that the sight and smell of an alcoholic drink are powerful cues that activate cravings among alcoholics, there is also the danger that cue exposure to alcohol could backfire and increase the likelihood of relapse. It is crucial that clients receive careful explanations as to why they are being exposed to the sight of alcoholic beverages and strong cautions not to engage in such activities on their own, such as by visiting bars without supervision (Baker, Cooney, & Pomerleau, 1987). By exposing alcoholics to alcohol cues in a treatment setting where they are prevented from consuming the alcohol, alcoholics can be taught coping techniques to deal with such cues when they are later discharged (Laberg, 1990). In addition, the cues should become weakened through extinction.

Pharmacological Methods

If alcoholics cannot stop drinking or maintain sobriety by cognitive and social means, is there a pharmacological approach? In recent years, attention has been directed toward the reduction of craving for alcohol by pharmacological means such as naltrexone to reduce relapse. Naltrexone, an opiate antagonist, blocks the ability of opioids such as alcohol and morphine to stimulate areas of brain receptors normally activated by these drugs. Prevention of the pleasurable responses in the brain ordinarily generated by alcohol's release of endogenous opioids may reduce alcohol consumption.

Naltrexone was evaluated in a clinical trial with 70 male veterans who had been drinking an average of 20 years (Volpicelli, Alterman, Hayashida, & O'Brian, 1992). Half received a 50 mg dose of naltrexone, and half received a placebo over a 12-week outpatient treatment. A double-blind procedure was used to minimize any bias. The men also were referred to Alcoholics Anonymous (AA) meetings and received alcoholism counseling and relapse prevention therapy.

Self-reports of alcohol drinking and craving were used. Relapse was defined in several ways: having five or more drinks on one occasion, consuming alcohol five or more times during the previous week, and having a blood alcohol concentration (BAC) of .10 mg % or greater when coming for treatment.

Naltrexone-treated patients were approximately half as likely to relapse as the placebo patients. Craving for the placebo group was maintained, but the naltrexone group had a gradual decline in self-reported craving.

A double-blind, 12-week outpatient clinical trial on 97 patients (72 men and 25 women), predominantly White and employed full-time (O'Malley et al., 1992), gave patients either a 50 mg dose of naltrexone or a placebo. Patients received one of two different types of therapy, coping skills or supportive therapy (nondirective).

Naltrexone reduced relapse rates by about one half, as naltrexone patients reported drinking on 4.3% of the study days, whereas placebo patients reported drinking on 9.9% of the study days. Those who received naltrexone and supportive therapy were less likely to sample a drink for the first time after beginning treatment as compared to other treatment groups. Patients treated with naltrexone and coping skills therapy were just as likely to slip as the controls were, but they were less likely to relapse. Results suggest that naltrexone, combined with coping skills therapy, is an effective treatment approach to reducing craving and relapse.

ACTIVE METHODS

Motivation and Commitment

Effective relapse prevention strategies might vary with the stage of recovery (Brownell et al., 1986). At the first stage, developing motivation and obtaining commitment should be the primary goals. Use of contracts involving contingencies of monetary rewards for sobriety have been tried widely but may work only for a self-selected sample because others may drop out or not even participate.

Screening, a strategy to deliberately choose those alcoholics for admission to treatment who seem more motivated or likely to succeed, is an approach that might seem to abandon the more difficult cases. Although this approach may seem to load the deck in favor of a treatment program, one argument in its behalf is that no one is doing a favor to alcoholics who are highly likely to fail the program by trying to treat them. They may only become further demoralized, even to the point of not accepting other forms of treatment that might prove more palatable and effective for them. Failure patients also may adversely affect other patients who otherwise are more likely to succeed.

One influential relapse prevention program (Marlatt & Gordon, 1985) involves an intensive set of about eight sessions. One of the first goals for the therapist is to determine which situations involve higher risk of relapse for each individual client (Marlatt & Gordon, 1985). Counselors are then in a better position to intervene by helping clients avoid dangerous situations with appropriate problem-solving and coping skills.

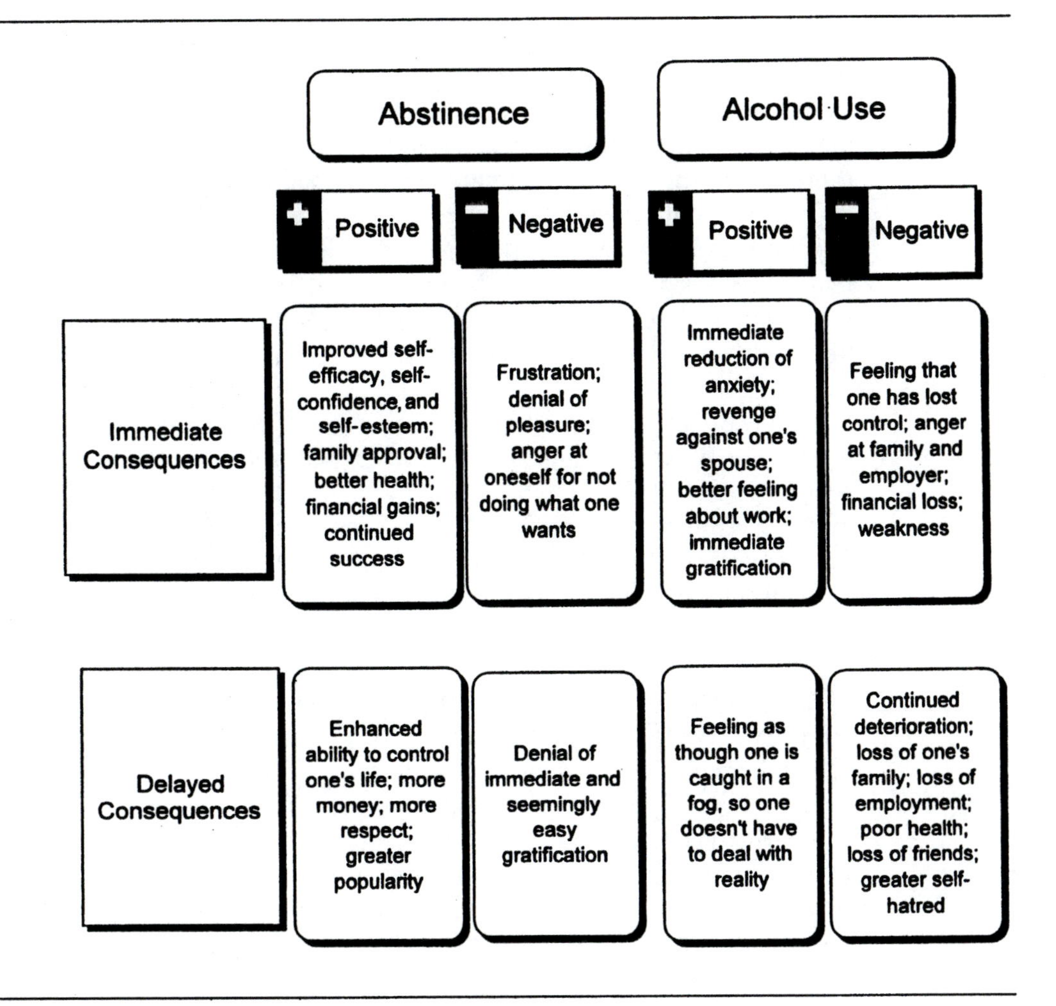

Figure 16.5. Decision Matrix for Resumption of Alcohol Use
SOURCE: Dimeff and Marlatt (1995). Copyright 1995 by Allyn & Bacon. Reprinted with permission.

Initial Behavior Change

The second stage, in which initial changes in behavior occur, has a low likelihood of relapse because the patient is still optimistic and motivated. Three important tasks are called for at this stage: decision making, cognitive restructuring, and coping skills (Brownell et al., 1986). Decision making entails helping the patient identify the immediate as well as long-term positive and negative consequences of either controlled moderate drinking or abstinence versus relapse. Figure 16.5 illustrates a decision matrix in which the alcohol-dependent person identifies the positive and negative consequences, both short and long term, of being abstinent or continuing to drink.

Cognitive restructuring involves rational interpretation of attitudes and feelings. For example, instead of blaming a lapse on their own lack of willpower or character, individuals may be helped to see that the situation they were in involved too much social pressure. They might be taught to think of craving as a normal part of recovery that can be treated rather than as a sign of hopelessness. The cognitive appraisal of the individual is a major factor of whether a slip or lapse inevitably leads to relapse. More relapse occurred among those persons who attributed their lapses to internal factors than for those who recognized the influences of external factors (Marlatt, 1985a).

Acquiring Coping Skills. Coping skills are needed for dealing with cravings when alcoholics are at high risk for relapse. Being able to refuse a drink in a social setting where there is high pressure to be a part of the group, for example, is much more difficult than a "Just say no" slogan might suggest. Such coping is critical for resisting temptation. Coping involves doing "something" as opposed to doing "nothing," but it need not involve complex reasoning or problem-solving skills (Shiffman, 1987). Cognitive forms of coping could entail distraction, thoughts involving delay, or thinking about the positive benefits of not drinking and the negative consequences of drinking. Behavioral forms of coping include eating, physical activity, escape, delay of action, and relaxation. However, this definition of coping includes so many activities that it is difficult to see how anyone could ever be described as "doing nothing."

Coping responses to relapse at 6 to 12 months following inpatient treatment were studied (Litman, Eiser, Rawson, & Oppenheim, 1984). Four types of responses were identified: positive thinking, negative thinking, avoidance/distraction, and seeking social supports. Scores on these behaviors did not differentiate eventual relapsers and nonrelapsers at intake. However, at 6 to 12 months after treatment, positive thinking and avoidance/distraction were associated with nonrelapse.

Clinical observations (Ludwig, 1988) support the view that alcoholics use various ways of "self-talk" or sobriety scripts to avoid relapse. A few examples from Ludwig (1988) will illustrate how alcoholics cope.

The negative consequences script:

> Every time I get the urge to drink, I immediately think of being sick, vomiting, shakes, being miserable.

The benefits of sobriety script:

> For the simple reason that I've got too much at stake. I've got a new home now, I've got a wife and family—three partners and a going concern—and one drink stands between me and all that.

The rationality script:

> I can stay sober if I want to. It's my decision. A man has a responsibility, and he's got to face it. A man has some kind of control over everything.

The avoid-the-first-drink script:

> I'm really an alcoholic and I can't handle it. One drink is all it takes.

The prayer script:

> The wine on the grocery shelf said, "Man you want me—you'd better buy me. You can really feel good on me." I prayed, "God, I'm really miserable. You've got to get me though this."

Developing Self-Efficacy. One relapse prevention study (Annis & Davis, 1988, 1991) focused on strengthening self-efficacy in problem drinkers so they could handle high-risk real-life situations. The therapist first identifies the client's coping skills and the environmental resources available for dealing with these situations. Then homework assignments are designed that help build this self-confidence.

Inasmuch as different problem drinkers are not equally susceptible to relapse in the same situations, a hierarchy of situations ranked by risk for relapse is identified for each client using the Inventory of Drinking Situations, which consists of eight major drinking situations: unpleasant emotions, pleasant emotions, physical discomfort, testing personal control, urges/temptations to drink, conflict with others, social pressure to drink, and pleasant times with others.

Clients performed a set of homework exercises starting with situations with the lowest risk for drinking (Annis & Davis, 1991). As the clients developed a sense of self-efficacy with success in these situations, they gradually received riskier situations. Homework assignments served several important goals: increasing awareness of events that trigger drinking, anticipating problem situations so that coping responses can be prepared, planning and rehearsing alternative coping responses, practicing new behaviors in increasingly more difficult situations, and noticing improved competency.

A study (Solomon & Annis, 1989) of the relationship between self-efficacy and treatment outcomes showed that successful abstinence up to 3 to 6 months posttreatment was greater for those with higher self-efficacy. Another study (Rychtarik, Prue, Rapp, & King, 1992) measured self-efficacy in male alcoholics at intake, discharge, and several times over the following year. Self-efficacy increased over this period. Those with lower gains were more likely to relapse.

Maintenance

Beyond these initial stages, sobriety must be maintained on a long-term basis, requiring continued monitoring, social support, and general lifestyle changes (Brownell et al., 1986). Monitoring could be done by the patient or by professionals, although in the latter instance, the line between the end of treatment and the beginning of maintenance becomes blurred.

Counselors must be aware of their role in dealing with lapses by their clients (Daley, 1989). If they become angry or give up on the clients when lapses occur, counselors may unwittingly contribute to relapse.

Social support is helpful for most individuals, although the source of the support may be a critical factor in its effectiveness. Lifestyle changes that allow other forms of gratification to replace the addiction may be helpful. Alternatives such as exercise, meditation, and relaxation training can be used as aids against relapse (Brownell et al., 1986).

Easing Reentry

A treated alcohol- or other drug-dependent individual moving from a hospital setting back into society might find an easier adjustment and lower likelihood of relapse if the reentry is gradual. Halfway houses were introduced in the 1950s as a means of providing a small, homelike environment in which residents could live for about 3 to 6 months following hospital treatment while developing self-sufficiency before returning to the community. Halfway house programs generally deal with alcoholics who are chronic abusers and have no homes or jobs to return to, so conclusions about their value may not apply to all alcoholics.

A controlled study (Sanchez-Craig & Walker, 1982) of the effectiveness of such facilities compared male and female alcoholics in halfway houses with other groups of alcoholics provided with either covert sensitization or discussion. Although relapse was not the specific focus of the study, the researchers found comparable risks of relapse for all groups because they all scored poorly on a number of drinking and nondrinking outcomes after 6, 12, and 18 months following treatment.

Polydrug Abusers and Relapse

The discussion in this chapter has dealt with relapse in which problems are limited to one drug. Unfortunately, polydrug abuse and dependency are commonplace. For example, smoking and drinking often occur together; among adult alcohol abusers, more than 85% also smoke (Abrams,

Monti, Niaura, Rohsenow, & Colby, 1996). Alcohol is frequently combined with illicit drugs such as cocaine or heroin. Cocaine and heroin also are used together by the same individuals.

A practical and theoretical concern is how to deal with the treatment and prevention of relapse of polydrug abusers (Miller & Bennett, 1996). Some polydrug users may be willing to quit using one drug but not the other. For example, some drinking smokers might be willing to try to stop drinking but wish to continue smoking, whereas the opposite preferences may hold for other individuals.

Aside from the preferences of the user, is it more efficacious to try to treat two different drug addictions concurrently or in succession? Some argue that dealing with one addiction may be easier because polydrug abusers might be more willing to try because they would still have the other drug to help cope with problems. On the other hand, given that relapse from one treated drug might be triggered by the use of other drugs, it could be argued that all drug problems should be addressed together.

There are arguments in favor of both approaches in treating smoking drinkers. Smoking may trigger drinking (Shiffman & Balabanis, 1996). Thus, if you treat only the alcoholism, the smoking may increase the likelihood of relapse. Some studies indicate that alcoholism treatment is more successful if alcoholics also quit smoking.

SUMMARY

The battle for recovery from alcohol and other drug dependencies does not end when a patient is discharged from a treatment program. As with other addictive behaviors, relapse occurs all too frequently. Retrospective self-reports are the primary source of evidence about the factors precipitating relapse, but there are limitations such as accuracy of recall as well as deliberate distortions, lies, or excuses. Retrospective reports that relapses occurred because of crises and emotional distress may be overstated because they could be means of seeking sympathy or avoiding blame.

Models of relapse such as the positive appetitional, compensatory response, opponent process, and conditioned withdrawal are based on concepts from classical conditioning theory in which originally neutral stimuli can become conditioned stimuli (CS) by association with an unconditioned stimulus (UCS). Thus, the sight, smell, or other cues (CS) that are paired with drugs (UCS) can come to elicit the reactions (UCR) that ordinarily occur in response to drugs.

Thus, over time, cues (CS) associated with drug use might themselves trigger the urge or craving (CR) to use the drug.

The opponent process model focuses on affective and conditioned determinants of drug use. It explains the development of tolerance as well as the difficulty of eliminating addictions. The incentive sensitization model takes a different approach in explaining the basis of dependency by distinguishing between two processes: wanting and liking. With prolonged drug use, changes occur in the brain that serve to maintain or increase the "wanting" while reducing the "liking" of the drug.

The social learning theory, with its emphasis on cognitive and behavioral coping, offers more opportunities for active involvement by the user. By identifying high-risk situations for lapse, it is hoped that one may stay out of such situations. When unavoidably placed in such situations, resistance to temptation is greater if individuals have good coping skills and alternative behaviors. Social learning theory emphasizes the need for alcoholics to gain a sense of self-efficacy, the feeling that one can control outcomes, to deal effectively with the urges to drink. Resistance to temptation also may be strengthened further by the attitudes and behaviors of significant others who can provide social support and reinforcement to the recovering alcoholic.

Different approaches for preventing relapse reflect different assumptions about the factors responsible for relapse. One method exposes alcoholics to alcohol-related cues, but drinking is not allowed. This technique delays the relapse of heavy drinking and leads to less total alcohol consumption. But there is also the danger that exposure to alcohol-related cues can backfire and increase the likelihood of relapse.

Pharmacological approaches to alcoholism treatment include the use of naltrexone, an antagonist of neurotransmitters ordinarily released by alcohol. By offsetting alcohol's effect on neurotransmission, naltrexone, combined with coping skills therapy, can be effective in reducing craving and relapse.

Polydrug treatment presents a difficult problem because cues associated with one drug may trigger relapse following successful treatment of a different drug. It may be difficult to persuade users to give up several drugs simultaneously, but it may be a more effective approach to minimizing relapse.

KEY TERMS

Abstinence violation effect
Attributions
Compensatory response model
Conditioned withdrawal (model)
Craving
Cue extinction
Incentive sensitization
Lapse
Opponent process theory
Positive appetitional model
Relapse

STIMULUS/RESPONSE

1. How can the adage "learn from your mistakes" be useful in helping prevent relapse for individuals who have stopped using alcohol and other drugs?
2. Once a small slip into resumed use of a drug occurs, a full relapse may follow. Do you think this outcome is due to a pharmacological or psychological reaction to making the slip?
3. Seemingly irrelevant decisions refer to behaviors that place the recovering individual at higher risk for relapse. For example, alcohol- or drug-dependent persons may suddenly find themselves in a drinking situation even though there was no conscious intent to go drinking. Have you ever tried to reduce or stop using some drug and found yourself in the same situation?
4. If you know someone who is trying to quit using some drug, what are some behaviors that you might unwittingly do that might increase his or her risk of relapse? What are some things that you could do to help this person maintain abstinence?

Prevention of Alcohol and Other Drug Problems 17

A tremendous toll of pain and suffering is inflicted on many people by the misuse of alcohol and many other drugs. Alcohol and drug dependency devastate the lives of many users and their families and friends who experience emotional, financial, and social damage. The types of problems associated with drugs differ in the extent to which harm occurs only to the user or also to innocent bystanders. Thus, physical health impairment caused by smoking or drinking mainly affects the user, whereas drinking and driving or second-hand smoke threaten others as well. Some problems such as impaired driving can be direct effects of drug use, but many other problems such as violence or depression may only be indirect consequences of drug use (Moskowitz, 1989). In addition, even casual or "recreational" drug users can cause serious physical harm from accidents due to a single-use episode. Whether drinking leads to a "social problem" also must depend on social norms and definitions (e.g., the extent to which public drunkenness is viewed as a problem varies in different societies). The concern of this chapter is with approaches to the prevention of alcohol and other drug-related problems.

In our society, people use licit drugs such as alcoholic beverages and, to a lesser extent, cigarettes in many homes as well as in public places such as parks, stores, bars, and restaurants. Drinking is permissible in many public facilities such as parks, theaters, and stadiums. Distillers, wineries, breweries, and cigarette manufacturers spend vast sums of money to advertise in newspapers, magazines, and television with messages implying that life without these substances is incomplete. Good times, glamorous friends, and personal success are depicted as part of the image of what people experience with alcoholic beverages and cigarettes.

Illegal drugs, on the other hand, are not as readily available as licit drugs are because their possession, sale, or use can lead to severe penalties, including incarceration. The locations where they can be obtained are less numerous, usually hidden, and often dangerous. The price of illicit drugs is also much higher than for licit drugs. Nonetheless, those who want to acquire these drugs do manage to find a way.

The tasks of prevention for licit and illicit drug use are quite different. With licit drugs, the influences of education, health, legal, and moral forces compete against the promotion and advertising of the alcohol and tobacco industries. Education about the health risks of cigarette smoking and alcohol consumption aims to reduce usage. Legal and economic disincentives include increased alcohol and cigarette taxes, zoning regulations for alcohol outlets, legal minimum drinking age for purchase and use, and restrictions on advertising.

Although educational, health, and moral influences against use also exist for illicit drugs, the advertising, marketing promotions, and subsidies from the federal government for licit drugs are absent. Heavy reliance is placed on legal means to control availability of illicit drugs. Educational and informational campaigns against illicit drugs aim to reduce the desire or demand for illicit drugs. Nonetheless, illicit drugs hold high attraction to many users, and the profit motive for drug sellers is even greater than for those who market legal drugs.

Prevention is a difficult task, given the strong desires of many to consume alcohol and other drugs. In general, society has failed to deal with the prevention of the root of the problems. The focus is on creating reasons for individuals not to use the substances rather than identifying why people use them in the first place or seeking alternatives.

Social Policy and Drugs

The goals and methods adopted by a society to deal with problems associated with alcohol and other drug use, abuse, and dependency are issues of intense controversy and heated debate. Social policy refers to the laws and programs that regulate the use of these substances. In the past, drug policy decisions have been based on many factors, including historical, philosophical, moral-religious, political, and economic considerations. Beliefs about fundamental issues of right and wrong, personal freedom, individual control, and social responsibility exert strong influences on how people feel about the proper place of alcohol and other drugs in our society. Firmly entrenched traditions are not easily changed. Politicians both play to and are controlled by their constituents. Lobbies for legal drugs have considerable political and economic power to fight for social policies and laws that favor their drugs and rule against illegal drugs. We will examine several divergent views about what our social policy about drugs should be.

ALL DRUGS SHOULD BE BANNED

At one extreme is the zero-tolerance position that all psychoactive drugs are undesirable. All drugs are viewed as evil and should be banned because they serve hedonistic goals such as the experience of pleasure. A puritanical attitude and longstanding American ideology that pleasure is selfish or incompatible with work have fostered a negative attitude toward all psychoactive drug use.

Any distinction between drug use and abuse is ignored because all drug use is seen as equivalent to abuse and addiction, sooner or later. The argument is that even if most abusers did not engage in any behaviors harmful to self or to others, they would eventually experience and suffer serious physical health hazards.

A common tactic is to arouse fear by creating the impression that the drug causes antisocial and criminal behavior among users. Usually the evidence is inconclusive but is portrayed as if it were. Thus, the finding that criminals tend to use certain drugs does not prove that the drug use caused the criminal behavior. Alternatively, it may be that living a life of crime fosters drug use, or some common third factor is responsible. Another tactic is to argue that use of one drug may cause the subsequent use of more dangerous drugs. This gateway or stepping-stone theory is highly similar to the domino theory for international relations, in which a strategy of containment of evil communism in far-off lands is advocated to prevent the evil forces from coming to our shores. Similarly, the association of certain drugs with immigrant populations such as opium with the Chinese, marijuana with Mexicans, and opiates with Italian immigrants is apt to increase support for bans against the drugs of disfavored immigrant groups.

ALL DRUGS SHOULD BE AVAILABLE

From an alternative perspective, individuals should have the choice to decide what course of action to take rather than be controlled by a paternalistic government. Individuals may be irrational in deceiving themselves as to the actual risk involved in using drugs, but they should be the ones to decide.

Some users do not seem to suffer harmful effects and feel it is their right to continue to enjoy their drugs. Some individuals may realize that potential dangers exist but feel they should be allowed to make the trade-off of possible future harm in return for immediate gratification. The life philosophy and values that worked a generation or two ago are not seen as viable in current society with its pleasure orientation and focus on immediate gratification. By outlawing a drug, society takes the choice away from the user.

An argument in favor of most psychoactive drugs is the fact that many drugs originated as medicines and have been used for such purposes over the course of their history, despite the fact that they also have been used for nonmedical purposes, often with harmful effects. Painkilling drugs such as ether, sedatives, morphine, opioids, and marijuana have been used for analgesic purposes in surgery. Stimulants such as cocaine have been offered as treatment for depression, melancholy, and weight control (amphetamines).

SOME DRUGS SHOULD BE BANNED, OTHERS NOT

A more temperate position is that some drugs are beneficial, on balance, and although their use should be controlled or limited, they should not be totally banned. Other drugs that, on balance, are harmful can justifiably be more controlled with sanctions for use or possession. Legal drugs are regarded by their advocates as the ones that most people can use without harm or risk of addiction. The unfortunate minority of users of drugs (e.g., alcohol) who do become addicted are seen as suffering a disease, and medical treatment is available to help them. Thus, they see no need to ban these substances because most of us do not have problems using them.

POLITICS VERSUS SCIENCE

As scientific evidence on the effects of drugs has accumulated, researchers have attempted to inform social planners and policymakers with objective data about the impact of alcohol and other drugs on physical health, psychological well-being, crime, and other social problems. Unfortunately, policymakers and voters often have not been persuaded by scientific findings so much as by personal beliefs and emotional feelings, often powered by stereotypes and misconceptions about the causes and consequences of substance abuse.

In part, the failure of the scientific evidence to affect social policy has been that research is often too complicated for nonscientists to comprehend. In addition, the scientific evidence has not always yielded clear conclusions, either because of the complexity of the problem or because of the unreliability or invalidity of some scientific studies. Finally, science can only provide part of the input that determines effective social policy, which is also a political and economic decision.

Much of the continuing debate over the effects of drugs is not based on scientific and objective research but reflects biases and prejudices on both sides. On one side is a tendency to demonize most if not all drugs. Scare tactics and fear are used to intimidate users; drugs are portrayed as "the bogeyman" who will get you if you don't watch out. The message is that once you use an illicit drug, you will get "hooked," and you won't be able to stop and will experience all kinds of unpleasant consequences, social and physical.

On the other side, one argument is that not everyone who uses a drug gets "addicted" or experiences harm. It is believed that people can learn how to use a drug in a manner that is not harmful and that penalties against use are unjustified because drug use is a "victimless crime." Proponents of more liberal drug policies in the United States point to other nations such as the Netherlands, where use of illicit drugs such as marijuana and heroin is tolerated without the widespread harm feared by drug opponents here (Nadelmann, 1997). At the same time, it must be cautioned that many other differences exist between the United States and other nations and that the societal effect of one drug will not necessarily be the same in different social settings. The history of drugs in a nation, along with its values, demographic characteristics, economic conditions, and political orientation, all combine with the drug to produce its eventual impact on a society.

Could it be that both views about drugs are defensible? One view may apply to some users, but the other view is valid for other users. Instead of assuming that all users will be affected in the same manner by drugs, we must recognize the possibility that the characteristics of the user and the setting in which the drug is used may be important additional determinants of what effect a drug has. In other words, the effects of drugs have a pharmacological basis, but the effects also depend on the social and psychological aspects of users such as their personalities, past experiences, social situation, and expectations (Zinberg, 1984).

The Public Health Model

A useful model for the analysis of public health problems considers the interactions of the *agent, host,* and *environment,* as shown in Figure 17.1. For drug issues, the *agent* is the "germ" or substance. Prevention efforts

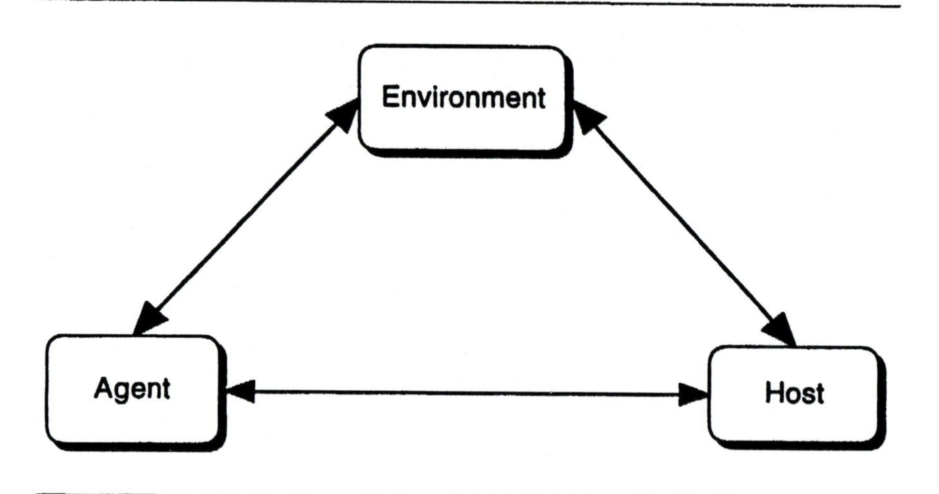

Figure 17.1. Diagram of Three Components of the Public Health Model

directed toward the agent focus on restricting its availability through means such as pricing, limiting the hours when it can be sold or served publicly, and establishing minimum drinking age laws. Such approaches emphasize external factors that might control the level of drug use and associated problems.

The *host* represents the potential or actual user who may eventually suffer harmful effects. Prevention efforts in this area might attempt to reduce the individual's desire or incentive to drink through means such as education and persuasion. In other words, if one can reduce the desire to use specific drugs, problems may be avoided, even if drugs are available.

Finally, the *environment* includes both the physical and social context in which the agent and host reside. A prevention focus on the environment might include the shaping of social attitudes and norms about drug use or the regulation of the physical environment in which drugs might be consumed.

Successful prevention strategies may need to consider all of these components of the system of interrelated factors rather than focusing on only one. The multiplicity of social and environmental forces, often beyond the control of individuals, that affects drug use must be recognized. In the case of alcohol, as Figure 17.2 indicates, laws and their enforcement, marketing and pricing, and media depictions are some of the environmental factors that must be considered in addition to any individual genetic or psychological factors when designing prevention strategies. We will take a closer look at these contextual factors in the following pages.

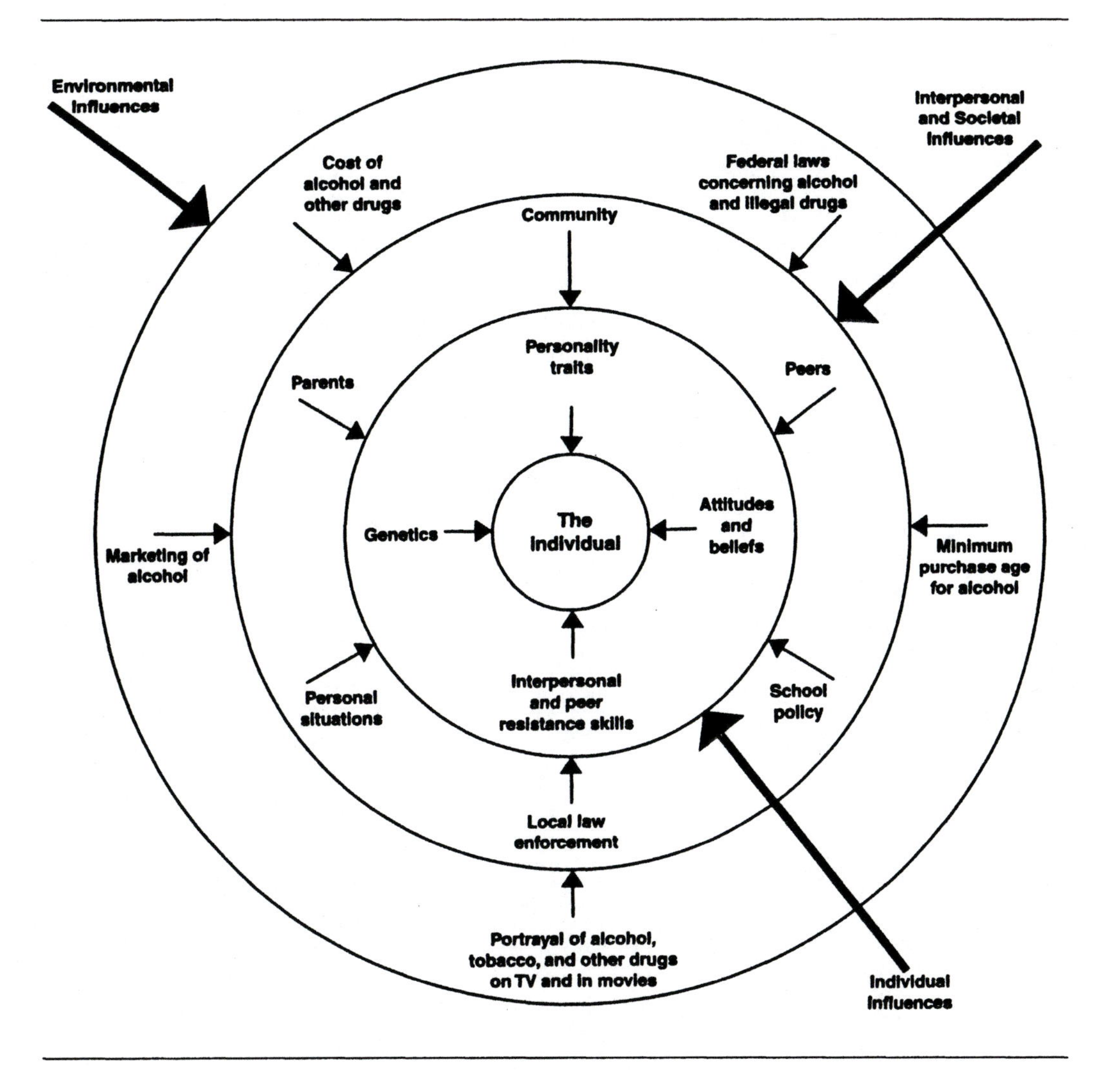

Figure 17.2. A Complex Set of Factors Affects Alcohol Use
SOURCE: National Clearinghouse for Alcohol Information (1989).

Control of Availability

Obviously, alcohol or any other drug must be physically available in the environment before it can cause problems. From this premise, many prevention efforts attempt to limit the physical availability of drugs (the agent). The assumption is that if drugs were less readily available in the environment, they would be consumed to a lesser extent and, it is hoped, with fewer related problems.

An underlying theoretical basis for this assumption is the **single distribution of consumption model** (Ledermann, 1956), which is based on comparisons in many nations of the relationship between per capita consumption of alcohol and rates of heavy drinking, as inferred from deaths due to liver cirrhosis. The frequency distribution for the amount of alcohol different people drink is one in which most citizens drank at either low or moderate levels, with a small percentage consuming alcohol at the high end of the continuum. Variants of the distribution of consumption model are possible, such as one involving a threshold, a certain use level below which there is little or no harm. Still, these models generally agree that if the availability of alcohol in the society as a whole can be reduced, the societal level of alcohol problems also should decrease.

However, social policy must consider other factors than the total consumption summed over all users in a society. A measure of total consumption cannot distinguish between acute or short-term and chronic or long-term use. This distinction is important in setting social drug policies because the consequences of acute and chronic use levels are not the same. Whereas high levels of acute use can cause accidents, violence, and loss of productivity, chronic use also is more likely associated with harmful physical effects such as liver cirrhosis, even at low levels per drinking episode.

Aggregrate use levels ignore how total use is distributed over the entire population (i.e., how many drinkers are heavy, moderate, and light drinkers and abstainers). This variable may be related to the extent of harm from use. Also, the risks of harm may not be linearly related to consumption level, as noted earlier. If risks are exponentially related, for example, the heavy drinkers, even if they are a minority of the population, contribute more to the overall or aggregate risk in the society. The light drinkers, although they would represent a larger percentage of the population, would contribute a smaller risk of problems.

Aggregate measures of consumption such as per capita consumption, which reflect the overall amount of use in society, also may not predict risks of harm for individuals. Aggregate measures are convenient summaries, but they are not sensitive to individual variations in use. Regardless of the total use level in society as a whole, individual use levels are better predictors of each individual's risk level for a particular problem.

Primary Prevention

Primary prevention involves methods for stopping drug use-related problems before they start. The benefits of primary prevention are often difficult to prove or require many years before they are evident. Consequently, this goal often has received a lower priority than the task of solving more immediate problems in which adverse consequences of drug abuse are more readily apparent. Diagnosing and identifying present drug abusers (secondary prevention) and treating persons already suffering from drug problems (tertiary prevention) usually demand priority over primary prevention of future problems.

Control of the availability of drugs is an important aspect of primary prevention and involves many different methods, but most can be classified as **supply reduction** or **demand reduction.** Supply reduction methods, aimed at restricting or eliminating the physical presence of drugs, differ for licit and illicit drugs. For licit drugs, availability can be lowered by increased taxes and pricing as well as by regulations about conditions for sale and use. For illicit drugs, supply reduction involves destruction of existing sources, interdiction of supplies crossing national borders, and confiscation. Demand reduction methods for both licit and illicit drugs include education and persuasion attempts to reduce the attractiveness of drugs among potential users. In the case of illicit drugs, even though the demand or desire may be high, threats of incarceration and fines aim to suppress actual use. An overview of different methods of primary prevention is presented now.

MASS MEDIA INFLUENCES

Mass media focus on demand reduction by promoting awareness and factual knowledge about drugs through public service announcements. Such programs are assumed to persuade audiences to avoid these substances, but they may have limited effectiveness (Wallack, 1981). The indirect nature of mass media, as compared to the personal touch of in-person communication, may limit their impact. The advantage of mass media is that in theory they can reach large numbers of people rapidly, but in practice people may not attend to, remember, or even correctly interpret many messages in the presentations. Even if they learn the information, they may not modify their drinking behavior because many other factors help maintain its level.

Moreover, there is the possibility of reactance, created by strong messages that backfire by increasing motivation to experiment with or try drugs. This effect was shown in a study (Bensley & Wu, 1991) that presented college students with either a high- or low-threat message against drinking. Later, they participated in a beer taste rating task designed to unobtrusively measure consumption. Those who had received the high-threat message, especially among male heavy drinkers, consumed more beer than those who had received the low-threat message.

The images of alcohol use and its effects portrayed in mass media entertainment programming are potentially a major environmental influence on the drug attitudes and use of viewers. For example, a study (Breed, Defoe, & Wallack, 1984) that examined the content of television programs to determine the number of acts of drinking of alcoholic beverages found an increase from the 1976-1977 season to the 1981-1982 season from about 5 to more than 8 acts per hour. By 1987, the number had risen to more than 10 acts per hour (Wallack, Breed, & Cruz, 1987). It is difficult to evaluate the effects of such programming because the types of individuals who view different types and amounts of programs are not equivalent. Whether exposure to such content actually has a causal influence on the level of alcohol use is conjectural. An alternative view is that media presentations reflect societal norms. In addition, it is important to consider whether the depictions placed drug use in a favorable or unfavorable light rather than measure only the total depictions shown.

IMPACT OF ADVERTISING

Advertising of drug products, of course, applies only to licit drugs. In contrast to mass media public information health messages, commercial messages about alcohol and tobacco often involve distorted and misleading glamorization about their effects. The goal is to market alcohol and tobacco products for profit through the creation of images and fantasies associated with these products rather than to impart factual information.

Huge sums of money, more than $1 billion each year since 1984, have been spent to advertise alcoholic beverages in the United States. After reaching a peak in 1986 of about $1.4 billion, the amount has since declined gradually (National Institute on Alcohol Abuse and Alcoholism, 1992). One might assume that advertising is highly effective in encouraging alcohol consumption to justify such expenditures. However, a review (Frankena et al., 1985) of existing research assessing the effects of brand-specific advertising found no strong effects on overall consumption levels.

Bans on alcohol advertising do not reduce sales, nor are total advertising expenditures reliably related to increased sales (Smart, 1988). Correlational studies that examined the relationship between the amount of consumption and exposure to alcohol advertising yielded mixed findings. Furthermore, the direction of causality was not clear with this type of evidence. Thus, people who like to drink also may enjoy watching advertisements for alcoholic beverages more than lighter or nondrinkers.

However, one analysis (Saffer, 1991) of data from 17 developed nations from 1970 to 1983 found that per capita alcohol consumption where there was a ban on alcohol advertising was only 84% as high as it was in countries without such restrictions. Moreover, alcohol abuse, as indexed by cirrhosis mortality and motor vehicle fatality rates, was lower in countries with the advertising bans.

ECONOMIC CONTROLS

One assumption is that higher costs of a drug may lead to reduced consumption because the user would have less disposable income, hence reducing availability of a drug. In support of this view, as noted earlier, increased liquor taxes between 1960 and 1975 in many states were associated with a decline in alcohol consumption (Cook, 1981). However, differences in the effectiveness of pricing may exist for different beverage types. Beer is price inelastic (i.e., its consumption level did not vary much with the price, whereas consumption of distilled spirits and, to some extent, wine was price elastic and reduced by higher prices) (Ornstein & Levy, 1983).

Although this reasoning might apply to many light drinkers, it is less likely to be effective with the highly addicted drinker who might forego other needs to spend economic resources on alcohol. Aggregate comparisons do not allow us to identify which persons are drinking less. As price goes up, does drinking decline evenly across the whole population or more so for some groups than for others? If social policy leads to higher prices that affect only lighter drinkers, it will not reduce the alcohol-related problems of heavier drinkers.

State and federal alcohol taxes have been relatively stable or have had small increases since the 1950s (Coate & Grossman, 1987). When adjusted for inflation, the real price of alcoholic beverages actually declined between 1960 and 1980 (Cook, 1981). Small price increases should lead to moderate reductions in alcohol consumption by young people, which in turn could conceivably reduce their involvement in automobile accidents and fatalities involving alcohol (Grossman, Coate, & Arluck, 1987).

A review of research (Leung & Phelps, 1993) on the effect of the price of alcohol on consumers found that higher prices are related to less consumption, after controlling for other factors such as income. This effect occurred for all types of alcoholic beverages, although beer had the least reduction in relation to price increases.

In contrast to the relationship of cost to use for licit drugs, a different situation may exist for illicit drugs. A major problem associated with the high price of illicit drugs is that heavy users may resort to various criminal activities to support their expensive drug habits. Price does not appear to deter the use of these drugs for those who are already dependent on them.

EDUCATIONAL CONTROLS

School-based alcohol and other drug prevention programs have tried numerous curricula that usually involve several components aimed at different goals. Normative beliefs have had the strongest correlation with alcohol use and would appear to be an important task for educational programs to address. On the other hand, tasks such as life skills, stress skills, and self-esteem have had a weak relationship with alcohol use and might seem to be less relevant for purposes of reducing risk for alcohol use.

Most school-based alcohol and other drug prevention programs focus on helping children resist peer influences by teaching coping skills and, through normative education, correcting the misperception that everyone is using drugs. Both of these objectives deal with factors that are among those having a strong relationship with alcohol use.

Many programs attempt to work with parents, encouraging them to work with their children. Universal programs are directed at all students to modify their alcohol and other drug use, and other programs target students who are already using drugs or are at higher risk.

Self-Esteem Programs

A kindergarten through 12th-grade curriculum of 15 sessions distributed over a year was designed to provide alcohol knowledge, shape positive alcohol attitudes, and build self-esteem (Hopkins, Mauss, Kearney, & Weisheit, 1988). The study involved 6,808 students, 75% White, from different school districts. Two- and 3-year follow-ups showed minimal benefits of these programs for students in comparison to students in control schools who did not participate. Random assignment of schools to the two treatments was not possible.

Resistance Skills Programs

Some school programs emphasize the development of **resistance skills** and social competence (Botvin, Baker, Dusenbury, Tortu, & Botvin, 1990). These models assume that resistance can be developed with experience just as inoculation can improve immunity to diseases. The Life Skills

Training (Botvin, Schinke, Epstein, Diaz, & Botvin, 1995) classroom program is designed to teach general personal and social skills as well as drug resistance skills. This 3-year curriculum, designed for middle school or junior high students, had a combination of techniques, including instruction, demonstration, feedback, reinforcement, behavioral rehearsal, and homework assignments.

Different schools received either the prevention program with formal provider training and feedback, the prevention program with videotaped provider training and no feedback, or no treatment. The curriculum included general as well as drug-specific problem-solving and decision-making skills, critical thinking skills for resisting peer and media influences, skills for increasing self-control and self-esteem, coping strategies for relieving stress and anxiety, and information about the drug use norms of peers.

Significant reductions ranging from 59% to 75% in comparison to controls occurred for cigarette smoking, marijuana use, and immoderate alcohol use. Prevention effects also were found for normative expectations and knowledge concerning substance use, interpersonal skills, and communication skills. A follow-up 6 years later showed that the prevalence of cigarette smoking, alcohol use, and marijuana use for students in the Life Skills Training program was 44% lower than for control students.

Normative Education

Many students believe that peers use drugs at higher levels than they actually do, a misperception that might encourage them to use drugs. To counter this tendency, a **normative education** curriculum teaches students that their peers do not use drugs at levels as high as they might think they do.

One study (Hansen, Graham, Wolkenstein, & Rohrbach, 1991) combined two types of programs, one involving resistance training and one focusing on influences of peer use norms in which the students learned that many other students did not use drugs. Four conditions—normative education curriculum only, resistance training curriculum only, both curricula, and neither curriculum—were compared among about 3,600 fifth graders in 128 different classes in 45 different schools. The results showed that receiving both normative education and resistance skills training was the most effect curriculum. In addition, the quality of program delivery, enthusiasm of the teachers, receptiveness of the students, and proper delivery of the program components, as judged by trainers, observers, and program specialists, contributed to the success of the students in acquiring resistance skills and perceived self-efficacy.

Project DARE

A drug education program for elementary schools that has been highly visible but also very controversial is the Drug Abuse Resistance Education (DARE) project. Initiated in 1983 in Los Angeles schools through the Los Angeles Police Department, DARE has been widely accepted and spread throughout the nation and taught in more than half of all schools in the United States. The orientation of the curriculum was to teach resistance skills ("Just say no") to millions of schoolchildren using police officers from the community. **Project DARE** receives funding currently under the Safe and Drug-Free Schools and Communities Act of 1994, which provides more than $400 million annually for DARE and other programs.

Despite its popular appeal and support, independent evaluators found that the program did not do what it was supposed to do. Although DARE raised children's self-esteem, taught them skills to resist peer pressures to use drugs, and improved their attitudes toward police, it did not appear to lower drug use (Ennett, Tobler, Ringwalt, & Flewelling, 1994). The critics argued that DARE grew into what resembles a government-sanctioned monopoly, operating in 8,000 communities and more than half of the nation's schools, despite a lack of convincing evidence that it lowered drug use.

Community-Based Approach

One attempt (Johnson et al., 1990; Pentz, 1995) to go beyond the school-based curricula to include efforts to improve community attitudes about alcohol involved the large-scale 3-year longitudinal Midwestern Prevention Project with sixth and seventh graders in 42 schools in the Kansas City metropolitan area.

This program used a school-based curriculum as well as a mass media community campaign. Different classes were randomly assigned to several different experimental treatment groups and one control group (mass media and community organization). Students who began the program in junior high showed significantly less use of marijuana (approximately 30%), cigarettes (about 25%), and alcohol (about 20%) in their senior year than children in schools that did not offer the program. The most important factor found to have affected drug use among the students was increased perceptions of their friends' intolerance of drug use.

LEGAL CONTROLS

Licit Drugs

Laws are intended to be stronger methods than education or economics for altering alcohol-related behaviors. Prohibition of alcohol is the most extreme example of government policy directed at reducing availability of a drug, but it did not prove viable because it created other problems even though it was effective in its goals when tried in the United States between 1919 and 1932.

Licensing of retail outlets is a less extreme control aimed at regulating or controlling availability of alcohol. A larger number of retail liquor outlets in a community should be directly correlated with the amount of alcohol sales and, presumably, consumption of alcohol. A review (MacDonald & Whitehead, 1983) of studies concluded that a larger number of retail outlets involving off-premises consumption in a community were associated with increased consumption, but this relationship was not found for on-premises drinking outlets.

This difference may be due to the fact that servers can restrict or limit alcohol that is purchased on the premises to intoxicated patrons, whereas the purchaser has control over the off-premises use of alcohol. Thus, if a drinker continues to drink beyond a safe level, servers can intervene and stop serving. The recognition that servers in commercial establishments can help keep alcohol availability at socially and legally acceptable levels for patrons has led to the development of programs to teach servers how to help maintain safer drinking environments for their customers (Saltz, 1986; Vegega, 1986).

States have passed stringent laws, imposed heavy sanctions, and applied strong enforcement in dealing with drinking and driving behavior (Farrell, 1989). Stronger laws instituted in several countries had immediate benefits (Ross, 1984), but the gains were often short-lived after the initial publicity (Epperlein, 1987).

Illicit Drugs

In the case of illicit drugs, the assumption is held that laws against the sale and use of these drugs are needed to keep the problem under control. It is further assumed that without these laws, the already substantial problems associated with illicit drug abuse would be much higher. Some might agree with the prediction but object to the methods used to enforce these laws, which often may infringe on civil liberties.

Although substantial funds have been allocated to law enforcement, incarceration, and rehabilitation, the efforts do not seem to have appreciably reduced the demand for many illicit drugs. The federal budget for fiscal year 2000 calls for $17.8 billion, a 4.3% increase over 1999. About two thirds of the budget is for law enforcement, interdiction of supplies at borders, crop eradication, and substitution in other countries. Only about one third of the budget is for demand reduction through education and persuasion programs. However, the evidence on the effect of reduced supplies of illegal drugs on the demand for them is not convincing (Institute of Medicine, 1996). Demand for many drugs is price elastic; use levels for many users are not closely related to the price (Reuter & Caulkins, 1995).

In addition to legal methods of reducing supplies of illicit drugs, increased attempts have been made to reduce demand through the legal system by arrests for federal drug offenses (Zimring & Hawkins, 1992). Mandatory jail time for certain drug offenses exists in almost all states, and in the past decade, there has been an increase in lengthy prison sentences (U.S. Bureau of Justice Statistics, 1992).

But the question still remains: How effective are severe penalties for drug offenses as deterrents? For example, increased enforcement against illicit drugs might have an unintended and ironic effect (MacCoun & Caulkins, 1996). As more dealers get arrested, the cost of dealing drugs becomes higher. Consequently, the selling price of drugs rises to compensate surviving dealers for their higher risk. The lure of more sizable profits for dealers from selling illicit drugs, coupled perhaps also by their underestimates of the objective risk of their arrest, could motivate more rather than less drug trafficking.

The impact of increased law enforcement on illicit drug consumers also seems to be limited. Illicit drug use is still high despite a large increase of drug offenders in prison populations. In New York and California and federal prisons, for example, drug offenders are the largest inmate population (U.S. Bureau of Justice Statistics, 1995).

Secondary Prevention

If we cannot "prevent" drug problems from occurring due to the many factors in the environment that make drug use attractive, we can and must still develop countermeasures for the reduction and minimization of existing problems stemming from excessive drug use. Secondary prevention refers to methods to reduce ongoing problems that drugs have created for society. How this task is achieved will be illustrated with three pervasive problems: heavy drinking among college students, driving while intoxicated (DWI), and drugs in the workplace.

HEAVY-DRINKING COLLEGE STUDENTS

As noted in Chapter 7, many college students, especially those in campus residential settings, often live up to the stereotype of the party animal by indulging in heavy drinking. Many will mature out of this pattern, as this behavior is sustained during college years by the peer influence of other heavy-drinking students. However, others will continue to drink at problematic levels after leaving college, and early intervention would be a form of secondary prevention.

However, few drinking students view themselves as having alcohol problems, preferring to regard their drinking as appropriate of college students. Secondary prevention might reduce drinking and related problems during college as well as in later life. Thus, teaching coping skills as alternatives to drinking and encouraging moderation in using alcohol may be more acceptable to heavy-drinking students than trying to persuade them that they have drinking problems.

In one study (Kivlahan, Marlatt, Fromme, Coppel, & Williams, 1990), three randomly assigned groups of college students were given an 8-week program. One group had a traditional lecture program based on the disease model of alcoholism that stressed the negative effects of alcohol abuse. Another group received a cognitive-behavioral coping skills course that included identification of situations with high risk for alcohol abuse and how to deal with them without drinking, and a third group was a control group that had completed daily records of their alcohol use.

Follow-ups conducted over a 1-year period showed reductions in self-reported drinking, with the coping skills group best, followed by the information-only group and then the control group. Still, about half of the students occasionally engaged in heavy drinking.

This approach led to the development of a program (Marlatt, Bear, & Larimer, 1995) to reduce drinking with entering freshmen at the University of Washington in 1990. Two groups of heavy-drinking students were randomly assigned to either the intervention or to the no-treatment control condition. A third group was a random sample of the screened pool of students that included drinkers of varying use levels. All students completed an extensive set of questionnaires when they entered the university to assess their alcohol and drug history, problems related to alcohol and drug use, and measures of other psychosocial variables such as life stressors, perceived drinking norms, and sexual behavior.

Over the first term, students in the intervention group met individually with interviewers who discussed their questionnaire responses with them in a nonjudgmental manner. The goal was to get the students to think about their behaviors by giving them feedback about their drinking relative to other students and to make choices for themselves about their use of drugs rather than for the interviewers to attempt to directly change student drinking behavior. Later in the year, students received feedback showing how their pattern of drinking and drinking-related problems changed over the year. The results, through the second year, were promising as more students in the intervention group showed modest reductions in drinking as compared to the control groups.

DRIVING WHILE INTOXICATED

In our highly mobile society with the widespread availability and popularity of alcoholic beverages, it is almost impossible to prevent many drinkers from driving vehicles while still under the influence of alcohol. People socialize, dine in restaurants, and engage in other activities that often involve consumption of alcoholic beverages. Lacking other attractive means of transportation to get home, many people end up driving under varying degrees of intoxication.

It is impossible for law enforcement personnel to apprehend every person driving under the influence of alcohol, and people realize that they may have a good chance of not being detected. If, of course, they have a traffic accident, they are likely to face stiff penalties and possibly injuries, assuming they are not killed outright. Nonetheless, these fears are usually minimized or rationalized because the driver who has been drinking needs to get home and knows that every drinking driver on the road cannot be detected or apprehended.

Secondary prevention deals with preventing recurrences of this type of behavior among those who are apprehended for **driving while intoxicated** (DWI) or **driving under the influence** (DUI). One countermeasure involves education and didactic presentation of information coupled with some small-group interactions to increase awareness. Another focus on deterrence uses the threat of punishment such as loss of license and driving privileges as well as a fine. Deterrence programs attempt to reduce the likelihood of future drinking-and-driving behavior of those apprehended for this offense as well as those who have not yet committed or been detected for such practices. These programs must be perceived as holding a reasonably high probability of apprehension for violations to be effective.

Some DWIs may need alcoholism treatment. One study (Wilson & Jonah, 1985) found that drinkers who admitted driving under the influence of alcohol reported more prior accidents and convictions. In addition, they drank more alcohol, used seat belts less, and reported being less likely to cut down drinking at a party before driving than those who did not report drinking and driving. There may be a risk behavior syndrome that involves risky driving behaviors, including the use of alcohol, especially for young drivers (Jonah & Dawson, 1987). However, it is dangerous to overgeneralize and treat all DWIs as if they were alcohol abusers. Referrals to treatment programs, psychotherapy, or Alcoholics Anonymous (AA) may be unnecessarily costly, ineffective, and unwarranted for DWIs who are not abusers of alcohol (Armor et al., 1978).

Subtypes of DWI Offenders

Several subtypes of DWI offenders in terms of personality traits and accident-related driving attitudes may exist (Donovan & Marlatt, 1982). The most common subtype involves individuals with infrequent and light drinking, a good driving record, good emotional adjustment, and the least driving-related aggression. A less frequent subtype shows depression, resentment, and low assertiveness.

Using this taxonomy, different secondary prevention approaches may be designed. For the first type, a controlled drinking emphasis may help these offenders identify situations with high risk for DWI and how to cope with them. For the second type, a program focusing on self-management training might help them improve their feelings of control and efficacy.

High-Risk and Repeat Offenders. High-risk "bad" drivers (many traffic arrests and violations) were studied prospectively over a 3-year period (Donovan, Umlauf, & Salzberg, 1991). This group was similar at the outset of the study in demographics, personality, and risk-enhancing driver attitudes. At the 3-year follow-up, they were more likely to be arrested for DWI (11.4% vs. 2.0%) than the general driving population. The subgroup of "bad" drivers who became DWI drank more often than the other high-risk drivers. These results imply that high-risk drivers should be a target group for early intervention for alcohol problems.

There may be personality differences between first and multiple DWI offenders. A total of 358 first offenders and 141 multiple offenders for driving under the influence of alcohol were compared on personality traits, drinking behavior and problems, and driving history based on official driving records (McMillen, Adams, Wells Parker, Pang, & Anderson, 1992). Multiple offenders were higher in hostility, sensation seeking, psychopathic deviance, mania, and depression than first offenders. They were significantly lower in emotional adjustment and assertiveness but higher in nontraffic arrests, accidents, and traffic tickets. Multiple offenders also consumed more alcohol, had more alcohol problems, and had higher blood alcohol concentrations at the time of arrest. Because this was not a longitudinal study, it is uncertain if the results show that personality differences preceded the differences in drinking-and-driving behavior or vice versa.

Implementation Problems

One problem facing these programs is poor or slow punishment of offenders. Higher recidivism rates in New York occurred among offenders whose alcohol tickets were not disposed in a timely manner and among offenders who were able to avoid a conviction even though their tickets were disposed (Yu & Williford, 1995). Time of arrest and blood alcohol content reading at the arrest did not predict drinking-and-driving recidivism. It appears important to swiftly and effectively convict drinking-and-driving offenders.

Another reason why programs may not be more effective is that when repeat DWI offenders have their licenses suspended, they do not always have to prove that they have gained control of their drinking problem for their licenses to be reinstated (Nichols, 1990). Also, many jurisdictions have diversionary programs that allow first-time DWIs to attend "traffic school" (education/treatment programs) to avoid having their arrests appear on their records or getting their licenses suspended (National Transportation Safety Board, 1987).

Whether this option is justifiable depends on numerous factors such as its impact on subsequent traffic violations involving alcohol. A comparison (Perrine & Sadler, 1987) of California DWI offenders given license actions (suspensions, fines) versus referral to rehabilitation programs found fewer crashes subsequently by those who received traffic citations, suggesting that the harsher policy may be more effective.

DRUGS IN THE WORKPLACE

The adverse effects of drug abuse and dependence often extend beyond the drinker's personal activities and carry over to the workplace, impairing performance and productivity. Absenteeism and tardiness, work productivity, workplace safety, and liability are major concerns about the detrimental effects of drugs among employees in the workplace.

Prior to the temperance movements of the 19th century, alcohol use on the job was not always regarded as undesirable but was commonly accepted. As the hazards of drinking on work quality became recognized, management's "solution" was typically to discharge such personnel. In the 1940s, a movement arose to provide **employee assistance programs** (EAPs) in which supervisors were taught to use poor or deteriorating work performance as a sign of possible alcohol problems. Then attempts to counsel and refer the employee to alcoholism treatment would be made. The idea of EAPs was more humane than firing employees, but it was also hoped that the programs would be cost-effective by avoiding the expense of retraining, new hiring, work site accidents, poor productivity, and litigation. However, EAPs were often difficult to implement due to resistance from both employers and employees.

It was not until the late 1980s that EAPs finally became widely accepted (Nathan, 1984; Roman, 1987; Trice & Staudemeier, 1989). Although companies were not legally required to have EAPs, they increased due to concerns about possible legal actions of discrimination if they fired alcoholics on grounds other than poor work performance. A national survey of health promotion activities on work sites conducted by the Office of Disease Prevention and Health Promotion (ODPHP; 1987) reported that 24% of work sites with 50 or more workers and more than half of those with 750 or more employees had EAPs.

At the same time that EAPs became more commonplace, they also adopted a more "broad-brush" approach that extends beyond intervention for alcohol problems to include referral and treatment for illegal drug abuse as well as other psychological problems that might hamper work to improve work site performance, reduce turnover, and cut absenteeism. The potential of EAPs to motivate drug abusers and dependents to seek treatment rests in the fact that employers have one important leverage that family members and friends lack—namely, control over the employee's job. However, threats of dismissals and penalties are less effective than "constructive confrontation" (Trice & Sonnenstuhl, 1988) and peer referral in motivating help seeking.

In theory, EAPs promise a means of early intervention, but in practice, a number of problems exist in their implementation such as risks of loss of confidentiality, coerced treatment, and invasion of privacy. Although employers have a right to expect work performance to meet certain criteria, it is only when alcohol abuse interferes with these goals that employers can legitimately attempt to urge employees to accept alcoholism treatment. However, overzealous employers sometimes exceed these limits and monitor employee behaviors that employers and supervisors find unacceptable, even when they do not interfere with work performance

(Fillmore, 1987). In addition to these political concerns, the effectiveness of EAPs in modifying drinking problems has not been adequately evaluated (Babor, Ritson, & Hodgson, 1986). Such evaluation is difficult because cooperation of companies and employees is not easy to obtain, and there is typically an absence of control groups.

Drug Testing

Drug testing is one objective approach that is aimed at preventing work impairment and accidents that may harm employees using drugs as well as those around them. Several issues arise that complicate the use of drug-testing policies. First, there is the assumption that the employee is presumed guilty until proven innocent. That is, by requiring drug tests, the burden of proof is on the employee. Given the potential safety problems created by employees under the influence of drugs in the workplace, it may be conceded that drug testing may be defensible as a lesser evil in jobs where there is high risk for substantial harm from accidents. However, this concession presumes that drug tests such as urinalysis are highly accurate, an assumption that is debatable (Hanson, 1993; Kapur, 1993; Zwerling, 1993).

There is also the issue of an employee's rights to a private life when not at work. If employees choose to engage in drug use when they are not at work, assuming they perform their job duties competently when they are at work, should they be required to be tested for drugs? Other issues involve invasion of privacy, confidentiality, and trust.

Harm Reduction Approach

As noted earlier, one philosophy of alcohol and drug prevention efforts has involved *supply reduction* through strict legal enforcement, interdiction, and taxation to reduce the availability of drugs in the environment. A second approach, *demand reduction,* focuses on users through education and treatment to change their behaviors and motivations. Although these methods start with different immediate goals and methods, as shown in Figure 17.3, both approaches aim for the same long-term goal, *prevalence reduction* or fewer users.

Harm reduction approaches—started in the 1980s in the Netherlands and England, primarily in connection with the use of methadone maintenance to deal with the heroin epidemic—hold the view that drug prob-

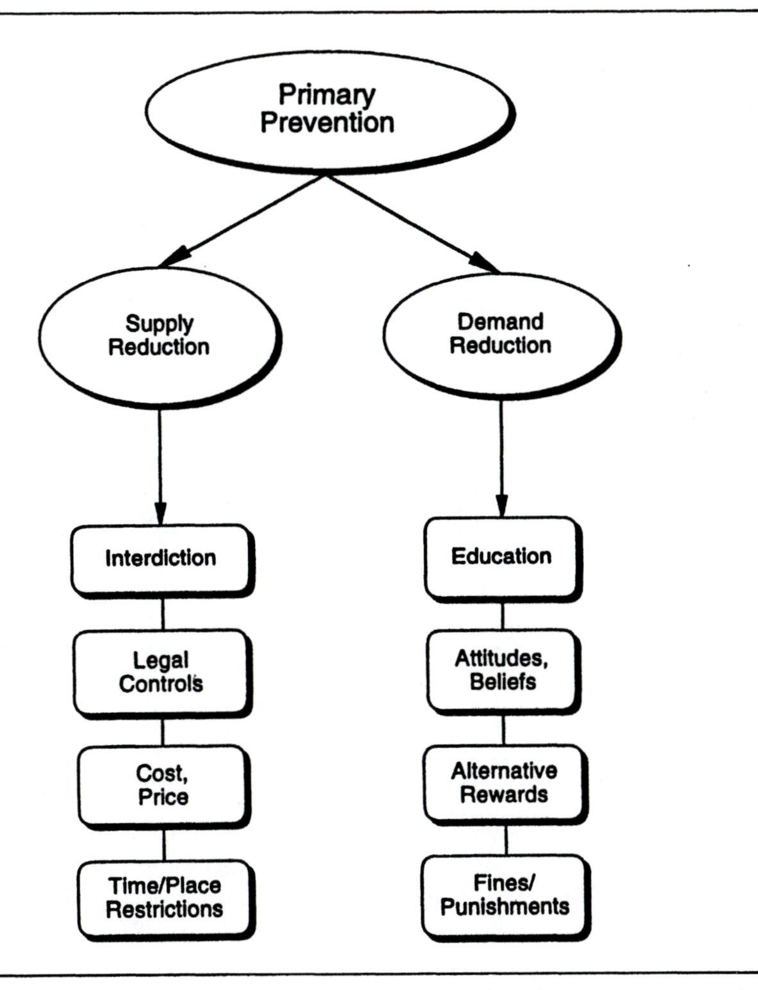

Figure 17.3. Key Aspects of Supply Versus Demand Reduction Strategies for Prevention of Drug Problems

lems may never be "prevented" in any absolute manner (Marlatt, 1998). The harm reduction approach is less ambitious than the "war on drugs" campaigns waged by the federal government. It concedes that we cannot readily prevent drug abuse, but meanwhile we can at least try to minimize its harms. In some European cities such as Amsterdam, faced with widespread illicit drug problems, attempts were made to make the use of drugs less risky to users as well as nonusers. The rapid spread of the HIV virus by heroin injectors prompted efforts to minimize the harm by clean needle exchange programs. The goal of this approach was not to condone or encourage heroin use but to contain or reduce the extent of health problems associated with its use.

For example, harm reduction advocates do not see methadone programs as an ideal solution for heroin addiction. Methadone is a longer-acting replacement for heroin that is taken orally so there is no risk for HIV exposure from using needles for injecting heroin. Its proponents see it as a drug of "lesser harm" than heroin and defend it on the grounds that methadone-treated heroin patients under medical supervision are less likely to experience cravings for heroin or commit crimes to gain drug money.

Figure 17.4 shows that the use reduction approach is primarily aimed at reducing levels of use (arrow b), whereas the harm reduction approach focuses on reducing the "average harm" to both users and nonusers (MacCoun, 1998). In addition, it is important to note that there may be some unintended effects of each approach. Trade-offs are involved when gains toward one goal may be offset by losses toward other goals. Use reduction efforts, when successful, might reduce the direct harm of a specific drug. However, drug use reduction also might unintentionally increase other forms of harm on average (dashed arrow c). Thus, increasing the price of a drug by making it illegal might lead users to criminal activities to obtain the drug. Similarly, the lack of clean needles for heroin users from a needle exchange program might not reduce use, yet it increases the risk of HIV infection.

Harm reduction, when successful at the individual level, might (arrow d) send "a wrong message" that a specific drug is not that dangerous. Consequently, at the societal level, there is an increase in the overall use of a risky drug. For example, a clean needle exchange program might make intravenous drugs appear safer (less risky) than users previously thought so they end up engaging in more harmful use levels. By making clean needles available, the use of intravenous drugs is less risky so the user might be less motivated to quit or to never start using heroin.

By lowering the actual or perceived risk of harm from a drug, there could be an unintended actual increase in use levels as a form of risk compensation by users (dashed arrow e). Thus, putting filters on cigarettes to make them "safer" might encourage smokers to continue their use. Similarly, drivers wearing seat belts may feel safer, so they drive more recklessly. Giving condoms to adolescents could make them feel less risk in engaging in sexual intercourse. Hence, microlevel harm reduction among individuals ironically increases macrolevel harm for society as a whole.

Other factors must be considered in the development of acceptable and viable prevention strategies. Total harm, as shown in Figure 17.4, is a joint outcome of the average harm per use and the total use (total harm equals the number of users multiplied by the quantity each user consumes). Average harm per use includes harm to users (overdoses, AIDS) and harm to nonusers (crime victimization, HIV infection).

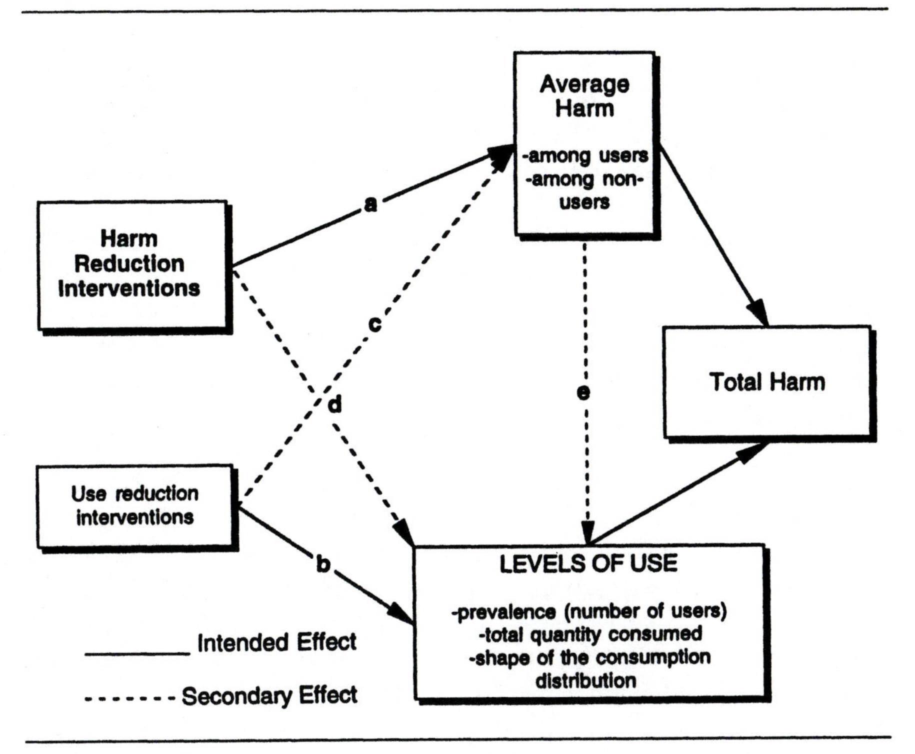

Figure 17.4. Comparison of Use Reduction Versus Harm Reduction Strategies for Prevention

SOURCE: MacCoun (1998). Copyright 1998 by the American Psychological Association. Used with permission.

QUANTITY REDUCTION AS A MIDDLE GROUND

Our national drug policy insists on making a sharp distinction between users and nonusers, and indices of the drug problems are *prevalence-oriented* indices based on rates of use during some specific time period. However, harm stemming from drug use may be more closely linked to the total quantity of a drug consumed in society than to the total number of individual users. The smaller percentage of the population that engages in heavy use contributes more harm than the much more numerous light or infrequent users. Consequently, a focus on methods of quantity reduction for individual users may be a more fruitful strategy, one that falls between strategies of prevalence reduction and harm reduction. Exactly how to best achieve this goal is less clear. One could target the heaviest users and try to get them to reduce their consumption levels. An example with alcohol is controlled drinking—a position not well accepted currently in the United States, although it is employed in England and in some European countries—which tries to get heavy drinkers to drink at lower levels. Opponents object to this approach because they feel that abstinence is necessary for recovery.

Harm reduction has had some success, especially with needle exchange programs for heroin users. It would be more likely to gain acceptance if there were not only reduced average harm but also no increased overall drug use levels. Harm reduction goals aimed at total consumption might be more effective by aiming efforts at drinkers in the middle of the consumption distribution than by focusing on problem drinkers. Lowering consumption in this larger subpopulation may reduce the total social costs of alcohol more than by concentrating on the smaller group at the high end of use.

Opponents of harm reduction reject this philosophy as condoning drug use and "sending the wrong message." Uncompromising in its war on drugs, the absolute position calls for zero tolerance. However, unlike the situation for illicit drugs, the resistance to the harm reduction approach is much weaker when the drugs involved are legal. For drugs such as tobacco and alcohol, concern over public health seems to prevail over moralistic condemnation. Thus, no one seriously proposes prohibition of the production, sale, and consumption of alcoholic beverages or cigarettes. For legal drugs, it seems acceptable to tolerate use and try to keep use and harm under control by imposing high taxes, using warning labels, and placing restrictions on times and places of sale and consumption.

Harm reduction strategies have not been as widely acceptable as prevalence reduction plans. Most people believe they can control their own use of drugs, especially alcohol, so they find it difficult to think that others cannot do likewise. Attitudes about drug policy reflect core values. Many feel that drug abusers "made their own bed, so they should be made to lie in it," even if they must suffer.

Promoting Social Change

Social change with respect to licit and illicit drugs is impossible for individuals to achieve on their own because the tasks are overwhelming. Working together, however, well-organized groups of individuals have been effective in goading federal, state, and local governments to plan and implement acceptable social policies to deal with drug use-related problems.

COMMUNITY ACTIVISM

In the 1970s, grassroots organizations such as Mothers Against Drunk Driving (MADD), Students Against Drunk Driving (SADD), and Remove Intoxicated Drivers (RID) forced national attention to the highway carnage created by drug-impaired drivers. They demonstrated that citizens could mobilize to deal with the societal inertia to confront the dangers created by drunk driving. These forces helped pressure the federal government to create the Presidential Commission on Drunk Driving in 1982, which has helped states and local communities take a tougher stance to enforce laws pertaining to drinking and driving. The withholding of federal highway funds from uncooperative states also served to motivate compliance.

Similarly, increased publicity, education, and awareness about the risks of fetal alcohol syndrome and other birth defects created by drinking among pregnant women illustrate how research can change public attitudes and concern about the health-related dangers of drinking. In some states, laws require establishments serving alcohol to post prominent signs warning patrons of other health risks of alcohol. Warning labels on alcoholic beverage containers also have been proposed as an effective method of reducing alcohol consumption (U.S. Department of Health and Human Services, 1987) by activist organizations such as the nonprofit Center for Science in the Public Interest.

In the past, prevention strategies for alcohol problems centered on controlling the agent, alcohol, as with Prohibition (Langton, 1991). The focus then shifted to the host, or individual drinker, during the alcoholism movement of the 1970s. The concept of responsible drinking, initially promoted but later abandoned in 1977 by the National Institute on Alcohol Abuse and Alcoholism, illustrates this approach. In the 1990s, the emphasis in prevention strategies again shifted, this time toward an emphasis on the environment. Programs to increase early detection and counseling can be seen as making the environment safer for others by reducing the chances that the drug user might harm others. For example, diversion programs for DWI offenders represented an early intervention to pressure individuals into alcoholism counseling and treatment sooner than they would otherwise seek. A positive aspect of drinking-and-driving diversion programs was the possible prevention of more serious drinking problems.

Similarly, as noted earlier in this chapter, many work organizations have recognized the impact of the work environment in creating drug problems. Historically, employers resisted the view that the workplace environment could itself be a factor contributing to alcohol problems among employees (Ames, 1989). Growing recognition that the physical, social, or ideological working conditions contributed to alcohol problems called for improvements in the work environment as well as early intervention to motivate the alcohol-dependent worker to seek treatment.

However, a negative feature of both drinking-and-driving diversion programs and EAP programs is the sometimes coercive nature of the interventions, which often threatens civil rights. Coerced treatment is problematic not only for those given the "choice" between treatment and going to jail (for DWI) or being fired (for alcohol-related work impairment) but also for the climate in alcoholism treatment and recovery facilities. For example, traditionally participants at AA meetings were individuals who had reached "rock bottom" and were ready to admit they were powerless. However, with the large influx of coerced participants in AA and in public treatment facilities, many of whom are hostile and uncooperative, the situation is drastically altered in ways that may impair the effectiveness of these programs for voluntary participants (Weisner, 1987).

Furthermore, it is difficult to prove that individuals who are coerced into treatment benefit because it is not possible to include control groups of alcohol-dependent workers or DWI offenders who do not receive treatment (Weisner, 1990). The difficulty of proving that prevention is effective is also due to the lengthy interval needed before an intervention takes hold. When preventive measures are successful, they are not so readily acknowledged because nothing dreadful happened to alarm us. We do not realize that we have been saved because we did not observe the danger firsthand—"it is easy to count the numbers we have pulled out of the stream, but it is hard to count the numbers who would have fallen in if more effective control programs had not been adopted" (Cahalan, 1987, p. 124). Unfortunately, most people are galvanized to take action only after serious damage has occurred. An ounce of prevention may be worth the proverbial pound of cure, but most people apparently would rather not spend the ounce on the chance that no treatment will ever be required.

A Tale of Two Drugs

These are most interesting times as we enter the 21st century. Public attitudes about tobacco and marijuana have changed in almost opposite directions over the past generation. During the 1940s, cigarettes were widely accepted even though there was some suspicion of their health hazards. Since the U.S. Surgeon General's report of 1964 (U.S. Department of Health, Education, and Welfare, 1964), there has been increased public rejection of smoking as a desirable or healthy behavior. Although smoking tobacco may not become illegal, it certainly has become increasingly stigmatized.

The first medical report of tobacco's ill effects dates as far back as 1665, when Samuel Pepys witnessed a Royal Society experiment in which a cat quickly expired when fed "a drop of distilled oil of tobacco." However, the modern scientific evidence that tobacco causes disease did not progress until the 1940s. Epidemiological and experimental evidence that smoking causes cancer led to the "cancer scares" in the 1950s and, ultimately, to the 1964 Surgeon General's report on smoking and health, which concluded that smoking causes lung cancer.

TOBACCO AND POLITICS

Yet until the 1990s, the tobacco industry was largely successful in protecting itself through aggressive legal, public relations, and political strategies. A turning point occurred in 1994 when a scientist working at the Brown and Williamson (B&W) Tobacco Corporation, the second-largest private cigarette manufacturer in the world in 1992, became a whistleblower by releasing incriminating internal documents that revealed that the tobacco industry had deceived the public for at least 30 years. According to their own documents, B&W knew of nicotine's pharmacological (drug) impact. By the 1960s, the tobacco industry had proven in its own laboratories that cigarette tar causes cancer in animals. In addition, B&W's lawyers were acting on the assumption that nicotine is addictive as the documents revealed their strategies to minimize the industry's exposure to litigation liability and additional government regulation.

In the past, tobacco companies have defended themselves on the grounds that there is no conclusive proof that smoking causes diseases. They staunchly held that smoking is not addictive but involves free choice by smokers. By not promoting cigarettes as a drug for the medication of disease, the tobacco industry managed to avoid control and regulation by the Food and Drug Administration (FDA). However, rapidly changing attitudes about cigarettes that have occurred since the mid-1960s, with the growing evidence of the health risks and dangers of dependency from cigarettes, have brought tobacco under intense governmental and public scrutiny. During the 1980s, higher excise taxes and restrictions on advertising of cigarettes were imposed. Restrictions on indoor smoking became widely imposed during the 1990s.

What was previously seen as a perhaps dirty but harmless habit has increasingly come to be viewed negatively as new evidence of the health risks from smoking accrue. The above-mentioned revelations, leaked from within the industry that additives and higher doses of nicotine were deliberately designed by manufacturers to create stronger addictions, further damaged the credibility and acceptance of cigarettes.

In 1996, the FDA was able to successfully reclassify tobacco as a drug, depicting the cigarette as a highly efficient nicotine delivery mechanism. This development seemingly justified more restrictions on tobacco, although far short of making it illegal (Kessler et al., 1997). At the end of 1999, however, the U.S. Supreme Court (Savage, 1999) decided not to support the argument that cigarettes were classifiable as drugs for medical purposes. Hence, the case for the FDA to make rulings affecting the sale and distribution of cigarettes is considerably weakened and in doubt.

MARIJUANA AND POLITICS

In contrast, the trend for marijuana's image has been in the opposite direction from that of tobacco. Marijuana is still not a legalized drug, and the efforts to decriminalize it since the late 1960s have been far from successful. From the demonized depictions of marijuana as a source of "reefer madness" prevalent in the 1930s, marijuana became a hip drug popularized in the 1960s by hippies and college students. During the 1970s, there was considerable pressure to "decriminalize" marijuana use. If decriminalized, marijuana would still be illegal, but users would be treated more leniently if arrested for possession or use. The National Commission on Marijuana and Health (1978) concluded that such changes were appropriate in view of the lack of evidence that marijuana was as dangerous as previously believed. However, President Nixon rejected the commission's report.

During the 1990s, marijuana has been promoted for possible medical uses. Although considerable controversy still rages, some research has shown it could have medical value for the terminally ill and for certain diseases. The federal government commissioned a report to evaluate the potential medical uses of marijuana. The Commission on Medical Marijuana (Institute of Medicine, 1998) arrived at a cautious conclusion that admitted there were some potential medical benefits, but they were offset by the health hazards created by the smoking involved with marijuana delivery. The commission felt that a safer method of obtaining the active pharmacological ingredients of marijuana was needed.

It is instructive to see the parallels in the arguments used for and against the legalization or decriminalization of marijuana with those used for and against the criminalization of tobacco. In Table 17.1, it can be seen that essentially the same issues arise for both drugs. Civil liberties and individuals' rights are used by proponents of each drug to defend its use, whereas health threats are used by opponents of each drug to attack its use. Interestingly, for tobacco as well as for marijuana, both sides use eco-

TABLE 17.1 Similarities in the pros and cons of legalizing a current illicit drug, marijuana, and the pros and cons of criminalizing a current legal drug, tobacco

Legalize Marijuana		*Criminalize Tobacco*	
Pros	*Cons*	*Pros*	*Cons*
Increase civil liberties	Open gateway to more illicit drugs	Close gateway to illicit drugs	Restrict civil liberties
Jobs created in marijuana industry	More health problems for marijuana users	Fewer health problems for cigarette users	Jobs lost in tobacco industry
More tax revenues	More treatment costs	Less treatment costs	Less tax revenues
Fewer legal and police costs	Increased use of marijuana	Decreased use of marijuana	More legal and police costs
Less crimes related to drug gangs	Sends "wrong message" that drugs can be harmless	Sends "right message" that drugs can be harmful	More crimes related to drug gangs

nomic consequences to support their opposing views. Tax revenues and employment motivate support for both drugs, but costs of treatment and loss of productivity warrant opposition to both drugs.

One lesson to be learned from this comparison of the recent history of attitudes and social policy regarding tobacco and marijuana is that it is easier to defend a legal drug from becoming illegal than it is to move an illegal drug to legal status. A legal drug is backed by a powerful industry with money and political influence, coupled with a larger constituency of addicted users to fight any legislative or economic regulations against the drug. In contrast, supporters of illegal drugs are afraid to show their support without risk of fines and imprisonment, and they have no large financial lobby to fight on the behalf of their drug of choice. The burden of proving that an illegal drug is benign is very difficult because a type of "Catch-22" is involved. Because it is illegal, it cannot be tested, and without tests, it cannot be vindicated. In contrast, substantial evidence that tobacco is very harmful seems insufficient to make much headway into making it illegal.

TO LEGALIZE OR NOT TO LEGALIZE

It is worth speculating what would happen if a currently illicit drug such as marijuana or cocaine were to become reclassified as legal or at least become decriminalized. How many law-abiding citizens who previously rejected these substances would then become users? And would the problems associated with use of these drugs when they were illegal, such as criminal activities to raise money to support these drug habits, be reduced once these drugs were legalized?

If large corporations could manufacture, advertise, and sell products from formerly illegal drugs in large volume for high profits, would the cost come down, thus leading to even greater use? And as tax revenues from sales of these now legal drugs pour into government coffers, would the sales and use of these drugs become more "acceptable" to society, as alcohol and tobacco are? It is not surprising, faced with the possible effects that a change in legal status of drugs could have on use, that opponents of currently illegal drugs want to draw a firm line in the sand between legal and illegal drugs.

In other words, are problems associated with illicit drugs due to their illegal status or to their pharmacological effects? Of course, changing the status of any drug from illegal to legal would not prevent problems associated with its use; certainly, the availability of alcohol has never been problem free. The issue here is not to decide which specific drugs should or should not be legal but to point out that the legal status of a drug itself has a major impact on the types and amounts of problems associated with its use.

SOCIETAL ROOTS OF DRUG PROBLEMS

Social class wars over legal and illegal drugs exist, with the middle class condemning illegal drugs that are often initially associated with the lower class. The middle and upper classes indulge in the use of currently legal drugs such as alcohol and tobacco, which are widely available even though they are harmful to individuals as well as to society.

Prejudices against some immigrant groups may have had more to do with the ban of drugs associated with these groups than clear evidence that these drugs are more dangerous than the "legal ones." In addition, manufacturers of products containing the "legal" drugs have defended their turf by attributing to the "illegal drugs" undesirable outcomes that could more readily stem from the marginalization in society faced by the users of these drugs that "forces" them into unrespectable forms of conduct.

Placing the blame on the drug or on the user overlooks how societal conditions foster and maintain a drug lifestyle among many disenfranchised members of society. To give one example, long-term changes in the economy have led to fewer manufacturing jobs and greater unemployment among those whose limited education and training prevent them from obtaining jobs requiring professional or technical skills. With nothing but time on their hands, doing drugs is a way of coping with lives with no hope. And with legitimate economic avenues closed, engaging in lucrative activities such as drug dealing becomes attractive. Consequently, it is hardly surprising that the war on drugs has led to an increasingly larger prison population from the inner cities, especially African Americans (Duster, 1997). Drugs, as well as those who abuse them, are only part of the problem. Until and unless social institutions can improve living conditions and provide economic opportunities for all, there will be no winners in the war on drugs, only losers.

The Future of Prevention

Prevention of alcohol and other drug problems is a Herculean task. The powerful alcohol and tobacco industries, backed by their constituency of users, are formidable opponents to changes in social policies restricting the availability of these legal drugs (Mosher & Jernigan, 1989). Alcoholic beverage and tobacco companies have skillfully influenced legislators through financial donations and lobbyists, derogated industry critics, and formed powerful alliances with other groups that also face the threat of increased excise taxes. They have tried to create a favorable public image by providing research funds for scientific investigators and also improved public relations by funding public service campaigns—such as warnings against drinking and driving, as well as product labels warning of health risks of smoking and drinking—and sponsoring sporting activities and cultural events.

Public recognition or opposition to these industries has been blunted by the prevailing tendency to regard use problems as the fault of the individual while overlooking the sophisticated marketing practices of the alcohol and tobacco pitchmen that promote and encourage drinking. However, public health proponents can form coalitions at the state and federal levels to affect legislation and also organize local constituencies to combat alcohol problems. Efforts to pass legislation to require warning labels, increase excise taxes, and obtain equal broadcast media time for counteradvertising are examples of campaigns involving the joint efforts and support of health, consumer advocate, educational, religious, and alcohol treatment groups.

The **public health model** illustrates the complex interplay between several components—host, agent, and environment—that must be examined when planning prevention programs. Attempted restriction of alcohol availability to a zero level during Prohibition proved unworkable because it was too unpopular and impossible to enforce. Educational attempts have proved inadequate and often irrelevant to prevention because mere ignorance does not fully account for alcohol abuse.

Because most drinkers seem to have the benefits of drinking without suffering any apparent harm, society appears willing to tolerate the price of having a certain number of alcohol-dependent individuals. As long as they are viewed as not harming anyone but themselves, the public seems willing to allow them to pay the price for their excesses. But, as witnessed by the increased public reaction against drinking drivers, the line is drawn when the alcohol abuser begins to victimize the innocent. More awareness and concern about fetal alcohol syndrome may similarly arouse public attention to the dangers that a drinking mother may create for her unborn fetus. The message may be that instead of trying to motivate the drinker to control his or her drinking, we may be more successful in preventing problems if we can increase awareness of the dangers that alcoholics and alcohol abusers create for everyone. Once alerted to these dangers, people will be motivated to protect themselves and, indirectly, everyone else.

A clash between individual rights and the well-being and safety of the public occurs in many situations when government attempts to act on the public's behalf. There is often resistance when there is the perception that the government is meddling with individual freedoms to decide the personal lives of its citizens. Therefore, laws and social policies that restrict access to alcohol or tobacco to minimize the threat to others from excessive use of these drugs are opposed vigorously by those who want to preserve their rights to use alcohol and tobacco as they wish.

Society is "co-opted," however, because the legal drugs create thousands of jobs for workers in the drug and drug-related industries, with spillover to marketing, advertising, distribution, and sales of these drugs. A cynic would even note that alcoholism and smoking cessation treatment providers constitute large and profitable industries themselves. The profit motive sustains the growth and continuation of the sales and consumption of licit drugs.

The government also is co-opted because it gains tax revenues from the sales of the legal drugs. Of course, the tax revenues may have to be spent treating and rehabilitating people suffering from psychological and physical damage from these drugs. By increasing taxes in attempts to discourage licit drug consumption, the government could end up reducing their incoming revenues in the long run, if they are successful. Hence, the government may be reluctant or ambivalent in regulating licit drug availability too strictly.

As a society, we are in conflict over the proper use of drugs. Almost everyone wants freedom to pursue his or her own objectives. For some, these goals include the right to use the drugs of their choice. For others, these goals include opposite objectives—to prevent others from using drugs they find objectionable. Exactly how all interests can be satisfied is a real dilemma. Somehow, society must achieve a balance—using legal, educational, economic, and moral controls—to regulate drug consumption so that those who benefit from such use do not create psychological and physical harm to either the users or those around them.

SUMMARY

The prevention of using alcohol and other drugs and the problems associated with their use involves a combination of educational, legal, and moral forces against the promotion, advertising, and sale of products from the alcohol and tobacco industries. For illicit drugs, heavy reliance is placed on legal means to control their availability in addition to educational and informational campaigns against their use.

Primary prevention tries to stop alcohol and other drug use-related problems before they start. Diagnosing and identifying present drug abusers (secondary prevention) and treatment of persons already suffering from drug problems (tertiary prevention) usually take priority over primary prevention because they are such immediate problems.

One approach to prevention is to reduce the availability of drugs. Creating conditions that raise costs of a legal drug due to pricing and taxes might reduce consumption, at least for lighter users. A different situation may exist with illicit drugs because heavy users may resort to criminal activities to support their expensive drug habits.

Another strategy involves demand reduction, as exemplified by school-based alcohol and other drug prevention programs that focus on teaching skills to children so they can cope without resorting to drugs. Normative education can help children resist peer influences to use drugs by correcting any misperception that most peers use drugs.

Drug testing is one objective approach used to reduce drug use that may lead to work impairment and accidents in the workplace. However, drug testing is not infallible and also may infringe on employees' privacy.

Another approach in alcohol and drug prevention efforts involves *supply reduction* through strict legal enforcement, interdiction, and taxation to reduce the availability of drugs. Use reduction efforts, when successful, might reduce the direct harm of a specific drug but also might unintentionally increase other forms of harm.

Harm reduction efforts, which concede that some drug use is unavoidable, try to minimize the harm created by use. Some success has been achieved, as with needle exchange programs for heroin users, which does not prevent heroin use but reduces the harm from infectious diseases conveyed by shared needles. Opponents of harm reduction reject this philosophy as condoning drug use and "sending the wrong message."

Society is compromised in its ability and desire to control alcohol and other drugs, however, because the legal drugs generate large excise tax revenues and create thousands of jobs in the drug industries, with spillover to marketing, advertising, distributing, and sales of these drugs. We also must acknowledge that our drug problem does not rest entirely on the characteristics of drugs or their users. Societal conditions may be among the root causes that contribute to drug abuse and dependency, and they also must be addressed if drug abuse and related problems are to be reduced in a just manner.

KEY TERMS

Demand reduction
Driving under the influence
Driving while intoxicated
Employee assistance programs (EAPs)
Harm reduction
Normative education
Project DARE
Public health model
Quantity reduction
Resistance skills
Single distribution of consumption model
Supply reduction
Use reduction

STIMULUS/RESPONSE

1. In most high schools with a zero-tolerance drug policy, students caught drinking are usually suspended or banned from extracurricular activities. Do you think these responses are adequate or appropriate? Do you think these punishments will prevent drinking? Some feel that these punishments only give offenders more free time to drink outside of school. Researchers have recommended that school officials talk to teens instead to determine if they have a drinking or drug problem and then refer students

to counselors and doctors for help. Do you think school officials should take this approach? How effective do you think it would be?

2. Experts feel that warning signs of substance abuse problems include changes in grades, more family fights, stealing, dropping friends, and lying. Do you agree that these are valid signs of substance abuse problems? Why or why not?

3. A study, released by the White House Office of National Drug Control Policy and the U.S. Department of Health and Human Services' Substance Abuse and Mental Health Services Administration, examined the most popular movie rentals and the most popular songs from 1996 and 1997. Illicit drugs appeared in 22% of the movies studied, and 27% of the songs had a clear reference to either alcohol or illicit drugs. Do you think the content is a cause or a reflection of attitudes and behavior? What studies need to be done to answer some of these questions? What do you think the policy of the entertainment industry should be regarding alcohol and drug depictions?

4. The consequences of substance use were depicted in about half of the movies in which they appeared and in about one fifth of the songs. In 26% of the movies, illicit drug use was shown in a humorous context. No report was given about what these consequences were and how they might have affected viewers. From your own experience, identify the major types of consequences you have seen in movies depicting drugs and speculate about the effects of such "messages" that viewers may have received.

5. Illicit drug use was associated with wealth or luxury in 20% of the songs in which drugs appeared, with sexual activity in 30% and with crime or violence in 20%. These results also mean that illicit drug use was *not* portrayed with wealth in 80% of the songs, with sexual activity in 70%, or with crime in 80%. What conclusions do you make from these statistics? Are the rates high or low?

6. Drug attitudes formed in 7th grade do not seem to affect use patterns in 12th grade. Do you think this evidence suggests that drug education was ineffective because it started too soon, before most children were ready to think about drugs, or that it started too late?

7. Are the attitudes and values of our society related to alcohol and other drugs consistent with the information presented in school drug education curricula? If not, how does this disparity affect the success of the school-based drug education?

8. How does marketing and advertising of alcohol and tobacco work against educational attempts to prevent alcohol and tobacco problems?

9. Controversy exists about the attempts of the alcohol and tobacco industries to increase drinking and smoking with advertising campaigns and promotions. A promotion by a brewery described a fictitious college course, "Drinking 101," which featured drinking games and recipes. Critics said the catalog encouraged binge drinking and underage drinking (because most college students are under the legal drinking age). Do you think these marketing tactics will affect the drinking of college students? Why or why not?
10. Many college athletic programs may receive support and funds from the alcohol industry. Should colleges continue or sever ties between their athletic programs and alcohol industry sponsors?
11. Should the alcohol and tobacco industries be allowed to sponsor ethnic community events, such as the popular annual Cinco de Mayo festivals in Latino communities?
12. The Work Site Alcohol Study, involving 14,000 employees at seven major U.S. companies, found that casual drinkers had more incidents of absenteeism and tardiness than did alcohol-dependent persons. Casual drinkers were responsible for 59% of total alcohol-related productivity problems, compared to 41% for alcohol-dependent workers. Do these findings mean that prevention should be directed more at the casual or social drinker than those with alcohol dependency? Do the data present a fair comparison, because there is a large disparity in the size of the two groups being compared?

References

Abbey, A. (1991). Acquaintance rape and alcohol consumption on college campuses: How are they linked? *Journal of American College Health, 39,* 165-169.

Abbey, A., Ross, L. T., and McDuffie, D. (1994). Alcohol's role in sexual assault. In R. R. Watson (Ed.), *Drug and alcohol abuse reviews: Vol. 5. Addictive behaviors in women* (pp. 97-123). Totowa, NJ: Humana.

Abel, E. L., & Sokol, R. J. (1987). Incidence of fetal alcohol syndrome and economic impact of FAS-related anomalies. *Drug and Alcohol Dependence, 19,* 51-70.

Ablon, J. (1984). Family research and alcoholism. In M. Galanter (Ed.), *Recent developments in alcoholism* (Vol. 2, pp. 383-395). New York: Plenum.

Abrams, D. B., Monti, P. M., Niaura, R. S., Rohsenow, D. J., & Colby, S. M. (1996). Interventions for alcoholics who smoke. *Alcohol Health & Research World, 20,* 111-117.

Ackerman, N. (1958). *The psychodynamics of family life.* New York: Basic Books.

Akutsu, P. D., Sue, S., Zane, N. W. S., & Nakamura, C. Y. (1989). Ethnic differences in alcohol consumption among Asians and Caucasians in the United States: An investigation of cultural and physiological factors. *Journal of Studies on Alcohol, 50,* 261-267.

Al-Anon. (1984). *Al-Anon family groups.* New York: Author.

Al-Anon. (1986). *First steps: Al-Anon . . . 35 years of beginnings.* New York: Author.

Alcocer, A. (1982). Alcohol use and abuse among the Hispanic American population. In National Institute on Alcohol Abuse and Alcoholism (Ed.), *Alcohol and health monograph: Special population issues* (Vol. 4, pp. 361-382). Rockville, MD: National Institute on Alcohol Abuse and Alcoholism.

Alcoholics Anonymous. (1952). *Twelve steps and twelve traditions.* New York: Author.

Alcoholics Anonymous. (1985). *Twelve steps and twelve traditions* (Rev. ed.). New York: Author.

Alcoholics Anonymous. (1987). *AA membership survey.* New York: Author.

Alcoholics Anonymous World Services. (1935). *Alcoholics Anonymous.* New York: Author.

Algan, O., Furedy, J. J., Demirgoeren, S., Vincent, A., & Poeguen, S. (1997). Effects of tobacco smoking and gender on interhemispheric cognitive function: Performance and confidence measures. *Behavioural Pharmacology, 8*(5), 416-428.

Allen, J. P., & Columbus, M. (Eds.). (1995). *Assessing alcohol problems: A guide for clinicians and researchers.* Bethesda, MD: National Institute on Alcohol Abuse and Alcoholism.

Alterman, A. I., Bedrick, J., Cacciola, J. S., Rutherford, M. J., Searles, J. S., McKay, J. R., & Cook, T. G. (1998). Personality pathology and drinking in young men at high and low familial risk for alcoholism. *Journal of Studies on Alcohol, 59,* 495-502.

American Psychiatric Association. (1980). *Diagnostic and statistical manual of mental disorders* (3rd ed.). Washington, DC: Author.

American Psychiatric Association. (1987). *Diagnostic and statistical manual of mental disorders* (3rd ed., rev.). Washington, DC: Author.

American Psychiatric Association. (1994). *Diagnostic and statistical manual of mental disorders* (4th ed.). Washington, DC: Author.

Ames, G. M. (1989). Alcohol-related movements and their effects on drinking policies in the American workplace: An historical review. *Journal of Drug Issues, 19,* 489-510.

Amir, M. (1967). Alcohol and forcible rape. *British Journal of Addiction, 62,* 219-232.

Andreatini, R., Galduroz, J. C. F., Ferri, C. P., & Oliveira De Souza Formigioni, M. L. (1994). Alcohol dependence criteria in *DSM-III-R*: Presence of symptoms according to degree of severity. *Addiction, 89,* 1129-1134.

Andrews, J. A., & Duncan, S. C. (1997). Examining the reciprocal relation between academic motivation and substance use: Effects of family relationships, self-esteem, and general deviance. *Journal of Behavioral Medicine, 20,* 523-549.

Anglin, M. D., & Hser, Y. (1992). Drug abuse treatment. In R. R. Watson (Ed.), *Drug and alcohol abuse reviews: Drug abuse treatment* (Vol. 4, pp. 1-36). Totowa, NJ: Humana.

Anglin, M. D., Hser, Y. I., & Booth, M. W. (1987). Sex differences in addict careers: 4. Treatment. *American Journal of Drug and Alcohol Abuse, 13,* 253-280.

Annis, H. M., & Davis, C. S. (1988). Assessment of expectancies in alcohol dependent clients. In D. M. Donovan & G. A. Marlatt (Eds.), *Assessment of addictive behaviors* (pp. 84-111). New York: Guilford.

Annis, H. M., & Davis, C. S. (1991). Relapse prevention. *Alcohol Health & Research World, 15,* 204-212.

Anthenelli, R. M., & Tabakoff, B. (1995). The search for biological markers. *Alcohol Health & Research World, 19,* 176-181.

Anthony, J. C., Warner, L. A., & Kessler, R. C. (1994). Comparative epidemiology of dependence on tobacco, alcohol, controlled substances, and inhalants: Basic findings from the National Comorbidity Survey. *Experimental Clinical Psychopharmacology, 2,* 244-268.

Anti-Drug Abuse Act, H.R. 5484 (1986).

Anti-Drug Abuse Act, 21 U.S.C. 862 (1988).

Apte, M. V., Wilson, J. E., & Korsten, M. A. (1997). Alcohol-related pancreatic damage: Mechanisms and treatment. *Alcohol and Health Research World, 21,* 13-20.

Armor, D. J., Polich, J. M., & Stambul, H. B. (1978). *Alcoholism and treatment.* New York: John Wiley.

Babor, T. F., Dolinsky, Z. S., Meyer, R. E., Hesselbrock, M. M., Hofmann, M., & Tennen, H. (1992). Types of alcoholics: Concurrent and predictive validity of some common classification schemes. *British Journal of Addiction, 87,* 1415-1431.

Babor, T. F., Kranzler, H. R., & Lauerman, R. J. (1989). Early detection of harmful alcohol consumption: Comparison of clinical, laboratory, and self-report screening procedures. *Addictive Behaviors, 14,* 139-157.

Babor, T. F., Ritson, E. B., & Hodson, R. J. (1986). Alcohol-related problems in the primary health care setting: A review of early intervention strategies. *British Journal of Addiction, 81,* 23-46.

Bachman, J. G., Wadswirth, K. N., O'Malley, P. M., Johnston, L. D., & Schulenberg, J. E. (1997). *Smoking, drinking, and drug use in young adulthood: The impacts of new freedoms and new responsibilities.* Mahwah, NJ: Lawrence Erlbaum.

Baer, J. S., Barr, H. M., Bookstein, F. L., Sampson, P. D., & Streissguth, A. P. (1998). Prenatal alcohol exposure and family history of alcoholism in the eitiology of adolescent alcohol problems. *Journal of Studies on Alcohol, 59,* 533-543.

Baer, J. S., Kivlahan, D. R., & Marlatt, G. A. (1995). High-risk drinking across the transition from high school to college. *Alcoholism, Clinical and Experimental Research, 19,* 54-61.

Bailey, M. B., Haberman, P. W., & Alksne, H. (1965). The epidemiology of alcoholism in an urban residential area. *Quarterly Journal of Studies on Alcohol, 26,* 19-40.

Baker, L. H., Cooney, N. L., & Pomerleau, O. F. (1987). Craving for alcohol: Theoretical processes and treatment procedures. In W. M. Cox (Ed.), *Treatment and prevention of alcohol problems: A resource manual* (pp. 184-202). Orlando, FL: Academic Press.

Baldwin, A. (1967). *Theories of development.* New York: John Wiley.

Bales, R. F. (1946). Cultural differences in rates of alcoholism. *Quarterly Journal of Studies on Alcohol, 6,* 480-499.

Ballard, H. S. (1997). The hematolical complications of alcoholism. *Alcohol Health & Research World, 21,* 42-52.

Ballenger, J. C., Goodwin, F. K., Major, L. F., & Brown, G. (1979). Alcohol and central serotonin metabolism in man. *Archives of General Psychiatry, 36,* 224-227.

Bandura, A. (1977). *Social learning theory.* Englewood Cliffs, NJ: Prentice Hall.

Bandura, A. (1999). A sociocognitive analysis of substance abuse. *Psychological Science, 10,* 214-217.

Bank, B. J., Biddle, B. J., Anderson, D. S., Hauge, R., Keats, D. M., Keats, J. A., Marlin, M. M., & Valentin, S. (1985). Comparative research on the social determinants of adolescent drinking. *Social Psychology Quarterly, 48,* 164-177.

Barnes, G. M., & Welte, J. W. (1990). Prediction of adults' drinking patterns from the drinking of their parents. *Journal of Studies on Alcohol, 51,* 523-527.

Baron, R. M., & Kenny, D. D. (1986). The moderator-mediator distinction in social psychological research: Conceptual, strategic and statistical considerations. *Journal of Personality and Social Psychology, 51,* 1173-1182.

Barrett, D. H., Anda, R. F., Croft, J. B., Serdula, M. K., & Lane, M. J. (1995). The association between alcohol use and health behaviors related to the risk of cardiovascular disease: The South Carolina Cardiovascular Disease Prevention Project. *Journal of Studies on Alcohol, 56,* 9-15.

Bates, M. E., & Tracy, J. I. (1990). Cognitive functioning in young social drinkers: Is there impairment to detect? *Journal of Abnormal Psychology, 99,* 242-249.

Bauman, K. E., Fisher, L. A., Bryan, E. S., & Chenoweth, R. L. (1985). Relationship between subjective expected utility and behavior: A longitudinal study of adolescent drinking behavior. *Journal of Studies on Alcohol, 46,* 32-38.

Beardslee, W. R., Son, L., & Vaillant, G. E. (1986). Exposure to parental alcoholism during childhood and outcome in adulthood: A prospective longitudinal study. *British Journal of Psychiatry, 149,* 584-591.

Beattie, M. (1987). *Codependent no more: How to stop controlling others and start caring for yourself.* New York: Harper/Hazelden.

Becker, H. (1963). *Outsiders: Studies in the sociology of deviance.* New York: Free Press.

Beckman, L. J. (1979). Reported effects of alcohol on the sexual feelings and behavior of women alcoholics and nonalcoholics. *Journal of Studies on Alcohol, 40,* 272-282.

Beckman, L. J. (1980). An attributional analysis of Alcoholics Anonymous. *Journal of Studies on Alcohol, 41,* 714-726.

Beckman, L. J. (1993). Alcoholics Anonymous and gender issues. In B. S. McCrady & W. R. Miller (Eds.), *Research on Alcoholics Anonymous: Opportunities and alternatives* (pp. 233-250). Piscataway, NJ: Rutgers Center of Alcohol Studies.

Begleiter, H., Porjesz, B., Bihari, B., & Kissin, B. (1984). Event-related potentials in boys at risk for alcoholism. *Science, 225,* 1493-1496.

Bell, R., Wechsler, H., & Johnston, L. D. (1997). Correlates of college student marijuana use: Results of a U.S. national survey. *Addiction, 92,* 571-581.

Bennett, L. A., & Wolin, S. J. (1990). Family culture and alcoholism transmission. In R. L. Collins, K. E. Leonard, & J. S. Searles (Eds.), *Alcohol and the family: Research and clinical perspectives* (pp. 194-219). New York: Guilford.

Bensley, L. S., Spieker, S. J., & McMahon, R. J. (1994). Parenting behavior of adolescent children of alcoholics. *Addiction, 89,* 1265-1276.

Bensley, L. S., Spieker, S. J., Van Eenwyk, J., & Schoder, J. (1999). Self-reported abuse history and adolescent problem behaviors: II. Alcohol and drug use. *Journal of Adolescent Health, 24,* 173-180.

Bensley, L. S., & Wu, R. (1991). The role of psychological reactance on drinking following alcohol prevention messages. *Journal of Applied Social Psychology, 21,* 1111-1124.

Berglas, S., & Jones, E. E. (1978). Drug choice as a self-handicapping strategy in response to noncontingent success. *Journal of Personality and Social Psychology, 36,* 405-417.

Berman, M. O. (1990). Severe brain dysfunction. *Alcohol Health & Research World, 14,* 120-129.

Berridge, K. C., & Robinson, T. E. (1995). The mind of an addicted brain: Neural sensitization of wanting versus liking. *Current Directions in Psychological Science, 4,* 71-76.

Biernacki, P. (1986). *Pathways from heroin addiction: Recovery without treatment.* Philadelphia, PA: Temple University Press.

Bierut, L. J., Dinwiddie, S. H., Begleiter, H., Crowe, R. R., Hesselbrock, V., Nurnberger, J. I., Porjesz, B., Schuckit, M. A., & Reich, T. (1998). Familial transmission of substance dependence: Alcohol, marijuana, cocaine, and habitual smoking: A report from the Collaborative Study on the Genetics of Alcoholism. *Archives of General Psychiatry, 55,* 982-988.

Black, C. (1981). *It will never happen to me.* Denver, CO: MAC.

Blane, H. T. (1977). Acculturation and drinking in an Italian American community. *Journal of Studies on Alcohol, 38,* 1324-1346.

Blane, H. T. (1988). Prevention issues with children of alcoholics. *British Journal of Addiction, 83,* 793-798.

Blum, K., Briggs, A. H., & Trachtenberg, M. C. (1989). Ethanol ingestive behavior as a function of central neurotransmission. *Experientia, 46,* 444-452.

Blum, K., & Payne, J. E. (1991). *Alcohol and the addictive brain: New hope for alcoholics from biogenetic research.* New York: Free Press.

Blum, K., Sheridan, P. J., Wood, R. C., Braverman, E. R., Chen, T. J., & Comings, D. E. (1995). Dopamine D2 receptor gene variants: Association and linkage studies in impulsive-addictive-compulsive behaviour. *Pharmacogenetics, 5,* 121-141.

Blume, S. B. (1994). Gender differences in alcohol-related disorders. *Harvard Review of Psychiatry, 2,* 7-14.

Boffey, P. M. (1982, June 28). Alcoholism study under new attack. *New York Times,* p. A12.

Boggs Act, Pub. L. No. 82-255 (1951).

Bohman, M. (1978). Some genetic aspects of alcoholism and criminality: A population of adoptees. *Archives of General Psychiatry, 35,* 269-276.

Bohman, M., Sivardsson, S., & Cloninger, C. R. (1981). Maternal inheritance of alcohol abuse: Cross fostering analysis of adopted women. *Archives of General Psychiatry, 38,* 965-969.

Bolter, J. F., & Hannon, R. (1986). Lateralized cerebral dysfunction in early and late stage alcoholics. *Journal of Studies on Alcohol, 47,* 213-218.

Botvin, G. J., Baker, E., Dusenbury, L., Tortu, S., & Botvin, E. M. (1990). Preventing adolescent drug abuse through a multimodal cognitive-behavioral approach: Results of a 3-year study. *Journal of Consulting and Clinical Psychology, 58,* 437-446.

Botvin, G. J., Schinke, S. P., Epstein, J. A., Diaz, T., & Botvin, E. M. (1995). Effectiveness of culturally focused and generic skills training approaches to alcohol and drug abuse prevention among minority adolescents: Two-year follow-up results. *Psychology of Addictive Behaviors, 9,* 183-194.

Bowen, M. (1974). Alcoholism as viewed through family systems theory and family psychotherapy. *Annals of the New York Academy of Sciences, 128,* 115-122.

Bowen, M. (1978). Alcoholism and the family. In M. Bowen (Ed.), *Family therapy in clinical practice* (pp. 259-268). New York: Jason Aronson.

Bradley, A. M. (1988). Keep coming back: The case for a valuation of Alcoholics Anonymous. *Alcohol Health & Research World, 12,* 192-201.

Bradley, K. A., Badrinath, S., Bush, K., Boyd-Wickizer, J., & Anawalt, B. (1998). Medical risks for women who drink alcohol. *Journal of General Internal Medicine, 13,* 627-639.

Brandsma, J. M., Maultry, M. C., & Welsh, R. J. (1980). *Outpatient treatment of alcoholism: A review and comparative study.* Baltimore, MD: University Park Press.

Breed, W., Defoe, J. R., & Wallack, L. (1984). Drinking in the mass media: A nine year project. *Journal of Drug Issues, 14,* 655-664.

Brennan, P., & Moos, R. H. (1990). Life stressors, social resources, and late-life problem drinking. *Psychology and Aging, 5,* 491-501.

Brennan, P., & Moos, R. H. (1996). Late-life drinking behavior: The influence of personal characteristics, life context, and treatment. *Alcohol Health & Research World, 20,* 197-204.

Brennan, P. L., Moos, R. H., & Kim, J. Y. (1993). Gender differences in the individual characteristics and life contexts of late-middle-aged and older problem drinkers. *Addiction, 88,* 781-790.

Brennan, P. L., Moos, R. H., & Mertens, J. R. (1994). Personal and environmental risk factors as predictors of alcohol use, depression, and treatment-seeking: A longitudinal analysis of late-life problem drinkers. *Journal of Substance Abuse, 6,* 191-208.

Brewer, C. (1993). Recent developments in disulfiram treatment. *Alcohol and Alcoholism, 28,* 383-395.

Brick, J. B., Nathan, P. E., Westrick, E., & Frankenstein, W. (1986). Effect of menstrual cycle phase on behavioral and physiological responses to alcohol. *Journal of Studies on Alcohol, 47,* 472-477.

Brisbane, F. L., & Wells, R. C. (1989). Treatment and prevention of alcoholism among Blacks. In T. D. Watts & J. R. Wright (Eds.), *Alcoholism in minority populations* (pp. 33-52). Springfield, IL: Charles C Thomas.

Brook, J. S., Brook, D. W., Gordon, A. S., Whiteman, M., & Cohen, P. (1990). The psychosocial etiology of adolescent drug use: A family interactional approach. *Genetic, Social, and General Psychology Monographs, 116,* 111-267.

Brown, J., Babor, T. F., Litt, M. D., & Kranzler, H. R. (1994). The Type A/Type B distinction: Subtyping alcoholics according to indicators of vulnerability and severity. *Annals of the New York Academy of Sciences, 708,* 23-33.

Brown, S. A., Goldman, M. S., Inn, A., & Anderson, L. R. (1980). Expectations of reinforcement from alcohol: Their domain and relation to drinking patterns. *Journal of Consulting and Clinical Psychology, 48,* 419-426.

Brown, S. A., Vik, P. W., Patterson, T. L., Grant, I., & Schuckit, M. (1995). Stress, vulnerability and adult alcohol relapse. *Journal of Studies on Alcohol, 56,* 538-545.

Brownell, K., Marlatt, G. A., Lichenstein, E., & Wilson, G. (1986). Understanding and preventing relapse. *American Psychologist, 41,* 765-782.

Burk, J. P., & Sher, K. J. (1988). The "forgotten children" revisited: Neglected areas of COA research. *Clinical Psychology Review, 8,* 285-302.

Burk, J. P., & Sher, K. J. (1990). Labeling the child of an alcoholic: Negative stereotyping by mental health professionals and peers. *Journal of Studies on Alcohol, 51,* 156-163.

Burnham, A. (1985, September). *Prevalence of alcohol abuse and dependence among Mexican Americans and non-Hispanic Whites in the community.* Paper presented at the NIAAA Conference on Epidemiology of Alcohol Use and Abuse Among U.S. Ethnic Minorities, Bethesda, MD.

Burton, R., Johnson, R. J., Ritter, C., & Clayton, R. R. (1996). The effects of role socialization on the initial use: An event history analysis from adolescence into middle adulthood. *Journal of Health and Social Behavior, 37,* 75-90.

Bushman, B. J., & Cooper, H. M. (1990). Effects of alcohol on human aggression: An integrative research review. *Psychological Bulletin, 107,* 341-354.

Buss, A. H. (1961). *The psychology of aggression.* New York: John Wiley.

Bux, D. A., Jr. (1996). The epidemiology of problem drinking in gay men and lesbians: A critical review. *Clinical Psychology Review, 16,* 277-298.

Caces, M. F., Harford, T. C., Williams, G. D., & Hanna, E. Z. (1999). Alcohol consumption and divorce rates in the United States. *Journal of Studies on Alcohol, 60,* 647-652.

Cadoret, R. J., & Gath, A. (1978). Inheritance of alcoholism in adoptees. *British Journal of Psychiatry, 132,* 252-258.

Cadoret, R. J., Traughon, R., & O'Gorman, E. T. (1987). Genetic and environmental factors in alcohol abuse and antisocial personality. *Journal of Studies on Alcohol, 48,* 1-8.

Caetano, R. (1984). Ethnicity and drinking in Northern California: A comparison among Whites, Blacks, and Hispanics. *Alcohol and Alcoholism, 18,* 1-14.

Caetano, R. (1988). Drinking patterns and alcohol problems in a national sample of U.S. Hispanics. In National Institute on Alcohol Abuse and Alcoholism (Ed.), *Alcohol use among U.S. ethnic minorities* (Research Monograph No. 18, DHHS Publication No. [ADM]87-1435). Washington, DC: Government Printing Office.

Caetano, R. (1990). Hispanic drinking in the U.S.: Thinking in new directions. *British Journal of Addiction, 85,* 1231-1235.

Caetano, R. (1993). Ethnic minority groups and Alcoholics Anonymous: A review. In B. S. McCrady & W. R. Miller (Eds.), *Research on Alcoholics Anonymous: Opportunities and alternatives* (pp. 209-232). Piscataway, NJ: Rutgers Center of Alcohol Studies.

Caetano, R., & Clark, C. L. (1998). Trends in alcohol consumption patterns among Whites, Blacks and Hispanics. *Journal of Studies on Alcohol, 59,* 659-668.

Caetano, R., & Mora, M. E. (1988). Acculturation and drinking among people of Mexican descent in Mexico and the United States. *Journal of Studies on Alcohol, 49,* 462-471.

Cahalan, D. (1970). *Problem drinkers: A national survey.* San Francisco: Jossey-Bass.

Cahalan, D. (1987). *Understanding America's drinking problem: How to combat the hazards of alcohol.* San Francisco: Jossey-Bass.

Cahalan, D., Cisin, I. H., & Crossley, H. M. (1969). *American drinking practices: A national study of drinking behavior.* New Brunswick, NJ: Rutgers Center of Alcohol Studies.

Caracci, G., & Miller, N. S. (1991). Alcohol and drug addiction in the elderly. In N. S. Miller (Ed.), *Comprehensive handbook of drug and alcohol addiction* (pp. 179-191). New York: Dekker.

Carroll, J. L., & Carroll, L. M. (1995). Alcohol use and risky sex among college students. *Psychological Reports, 76,* 723-726.

Catalano, R. F., Morrison, D. M., Wells, E. A., Gillmore, M. R., Iritani, B., & Hawkins, J. D. (1992). Ethnic differences in family factors related to early drug initiation. *Journal of Studies on Alcohol, 53,* 208-217.

Cermak, T. L. (1986). *Diagnosing and treating codependency: A guide for professionals.* Minneapolis, MN: Johnson Institute.

Cermak, T. L. (1989). Al-Anon and recovery. In M. Galanter (Ed.), *Recent developments in alcoholism: Emerging issues in treatment* (Vol. 7, pp. 91-104). New York: Plenum.

Cervantes, R. C., Gilbert, M. J., de Snyder, N. S., & Padilla, A. M. (1990-1991). Psychosocial and cognitive correlates of alcohol use in younger adult immigrant and U.S.-born Hispanics. *International Journal of the Addictions, 25,* 687-708.

Chao, H. M., & Foudin, L. (1986). Symposium on imaging research in alcoholism. *Alcoholism, 10,* 223-225.

Chapman, P. L. H., & Huygens, I. (1988). An evaluation of three treatment programmes for alcoholism: An experimental study with 6- and 18-month follow-ups. *British Journal of Addiction, 83,* 67-81.

Charette, L., Tate, D. L., & Wilson, A. (1990). Alcohol consumption and menstrual distress in women at higher and lower risk for alcoholism. *Alcoholism, Clinical and Experimental Research, 14,* 152-157.

Charness, M. E. (1990). Alcohol and the brain. *Alcohol Health & Research World, 14,* 85-89.

Chasnoff, I. J. (1991). Cocaine and pregnancy: Clinical and methodologic issues. *Clinics in Perinatology, 18,* 113-123.

Chasnoff, I. J., Griffith, D. R., Freier, C., & Murray, J. (1992). Cocaine/polydrug use in pregnancy: Two-year follow-up. *Pediatrics, 89,* 284-289.

Chassin, L., Curran, P. J., Hussong, A. M., & Colder, C. R. (1996). The relation of parent alcoholism to adolescent substance use: A longitudinal follow-up study. *Journal of Abnormal Psychology, 105*, 70-80.

Chassin, L., Presson, C. C., Sherman, S. J., & Mulvenon, S. (1994). Family history of smoking and young adult smoking behavior. *Psychology of Addictive Behaviors, 8*, 102-110.

Chassin, L., Rogosch, F., & Barrera, M. (1991). Substance use and symptomatology among adolescent children of alcoholics. *Journal of Abnormal Psychology, 100*, 449-463.

Chermack, S. T., & Giancola, P. R. (1997). The relation between alcohol and aggression: An integrated biopsychosocial conceptualization. *Clinical Psychology Review, 17*, 621-649.

Chermack, S. T., & Taylor, S. P. (1995). Alcohol and human physical aggression: Pharmacological versus expectancy effects. *Journal of Studies on Alcohol, 56*, 449-456.

Cheung, Y. W. (1993). Approaches to ethnicity: Clearing roadblocks in the study of ethnicity and substance abuse. *International Journal of the Addictions, 28*, 1209-1226.

Chi, I., Lubben, J., & Kitano, H. H. L. (1989). Differences in drinking behavior among three Asian-American groups. *Journal of Studies on Alcohol, 50*, 15-23.

Chiat, L. D., & Perry, J. L. (1994). Acute and residual effects of alcohol and marijuana, alone and in combination, on mood and performance. *Psychopharmacology, 115*, 340-349.

Chiriboga, C. A. (1998). Neurological correlates of fetal cocaine exposure. *Annals of the New York Academy of Sciences, 846*, 109-125.

Cicero, T. (1982). Alcohol-induced deficits in the hypothalamic-pituitary-luteining hormone axis in the male. *Alcoholism, 6*, 207-215.

Clair, D., & Genest, M. (1987). Variables associated with the adjustment of offspring of alcoholic fathers. *Journal of Studies on Alcohol, 48*, 345-358.

Clark, W. B. (1981). Public drinking contexts: Bars and taverns. In T. C. Harford & L. S. Gaines (Eds.), *Social drinking contexts, National Institute on Alcohol Abuse and Alcoholism* (Research Monograph No. 7, DHHS Publication No. [ADM]81-1097, pp. 8-33). Washington, DC: Government Printing Office.

Clark, W. B., & Midanik, L. (Eds.). (1982). *Alcohol use and alcohol problems among U.S. adults: Results of the 1979 national survey* (Research Monograph No. 1, DHHS Publication No. [ADM]82-1190). Washington, DC: Government Printing Office.

Clayton, R. R., Voss, H. L., Robbins, C., & Skinner, W. F. (1986). Gender differences in drug use: An epidemiological perspective. In B. A. Ray & M. C. Braude (Eds.), *Women and drugs: A new era for research* (NIDA Research Monograph No. 65, pp. 80-99). Washington, DC: Government Printing Office.

Cloninger, C. R. (1987). Neurogenetic adaptive mechanisms in alcoholism. *Science, 236*, 410-416.

Cloninger, C. R., Bohman, M., & Sigvardsson, S. (1981). Inheritance of alcohol abuse: Cross fostering analysis of adopted men. *Archives of General Psychiatry, 38,* 861-868.

Coate, D., & Grossman, M. (1987). Change in alcoholic beverage prices and legal drinking ages: Effects on youth alcohol use and motor vehicle mortality. *Alcohol Health & Research World, 12,* 22-26.

Cohen, S., & Shiffman, S. (1989). Debunking myths about self quitting. *American Psychologist, 44,* 1355-1365.

Coles, R., & Stokes, G. (1985). *Sex and the American teenager.* New York: HarperCollins.

Collins, J. J. (1986). The relationship of problem drinking to individual offending sequences. In A. Blumstein, J. Cohen, J. A. Roth, & C. Visher (Eds.), *Criminal careers and "career criminals"* (Vol. 2, pp. 89-120). Washington, DC: National Academy Press.

Collins, J. J., & Schlenger, W. E. (1988). Acute and chronic effects of alcohol use on violence. *Journal of Studies on Alcohol, 49,* 532-537.

Comings, E. E., Ferry, L., Bradshaw-Robinson, S., Burchette, R., Chiu, C., & Muhleman, D. (1996). The dopamine D2 receptor (DRD2) gene: A genetic risk factor in smoking. *Pharmacogenetics, 6,* 73-79.

Community Mental Health Centers Act, Pub. L. No. 88-164, 77 Stat. 282 (1963).

Community Mental Narcotic Addict Rehabilitation Act, Pub. L. No. 89-273 (1966).

Comprehensive Crime Control Act, 21 U.S.C. 811(1) (1984).

Comprehensive Drug Act and Control Action, Pub. L. No. 91-513 (1970).

Controlled Substances Act, Pub. L. No. 91-513, Title II (1970).

Cook, P. J. (1981). The effects of liquor taxes on drinking, cirrhosis and auto accidents. In M. H. Moore & D. R. Gerstein (Eds.), *Alcohol and alcohol policy: Beyond the shadow of prohibition* (pp. 255-285). Washington, DC: National Academy Press.

Cook, R. T. (1998). Alcohol abuse, alcoholism, and damage to the immune system—a review. *Alcoholism, Clinical and Experimental Research, 22,* 1927-1942.

Cooney, N. L., Gillespie, R. A., Baker, L. H., & Kaplan, R. F. (1987). Cognitive changes after alcohol cue exposure. *Journal of Consulting and Clinical Psychology, 55,* 150-155.

Cooney, N. L., Kadden, R. M., Litt, M. D., & Getter, H. (1991). Matching alcoholics to coping skills or interactional therapies: Two-year follow-up results. *Journal of Consulting and Clinical Psychology, 59,* 598-601.

Cooper, M. L., Frone, M. R., Russell, M., & Mudar, P. (1995). Drinking to regulate positive and negative emotions: A motivational model of alcohol use. *Journal of Personality and Social Psychology, 69,* 990-1005.

Cooper, M. L., Peirce, R. S., & Tidwell, M. O. (1995). Parental drinking problems and adolescent offspring substance use: Moderating effects of demographic and familial factors. *Psychology of Addictive Behaviors, 9,* 36-52.

Cooper, M. L., Russell, M., Skinner, J. B., Frone, M. R., & Mudar, P. (1992). Stress and alcohol use: Moderating effects of gender, coping, and alcohol expectancies. *Journal of Abnormal Psychology, 101,* 139-152.

Cotton, N. S. (1979). The familial transmission of alcoholism: A review. *Journal of Studies on Alcohol, 40,* 89-116.

Cox, W. M. (1987). Personality theory and research. In H. T. Blane & K. E. Leonard (Eds.), *Psychological theories of drinking and alcoholism* (pp. 55-89). New York: Guilford.

Cox, W. W., & Klinger, E. (1988). A motivational model of alcohol use. *Journal of Abnormal Psychology, 97,* 168-180.

Craik, F. I. M. (1977). Similarities between the effects of aging and alcoholic intoxication on memory performance construed within a "levels of processing" framework. In I. M. Birnbaum & E. S. Parker (Eds.), *Alcohol and human memory* (pp. 9-21). Hillsdale, NJ: Lawrence Erlbaum.

Criqui, M. (1990). Comments on Shaper's "Alcohol and mortality: A review of prospective studies": The reduction of coronary heart disease with light to moderate alcohol consumption: Effect or artifact? *British Journal of Addiction, 85,* 854-857.

Crowe, L. C., & George, W. H. (1989). Alcohol and human sexuality: Review and integration. *Psychological Bulletin, 105,* 374-386.

Crowley, J. E. (1991). Educational status and drinking patterns: How representative are college students? *Journal of Studies on Alcohol, 52,* 10-16.

Cummings, C., Gordon, J. R., & Marlatt, G. A. (1980). Relapse: Strategies of prevention and prediction. In W. R. Miller (Ed.), *The addictive behaviors: Treatment of alcohol, drug addiction, smoking and obesity* (pp. 291-321). New York: Pergamon.

Cummings, C., & Marlatt, G. A. (1983, August). *Stress-induced alcohol consumption in high-risk drinkers.* Paper presented at the annual meeting of the American Psychological Association, Anaheim, CA.

Curran, P. J., & Chassin, L. (1996). A longitudinal study of parenting as a protective factor for children of alcoholics. *Journal of Studies on Alcohol, 57,* 305-313.

Daley, D. C. (1989). *Relapse prevention: Treatment alternatives and counseling aids.* Blue Ridge Summit, PA: Tab Books.

Darrow, S. L., Russell, M., Cooper, M. L., Midar, P., & Frone, M. R. (1992). Sociodemographic correlates of alcohol consumption among African-American and White women. *Women and Health, 18,* 35-51.

Davidson, E. S., Finch, J. F., & Schenk, S. (1993). Variability in subjective responses to cocaine: Initial experiences of college students. *Addictive Behaviors, 18*(4), 445-453.

Davidson, E. S., & Schenk, S. (1994). Variability in subjective responses to marijuana: Initial experiences of college students. *Addictive Behaviors, 19*(5), 531-538.

Davies, D. L. (1962). Normal drinking in recovered alcohol addicts. *Journal of Studies on Alcohol, 23,* 94-104.

Dawson, D. A. (1994). Consumption indicators of alcohol dependence. *Addiction, 89,* 345-350.

Dawson, D. A., Grant, B. F., & Chou, P. S. (1995). Gender differences in alcohol intake. In W. A. Hunt & S. Zakhari (Eds.), *Stress, gender, alcohol-seeking behavior* (pp. 3-21). Washington, DC: Government Printing Office.

Dawson, D. A., Grant, B. F., & Harford, T. C. (1995). Variation in the association of alcohol consumption with five *DSM-IV* alcohol problem domains. *Alcoholism, Clinical and Experimental Research, 19,* 66-74.

Dawson, D. A., Harford, T. C., & Grant, B. F. (1992). Family history as a predictor of alcohol dependence. *Alcoholism, Clinical and Experimental Research, 16*(3), 572-575.

Day, N. L., Goldschmidt, L., Robles, N., Richardson, G., Cornelius, M., Taylor, P., Geva, D., & Stoffer, D. (1991). Prenatal alcohol exposure and offspring growth at 18 months of age: The predictive validity of two measures of drinking. *Alcoholism, Clinical and Experimental Research, 15,* 914-918.

Day, N. L., & Richardson, G. A. (1991). Prenatal alcohol exposure: a continuum of effects. *Seminars in Perinatology, 15,* 271-279.

deBlois, C. S., & Stewart, M. A. (1983). Marital histories of women whose first husbands were alcoholic or antisocial. *British Journal of Addictions, 78,* 205-213.

Deery, H. A., & Love, A. W. (1996). The effect of a moderate dose of alcohol on the traffic hazard perception profile of young drink-drivers. *Addiction, 91*(6), 815-827.

Denzin, N. (1987). *The alcoholic self.* Beverly Hills, CA: Sage.

Desiderato, L. L., & Crawford, H. J. (1995). Risky sexual behavior in college students: Relationships between number of sexual partners, disclosure of previous risky behavior, and alcohol use. *Journal of Youth and Adolescence, 24*(1), 55-68.

Devane, W. A., Hanus, L., Breuer, A., Pertwee, R. G., Stevenson, L. A., Griffin, G., Gibson, D., Mandelbaum, A., Etinger, A., & Mechoulam, R. (1992). Isolation and structure of a brain constituent that binds to the cannabinoid receptor. *Science, 258,* 1946-1949.

Di Chiara, G. (1997). Alcohol and dopamine. *Alcohol & Health Research World, 21,* 108-114.

Dickens, B. M., Doob, A. N., Warwick, O. H., & Winegard, W. C. (1982). *Report of the Committee of Enquiry into Allegations Concerning Drs Linda and Mark Sobell.* Toronto, Canada: Addiction Research Foundation.

DiClemente, C. C. (1993). Alcoholics Anonymous and the structure of change. In B. S. McCrady & W. R. Miller (Eds.), *Research on Alcoholics Anonymous: Opportunities and alternatives* (pp. 79-98). Piscataway, NJ: Rutgers Center of Alcohol Studies.

DiClemente, C. C., Prochaska, J. O., Fairhurst, S. K., Velicer, W. F., Velasquez, M. M., & Rossi, J. (1991). The process of smoking cessation: An analysis of precontemplation, contemplation, and preparation stages of change. *Journal of Consulting and Clinical Psychology, 59,* 295-304.

Dimeff, L. A., & Marlatt, G. A. (1995). Relapse prevention. In R. K. Hester & W. R. Miller (Eds.), *Handbook of alcoholism treatment approaches: Effective alternatives* (2nd ed., pp. 176-194). Needham Heights, MA: Allyn & Bacon.

Domenico, D., & Windle, M. (1993). Intrapersonal and interpersonal functioning among middle-aged female adult children of alcoholics. *Journal of Consulting and Clinical Psychology, 61,* 659-666.

Donovan, C., & McEwan, R. (1995). A review of the literature examining the relationship between alcohol use and HIV-related sexual risk-taking in young people. *Addiction, 90*(3), 319-328.

Donovan, D. M., & Marlatt, G. A. (1982). Reasons for drinking among DWI arrestees. *Addictive Behaviors, 7,* 423-426.

Donovan, D. M., Umlauf, R. L., & Salzberg, P. M. (1991). Bad drivers: Identification of a target group for alcohol-related prevention and early intervention. *Journal of Studies on Alcohol, 51,* 136-141.

Donovan, J., Jessor, R., & Jessor, L. (1983). Problem drinking in adolescence and young adulthood: A followup study. *Journal of Studies on Alcohol, 44,* 109-137.

Douglass, R. L. (1984). Aging and alcohol problems: Opportunities for socioepidemiological research. In M. Galanter (Ed.), *Recent developments in alcoholism* (Vol. 2, pp. 251-256). New York: Plenum.

Driver, H. E., & Swann, P. F. (1987). Alcohol and human cancer (review). *Anticancer Research, 7,* 309-320.

Drug Abuse Office and Treatment Act, Pub. L. No. 92-255 (1972).

Drug Enforcement Administration. (1989). *Drugs of abuse.* Washington, DC: U.S. Department of Justice.

Drummond, D. C., & Glautier, S. (1994). A controlled trial of cue exposure treatment in alcohol dependence. *Journal of Consulting and Clinical Psychology, 62,* 809-817.

Duncan, S. C., Strycker, L. A., & Duncan, T. E. (1999). Exploring associations in developmental trends of adolescent substance use and risky sexual behavior in a high-risk population. *Journal of Behavioral Medicine, 22,* 21-34.

Duster, T. S. (1997). Pattern, purpose, and race in the drug war: The crisis of credibility in criminal justice. In C. Reinarman & H. G. Levine (Eds.), *Crack in America: Demon drugs and social justice* (pp. 260-288). Berkeley: University of California Press.

Earleywine, M., & Martin, C. S. (1993). Anticipated stimulant and sedative effects of alcohol vary with dosage and limb of the blood alcohol curve. *Alcoholism, Clinical and Experimental Research, 17,* 135-139.

Edwards, G., & Gross, M. M. (1976). Alcohol dependence: Provisional descriptions of a clinical syndrome. *British Medical Journal, 1,* 1058-1061.

Ekerdt, D. J., Labry, L. O., Glynn, R. J., & Davis, R. W. (1989). Change in drinking behaviors with retirement: Findings from the Normative Aging Study. *Journal of Studies on Alcohol, 50,* 347-353.

Elkins, R. L. (1991). An appraisal of chemical aversion (emetic therapy) approaches to alcoholism treatment. *Behaviour Research and Therapy, 29,* 387-418.

Ellis, A., McInerney, J. F., DiGuiseppe, R., & Yeager, R. J. (1988). *Rational-emotive therapy with alcoholics and substance abusers.* New York: Permagon.

Ellis, D. A., Zucker, R. A., & Fitzgerald, H. E. (1997). The role of family influences in development and risk. *Alcohol Health & Research World, 21,* 218-226.

Ellis, R. J., & Oscar-Berman, M. (1989). Alcoholism, aging, and functional cerebral asymmetries. *Psychological Bulletin, 106,* 128-147.

Elwood, J. M., Pearson, J. C. G., Skippen, D. H., & Jackson, S. M. (1984). Alcohol, smoking, social and occupational factors in the aetiology of cancer of the oral cavity, pharynx, and larynx. *International Journal of Cancer, 34,* 603-612.

Emanuele, N., & Emanuele, M. A. (1997). The endocrine system: Alcohol alters critical hormonal balance. *Alcohol Health & Research World, 21,* 53-64.

Emrick, C. (1987). Alcoholics Anonymous: Affiliation processes and effectiveness as treatment. *Alcoholism, Clinical and Experimental Research, 11,* 416-423.

Emrick, C. D. (1989). Alcoholics Anonymous: Membership characteristics and effectiveness of treatment. In M. Galanter (Ed.), *Recent developments in alcoholism: Emerging issues in treatment* (Vol. 7, pp. 37-53). New York: Plenum.

Emrick, C. D., & Hansen, J. (1983). Assertions regarding effectiveness of treatment for alcoholism: Fact or fantasy? *American Psychologist, 38,* 1078-1088.

Engs, R. C. (1990). Family background of alcohol abuse and its relationship to alcohol consumption among college students: An unexpected finding. *Journal of Studies on Alcohol, 51,* 542-547.

Ennett, S. T., Tobler, N. S., Ringwalt, C. L., & Flewelling, R. L. (1994). How effective is drug abuse resistance education? A meta-analysis of Project DARE outcome evaluations. *American Journal of Public Health, 84,* 1394-1401.

Epperlein, T. (1987). Initial effects of the crackdown on drinking drivers in the state of Arizona. *Accident Analysis and Prevention, 19,* 285-303.

Erickson, P. G., Aldaf, E. M., Murray, G. F., & Smart, R. G. (1987). *The steel drug: Cocaine in perspective.* Lexington, MA: Lexington Books.

Etheridge, R. M., Hubbard, R. L., Anderson, J., Craddock, S. G., & Flynn, P. M. (1997). Treatment structure and program services in the drug abuse treatment outcome study (DATOS). *Psychology of Addictive Behaviors, 11,* 244-260.

Evans, D. M., & Dunn, N. J. (1995). Alcohol expectancies, coping responses and self-efficacy judgments: A replication and extension of Cooper et al.'s 1988 study in a college sample. *Journal of Studies on Alcohol, 56,* 186-193.

Evert, D. L., & Oscar-Berman, M. (1995). Alcohol-related cognitive impairments. *Alcohol Health & Research World, 19,* 89-96.

Farkas, G., & Rosen, R. C. (1976). The effects of ethanol on male sexual arousal. *Journal of Studies on Alcohol, 37,* 265-272.

Farrell, A. D. (1994). Structural equation modeling with longitudinal data: Strategies for examining group differences and reciprocal relationships. *Journal of Consulting and Clinical Psychology, 62,* 477-487.

Farrell, S. (1989). Policy alternatives for alcohol-impaired driving. *Health Education Quarterly, 16,* 413-427.

Faulkner, D. L., & Merritt, R. K. (1998). Race and cigarette smoking among United States adolescents: The role of lifestyle behaviors and demographic factors. *Pediatrics, 101,* E4.

Feinstein, A. R. (1988). Scientific standards in epidemiologic studies of the menace of daily life. *Science, 242,* 1257-1263.

Fell, J. C., & Nash, C. E. (1989). The nature of the alcohol problem in U.S. fatal crashes. *Health Education Quarterly, 16,* 335-343.

Ferguson, F. N. (1968). Navajo drinking: Some tentative hypotheses. *Human Organizations, 27,* 159-167.

Ferrence, R. G. (1980). Sex differences in the prevalence of problem drinking. In O. J. Kalant (Ed.), *Alcohol and drug problems in women: Recent advances in alcohol and drug problems* (Vol. 5, pp. 69-124). New York: Plenum.

Fillmore, K. M. (1975). Relationships between specific drinking patterns in early adulthood and middle age: An exploratory 20-year follow-up study. *Journal of Studies on Alcohol, 36,* 882-907.

Fillmore, K. M. (1984). "When angels fall": Women's drinking as cultural preoccupation and as reality. In S. C. Wilsnack & L. J. Beckman (Eds.), *Alcohol problems in women: Antecedents, consequences, and intervention* (pp. 7-36). New York: Guilford.

Fillmore, K. M. (1985). The social victims of drinking. *British Journal of Addiction, 80,* 307-314.

Fillmore, K. M. (1986). Issues in the changing drinking patterns among women in the last century. In National Institute on Alcohol Abuse and Alcoholism (Ed.), *Women and alcohol: Health-related issues* (Research Monograph No. 16, DHHS Publication No. [ADM]86-1139, pp. 69-77). Washington, DC: Government Printing Office.

Fillmore, K. M. (1987). Prevalence, incidence and chronicity of drinking patterns and problems among men as a function of age: A longitudinal and cohort analysis. *British Journal of Addiction, 82,* 77-83.

Fillmore, K. M., & Kelso, D. (1987). Coercion into alcoholism treatment: Meanings for the disease concept of alcoholism. *Journal of Drug Issues, 17,* 301-319.

Fillmore, K. M., & Midanik, L. (1984). Chronicity of drinking problems among men: A longitudinal study. *Journal of Studies on Alcohol, 45,* 228-236.

Fillmore, M. T., & Vogel Sprott, M. (1995). Expectancies about alcohol-induced motor impairment predict individual differences in responses to alcohol and placebo. *Journal of Studies on Alcohol, 56,* 90-98.

Fingarette, H. (1988). *Heavy drinking: The myth of alcoholism as a disease.* Berkeley: University of California Press.

Finlayson, R. E. (1995). Misuse of prescription drugs. *International Journal of the Addictions, 30,* 1871-1901.

Finn, P. R., & Pihl, R. O. (1987). Men at high risk for alcoholism: The effect of alcohol on cardiovascular reactivity and sensitivity to alcohol. *Journal of Abnormal Psychology, 96,* 230-236.

Finn, P. R., & Pihl, R. O. (1988). Risk for alcoholism: A comparison between two different groups of sons of alcoholics on cardiovascular reactivity and sensitivity to alcohol. *Alcoholism, Experimental and Clinical Research, 12,* 742-747.

Finney, J. W., & Moos, R. H. (1984). Life stressors and problem drinking among older adults. In M. Galanter (Ed.), *Recent developments in alcoholism* (Vol. 2, pp. 267-288). New York: Plenum.

Finney, J. W., & Moos, R. H. (1986). Matching patients with treatments: Conceptual and methodological issues. *Journal of Studies on Alcohol, 47,* 122-134.

Finney, J. W., & Moos, R. H. (1991). The long-term course of treated alcoholism: I. Mortality, relapse and remission rates and comparisons with community controls. *Journal of Studies on Alcohol, 52,* 44-54.

Finney, J. W., & Moos, R. H. (1992). The long-term course of treated alcoholism: II. Predictors and correlates of 10-year functioning and mortality. *Journal of Studies on Alcohol, 53,* 142-153.

Finnigan, F., Hammersley, R., & Millar, K. (1995). The effects of expectancy and alcohol on cognitive-motor performance. *Addiction, 90,* 661-672.

Fleming, J., Mullen, P. E., Sibthorpe, B., & Bammer, G. (1999). The long-term impact of childhood sexual abuse in Australian women. *Child Abuse & Neglect, 23,* 145-159.

Fletcher, B. W., Tims, F. M., & Brown, B. S. (1997). The drug abuse treatment outcome study (DATOS): Treatment evaluation research in the United States. *Psychology of Addictive Behaviors, 11,* 216-229.

Flynn, P. M., Craddock, S. G., Hubbard, R. L., Anderson, J., & Etheridge, R. (1997). Methodological overview and research design for the drug abuse treatment outcome study (DATOS). *Psychology of Addictive Behaviors, 11,* 230-243.

Foy, D. W., Nunn, L. B., & Rychtarik, R. G. (1984). Broad-spectrum behavioral treatment for chronic alcoholics: Effect of training controlled drinking skills. *Journal of Consulting and Clinical Psychology, 52,* 218-230.

Frankena, M., Cohen, M., Daniel, T., Ehrlich, L., Greenspun, N., & Kelman, D. (1985). Alcohol advertising, consumption and abuse. In *Recommendations of the staff of the Federal Trade Commission: Omnibus petition for regulation of unfair and deceptive alcoholic beverage marketing practices* (Docket No. 209-46). Washington, DC: Federal Trade Commission.

Freud, S. (1962). *Three essays on the theory of sexuality* (J. Strachey, Trans.). New York: Norton. (Original publication 1905)

Frezza, M., DiPadova, C., Pozzato, G., Terpin, M., Baraona, E., & Lieber, C. S. (1990). High blood alcohol levels in women: The role of decreased gastric alcohol dehydrogenase. *New England Journal of Medicine, 322,* 95-99.

Frieze, I. H., & Schafer, P. C. (1984). Alcohol use and marital violence: Female and male differences in reactions to alcohol. In S. C. Wilsnack & L. J. Beckman (Eds.), *Alcohol problems in women: Antecedents, consequences, and intervention* (pp. 260-279). New York: Guilford.

Gabrieli, W. F., Jr., Nagoshi, C. T., Rhea, S. A., & Wilson, J. R. (1991). Anticipated and subjective sensitivities to alcohol. *Journal of Studies on Alcohol, 52,* 205-214.

Gaines, A. D. (1985). Cultural conceptions and social behavior among urban Blacks. In L. A. Bennett & G. M. Ames (Eds.), *The American experience with alcohol: Contrasting cultural perspectives* (pp. 171-197). New York: Plenum.

Gebhard, P. H., Gagnon, J. H., Pomeroy, W. B., & Christianson, C. V. (1965). *Sex offenders.* New York: Harper & Row.

George, W. H., & Marlatt, G. A. (1986). The effects of alcohol and anger on interest in violence, erotica, and deviance. *Journal of Abnormal Psychology, 95,* 150-158.

George, W. H., & Norris, J. (1991). Alcohol, disinhibition, sexual arousal, and deviant sexual behavior. *Alcohol Health & Research World, 15,* 133-138.

Gfroerer, J., & Brodsky, M. (1992). The incidence of illicit drug use in the United States, 1962-1989. *British Journal of Addiction, 87,* 1345-1351.

Giancola, P. R., & Zeichner, A. (1995). Alcohol-related aggression in males and females: Effects of blood alcohol concentration, subjective intoxication, personality, and provocation. *Alcoholism, Clinical and Experimental Research, 19,* 130-134.

Giancola, P. R., & Zeichner, A. (1997). The biphasic effects of alcohol on human physical aggression. *Journal of Abnormal Psychology, 106,* 598-607.

Gianetti, V. (1981). Alcoholics Anonymous and the recovering alcoholic: An exploratory study. *American Journal of Drug and Alcohol Abuse, 8,* 363-370.

Gilbert, D. G., McClernon, F. J., Rabinovich, N. E., Plath, L. C., Jensen, R. A., & Meliska, C. J. (1998). Effects of smoking abstinence on mood and craving in men: Influences of negative-affect-related personality traits, habitual nicotine intake and repeated measurements. *Personality and Individual Differences, 25,* 399-423.

Gilbert, M. J., & Cervantes, R. C. (1987). *Mexican Americans and alcohol.* Los Angeles: University of California, Los Angeles.

Gilbert, M. J., & Cervantes, R. C. (1989). Alcohol treatment for Mexican Americans: A review of utilization patterns and therapeutic approaches. In M. J. Gilbert (Ed.), *Alcohol consumption among Mexicans and Mexican-Americans: A bi-national perspective.* Los Angeles: UCLA Spanish Speaking Mental Health Research Center.

Gilbert, O. G. (1979). Paradoxical tranquilizing and emotion reducing effects of nicotine. *Psychological Bulletin, 86,* 643-662.

Gill, J. (1997). Women, alcohol and the menstrual cycle. *Alcohol and Alcoholism, 32,* 435-441.

Ginsburg, H. M. (1978). Defensive research: The treatment outcome prospective study (TOPS). *Annals of the New York Academy of Sciences, 311,* 265-269.

Glantz, M. D. (1992). A developmental psychopathology model of drug abuse vulnerability. In M. D. Glantz & R. Pickens (Eds.), *Vulnerability to drug abuse* (pp. 389-418). Washington, DC: American Psychological Association.

Glaser, F., & Ogborne, A. C. (1982). Does A. A. really work? *British Journal of Addictions, 77,* 123-129.

Glass, T. A., Prigerson, H., Kasl, S. V., & Mendes-de-Leon, C. F. (1995). The effects of negative life events on alcohol consumption among older men and women. *Journal of Gerontology Series B Psychological Sciences and Social Sciences, 4,* S205-S216.

Glenn, S. W., & Parsons, O. A. (1989a). Alcohol abuse and familial alcoholism: Psychosocial correlates in men and women. *Journal of Studies on Alcohol, 50,* 116-127.

Glenn, S. W., & Parsons, O. A. (1989b). Effects of alcohol abuse and familial alcoholism on physical health in men and women. *Health Psychology, 8,* 325-341.

Glueck, S., & Glueck, E. (1950). *Unraveling juvenile delinquency.* New York: Commonwealth Fund.

Glynn, S. A., Albanes, D., Pietinen, P., Brown, C. C., Rautalahti, M., Tangrea, J. A., Taylor, P. R., & Virtamo, J. (1996). Alcohol consumption and risk of colorectal cancer in a cohort of Finnish men. *Cancer Causes and Control, 7*, 214-223.

Goldman, E., & Najman, J. M. (1984). Lifetime abstainers, current abstainers and imbibers: A methodological note. *British Journal of Addiction, 79*, 309-314.

Goldman, M. S. (1983). Cognitive impairment in chronic alcoholics: Some cause for optimism. *American Psychologist, 38*, 1045-1054.

Gomberg, E. (1980). *Drinking and problem drinking among the elderly.* Ann Arbor: University of Michigan, Institute of Gerontology.

Gomberg, E. (1982). Alcohol use and problems among the elderly. In National Institute on Alcohol Abuse and Alcoholism (Ed.), *Alcohol and health monograph: Special population issues* (Vol. 4, pp. 263-292). Washington, DC: Government Printing Office.

Gomberg, E. (1984, August). *Femininity issues in women's alcohol use.* Paper presented at American Psychological Association Convention, Toronto, Ontario.

Gomberg, E. (1990). Drugs, alcohol, and aging. In L. Kozlowski, H. M. Annis, H. D. Cappell, F. B. Glaser, M. S. Goodstadt, Y. Isreal, H. Kalant, E. M. Sellers, & E. R. Vingilis (Eds.), *Recent advances in alcohol and drug problems* (Vol. 10, pp. 171-213). New York: Plenum.

Gomberg, E. (1993). Women and alcohol: Use and abuse. *Journal of Nervous and Mental Disease, 181*, 211-219.

Gomberg, E. (1994). Risk factors for drinking over a woman's life span. *Alcohol Health & Research World, 18*, 220-227.

Gomberg, E. (1995). Older women and alcohol: Use and abuse. In M. Galanter (Ed.), *Recent developments in alcoholism: Women and alcohol* (Vol. 12, pp. 61-79). New York: Plenum.

Gomberg, E. (1996). Men, women and prescribed psychoactive drugs. In M. V. Seeman (Ed.), *Gender and psychopathology.* Washington, DC: American Psychiatric Association.

Gomberg, E. S. L., & Lisansky, J. M. (1984). Antecedents of alcohol problems in women. In S. Wilsnack & L. J. Beckman (Eds.), *Alcohol problems in women* (pp. 233-255). New York: Guilford.

Goodwin, D. W., Schulsinger, F., Hermansen, L., Guze, S. B., & Winokur, G. (1973). Alcohol problems in adoptees raised apart from biological parents. *Archives of General Psychiatry, 28*, 238-243.

Goodwin, D. W., Schulsinger, F., Moller, N., Hermansen, L., Winokur, G., & Guze, S. B. (1974). Drinking problems in adopted and nonadopted sons of alcoholics. *Archives of General Psychiatry, 31*, 164-169.

Goodwin, D. W., Schulsinger, F., Moller, N., Mednick, S., & Guze, S. B. (1977). Psychopathology in adopted and nonadopted daughters of alcoholics. *Archives of General Psychiatry, 34*, 1005-1009.

Gordon, J. R., & Barrett, K. (1993). The codependency movement: Issues of context and differentiation. In J. S. Baer, G. A. Marlatt, & R. J. McMahon (Eds.), *Addictive behaviors across the life span* (pp. 307-339). Newbury Park, CA: Sage.

Gorman, J. M., & Rooney, J. F. (1979). The influence of Al-Anon on the coping behavior of wives of alcoholics. *Journal of Studies on Alcohol, 40*, 1030-1038.

Gottesman, I. I., & Prescott, C. A. (1989). Abuses of the MacAndrew MMPI Alcoholism Scale: A critical review. *Clinical Psychology Review, 9,* 223-242.

Graham, J. R., & Strenger, V. E. (1988). MMPI characteristics of alcoholics: A review. *Journal of Consulting and Clinical Psychology, 56,* 197-205.

Graham, K., Carver, V., & Brett, P. J. (1995). Alcohol and drug use by older women: Results of a national survey. *Canadian Journal of Aging, 14,* 769-791.

Granfield, R., & Cloud, W. (1996). The elephant that no one sees: Natural recovery among middle-class addicts. *Journal of Drug Issues, 26,* 45-61.

Grant, B. F. (1993). *ICD-10* harmful use of alcohol and the alcohol dependence syndrome: Prevalence and implications. *Addiction, 88,* 413-420.

Grant, B. F. (1996). Prevalence and correlates of drug use and *DSM-IV* drug dependence in the United States: Results of the National Longitudinal Alcohol Epidemiologic Survey. *Journal of Substance Abuse, 8,* 195-210.

Grant, B. F. (1997). Barriers to alcoholism treatment: Reasons for not seeking treatment in a general population sample. *Journal of Studies on Alcohol, 58,* 365-371.

Grant, B. F., Harford, T. C., Chou, P., Pickering, R., Dawson, D. A., Stinson, F. S., & Noble, J. (1991). Prevalence of *DSM-III-R* alcohol abuse and alcoholism: United States, 1988. *Alcohol Health and Research World, 15,* 91-96.

Grant, B. F., Harford, T. C., Dawson, D. A., Chou, P., DuFour, M., & Pickering, R. P. (1994). Prevalence of *DSM-IV* alcohol abuse and dependence: United States, 1992. *Alcohol Health and Research World, 18,* 243-248.

Grant, B. F., Harford, T. C., & Grigson, M. B. (1988). Stability of alcohol consumption among youth: A national longitudinal survey. *Journal of Studies on Alcohol, 49,* 253-260.

Grant, I. (1987). Alcohol and the brain's neuropsychological correlates. *Journal of Consulting and Clinical Psychology, 55,* 310-324.

Graves, K. L., & Leigh, B. C. (1995). The relationship of substance use to sexual activity among young adults in the United States. *Family Planning Perspectives, 27,* 18-22, 33.

Greeley, A., McCready, W. C., & Theisen, G. (1980). *Ethnic drinking subcultures.* New York: Praeger.

Greenson, R. R. (1967). *The technique and practice of psychoanalysis.* New York: International Universities Press.

Grossman, M., Coate, D., & Arluck, G. M. (1987). Price sensitivity of alcoholic beverages in the United States: Youth alcohol consumption. In H. D. Holder (Ed.), *Control issues in alcohol abuse prevention: Strategies for states and communities* (pp. 169-198). Greenwich, CT: JAI.

Gruenewald, P. J., Ponicki, W. R., & Mitchell, P. R. (1995). Suicide rates and alcohol consumption in the United States, 1970-89. *Addiction, 90,* 1063-1075.

Grunberg, N. E., Winders, S. E., & Wewers, M. E. (1991). Gender differences in tobacco use. *Health Psychology, 10,* 143-153.

Gusfield, J. R. (1963). *Symbolic crusade: Status politics and the American temperance movement.* Urbana: University of Illinois Press.

Gustafson, R. (1993). What do experimental paradigms tell us about alcohol-related aggressive responding? *Journal of Alcohol Studies, 11*(Suppl.), 20-29.

Hajek, P. (1994). Treatments for smokers. *Addiction, 89,* 1543-1549.

Hajek, P. (1996). Current issues in behavioral and pharmacological approaches to smoking cessation. *Addictive Behaviors, 21*(6), 699-707.

Ham, H. P., & Parsons, O. A. (1997). Organization of psychological functions in alcoholics and nonalcoholics: A test of the compensatory hypothesis. *Journal of Studies on Alcohol, 58,* 67-74.

Hanna, E. Z., Faden, V. B., & Harford, T. C. (1993). Marriage: Does it protect young women from alcoholism? *Journal of Substance Abuse, 5,* 1-14.

Hansen, W. B., Graham, J. W., Wolkenstein, B. H., & Rohrbach, L. A. (1991). Program integrity as a moderator of prevention program effectiveness: Results for fifth-grade students in the Adolescent Alcohol Prevention Trial. *Journal of Studies on Alcohol, 52,* 568-579.

Hanson, M. (1993). Overview on drug and alcohol testing in the workplace. *Bulletin on Narcotics, 45,* 3-44.

Harburg, E., Davis, D. R., & Caplan, R. (1982). Parent and offspring alcohol use: I. Imitative and aversive transmission. *Journal of Studies on Alcohol, 43,* 497-516.

Harburg, E., DiFranceisco, W., Webster, D., Gleiberman, L., & Schork, A. (1990). Familial transmission of alcohol use: II. Imitation of and aversion to parent drinking (1960) by adult offspring (1977)—Tecumseh, Michigan. *Journal of Studies on Alcohol, 51,* 245-256.

Harford, T. C. (1993). Stability and prevalence of drinking among young adults. *Addiction, 88,* 273-277.

Harris, R. A., & Buck, K. J. (1990). The processes of alcohol tolerance and dependence. *Alcohol Health & Research World, 14,* 105-110.

Harrison Anti-Narcotic Act, Pub. L. No. 63-233, 38 Stat. 785 (1914).

Hashtroudi, S., & Parker, E. S. (1986). Acute alcohol amnesia. In H. D. Cappell, F. B. Glaser, Y. Isreal, H. Kalant, W. Schmidt, E. Sellers, & R. C. Smart (Eds.), *Research advances in alcohol and drug problems* (Vol. 9, pp. 179-209). New York: Plenum.

Hasin, D., Grant, B., Harford, T., Hilton, M. E., & Endicott, J. (1990). Multiple alcohol-related problems in the United States: On the rise? *Journal of Studies on Alcohol, 51,* 485-493.

Hawkins, J. D., & Weis, J. G. (1985). The social development model: An integrated approach to delinquency prevention. *Journal of Primary Prevention, 6,* 73-97.

Haxby, D. G. (1995). Treatment of nicotine dependence. *American Journal of Health System Pharmacology, 52,* 265-281.

Heath, A. C., Jardine, R., & Martin, N. G. (1989). Interactive effects of genotype and social environment on alcohol consumption in female twins. *Journal of Studies on Alcohol, 50,* 38-48.

Heath, D. B. (1989). American Indians and alcohol: Epidemiological and sociocultural relevance. In D. L. Spiegler, D. A. Tate, S. S. Aitken, & C. M. Christian (Eds.), *Alcohol use among U.S. ethnic minorities* (Research Monograph No. 18, DHHS Publication No. [ADM]87-1435). Washington, DC: National Institute on Alcohol Abuse and Alcoholism.

Heishman, S. J., Arasteh, K., & Stitzer, M. L. (1997). Comparative effects of alcohol and marijuana on mood, memory, and performance. *Pharmacology, Biochemistry and Behavior, 58,* 93-101.

Heller, K., Sher, K. J., & Benson, C. S. (1982). Problems associated with risk overprediction in studies of offspring of alcoholics: Implications for prevention. *Clinical Psychology Review, 2,* 183-200.

Helzer, J. E. (1987). Epidemiology of alcoholism. *Journal of Consulting and Clinical Psychology, 55,* 284-292.

Helzer, J. E., & Burnam, M. A. (1990). Alcohol abuse and dependence. In L. N. Robins & D. A. Regnier (Eds.), *Psychiatric disorders in America.* New York: Free Press.

Helzer, J. E., Robins, L. E., & Taylor, J. R. (1986). Moderate drinking in ex-alcoholics: Recent studies. *Journal of Studies on Alcohol, 47,* 115-120.

Herd, D. (1985). Ambiguity in Black drinking norms. In L. A. Bennett & G. M. Ames (Eds.), *The American experience with alcohol: Contrasting cultural perspectives* (pp. 149-170). New York: Plenum.

Herd, D. (1987). Rethinking Black drinking. *British Journal of Addiction, 82,* 219-223.

Herd, D. (1989). The epidemiology of drinking patterns and alcohol-related problems among U.S. Blacks. In D. L. Spiegler, D. A. Tate, S. S. Aitken, & C. M. Christian (Eds.), *Alcohol use among U.S. ethnic minorities* (Research Monograph No. 18, DHHS Publication No. [ADM]89-1435, pp. 3-50). Rockville, MD: National Institute on Alcohol Abuse and Alcoholism.

Herd, D. (1990). Subgroup differences in drinking patterns among Black and White men: Results from a national survey. *Journal of Studies on Alcohol, 51,* 221-232.

Herd, D. (1994). The effects of parental influences and respondents' norms and attitudes on Black and White adult drinking patterns. *Journal of Substance Abuse, 6,* 137-154.

Herd, D. (1997). Sex ratios of drinking patterns and problems among Blacks and Whites: Results from a national survey. *Journal of Studies on Alcohol, 58*(1), 75-82.

Herd, D., & Grube, J. (1993). Drinking contexts and drinking problems among Black and White women. *Addiction, 88,* 1101-1110.

Herd, D., & Grube, J. (1996). Black identity and drinking in the US: A national study. *Addiction, 91,* 845-857.

Hesselbrock, V. M., Hesselbrock, M. N., & Stabenau, J. R. (1985). Alcoholism in men patients subtyped by family history and antisocial personality. *Journal of Studies on Alcohol, 46,* 59-64.

Hill, S. Y. (1995). Neurobiological and clinical markers for a severe form of alcoholism in women. *Alcohol Health & Research World, 19*(3), 249-256.

Hill, S. Y., & Steinhauer, S. R. (1993). Assessment of prepubertal and postpubertal boys and girls at risk for developing alcoholism with P300 from a visual discrimination task. *Journal of Studies on Alcohol, 54,* 350-358.

Hilton, M. E. (1986). Abstention in the general population of the U.S.A. *British Journal of Addiction, 81,* 95-112.

Hilton, M. E. (1988). Trends in U.S. drinking patterns: further evidence from the past 20 years. *British Journal of Addiction, 83,* 269-278.

Hinshaw, S. P. (1987). On the distinction between attention deficits/hyperactivity and conduct problems/aggression in child psychopathology. *Clinical Psychology Review, 101,* 443-463.

Hodgins, D. C., el-Guebaly, N., & Armstrong, S. (1995). Prospective and retrospective reports of mood states before relapse to substance use. *Journal of Consulting and Clinical Psychology, 63,* 400-407.

Hoffmann, D., & Hoffmann, I. (1997). The changing cigarette, 1950-1995. *Journal of Toxicology and Environmental Health, 50,* 307-364.

Hopkins, R. H., Mauss, A. L., Kearney, K. A., & Weisheit, R. A. (1988). Comprehensive evaluation of a model alcohol education curriculum. *Journal of Studies on Alcohol, 49,* 38-50.

Horwitz, A. V., White, H. R., & Howell-White, S. (1996). Becoming married and mental health: A longitudinal study of a cohort of young adults. *Journal of Marriage and Family, 58,* 895-907.

Hotaling, G. T., & Sugarman, D. B. (1986). An analysis of risk markers in husband to wife violence: The current state of knowledge. *Violence and Victimology, 1,* 101-124.

Hser, Y. I., Anglin, M. D., & Booth, M. W. (1987). Sex differences in addict careers: 3. Addiction. *American Journal of Drug and Alcohol Abuse, 13,* 231-251.

Hubbard, R. L., Craddock, S. G., Flynn, P. M., Anderson, J., & Etheridge, R. M. (1997). Overview of 1-year followup in the drug abuse treatment outcome study (DATOS). *Psychology of Addictive Behaviors, 11,* 261-278.

Hubbard, R. L., Marsden, M. E., Rachal, J. V., Harwood, H. J., Cavanaugh, E. R., & Ginsburg, H. M. (1989). *Drug abuse treatment: A national study of effectiveness.* Chapel Hill: University of North Carolina Press.

Hughes, J. R. (1992). Tobacco withdrawal in self-quitters. *Journal of Consulting and Clinical Psychology, 60,* 689-697.

Hugues, J. N., Cofte, T., Perret, G., Jayle, M. S., Sebaoun, J., & Modigliani, E. (1980). Hypothalamo-pituitary ovarian function in 31 women with chronic alcoholism. *Clinical Endocrinology, 12,* 543-551.

Hull, C. (1943). *Principles of behavior.* New York: Appleton-Century-Crofts.

Hull, J. (1987). Self-awareness model. In H. T. Blane & K. E. Leonard (Eds.), *Psychological theories of drinking and alcoholism* (pp. 272-304). New York: Guilford.

Hull, J., & Bond, C. F. (1986). Social and behavioral consequences of alcohol consumption and expectancy: A meta-analysis. *Psychological Bulletin, 99,* 347-360.

Hull, J., Levenson, R. W., Young, R. D., & Sher, K. J. (1983). Self-awareness reducing effects of alcohol. *Journal of Personality and Social Psychology, 44,* 461-473.

Hull, J., & Young, R. D. (1983). Self-consciousness, self-esteem, and success-failure as determinants of alcohol consumption in male social drinkers. *Journal of Personality and Social Psychology, 44,* 1097-1109.

Hunt, W. A., & Matarazzo, J. E. (1973). Three years later: Recent developments in the experimental modification of smoking behavior. *Journal of Abnormal Psychology, 81,* 107-114.

Hurlburt, G., Gade, G., & Fuqua, D. (1984). Personality differences between Alcoholics Anonymous members and nonmembers. *Journal of Studies on Alcohol, 45,* 170-171.

Husten, C. G., Shelton, D. M., Chrismon, J. H., Lin, Y. C., Mowery, P., & Powell, F. A. (1997). Cigarette smoking and smoking cessation among older adults: United States, 1965-94. *Tobacco Control, 6,* 175-180.

Indian Health Service. (1982). *Analysis of fiscal year 1981: Indian Health Service and U.S. hospital discharge rates by age and primary diagnosis.* Rockville, MD: Author.

Institute of Medicine. (1990). *Broadening the base of treatment for alcohol problems.* Washington, DC: National Academy Press.

Institute of Medicine. (1996). *Pathways of addiction: Opportunities in drug abuse research.* Washington, DC: National Academy Press.

Institute of Medicine. (1998). *Marijuana and medicine: Assessing the science base.* Washington, DC: Office of National Drug Control Policy.

Ito, T. A., Miller, N., & Pollock, V. E. (1996). Alcohol and aggression: A meta-analysis on the moderating effects of inhibitory cues, triggering events, and self-focused attention. *Psychological Bulletin, 120,* 60-82.

Jackson, J. K. (1954). The adjustment of the family to the crisis of alcoholism. *Quarterly Journal of Studies on Alcohol, 15,* 562-586.

Jackson, J. K. (1962). Alcoholism and the family. In J. Pittman & C. R. Snyder (Eds.), *Society, culture, and drinking patterns* (pp. 472-492). New York: John Wiley.

Jacob, T., Krahn, G. L., & Leonard, K. (1991). Parent-child interactions in families with alcoholic fathers. *Journal of Consulting and Clinical Psychology, 59,* 176-181.

Jacob, T., & Leonard, K. (1988). Alcoholic-spouse interaction as function of alcoholism subtype and alcohol consumption. *Journal of Abnormal Psychology, 97,* 231-237.

Jacob, T., & Leonard, K. (1992). Sequential analysis of marital interactions involving alcoholic, depressed, and nondistressed men. *Journal of Abnormal Psychology, 101,* 647-656.

Jacob, T., Ritchey, D., Cvitkovic, J., & Blane, H. (1981). Communication styles of alcoholic and nonalcoholic families when drinking and not drinking. *Journal of Studies on Alcohol, 43,* 466-482.

Jacob, T., & Seilhamer, R. A. (1989). Alcoholism and family interaction. In M. Galanter (Ed.), *Recent developments in alcoholism* (Vol. 7, pp. 129-145). New York: Plenum.

James, W. (1890). *Principles of psychology.* New York: Holt.

Jarvik, M. E. (1979). Biological influences on cigarette smoking. In N. A. Krasnegor (Ed.), *The behavioral aspects of smoking* (National Institute on Drug Abuse Research Monograph 26, pp. 7-45). Washington, DC: U.S. Department of Health, Education, and Welfare.

Jellinek, E. M. (1943). Benjamin Rush's "An inquiry into the effects of ardent spirits upon the human body and mind, with an account of the means of preventing and of the remedies for curing them." *Quarterly Journal of Studies on Alcohol, 4,* 321-341.

Jellinek, E. M. (1946). Phase in the drinking history of alcoholics: An analysis of a survey conducted by the official organization of Alcoholics Anonymous. *Quarterly Journal of Alcohol Studies, 1,* 1-88.

Jellinek, E. M. (1952). Phases of alcohol addiction. *Quarterly Journal of Studies on Alcohol, 13,* 673-684.

Jellinek, E. M. (1960). *The disease conception of alcoholism.* New Brunswick, NJ: Hillhouse.

Jessor, R., & Jessor, S. (1975). Adolescent development and the onset of drinking: A longitudinal study. *Journal of Studies on Alcohol,* 27-51.

Jessor, R., & Jessor, S. (1977). *Problem behavior and psychosocial development: A longitudinal study.* New York: Academic Press.

Johnson, C. A., Pentz, M. A., Weber, M. D., Dwyer, J. H., Baer, N., MacKinnon, D. P., Hansen, W. B., & Flay, B. R. (1990). Relative effectiveness of comprehensive community programming for drug abuse prevention with high-risk and low-risk adolescents. *Journal of Consulting and Clinical Psychology, 58,* 447-456.

Johnson, F. W., Gruenewald, P. J., Treno, A. J., & Taff, G. A. (1998). Drinking over the life course within gender and ethnic groups: A hyperparametric analysis. *Journal of Studies on Alcohol, 59,* 568-580.

Johnson, P. B. (1982). Sex differences: Women's roles and alcohol use: Preliminary national data. *Journal of Social Issues, 39,* 93-116.

Johnston, L. D., O'Malley, P. M., & Bachman, J. G. (1996). *National survey results on drug use from the Monitoring the Future Study, 1975-1995: Vol. 1. Secondary school students* (DHHS Publication No. NIH 97-4139). Rockville, MD: National Institute on Drug Abuse.

Johnston, L. D., O'Malley, P. M., & Bachman, J. G. (1997). *Drug use among American high school seniors, college students and young adults, 1975-1995: Vol. 1. Secondary school students* (DHHS Publication No. NIH 97-4139). Rockville, MD: National Institute on Drug Abuse.

Johnston, L. D., Wadsworth, K. N., O'Malley, P. M., Bachman, J. G., & Schulenberg, J. E. (1997). *Smoking, drinking, and drug use in young adulthood: The impacts of new freedoms and new responsibilities.* Mahwah, NJ: Lawrence Erlbaum.

Jonah, B. A., & Dawson, N. E. (1987). Youth and risk: Age differences in risky driving, risk perception, and risk utility. *Alcohol, Drugs, and Driving, 3,* 13-29.

Jones, B. M., & Parsons, O. A. (1971). Impaired abstracting ability in chronic alcoholics. *Archives of General Psychiatry, 24,* 71-75.

Jones, B. T., & McMahon, J. (1994). Negative alcohol expectancy predicts post-treatment abstinence survivorship: The whether, when and why of relapse to a first drink. *Addiction, 89,* 1653-1665.

Jones, K. L., Smith, D. W., Ulleland, C. N., & Streissguth, A. P. (1973). Pattern of malfunction in offspring of chronic alcoholic mothers. *Lancet, 1,* 1267-1271.

Jones, M. C. (1968). Personality antecedents and correlates of drinking patterns in adult males. *Journal of Consulting and Clinical Psychology, 32,* 2-12.

Jones, M. C. (1971). Personality antecedents and correlates of drinking patterns in women. *Journal of Consulting and Clinical Psychology, 36,* 61-69.

Jones, M. C., Webb, R. J., Hsiao, C. Y., & Hannan, P. (1995). Relationships between socioeconomic status and drinking problems among Black and White men. *Alcoholism, Clinical and Experimental Research, 19,* 623-627.

Josephs, R. A., & Steele, C. M. (1990). The two faces of alcohol myopia: Attentional mediation of psychological stress. *Journal of Abnormal Psychology, 99,* 115-126.

Julien, R. M. (1995). *A primer of drug action* (7th ed.). San Francisco: Freeman.

Julien, R. M. (1998). *A primer of drug action* (8th ed.). San Francisco: Freeman.

Jung, J. (1995). Parent-child closeness affects the similarity of drinking levels between parents and their college-age children. *Addictive Behaviors, 20,* 61-67.

Kadden, R. M., Getter, H., Cooney, N. L., & Litt, M. D. (1989). Matching alcoholics to coping skills or interactional therapies: Posttreatment results. *Journal of Consulting and Clinical Psychology, 57,* 698-704.

Kalant, H. (1997). Opium revisited: A brief review of its nature, composition, non-medical use and relative risks. *Addiction, 92,* 267-277.

Kalant, H. (1998). Pharmacological interactions of aging and alcohol. In U.S. Department of Health and Human Services (Ed.), *Alcohol problems and aging* (pp. 99-116). Washington, DC: Government Printing Office.

Kandall, S. R. (1998a). Women and addiction in the United States—1850-1920. In C. L. Wetherington & A. B. Roman (Eds.), *Drug addiction research and the health of women* (pp. 33-52). Rockville, MD: National Institute on Drug Abuse.

Kandall, S. R. (1998b). Women and addiction in the United States—1920 to present. In C. L. Wetherington & A. B. Roman (Eds.), *Drug addiction research and the health of women* (pp. 53-80). Rockville, MD: National Institute on Drug Abuse.

Kandel, D. B., & Andrews, K. (1987). Processes of adolescent socialization by parents and peers. *International Journal of the Addictions, 22,* 319-342.

Kandel, D. B., Davies, M., Karus, D., & Yamaguchi, K. (1986). The consequences in young adulthood of adolescent drug involvement. *Archives of General Psychiatry, 43,* 746-754.

Kandel, D. B., Johnson, J., Bird, H. R., Canino, G., Goodman, S., Lahey, B., Regier, D., & Schwab-Stone, M. (1997). Psychiatric disorders associated with substance use among children and adolescents: Findings from the Methods for the Epidemiology of Child and Adolescent Mental Disorders (MECA) Study. *Journal of Abnormal Child Psychology, 25,* 121-132.

Kandel, D. B., Warner, L. A., & Kessler, R. C. (1998). The epidemiology of substance use and dependence among women. In C. L. Wetherington & A. B. Roman (Eds.), *Drug addiction research and the health of women* (pp. 105-130). Washington, DC: National Institute on Drug Abuse.

Kaprio, J., Koskenvuo, M., Langinvaino, H., Ramonov, K., Sarna, S., & Rose, R. J. (1987). Genetic influences on use and abuse of alcohol: A study of 5638 adult

Finnish twin brothers. *Alcoholism, Clinical and Experimental Research, 11*, 349-356.

Kaprio, J., Viken, R., Koskenvuo, M., Romanov, K., & Rose, R. J. (1992). Consistency and change in patterns of social drinking: A 6-year follow-up of the Finnish Twin Cohort. *Alcoholism, Clinical and Experimental Research, 16*, 234-240.

Kapur, B. M. (1993). Drug-testing methods and clinical interpretations of test results. *Bulletin on Narcotics, 45*(2), 115-154.

Kaskutas, L. A. (1996). A road less traveled: Choosing the "Women for Sobriety" program. *Journal of Drug Issues, 26*, 77-94.

Kaslow, R. A., Blackwelder, W. C., Ostrow, D. C., Yerg, D., Palenicek, J., Coulson, A. H., & Valdiserri, R. O. (1989). No evidence for a role of alcohol or other psychoactive drugs in accelerating immunodeficiency in HIV-1 positive individuals. *Journal of the American Medical Association, 261*, 3424-3429.

Kassel, J. D. (1997). Smoking and attention: A review and reformulation of the stimulus-filter hypothesis. *Clinical Psychology Review, 17*, 451-478.

Kaufman, E. (1985). Family therapy in the treatment of alcoholism. In T. E. Bratter & G. G. Forrest (Eds.), *Alcoholism and substance abuse: Strategies for clinical intervention* (pp. 376-397). New York: Free Press.

Keller, D. S. (1996). Exploration in the service of relapse prevention: A psychoanalytic contribution to substance abuse treatment. In F. Rotgers, D. S. Keller, & J. Morgenstern (Eds.), *Treating substance abuse: Theory and technique* (pp. 84-116). New York: Guilford.

Keller, E. L. (1996). Invisible victims: Battered women in psychiatric and medical emergency rooms. *Bulletin of the Menninger Clinic, 60*, 1-21.

Kendall, R. E. (1991). Relationship between the *DSM-IV* and the *ICD-10*. *Journal of Abnormal Psychology, 100*, 297-301.

Kendler, K. S., Heath, A. C., Neale, M. C., Kessler, R. C., & Eaves, L. J. (1992). A population-based twin study of alcoholism in women. *Journal of the American Medical Association, 268*, 1877-1882.

Kessler, D. A., Barnett, P. S., Witt, A., Zeller, M. R., Mande, J. R., & Schultz, W. B. (1997). The legal and scientific basis for FDA's assertion of jurisdiction over cigarettes and smokeless tobacco. *Journal of the American Medical Association, 277*, 405-408.

Kessler, R. C., McGonagle, K. A., Zhao, S., Nelson, C. B., Eshelman, S., Wittchen, H. U., & Kandler, K. S. (1994). Lifetime and 12-month prevalence of *DSM-III-R* psychiatric disorders in the United States. *Archives of General Psychiatry, 51*, 8-19.

Kessler, R. C., Nelson, C. B., McGonagle, K. A., Edlund, M. J., Frank, R. G., & Leaf, P. J. (1996). The epidemiology of co-occurring mental disorders and substance use disorders in the National Comorbidity Study: Implications for prevention and service utilization. *American Journal of Orthopsychiatry, 66*, 17-31.

Kilpatrick, D. G., Resnick, H. S., Saunders, B. E., & Best, C. L. (1998). Victimization, posttraumatic stress disorder, and substance use and abuse among women. In C. L. Wetherington & A. B. Roman (Eds.), *Drug addiction research and the health of women* (pp. 285-307). Rockville, MD: National Institute on Drug Abuse.

Kitano, H., & Chi, I. (1986-1987). Asian Americans and alcohol use. *Alcohol Health & Research World, 11,* 42-46.

Kitano, H., Chi, I., Rhee, S., Law, C. K., & Lubben, J. E. (1992). Norms and alcohol consumption: Japanese in Japan, Hawaii, and California. *Journal of Studies on Alcohol, 53,* 33-39.

Kitano, H. H. L., Hatanaka, H., Yeung, W., & Sue, S. (1985). Japanese-American drinking patterns. In L. A. Bennett & G. M. Ames (Eds.), *The American experience with alcohol: Contrasting cultural perspectives* (pp. 335-357). New York: Plenum.

Kivlahan, D. R., Marlatt, G. A., Fromme, K., Coppel, D. B., & Williams, E. (1990). Secondary prevention with college drinkers: Evaluation of an alcohol skills training program. *Journal of Consulting and Clinical Psychology, 58,* 805-810.

Klassen, A. D., & Wilsnack, S. C. (1986). Sexual experiences and drinking among women in a U.S. national survey. *Archives of Sexual Behavior, 15,* 363-392.

Klatsky, A. L., Armstrong, M. A., & Friedman, G. D. (1986). Relations of alcoholic beverage use to subsequent coronary artery disease hospitalization. *American Journal of Cardiology, 58,* 710-714.

Klatsky, A. L., Armstrong, M. A., & Friedman, G. D. (1990). Risk of cardiovascular mortality in alcohol drinkers, ex-drinkers and nondrinkers. *American Journal of Cardiology, 66,* 1237-1242.

Klatsky, A. L., Armstrong, M. A., & Kipp, H. (1990). Correlates of alcoholic beverage preference: Traits of persons who choose wine, liquor or beer. *British Journal of Addiction, 85,* 1279-1289.

Klatsky, A. L., Friedman, G. D., & Siegelaub, A. B. (1979). Alcohol use, myocardial infarction, sudden cardiac death, and hypertension. *Alcoholism, Experimental and Clinical Research, 3,* 33-39.

Knupfer, G. (1972). Ex-problem drinkers. In M. Roff, L. Robins, & M. Pollack (Eds.), *Life history research in psychopathology* (Vol. 2, pp. 256-280). Minneapolis: University of Minnesota Press.

Koob, G. F., & Le Moal, M. (1996). Drug abuse: Hedonic homeostatic dysregulation. *Science, 278,* 52-58.

Koss, M. P., Gidycz, C. A., & Wisniewski, N. (1987). The scope of rape: Incidence and prevalence of sexual aggression and victimization in a national sample of higher education students. *Journal of Consulting and Clinical Psychology, 55,* 162-170.

Kozlowski, L. T., Pillitteri, J. L., & Sweeney, C. T. (1994). Misuse of "light" cigarettes by vent blocking. *Journal of Substance Abuse, 6,* 333-336.

Kranzler, H. R. (Ed.). (1995). *The pharmacology of alcohol abuse.* New York: Springer-Verlag.

Krogh, D. (1991). *Smoking: The artificial passion.* New York: Freeman.

Kushner, M. G., & Sher, K. J. (1993). Comorbidity of alcohol and anxiety disorders among college students: Effects of gender and family history of alcoholism. *Addictive Behaviors, 18,* 543-552.

Kushner, M. G., Sher, K. J., Wood, M. D., & Wood, P. K. (1994). Anxiety and drinking behavior: Moderating effects of tension-reduction alcohol outcome expectancies. *Alcoholism, Clinical & Experimental Research, 18,* 852-860.

Laberg, J. C. (1986). Alcohol and expectancy: Subjective, psychophysiological and behavioral responses to alcohol stimuli in severely, moderately and non-dependent drinkers. *British Journal of Addiction, 81,* 797-808.

Laberg, J. C. (1990). What is presented, and what prevented, in cue exposure and response prevention with alcohol dependent subjects. *Addictive Behaviors, 15,* 367-386.

Laberg, J. C., & Ellertson, B. (1987). Psychophysiological indicators of craving in alcoholics: Effects of cue exposure. *British Journal of Addiction, 82,* 1341-1348.

Landrine, H., & Klonoff, E. A. (1998, December). *Culture change, tobacco and alcohol use among U.S. ethnic minorities: An operant model of acculturation.* Paper presented at the Conference on Acculturation: Advances in Theory, Measurement, and Applied Research, San Francisco.

Lange, L. G., & Kinnunen, P. M. (1987). Cardiovascular effects of alcohol. *Advances in Alcohol and Substance Abuse, 6,* 47-52.

Langeland, W., & Hartgers, C. (1998). Child sexual and physical abuse and alcoholism: A review. *Journal of Studies on Alcohol, 59,* 336-348.

Langenbucher, J. W., & Chung, T. (1995). Onset and staging of *DSM-IV* alcohol dependence using mean age and survival-hazard methods. *Journal of Abnormal Psychology, 104,* 346-354.

Langton, P. A. (1991). *Drug use and the alcohol dilemma.* Needham Heights, MA: Allyn & Bacon.

Lau, M. A., Pihl, R. O., & Peterson, J. B. (1995). Provocation, acute alcohol intoxication, cognitive performance, and aggression. *Journal of Abnormal Psychology, 104,* 150-155.

Ledermann, S. (1956). *Alcool, Alcoolisme, Alcoolisation, Donné scientifiques de Caractère Physiologique Économique et Social* (National d'Études Demographiques, Travaux et Documents, Cahier No. 29). Paris: Presses Universitaires de France.

Leeds, J., & Morgenstern, J. (1996). Psychoanalytic theories of substance abuse. In F. Rotgers, D. S. Keller, & J. Morgenstern (Eds.), *Treating substance abuse: Theory and technique* (pp. 68-83). New York: Guilford.

Leigh, B. C. (1987a). Beliefs about the effects of alcohol on self and others. *Journal of Studies on Alcohol, 48,* 467-475.

Leigh, B. C. (1987b). Evaluations of alcohol expectancies: Do they add to prediction of drinking pattern? *Psychology of Addictive Behaviors, 1,* 135-139.

Leigh, B. C. (1993). Alcohol consumption and sexual activity as reported with a diary technique. *Journal of Abnormal Psychology, 102,* 490-493.

Leigh, B. C., & Morrison, D. M. (1991). Alcohol consumption and sexual risk-taking in adolescents. *Alcohol Health & Research World, 15,* 58-63.

Leigh, B. W. (1990). Alcohol and unsafe sex: An overview of research and theory. In D. Seminara, A. Pawlowski, & R. Watson (Eds.), *Alcohol, immunomodulation, and AIDS* (pp. 35-46). New York: Alan R. Liss.

Lemere, F., & Smith, J. W. (1973). Alcohol-induced sexual impotence. *American Journal of Psychiatry, 130,* 212-213.

Leonard, K. E. (1990). Summary: Family processes and alcoholism. In R. L. Collins, K. E. Leonard, & J. S. Searles (Eds.), *Alcohol and the family: Research and clinical perspectives* (pp. 272-281). New York: Guilford.

Leonard, K. E., & Roberts, L. J. (1998). Marital aggression, quality, and stability in the first year of marriage: Findings from the Buffalo Newlywed Study. In T. N. Bradbury (Ed.), *The developmental course of marital dysfunction* (pp. 44-73). New York: Cambridge University Press.

Leonard, K. E., & Rothbard, J. C. (1999). Alcohol and the marriage effect. *Journal of Studies on Alcohol, 13*(Suppl.), 139-146.

Leonard, K. E., & Senchak, M. (1996). Prospective prediction of husband marital aggression within newlywed couples. *Journal of Abnormal Psychology, 105,* 369-380.

Leung, S. F., & Phelps, C. E. (1993). My kingdom for a drink. . . ? A review of estimates of the price sensitivity of demand for alcoholic beverages. In M. E. Hilton & G. Bloss (Eds.), *Economics and the prevention of alcohol-related problems* (NIAAA Research Monograph No. 25, NIH Publication No. 93-3513, pp. 1-31). Bethesda, MD: National Institutes of Health, National Institute on Alcohol Abuse and Alcoholism.

Levenson, M. R., Aldwin, C. M., & Spiro, A., III. (1998). Age, cohort, and period effects on alcohol consumption and problem drinking: Findings from the Normative Aging Study. *Journal of Studies on Alcohol, 59,* 712-722.

Leventhal, H., & McCleary, P. D. (1980). The smoking problem: A review of the research and theory in behavioral risk modification. *Psychological Bulletin, 88,* 370-405.

Lévi-Strauss, C. (1966). *The savage mind.* Chicago: University of Chicago Press.

Lex, B. W. (1985). Alcohol problems in special populations. In J. H. Mendelsohn & N. K. Mello (Eds.), *The diagnosis and treatment of alcoholism* (pp. 89-187). New York: McGraw-Hill.

Lex, B. W. (1987). Review of alcohol problems in ethnic minority groups. *Journal of Consulting and Clinical Psychology, 55,* 293-300.

Lex, B. W. (1991). Some gender differences in alcohol and polysubstance users. *Health Psychology, 10,* 121-132.

Lex, B. W. (1994). Alcohol and other drug abuse among women. *Alcohol Health & Research World, 18,* 212-219.

Li, H. Z., & Rosenblood, L. (1994). Exploring factors influencing alcohol consumption patterns among Chinese and Caucasians. *Journal of Studies on Alcohol, 55,* 427-433.

Liberto, J. G., & Oslin, D. W. (1995). Early versus late onset of alcoholism in the elderly. *International Journal of the Addictions, 30,* 1799-1818.

Lidberg, L., Tuck, J. R., Asberg, M., Scalia-Tomba, G. P., & Bertilsson, L. (1985). Homicide, suicide and CSF 5-HIAAA. *Acta Psychiatrica Scandinavica, 71,* 230-236.

Lieber, C. S. (1984). Alcohol and the liver: 1984 update. *Hepatology, 4,* 1243-1260.

Lieber, C. S. (1994). Susceptibility to alcohol-related liver injury. *Alcohol and Alcoholism, 2*(Suppl.), 315-326.

Lieber, C. S., Garro, A. J., Leo, M. A., & Worner, T. M. (1986). Mechanisms for the interrelationship between alcohol and cancer. *Alcohol Health & Research World, 10,* 10-17.

Lieber, C. S., Seitz, H. K., Garro, A. J., & Worner, T. M. (1979). Alcohol-related diseases and carcinogenesis. *Cancer Research, 39,* 2863-2886.

Liguori, A., Gatto, C. P., & Robinson, J. H. (1998). Effects of marijuana on equilibrium, psychomotor performance, and simulated driving. *Behavioural Pharmacology, 9,* 599-609.

Liljestrand, P. (1993). Quality in college student drinking research: Conceptual and methodological issues. *Journal of Alcohol and Drug Education, 38,* 1-36.

Lin, T. Y. (1982). Alcoholism among the Chinese: Further observations of a low-risk population. *Culture, Medicine, and Psychiatry, 6,* 109-116.

Lipsey, M. W., Wilson, D. B., Cohen, M. A., & Derzon, J. H. (1997). Is there a causal relationship between alcohol use and violence? A synthesis of evidence. In M. Galanter (Ed.), *Recent developments in alcoholism: Alcohol and violence* (Vol. 13, pp. 245-282). New York: Plenum.

Liskow, B. I., & Goodwin, D. W. (1987). Pharmacological treatment of alcohol intoxication, withdrawal and dependence: A critical review. *Journal of Studies on Alcohol, 48,* 356-370.

Litman, G., Eiser, J. R., Rawson, N. S. B., & Oppenheim, A. N. (1984). The relationship between coping behaviours, their effectiveness and alcoholism relapse and survival. *British Journal of Addiction, 79,* 281-293.

Lloyd, H. M., & Rogers, P. J. (1997). Mood and cognitive performance improved by a small amount of alcohol given with a lunchtime meal. *Behavioural Pharmacology, 8,* 188-195.

Lohrenz, L. J., Connelly, J. C., Coyne, L., & Spare, K. E. (1978). Alcohol problems in several Midwestern homosexual communities. *Journal of Studies on Alcohol, 39,* 1959-1963.

Longabaugh, R., Wirtz, P. W., Beattie, M. C., Noel, N., & Stout, R. (1995). Matching treatment focus to patient social investment and support: 18-month follow-up results. *Journal of Consulting and Clinical Psychology, 63,* 296-307.

Lovibond, S., & Caddy, G. (1970). Discriminated aversive control in the moderation of alcoholics' drinking behaviour. *Behavior Therapy, 1,* 437-444.

Lowe, G. (1986). State-dependent learning effects with a combination of alcohol and nicotine. *Psychopharmacology, 89,* 105-107.

Lowry, R., Holtzman, D., Truman, B. I., Kann, L., Collins, J. L., & Kolbe, L. J. (1994). Substance use and HIV-related sexual behaviors among US high school students: Are they related? *American Journal of Public Health, 84,* 1116-1120.

Lubben, J., Chi, I., & Kitano, H. (1988a). Exploring Filipino-American drinking behavior. *Journal of Studies on Alcohol, 49,* 26-29.

Lubben, J., Chi, I., & Kitano, H. (1988b). The relative influence of selected social factors on Korean drinking behavior in Los Angeles. *Advances in Alcohol and Substance Abuse, 8,* 1-17.

Ludwig, A. M. (1986). Pavlov's "bells" and alcohol craving. *Addictive Behaviors, 11,* 87-91.

Ludwig, A. M. (1988). *Understanding the alcoholic's mind: The nature of craving and how to control it.* New York: Oxford University Press.

Lynskey, M. T., Fergusson, D. M., & Horwood, L. J. (1994). The effect of parental alcohol problems on rates of adolescent psychiatric disorders. *Addiction, 89,* 1277-1286.

MacAndrew, C. (1965). The differentiation of male alcoholic outpatients from nonalcoholic psychiatric outpatients by means of the MMPI. *Quarterly Journal of Studies on Alcohol, 26,* 238-246.

MacAndrew, C., & Edgerton, R. B. (1969). *Drunken comportment: A social explanation.* Chicago: Aldine.

MacCoun, R. J. (1998). Toward a psychology of harm reduction. *American Psychologist, 53,* 1199-1208.

MacCoun, R. J., & Caulkins, J. (1996). Examining the behavioral assumptions of national drug control policy. In W. K. Bickel & R. J. DeGrandpre (Eds.), *Drug policy and human nature: Psychological perspectives on the prevention, management, and treatment of illicit drug use* (pp. 177-197). New York: Plenum.

MacDonald, S., & Whitehead, P. (1983). Availability of outlets and consumption of alcoholic beverages. *Journal of Drug Issues, 13,* 477-486.

MacMahon, S. (1987). Alcohol consumption and hypertension. *Hypertension, 9,* 111-121.

Maher, J. J. (1997). Exploring alcohol's effects on liver function. *Alcohol Health & Research World, 21,* 5-12.

Maisto, S. A., & Carey, K. B. (1987). Treatment of alcohol abuse. In T. D. Nirenberg & S. A. Maisto (Eds.), *Developments in the assessment and treatment of addictive behaviors* (pp. 173-212). Norwood, NJ: Ablex.

Maisto, S. A., Galizio, M., & Conners, G. J. (1995). *Drug use and misuse* (2nd ed.). New York: Holt, Rinehart, & Winston.

Malin, H., Croakley, J., Kaelber, C., Munch, N., & Holland, W. (1982). An epidemiologic perspective on alcohol use and abuse in the United States. In National Institute on Alcohol Abuse and Alcoholism (Ed.), *Alcohol consumption and related problems* (Alcohol and Health Monograph No. [ADM]82-1190, pp. 99-153). Washington, DC: Government Printing Office.

Marijuana Stamp Tax Act, Pub. L. No. 75-238 (1937).

Marin, G., Posner, S. F., & Kinyon, J. B. (1993). Alcohol expectancies among Hispanics and non-Hispanic Whites: Role of drinking status and acculturation. *Hispanic Journal of Behavioral Sciences, 15,* 373-381.

Marlatt, G. A. (1978). Craving for alcohol, loss of control, and relapse: A cognitive-behavioral analysis. In P. E. Nathan, G. A. Marlatt, & T. Loberg (Eds.), *Alcoholism: New directions in behavioral research and treatment* (pp. 271-314). New York: Plenum.

Marlatt, G. A. (1985a). Cognitive assessment and intervention procedures for relapse preventions. In G. A. Marlatt & J. R. Gordon (Eds.), *Relapse prevention: Maintenance strategies in the treatment of addictive behaviors* (pp. 201-279). New York: Guilford.

Marlatt, G. A. (1985b). Relapse prevention: Theoretical rationale and overview of the model. In G. A. Marlatt & J. R. Gordon (Eds.), *Relapse prevention: Mainte-*

nance strategies in the treatment of addictive behaviors (pp. 3-70). New York: Guilford.

Marlatt, G. A. (Ed.). (1998). *Harm reduction: Pragmatic strategies for managing high-risk behaviors.* New York: Guilford.

Marlatt, G. A., Bear, J. S., & Larimer, M. E. (1995). Preventing alcohol abuse in college students: A harm reduction approach. In G. M. Boyd, J. Howard, & R. Zucker (Eds.), *Alcohol problems among adolescents: Current directions in prevention research* (pp. 147-172). Northvale, NJ: Lawrence Erlbaum.

Marlatt, G. A., Demming, B., & Reid, J. (1973). Loss of control drinking in alcoholics: An experimental analogue. *Journal of Abnormal Psychology, 81,* 233-241.

Marlatt, G. A., & Gordon, J. R. (Eds.). (1985). *Relapse prevention: Maintenance strategies in the treatment of addictive behaviors.* New York: Guilford.

Marlatt, G. A., Kosturn, C. F., & Lang, A. R. (1975). Provocation to anger and opportunity for retaliation as determinants of alcohol consumption in social drinkers. *Journal of Abnormal Psychology, 84,* 652-659.

Marlatt, G. A., & Rohsenow, D. J. (1980). Cognitive processes in alcohol use: Expectancy and the balanced placebo design. In N. K. Mello (Ed.), *Advances in substance abuse: Behavioral and biological research* (pp. 159-199). Greenwich, CT: JAI.

Martin, C. S., Clifford, P. R., Maisto, S. A., Earleywine, M., Kirisci, L., & Longabaugh, R. (1996). Polydrug use in an inpatient treatment sample of problem drinkers. *Alcohol, Clinical and Experimental Research, 20,* 413-417.

Martin, C. S., Earleywine, M., & Finn, P. (1990). Some boundary conditions for effective use of alcohol placebos. *Journal of Studies on Alcohol, 51,* 500-505.

Martin, C. S., Earleywine, M., Musty, R. E., Perrine, M. W., & Swift, R. M. (1993). Development and validation of the Biphasic Alcohol Effects Scale. *Alcoholism, Clinical and Experimental Research, 17,* 140-146.

Martin, C. S., Kaczynski, N. A., Maisto, S. A., Bukstein, O. M., & Moss, H. B. (1995). Patterns of *DSM-IV* alcohol abuse and dependence symptoms in adolescent drinkers. *Journal of Studies on Alcohol, 56,* 672-680.

Masters, W. H., & Johnson, V. E. (1966). *Human sexual response.* Boston: Little, Brown.

Mattson, M. E., & Allen, J. P. (1991). Research on matching alcoholic patients to treatments: Findings, issues, and implications. *Journal of Addictive Diseases, 11,* 33-49.

Mattson, S. N., & Riley, E. P. (1998). A review of the neurobehavioral deficits in children with fetal alcohol syndrome or prenatal exposure to alcohol. *Alcoholism, Clinical and Experimental Research, 22,* 279-294.

May, P. A. (1982). Substance abuse and American Indians: Prevalence and susceptibility. *International Journal of the Addictions, 17,* 1185-1209.

May, P. A. (1995). A multiple-level comprehensive approach to the prevention of fetal alcohol syndrome (FAS) and other alcohol-related birth defects (ARBD). *International Journal of Addictions, 30,* 1549-1602.

McCauley, J., Kern, D. E., Kolodner, K., Dill, L., Schroeder, A. F., DeChant, H. K., Ryden, J., Derogatis, L. R., & Bass, E. B. (1997). Clinical characteristics of women with a history of childhood abuse: Unhealed wounds. *Journal of the American Medical Association, 277,* 1362-1368.

McClelland, D. C., Davis, W. N., Kalin, R., & Wanner, E. (1972). *The drinking man.* New York: Free Press.

McCord, J. (1988). Identifying developmental paradigms leading to alcoholism. *Journal of Studies on Alcohol, 49,* 357-362.

McCord, W., & McCord, J. (1960). *Origins of alcoholism.* Stanford, CA: Stanford University Press.

McCrady, B. S. (1987). Implications of neuropsychological research findings for the treatment and rehabilitation of alcoholics. In O. A. Parsons, N. Butters, & P. E. Nathan (Eds.), *Neuropsychology of alcoholism: Implications for diagnosis and treatment* (pp. 381-391). New York: Guilford.

McCrady, B. S. (1989). Outcomes of family-involved alcoholism treatment. In M. Galanter (Ed.), *Recent developments in alcoholism* (Vol. 7, pp. 165-182). New York: Plenum.

McCrady, B. S. (1994). Alcoholics anonymous and behavior therapy: Can habits be treated as diseases? Can diseases be treated as habits? *Journal of Consulting and Clinical Psychology, 62,* 1159-1166.

McCrady, B. S., & Delaney, S. I. (1995). Self-help groups. In R. K. Hester & W. R. Miller (Eds.), *handbook of alcoholism treatment approaches: Effective alternatives* (2nd ed., pp. 160-175). Needham Heights, MA: Allyn & Bacon.

McCrady, B. S., & Epstein, E. E. (1995). Directions for research on alcoholic relationships: Marital- and individual-based models of heterogeneity. *Psychology of Addictive Behaviors, 9,* 157-166.

McCrady, B. S., & Miller, W. R. (1993). *Research on Alcoholics Anonymous: Opportunities and alternatives.* Piscataway, NJ: Rutgers Center of Alcohol Studies.

McCubbin, H. I., McCubbin, M. A., Thompson, A. I., & Han, S. Y. (1999). Contextualizing family risk factors for alcoholism and alcohol abuse. *Journal of Studies on Alcohol, 13*(Suppl.), 75-78.

McGrath, P. J., Nunes, E. V., & Stewart, J. W. (1996). Imipramine treatment of alcoholics with primary depression. *Archives of General Psychiatry, 53,* 232-240.

McGue, M., Sharma, A., & Benson, P. (1996). Parent and sibling influence on adolescent alcohol use and misuse: Evidence from a U.S. adoption cohort. *Journal of Studies on Alcohol, 57,* 8-18.

McKay, J. (1999). Studies of factors in relapse to alcohol, drug and nicotine use: A critical review of methodologies and findings. *Journal of Studies on Alcohol, 60,* 566-576.

McKim, W. A. (1997). *Drugs and behavior: An introduction to behavioral pharmacology* (3rd ed.). Upper Saddle River, NJ: Prentice Hall.

McKirnan, D. J., & Peterson, P. L. (1989). Alcohol and drug use among homosexual men and women: Epidemiology and population characteristics. *Addictive Behaviors, 14,* 545-553.

McMahon, J., & Jones, B. T. (1994). Social drinkers' negative alcohol expectancy relates to their satisfaction with current consumption: Measuring motivation for change with the NAEQ. *Alcohol and Alcoholism, 29,* 687-690.

McMillen, D. L., Adams, M. S., Wells Parker, E., Pang, M. G., & Anderson, B. J. (1992). Personality traits and behaviors of alcohol-impaired drivers: A comparison of first and multiple offenders. *Addictive Behaviors, 17,* 407-414.

Mechoulam, R., Hanus, L., & Martin, B. R. (1994). Search for endogenous ligands of the cannabinoid receptor. *Biochemical Pharmacology, 48,* 1537-1544.

Meilman, P. W. (1993). Alcohol-induced sexual behavior on campus. *Journal of American College Health, 42,* 27-31.

Meilman, P. W., Cashin, J. R., McKillip, J., & Presley, C. A. (1998). Understanding the three national databases on collegiate alcohol use. *Journal of American College Health, 46,* 159-162.

Meilman, P. W., Stone, J. E., Gaylor, M. S., & Turco, J. H. (1990). Alcohol consumption by college undergraduates: Current use and 10-year trends. *Journal of Studies on Alcohol, 51,* 389-395.

Mellinger, G. D., Balter, M. B., & Manheimer, D. I. (1971). Patterns of psychotherapeutic drug use among adults in San Francisco. *Archives of General Psychiatry, 25,* 385-394.

Mello, N. K. (1988). Effects of alcohol abuse on reproductive function in women. In M. Galanter (Ed.), *Recent developments in alcoholism* (Vol. 6, pp. 253-276). New York: Plenum.

Mello, N. K., Mendelsohn, J. H., & Lex, B. W. (1990). Alcohol use and premenstrual symptoms in social drinkers. *Psychopharmocology, 101,* 448-455.

Mello, N. K., Mendelsohn, J. H., & Teoh, S. K. (1989). Neuroendocrine consequences of alcohol abuse in women. *Annals of the New York Academy of Sciences, 562,* 211-240.

Mello, N. K., Mendelsohn, J. H., & Teoh, S. K. (1993). An overview of the effects of alcohol on neuroendocrine function in women. In S. Zakhari (Ed.), *Alcohol and the endocrine system* (Research Monograph No. 23, NIH Publication No. 93-3533, pp. 139-169). Bethesda, MD: National Institute on Alcohol Abuse and Alcoholism.

Mercer, P. W., & Khavari, K. A. (1990). Are women drinking more like men? An empirical examination of the convergence hypothesis. *Alcoholism, Clinical and Experimental Research, 14,* 461-466.

Merikangas, K. R., Stolar, M., Stevens, D. E., Goulet, J., Preisig, M. A., Fenton, B., Zhang, H., O'Malley, S. S., & Rounsaville, B. J. (1998). Familial transmission of substance use disorders. *Archives of General Psychiatry, 55,* 973-979.

Mette, P., & Crabbe, J. C. (1996). Dependence and withdrawal. In R. A. Dietrich & V. G. Erwin (Eds.), *Pharmacological effects of alcohol on the nervous system* (pp. 269-290). Boca Raton, FL: CRC.

Mezzich, C. A., Tarter, R. E., Giancola, P. R., Lu, S., Kirisci, L., & Parks, S. (1997). Substance use and risky sexual behavior in female adolescents. *Drug and Alcohol Dependence, 44*(2/3), 157-166.

Midanik, L. T., Klatsky, A. L., & Armstrong, M. A. (1989). A comparison of 7-day recall with two summary measures of alcohol use. *Drug and Alcohol Dependence, 24,* 127-134.

Miller, B. A., & Downs, W. R. (1993). The impact of family violence on the use of alcohol by women. *Alcohol Health & Research World, 17,* 137-143.

Miller, B. A., & Downs, W. R. (1995). Violent victimization among women with alcohol problems. In M. Galanter (Ed.), *Recent developments in alcoholism* (Vol. 12, pp. 81-101). New York: Plenum.

Miller, B. A., Downs, W. R., & Gondoli, D. M. (1989). Delinquency, childhood violence, and the development of alcoholism in women. *Crime and Delinquency, 35*(1), 94-108.

Miller, B. A., Downs, W. R., & Testa, M. (1993). Interrelationships between victimization experiences and women's alcohol use. *Journal of Studies on Alcohol, 11*(Suppl.), 109-117.

Miller, B. A., Maguin, E., & Downs, W. R. (1997). Alcohol, drugs, and violence in children's lives. In M. Galanter (Ed.), *Recent developments in alcoholism* (Vol. 13, pp. 357-385). New York: Plenum.

Miller, B. A., Smyth, N. J., & Mudar, P. J. (1999). Mothers' alcohol and other drug problems and their punitiveness toward their children. *Journal of Studies on Alcohol, 60,* 632-642.

Miller, M. M. (1998). Traditional approaches to the treatment of addiction. In A. W. Graham & T. K. Schultz (Eds.), *Principles of addiction medicine* (2nd ed., pp. 315-326). Chevy Chase, MD: American Society of Addiction Medicine.

Miller, N. S., & Gold, M. S. (1994). Dissociation of conscious desire (craving) from and relapse in alcohol and cocaine dependence. *Annals of Clinical Psychiatry, 6,* 99-106.

Miller, P. M., Smith, G. T., & Goldman, M. S. (1990). Emergence of alcohol expectations in childhood: A possible critical period. *Journal of Studies on Alcohol, 51,* 343-349.

Miller, W. (1983). Controlled drinking: A history and a critical review. *Journal of Studies on Alcohol, 44,* 68-82.

Miller, W. R. (1985). Motivation for treatment: A review with special emphasis on alcoholism. *Psychological Bulletin, 98,* 84-107.

Miller, W. R. (1990). Alcohol treatment alternatives: What works? In H. B. Milkman & L. I. Sederer (Eds.), *Treatment choices for alcoholism and substance abuse* (pp. 253-264). Lexington, MA: Lexington Books.

Miller, W. R. (1995). Increasing motivation for change. In R. K. Hester & W. R. Miller (Eds.), *Handbook of alcoholism treatment approaches: Effective alternatives* (2nd ed., pp. 89-104). Needham Heights, MA: Allyn & Bacon.

Miller, W. R. (1996). Motivational interviewing: Research, practice, and puzzles. *Addictive Behaviors, 21,* 835-842.

Miller, W. R., Benefield, R. G., & Tonigan, J. S. (1993). Enhancing motivation for change in problem drinking: A controlled comparison of two therapist styles. *Journal of Consulting and Clinical Psychology, 61,* 455-460.

Miller, W. R., & Bennett, M. E. (1996). Treating alcohol problems in the context of other drug abuse. *Alcohol Health & Research World, 20,* 118-123.

Miller, W. R., Brown, J. M., Simpson, T. L., Handmaker, N. S., Bien, T. H., Luckie, L. F., Montgomery, H. A., Hester, R. K., & Tonigan, J. S. (1995). What works: A methodological analysis of the alcoholism treatment literature. In R. K. Hester & W. R. Miller (Eds.), *Handbook of alcoholism treatment approaches: Effective alternatives* (2nd ed., pp. 12-44). Needham Heights, MA: Allyn & Bacon.

Miller, W. R., & Hester, R. K. (1986a). The effectiveness of alcoholism treatment: What research reveals? In W. R. Miller & N. Heather (Eds.), *The addictive behaviors: Processes of change* (pp. 121-174). New York: Plenum.

Miller, W. R., & Hester, R. K. (1986b). Matching problem drinkers with optimal treatments. In W. R. Miller & N. Heather (Eds.), *The addictive behaviors: Processes of change* (pp. 175-203). New York: Plenum.

Miller, W. R., Leckman, A. L., Delaney, H. D., & Tinkcom, M. (1992). Long-term follow-up of behavioral self-control training. *Journal of Studies on Alcohol, 53,* 249-261.

Miller, W. R., & Taylor, C. A. (1980). Relative effectiveness of bibliotherapy, individual and group self-control training in the treatment of problem drinkers. *Addictive Behaviors, 15,* 13-24.

Miller, W. R., Zweben, D. S. W., DiClemente, C. C., & Rychtarik, R. G. (1995). *Motivational enhancement therapy manual* (Vol. 2). Rockville, MD: National Institute on Alcohol Abuse and Alcoholism.

Miller-Tutzauer, C., Leonard, K. E., & Windle, M. (1991). Marriage and alcohol use: A longitudinal study of "maturing out." *Journal of Studies on Alcohol, 52,* 434-440.

Moncrieff, J., Drummond, D. C., Candy, B., Checinski, K., & Farmer, R. (1996). Sexual abuse in people with alcohol problems: A study of the prevalence of sexual abuse and its relationship to drinking behaviour. *British Journal of Psychiatry, 169,* 355-360.

Monti, P. M., Binkoff, J. A., Abrams, D. B., Zwick, W. R., Nirenberg, T. D., & Liepman, M. R. (1987). Reactivity of alcoholics and nonalcoholics to drinking cues. *Journal of Abnormal Psychology, 96,* 1-5.

Monti, P. M., Gulliver, S. B., & Myers, M. G. (1994). Social skills training for alcoholics: Assessment and treatment. *Alcohol and Alcoholism, 29,* 627-637.

Monti, P. M., Rohsenow, D. J., Colby, S. M., & Abrams, D. B. (1995). Coping and social skills training. In R. K. Hester & W. R. Miller (Eds.), *Handbook of alcoholism treatment approaches: Effective alternatives* (2nd ed., pp. 221-241). Needham Heights, MA: Allyn & Bacon.

Mooney, D. K., Fromme, K., Kivlahan, D. R., & Marlatt, G. A. (1987). Correlates of alcohol consumption: Sex, age, and expectancies relate differentially to quantity and frequency. *Addictive Behaviors, 12,* 235-240.

Moore, K. L., and Persaud, T. V. N. (1993). *The developing human: Clinically oriented embryology* (3rd ed.). Philadelphia, PA: Saunders.

Moos, R., & Billings, A. G. (1982). Children of alcoholics during the recovery process: Alcoholic and matched control families. *Addictive Behaviors, 7,* 155-163.

Moos, R., Brennan, P., & Schutte, K. (1998). Life context factors, treatment, and late-life drinking behavior. In U.S. Department of Health and Human Services (Ed.), *Alcohol problems and aging* (pp. 261-280). Washington, DC: Government Printing Office.

Moos, R. H., Finney, J. W., & Chan, A. D. (1981). The process of recovery from alcoholism: I. Comparing alcoholic patients and matched community controls. *Journal of Studies on Alcohol, 42,* 383-402.

Morgenstern, J., & McCrady, B. S. (1993). Cognitive processes and change in disease-model treatment. In B. S. McCrady & W. R. Miller (Eds.), *Research on Alcoholics Anonymous: Opportunities and alternatives* (pp. 153-166). Piscataway, NJ: Rutgers Center of Alcohol Studies.

Mosher, J. F., & Jernigan, D. H. (1989). New directions in alcohol policy. In L. Breslow, J. E. Fielding, & L. B. Lave (Eds.), *Annual review of public health* (Vol. 10, pp. 245-279). Palo Alto, CA: Annual Reviews.

Moskowitz, H., & Burns, M. (1971). The effect of alcohol upon the psychological refractory period. *Quarterly Journal of Studies on Alcohol, 32,* 782-790.

Moskowitz, H., Burns, M. M., & Williams, A. F. (1985). Skills performance at low blood alcohol levels. *Journal of Studies on Alcohol, 46,* 482-485.

Moskowitz, H., & DePry, D. (1968). The effect of alcohol on auditory vigilance and divided-attention tasks. *Quarterly Journal of Studies on Alcohol, 29,* 54-63.

Moskowitz, J. M. (1989). The primary prevention of alcohol prolems: A critical review of the research literature. *Journal of Studies on Alcohol, 50,* 54-88.

Mumola, C. J. (1999). Substance abuse and treatment, state and federal prisoners, 1997. In U.S. Department of Justice (Ed.), *U S. Bureau of Justice Statistics special report* (p. 1). Washington, DC: U.S. Department of Justice.

Murdoch, D., Pihl, R. O., & Ross, D. (1990). Alcohol and crimes of violence: Present issues. *International Journal of the Addictions, 25,* 1065-1081.

Murphy, C. M., & O'Farrell, T. J. (1994). Factors associated with marital aggression in male alcoholics. *Journal of Family Psychology, 8,* 321-335.

Murphy, C. M., & O'Farrell, T. J. (1996). Marital violence among alcoholics. *Current Directions in Psychological Science, 5,* 183-186.

Murphy, C. M., & O'Farrell, T. J. (1997). Couple communication patterns of maritally aggressive and nonaggressive male alcoholics. *Journal of Studies on Alcohol, 58,* 83-90.

Murray, A. L., & Lawrence, P. S. (1984). Sequelae to smoking cessation. *Clinical Psychology Review, 4,* 143-157.

Musto, D. F. (1987). *The American disease: Origins of narcotic control* (Expanded ed.). New York: Oxford University Press.

Myers, J. K., Weissman, M. M., Tischler, G. L., Holzer, C. E., III, Leaf, P. J., Orvaschel, H., Anthony, J. C., Boyd, J. H., Burke, J. D., Jr., Kramer, M., & Stoltzman, R. (1984). Six month prevalence of psychiatric disorders in three communities. *Archives of General Psychiatry, 41,* 959-967.

Nadelmann, E. A. (1997). Drug prohibition in the U.S.: Costs, consequences, and alternatives. In C. Reinarman & H. G. Levine (Eds.), *Crack in America: Demon drugs and social justice* (pp. 288-316). Berkeley: University of California Press.

Nagoshi, C. T., & Wilson, J. R. (1987). Influence of family alcoholism history on alcohol metabolism, sensitivity, and tolerance. *Alcoholism, Clinical and Experimental Research, 11,* 392-398.

Narcotics Control Act, Pub. L. No. 84-728 (1956).

Nathan, P. E. (1984). Alcohol prevention in the workplace. In P. M. Miller & T. D. Nirenberg (Eds.), *Prevention of alcohol abuse* (pp. 387-406). New York: Plenum.

Nathan, P. E. (1992). Peele hasn't done his homework—again: A response to "Alcoholism, politics, and bureaucracy: The consensus against controlled-drinking therapy in America." *Addictive Behaviors, 17,* 63-65.

National Clearinghouse for Alcohol Information. (1989). *Prevention Plus II: Tools for creating and sustaining drug-free communities.* Rockville, MD: Author.

National Commission on Marijuana and Health. (1978). *Marijuana and health.* Washington, DC: Author.

National Institute of Justice. (1995). *Drug use forecasting: Annual report on adult and juvenile arrestees.* Washington, DC: Author.

National Institute on Alcohol Abuse and Alcoholism. (1981). *Indian clients treated in NIAAA-funded programs.* Rockville, MD: Author.

National Institute on Alcohol Abuse and Alcoholism. (1990). *Seventh special report to U.S. Congress.* Washington, DC: Government Printing Office.

National Institute on Alcohol Abuse and Alcoholism. (1992). *Epidemiologic report.* Rockville, MD: Author.

National Institute on Alcohol Abuse and Alcoholism. (1997). Matching alcoholism treatments to client heterogeneity: Project MATCH posttreatment drinking outcomes. *Journal of Studies on Alcohol, 58,* 7-29.

National Institute on Drug Abuse/National Institute on Alcoholism and Alcohol Abuse (NIDA/NIAAA). (1990). *National Drug and Alcoholism Treatment Unit Survey (NDATUS) 1989: Main findings report.* Rockville, MD: Author.

National Transportation Safety Board. (1987). Deficiencies in enforcement, judicial, and treatment programs related to repeat offender drunk drivers. *Alcohol, Drugs and Driving, 3,* 31-42.

Neff, J. A., & Hoppe, S. K. (1992). Acculturation and drinking patterns among U.S. Anglos, Blacks, and Mexican Americans. *Alcohol and Alcoholism, 27,* 293-308.

Neff, J. A., Hoppe, S. K., & Perea, P. (1987). Acculturation and alcohol use: Drinking patterns and problems among Anglo and Mexican American male drinkers. *Hispanic Journal of Behavioral Sciences, 9,* 151-181.

Nelson, D. E., Giovino, G. A., Shopland, D. R., Mowery, P. D., Mills, S. L., & Eriksen, M. P. (1995). Trends in cigarette smoking among US adolescents, 1974 through 1991. *American Journal of Public Health, 85*(1), 34-40.

Newlin, D. B., & Thomson, J. B. (1990). Alcohol challenge with sons of alcoholics: A critical review and analysis. *Psychological Bulletin, 108,* 383-402.

Niaura, R. S., Rohsenow, D. J., Binkoff, J. A., Monti, P. M., Pedraza, M., & Abrams, D. B. (1988). Relevance of cue reactivity to understanding alcohol and smoking relapse. *Journal of Abnormal Psychology, 97,* 133-152.

Nichols, J. L. (1990). Treatment versus deterrence. *Alcohol Health & Research World, 14,* 44-51.

Nixon, S. J. (1995). Assessing cognitive impairment. *Alcohol Health & Research World, 19,* 97-103.

Nixon, S. J., & Parsons, O. A. (1991). Alcohol-related efficiency deficits using an ecologically valid test. *Alcoholism, Clinical and Experimental Research, 15,* 601-606.

Nixon, S. J., & Parsons, O. A. (1993). Neurobehavioral sequelae of alcoholism. *Neurologic Clinics, 11,* 205-218.

Nixon, S. J., Tivis, R., & Parsons, O. A. (1995). Behavioral dysfunction and cognitive efficiency in male and female alcoholics. *Alcoholism, Clinical and Experimental Research, 19,* 577-581.

Noble, E. P., Blum, K., Khalsa, M. E., Ritchie, T., Montgomery, A., Wood, R. C., Fitch, R. J., Ozkaragoz, T., Sheridan, P. J., Anglin, M. D., Paredes, A., Treiman, L. J., & Sparks, R. S. (1993). Allelic association of the D2 dopamine receptor gene with cocaine dependence. *Drug and Alcohol Dependence, 83,* 271-285.

Noble, E. P., Jeor, S. T., Ritchie, T., Syndulko, K., Jeor, S. C., Fitch, R. J., Brunner, R. L., & Sparkes, R. S. (1994). D2 dopamine receptor gene and cigarette smoking: A reward gene? *Medical Hypothesis, 42,* 257-260.

Nordstrom, G., & Berglund, M. (1987). A prospective study of successful long-term adjustment in alcohol dependence: Social drinking vs. abstinence. *Journal of Studies on Alcohol, 48,* 95-103.

Norris, J., & Kerr, K. L. (1993). Alcohol and violent pornography: Responses to permissive and nonpermissive cues. *Journal of Studies on Alcohol, 11,* 118-127.

Oetting, E. R., & Beauvais, F. (1987). Peer cluster theory, socialization characteristics, and adolescent drug use: A path analysis. *Journal of Counseling Psychology, 34,* 205-213.

O'Farrell, T. J. (1995). Marital and family therapy. In R. K. Hester & W. R. Miller (Eds.), *Handbook of alcoholism treatment approaches: Effective alternatives* (2nd ed., pp. 195-220). Needham Heights, MA: Allyn & Bacon.

O'Farrell, T. J., Choquette, K. A., Cutter, H. S., & Birchler, G. R. (1997). Sexual satisfaction and dysfunction in marriages of male alcoholics: Comparison with nonalcoholic maritally conflicted and nonconflicted couples. *Journal of Studies on Alcohol, 58,* 91-99.

O'Farrell, T. J., & Murphy, C. M. (1995). Marital violence before and after alcoholism treatment. *Journal of Consulting and Clinical Psychology, 63,* 256-262.

Office of Disease Prevention and Health Promotion (ODPHP). (1987). *National survey of worksite health promotion activities: A summary.* Silver Springs, MD: ODPHP National Health Information Center.

Ogborne, A. C. (1989). Some limitations of Alcoholics Anonymous. In M. Galanter (Ed.), *Recent developments in alcoholism* (Vol. 7, pp. 55-67). New York: Plenum.

Ogborne, A. C. (1993). Assessing the effectiveness of Alcoholics Anonymous in the community: Meeting the challenges. In B. S. McCrady & W. R. Miller (Eds.), *Research on Alcoholics Anonymous: Opportunities and alternatives* (pp. 339-356). Piscataway, NJ: Rutgers Center of Alcohol Studies.

Ogborne, A., & Glaser, F. (1981). Characteristics of affiliates of Alcoholics Anonymous. *Journal of Studies on Alcohol, 42,* 661-675.

O'Hare, T. M. (1990). Drinking in college: Consumption patterns, problems, sex differences and legal drinking age. *Journal of Studies on Alcohol, 51,* 536-541.

Olenick, N. L., & Chalmers, D. K. (1991). Gender specific drinking styles in alcoholics and nonalcoholics. *Journal of Studies on Alcohol, 52,* 325-330.

O'Malley, S. S., Jaffe, A. J., Chang, G., Schottenfeld, R. S., Meyer, R. E., & Rounsaville, B. (1992). Naltrexone and coping skills therapy for alcohol dependence: A controlled study. *Archives of General Psychiatry, 49,* 881-887.

Omnibus Budget Reconciliation Act, Pub. L. No. 97-35, 95 Stat. 357 (1981).

Orford, J., & Edwards, G. (1977). *Alcoholism: A comparison of treatment and advice, with a study of the influence of marriage.* Oxford, UK: Oxford University Press.

Orford, J., Guthrie, S., Nicholls, P., Oppenheimer, E., Egert, S., & Hensman, C. (1975). Self-reported coping behaviour of wives of alcoholics and its association with drinking outcome. *Journal of Studies on Alcohol, 36,* 1254-1267.

Orford, J., & Velleman, R. (1991). The environmental intergenerational transmission of alcohol problems: A comparison of two hypotheses. *British Journal of Medical Psychology, 64,* 189-200.

Ornstein, S., & Levy, D. (1983). Price and income elasticities of demand for alcoholic beverages. In M. Galanter (Ed.), *Recent developments in alcoholism* (Vol. 1, pp. 303-345). New York: Plenum.

Oscar-Berman, M. (1988). Normal functional asymmetries in alcoholism? *Aphasiology, 2,* 369-374.

Pandey, G. N., Fawcett, J., Gibbons, R., Clark, C. D., & Davis, J. M. (1988). Platelet monoamine oxidase in alcoholism. *Biological Psychiatry, 24,* 15-24.

Pandina, R. J., & Johnson, V. (1989). Familial drinking history as a predictor of alcohol and drug consumption among adolescent children. *Journal of Studies on Alcohol, 50,* 245-253.

Parker, D. A., & Harford, T. C. (1992). Gender-role attitudes, job competition and alcohol consumption among women and men. *Alcoholism, Clinical and Experimental Research, 16,* 159-165.

Parker, D. A., Harford, T. C., & Rosenstock, I. M. (1994). Alcohol, other drugs, and sexual risk-taking among young adults. *Journal of Substance Abuse, 6,* 87-93.

Parker, E. S., & Noble, E. (1977). Alcohol consumption and cognitive functioning in social drinkers. *Journal of Studies on Alcohol, 38,* 1224-1232.

Parrott, A. C., & Garnham, N. J. (1998). Comparative mood states and cognitive skills of cigarette smokers, deprived smokers and nonsmokers. *Human Psychopharmacology Clinical and Experimental, 13,* 367-376.

Parsons, O. A. (1986). Cognitive functioning in sober social drinkers: A review and critique. *Journal of Studies on Alcohol, 47,* 101-114.

Parsons, O. A., & Leber, W. R. (1981). The relationship between cognitive dysfunction and brain damage in alcoholics. *Alcoholism, 5,* 326-343.

Partanen, J., Bruun, K., & Markkanens, T. (1966). *Inheritance of drinking behavior* (Vol. 14). Helsinki: Finnish Foundation for Alcohol Studies.

Patterson, B. W., Williams, H. L., McLean, G. A., Smith, L. T., & Schaffer, K. W. (1987). Alcoholism and family history of alcoholism: Effects on visual and auditory event-related potentials. *Alcohol, 4,* 265-269.

Paul, J. P., Stall, R., & Bloomfield, K. A. (1991). Gay and alcoholic: Epidemiologic and clinical issues. *Alcohol Health & Research World, 15,* 151-160.

Paul, J. P., Stall, R. D., Crosby, G. M., Barrett, D. C., & Midanik, L. T. (1994). Correlates of sexual risk-taking among gay male substance abusers. *Addiction, 89,* 971-983.

Pavlov, I. P. (1927). *Conditioned reflexes.* Oxford, UK: Oxford University Press.

Peele, S. (1989). *Diseasing of America: Addiction treatment out of control.* Lexington, MA: Lexington Books.

Peele, S. (1992). Alcoholism, politics, and bureaucracy: The consensus against controlled-drinking therapy in America. *Addictive Behaviors, 17,* 49-62.

Pendery, M., Maltzman, I., & West, J. (1982). Controlled drinking by alcoholics? New findings and a reevaluation of a major affirmative study. *Science, 217,* 169-175.

Penick, E. C., Powell, B. J., Bingham, S. F., Liskow, B. I., Miller, N. S., & Read, M. R. (1987). A comparative study of familial alcoholism. *Journal of Studies on Alcohol, 48,* 136-146.

Pennsylvania Liquor Control Board. (1995). *Alcohol impairment chart* [Online]. Available: www.lcb.state.pa.us/edu/adult-chart.htm

Pentz, M. A. (1995). Prevention research in multiethnic communities. In G. J. Botvin, S. Schinke, & M. A. Orlandi (Eds.), *Drug abuse prevention with multiethnic youth* (pp. 193-214). Thousand Oaks, CA: Sage.

Pernanen, K. (1981). Theoretical aspects of the relationship between alcohol use and crime. In J. J. Collins (Ed.), *Drinking and crime: Perspectives on the relationships between alcohol consumption and criminal behavior* (pp. 1-69). New York: Guilford.

Pernanen, K. (1991). *Alcohol and human violence.* New York: Guilford.

Perrine, M. W. (1990). Who are the drinking drivers? The spectrum of drinking drivers revisited. *Alcohol Health & Research World, 14,* 26-35.

Perrine, M. W., & Sadler, D. D. (1987). Alcohol treatment program versus license suspension for drunken drivers: The four-year traffic safety impact. In P. C. Noordzij & R. Roszbach (Eds.), *Alcohol, drugs, and traffic safety.* New York: Elsevier.

Pert, C., & Snyder, S. H. (1973). Opiate receptor: Demonstration in central nervous system tissue. *Science, 179,* 1011-1014.

Peterson, J. B., Rothfleisch, J., Zelazo, P. D., & Pihl, R. O. (1990). Acute alcohol intoxication and cognitive functioning. *Journal of Studies on Alcohol, 51,* 114-122.

Peterson, P. L., Hawkins, J. D., Abbott, R. D., & Catalano, R. F. (1994). Disentangling the effects of parental drinking, family management, and parental alcohol norms on current drinking by Black and White adolescents. *Journal of Research on Adolescence, 4,* 203-227.

Pfefferbaum, A., & Rosenbloom, M. J. (1990). Brain-imaging tools for the study of alcoholism. *Alcohol Health & Research World, 14,* 219-231.

Pickens, R. W., Svikis, D. S., McGue, M., Lykken, D. T., Heston, L. L., & Clayton, P. J. (1991). Heterogeneity in the inheritance of alcoholism: A study of male and female twins. *Archives of General Psychiatry, 48,* 19-28.

Pierce, J. P., Fiore, M. C., Novotny, T. E., Hatziandreu, E. J., & Davis, R. M. (1989). Trends in cigarette smoking in the United States: Projections to the year 2000. *Journal of the American Medical Association, 261*(1), 61-65.

Pihl, R. O., & Peterson, J. (1991). Attention-deficit hyperactivity disorder, childhood conduct disorder, and alcoholism. *Alcohol Health & Research World, 15,* 25-31.

Pihl, R. O., Peterson, J., & Finn, P. (1990a). An heuristic model for the inherited predisposition to alcoholism. *Psychology of Addictive Behaviors, 4,* 12-25.

Pihl, R. O., Peterson, J., & Finn, P. (1990b). Inherited predisposition to alcoholism: Characteristics of sons of male alcoholics. *Journal of Abnormal Psychology, 99,* 291-301.

Pihl, R. O., & Yankofsky, L. (1979). Alcohol consumption in male social drinkers as a function of situationally induced depressive affect and anxiety. *Psychopharmology, 65,* 251-257.

Podolsky, D. M. (1986). Alcohol consumption and the risk of breast cancer. *Alcohol Health & Research World, 10,* 40-43.

Polich, J. M., Armor, D. J., & Braiker, H. B. (1981). *The course of alcoholism: Four years after treatment.* New York: John Wiley.

Pomerleau, C. S., Cole, P. A., Lumley, M. A., Marks, J. L., & Pomerleau, O. F. (1994). Effects of menstrual phase on nicotine, alcohol, and caffeine intake in smokers. *Journal of Substance Abuse, 6,* 227-234.

Pomerleau, C. S., Pomerleau, O. F., & Garcia, A. W. (1991). Biobehavioral research on nicotine use in women. *British Journal of Addiction, 86,* 527-531.

Pomerleau, O., Pertschuk, M., Adkins, D., & Brady, J. P. (1978). A comparison of behavioral and traditional treatment for middle income problem drinkers. *Journal of Behavioral Medicine, 1,* 187-200.

Pontieri, F. E., Tanda, G., Orzi, F., & Di Chiara, G. (1996). Effects of nicotine on the nucleus accumbens and similarity to those of addictive drugs. *Nature, 382,* 255-257.

Porjesz, B., & Begleiter, H. (1997). Event-related potentials in COA's. *Alcohol Health & Research World, 21,* 236-240.

Powell, B. J., Penick, E. C., Read, M. R., & Ludwig, A. M. (1985). Comparison of three outpatient treatment interventions: A twelve-month followup of men alcoholics. *Journal of Studies on Alcohol, 46,* 309-312.

Power, C., & Estaugh, V. (1990). The role of family formation and dissolution in shaping drinking behaviour in early adulthood. *British Journal of Addiction, 85,* 521-530.

Prescott, C. A., & Kendler, K. S. (1995). Twin study design. *Alcohol Health & Research World, 19,* 200-205.

Prest, L. A., Benson, M. J., & Protinsky, H. O. (1998). Family of origin and current relationship influences on codependency. *Family Process, 37,* 513-528.

Prochaska, J. O., DiClemente, C. C., & Norcross, J. C. (1992). In search of how people change: Applications to addictive behaviors. *American Psychologist, 47,* 1102-1114.

Pure Food and Drug Act, U.S. Statutes at Large 59th Congr., Sess. I, Chp. 3915, pp. 768-722 (1906).

Rachman, S., & Teasdale, J. (1969). *Aversion therapy: Appraisal and status.* Coral Gables, FL: University of Miami Press.

Randall, C. L., Roberts, J. S., Del Boca, F. K., Carroll, K. M., Connors, G. J., & Mattson, M. E. (1999). Telescoping of landmark events associated with drinking: A gender comparison. *Journal of Studies on Alcohol, 60,* 252-260.

Ray, O., & Ksir, C. (1993). *Drugs, society, and human behavior.* St. Louis, MO: Mosby.

Reed, R. J., Grant, I., & Rourke, S. B. (1992). Long-term abstinent alcoholics have normal memory. *Alcoholism, Clinical and Experimental Research, 16,* 677-683.

Regan, T. J. (1990). Alcohol and the cardiovascular system. *Journal of the American Medical Association, 264,* 377-381.

Regier, D. A., Myers, J. K., Kramer, M., Robins, L. N., Blazer, D. G., Hough, R. L., Eaton, W. W., & Locke, B. Z. (1984). The NIMH Epidemiologic Catchment Area Program: Historical context, major objectives, and study population characteristics. *Archives of General Psychiatry, 41,* 934-941.

Rehm, J., Ashley, M. J., Room, R., Single, E., Bondy, S., Ferrence, R., & Giesbrecht, N. (1996). On the emerging paradigm of drinking patterns and their social and health consequences. *Addiction, 91,* 1615-1621.

Rehm, J., & Sempos, C. T. (1995). Alcohol consumption and all-cause mortality. *Addiction, 90,* 471-480.

Reich, T., Cloninger, C. R., Van Eerdewegh, P., Rice, J. P., & Mullaney, J. (1988). Secular trends in the familial transmission of alcoholism. *Alcoholism, Clinical and Experimental Research, 12,* 458-464.

Reuter, P., & Caulkins, J. P. (1995). Redefining the goals of national drug policy: Recommendations from a working group. *American Journal of Public Health, 85,* 1059-1063.

Risberg, J., & Berglund, M. (1987). Cerebral blood flow and metabolism in alcoholics. In O. A. Parsons, N. Butters, & P. E. Nathan (Eds.), *Neuropsychology of alcoholism: Implications for diagnosis and treatment* (pp. 64-75). New York: Guilford.

Robbins, C. (1989). Sex differences in psychosocial consequences of alcohol and drug abuse. *Journal of Health and Social Behavior, 30,* 117-130.

Robertson, J. A., & Plant, M. A. (1988). Alcohol, sex, and risks of HIV infection. *Drug and Alcohol Dependence, 22,* 75-78.

Robins, L. N., Helzer, J. E., Weissman, M. M., Orvascel, H., Gruenberg, E., Burker, J. D., Jr., & Regier, D. A. (1984). Lifetime prevalence of specific psychiatric disorders in three sites. *Archives of General Psychiatry, 41,* 949-958.

Robinson, T. E., & Berridge, K. C. (1993). The neural basis of drug craving: An incentive-sensitization theory of addiction. *Brain Research Review, 18,* 247-291.

Rodriguez, M. (1994). Influence of sex and family history of alcoholism on cognitive functioning in heroin users. *European Journal of Psychiatry, 8,* 29-36.

Rogosch, F., Chassin, L., & Sher, K. J. (1990). Personality variables as mediators and moderators of family history for alcoholism: Conceptual and methodological issues. *Journal of Studies on Alcohol, 51,* 310-318.

Roizen, J. (1997). Epidemiological issues in alcohol-related violence. In M. Galanter (Ed.), *Recent developments in alcoholism: Alcohol and violence* (Vol. 13, pp. 7-40). New York: Plenum.

Roizen, R. (1983). *Alcohol dependence symptoms in cross-cultural perspective: A report of findings from the World Health Organization study of community response to alcoholism.* Berkeley, CA: Alcohol Research Group.

Roman, P. M. (1987). Growth and transformation in workplace alcoholism programming. In M. Galanter (Ed.), *Recent developments in alcoholism* (Vol. 6, pp. 131-158). New York: Plenum.

Roosa, M. W., Sandler, I. N., Beals, J., & Short, J. L. (1988). Risk status of adolescent children of problem-drinking parents. *American Journal of Community Psychology, 16,* 225-239.

Rose, G., Bengtsson, C., Dimberg, L., Kumlin, L., & Eriksson, B. (1998). Life events, mood, mental strain and cardiovascular risk factors in Swedish middle-aged men: Data from the Swedish part of the Renault/Volvo Coeur Study. *Occupational Medicine, 48,* 329-336.

Rose, J. E. (1988). The role of upper airway stimulation in smoking. In O. F. Pomerleau & C. S. Pomerleau (Eds.), *Nicotine replacement: A critical evaluation* (pp. 95-96). New York: Alan R. Liss.

Rosenberg, H. (1995). The elderly and the use of illicit drugs: Sociological and epidemiological considerations. *International Journal of the Addictions, 30,* 1925-1951.

Ross, H. L. (1984). *Deterring the drinking driver: Legal policy and social control.* Lexington, MA: D. C. Heath.

Rubin, E. (1979). Alcoholic myopathy in heart and skeletal muscle. *New England Journal of Medicine, 301,* 28-33.

Rubin, E., & Lieber, C. S. (1968). Alcohol, other drugs, and the liver. *Annals of Internal Medicine, 69,* 1063-1067.

Ryan, C. (1980). Learning and memory deficits in alcoholics. *Journal of Studies on Alcohol, 41,* 437-447.

Ryan, C., & Butters, N. (1983). Cognitive deficits in alcoholics. In B. Kissin & H. Begleiter (Eds.), *The pathogenesis of alcoholism* (pp. 485-538). New York: Plenum.

Ryan, C., & Butters, N. (1984). Alcohol consumption and premature aging: A critical review. In M. Galanter (Ed.), *Recent developments in alcoholism* (pp. 223-250). New York: Plenum.

Ryan, C., & Butters, N. (1986). Neuropsychology of alcoholism. In D. Wedding, A. M. Norton, & J. S. Webster (Eds.), *The neuropsychology handbook* (pp. 376-409). New York: Springer.

Ryan, R. M., Plant, R. W., & O'Malley, S. (1995). Initial motivations for alcohol treatment: Relations with patient characteristics, treatment involvement, and dropout. *Addictive Behaviors, 20,* 279-297.

Rychtarik, R. G., Foy, D. W., Scott, T., Lokey, L., & Prue, D. M. (1987). Five-six year follow-up broad-spectrum behavioral treatment for alcoholism: Effects of training controlled drinking skills. *Journal of Consulting and Clinical Psychology, 55,* 106-108.

Rychtarik, R. G., Prue, D. M., Rapp, S. R., & King, A. C. (1992). Self-efficacy, aftercare and relapse in a treatment program for alcoholics. *Journal of Studies on Alcohol, 53,* 435-440.

Safe and Drug-Free Schools and Communities Act, H.R. 6, Title IV (1994).

Saffer, H. (1991). Alcohol advertising and alcohol abuse. *Journal of Health Economics, 10,* 65-79.

Saltz, R. (1986). Server intervention: Will it work? *Alcohol Health & Research World, 10,* 12-19, 35.

Sanchez-Craig, M., Leigh, G., Spivak, K., & Lei, H. (1989). Superior outcome of females over males after brief treatment for reduction of heavy drinking. *British Journal of Addiction, 84,* 395-404.

Sanchez-Craig, M., & Walker, K. (1982). Teaching coping skills to chronic alcoholics in a coeducational halfway house: I. Assessment of programme effects. *British Journal of Addiction, 77,* 35-50.

Savage, D. G. (1999, December 2). High court wary of classifying tobacco as drug. *Los Angeles Times,* p. A-1.

Sayette, M. A., Breslin, F. C., Wilson, G. T., & Rosenblum, G. D. (1994). An evaluation of the balanced placebo design in alcohol administration research. *Addictive Behaviors, 19,* 333-342.

Sayette, M. A., & Wilson, G. T. (1991). Intoxication and exposure to stress: Effects of temporal patterning. *Journal of Abnormal Psychology, 100,* 56-62.

Schachter, S. (1982). Recidivism and self-cure of smoking and obesity. *American Psychologist, 37,* 436-444.

Schachter, S., Silverstein, B., Kozlowski, L. T., Perlick, D., Herman, C. P., & Liebling, B. (1977). Studies of the interaction of psychological or pharmacological determinants of smoking. *Journal of Experimental Psychology: General, 106,* 3-12.

Schafer, J., & Brown, S. A. (1991). Marijuana and cocaine effect expectancies and drug use patterns. *Journal of Consulting and Clinical Psychology, 59,* 558-565.

Schatzkin, A., & Longnecker, M. P. (1994). Alcohol and breast cancer: Where are we now and where do we go from here? *Cancer, 74*(3, Suppl.), 1101-1110.

Scher, M. S., Richardson, G. A., Coble, P. A., Day, N. L., & Stoffer, D. S. (1988). The effects of prenatal alcohol and marijuana exposure: Disturbances in neonatal sleep cycling and arousal. *Pediatric Research, 24,* 101-105.

Schmidt, C., Klee, L., & Ames, G. (1990). Review and analysis of literature on indicators of women's drinking problems. *British Journal of Addiction, 85,* 179-192.

Schuckit, M. (1981). Peak blood alcohol levels in men at high risk for future development of alcoholism. *Alcoholism, Clinical and Experimental Research, 5,* 64-66.

Schuckit, M. (1987). Biological vulnerability to alcoholism. *Journal of Consulting and Clinical Psychology, 55,* 301-309.

Schuckit, M. A., Anthenelli, R. M., Bucholz, K. K., Hesselbrock, V. M., & Tipp, J. (1995). The time course of development of alcohol-related problems in men and women. *Journal of Studies on Alcohol, 56*(2), 218-225.

Schuckit, M. A., Daeppen, J. B., Tipp, J. E., Hesselbrock, M., & Bucholz, K. K. (1998). The clinical course of alcohol-related problems in alcohol dependent and nonalcohol dependent drinking women and men. *Journal of Studies on Alcohol, 59,* 581-590.

Schuckit, M. A., Hesselbrock, V., Tipp, J., Anthenelli, R., Bucholz, K., & Radziminski, S. (1994). A comparison of *DSM-III-R, DSM-IV* and *ICD-10* substance use disorders diagnoses in 1922 men and women subjects in the COGA study. *Addiction, 89,* 1629-1638.

Schulenberg, J., O'Malley, P. M., Bachman, J. G., Wadsworth, K. N., & Johnston, L. D. (1996). Getting drunk and growing up: Trajectories of frequent binge drinking during the transition to young adulthood. *Journal of Studies on Alcohol, 57,* 289-304.

Schutte, K. K., Moos, R. H., & Brennan, P. L. (1995). Depression and drinking behavior among women and men: A three-wave longitudinal study of older adults. *Journal of Consulting and Clinical Psychology, 63,* 810-822.

Searles, J. S. (1988). The role of genetics in the pathogenesis of alcoholism. *Journal of Abnormal Psychology, 97,* 153-167.

Searles, J. S., Perrine, M. W., Mundt, J. C., & Helzer, J. E. (1995). Self-report of drinking using touch-tone telephone: Extending the limits of reliable daily contact. *Journal of Studies on Alcohol, 56,* 375-382.

Searles, J. S., & Windle, M. (1990). Introduction and overview: Salient issues in the children of alcoholics literature. In M. Windle & J. S. Searles (Eds.), *Children of alcoholics: Critical perspectives* (pp. 1-8). New York: Guilford.

Seitz, H. K., Gärtner, U., Egerer, G., & Simanowski, U. A. (1994). Ethanol metabolism in the gastrointestinal tract and its possible consequences. *Alcohol and Alcoholism, 2*(Suppl.), 157-162.

Seitz, H. K., Pöschl, G., & Simanowski, U. A. (1998). Alcohol and cancer. *Recent Developments in Alcoholism, 14,* 67-95.

Selzer, M. L. (1971). The Michigan Alcohol Screening Test: The quest for a new diagnostic instrument. *American Journal of Psychiatry, 27,* 1653-1658.

Senchak, M., Leonard, K. E., Greene, B. W., & Carroll, A. (1995). Comparisons of adult children of alcoholic, divorced, and control parents in four outcome domains. *Psychology of Addictive Behaviors, 9,* 147-156.

Shaper, A. G. (1990). Alcohol and mortality: A review of prospective studies. *British Journal of Addiction, 85,* 837-847.

Shedler, J., & Block, J. (1990). Adolescent drug use and psychological health. *American Psychologist, 45,* 612-630.

Sher, K. J. (1987). Stress response dampening. In H. T. Blane & K. E. Leonard (Eds.), *Psychological theories of drinking and alcoholism* (pp. 227-271). New York: Plenum.

Sher, K. J. (1991). *Children of alcoholics: A critical approach of theory and research.* Chicago: University of Chicago Press.

Sher, K. J. (1997). Psychological characteristics of children of alcoholics. *Alcohol Health & Research World, 21,* 247-254.

Sher, K. J., & Levenson, R. W. (1982). Risk for alcoholism and individual differences in the stress-response-dampening effect of alcohol. *Journal of Abnormal Psychology, 91,* 350-368.

Sher, K. J., & Trull, T. J. (1994). Personality and disinhibitory psychopathology: Alcoholism and antisocial personality disorder. *Journal of Abnormal Psychology, 103,* 92-102.

Sher, K. J., Walitzer, K. S., Wood, P. K., & Brent, E. E. (1991). Characteristics of children of alcoholics: Putative risk factors, substance use and abuse, and psychopathology. *Journal of Abnormal Psychology, 100,* 427-448.

Sherwood, N. (1993). Effects of nicotine on human psychomotor performance. *Human Psychopharmacology Clinical and Experimental, 8,* 155-184.

Sherwood, N. (1995). Effects of cigarette smoking on performance in a simulated driving task. *Neuropsychobiology, 32,* 161-165.

Shiffman, S. (1987). Maintenance and relapse: Coping with temptation. In T. D. Nirenberg & S. A. Maisto (Eds.), *Developments in the assessment and treatment of addictive behaviors* (pp. 353-385). Norwood, NJ: Ablex.

Shiffman, S., & Balabanis, M. (1996). Do drinking and smoking go together? *Alcohol Health & Research World, 20,* 107-110.

Shiffman, S., Fischer, L. A., Paty, J. A., Gnys, M., Kassel, J. D., Hickcox, M., & Perz, W. (1994). Drinking and smoking: A field study of their association. *Annals of Behavioral Medicine, 16,* 203-209.

Shrier, L. A., Emans, S. J., Woods, E. R., & DuRant, R. H. (1997). The association of sexual risk behaviors and problem drug behaviors in high school students. *Journal of Adolescent Health, 20,* 377-383.

Siegel, S. (1983). Classical conditioning, drug tolerance, and drug dependence. In Y. Isreal, F. B. Glaser, H. Kalant, R. E. Popham, W. Schmidt, & R. G. Smart (Eds.), *Research advances in alcohol and drug problems* (pp. 207-246). New York: Plenum.

Silverman, D. T., Brown, L. M., Hoover, R. N., Schiffman, M., Lillemoe, K. D., Schoenberg, J. B., Swanson, G. M., Hayes, R. B., Greenberg, R. S., Benichou, J., et al. (1995). Alcohol and pancreatic cancer in Blacks and Whites in the United States. *Cancer Research, 55,* 4899-4905.

Simpson, D. D., Chatham, L. R., & Brown, B. (1995). The role of evaluation research in drug abuse policy. *Current Directions in Psychological Science, 4,* 123-126.

Simpson, D. D., Joe, G. W., Fletcher, B. W., Hubbard, R. L., & Anglin, M. D. (1999). A national evaluation of treatment outcomes for cocaine dependence. *Archives of General Psychiatry, 56,* 507-514.

Singleton, E. G., & Gorelick, D. A. (1998). Mechanisms of alcohol craving and their clinical implications. In M. Galanter (Ed.), *Recent developments in alcoholism* (Vol. 14, pp. 177-195). New York: Plenum.

Skager, R., Frifth, S. L., & Maddahian, E. (1989). *Biennial survey of drug and alcohol use among California students in Grades 7, 9, and 11: Winter 1987-1988.* Sacramento, CA: Office of the Attorney General, Crime Prevention Center.

Skinner, B. F. (1938). *The behavior of organisms.* New York: Appleton-Century-Crofts.

Slotkin, T. A. (1998). Fetal nicotine or cocaine exposure: Which one is worse? *Journal of Pharmacology and Experimental Therapeutics, 285,* 931-945.

Smart, R. G. (1978). Do some alcoholics do better in some types of treatment than others? *Drug and Alcohol Dependence, 3,* 65-75.

Smart, R. G. (1988). Does alcohol advertising affect overall consumption? A review of empirical studies. *Journal of Studies on Alcohol, 49,* 314-323.

Smith, D. W. (1982). Fetal alcohol syndrome: A tragic and preventable disorder. In N. J. Estes & M. E. Heinemann (Eds.), *Alcoholism: Development, consequences, and interventions* (pp. 187-192). St. Louis, MO: C. V. Mosby.

Smith, G. T., Goldman, M. S., Greenbaum, P. E., & Christiansen, B. A. (1995). Expectancy for social facilitation from drinking: The divergent paths of high-expectancy and low-expectancy adolescents. *Journal of Abnormal Psychology, 104,* 32-40.

Smith-Warner, S. A., Spiegelman, D., Yaun, S. S., van den Brandt, P. A., Folsom, A. R., Goldbohm, R. A., Graham, S., Holmberg, L., Howe, G. R., Marshall, J. R., Miller, A. B., Potter, J. D., Speizer, F. E., Willett, W. C., Wolk, A., & Hunter, D. J. (1998). Alcohol and breast cancer in women: A pooled analysis of cohort studies. *Journal of the American Medical Association, 279,* 535-540.

Snodgrass, S. R. (1994). Cocaine babies: A result of multiple teratogenic influences. *Journal of Child Neurology, 9,* 227-233.

Sobell, L. C., Sobell, M. B., & Toneatto, T. (1991). Recovery from alcohol problems without treatment. In N. Heather, W. R. Miller, & J. Greeley (Eds.), *Self-control and addictive behaviors* (pp. 198-242). New York: Pergamon.

Sobell, M. B., & Sobell, L. C. (1973). Alcoholics treated by individualized behavior therapy: One year treatment outcome. *Behavior Research Therapy, 11,* 599-618.

Sobell, M. B., & Sobell, L. C. (1993). *Problem drinkers: Guided self-change treatment.* New York: Guilford.

Solomon, K. E., & Annis, H. M. (1989). Development of a scale to measure outcome expectancy in alcoholics. *Cognitive Therapy and Research, 13,* 409-421.

Solomon, R. L. (1980). The opponent-process theory of acquired motivation: The costs and pleasure and the benefits of pain. *American Psychologist, 35,* 691-712.

Southwick, L., & Steele, C. (1987). Restrained drinking: Personality correlates of a control style. *Journal of Drug Issues, 17,* 349-358.

Southwick, L., Steele, C., Marlatt, A., & Lindell, M. (1981). Alcohol-related expectancies: Defined by phase of intoxication and drinking experience. *Journal of Consulting and Clinical Psychology, 49,* 713-721.

Spencer, G. (1989). Projections of the population of the United States, by age, sex, and race: 1988 to 2080. In U.S. Bureau of the Census (Ed.), *1989 current population reports* (Series P-25, No. 1018). Washington, DC: Government Printing Office.

Steele, C. M., & Josephs, R. A. (1988). Drinking your troubles away: II. An attention-allocation model of alcohol's effect on psychological stress. *Journal of Abnormal Psychology, 97,* 196-205.

Steele, C. M., & Southwick, L. (1985). Alcohol and social behavior: I. The psychology of drunken excess. *Journal of Personality and Social Psychology, 48,* 18-34.

Steinglass, P. (1981). The alcoholic family at home: Patterns of interaction in dry, wet, and transitional stages of alcoholism. *Archives of General Psychiatry, 38,* 578-584.

Steinglass, P., Bennett, L. A., Wolin, S. J., & Reiss, D. (1987). *The alcoholic family.* New York: Basic Books.

Stewart, J., deWit, H., & Eikelboom, R. (1984). The role of unconditioned and conditioned drug effects in the self-administration of opiates and stimulants. *Psychological Review, 91,* 251-268.

Stewart, M. A., & duBlois, C. S. (1981). Wife abuse among families attending a child psychiatry clinic. *Journal of the American Academy of Child Psychiatry, 20,* 845-862.

Stockwell, T. R., Hodgson, R. J., Rankin, H. J., & Taylor, C. (1982). Alcohol dependence, beliefs and the priming effect. *Behavior Research and Therapy, 20,* 513-522.

Storgaard, H., Nielsen, S. D., & Gluud, C. (1994). The validity of the Michigan Alcoholism Screening Test (MAST). *Alcohol and Alcoholism, 29,* 493-502.

Straus, R., & Bacon, S. (1953). *Drinking in college.* New Haven, CT: Yale University Press.

Strecher, V. J. (1983). A minimal-contact smoking cessation program in a health care setting. *Public Health Reports, 98,* 497-502.

Streissguth, A. P., Clarren, S. K., & Jones, K. L. (1985). Natural history of the fetal alcohol syndrome: A 10-year followup of eleven patients. *Lancet, 2,* 85-91.

Streissguth, A. P., Herman, C. S., & Smith, D. W. (1978). Intelligence, behavior, and dysmorphogenesis in the fetal alcohol syndrome: A report on 20 patients. *Journal of Pediatrics, 92,* 363-367.

Streissguth, A. P., Martin, D. C., Barr, H. M., Sandman, B. M., Kirchner, G. L., & Darby, B. L. (1984). Intrauterine alcohol and nicotine exposure: Attention and reaction time in four-year-old children. *Developmental Psychology, 20,* 533-541.

Substance Abuse and Mental Health Services Administration. (1995). *National household survey on drug abuse: Main findings 1995.* Rockville, MD: U.S. Department of Health and Human Services.

Substance Abuse and Mental Health Services Administration. (1997). *National household survey on drug abuse: Main findings 1997.* Rockville, MD: U.S. Department of Health and Human Services.

Substance Abuse and Mental Health Services Administration. (1998). *National household survey on drug abuse: Main findings 1998.* Rockville, MD: U.S. Department of Health and Human Services.

Sue, S., Kitano, H. H. L., Hatanaka, H., & Yeung, W. (1985). Alcohol consumption among Chinese in the United States. In L. A. Bennett & G. M. Ames (Eds.), *The American experience with alcohol: Contrasting cultural perspectives* (pp. 359-371). New York: Plenum.

Sutker, P. B., Allain, A. N., Brantley, P. J., & Randall, C. L. (1982). Acute alcohol intoxication, negative affect, and autonomic arousal in women and men. *Addictive Behaviors, 7,* 17-25.

Sutker, P. B., Tabakoff, B., Goist, K. C., Jr., & Randall, C. L. (1983). Acute alcohol intoxication, mood states and alcohol metabolism in women and men. *Pharmacology, Biochemistry and Behavior, 18,* 349-354.

Sutocky, J. W., Shultz, J. M., & Kizer, K. W. (1993). Alcohol-related mortality in California, 1980 to 1989. *American Journal of Public Health, 83,* 817-823.

Swan, G. E., Carmelli, D., & Cardon, L. R. (1997). Heavy consumption of cigarettes, alcohol and coffee in male twins. *Journal of Studies on Alcohol, 58,* 182-190.

Swanson, J. W. (1993). Alcohol abuse, mental disorder, and violent behavior: An epidemiologic inquiry. *Alcohol Health & Research World, 17,* 123-132.

Szabo, G. (1998). Monocytes, alcohol use, and altered immunity. *Alcoholism, Clinical and Experimental Research, 22*(5, Suppl.), 216S-219S.

Szasz, T. (1987). *Ceremonial chemistry: The ritual persecution of drugs, addicts, and pushers* (Rev. ed.). Holmes Beach, FL: Learning Publications.

Tabakoff, B., & Hoffman, P. L. (1987). Biochemical pharmacology of alcohol. In H. Y. Meltzer (Ed.), *Psychopharmacology of alcohol: The third generation of progress* (pp. 1521-1526). New York: Raven.

Tabakoff, B., Hoffman, P. L., & Petersen, R. C. (1990). Advances in neurochemistry: A leading edge of alcohol research. *Alcohol Research & Health World, 14,* 138-143.

Tarter, R. E. (1988). Are there inherited behavioral traits that predispose to alcohol abuse? *Journal of Consulting and Clinical Psychology, 56,* 189-196.

Tarter, R. E., Alterman, A. I., & Edwards, K. L. (1985). Vulnerability to alcoholism in men: A behavior-genetic perspective. *Journal of Studies on Alcohol, 46,* 329-356.

Tarter, R. E., & Edwards, K. (1988). Psychological factors associated with the risk for alcoholism. *Alcoholism, Clinical and Experimental Research, 12,* 471-480.

Tarter, R. E., Moss, H., Arria, A. M., Mezzich, A. C., & Vanyukov, M. M. (1992). The psychiatric diagnosis of alcoholism: Critique and proposed reformulation. *Alcoholism, Clinical and Experimental Research, 16,* 106-121.

Tarter, R. E., Moss, H., & Laird, S. B. (1990). Biological markers for vulnerability to alcoholism. In R. L. Collins, K. E. Leonard, & J. S. Searles (Eds.), *Alcohol and the family: Research and clinical perspectives* (pp. 79-106). New York: Guilford.

Tate, D. L., & Charette, L. (1991). Personality, alcohol consumption, and menstrual distress in young women. *Alcoholism, Clinical and Experimental Research, 15,* 647-652.

Taylor, S. P. (1967). Aggressive behavior and physiological arousal as a function of provocation and the tendency to inhibit aggression. *Journal of Personality, 35,* 297-310.

Taylor, S. P., & Chermack, S. T. (1993). Alcohol, drugs and human physical aggression. *Journal of Studies on Alcohol, 11*(Suppl.), 78-88.

Taylor, S. P., & Hulsizer, M. R. (1998). Psychoactive drugs and human aggression. In R. G. Geen, & E. Donnerstein (Eds.), *Human aggression: Theories, research, and implications for social policy* (pp. 139-165). San Diego, CA: Academic Press.

Taylor, S. P., & Leonard, K. E. (1983). Alcohol and human physical aggression. In R. G. Geen & E. I. Donnerstein (Eds.), *Aggression: Theoretical and empirical reviews* (Vol. 2, pp. 77-101). New York: Academic Press.

Temple, M. (1987). Alcohol use among male and female college students: Has there been a convergence? *Youth and Society, 19,* 44-72.

Temple, M. T., & Leigh, B. C. (1992). Alcohol consumption and unsafe sexual behavior in discrete events. *Journal of Sex Research, 29,* 207-219.

Temple, M. T., & Leino, V. (1989). Long-term outcomes of drinking: A 20-year longitudinal study of men. *British Journal of Addiction, 84,* 889-900.

Thomas, D. B. (1995). Alcohol as a cause of cancer. *Environmental Health Perspectives, 103*(Suppl. 8), 153-160.

Thomas, J. C. (1989). An overview of marital and family treatments with substance abusing populations. *Alcoholism Treatment Quarterly, 6,* 91-102.

Thompson, K. M., & Wilsnack, R. W. (1987). Parental influence on adolescent drinking: Modeling, attitudes, or conflict. *Youth and Society, 19,* 22-43.

Thorndike, E. L. (1911). *Animal intelligence.* New York: Macmillan.

Tiffany, S. T. (1990). A cognitive model of drug urges and drug-use behavior: Role of automatic and nonautomatic processes. *Psychological Review, 97,* 147-168.

Tomkins, S. S. (1966). Psychological model for smoking behavior. *American Journal of Public Health & the Nation's Health, 56*(12, Suppl.), 17-20.

Trice, H., & Sonnenstuhl, W. (1988). Constructive confrontation and other referral processes. In M. Galanter (Ed.), *Recent developments in alcoholism* (Vol. 6, pp. 159-170). New York: Plenum.

Trice, H. M., & Staudemeier, W. J. (1989). A sociocultural history of Alcoholics Anonymous. In M. Galanter (Ed.), *Recent developments in alcoholism: Emerging issues in treatment* (Vol. 7, pp. 11-35). New York: Plenum.

Trimble, J. E. (1991). Ethnic specification, validation prospects, and the future of drug use research. *International Journal of the Addictions, 25,* 149-170.

Trimpey, J. (1992). *Rational recovery from alcoholism* (4th ed.). New York: Delacorte.

Tsuang, M. T., Lyons, M. J., Meyer, J. M., Doyle, T., Eisen, S. A., Goldberg, J., True, W., Lin, N., Toomey, R., & Eaves, L. (1998). Co-occurrence of abuse of different drugs in men: The role of drug-specific and shared vulnerabilities. *Archives of General Psychiatry, 55,* 967-972.

Tuchfield, B. S. (1981). Spontaneous remission in alcoholics: Empirical observations and theoretical implications. *Journal of Studies on Alcohol, 42,* 626-640.

Tucker, J. A., Vuchinich, R. E., & Sobell, M. B. (1982). Alcohol's effects on human emotions: A review of the stimulation/depression hypothesis. *International Journal of the Addictions, 17,* 155-180.

Tulving, E. (1983). *Elements of episodic memory.* New York: Oxford University Press.

Tweed, S. H., & Ryff, C. D. (1991). Adult children of alcoholics: Profiles of wellness. *Journal of Studies on Alcohol, 52,* 133-141.

U.S. Bureau of Justice Statistics. (1992). *Drugs, crime, and the justice system: A national report from the Bureau of Justice Statistics* (Rep. No. NCJ-133652). Washington, DC: Government Printing Office.

U.S. Bureau of Justice Statistics. (1995). *Census of state and federal adult correctional facilities* (Rep. No. NCJ 164266). Washington, DC: Government Printing Office.

U.S. Bureau of the Census. (1992). *1990 census of population, general population characteristics, United States.* Washington, DC: U.S. Department of Commerce, Economics and Statistics Administration, Bureau of the Census.

U.S. Department of Commerce. Office of Federal Statistical Policy and Standards. (1978). *Statistical policy handbook.* Washington, D.C.: U.S. Government Printing Office.

U.S. Department of Education. (1994). *1990 census data on the condition of education of racial/ethnic groups* (National Center for Educational Statistics, Publication No. 94-243). Washington, DC: Author.

U.S. Department of Health and Human Services. (1987). *Review of the research literature on the effects of health warning labels: A report to the U.S. Congress.* Rockville, MD: National Institute on Alcohol Abuse and Alcoholism.

U.S. Department of Health and Human Services. (1990). *Health benefits of smoking cessation: A report of the surgeon general* (DHHS Publication No. [CDC]90-8416). Washington, DC: Government Printing Office.

U.S. Department of Health and Human Services. (1995). *Substance use among women in the United States.* Washington, DC: Government Printing Office.

U.S. Department of Health and Human Services. (1997a). *National household survey on drug abuse: Population estimates 1996.* Rockville, MD: Substance Abuse and Mental Health Services Administration, Office of Applied Studies.

U.S. Department of Health and Human Services. (1997b). *Ninth special report to U.S. Congress: Alcohol and health.* Washington, DC: Government Printing Office.

U.S. Department of Health and Human Services. (1997c). *Preliminary results from the 1996 National Household Survey on Drug Abuse.* Rockville, MD: Substance Abuse and Mental Health Services Administration, Office of Applied Studies.

U.S. Department of Health and Human Services. (1997d). *Substance use among women in the United States.* Washington, DC: Government Printing Office.

U.S. Department of Health, Education, and Welfare. (1964). *Smoking and health: Report of the Advisory Committee to the Surgeon General of the Public Health Service* (DHEW Publication No. [PHS]1103). Washington, DC: Government Printing Office.

U.S. Surgeon General. (1998). *Tobacco use among U.S. racial/ethnic minority groups.* Washington, DC: U.S. Department of Health and Human Services.

Vaillant, G. E. (1988). What can long-term follow-up teach us about relapse and prevention of relapse in addiction? *British Journal of Addiction, 83,* 1147-1157.

Vaillant, G. E. (1992). Is there a natural history of addiction? In C. P. O'Brien & J. H. Jaffe (Eds.), *Addictive states* (Vol. 70, pp. 41-58). New York: Raven.

Vaillant, G. E., & Milofsky, E. S. (1982). The etiology of alcoholism: A prospective viewpoint. *American Psychologist, 37,* 494-503.

Van Hesselt, V. B., Morrison, R. L., & Bellack, A. S. (1985). Alcohol use in wife abusers and their spouses. *Addictive Behaviors, 10,* 127-135.

Van Thiel, D. H. (1983). Ethanol: Its adverse effects on the hypothalamic-pituitary-gonadal axis. *Journal of Laboratory Clinical Medicine, 101,* 21-33.

Vegega, M. E. (1986). NHTSA responsible beverage service research and evaluation project. *Alcohol Health & Research World, 10,* 20-23.

Velicer, W. F., Prochaska, J. O., Rossi, J. S., & Snow, M. G. (1992). Assessing outcome in smoking cessation studies. *Psychological Bulletin, 111,* 23-41.

Velleman, R. (1992a). A review of environmentally oriented studies concerning the relationship between parental alcohol problems and family disharmony in the genesis of alcohol and other problems: I. The intergenerational effects of alcohol problems. *International Journal of the Addictions, 27,* 253-280.

Velleman, R. (1992b). A review of environmentally oriented studies concerning the relationship between parental alcohol problems and family disharmony in the genesis of alcohol and other problems: II. The intergenerational effects of family disharmony. *International Journal of Addictions, 27,* 367-389.

Vogel-Sprott, M., & Barrett, B. (1984). Age, drinking habits and the effects of alcohol. *Journal of Studies on Alcohol, 45,* 517-521.

Volavka, J., Pollack, V., Gabrielli, W. F., & Mednick, S. A. (1985). The EEG in persons at risk for alcoholism. In M. Galanter (Ed.), *Recent developments in alcoholism* (Vol. 3, pp. 21-36). New York: Plenum.

Volpicelli, J. R. (1987). Uncontrollable events and alcohol drinking. *British Journal of Addiction, 82,* 381-392.

Volpicelli, J. R., Alterman, A. I., Hayashida, M., & O'Brian, C. P. (1992). Naltrexone in the treatment of alcohol dependence. *Archives of General Psychiatry, 49,* 876-880.

Volpicelli, J. R., Clay, K. L., Watson, N. T., & Volpicelli, L. A. (1995). Naltrexone and the treatment of alcohol dependence. *Alcohol Health & Research World, 18*(4), 272-278.

Volpicelli, J. R., Watson, N. T., King, A. C., Sherman, C. E., & O'Brien, C. P. (1995). Effect of naltrexone on alcohol "high" in alcoholics. *American Journal of Psychiatry, 152,* 613-615.

Volstead Act of 1920, 18th Amendment to the U.S. Constitution (ratified January 29, 1919).

Von Knorring, A. L., Bohman, M., Von Knorring, L., & Oreland, L. (1985). Platelet MAO activity as a biolgical marker in subgroups of alcoholism. *Acta Scandinavica, 72,* 51-58.

Wagenknecht, L. E., Craven, T. E., Preisser, J. S., Manolio, T. A., Winders, S., & Hulley, S. B. (1998). Ten-year trends in cigarette smoking among young adults, 1986-1996: The CARDIA study. Coronary Artery Risk Development in Young Adults. *Annals of Epidemiology, 8,* 301-307.

Waldorf, D., Reinarman, C., & Murphy, S. (1991). *Cocaine changes: The experience of using and quitting.* Philadelphia, PA: Temple University Press.

Walker, R. D., Donovan, D. M., Kivlahan, D. R., & O'Leary, M. R. (1983). Length of stay, neuropsychological performance, and aftercare: Influence on alcohol treatment outcome. *Journal of Consulting and Clinical Psychology, 51,* 900-911.

Wall, T. L., Thomasson, H. R., & Ehlers, C. L. (1996). Investigator-observed alcohol-induced flushing but not self-report of flushing is a valid predictor of ALDH2 genotype. *Journal of Studies on Alcohol, 57,* 267-272.

Wallace, J. (1985). Critical issues in alcoholism therapy. In S. Zimberg, J. Wallace, & S. B. Blume (Eds.), *Practical approaches to alcoholism psychotherapy* (pp. 37-49). New York: Plenum.

Wallace, J. (1996). Theory of 12-step-oriented treatment. In F. Rotgers, D. S. Keller, & J. Morgenstern (Eds.), *Treating substance abuse: Theory and technique* (pp. 13-36). New York: Guilford.

Wallack, L. (1981). Mass media campaigns: The odds against finding behavior change. *Health Education Quarterly, 8,* 209-260.

Wallack, L., Breed, W., & Cruz, J. (1987). Alcohol on prime-time television. *Journal of Studies of Alcohol, 48,* 33-38.

Weatherspoon, A. J., Danko, G. P., & Johnson, R. C. (1994). Alcohol consumption and use norms among Chinese Americans and Korean Americans. *Journal of Studies on Alcohol, 55,* 203-206.

Webster, D. W., Harburg, E., Gleiberman, L., Schork, A., & DiFranceisco, W. (1989). Familial transmission of alcohol use: I. Parent and adult offspring alcohol use over 17 years—Tecumseh, Michigan. *Journal of Studies on Alcohol, 50,* 557-566.

Webster, L. A., Wingo, P. A., Layde, P. M., & Ory, H. W. (1983). Alcohol consumption and risk of breast cancer. *Lancet, 2,* 724-726.

Wechsler, H., Dowdall, G. W., Davenport, A., & Castillo, S. (1995). Correlates of college student binge drinking. *American Journal of Public Health, 85,* 921-926.

Wechsler, H., Dowdall, G. W., Davenport, A., & DeJong, W. (1995). *Binge drinking on campus: Results of a national study.* Bethesda, MD: Higher Education Center for Alcohol and Other Drug Prevention.

Wechsler, H., Dowdall, G. W., Davenport, A., & Rimm, E. B. (1995). A gender-specific measure of binge drinking among college students. *American Journal of Public Health, 85,* 982-985.

Wechsler, H., & McFadden, M. (1979). Drinking among college students in New England. *Journal of Studies on Alcohol, 40,* 969-996.

Wechsler, H., Moeykens, B., Davenport, A., Castillo, S., & Hanson, J. (1995). The adverse impact of heavy episodic drinkers on other college students. *Journal of Studies on Alcohol, 56,* 628-634.

Wegsheider, S. (1981). *Another chance: Hope and health for the alcoholic family.* Palo Alto, CA: Science and Behavior Books.

Weibel, J., & Weisner, T. (1980). *An ethnography of urban Indian drinking patterns in California.* Sacramento: California State Department of Alcohol and Drug Problems.

Weibel-Orlando, J. (1985). Indians, ethnicity, and alcohol: Contrasting perceptions of the ethnic self and alcohol use. In L. A. Bennett & G. M. Ames (Eds.), *The American experience with alcohol: Contrasting cultural perspectives* (pp. 201-226). New York: Plenum.

Weiner, B. (1985). An attributional analysis of achievement motivation and emotion. *Psychological Review, 92,* 548-573.

Weingartner, H., & Faillace, L. A. (1971). Alcohol state dependent learning in man. *Journal of Nervous and Mental Disease, 153,* 395-406.

Weisner, C. (1987). The social ecology of alcohol treatment in the U.S. In M. Galanter (Ed.), *Recent developments in alcoholism* (Vol. 5, pp. 203-243). New York: Plenum.

Weisner, C. M. (1990). Coercion in alcohol treatment. In Institute of Medicine (Ed.), *Broadening the base of treatment for alcohol problems* (pp. 579-609). Washington, DC: National Academy Press.

Welte, J., Hynes, G., Sokolov, L., & Lyons, J. P. (1981b). Effect of length of stay in inpatient alcoholism treatment on outcome. *Journal of Studies on Alcohol, 42,* 483-491.

Welte, J., Hynes, G., Sokolov, L., & Lyons, J. P. (1981a). Comparison of clients completing inpatient alcoholism treatment with clients who left prematurely. *Alcoholism, Clinical and Experimental Research, 5,* 393-399.

Welte, J. W. (1998). Stress and elderly drinking. In U.S. Department of Health and Human Services (Ed.), *Alcohol problems & aging* (pp. 229-246). Washington, DC: Government Printing Office.

Welte, J. W., & Abel, E. L. (1989). Homicide: Drinking by the victim. *Journal of Studies on Alcohol, 50,* 197-201.

Welte, J. W., & Barnes, G. M. (1987). Alcohol use among adolescent minority groups. *Journal of Studies on Alcohol, 48,* 329-336.

Werler, M. M., Pober, B. R., & Holmes, L. B. (1985). Smoking and pregnancy. *Teratology, 32,* 473-481.

Werner, E. E. (1986). Resilient offspring of alcoholics: A longitudinal study from birth to age 18. *Journal of Studies on Alcohol, 47,* 34-40.

West, M. O., & Prinz, R. J. (1987). Parental alcoholism and childhood psychopathology. *Psychological Bulletin, 102,* 204-218.

Westermeyer, J. (1972). Chippewa and majority alcoholism in the Twin Cities: A comparison. *Journal of Nervous and Mental Disorders, 155,* 322-327.

White, H. R., Brick, J., & Hansell, S. (1993). A longitudinal investigation of alcohol use and aggression in adolescence. *Journal of Studies on Alcohol, 11*(Suppl.), 62-77.

Widiger, T. A., Frances, A. J., Pincus, H. A., Davis, W. W., & First, M. B. (1991). Toward an empirical classification for the *DSM-IV. Journal of Abnormal Psychology, 100,* 280-288.

Widom, C. S., Ireland, T., & Glynn, P. J. (1995). Alcohol abuse in abused and neglected children followed-up: Are they at increased risk? *Journal of Studies on Alcohol, 56,* 207-217.

Wikler, A. (Ed.). (1965). *Conditioning factors in opiate addiction and relapse.* New York: McGraw-Hill.

Wikler, A. (1973). Dynamics of drug dependence. *Archives of General Psychiatry, 28,* 611-616.

Wilks, J., Callan, V. J., & Austin, D. A. (1989). Parent, peer and personal determinants of adolescent drinking. *British Journal of Addiction, 84,* 619-630.

Willett, W. C., Green, A., Stampfer, M. J., Speizer, F. E., Colditz, G. A., Rosner, B., Monson, R. R., Stason, W., & Hennekens, C. H. (1987). Relative and absolute excess risks of coronary heart disease among women who smoke cigarettes. *New England Journal of Medicine, 317,* 1303-1309.

Williams, C. M., & Skinner, A. E. (1990). The cognitive effects of alcohol abuse: A controlled study. *British Journal of Addiction, 85,* 911-917.

Williams, G. D., Grant, B. F., Harford, T. C., & Noble, J. (1989). Population projections using *DSM-III* criteria: Alcohol abuse and dependence, 1990-2000. *Alcohol Health & Research World, 13,* 366-370.

Williams, J. G., & Morrice, A. (1992). Measuring drinking patterns among college students. *Psychological Reports, 70,* 231-238.

Williams, R. R., & Horm, J. W. (1977). Association of cancer sites with tobacco and alcohol consumption and socioeconcomic status of patients: Interview study from the Third National Cancer Survey. *Journal of the National Cancer Institute, 58,* 527-547.

Wills, T. A., DuHamel, K., & Vaccaro, D. (1995). Activity and mood temperament as predictors of adolescent substance use: Test of a self-regulation mediational model. *Journal of Personality and Social Psychology, 68,* 901-916.

Wilsnack, R. W., & Cheloha, R. (1987). Women's roles and problem drinking across the lifespan. *Social Problems, 34,* 231-248.

Wilsnack, S. (1973). Sex role identity in female alcoholism. *Journal of Abnormal Psychology, 82,* 253-261.

Wilsnack, S. C. (1974). The effects of social drinking on women's fantasy. *Journal of Personality, 42,* 43-61.

Wilsnack, S. C. (1976). The impact of sex roles on women's alcohol use and abuse. In M. Greenblatt & M. A. Schuckit (Eds.), *Alcoholism problems in women and children* (pp. 37-63). New York: Grune & Stratton.

Wilsnack, S. C. (1984). Drinking, sexuality, and sexual dysfunction in women. In S. C. Wilsnack & L. J. Beckman (Eds.), *Alcohol problems in women: Antecedents, consequences, and intervention* (pp. 189-227). New York: Guilford.

Wilsnack, S. C. (1996). Patterns and trends in women's drinking: Recent findings and some implications for prevention. In J. M. Howard, S. E. Martin, P. D. Mail, M. E. Hilton, & E. D. Taylor (Eds.), *Women and alcohol: Issues for prevention research* (Research Monograph No. 32, pp. 19-63). Washington, DC: Government Printing Office.

Wilsnack, S. C., Klassen, A. D., Schur, B. E., & Wilsnack, R. W. (1991). Predicting onset and chronicity of women's problem drinking: A five-year longitudinal analysis. *American Journal of Public Health, 81,* 305-318.

Wilsnack, S. C., Vogeltanz, N. D., Klassen, A. D., & Harris, T. R. (1997). Childhood sexual abuse and women's substance abuse: National survey findings. *Journal of Studies on Alcohol, 58,* 264-271.

Wilsnack, S. C., & Wilsnack, R. W. (1978). Sex roles and drinking among adolescent girls. *Journal of Studies on Alcohol, 39,* 1855-1874.

Wilsnack, S. C., & Wilsnack, R. W. (1992). Women, work, and alcohol: Failures of simple theories. *Alcoholism, Clinical and Experimental Research, 16,* 172-179.

Wilsnack, S. C., Wilsnack, R. W., & Klassen, A. D. (1984). Women's drinking and drinking problems: Patterns from a 1981 national survey. *American Journal of Public Health, 74,* 1231-1238.

Wilsnack, S. C., Wilsnack, R. W., & Klassen, A. D. (1986). Epidemiological research on women's drinking, 1978-1984. In National Institute on Alcohol

Abuse and Alcoholism (Ed.), *Women and alcohol: Health-related issues* (Research Monograph No. 16, DHHS Publication No. [ADM]86-1139, pp. 1-68). Washington, DC: Government Printing Office.

Wilson, G. T. (1987). Chemical aversion conditioning as a treatment for alcoholism: A re-analysis. *Behavior Research and Therapy, 25,* 503-515.

Wilson, G. T., & Lawson, D. W. (1976a). The effects of alcohol on sexual arousal in women. *Journal of Abnormal Psychology, 85,* 489-497.

Wilson, G. T., & Lawson, D. W. (1976b). Expectancies, alcohol, and sexual arousal in male social drinkers. *Journal of Abnormal Psychology, 85,* 587-594.

Wilson, G. T., & Lawson, D. M. (1978). Expectancies, alcohol, and sexual arousal in women. *Journal of Abnormal Psychology, 87,* 358-367.

Wilson, R. J., & Jonah, B. A. (1985). Identifying impaired drivers among the general driving population. *Journal of Studies on Alcohol, 46,* 531-537.

Windle, M. (1997). Mate similarity, heavy substance use and family history of problem drinking among young adult women. *Journal of Studies on Alcohol, 58,* 573-580.

Windle, M., Windle, R. C., Scheidt, D. M., & Miller, G. B. (1995). Physical and sexual abuse and associated mental disorders among alcoholic inpatients. *American Journal of Psychiatry, 152,* 1322-1328.

Winokur, G., Reich, T., Rimmer, J., & Pitts, F. N. (1970). Alcoholism III: Diagnosis and family psychiatric illness. *Archives of General Psychiatry, 23,* 104-111.

Wiseman, J. (1970). *Stations of the lost: The treatment of skid row alcoholics.* Englewood Cliffs, NJ: Prentice Hall.

Woititz, J. (1983). *Adult children of alcoholics.* Deerfield, FL: Health Communications.

Wolchik, S. A., Braver, S. L., & Jensen, K. (1985). Volunteer bias in erotica research: Effects of intrusiveness of measure and sexual background. *Archives of Sexual Behavior, 14,* 93-107.

Wolff, P. (1972). Ethnic differences in alcohol sensitivity. *Science, 125,* 449-451.

Wolin, S. J., Bennett, L. A., & Jacobs, J. (1988). Assessing family rituals in alcoholic families. In E. Imber-Black, J. Roberts, & R. A. Whiting (Eds.), *Rituals in families and family therapy* (pp. 230-256). New York: Norton.

Wolin, S. J., Bennett, L. A., Noonan, D. L., & Teitelbaum, M. A. (1980). Disrupted family rituals: A factor in the intergenerational transmission of alcoholism. *Journal of Studies on Alcohol, 41,* 199-214.

Workman-Daniels, K. L., & Hesselbrock, V. M. (1987). Childhood problem behavior and neuropsychological functioning in persons at risk for alcoholism. *Journal of Studies on Alcohol, 48,* 187-193.

World Health Organization (WHO). (1978). *Mental disorders: Glossary and guide to their classification in accordance with the ninth revision of the international classification of diseases.* Geneva, Switzerland: Author.

World Health Organization (WHO). (1990). *International classification of diseases* (10th rev.). Geneva, Switzerland: Author.

Wright, D. M., & Heppner, P. P. (1991). Coping among nonclinical college-age children of alcoholics. *Journal of Counseling Psychology, 38,* 465-472.

Wright, D. M., & Heppner, P. P. (1993). Examining the well-being of nonclinical college students: Is knowledge of the presence of parental alcoholism useful? *Journal of Counseling Psychology, 40,* 324-334.

Yamaguchi, K., & Kandel, D. B. (1984). Patterns of drug use from adolescence to young adulthood: Sequences of progression. *American Journal of Public Health, 74,* 668-672.

Yazaki, K., Haida, M., Kurita, D., & Shinohara, Y. (1996). Effect of chronic alcohol intake on energy metabolism in human muscle. *Alcoholism, Clinical and Experimental Research, 20*(9, Suppl.), 360A-362A.

York, J. L. (1995). Progression of alcohol consumption across the drinking career in alcoholics and social drinkers. *Journal of Studies on Alcohol, 56,* 328-336.

Yu, J., & Williford, W. R. (1995). Drunk-driving recidivism: Predicting factors from arrest context and case disposition. *Journal of Studies on Alcohol, 56*(1), 60-66.

Zeiner, A., & Paredes, A. (1978). Differential biological sensitivity to ethanol as a predictor of alcohol abuse. In D. Smith (Ed.), *Multi-cultural view of drug abuse* (pp. 591-599). Cambridge, MA: Schenkman.

Zimring, F. E., & Hawkins, G. (1992). *The search for rational drug control.* Cambridge, UK: Cambridge University Press.

Zinberg, N. E. (1984). *Drug, set, and setting: The basis for controlled intoxicant use.* New Haven, CT: Yale University Press.

Zucker, R. A. (1987). The four alcoholisms: A developmental account of the etiologic process. In P. C. Rivers (Ed.), *Alcohol and addictive behavior: Vol. 34. Nebraska symposium on motivation* (pp. 27-83). Lincoln: University of Nebraska Press.

Zucker, R. A., Ellis, D. A., Bingham, C. R., & Fitzgerald, H. E. (1996). The development of alcoholic subtypes: Risk variation among alcoholic families during the early childhood years. *Alcohol Health & Research World, 20,* 46-55.

Zucker, R. A., & Gomberg, E. L. (1986). Etiology of alcoholism reconsidered: The case for a biopsychosocial process. *American Psychologist, 41,* 783-793.

Zwerling, C. (1993). Current practice and experience in drug and alcohol testing in the workplace. *Bulletin on Narcotics, 45,* 155-196.

Glossary

AA *See* Alcoholics Anonymous.

Absolute alcohol Measure that adjusts for different concentrations of alcohol in different beverages (beer is about 5%, wine 13%, and distilled spirits 41% alcohol).

Abstainers Nonusers of a drug; may be lifelong or only for a specified period.

Abstinence Condition of not using a drug.

Abstinence violation effect (AVE) A major relapse follows a minor slip after a period of abstinence.

Abuse A condition in which the user has many drug use-related problems, including work or school performance and social, financial, legal, physical, and mental health problems.

Acculturation Process by which immigrants acquire knowledge of the customs of the host culture.

Acetylcholine Neurotransmitter found in the parasympathetic nervous system.

Action potential Electrical changes produced when a cell membrane is polarized and ion movement occurs through the cell.

Addiction Commonly refers to dependency on drugs; the term is not as widely used by researchers.

Addictive personality Notion that certain types of persons are prone to have addictions.

Age effect When differences in behavior are due to age differences per se.

Age of onset Age when a person starts using a drug; early- and late-onset drinkers differ.

Aggregate indices A total score of some outcome summed over a whole group, as opposed to an index based on individuals.

Agonistic Facilitative effects of a psychoactive drug on receptor binding.

Al-Anon Self-help group modeled after Alcoholics Anonymous, typically for the wives and families of alcoholics.

Alcohol dependence syndrome Alcoholism viewed as a continuum rather than a dichotomy of impairment. Problems related to alcohol use are included as a separate dimension. *See also* Dependence.

Alcohol myopia Term refers to alcohol's effect to restrict attention.

Alcoholics Anonymous (AA) World-wide mutual support recovery program for alcoholics developed in the United States in the late 1930s and based on disease conception of alcoholism.

Alcoholism Commonly used term for dependency; the term is not as widely used by researchers.

Alcohol-related birth defects Impaired development and function attributed to alcohol use during pregnancy; broader in scope than the fetal alcohol syndrome.

Amphetamine Stimulant drug (called speed, if injected); originally thought useful for increasing alertness and work productivity but also widely abused.

Antabuse Drug sometimes used in alcoholism treatment because it produces an adverse physical reaction with metabolic chemicals produced by drinking alcohol.

Antagonistic Inhibitory effects of a psychoactive drug on receptor binding.

Anterograde amnesia Memory loss in alcoholics of recent events following drinking.

Antisocial personality disorder Pathological condition involving hostility and aggression toward others.

Ascending limb The portion of the blood alcohol curve from zero to its peak level after drinking.

Attributions Causal explanations for outcomes, as in accounts for relapse by persons who resume drug use following abstinence.

Attrition Dropping out or not continuing in an alcohol or other drug treatment program.

Autonomic nervous system Part of the nervous system that governs involuntary responses such as emotions and emergency responses.

AVE *See* Abstinence violation effect.

Aversion The tendency of children of alcoholics to develop an aversion to drinking. themselves.

Aversion (conditioning) Treatment involving pairing of aversive outcomes such as pain or nausea with a drug so that future use may be stopped by thoughts of the aversive experiences.

BAC *See* Blood alcohol concentration.

BAL *See* Blood alcohol level.

Balanced placebo Research design used to separate expectancy from the pharmacological effect of drugs. Half of the participants are told they will receive alcohol; half of these two groups actually do receive alcohol, and the other half do not.

Barbiturates Depressant drug used for sedative effects such as in sleeping pills.

Behavioral approach to treatment Objective approach based on learning theory; uses reinforcement, modeling, and role-playing to develop coping skills for high-risk situations for drug use.

Benzodiazepines Prescription drugs used to reduce anxiety.

Binge drinking Taking five or more drinks on one occasion by men, four or more on one occasion by women.

Biphasic When an affective state created by use of some drugs gives way to an opposite affect over time.

Blackout Later lack of memory for events that happened while drinking. *See also* State-dependent learning.

Blood alcohol concentration (BAC) Measure of alcohol from blood or breath samples that is correlated with how much alcohol has been consumed in the past hour or two.

Blood alcohol level (BAL) *See* Blood alcohol concentration.

Central nervous system Part of the nervous system involved with conscious and voluntary behaviors; includes brain and spinal cord.

Cerebellum Part of the brain above the medulla that acts as a reflex center and controls coordination.

Cerebrum Large top section of the nervous system consisting of two hemispheres; it integrates incoming and outgoing stimuli.

Child abuse Physical or psychological harm to a child, nonsexual or sexual, caused by an adult.

Children of alcoholics Self-help organization or individuals who feel they are dysfunctional from having an alcoholic parent.

Cirrhosis (of the liver) Disease related to alcoholism that impairs the liver's ability to detoxify alcohol and other drugs.

Classical conditioning Association of two otherwise unrelated events enables one to elicit the other in the future; Pavlov's bell and dog salivation experiment is the model.

Cocaine Central nervous system stimulant, obtained from coca bush leaves.

Codependency When someone close to the drug-dependent individual contributes to that dependency.

Cognitive-behavioral coping Techniques based on social learning theory, with emphasis on modeling and rehearsal of specific behaviors to obtain positive reinforcement.

Cohort A group that shares similar experiences such as those of a given age.

Cohort effect If results vary for different groups, such as age groups, they may reflect a cohort effect.

Comorbidity Two or more disorders occur together in the same individuals; abuse of two different drugs or abuse of a drug and having a psychiatric disorder.

Compensatory response model A model of relapse focusing on cues associated with a drug's reduced effect or tolerance to prolonged use.

Conditioned withdrawal model A model of relapse focusing on cues associated with prior distress from lacking an accustomed drug to trigger relapse.

Controlled drinking Idea that a recovering alcoholic can drink in moderation without relapse.

Controlled observation When data are collected under conditions that allow sound causal inferences such as in an experiment.

Controlled substance Any illegal drug.

Convergence view Idea that alcohol use of men and women is becoming more similar.

Crack cocaine Smokable form of concentrated cocaine.

Craving Intense desire to use a drug.

Cross sectional Research design in which age comparisons are made of individuals who vary in age.

Cross tolerance When tolerance developed for one drug carries over to a different drug, making it easier for the user to adapt to it.

Cue extinction Attempt to expose alcoholics to cues related to alcohol without letting them drink to see if the desire to drink will diminish or extinguish.

DA *See* Dopamine.

DARP *See* Drug Abuse Reporting Program.

DATOS *See* Drug Abuse Treatment Outcome Study.

DA transporter gene Genetic basis for individual differences in dopamine (DA) levels.

Decriminalization Reducing enforcement of laws against the use of illegal drugs but maintaining their illegal status.

Delirium tremens Part of the alcohol withdrawal syndrome that occurs during abstinence from drinking by alcoholics; involves agitation, shakes, tremors, hallucinations.

Delta 9 THC Delta 9 tetrahydrocannabinol, the active ingredient in marijuana.

Demand reduction Social policy to reduce population desire for a drug.

Denial Psychodynamic theory term refers to a failure to admit a problem or to accept treatment; often used in a circular manner so that anyone who has a problem but is not being treated is said to be in denial.

Dependence Condition formerly called addiction in which users develop impaired control of using some drug.

Depolarization Electrical potential of the cell membrane to become more neutral as the message traverses through the neuron to the synapse.

Descending limb The portion of the blood alcohol curve from its peak level back to zero after drinking.

Detoxification Process of eliminating a drug from the body by the liver; medical intervention may be involved for heavy users.

Developmental typology Types of alcoholics according to age of onset and duration.

Diagnostic and Statistical Manual (DSM) Major classification system for defining clinical problems, including substance abuse and dependency.

Differential attrition Dropping out of treatment is selective, occurring more for some groups than for others.

Differential remission Improvement from dependency occurs faster for some than for others.

Differentiator Model A model suggesting that sons of alcoholics experience stronger arousing effects of alcohol than sons of nonalcoholics on the ascending limb of the blood alcohol curve as well as faster tolerance to alcohol on the descending limb.

Diffuse/generalized effects hypothesis View that the amount of general brain damage determines the amount of cognitive impairment in alcoholics.

Disease conception An influential medical model of alcoholism proposed by Jellinek and a cornerstone of Alcoholics Anonymous and many hospital treatment programs.

Distribution of consumption theory A theory that reducing alcohol availability would reduce alcohol-related problems because higher rates of alcohol consumption in a society are related to the degree of alcohol-related problems.

Dizygotic (DZ) twins Fraternal twins who come from separate eggs.

Domestic violence Physical or psychological harm inflicted by marital partners.

Dopamine (DA) Neurotransmitter affecting reward states from most psychoactive drugs.

Dose response curve The relationship between the amount of a drug and its effect on some behavior.

Drinking style The pattern, physical and social context, and meaning of drinking.

Driving under the influence (DUI) Alcohol or other drug impaired operation of a motor vehicle.

Driving while intoxicated (DWI) Alcohol or other drug impaired operation of a motor vehicle.

Drug Abuse Reporting Program (DARP) A large-scale survey of the prevalence of drug abuse and treatment conducted in the early 1970s, showing reduced crime and other benefits from treatment programs.

Drug Abuse Treatment Outcome Study (DATOS) A large scale national study to evaluate the effectiveness of different treatment programs for drug abusers.

DSM *See Diagnostic and Statistical Manual.*

DUI *See* Driving under the influence.

DWI *See* Driving while intoxicated.

EAPs *See* Employee assistance programs.

Ecstasy A popular, but illegal, amphetamine (MDMA) used at "rave parties."

EEG See Electroencephalogram.

Electroencephalogram (EEG) Instrument for measuring brain wave activity from electrodes placed on the scalp.

Employee assistance programs (EAPs) Guidance, information, counseling, and referral services for employees with alcohol- and other drug-related problems.

Endogenous opiates Pain-alleviating opiates generated in the body. *See also* Endorphins.

Endorphins The body's own opiate substance for reducing pain.

Enkephalins Peptides involved with pain control.

Enzyme A protein that accelerates a chemical reaction but does not itself undergo a net change.

Epidemiology Study of factors associated with the occurrence of different drug use patterns and consequences.

Epinephrine Neurotransmitter found in the sympathetic nervous system.

Episodic drinking Drinking on an unpredictable basis in amount or intervals.

ERP *See* Event-related potentials.

Estrogen Female sex hormone regulator of the menstrual cycle and ovulation.

Ethanol Scientific name for alcohol (actually ethyl alcohol).

Ethnography Field research under natural rather than laboratory conditions.

Event-related potentials (ERP) Electrical activity measured from a region of the brain assumed to involve attention.

Expectancy(ies) Belief(s) about outcomes of the use of a drug.

Expectancy controls Comparison groups that do not receive but think they are getting alcohol to drink; their behavior is compared with those who do receive alcohol to see if mere expectancy can produce similar effects to alcohol.

Facial flushing A tendency for the face to blush when alcohol is consumed; more prevalent among Asians and thought to serve as a protection against alcohol abuse.

FAE *See* Fetal alcohol effects.

Family rituals Traditional patterns of family interaction assumed to be disrupted by alcoholism.

Family systems Approach emphasizing the impact of each family member on other members.

FAS *See* Fetal alcohol syndrome.

Fetal alcohol effects (FAE) Less apparent impairments than fetal alcohol syndrome found in children due to drinking during pregnancy.

Fetal alcohol syndrome (FAS) A pattern of physical and psychological impairments found in children whose mothers drank excessively during pregnancy.

FH+ families Families in which one or more members have been alcohol dependent.

FH- families Families in which none of its members has been alcohol dependent.

Frontal lobe Front area of the cerebrum.

Frontal lobe hypothesis View that alcoholism damages the frontal lobe to impair cognitive functions.

GABA *See* Gamma aminobutyric acid.

G proteins Molecules within neurons that bind receptors to ion channels or enzymes.

Gamma aminobutyric acid (GABA) The primary inhibitory neurotransmitter in the nervous system.

Gateway drugs Drugs which, if used regularly, are related to eventual use of more harmful drugs.

General population survey Survey uses a random sample of the general population; also called a household survey.

Genetic marker Physiological variable associated with a specific gene that is highly associated with a specific disease outcome.

Glutamate Amino acid that is the primary excitatory neurotransmitter.

Half-life Amount of time needed for a specific drug to be eliminated by half.

Hallucinogen Drug capable of creating hallucinogenic-like altered states of consciousness.

Harm reduction An approach to drug policy that falls between prohibition and legalization; tries to minimize harm that may occur for those who cannot be prevented from using drugs.

Harrison Narcotics Act Major legislation in 1914 that made narcotics and many other drugs illegal.

Hashish Psychoactive drug; concentrated resin from the cannabis plant.

Heavy drinking Arbitrarily defined as having five or more drinks several times a month.

Heroin Synthetic drug derived from morphine that is a more potent opiate.

Higher power Alcoholics Anonymous concept that recovery requires that alcoholics acknowledge some factor more powerful than themselves.

Hippocampus Brain region in the temporal lobe related to memory and learning.

Hypothalamus Small structure in the limbic system that regulates many functions, including eating, drinking, and sexual behavior.

ICD *See International Classification of Diseases.*

Impaired control View that dependence involves a continuum of inability to refrain from using a drug.

Incentive sensitization Heightened attention to and wanting of a drug by a long-term user.

Incidence The number or rate of new cases of some outcome in a given time period. *See also* Prevalence.

Increased vulnerability hypothesis View that older persons are cognitively impaired by alcohol more than younger persons.

Indigenous reports Information about the nature and function of drug use from a population under study rather than the observation of outsiders.

Inhalation A method of taking drugs by breathing deeply; for example, "snorting" cocaine to get faster and stronger impact.

Interactions (of drugs) The effect of a drug may vary with other drugs used or with different contexts of use.

International Classification of Diseases (ICD) A classification system developed by the World Health Organization for identifying major diseases, including disorders related to substances.

Invulnerables Term referring to those children of alcoholics who avoid alcohol abuse and dependency despite being at risk for these problems.

Ions Electrically charged particles that enter and exit the neuron to send nerve impulses.

Ion channel Areas on the neuron membrane that admit specific ions into the cell.

Jellinek's subtypes of alcoholism A taxonomy of alcoholics in terms of use patterns and the physical reactions experienced such as tolerance and withdrawal.

LAAM (levo-alpha-acetylmethadol) Synthetic narcotic similar to methadone but longer lasting; is used to treat heroin addicts.

Lapse Commonly called a "slip," referring to a momentary return to drug use following a period of abstinence.

Longitudinal studies Research design in which age comparisons are made of the same individuals over time as they get older.

Loss of control View under the disease model of alcoholism that alcoholics experience an inability to stop drinking once they start and should abstain.

LSD *See* Lysergic acid diethylamide.

Lysergic acid diethylamide (LSD) Hallucinogenic drug popularized during the 1960s.

Machismo Latino/Hispanic concept of masculinity as a factor motivating drinking.

MAO inhibitors *See* Monoamine oxidase inhibitors.

Marijuana Smoked drug from leaves of cannabis plant and most widely used illegal drug.

Marital family therapy Treatment emphasizing couples both being involved in change.

Marital family treatment Therapy approach that includes the nondependent spouse and family members in the treatment of alcohol and other drug dependents.

Marker variables Factors that can help identify or predict users and nonusers of drugs; they may or may not cause the differences in use.

Marriage effect Term that describes but does not explain the finding that lower rates of alcohol problems occur with married than with single persons.

Matching Assigning patients to treatments assumed to be more effective for them.

Medical model Belief that addictions and dependency are physical diseases.

MEOS *See* Microsomal ethanol oxidizing system.

MET *See* Motivational enhancement treatment.

Meta-analysis A statistical method for combining the results of many independent studies by different researchers on a specific topic to allow conclusions based on a larger sample than is usually possible for individual studies.

Metabolic (indices of drug use) Blood and urine samples contain metabolic by-products of drug use, including gamma-glutamyltransferase (GGT) for alcohol and cotinine for nicotine.

Methadone A synthetic opiate that is slower acting and taken by tablets; used to treat heroin addicts.

Methadone maintenance A program designed to help heroin addicts by giving them a replacement drug therapy, methadone, considered to be less addictive.

Methamphetamine Variant of amphetamine that is easily made at home.

Microsomal ethanol oxidizing system (MEOS) Major enzyme system for alcohol metabolism by the liver.

Minnesota Model of Treatment The traditional 28-day hospital or clinic treatment program for addictions based on a disease model.

Minnesota Multiphasic Personality Inventory A leading test instrument for measuring different dimensions of psychopathology.

Modeling Process of learning skills and behaviors from observing a model performing these responses.

Moderator variable Whether or not one factor is related to another may depend on a third variable, called a moderator variable. For example, if a positive family history of alcoholism that leads to behavior problems depends on the child's self-esteem, then self-esteem is the moderator variable.

Monitoring the Future (MTF) survey An annual national survey conducted at the University of Michigan to assess alcohol and other drug use of high school students.

Monoamine oxidase (MAO) inhibitors Drugs that block a specific enzyme, monoamine oxidase, so that an antidepressant drug can relieve depression.

Monozygotic (MZ) twins Identical twins who come from a single egg.

Motivational enhancement treatment (MET) Treatment approach emphasizing motivating the client to want to change and to assume responsibility.

Motivational interviewing A method of structured nonconfrontational interviewing aimed at creating awareness and motivation in the alcohol or drug abuser to reduce his or her substance abuse.

MTF *See* Monitoring the Future survey.

Multiple-regulation model Theory about the relationship of physiological and psychological factors on the control of smoking.

Multiple sex roles Having several functions expected because of one's sex.

MZ *See* Monozygotic twins.

Naltrexone An opiate antagonist that is believed to be useful in treating alcoholism.

Narcotic Drug capable of producing sleep state and pain relief.

National Drug and Alcoholism Treatment Unit Survey (NDATUS) Study to estimate the number and type of clients receiving alcohol and other drug treatment in federally funded centers across the United States.

National Household Survey on Drug Abuse (NHSDA) An annual national survey to assess alcohol and other drug use in the general population.

Natural recovery Recovery from addictions without formal treatment.

NDATUS *See* National Drug and Alcoholism Treatment Unit Survey

Neuron A nerve cell; sensory neurons carry messages to and motor neurons carry messages from the central nervous system.

Neurotransmitters Chemicals released by neurons that excite or inhibit adjacent neurons.

NHSDA *See* National Household Survey on Drug Abuse.

Nicotine The active ingredient in tobacco cigarettes.

Nicotine regulation The tendency of smokers to develop smoking patterns that achieve and maintain their preferred level of nicotine.

Norepinephrine Neurotransmitter important for waking and appetite regulation.

Normative education Approach for prevention in which children learn that there are not as many peers using drugs as they might think.

Nucleus accumbens A nucleus in the mid-brain related to positive reinforcement.

Operant conditioning Reinforcement procedures used to change behavior gradually; involves some trial-and-error active learning.

Opponent process theory Model of addictions focusing on the body's tendencies to produce an effect opposite to that of any drug; with repeated use, the drug effect is weaker, but the opponent process becomes stronger, leading to more use to produce the drug's earlier effects.

P300 wave A brain wave change occurring about 300 milliseconds after a research participant attends to a signal; is assumed to reflect the act of attending.

Parasympathetic Part of the autonomic nervous system that promotes a resting state.

Peer selection Process by which people choose those with whom they want to associate.

Period effect Results depend on the historical period when participants in a study lived.

Peripheral nervous system The part of the nervous system that coordinates input to and from the environment with central nervous system processes.

Perseveration A tendency to repeat the same incorrect response; assumed to be an indication of impairment.

pH scale A scale assessing the degree of alkalinity or acidity of chemicals.

Placebo A control condition in an experiment to assess psychological effects of drug taking. A substance is given that is not psychoactive to participants who believe it is.

Polarization The tendency of children of alcoholics to develop either extremely positive or negative alcohol attitudes and use patterns.

Polydrug abuse Abuse of more than one psychoactive drug together or in quick succession.

Positive appetitional model A model in which relapse is in response to the presence of stimuli associated with the user's prior experiences of desired effects from a drug.

Premature aging hypothesis View that cognitive deficits in alcoholics are due to premature aging from chronic use of alcohol.

Prevalence Number or rate of existing cases (old and new) of some outcome in some time period. *See also* Incidence.

Price elasticity Extent to which price affects drug use; elastic refers to large effects, whereas inelastic refers to little or no effect.

Primary prevention Prevention aimed at stopping a problem before it even starts.

Proband Person assumed to be at risk of alcohol or other drug abuse or dependency.

Profane separation Concept that deviant behavior such as drug use for some groups may involve a desire for distance from groups with other values.

Project DARE A school-based program of drug education led by community police officers.

Project MATCH A research study to evaluate the effectiveness of matching alcoholic clients to three different treatments to see if more effective outcomes would occur overall.

Prospective studies Research design in which data are collected at several points in time, starting with the present.

Protective factors Variables related to lower risk of alcohol and other drug problems.

Psychoanalytic approach Based on views of Freud and his followers, drugs are seen as involving unconscious unresolved conflicts.

Psychodynamic approaches Individual or group-structured therapy focusing on achieving insight.

Psychopathology Commonly called abnormal behavior but includes psychiatric disorders, including personality disorder and affective or mood disorders.

Public health model Approach emphasizing the need to consider the user or host, the agent or drug, and the environment in which the user takes the drug.

QF index of drinking Quantity and frequency of use are combined to provide a total use index.

Quantity reduction Approach to social policy that emphasizes the need to lower the amount used per person to minimize harm.

Random assignment Procedure of assigning participants to different treatments or procedures so each person has an equal chance to be in any treatment; essential for ruling out alternative explanations for experimental outcomes.

Random selection Procedure of selecting participants for a study that gives each person an equal chance of being selected.

Rational emotive therapy (RET) Based on methods of Albert Ellis, this approach focuses on reasoning and logic for guiding behavior.

Rational Recovery (RR) A for-profit organization emphasizing reason and personal responsibility for recovery from addictions.

Receptors Sites on neurons that accept different neurotransmitters arriving at the synapse from other neurons.

Relapse Resumption of using a drug following a period of abstinence.

Relapse prevention Approach based on social and cognitive processes to teach self-awareness and monitoring, as well as coping skills for managing high-risk situations for drug use.

Remission Recovery from abuse or dependency.

Resistance skills Refers to techniques for overcoming peer pressure to use drugs.

RET *See* Rational emotive therapy.

Retrospective studies Research design in which data are collected about behavior that occurred at some earlier time.

Reuptake Process of removing neurotransmitters from a synapse and recycling them for future use.

Right hemisphere hypothesis Theory that alcohol primarily affects functions controlled by the right hemisphere such as visual-spatial abilities.

Risk factors Variables that are predictive of some negative outcome such as drug abuse.

Rohypnol® A club drug popular at all-night dances or raves; also called "roofies" or "date rape" drug.

RR *See* Rational recovery.

Schedule of drugs Federal agency classification of controlled substances in terms of their medicinal value and risk of addiction.

Screening Process of identifying at-risk individuals in greater need of intervention or treatment.

Secondary prevention Treatment or intervention for individuals who have begun to develop alcohol and other drug problems.

Self-efficacy A sense of control where an individual feels competent to deal with specific situations.

Self-medication Attempt to treat one's own health problems, often with excess use of drugs.

Self-report A widely used method of obtaining information about alcohol and other drug use that is convenient but can be misleading, falsified, or inaccurate.

Self-selection Individuals who enter a treatment or engage in some specific behavior are different in important ways from those who do not.

Semantic versus episodic memory Semantic involves general knowledge, whereas episodic deals with specific incidents or facts.

Sensitivity Accurate index of drug use, with few false negatives in which users are misclassified as not using.

Serotonin Neurotransmitter found in raphe nuclei that affects depression and mood states.

Sex role conflict View that women feel conflict over traditional and modern views of their role.

Sex role deprivation View that women were restricted to traditional sex roles and had no other opportunities.

Sex roles The distinctive behaviors that society allows or expects from males and females.

Sex role theories A set of views about how sex roles affect behavior.

Sexual dysfunction Impaired sexual behavior or functioning, including impotence, lack of orgasm, infertility, and miscarriages.

Single distribution of consumption model A model that assumes most people drink moderately, or not at all, while a few drink heavily. Moreover, the higher the availability of alcohol in a society, the higher will be the total consumption and related problems.

Situational anxiety As opposed to generalized anxiety, this form is specific to given situations.

SMART Recovery A self-help organization emphasizing reason and personal responsibility for recovery from addictions.

Snowballing A nonrandom sampling method for obtaining participants for a study by using contacts referred by previous participants.

Social learning Theory about how observation of models affects behavior.

Solitary versus dyadic drinking Drinking alone versus with another person.

Somatization Tendency to explain psychological symptoms in terms of a physical problem.

Specificity Accurate index of drug use, with few false positives in which nonusers are misclassified as using.

Stable drinking Drinking in a predictable pattern of amount or time.

Stages of alcoholism Aspects of a disease model of alcoholism describing an invariant progression through several increasingly worse stages: prealcoholic, prodromal, crucial, and chronic.

Stages of change model Model of factors leading from precontemplation through several stages toward recovery from dependency.

State-dependent learning Learning acquired in a specific situation that is forgotten is more likely to be recalled in the original context. *See also* Blackout.

Supply reduction Drug policy approach focusing on reducing the available supply.

Surveillance indicators of use Indirect measures of use based on records such as sales tax revenue, health statistics, and alcohol-related driving accidents.

Sympathetic nervous system Part of the autonomic nervous system that promotes an emergency state reaction.

Synaptic junction The space, also called the synapse, between adjacent neurons in which neurotransmitters are passed from one neuron to others.

Temperament A general personality disposition, such as activity level, that is assumed to be biologically based or innate.

Temperance Movement, often associated with religious groups, to prevent alcohol use. Originally intended to reduce, it often called for total abstinence.

Tertiary prevention Prevention approach emphasizing changes in the environment that reduce the likelihood of drug-related problems.

Tolerance A form of habituation to drugs in which repeated use leads to smaller effects.

TOPS *See* Treatment Outcome Prospective Study.

Treatment Outcome Prospective Study (TOPS) A major evaluation study showing drug treatment effectiveness in the late 1970s; examined outcomes in relation to patient characteristics, program environments, and available treatment services.

Triangulation When two members of a family are in conflict, they may draw a third party into the conflict to take sides, adding to problems that family therapy must deal with.

12 steps A series of behaviors and attitudes that is the basis for recovery in Alcoholics Anonymous.

Type 1 and 2 (milieu and male limited alcoholism) Cloninger's typology of alcoholics focusing on age of onset and consequences.

Type A and B (alcoholism) Babor's typology of alcoholics focusing on age of onset and consequences.

Uncontrolled observations Natural observations or correlations that may have several possible interpretations. *See also* Controlled observation.

Use A descriptive term to refer to any use of a substance.

Use reduction A drug policy approach focusing on methods of reducing how much individuals use drugs.

Use-related problems Adverse consequences including health, social, financial, and legal problems stemming from use of alcohol and other drugs.

Vulnerability Susceptibility to becoming dependent on alcohol and other drugs.

Wernicke-Korsakoff syndrome Cognitive deficits, including memory loss and confusion, attributed to brain damage from alcoholism.

Wet versus dry family interaction How the family interacts when the alcoholic is drinking versus not drinking.

WHO *See* World Health Organization.

Withdrawal or abstinence syndrome Adverse syndrome of discomfort experienced when alcohol and drug abusers and dependents do not have access to their drug.

Women for Sobriety A self-help recovery from addictions to serve the needs of women.

World Health Organization (WHO) An international agency that deals with health issues and policy.

Name Index

Subject Index

About the Author

John Jung is Professor of Psychology at California State University, Long Beach. He has published several psychology textbooks covering topics such as research methods, ethical issues in the conduct of psychological experiments with humans, and laboratory methods in experimental psychology. He also has written textbooks on human memory, human motivation, and an earlier book on the psychology of alcohol use. He has served as an ad hoc member of the Study Section for the National Institute on Alcohol Abuse and Alcoholism. He also has published numerous journal articles on his research on alcohol use, social support, health psychology, and memory.

For the past 20 years, he has been funded by the National Institute of Mental Health to direct a mentoring program to recruit minority students into research careers. Dr. Jung also is the faculty research coordinator for the McNair Scholars Program, a mentoring program funded by the U.S. Department of Education to increase doctoral degrees among low-income students who are the first in their families to attend college or come from groups underrepresented in their fields of study.

in the United States
LVS00004B/117-148